The Intersexes

The Intersexes

A History of Similisexualism as a Problem in Social Life

Edward Irenaeus Prime-Stevenson

MINT EDITIONS

The Intersexes: A History of Similisexualism as a Problem in Social Life was first published in 1908.

This edition published by Mint Editions 2021.

ISBN 9781513295343 | E-ISBN 9781513295497

Published by Mint Editions®

MINT EDITIONS

minteditionbooks.com

Publishing Director: Jennifer Newens
Design & Production: Rachel Lopez Metzger
Project Manager: Micaela Clark
Typesetting: Westchester Publishing Services

Contents

I

INTRODUCTORY:
OLD IGNORANCES AND NEW PSYCHOLOGY

A special trait of the last quarter of the century lately ended was the subtle but general, decided change in what one may call psychologic perspectives. The thoughtful classes have studied their fellow men of late, from the standpoints of practical psychiatrics and of moral responsibility, with a clearness of insight and from a variety of angles not before our time so considered or attained. The changes in currents of religious belief, by which dogmas have been displaced in favour of more natural spiritual conclusions, changes through which the understructure of ethical systems have been questioned and often rebuilt, have served humanity profoundly. Social science, applied to the individual, has also wrought similar healthful details in everyday life.

The Medical Psychologist.

Perhaps no process in the category has been more valuable than the leverage of the medical psychologist. His studies of phases of human nature, and his conclusions as to its expressions, exercise now-a-days upon the social attitudes an influence for which we have no parallel unless we revert to the Middle-Ages and to the best aspects (troublesomely blended, as they were, with mischievous errors) of Ecclesiasticism as a factor in mediaeval society.

The Psychologic Physician as a Juryman to the World.

Today this pratical application of the psychologist to social science puts the physician, especially, in the place and responsability of being a sort of juryman to the whole world. He is brought into the court-room, the State-Commission, the Parliament. In all our dealings with psychologic analisys, sooner or later, we are likely to revert to him. The medico-psychologist has now not only the ancient or new fields of experimental research; for, along with them, he possesses the advantage of largest freedom of speech in giving out his theories and practices to any intelligent outsiders. His sounder conclusions are even "popularized" almost as swiftly as accepted by members of his profession. In fact, so soon do they become common property that one or another school of charlatanism, ever-ready with perilous tendences of argument, often injures the more conservative and riper convictions of responsible thinkers. But however much is the mischief of superficial medical psychology, here or there, the physician who is a true psychiater constantly effects admirable *rapports* between law and the individual; relationships which are not credited always rightly to the distinctly psycho-medical judgment.

Old Notions and Theories Dismissed by Modern Science.

Directly or indirectly, to the higher scope of medical psychology do we owe the fact, for instance, that nervous ailments of men and women are no longer ascribed to devils and to witchcraft. The days of burning helpless human creatures for sorcery are past; even the most persistent confession that some wretched "accused" could shriek forth would now be nothing to a judge or a churchman. The students of alienism have changed ancient ideas about insanity, and have corrected forever the hideous ignorances of Bedlam treatments. We are no longer instructed that mad people are so depraved that God has visited a special judgment on them, and that starvation and beatings are the fittest methods of restoring the lost reason. The drunkard is regarded in the light of a victim of alcoholism, often, rather than as a responsible member of the community.

The Criminal as a Scientific Problem.

To criminal classes the medical psychologist lately has been particularly attentive. We have learned from this devotion that there exists a profound and demonstrable connection of mystery between the Will and a nervous organism, rapports between heredity and tendency to crime. We are willing to believe that felony may be a process of disease; even to our perceiving murder, arson, theft as involuntary acts. We have grown into pitying the suicide as a creature who is far less a moral sinner than an unhappy monomaniac; his psychologic equilibrium is so impaired that there is merely a fraction of moral responsability in his hanging himself in a wood, or putting a bullet through his heart. The world no longer regards epidemics as having theological mysteries in their origins; as expressing any immediate visitation of divine wrath. Scientific plumbing, the sanitary care of water-supplies, the bacteriologist with his microscope, the antiseptic treatment of surgical operations; more than for these relatively outward results is the doctor, as a practical scientist, to be thanked. Taking such a school of medical thought at its best, we realize how vigorous, not to say supreme, a factor the psychologic doctor can be, and also that his higher and most modern influence is hardly more than begun as to many further processes affecting public opinion and intelligence. The just concepts of human nature, the traits of man as the psychical and temperamental product which he is, the analysis of his responsibility to himself and to his fellows, present topics immediate to our day, to be viewed with a clarity not hitherto achieved. The process is dual.

It brings destruction of many of the old fabrics, and a building-up of entirely new ones, through materials not earlilier in the hands of the social architect.

The Question of Intersexes.

Advanced theories and conclusions of medical psychologists have an important share in the following pages: therefore I have laid preliminary stress on such psychology in relation to general social-scientific progress. And with respect to the particular subject of the ensuing chapters, the existence of Intersexes in the human race, their various minor gradations as part of a series of fixed psychologic facts, the attributes of these Intersexes, and the social, moral and legal standpoints that are maintainable toward them, ideas of justice or injustice to them-in such considerations I shall be obliged to refer constantly to researches of distinguished medico-psychologists of our time. Hence what I shall write will be not much more than a summary of their decisions; apart from what is the share of personal exploration, in the lighter paths. As will be seen, the profound attention and discussions of psychiaters have been concentrating themselves more and more during many years, in spite of constant embasassments and perplexities, upon one of the most startling and obscure facts in human existence yet under scientific investigation. But of scientific theories of Intersexual life, and of what belongs to it by inalienable rights or is foreign to it, the intelligent lay-world is still far too ignorant, in spite of the vivid relation of the matter to millions of individuals. An enormous literature bearing upon it already exists: but not for the average lay-reader, and sparsely in English. The studies in print are chiefly in German, French, Italian and Russian. Their tone is not popular enough for ordinary readers. No adequate English work setting forth the topic exists in English at all, with easy accessibility. Indeed, such delicate and recondite chapters of

Undercurrents of Personal Interest in Understanding Sexual Impulses.

human existence are opened, so many painful moral questions recur, that one does not wonder at the reserved attitude of authours, editors and publishers.

I can offer myself on this occasion only as a finger-post to guide the reader along a road where shapes that will be startling mystic, beautiful, repulsive, tragic, commonplace, are continually to be seen. It is a highway of human-nature hourly traversed by millions, of all ranks; a road foot-worn, day by day, since humanity began. But the procession upon it is one extraordinarily, sternly reticent. Perhaps the very reader of these lines may long have been marching, or staggering, with the cortège, half-conscious of his companions far behind him, or at hand on the right or the left, or beyond him. Those who could unriddle the march to him are not likely to speak a word to him. Those who are willing to speak of one or another social or moral phase of the matter, particularly of the more obvious and vulgar aspects, are as a general rule, either insincere or wholly ignorant of the real psychology in what they discuss. And the reader may be the last person in his whole circle of friends to confess that he has a profound personal interest in the topic. Like the Spartan lad, with the gnawing fox hidden under his garment, he may have done nothing more instinctively and carefully, all his life long, than to try to hide from all interlocutors the anguish that is destroying his peace of mind and life.

II

Male and Female Human Nature as Theory and as Reality: The Theory of Intersexes

One of the most popular and long-rooted notions in society in the idea which makes a man, the male human species, as distinguished from woman, decidedly more consistent and symmetrical as a type than the female one. If we group together what we are likely to think the most usual and normal masculine traits, putting them into a kind of "property list," we are likely to fancy that the contents of that list quite completely is approached by the majority of men around us, right and left. But suppose we examine carefully how far this conviction is borne out by facts?

The Male Sex as Consistent, or as Unsymetrical.

The Ideal "Average" Man.

We will say, for istance, that the typic "average" man is likely to be possessed of an independent nature. He should have decided impulses, mental and physical, toward aggressive action, a due sense of the moral perspectives of things, self-reliance, self-control enough for his own good. He should tend to reticence rather than talkativeness, should disregard detail when a general result is in view, should be of firm nervous poise, such as the average woman does not exhibit. He should feel especially an inborn, instinctive drawing of his sexual nature toward woman as the mysterious, natural completion of his individuality, both physical and psychical. Shall we accept this as a fair summary? Other details can be added, of course; but this will suffice. I do not lay stress here on the moral equipment, so much as upon the temperamental understructure; the outline of a kind of masculine birthright. The reader will please note, too, that I am expressly avoiding any emphases that will create an "heroic" type, offering the sort of ideal man met in Greek drama, in classic history, or in modern romance.

Similarly, let the reader frame for himself a merely physical masculinity; virile enough, but not at all ideal. We will not busy ourselves with a male type that externally would suit the frieze of the Parthenon, or storm through the pages of Northern Sagas and Malory. Roughly made up, let us picture only a strong frame, that is to say, strong in comparison with a woman's frailer physique; with symmetry of outline, due proportion between head and body and limbs, ordinary aspects of a muscular development capable of endurance; and so on through the details of skin-texture, growth of hair and beard, quality of voice, gait, freedom of movement. All of these are traits that we take for granted as existing in a liberal preponderance among the members of a regiment, a club, or even a house-party, not to speak of the younger or older contingent at a cricket-match or in the crowd of a bank-holiday.

Reverting to the Actual Male Type.

Now, after figuring out this type of a normally manly personality, inward and outward, the reader will please let his mind run over the list of his more intimate male acquaintance. How many of the men that he knows show a decided "working majority" of those traits, fundamental to a normal man' identity? Of the traits that are non-corporeal, how often do we find this or that Mend falling short! Add to the list other qualifications; the discrepancies become plainer. True self-reliance, aggressiveness, moral perspective, self-control, manly silence, the sense of trifles, as trifles, of the important as the important, also the decided sexual instinct mentioned—does the widest circle of our acquaintance offer us many men that conform closely to these specifications? Is the reader of these pages a man? Let him review himself, to decide on his conscience, how far he is normal in the due measure. Is one at all struck by the fact that his Ego, even if he has never remarked it before, is particularly deficient in essential details of psychical masculinity? With the same thoughtfulness, will the reader think over this or that group of his friends?—analyzing them narrowly, with regard to the outward and inward traits and manners I have set down. We are surprised to discover how continually we have friends and acquaintances that are more or less failures in the way of some plain characteristic that belongs to a manly personality. In fact, true, typical manliness, or, if the reader prefer another term, typical masculinity, seems all at once to be a far more elusive attribute than we had thought it. We are astonished to find how successfully a good many men pass for thoroughly masculine individualities who are imperfect examples of even quite commonplace models of men.

Historic Masculinity Examined as to Psychology.

From the circle of our own aquainthance, we will turn to the pages ot history, biography, memoirs, correspondence and travel. Also let us consider many sorts of literature, apart from obvious fiction, in which men have written themselves down in portraitures more or less sincere and true, or have so depicted others. The class of records I mean (and it is especially inclusive of the most intimate of human chronicles) is not to be mixed with conventional and secondhand studies of the kind, where the subject has been put into poses-plastiques by editors of more art than sincerity. Out of true human documents, what surprising divergencies from a fully masculine image in our minds do many men show!—having passed through the world, and into history as emphatically male, exercising great influence on their associates as absolute men! In all classes and all epochs we meet curious discrepancies, startling inconsistencies, especially as we go upward, in the scale of aesthetic sensitiveness. We meet with the prince in whose nature the arrogance of Lucifer is contrasted with a want of dignity of character that would put to shame a peasant in a pothouse. We find the great statesman who turns from the working-out of a treaty, or the fight over a great parliamentary measure, to adore his mirror, or to concoct a wash for his complexion. We smile at the brave soldier who hates to go to bed in the dark, who quivers before a cat or a dentist. We come upon the eloquent divine, apparently much nearer heaven than earth, who has avance as a master-passion, and to whom a gourmand's table is a necessity. The philosopher who loses his temper as he loses his game of cards; the jurist that, off his bench, is stocked with unjust and silly prejudices; the athlete who embroiders; and the pugilist to whom a touch of fur is a nervous distress—all these are to be encountered. And yet we can go on. For, in the more aesthetic walks of life occur striking temperamental inconsistencies from any perfect moulds of virility. There is the poet whose verse shakes the world with its vigor but who cannot look you in the eyes, and who relishes perfumes and sweets like a cocotte: the painter of roses and lilies whose greatest recreation is a prize-ring or a guillotining; the composer of delicate harmonies who loves the obscene oaths of bargees; the religious allegorist who haunts the bull-fight. So could we proceed through a thousand examples of inconsistent male making-up; met in all civilizations, and of record in every public library.

We begin to wonder, after we have thus reflected, exactly what is the proportion of really manly, masculine, symmetrical men in the world; if there ever has been so large a proportion of them as we have taken for granted. Does Nature so often stand up and say of her normal, usual male product, "This is a man!?" The achieved male, whether as to his bodily structure, or his mental and moral and temperamental equipment appears suddenly to grow vague. Yet we have not been searching for ideals, for extraordinary assemblages of distinctive male qualities. We are only trying to find a well-rounded consistency, measured by accepted tests the world over.

A Distinctively Effeminate Male Type Is Not in Question.

Let me anticipate a probable comment here: that an effeminated man, one effeminated mentally, morally, temperamentally and in his body, is never uncommon. But the reader must not confuse such distinctively, offensively effeminated types of man with a merely inconsistent one, as to this or that standard of male attributes. The man who in his physique, his intellect, his temperament, his tastes, his mannerisms and so on, peculiarly differs from the truer male standard, presenting obviously a general dissent, is not the personality meant here. We are dealing with one that departs more subtly from a true man-type. Effeminacy in the male, as usually depicted and understood, we may regard as an extreme. It is likely to be particularly associated with the outward man, embodied in his physique, to plain observation. We are dealing more with the psychologic failure of a man to be adequately virile. For that matter, we need not yet bring specially concrete examples into our analysis.

Of the Average Female Ideal and Divergencies from It.

Suppose that we now turn from the masculine to the feminine. Let us think of woman as she is typified and realized, either past or present, in commonplace life. We cannot fail to remark the same sort of divergence from what we call essential womanliness, in one respect or in another. Our study puts woman after woman more or less out of measure with the feminine symmetry we have a right to expect. Make the tests again, those of both physiology and psychology. Opposed, for instance, to the accepted idea that the great majority of women are "dependent" in their attitude toward social existence, we find that every walk of life offers types that dominate social life, as a matter of course; flouting many canons of intellectual, moral, and even physical relations to it; able to hold their own without struggle. Suppose we endow the "average woman" with theoretic characteristics marking her out. We expect her to be ordinarily not capable of dealing closely with the abstract; to act largely on impulse: to possess nervous energy rather than staying-power; to be uncombative; to have ideals as to moral attitudes rather than observances of them by herself; to shun responsibilities of severe sort; and (once more important) we endow her with the sexual impulse of seeking her unity with a man and her surrender to him. In place of this type, we constantly encounter a feminine creature of predisposition for what is abstract; governed in personal relations to life by calm reflection; full of physical and mental endurance; aggressive and with even a pleasure in stressful activity. We find women deeply ethical and philosophic. We meet many who are indifferent to much that is a traditional part of the feminine world, such as their personal beauty, its adornment, and their influence as to sex over men: including the more or less marked dissent from surrender to man, either physically or intellectually. We have analyses and intellectual independence in a corset; the battle of life ardently carried on in a petticoat! Especially, is to be noted the instinctive absence of sexual interest that such a woman shows toward a man.

The outward physique of such women often does not conform to a correct and ideal female anatomy. The example can incline toward masculinity, as to build, height, features, mannerisms, now as to another; occasionally going so far as to be hermaphroditic.

Some Instances of the Type of Masculinity in Woman.

We can select instances at random of the non-conforming woman that are historic; though we shall better understand the wide distribution of the variants when we come to ordinary and private-life examples, and to what they say of themselves. Deborah, Boadicea, Hypatia, Joan of Arc, Elizabeth, of England, Christina of Sweden, Mary Somerville, Angela Postovoitov, Franziska Skanagatta, Anna Maria Schurman, George Sand, George Eliot, give clear traits of the kind sought. The bar, the clinic, the pulpit, the editorial-room, every branch of trade, many of the responsible interests of finance: the university, the gymnasiums, hunting-fields, shooting-boxes, even the army and navy—we have only to look about us to recognize this sort of woman that is only nominally womanly, according to correct prejudices. Let me take pains to remind the reader that I am not laying weight here, any more than in speaking of the divergent and inconsistent male type, on what is essentially a *physical* departure.

The unwomanish woman is often wholly feminine in externals, and conforms to them with more or less care. Nevertheless outward unfeminineness of a woman, when it is marked, has rather more

significance in our study than has the externally unmasculine in a man.

The Emotional
Inconsistencies in
Men.

Whatever the other shortcomings from the correct standard of masculinity, it is in the emotional currents that a man shows to us often his most striking unconformity. These currents are the chief witnesses toward his male-sexual imperfection. Masculine geology is full of what are called "faults," discordant chemistry, mutinous strata. A man outwardly absolutely normal and regarded as of perfect normality of mind, can be a riddle to himself on account of his mysterious emotional eccentricity. A man conceals this, or anything else, far better than can a woman, because the method is less superficial. Shakespeare's exclamation, "O, what may man within him hide!" is newly understood, in considering the biographical studies and confessions making part of this study. A man's whole existence, his schoolboy-days, his university life, business or professional career, his deathbed hours, can easily be nothing so much as a concealment of all that is most himself, psychologically. To hide it becomes a second nature, or rather a first one. Indeed, the more carefully the student of masculine character makes a practical study, gives the right clews for it, of his own sex, in all ranks and phases accessible to the average observer, the sooner he reaches a conclusion that a man's emotional center of gravity is a great deal less definite and stable than current impressions locate it. We can even believe—sometimes—that masculine humanity is likely to be far more the victim of its emotional tendencies than are women. Under a well-sustained (frequently a spendidly sustained) dissimulation, beneath intense reserves, veiled by pride or policy, there can exist sufferings from inborn temperamental causes, with emotional crises, that are fearful to meet. The closest friend may be the last to suspect them; may be the last one that the sufferer would wish to find suspecting. In getting into touch with such veiled personal tragedies as even this book liberally offers, we shall realize that in nothing is a man more completely inconsistent than in his relation to common theories of male emotional nature.

We have thus alluded to the psychologic and physiologic discrepancies that exist now, that ever have existed, between received and popular ideals

A Principle in Nature.

of each of the two great sexual classes, and their current and real selves. With this, we come face to face with a matter of the first importance; of cosmic breadth of bearing. To point it out is not new; in enlarging on it here I follow the analyses and indeed the phrase of many a predecessor— of one brilliant German theorist in particular. There exists one striking principle of distinction between the works of Nature and the works of Art. Art completes what it undertakes, and therewith makes its products more or less independent from each other. But Nature never has made for us, and never will make, any one thing complete, detached from all other kinds, really independent and finished as a product, by itself. She refuses any labour that has nothing to do with the rest of her cosmic, cyclic, general scheme. Nature in all her work, here or there, is perpetually referring us back or forward to other creations; to things "the same yet not the same"; to the like but not the identical. Putting a little more into one expression of herself, a little less into another, often merely using the same materials in another recipe. Nature keeps on melting, fusing, half-melting, half-fusing one set of her principles and products with another, almost as if in capricious experiment, or as aiming toward some perfect and independent thing never to be realized. She works along an endless chain, full of interrelationships; gracefully playing with what are not detached performances from her fine hand but merely between-expressions. All is of mere degrees, all, along her vast system of organic life.

Between whitest of men and the blackest negro stretches out a vast line of intermediary races as to their colours; brown, olive, red tawny, yellow. Between a protozoan and the most perfect development of the mammalia, we trace a succession of dependent intersteps. From a fish to a giraffe we can establish a series of details that unites them as form of life; while each middle link has its own place. A trilobite is at one end of Nature's workshop; a Spinoza, a Shakespeare, a Beethoven is at the other; led-to by cunning gradations. Nature can "evolve" an onion into a philosopher, or a mollusk to a prime-minister. The spectrum is a chain. Prom violet and indigo into scarlet, there is nothing but a succession of gradient hues. Each link is, in paradox, both a matter of dependence on the whole system, yet of independence: part of its nearer neighbours, while having its right to be accounted relatively separate and responsible by itself. There is no absolute darkness: there is no absolute light. There is no absolute heat, no absolute cold. In fact, Nature abhors the absolute,

> Nature's Endless Unity.

delights in the fractional. We have no right to consider any of her works more than a link; though we are logically bound to give to it due fractional autonomy. Hence, equally by logic, we must be on our guard against quarrelling with it because it "ought to be" more complete toward genus, toward type, than it is. For, Nature is continually rebuking our narrow, proud, perverse definitism. She asks why, if we are so exact, we do not blame the dawn because it is rosy instead of glowing white, do not throw down in disgust the hedge-rose because it lacks the petals and colours of so many stately garden-beauties; do not ridicule the bull because he does not boast the antlers of a stag; do not despise the ostrich because it has not the eagle's wings; do not think that the terrible beauty of some tropical serpent is ruined since it has not even as many legs as the tiniest lizard; do not reject as disgracefully incomplete and hesitant in the evolution of existences such intermediaries as we find in the platypus, the porcupine, the whale, the quadrumana, in even the most superiour and complex and firmly-elaborated creations about us. Every where we encounter borrowings from one, loans from the other, strange but natural inter-relations, revolts against conforming to details that seem almost obligations in kind and taste and conduct, crossings of what seem natural boundaries, whole kingdoms of life instituted in an allowed and eternal rebellion from a common law.

The Human Species as Theoretic Extremes.

We must thus dismiss some popular notions of what constitutes sexual manhood and womanhood, and their indispensable system of attributes, as being other than two widely-parted extremes. Nature constantly demands of us why we have endowed our ideals of the two sexes with only such or such qualities; by what right we have gone on insisting that each specimen of sex in humanity must conform absolutely to two theories, must follow out two programmes only, or else be thought amiss, imperfect and degenerate. Why have we set up masculinity and femininity as processes that have not perfectly logical and respectable inter-steps? We have established, we have decked out, to our own ideas, just two sexes. Where presently we are confronted by what appears an abnormality in their expression we have said that that expression is imperfect, and to be repudiated. The fact is that have we lacked charter-right, guidance and warrant for our arrogance. Generation after generation, we have gone on, judging humanity sexually without full initial authority. Nature, on the contrary, all the while, ever has been striving patiently, silently, to remind us that we have been too narrow; that what we call the exceptional, the abnormal, may be perfectly normal; mature to itself and entlited to its own independent place and recognition in anthropology and society. In defining sex for instance, Nature would nut permit us to forget, that the physique of the unborn child so embodies for many weeks the traits of two sexes that the skilled anatomist cannot tell us whether the foetus should have been born a boy or a girl.

The Natural Intersexes.

Thus become clear the inference, the conviction, logical truth that cyclic Nature has always maintained in the human species a series of graduated and necessary Intersexes, between the two great major sexes that we recognize as distinctively "man" and "woman" i.e. as the extreme masculine and the extreme feminine. These Intersexes are not physically obvious in the frapjik degree that we have foolishly expected such natural differences would be expressed. The average eye and mind have never learned even how to look for them, though they are around us daily in their positive attributes. They are the less perceived because their physical differences from the one or the other removed sex toward which they incline, but to which they do not attain, are not necessarily readily visible. Their subtle separation from their Over-sex begins at a deeper plane, on that alone, constantly—the psychological, not physical. What masks particularly its presence is that even the psychology stays in hiding; the student must be trained to recognize its signs. Especially are these Intersexes established, determined and excused, by one supremely natural factor in them—the sexual instincts. This is their master-separation, although other traits are more or less concurrent and logical therein. Such Intersexes express the half-steps, the between-beings. Their existence is as irrefutable as immemorial. For centuries, the world has narrowed-down mankind into two sexes. There are at least two more than our traditional anthropological spectrum has perceived and recognized; each of primary importance always.

Certain Consequences of Admitting this Intersexual Theory.

The theory of these Intersexes is likely to be startling to the layman, as soon as he thinks of it otherwise than as a fantasy, and begins to perceive its practical bearings on the world's social systems. For, undeniably, by an unavoidable succession of its applications it has much in it revolutionary of social, moral and individual life. We must reconsider many old conclusions, especially many theories of the sexual instincts, in all races and civilizations. Lifelong ideas, rooted prejudices suddenly are sapped under its chemistry. Impulses in intersexual humanity, in the "between-man" or the "between-woman" working out their own emotional natures helplessly and independently even while mocked or denounced therefor, are not to be judged by pulpit or statute-book, but by medical psychology. By noting else so arbitrarily, because not otherwise so accurately. Particularly must we throw away one long-established notion as to sex in the human race, in general.

Sex is Never to be Determined by the Physique.

That special error is the idea that sex is to be *determined* by the physique. Physique is not, and never should be, determinative of sex in man or woman or intersex. No—the one determinative, putting the stress on the word *determinative*, is the sexual instinct. Nothing else. Not the bodily organs and structure, not the mental, the moral, the general emotional making-up of the human being, can stand out as a determinative before this one trait. Such details can coincide in a general effect; or they can (as so continually is the case) only help to conceal the true sex, to mislead us cunningly and elaborately; and, what is more, sometimes to deceive perfectly the very person most concerned, who is the unlucky subject of their masquerade.

Sex Determined by Sexual Instinct.

We repeat it; sex is determined by the sexual instinct; by the desire physical and psychical, of one human being for another, no matter what his or her bodily aspects and other endowment. In every other trait that we have been accustomed to accept as telling of what sex we or another fellow-creature may be, Nature hoodwinks and plays with us, or else gives us relatively superficial clues.

What are the Intersexes?

Taking this series of conclusions as our guidance, let us re-distribute the human race sexually. To the one extreme and perfect masculine sex, a man, and to the other extreme and perfect female sex, a woman, we will add at least two Intersexes. These Intersexes partake of the natures and temperaments and physiques of both the male and the female, now to one extent, now to another. Departing from the first sex a man, we establish a second and "intersexual" sex, known to European medico-psychologic literature as the Urning, or Uranian sex. The name is derived from the classic fable of the "Venus Urania," and from the Platonic discussions concerning a mystic "nobler Venus" the divine patroness of similisexual, passional loves, especially between males; reaffirming, the theory of there having been created only one single human sex of old; that only later came to subsist two types with their separate sexual instincts in mankind, each by divine insinuation. We next establish or proceed to re-establish, a third sex, or intersex, called the Uraniad, which refers to the feminine, but the feminine sexually masculinized; of which sex many "women-seeming" women are members. Last, we place the perfectly feminine sex, its extreme, the woman as we have long recognized her. The arrangement of these four sexes the sorting of the two "intersexes" thus, has been questioned. There are subtle and interesting arguments for putting the Uranian, or masculine intersex, absolutely as the first and completest of the sexes known, not simply as an intersex; at the same time relegating the man-type as commonly met, to the merely intersexual degree. There is also a considerable line of finer intersexual distinctions and types, adjusted by various psychiaters which makes the list of intersexes exceed the four here established. But for all ordinary purposes the restriction to four, and the foregoing adjustments are sufficient.

These two Intersexes named here as the Uranian and the Uraniad, the one partaking most of the outwardly and inwardly masculine yet not fully a man, the other leaning toward the typic feminine yet not fully woman, are each indisputably a blend of the two extreme sexes. Each is more or less indisputably entitled to recognition as to its individual rights; each exists now as ever in a most important proportion to the rest of mankind. These Intersexes are constantly working-out about us, with or without social recognition and sanction, their own sexual instincts. Too often such types are not only unknown to their fellow-men for what they are, but also too often not known to—themselves. Especially do we find them the victims of sexual repression, seekers after a sexual expression that they cannot obtain without disgraces, dangers, and crimes. Not less especially are they petitioners for at least a tentative, a cautious consideration and tolerance, social and legal; fugitives from miseries and injustices which an unreasoning and ill-informed world, with its tendency to generalize, has far too little suspected. It is true that they present inevitably and often painfully, whether taken as individuals or as classes, many traits, claims, theories, impulses, practices, deviations from the more or less normally human, which cannot be tolerated in ethics and social life by even philosophic justice however dispassionate. They have sex-idioms that repel and terrify us, no matter how elastic is our human sympathy. But admitting all which will deepen around them this undeniable shadow, the fact remains that a great proportion of Intersexual lives are led and probably for a long time to come must be led, under a sexual, social and moral ban that blots our human civilization. Day by day is continued about us, no matter with what outward serenity a chronicle of underserved martyrdom that can be dramatic beyond any description in its emotional currents; demanding relief by a psychiatric enlightenment not yet more than begun.

III

Alterosexual Love and Friendship: Similisexual Love and Friendship

Before we enter further upon analyses of the Uranian and Uraniad Intersexes, some consideration in this chapter and its successor

Love Defined.

will be of importance to readers who for the first time find themselves analyzing attentively sexual feelings.

Love, as distinguished from other human emotions, particularly as distinguished from friendship, is the attraction exerted on one human being over another through the quality of our aesthetic sensitiveness; the quality of our sentiment, more or less refined, for beauty. The feeling includes distinctively our wish to *possess* the object that we love by physical connection with ourselves. We desire to unite ourselves to the being that we love, as closely as possible by a physical nearness. At the same time, we seek often to give ourselves up, in an inevitable personal surrender. The two impulses, the wish to possess, and the impulse to surrender, are inextricably blent in real love, and as a rule cannot be parted. The seeking for possession, the impulse to give ourselves as we achieve it, must be both physical and psychical, if one wishes to feel the fullest mystery of love as a passion. If the sentiment be only physical it is not perfect love, though it is a love. If it be only psychologic, if we do not demand so much the physical possession, nor feel the wish to surrender ourselves as a matter of course in attaining it, then again we do not fully *love*. There must be the duality of feeling.

Friendship as Distinguished from Love.

Now, friendship, as that feeling is commonly understood, does not include this dual desire; this seeking for physical possession. Friendship sometimes hardly demands large psychical possession, or feels a profound spiritual self-surrender. The physical thrill is not of it, no matter how ardent may the friendship be. Logically and clearly, friendship is divorced from the sexual attraction so inseparable from love, and from love's great master-principle of attraction. Our intense admiration of the mere *beauty* of a man or woman, that is to say of what seems to us their beauty, is not determining in friendship. Hence friendship can never be as vivid and masterful a power, not to say passion, as love. The latter ever remains the most vivid, mysterious and elementary emotion of the human race.

If friendship be free from real love-emotion, then friendship will be found to reach truest expression between individuals of the same sex. It represents thus what we will call "similisexual friendship." I am not disparaging here warm and dispassionate friendships between the opposite sexes, constantly met, and so-called (by a term long mis-used) "Platonic" in their nature. In place of that phrase we will call these "heterosexual friendships." But, no matter how firm and deep are countless instances of heterosexual friendships between persons of the opposite sexes, they do not compare favourably with similisexual friendships. Too frequently they attack elementary purity of the sentiment. Frequently also are they more or less sustained with self-deceptions; no matter what arguments and examples may bring against such a charge. We shall find it needful presently to question nicely the nature of many heterosexual friendships. We shall be obliged also to question, even more sharply in the close study of the Uranian and Uraniad life, the character of many similisexual ties, whether between men and men, or women and women; and our conventional ideas of them are likely to be changed before the analysis of this study will be finished. The whole theory of so-called Platonic friendships, of psychic ties of heterosexual kind, is ill-sustained by realities in human-nature and social history. The finest, most unalloyed friendship must be similisexual; even if we admit presently, in a sort of paradox that many relationships seeming precisely friendship are not so; many that seem not so being precisely such.

There is no grossening of human-nature, no injustice to the finer psychic qualities in us, when we accept the idea that love from one human being toward another must include the wish to possess physically, and the yearning to give oneself, physically. Even if such a rule seems to accentuate the merely animal-nature in man, we cannot get far away from the conclusion. If we are honest with ourselves and humanity we ought not to try to get away from it. Love must contain the sexual desire, the wish for physical possession of beauty. So long as we cannot descry clearer than we do the place of the brute-world in the mysterious general scheme of Nature we need not be too conservative about admitting ourselves as animals in many instincts. Here may be noted, à-propos of the brute-world, that friendship between beasts is a sentiment much less often marked than is one or other degree of sexual admiration and attraction. Interesting examples of friendships between brutes, wild or domestic, are often met; but they are disproportionate to the tendency of animals toward companionship through heterosexual love, or similisexual love: as will be touched on later.

In speaking of human love, we must differentiate in it certain strong affections often called love—maternal love, filial love, fraternal

"Natural Affections."

love, and so on. Such sentiments however spontaneous, deep and pure, are not love, as that sentiment really is, and as it should be distinguished from all non-sexual phases of our regard. Parental, filial, fraternal affections are called "love" only by a thousand-year-old looseness of ideas and terms. Such sentiments ought to be classed more popularly as "natural affections" just as by that term they are classed legally. However beautiful, they are far less certain, less genuine less obscure and less mysterious than love. They refer rather to friendship. They lack the essential sexual note, the desire for *possessing* beauty. Indeed we may grade the various kindly human sentiments that we feel for our fellow-beings as thus: love, friendship, natural affection, friendly human interest.

Similisexual Love.

The instant that the physical desire, with or without a concurrent spiritual desire, springs up in us, stirred to life by a quickening sense of physical beauty in the object of our interest, then there cannot be logical question of our sentiment being more than mere strong friendship, or more than a minor "natural affection." We are in the presence of passional sexual love; of such love in its lighter or more vehement character perhaps, but of erotic love. It is love, no matter what are the real or supposed sexes of the persons concerned. The instant that even vaguely we want to possess, and even vaguely feel that we would be willing to surrender ourselves along with the possession, then no matter how "impossible" how terrifying, how bewildering such an impulse be to us we love, we love sexually. From friendship, we are already far afield.

"Similisexual Love not admitted as Legitimate in Man."

But with this logical and inevitable conLegitimate in elusion, we come lace to lace with a convention long-sustained in generally intelligent circles of human thought with which we are put into startling and bewildered warfare. During a long succession of centuries, including especially those influenced by Jewish and Christian theological systems of morals and law, has been affirmed and re-affirmed, has been asserted in public literature and in private conversation, has been held as as a basal truth, that a man should love, should be sexually drawn to, a woman only; never to another man. In like manner, that a woman should love, should be attracted sexually, only to a man; never to another woman.

We have been assured, peremptorily, argumentatively, for at least a couple of thousand years, that if a man do not feel his sexual nature going out toward a woman, then something is distinctly minus in his body or in his temperament. But if he goes a step farther, and not only feels no sexual attraction to woman, but by some mysterious psychologic processes finds himself sexually attracted toward men, feels an admiring physical desire for them and their beauty, feels concurrent yearning to surrender himself physically to a man, youthful or elder, then he is a diseased abnormality, a shocking degenerate from manhood, a monster or a maniac. During long centuries the statute-books of the majority of European nations have expressly recognized such a man only as a monster and anomaly: and in respect of his working-out his sexual impulses of the kind, he ranks legally as a felon, in even many countries today.

Similar has been the popular ethical attitude of mind toward those mysterious, ungovernable impulses by which a certain equally large proportion of women are, contrary to the generality of the sex, drawn toward other women by sexual love, often along with complete sexual coldness toward men.

Woman's Similisexual Love Less Rebunked by Society and Law.

But in the case of such abnormal impulses on the part of women, it is important to observe that both socially and legally the matter is far lighter regarded. In fact, it is often smiled at as a feminine peccadillo of perverseness, a womanish weakness or sentimental excess, neglectable compared with what is called " unnatural " love in a man. The organic and bodily expression of a woman's sexual passion for another woman is less concrete than is the erotic embrace of the male. This too, affects the general social sentiment. A woman giving way to similisexual temperament is not a felon. Scarcely ever is her impulse spoken of by law-codes. The Mosaic

Canon, so severe as to similisexual love between men, and made the basis of much of our modern system of ethical law, ignores women in its denunciations, wholly. The New Testament Canon, the continuation of the Mosaic system in large part, makes no references to female impulses of the sort, except in the Pauline pastoral to the Romans.

Established Intolerance of the Modern World toward Similisexual Love.

Such is a brief statement of similisexual love, and of its positive distinctions from friendships; whether heterosexual or similisexual. We are all of us familiar, from youth up, with the attitude of the world, intolerant, horrified, arbitrary, toward any mature phases of it. We have heard it mocked in our boyish school-days, often with boyish hypocrisy. We have grown to manhood and to womanhood, accepting it as a vice and perversion, rightfully opposed by law, by all sound social morality. We have turned marvelling from the examples incessantly coming to light, existing all the world over, of especially a man's sexual love for another man. We have also restrictedly, confused it with a phase of it that demands always a swift and a severe repression, the debauchery of immature and innocent youth. We have wondered over the revelations of medical specialists' pamphlets; or at the testimony in a police-court dock during some "scandal-trial." By our elementary moral education, we have been taught that such a passion today is a perverse lapse to pagan and barbarous morals. Homosexual love when met, for instance, in particularly the Oriental and Latin races, we are told should mean imperfect moral education and regrettable racial instincts that are inferior to, especially, the Anglo-Saxon temperament and to Anglo-Saxon ethics; a relic of sheer primitive Eastern and Latin depravity, to which the civilized world lapses, just as a child commits a nastiness or tells a lie, because he has not outgrown evil predispositions. That such similisexual love is, now as ever, capable of agreement with the finest and purest social and moral civilization, the most distinct aestetic superiority, with the strongest religious quality in the race or the individual—these ideas will not be endured for a moment by the average Anglo-Saxon. He regards them as out of discussion. He has not even found it worth while, as a special and ethical problem, to think twice about them seriously, in his life.

Certain More Intelligent Liberalized Admissions and Ideas on the Topic.

It is true that, gradually, a more thoughtful element in general society has reflected uneasily, unwillingly. Confronted with history, with broad anthropologic theories, with startling incidents in all classes of contemporary social life, and with the discussions of foreign psychologic physicians set before them, many men and women have altered their attitude of repugnance even to look into the topic. Some English psychologists have gone so far as to reach, and to remain in, a tolerantly conservative position toward it. They have met with too many facts for feeling honestly clear as to old theories, however long-established. But this conservative class has not gone much further than the admission that "a dark problem in morals," "an unexplainable element in psychology" is involved. If one argue with them against classifying all homosexual impulses with barbarism, pointing out that precisely this instinct of similisexual love between man and man has always existed, side by side, with the finest social life, with the most virile militarism, with the highest moral and aesthetic civilizations of the past, even to being recognized as a great factor for social good, the argument is not accepted for a moment.

Similisexual Love Especially Declared Contrary to Christian Morals.

For, one is assured that no ancient civilizations obeyed the Christian Dispensation, or compare well with it; that Christian morals as the basis of all sound social and moral law, abhor the homosexual impulse; that the Christian Scriptures have placed it in the category of gravest sins and felonies: and that homosexualism entered into the decadence of races and nations, as an essential factor. We are also informed that similisexual love "has relatively disappeared"; is more and more forgotten, has become vagabond a moral perversion from humanity today, in all "high civilizations" and all "superior moral life." We are assured that human nature has emphatically "changed," in this respect as in others thanks to especially the powerful influence of the contemporary Judaic-Christian basis of social ethics. To all such replies, or to others equally without foundation in fact, one can quote only Christopher Sly, and exclaim that for the sake of those who believe possible such an atrophy of human nature, and who ignore plain and too-often distressing facts—"'Tis an excellent piece of work; would it were done!" We shall in another chapter estimate more minutely this matter.

Salient Aspects of Masculine Friendships.

EDWARD IRENAEUS PRIME-STEVENSON

Let us now turn to what is generally accepted as friendship between men and men. We will revert to what has been termed "similisexual friendship as distinguished from love; and will narrow our terminology by calling such masculine friendships "homosexual" friendships. I use the word "friendship" in this connection subject to general ideas on the matter; only, in fact, till I can make clearer to the reader the true nature of its tie, in numerous examples about us.

In the deep, often unaccountable, friendships between men, whether historic or commonplace, whether observed in the instances of others or in our own personal experience, has the reader never questioned if there be not some warmer, often more obscure and irresistible impulse promoting the sentiment? Certainly the need of referring-back many intensely intimate, passionate and "reasonless" homosexual friendships, so-called, to some sexual mystery often impresses itself on the psychologist. Various traits in such relationships quicken our suspicion. Constantly, disconcertingly occurs a new version of the old school-boy rhyme about Dr. Fell: we do not know, after all, *why* we like Jack or Harry, we only know that we do like them. Much opposes our sentiment often. But nothing conquers it.

The Seeming "Contrariness of Types" in Male. Friendships Often makes Similisexual Friendship a Puzzle to Observers.

One frequent characteristic is that the two men are not obviously harmonious psychically: not in their classes, their temperaments, their educations, intelligences, tastes, prejudices, practical interests and speech. Another curious objection is met when the two men-friends are not spiritual enough to be influenced by recondite intellectual currents, and are peculiarly averse from giving way to finer sorts of sentimentalities; concealing from the world any lapse toward such "weakness," as it seems to them. Again one understands less the basis of certain "friendships" when the time has been too short to allow so strong a mutual attraction to be developed by a gradual knowledge and study of one another. For, often in homosexual friendship, as in alterosexual love, one man merely crosses the pathway of the other. A few words, a few glances—and lo, relations perhaps mutually in a perfect balance or perhaps quite unequal, but affecting henceforth whatever are life and character for each, or for one the two men, spring into irresistible activity. Scarcely yet quite aware of each other's existence and Ego, a mutuality still unreasoned-out, a flower of passion, vague or absolute, germinated and ripened like the Hindoo juggler's mango-tree illusion, such an emotion crystallizes to one of the most beautiful psychologic situation that human nature experiences. This suddenness, of friendship, as a thing illogical as sudden love, is an every-day phenomenon. The men concerned in it are of every class and type. The same conditions of mystery in such processes apply, of course, to many sudden, intimate friendships between women.

The word "passionate" was written a moment ago, in speaking of the intenser and more concentrated ardours of male homosexual friendships. With that quality we reach what sharply engages the attention of the explorer into psychology of the affections. For, ever and ever again, in these warm, profound, apparently normal homosexual friendships, can be divined, or else is outspoken, the relative incapability of any woman to be an important sentimental and sexual influence over such preoccupied natures. The men concerned, or one of them, may present the type of the firm "holder-off" from any relations to women except what are relatively secondary, even apathetic. That is, to woman as a sex. She seems to have no power over the deepest emotional nature, in such men. She plays only a superficial, tolerated, casual rôle in their lives from day to day. Such men seem to say of love for a woman:

> *"It is to be all made of fantasy,*
> *All made of passion, and all made of wishes,*
> *All adoration, duty and observance.*
>
> . . . .
>
> *And so am I for—no woman!"*

We can indeed separate men, roughly-classed, into three distinct groups as to their social attitudes toward woman. They are either woman-haters, or woman-tolerators, or woman worshippers. These three divisions take in pretty completely male humanity, past and present. The woman-worshipper, or gynolator, is the most frequently met, provided we can rely on the sincerity of his outward demeanor. But often he is more politic than sincere; appreciating the need socially of playing his deferential rôle to the

Men Classed According to their Standpoint toward Women: the Woman-Hater, the Woman-Tolerator, and the Woman-Worshipper.

full. For, just this type, the woman-worshipper, frequently is disclosed to us in history, biography and daily social life as in his most intimate relationship, only if united by friendship of passionate sort with some man-friend.

The same statement is more clearly true of the second-named class, the woman-tolerators. Their attitude—civil, graceful, reticent, dispassionate toward women-acquaintances protects them from critical rebuke from women about them: but includes no real homage to woman as an indispensable factor in the mental or physical well-being of such males. This attitude is not of the sort to bring reproach on such men as generally selfish or aesthetically unimpressionable. Often they are nothing of the sort.

The So-called Woman Hater.

The declared, or undeclared woman-hater, in all sorts of protean forms, Irequently exaggerates his pose and enmity. Sometimes, too, it is a jest with him. But the instances are countless when such aversion is neither his joke nor that of acquaintances. His gradations vary from downright boorish enmity to courteous scorn: and of course they may be the result of some painful experience: not enmity that springs out of an inborn repugnance or indifference. Succeding pages of this study can painfully illustrate this fact. But frequently the woman-hater, outspoken or tacit, is neither an eccentric nor a misanthrope; but a gynophobe by his inborn, unchangeable nature. With such women-haters, when men of finer mould and character, we are likely to meet often an interesting special type, the man born for friendship, for "friendship" only; with his own sex only. We discern that his emotional nature is anchored to that, is satisfied with that. Such a man's innermost soul is created to thrill in that masculine atmosphere, as in no other. "Friendship" becomes the secret fire and spirit-throb of his social existence. In such a sentiment arise his profoundest, his most sacred joys and griefs, his most vivid enthusiasms and repulsions. There pivot themselves instinctively his sharpest differences, his passionate dependencies, his most humbling reconciliations, his noblest sacrifices, fullest altruisms, even to utter self-forgetfulness. By this spell the man's Ego also can commit itself to melancholy errors, to cruel disillusions of sentiments; can become subjected to an hundred influences for good or harm in his character and life, all exactly as in that other more widely understood relation—that to a woman—the alterosexual love. This deep "friendship" (again I am using a term subject frequently to question) often develops when both parties, or one of the two men, can be set down distinctively as woman-tolerator, or woman-hater. Less frequently it comes to our notice with the woman-worshipper, though

Observation of Donnay.

we shall see presently how it can be consistent in a most significant degree, with the outward professions of some absolute Don Juan.

A happy medium between the womanhater and the woman-tolerator, one frequent in smart social life, is admirably defined by the brilliant French dramatist, Donnay, in a dialogue between two men, in his penetrating psychologic comedy "Amants," where the cynical de Sambré ridicules the woman-adoring Vétheuil for his servitude to the sex. De Sambré says:

"I have had commerce, that's the word, with different womenkind. Rut I've never *loved* any of them! . . . My dear fellow, its all very simple. The Orientals, they have perfectly understood woman; they have put her in the place where she belongs. We don't live in the Orient but in the Occident; so of course it isn't a matter of making our women wear veils, of keeping them shut up between four walls and eunuchs; but there is the necessity for us of shutting up the *moukère* morally, intellectually, in a harem. That is to say, we must not permit her to go wandering around in the domain of our thoughts, any more than in the avenues of our hearts the streets of our occupations. You understand? . . . Oh yes, you ask what is to be done if she deceives us? as is inevitable, for she will bore herself to death in the moral harem. Let her deceive! Ho you think I am bothering about mere contingencies? No, no, the thing is that in such conditions woman does not *trouble* a man any more that is the essential! Her power over a man is curiously reduced; *then* when she gives herself, whether to you or to your neighbour, you can put the fact down to real value, and not to a factitious value, the result of our prejudices, our pride, our fancies. . . You suppress idle gallantry, you suppress paying your court, jealousy, all such things which take up an enormous amount of time, when even they do not take up a man's entire life! Look at the sort of man who at twenty-five years of age is still influenced by women! He can do nothing really useful, serious, in life. How old are you, Vétheuil? I don't know—thirty-four perhaps. What have you done with your time?

You've lost it in women's bedrooms, till now you are fairly isolated under the skirts of the women, sunk in the middle of the, ocean of the world, like a diver under his glass bell, as Jean-Haul Richter says. Ah, my dear fellow! there are more interesting things to do, more interesting problems to solve, in any science you please!"

Historic Types of Deep Friendships Between Men of Various Temperaments and Attitudes toward Woman.

The types of great "friendships," of passionate intimacy, between two men oi sensitive mutuality through life, or long periods of life, have multiplied through the world's social history. Such male pairs have become household names; beloved ideals forever. We go back to the very nursery, to school-forms and our earliest personal interests in humanity to meet them. Legend, myth, history and religion blend in their circle. They are so frequent even in our own unromantic date, that they almost make it needless to mention here more than a few typical instances. Damon and Pythias, Orestes and Pylades, Harmodios and Aristogeiton, Nisus and Euryalus, Alexander the Great and Hephaestion, Julian the Apostate and Sallustius, stand forth out of Grecian and Roman classics. David and Jonathan, Christ and John, the beloved young Disciple, are familiar Biblical "friendships" of exceeding beauty and sentimental tenderness. Coming down into the light of common day the list shines brightly. All tempers, all races, all professions add to it, be its colouring now of one tinge, now of another. Michael Angelo Buonarrotti and Tommaso Cavalieri, Cinq-Mars (Henri d'Effiat) and François de Thou, Shakespeare and the young Earl of Southampton. Sir Philip Sydney and his three beloved friends Greville, Dyer and Languet; Montagne and Etienne de la Boetie, Erasmus of Rotterdam and "that one companion of my innermost life"; the learned Beza and his "other self," young Audebert: Edward II of England and Piers Gaveston; James I of England and those intimacies, so strangely passional which James maintained with Robert Carr, Villiers, (Buckingham) and others; Frederick the Great with Baron Trenck, Lieutenant Kette, Graf von Görz, and others; the dauntless Charles XII of Sweden with brother-soldiers sometimes far inferior in rank; the philanthropic Bishop Jocelyn of Clogher and the ill-fortuned soldier Henry Moverly; Lord Byron with Lord Clare, Nicolo Giraud and Eddleston; Horace Walpole in the one—perhaps—deep sentiment of Walpole's life, Sir Henry

Conway; Grillparzer and Georg Altmütter; the masterly historian Johannes Müller and Bonstetten; the unhappy Ludwig II of Bavaria with many men whose kingdoms were only of art or letters, including Richard Wagner, and the gifted and erratic actor Joseph Kainz: the fiery General Skobeleff and his mysterious "Vassilieff" not to mention two or three others; General Gordon brave, yet tender, with Lord Arthur Hamilton—but no need to cite further the record of typically profound "friendships." Worth noting is the fact that many of them refer us not only to aesthetic life, but to the military profession and temperament, to the most genuine and even stalwart masculinity of physiques and occupations, with no trace or possible shade of effeminacy, or of a degeneracy of mind or body in such men-types.

Nor are impressive and fine homosexual and similisexual "friendships" the property of cultivated natures only. The humblest circles of a country village, the rudest regiment of foot-soldiery, the ship, the factory, the shop, the prison-pen and the chain-gang, tell the same tale of one man's heart meeting another's heart, with a regard that the Scriptural words long ago ranked truthfully as "passing the love of women." And in natures otherwise immature we find striking examples of a ripened and profound sentiment. Between mere lads, youths in schools and colleges, are evolved sex-dramas of tragical force; the child the father of the man in this, as in other things.

The Illusive Element of Many Profound "Friendships" so-called: and certainty of Dispute.

In a large proportion of such typical "homosexual friendships" no third party is in a position to perceive the real origin and quality of the sentiment. The world takes for granted that it is based in a strictly intellectual process. It is regarded as a mental affiliation, primarily a result of tastes and circumstances more or less matter of fact. That it can be an absolutely or partially erotic impulse, an irresistible sexual attraction, a love, a sexual desire of the man, either completely or fractionally, this is frequently not perceived. Nor is popularly admitted that logical ground for such a construction of it can exist in normal and moral human natures. Little is the fact understood that while many, many such friendships do, indeed begin and progress as relatively spiritual and dispassionate relations, they can develop into a similisexual love: which love is their mystic *raison d'être*, without quite obvious attributes of it in natures concerned. Certainly into similisexual, homosexual loves, qualified as "friendships" can be fused much that is wholly intellectual, and unsexual. But when the subtle erotic quality wakens, either earlier or later in the bond, often it never loses its dominant chemical force in the tie till the bodily powers and sex-emotion alike decline with declining life, quite as in the case of alterosexual love. But let us observe that merely to suggest the presence of sexual passion on the part of either friend, the workings of a conscious or sub-conscious sexual nature, "the desire of beauty," is to meet a shocked, a disgusted incrudelity. "Surely we know better than that!" No, no! In such a friendship as So-and So with So-So, no such abominable perversion exists." So cries, perhaps, the reader of these lines, as he reflects on examples of close and tender masculine intimacies that he feels sure he "knows inside-out," either historic ones or as mere instances about him that are pertinent; or as he recalls his own friendships. The suggestion of physical impulses in them sets the average observer vis-à-vis with what he calls vile, monstrous and unnatural. In fact, the idea of a physical passion between man and man, as between women and women, he cannot "understand," cannot conceive its concrete satisfaction. It seems to him to outrage all sexualism, the logic of virility and femininity; especially virility. There will be time presently to discuss whether in masculine friendships the element of a satisfied physical desire offers anything unnatural and abnormal. With the study of the Uranian and Uraniad Intersexes we come upon that matter.

The "Sexual Germ" in Friendships.

Meantime, however displeasing to the reader, let it be affirmed that all real friendships between men have a sexual germ. Also can one declare it as a perfectly assured fact, in hundreds of instances of noble and honoured friendships, those suggesting the "model," the "ideal" sort, between men, that the concrete sexual tie and its satisfaction, have been of the first importance in the relation. That has been originally its master-factor. That has rendered such so-called "friendship" the most concentrated and absorbing of similisexual loves. No matter what have been the biographic glosses and subterfuges, no matter what have been the amiable fictions, no matter how indignant have been the denials, the real bond was welded by a profound, mysterious, noble, passionate sexualism. Such too, are examples that every day could disclose about us, right and left. Everywhere are the ties absolutely embodying the antique, eternal sentiment; yet trembling at revelation of it to the outside world. The link is a marriage of the body as well as of the soul. It is a love: not a friendship. It is the supremely virile love, expressing itself as human nature, naturally and inevitably, ever has expressed itself in a vast proportion of all races and grades of mankind. But such physical erotism in multitudinous instances has not a jot impaired the high spiritual quality of the relation. It has often enriched it. The psychic and the physical have been blent in it, in an harmonious chemistry, too subtle and natural for vulgar analysis. The bodily and the spiritual passion have been each the complement of the other, by Nature's initiative, and by Divine impulsion.

The "Instinctively" Conservative Attitude toward Women on the Part of Many Men: Its Unchanged Presence Subconsciously.

We may often be misled by one trait external to such mysterious passion in similisexual intimacies—the attitude of one or both friends toward women. Damon is not a woman-hater, not a mere woman-tolerator, perhaps: but a woman-amateur, even to being a *coureur des femmes* at least by repute. Pythias often plays his social role of woman-enthusiast, with the finest touches of art and nature. But the two friends knows what we do not know. Their comedy can be smiled at or deplored by them, according to its difficulties and necessities. Marriage can hide the real situation of the similisexual love. But marriage can try in vain to expel it. Damon remains Damon, Pythias remains Pythias, to one another, no matter what upper currents of their emotional life help them or oblige them to keep their secret. In the majority of such really similisexual bonds, the attitude toward women ranges from the generally cordial and admiring, but never self-committing, to the cold and aloof one. The man never wholly surrenders himself; even when he appears to do so. His real self, his full, absolute Ego, surrenders only with his male Mend. We shall understand shortly why this is inevitably of such intense personal significance to him, for his joy or grief, for his good or ill; why so often he feels, with a sentiment far deeper and more sexual than is guessed, the message in Emerson's vibrant lines on male friendships, and the "hidden life" in them:

"A ruddy drop of manly blood
The surging sea outweighs.
The world uncertain comes and goes,
The lover, rooted, stays.

. . . .

My careful heart was free again

"O, friend," my bosom said,
Through thee alone the sky is arched,
Through thee, the rose is red!
All things through thee take nobler form,
And look beyond the earth;
And is the mill-round of our fate,
A sun-path in thy worth!
Me, too, thy nobleness has taught
To master my despair;
The fountains of my hidden life
Are through thy friendship fair."

IV

Similisexual Love in the Brute World; in Primitive, Barbarous and Semi-Civilized Man; in Ancient Civilizations and Religions; and under Ancient and Modern Statutory Law

The distinctly individual and biographic contents of this study will be regarded by the less philosophic with more interest than these preliminary analyses of various aspects of similisexual passion. But only through these considerations can one enter with full intelligence on the narratives and other clinical memoranda of Uranian and Uraniad types.

Similisexual Love in the Brute Creation.

When we look into sexualism in the brute-world we soon discern that nothing could be more the misuse of a term than to speak of similisexual passion as "against nature," an an "unnatural" impulse, and so on. Everyday observation, wherever wild animals or tame are to be watched, convinces us of the in-rooted propensity. The entire chain of beasts, birds, fishes, reptiles, and rather in proportion to advances in fineness of nervous organism, practice similisexual habits, by inborn impulses and deliberate choice. By an odd contradiction of phrase, the tendency is called both an "unnatural" and a "bestial" one, In the mammals, the horse, the dog, the camel, the ass, the elephant, all members of the ursine, lupine, bovine and rodent families, the larger and the smaller felidae, and in particular the ape and monkey, entire genera are given to it. In Dr. Garnier's interesting work on Onanism he gives many instances. The preference on the part of the animal for sexual gratification with its own sex instead of with the opposite one, does not necessarily originate in the fact that the male, for instance, has no access to the female for heterosexual copulation. On the contrary his inclination seems deliberate, often to obstination.

In birds the tendency is also general. A great proportion of birds make no distinction whatever between copulating with the male or the female; actively or passively participating in it. The same obedience to either the active or passive role is observed in many common beasts. One of our domestic animals giving us every day the most common proof of making no distinction as to sexual passion, the dog, is rarely willing to be passive in the act; though the dog, occasionally, seems to prefer that form. The word "dog" in all oriental languages, especially in Scriptural usages, is synomous for sodomite, etc.

In the entomological kingdom most interesting habits of deliberate, preferred similisexual intercourse between male insects have been minutely observed and recorded. The reader, is referred to the notes of Professor Karsch of Berlin, and to Kelch, Noel, Osten-Sacken, Lacassagne and others, either directly or as cited by Moll, Ellis, and others when treating of human similisexualism. But the naturalist does not discover any new general principle when studying the instinct in the animal-world. Pliny and Aristotle noted it, and even argued from it toward the general problem.

We may also take note of the fact that botany is not altogether silent on the question of similisexual relations between plants. Something much like (strange as it seems) a deliberate similisexual intention has been studied by several botanists of authority in connection with researches into fertilization and cross-fertilizations.

In Primitive Man.

We turn to primitive man; or at least to far-away periods of human social and racial existence. What was the attitude of individuals or nations toward similisexual passion when men were uninfluenced by artificial cultures, and followed the lead of plain natural impulses?

That it was a primitive, natural predisposition in human nature, is hardly contestable, even if the scrawls of troglodytes and lacustrine savages do not speak of it. The oldest Oriental and Latin and Hellenic writers found it active in the barbarous nations with whom they came into contact, in war or peace. Today, the explorers in the wilds of the savage-world have found it rooted, contrary to theories of its relation to advanced esthetic life. The savage still regards it largely as of no import, morally or physiologically. Similisexual love, the will to satisfy it, has among its paradoxes this one, that it pervades quite uncultured natures, while also appearing to be to be a direct consequent of aesthetic and intellectual cultivation. To refined civilizations it is almost an inevitable accompaniment, ever working along the nervous lines of aesthetic susceptibility. But also it occurs distinctly where all society's concepts are rudimentary. The savages of Asia, Central Africa and East-Indian islands, the Esquimaux, the Patagonian and Red Indian tribesmen, the barbaric dwellers in the archipelagoes of the Pacific, are all given to similisexual practices, whether between men and men or between women and women, but especially in its male phases. Among that mystic and ever-primitive race, the Gipsies, the passion of the male for the male, and its frankest physical gratification is current, especially in Central-European *Zigeunerthum*. The ancient Scythians so accepted the instinct of sexual relations between males that a special class of well-conducted male prostitutes was organized by that warlike people. The primitive German and Gothic races were given to it, coincidental with their strongest military periods. Today it is one of the racial traits of their descendants. The Etruscans were peculiarly given to similisexualism and the Tuscans and Umbrians have inherited its passions. It was a part of the Aztec social system, and even of Aztec religions, and Central America and South America know it instinctively.

In Assyrian, Babylonian and Egyptian Races.

In the social life of those great past peoples, the Assyrian, Babylonian and Egyptian nations, similisexual love, at least between males, was more or less a recognized and even legitimate factor, physiologic and spiritual. The sexual charm of the male for the male, the influence of his beauty as an esthetic force on his own sex, appears to have been taken for granted as natural, and seldom was discountenanced. Of a prevalence of female similisexualism we have no historic record, but its existence is beyond doubt. Earliest legislation took little or no control of the, similisexual impulses and habits. In -Egypt there seems to have been no period when men were not accustomed to give free course, as by natural right, to the passion. In all dynasties, in all classes, in the army, the priesthood, in civil life, it was well-known.

Here we may notice a matter, referring to Egypt, that will be found significant; painfully so when presently we look at the attitudes of modern criminal-law toward the passion. In Egypt, at the time of Moses and the Jewish servitude, similisexualism could be easily

Why Similisexual Love was so Severely Denounced by the Mosaic Code.

a deterrent, of importance, to increase of population. It was especially a check of the male and "war-available." Sexual intercourse between men was a foe to normal sexual satisfaction, to heterosexual love, and so to early marriages and offspring. Undoubtedly the habit was rooted in the Hebrew people when, for generations captive to the Egyptian race, saturated with all that was Egyptian, morally, socially and religiously. Moses, or whoever, whatever, is typified by Moses, the shrewd, far-seeing law-giver, had his mind fixed on, not only the deliverance of his race hut on its uttermost expansion as a people, a fighting people. There were arduous campaigns before the Hebrews for their establishment as a dominant race. Hence Mosaic laws set severe penalties against masculine similisexualism. The new nation must be made populous as well as prosperous. Every individual male was to count. Every family was to be urged to increase and multiply, or the military occupation of the Promised Land would be impossible. Accordingly the early Hebrew legislation repudiated on a distinctly religious basis, and branded as a moral and religious offence, an impulse that has no natural, no spiritual reasons for such prohibition any more than has the classing of one or another beast as a "clean" or "unclean" article of diet. The Mosaic ban of semilisexualism had a direct relation to economy of sexual powers, and to population.

The "Sin of Sodom" never a Sin, and Never Established as Such by the Story of Lot, etc.

Naturally one is told by surprised objectors to this plain fact, that the "earlier," "ante-Mosaic," civilization opposed similisexual love; punished mercilessly sexual intercourse of the kind. So we have been informed, when especially the story of Lot and his mysterious guests in Sodom is cited. But such objectors will do well to understand once for all (likely for the first time) that the entire episode of Lot and the wicked men of Sodom does not afford any grounds for arguing that Sodom was destroyed on account of its similisexual tastes and practices, or that Sodom was really given to such. Further, we have no proof that homosexual intercourse was ever special to Sodom, ever was or is an offense to God, even to a Jehovistic concept of God; nor that what the world's statute-books, and pulpit-parlance especially, have so long termed "sodomy" should ever have such a meaning. The incident of Lot and his guests, and of the mob that attacked Lot's house in Sodom with the clamorous "Bring out the men, that we may *know* them!" correctly read, is simply a common civic episode of a suspicious Oriental town. A mob-element being excited, feared some political treachery; and violated the hospitality that Lot had offered to two strangers, supposed to be spies or what else, by the unfriendly crowd. There is no textual or other reason to give the verb "know" a sexual value, no warrant for sexual colouring of the affair. Almost exactly the same incident occurs in another defense of guests; set forth in Judges XIX, vv. 16–26 (retold in Chap. XX, vv. 4–5) in the night-attack of the curious and alarmed townsmen of the city of Gibeah. There, too, a stranger, a Levite, had been taken into a house, with the same Eastern hospitality, and saved his life by allowing his concubine to be the victim of the mob, precisely as Lot offered his virgin daughters. Both episodes are plainly tales of violated hospitality. The same devices to appease the citizens are mentioned; but there is no evidence even in this last detail of sexual insults to the guest. In the story of the Levite, we distinctly read that the object of the attack was because "they thought *to have slain*" him; and Sodom's mob included both "young and old, all the people from every quarter." The two stories are absolutely of Oriental "guest and host" duties and claims.

The Mosaic charge to Israel that similisexual love was an abomination in the sight of the Jewish Jehovah, a particular moral enormity meriting death, had no basis in any moral "revelation to Moses," any more than had other wise provisions of the Mosaic Code. The warning, the death-penalty, were inserted for directly practical motives, not theological nor ethical objections. (The very words that are used of similisexual relations as a *sin*, refer to many other matters often; to what we consider quite minor offenses). Let us note, for other example, the story of Onan. There is absolutely no ground in the incident of Onan and the spilled seed, for regarding masturbation as a moral obliquity. Onan was not punished for what was a moral sexual dereliction *per se;* but for unwillingness to marry his brother's widow, and to raise up a family for his brother's name; a breach of religion, of Oriental civil-custom, in Onan's early day. Onan, like many men, has his name used as a reproach against him and his posterity, by an injustice to the man and the action. We can admit that the Mosaic Code put similisexual passion and its gratification in line with grave moral, social, religious offenses, with rape, murder, idollatry, bestiality. But such a juxtaposition and the death-penalty for homosexual relations should never have been taken by later and non-Israelitish peoples as referring such sexual intercourse, between men and men, or women and women, to the unnatural, or to the ethically vicious.

There is interest in our also noticing here that though Moses so plainly includes bestiality as an offence, laying stress on feminine intercourse with a beast, he makes no allusion to similisexual passion between two women, general as it must have been in the Egyptian and Hebrew social life.

The Status of Mosaic—Judaic Law, and Canon Law through Christian Ethics, as an Unwarrantable Position.

We are thus brought all at once to a peculiarly important, a startling but irresistible conclusion. Our general fabric of modern and Christian law, directly and indirectly, being so considerably informed with ideas and provisions of the Mosaic Code, in spite of the weight of Roman and other legislative codes that enter into modern legislation and ethical feeling, we realize that the attitude of Christian civilization and of Christian morals toward similisexual love and its gratification is simply a relic of ancient Jewish, semi-civilized dispensations. Legislation against it utters a moral-social sentiment with which we have, today, rightfully, little or nothing to do.

More than this, however startling to us, let us observe also that similisexualism has never by right known any essential, even inferred, prohibition in the real Christian system. For, the position of the Gospel narratives, the attitude and expressions or silences of Christ as to it, point out differentially the fact that what the Apostles affirmed of it was on their own authority; merely part and parcel of the Judaism with which, from the very beginning, Christianity has been so loaded down. From that it suffers today only too much. The purest New Testament ethical dispensation ever should ignore homosexualism, when we look closely into the finer origins of gospel ethics. Our criminal laws, so much infused with old Canon Law, with mediaevally religious views, have perpetuated the hostile sentiment and error. In fact, the attitude of Christ toward many recondite human relations raises the question of how far Christ himself is an illustration of the emotion of similisexual love, with its concurrent reserve toward any warmer relationships to woman than that of son or friend or teacher. We also justly can infer that Apostolic Christianity pronounced against intersexualism through policy, quite as much as through moral antagonism of Jewish colour.

Similisexual Love in Greece in Classic Epochs.

We reach now the race and the civilization commonly most associated with similisexual love, as an open element of emotion and civil life. The passion early received one of its names, "Greek love" from significance in almost every period of Hellenic society. It was instinctive to the Greek temperament, a temperament at once rugged and yet aesthetically sensitive as in no other race. Similisexuality long-time has been spoken of also as "Greek friendship." This is a misleading term, since similisexualism often was distinguished by Greek psychists and philosophers and legislators from friendships between men and men, or women and women, on lines that have differentiated it in the preceding chapter. We may indeed say that certain of the finest epochs of Grecian military dominancy, and esthetic, sensitiveness were informed saturated, ruled by homosexualism. That a man should be sexually attracted, enthralled, by the corporeal beauty of another male being, as well as won to him by intellectual and moral attractions in the object of his passion, was regarded as wholly natural. The sentiment was outspoken exactly as the heterosexual love was outspoken. Often the freest and happiest mutual course was given it. It was admired, idealized and reverenced. Heroic Greece, warlike Greece, pacific Greece, philosophic Greece, aesthetic and ethic Greece recognized its natural impulses. A man's sexual love for a man or for a youth, at certain periods was accounted purer, more elevating and manly than love for woman. The Greek was a passional woman-lover, frequently. But the sentiment for mistress or betrothed or wife was, over again, ranked as inferior to the heroic and mysterious similisexual flame. This, instead, became a leaven and lever in statecraft. It strengthened the young warrior's spirit in battle, as he fought for, or beside, the "dear companion." It struck down tyrants, breathed life into art and letters, idealized human nature. It was prehistorically a part of the Olympian system of Hellenic mythology, from Jupiter downward. Especially it gave rise to the Platonic theory of the Two Venuses; Venus Pandemonia inspiring the heart with love for the other sex; the other a Venus Urania, the greater and more elementary Venus, that inspires a man's passion for a man. It endured through many Hellenic periods, though subject to important civil attitudes, including hostile ones. Greece today knows it, as does the rest of the modern world, though in its relatively clandestine relation to daily life. As Hellenic society and states declined, the phases of similisexual love altered; its quality abased, becoming vulgarized in tone and idealism. It transferred itself, under such derogatory phases, into the Roman social fabric, though it was not in the least new to Oscan, Etruscan and early Latin civilizations. Even to day, it survives in a particular frankness and purity in a spot near its original Grecian home. A similisexual love between men, that frequently offers much of the heroic and ideal, is found in the wild and reticent clans of the Albanians; honourably recognized by that warlike and imaginative race as a distinct sentimental factor; and there, too, as a sentiment by no means of the "disembodied" type.

Was Similisexual Love Primitive, and of the Heroic Age, in Greece?

Certain students of the similisexual instinct in Hellenic life have claimed that the earliest periods of Greek society, particularly the Heroic and Homeric Epochs recognized only a spiritual, intellectual love between man and man; a sentiment intensely romantic and absorbing, even to excluding love for woman, but without the wish for physical gratification. We are asked to recognize in the bond between, for instance, Achilles and Patroclus only this abstract and ideal love. The notion is incorrect. The mistake originated with the wish of later apologists to gloss over the true elements of such relationship. Especially did such a view become part of the aim of Judaic and Christian ethics to define similisexual love between men as a depraved pagan impulse; not compatible with elevated heathenism, or with finer heroic temperaments. The same insistence on such heroic "friendship" as having no physical undercurrent, has dealt dishonestly with Biblical and other Oriental male affinities; with thousands of modern historic examples. It has been accented by a sort of perverse suppression of biographical details; by following too reticent or too ignorant guides.

But we must point out that the Greeks themselves made at least three important distinctions as to homosexualism, during various periods of their social fabric. They did, indeed, recognize a merely spiritual passion and bond, untouched by physical desires. This type, however it was

The Distinctions in Hellenic Love.

confused with a much less ideal sentiment, existed and it was much lauded; as it deserved. But it was not love, but friendship, at its highest throb. As regards it we also have reason to believe that many aspects which the idealists in Greece permitted to this psychic relationship, as details of its spirituality, were blended with physical desires. A calmer sentiment bespeaks maturity of the ages, minds and tempers in the two friends. Second, we find current in Greece the similisexual physical love confessedly, or under a veil; including high idealism, intellectual companionships, completion of the friend's existence, along with the physical passion for him, and its natural satisfaction. This is a sort of similisexual passion and love-sentiment in which the friends are relatively of equal and fairly mature ages. It needs a ripened emotionality on both sides, a harmonious and balanced union. Last, we must record the fact that as Greek social civilization developed at the expense of its heroic quality, as Greek military spirit weakened, there increased in the aesthetic Hellene his sense of merely boyish beauty, with his desire of mere physical possession of a youth. This sentiment we know today under the phases of Pederasty, or boy-love, on the part of the man. Beyond dispute, this was and is a lower, in some sense a decadent aesthetic emotion. It was probably wrought into the Greek temperament by Oriental and outside influences; at least they developed it materially. It was the surrender of the Hellene to his more superficial sense of what is indeed, a peculiarly winning expression of human beauty; but one divorced in too large degree from the intellectual dignity and mature beauty that enters into fine similisexual love. In such a sentiment lurks contravention of childhood, damage to emotional tranquillity and innocence of youth. It becomes a baneful social influence, and a menace to national and individual well-being, whether in Greece or any other land, whether in past epochs, or about us to day.

Attitudes of Greek Society toward Pederasty.

Pederasty became a most influential sentiment in Greek life, during numerous periods of greater or lesser importance and interest. As its harmful relations to youth became clearer understood, it was directly legislated against, often most severely, by Greek lawgivers; sometimes was strongly repudiated socially. But this hostile attitude was a fluctuating matter. Through long epochs of all that was most Greek, boy-love was regarded as quite as legitimate and ideal a sentiment as the love of a man for a woman, or even more so. General was the passion of a man, not merely a young man, or a lad, for the loveliness of a boy just verging on manhood, and so uniting especially the first potency of the masculine physique with the grace of the feminine, and at the same time offering the spontaneous psychic charm of youthful, boyish natures. Pederastic admiration was outspoken and accepted by all classes, from philosophers and poets to statesmen or the humblest citizens. The Greek lyric and dramatic writers made it their theme. Theognis, Anacreon, Pindar, Meleager, Euripides, Plato, Lucian, Athenaeus, and so on in an endless succession, "married it to immortal verse," to noble prose or to learned study. Amusingly, we discover how Socratism juggled rhetorically with it. For, it is true that we find the Greek philosophers, eternal straw-splitters, often insisting on line distinctions in the quality of pederasty. They persisted in giving it as far as possible an intellectual

EDWARD IRENEAEUS PRIME-STEVENSON

and educational and other complexions. They draped elegantly its nudely physical quality, they made it what we might call pedophily, in place of pederasty. But it is not easy to believe in the sincerity of the average Greek pedophilist in vigorous and normal life, who repudiated all idea of bodily desire in his passion for a beautiful youth. Socrates cannot be acquitted of just this real and natural sort of similisexual love of the pederastic sort. His admirations and intimacies were not merely psycho-pedophilic: no matter what are specious counter-arguments or such occasional anecdotes as that well-known one by Alcibiades—a tale of dubious sincerity. Indeed much of what is written as "apologetic" and controversial of pederasty in Hellenic temperaments is rhetoric. The pages of Plutarch and of Athenaeus are lavish in instances of the fact that every phase of hellenic society was influenced by the physical passion of the male for the male. Grave political events could turn on such a sentiment, and even valuable national concomitants. In Plutarch's Life of Pelopidas, a considerable account occurs of the celebrated "Sacred Band," originated by Gorgias, exclusively composed of young warriors. Each one was the declared lover of some comrade, his associate in battle or peace, with whom his career and life were indissolubly united in a homosexual emotion, tending toward their mutual advance in bravery and virtue. The story of Aristides specially recognizes the fact that the life-long feud between Aristides and Themistocles took its course because of their early rivalry for the love of a certain youth called Stesilaos of Keos, spoken of "as the most beautiful young man of his time;" for the exclusive possession of whom the two men struggled obstinately. Plutarch says that this Stesilaos "was adored by them both with an affection that passed all bounds." Agesilaos the noble sovereign of Sparta, was highly susceptible to similisexual passions. His relationships to one or another beautiful boy, were famous. We read of his intimacy with Megabetes, the handsome son of Spithridates; of the swift attraction which he exercised on the beautiful young son of Pharnabazus; of his similisexual attitude toward the young king Agesipolis, his ward; indeed of his special approval of all such sentiments. Agesilaos seems to have transmitted his similisexualism to his son, Archidamos; for we have an account of Archidamos as the lover of a beautiful lad named Kleomenes, the same youth who presently died a glorious death in battle, and upon whose body another young man named Panteus committed suicide in his intense grief and love; an historical incident worthy the pen of a Vergil. Again, in the history of the tyrannical Demetrius comes the story of Damocles "the Beautiful." This boy was famed far and wide for his surpassing loveliness. Demetrius was determined to possess him, and laid all manner of plans to that end. The boy would none of him. One day, the tyrant, inflamed with his lust, surprised the boy alone, in a private bath; for Damocles had avoided all public places of the kind, so hateful to him was the passion of the prince. Finding that this time he was helpless, the lad threw himself into the boiling water, and so perished, rather than allow himself to be enjoyed by a man whom he loathed.

Many more historic passages to the point can be cited from Hellenic authours of history. We shall see later what belles-lettres afford, in the same key.

In short, similisexual love and its intercourse in Hellenic life was, for the most part, put on a footing with heterosexual love, even when it narrowed itself, not to say degenerated, to pederasty as a merely physical rather than spiritual impulse. When pederastic, it was not legislated-against nor frowned-down, except when dangers to the intellectual, moral and physical development of the lad and disturbance in the family were perceived, and properly made a serious consideration. It was satirized as a weakness, reproved as a lapse, by philosophers and poets when it was not excepted-against in any statutory manner.

Feminine Similisexualism in Greece.

The similisexual passion between women appears with distinctness in Greek social life, and enters into Hellenic literature with emphasis. It has, in fact, received a specific name, Lesbianism, from the relationship of the great woman-poet of Hellas to the passion. "Greek love" as a term has been long applied almost as particularly to female similisexualism, and to its grosser phases, as it has been to masculine passion. But no legislative notice was taken of feminine similisexualism by Greek statutory law. Society smiled at it, or ignored it; just as is the case today. It never acquired any dignified philosophic or other recognition in Greece, at any time; apparently being relegated to the indifference that was felt toward much that was feminine, by the Hellene.

Rooted in the primitive Etruscan and and Latin peoples, a covert passion in the earlier and less aesthetic Roman State, strengthened by

Similisexual Love in Rome.

Greek and Oriental influences in proportion to the progress of luxury and loss of idealism in later periods of Roman civilization, the sexual passion of the male for the male pervaded Rome with cumulative vigour. Throughout classic and pagan epochs, it was, successively, either tolerated; or merely spasmodically reprehended as a civil danger, rather than treated through any general moral question of it; or satirized, idealized, glorified; or simply taken for granted. We are often assured that *primitive* Latin society was a stranger to it, or regarded it as a moral disgrace. This is not the fact, any more than that it became first influential in Latin character through importation from Greece. It did however suffer shameful debasements from Greek ideals, when Roman corruption of social morals was at the fullest, along with the Roman grossness that distorted so much of what in Greek conditions was richly ideal and spiritual.

Rome republican and monarchical, Rome military and pacific, Rome m power and decadence, was a Rome similisexual as to love. Under the Republic, a certain vague attitude of rebuke to it seems to have existed, but not as to feminine similisexualism. Of the remote Scatinian Law that bore on it, we have vague data; that law appears to have referred to special pederastic practices and to the protection of innocent youth from debauchery. The Lex Julia, another early law dealing with the matter, is also obscure in its scope. We can note the presence of a special legislation of some sort that related to soldiers when in military service, needing a bodily vigour not to be impaired in camps and barracks. This latter detail, by the way, is today recognized by modern Italian law, which otherwise takes no notice of sexual passions or practices between men and men, men and youths, women and their own sex, unless public decency is openly outraged, force used, or minor youth debauched.

In Primitive Rome.

Under the Roman Empire, however, similisexual love reached a degree of open acceptance, stood on a sentimental footing, in Roman society that met almost no repudiation of it by popular notions. We have but to turn to the pages of the finest flower or the rankest weed-growth of Latin literature, to the historians and biographers of the golden-decadent Roman world, whether giving us pictures of the Palatine or the Suburra, to find it writ large. Legislation cared little for it, save now and then some protective laws for minors, among these Domitian's prohibitive laws against prostitution of young children, which Martial received with such fulsome praise in an epigram. The sentiment in the epoch of the first

In Imperial Rome.

Caesars degenerated repulsively. It became crudely pederastic, losing all quality of manly idealism. All phases of it obtained. Its prostitutes were legion. The Augustan Age was full of it. One has only to read his Vergil, and the pages of Suetonius, Tacitus, Dion Cassius, Tibullus, Catullus, Juvenal, Persius, Martial, where each has written part of the long record, showing us how gross or spiritual was the passion in the Roman temperament. The Empire was filled full with it. The attitudes of high Roman philosophy, did not affect the general views. Not till the Judo-Christian system of Apostolic ethics reached the Imperial throne, and became weighty in Roman statutory law and in the public mind, did the idea that similisexual love was contrary to nature, and to be rooted-out as an evil impulse in the human temperament, become fixed. Even as late as the reign of Alexander Severus (A.D. 222–236) the Roman law dealt only with debauchment of minors. The same reserve is noted under such late legislators as the Emperors Philip, and Aurelius Victor.

In Later Rome.

That in the voluptuous and decadent social whirlpool of the Twelve Caesars (the Neronian reign especially) the whole aspect of similisexual love became degraded even to outraging all sense of aesthetics, social decency and virility is only too plain. But it was no new matter; no product of mere late-Roman rottenness. The most august and warlike and philosophic and ethic Emperors, or private citizens, were given to homosexual passions, no matter what were their relations to women; and this, too, at a time when ordinary and heterosexual love had no limit to its open vehemence, and to honour or shame. Julius Caesar seems to have been in all years of his life an unqualified passive pederast; satirized as "every man's woman, and every woman's man." His relations to young Nicomedes, King of Bithynia, and to his favorite nephew, who later became the great Augustus, were coarse jests of his day. Augustus the noblest figure in the Roman imperial succession, was similisexual, and by no means confined his intimacies to those with his great predecessor. We find the theater-crowds joking, in the presence of Augustus, as to his habits of the sort; and there is one reference in Plutarch (in the life of Demetrius) to a certain youth called by a significant nick-name "Delicias," who had been a favourite of Augustus when the great emperor was only Octavianus. The conspiracy which ended tragically the career of Sertorius came to a climax because of the mixing in it of two beautiful young pederasts, Manlius and Aufidius: the lover of Manlius, a high officer in the army, was weak enough to disclose to his minion the plot against his commander, and the secret began to spread untimely. In the life of Caius Lucius, a valiant soldier, a nephew of Marius, we are told by Plutarch of the passion of Lucius for a certain young officer in his service named Trebonius. Trebonius would not yield himself. Caius Lucius contrived to lure the young man to his tent one night, and attempted to violate him. Trebonius killed Lucius with his sword. This affair made a great scandal. One of the earliest official acts of Cato the Censor was to degrade Lucius Quintus Flamininus, a brother of the great Titus Flamininus, from office, and from his seat at public spectacles, because of a most inhuman crime. Lucius Quintus Flamininus kept a beautiful boy, whom he loved out of measure as a similisexual plaything. The lad pettishly complained once that in the circus he "had never seen a man die." Flamininus ordered that a slave should be brought at once to the dining-room where they then sat; to be executed. Plutarch tells the same gruesome tale, in his account of Titus Flamininus. Plutarch mentions the homosexualism of Pompey. There are other references of more or less pertinence to a study of homosexualism in Rome, at various epochs that far precede the real decadence of the Roman character or State. With the social laxities and lost ideals of the imperial periods, the passion had full movement. Almost each succeeding Caesar, and his court, illustrated it. We trace it onward and onward, through the reigns of Caius, of Claudius, of Nero, and so on, to the immortal passion of Trajan for Antinous, and to princes and epochs far beyond. The emotion never fails of appearing. But it was, as I have pointed out, strikingly pederastic. Hence it deteriorated; even if we can justly believe that many Romans felt it with its noble and better-compounded elements; turning away from the merely physical passion.

The preponderance of the instinct of similisexual love among Roman women is a matter of clear data, either through historians or belleslettres inference. By merely the references in Juvenal, we can draw plain enough inferences. It must have been general, at least in the intimately smart circles of social Rome. It is not referred to as of emotional consequence by the lyric poets; but rebuked by satirists. No Latin Sappho has sung it. No statutory codes paid attention to it, till the Christian régime attacked it as a moral and religious offence, like the masculine passion.

But the change was great on the advance of a New Faith into the social and legal and spiritual fabric of the pagan world. With the sternly

Feminine Similisexualism in Rome.

prohibitory attitude toward so much that was *human*, assumed by a Christianity that was and remains Saturated with Judaism, similisexual love began to take-on swiftly, for the whole world a new aspect—that of a special and terrible sin. Hitherto it had been distinctively such—a sin *per se*, a sin by religious conviction—only to the Jew. But now that position was to be vastly strengthened in the new and yeasty social revolution, following the decline of Pagan Humanism. All earthly passions were looked at askance by the primitive and Apostolic teachers. Profane loves were snares that drew the heart from God, and from the working-out of personal salvation, during a short and delusive earthly life. The hermits and ascetics implored men and women to fight down all desires, save for Heaven. To love God and the agonized Redeemer must be man's absorbing passion. Thousands fled to the deserts and forests, to shut themselves away from the temptations and distractions of any human affections. The Mosaic position toward similisexual love was affirmed and reaffirmed by presbyter and priest, by apostle and bishop. The tale of Sodom and Gommorrha was blackened into wholly a special sexual warning. The words of the Jewish ex-voluptuary, who became a pillar of the New Faith, St. Paul, and the allusions of other teachers were cited as the Voice of God concerning a pagan sin of sins; an awful impulse against Nature as perfected by God.

That this sentiment should take such Patristic force is easily understood. Such love was a distinct tendency toward pagan aestheticism. That above all, must be rooted out, annihilated with other earthly interests, other indulgences of the fleshly instincts. There was no place for them under the new dispensation. All

profane love save altruistic benevolence to our neighbour, was a peril. Heterosexual love was pernicious enough; any other sort vastly worse. Woman was a snare. Had not Christ held aloof from her?—even if he had been the guest and friend of Martha and Mary. Marriage was tolerated for the laity; but the saintly must abide celibate, the holy-minded must have no personal knowledge of carnal lust.

This was not all. For the sentiment hostile to similisexual love, bent on making in the most depraved of instincts, increased just as the

EDWARD IRENAEUS PRIME-STEVENSON

Catholic Church exaggerated its respect for the humble mother of the Redeemer. The new Faith made the worship of the Feminine-Abstract, the Blessed Lady the Immaculate Virgin, a mysterious, strenuous cult; even to displacing by it the just adoration of Christ. Woman, as typified by the Virgin, was held up as the ideal of the world-heart. Mariolatry, the fine flower of feminine concepts became the special policy of the Roman Church, in shrewd concession to human, aesthetic impulses, and in a perpetual combat of male sexualism. Just as Christianity had darkened existence with the gloom and gore of the Cross, so the sentiment-of Mary-worship was to effeminize the social and sexual life of the male.

We have now to consider briefly other legal aspects. Under Constantine and Justinian the similisexual passion took its place in relation to civil law as a felony, punishable with great severity—castration and death included. With the breaking-up of the Empire, and the parting of Europe and the rest of the world into the Mediaeval States, each established its own criminal laws and moral systems; but almost all were influenced directly by Roman and Christian conceptions. Hence the intolerant attitude to similisexual love grew only the stronger. The Church, with its severe Canon Law, made it a special matter for ecclesiastical punishment, like heresy, apostasy and other spiritual felonies. It became abhorred as the vice of vices, the very hell-poison of the Beast in mankind. It was visited with death by fire and torture.

The Later Canon and Roman Law, and Similisexuality.

And yet, when the sentiment of the Christian code of morals and laws so characterized it, the homosexual passion persistently held firm place in humanity. It was continually coming to the surface. By curious irony, the Church became a special conservatory for its cultivation, in spite of law and gospel. Under the mask of spiritually loathing it, the finer society of the mediaeval Italian, Teutonic and Gallic world was riddled-through with similisexual love. Except when deteriorated to a vulgar pederasty, or when associated with moral and physical offence and danger to the individual, thoughtful laic minds held back from attack upon a passion that, if refined, never could injure the moral and spiritual nature any more than could the heterosexual love. How rebuke an impulse which indeed was often part of the finest idealism

The Persistence of the Passion despite all Legistation and Social Ban.

and altruism? as natural in demanding its expression as thirst and hunger and sleep!

Naturally the mediaeval period of Italy was outspoken both in civil and canon law, against the passion. But soon this attitude became nominal. The Renaissance especially revived the sentiment in the Italian soul, where it had never been lost, giving it renewed social force. The Italian-Hellenic psychos with its boundless aestheticism, declined to be coerced by any religious teachings as to this sort of love, or as to the other. It became a more or less open phase of Italy's social life in all classes, especially the aristocratic, in Tuscany, Rome, Apulia and Sicily. With such popes as the Borgias and such princes as the Medici it was very considerably pederastic. Laws against homosexual offences fell into disuse, or were abrogated. In the Statutes of Siena which set the most-cruel penalties for it, we find that their repeal was urged because otherwise "everybody" would suffer doom for it. Florence became enthusiastically pederastic: in vain Savonarola denounced it. Perugia, Verona, Venice, Milan, Naples, Rome, many towns of Sicily, were distinctively "Cities of Sodom" as they are today. And in Italy, at this time, it assumed frequently its ancient Greek dignity, its old-time heroic beauty; a sentiment, for life and death, between the two men bound together in it. Cloister and camp, palace and barrack, studio and shop, it nearly regained its old estate in Italy the Kind. There is somewhat of the ironical, too, in discovering that many indisputably similisexual loves have been glorified by biographers, poets and moralists for centuries, under the name of marvellous and warm "friendships," either in ignorance or in reluctance to look into and to confess their real complexions. Some of these instances we shall have occasion to clarity in later parts of this study.

In Mediaeval and Renaissance Italy.

The German, Austrian, Keltic and Scandinavian and Slavic races have always been instinctively similisexual. The Christian system, and its codes of law, secular and spiritual, took special notice in Teutonic and Gallic lands of an impulse that seemed so perverse as to be a social horror for punishment by axe and stake. Under the Karolingian Codes, Germany denounced similisexual love between men, in 289 A.D., as punishable with death, unless the criminal was peculiarly repentant. Later, the invasions of the Saracens and the

In Teutonic Countries and Laws: and in France and the North; during the Mediaeval Periods, etc.

plague were laid to its secret existence in Central Europe; to the direct visitation of the anger of God, as "on Sodom." The German Canon-Law took the offence under its care. So did early French codes. In some cases the offence between women is part of the legislation, but for the most part not particularized. It was visited with excommunication, confiscation of estate, castration, beheading, fire, and so on, according to the circumstances. Benefit of the clergy was sometimes given to the unfortunate offender, sometimes not allowed him. In France, nevertheless there was a milder attitude even if in many instances we find the accused man castrated, decapitated, or burned; or all three. In Scandinavia, Denmark and their vicinage, similisexualism was a rooted passion, alluded-to by the literature of the races; the attribute of their deities. It was regarded popularly according to one or another degree of aversion, or toleration, or legal reprehension, before the Christian epoch in the Northlands. With the acceptance of Christianity and of the Canon and Civil laws on that basis, such relations between men were, of course, defined as capital sins against God and natural instincts, and were made felonies to be punished with death; a penalty frequently paid.

The British Position, Social and Legal, prior to Contemporary Statutes: and Today.

In England, Ireland and Scotland, through all Great Britain with its complex blend of Teutonic, Keltic, Anglo-Saxon and other psychologic traits, along with a high-strung nervous organism, the impulse toward similisexual love between, especially, men has been a most vehement one. This in spite of all obstacles that religious, moral, social legal obstructions against it. In no country of Europe today (contrary to a general notion) is it more an undercurrent of masculine social life, whether elevated or deteriorated in its phases. Subterfuges and conventional hypocrisies do not alter the plain facts before medico-psychiaters. To the sensuous and sensual English organism homosexuality is innate. The iron-bound British social conventions and the perpetuated errors regarding it, whether from the spiritual or physical standpoints, sternly denounce it. The tendency of the Englishman to suppress or hide all emotions in him, makes easier his denial of it. Religion, moral convictions and strong statutory laws unite for this status in Britain. We find it denounced, from the first British-Christian period, as one of the supreme moral offences, and punished under the old laws of the land with death. In Scotland, where the instinct ever was and is strong, the formal death-penalties were abolished only recently. The Victorian Statutes are more human, as we shall see. But still the British, law knows no philosophic and questioning attitude toward homosexuality, such as we shall presently remark in the cases of other European States. Social England is horrified (or pretends to be) at the very existence of homosexual passion. The Englishman affects not to "understand" how classic and aesthetic Greece and Rome gave place to the feeling. Often he really refuses to believe that the references to it, which he reads in schooldays or in his study, refer to a concrete similisexual emotion, physically gratified. He construes the verses of Propertius and Tibullus and the Greek poets, he reads the sonnets of Michael Angelo or Shakespeare, as mere "idealism" or "allegory"! He declares the homosexual man to be a monstrosity, a freak of Nature, or un-nature, a vileness out of name; all this in solemn and grotesque ignorance or hypocrisy.

In the Oriental Civilization.

During all the social history of Asian and African and other Oriental civilizations, similisexual love, particularly between males, has flourished, side by side with alterosexual love; for the most part, accepted as a natural and lawful passion. It was never deemed a matter for legal rebuke under the finest Persian, Arabic, Saracenic, Turkish and other epochs. It was frequently disparaged and satirized, by the Eastern poets of alterosexual passion; but never was it morally taken to task except by severer, distinctly religious, minds of Islam. The Arab and Persian gave himself up to it with the romantic and esthetic and voluptuous *laissez-aller* of his temperament. The full glow of military supremacy, and the most brilliant epochs of letters and art in the East were witnesses to it. Hafiz, Omar-Khayam, Nafsawih, Abu-Nuwas, and others, have enshrined it in poetry of intense romanticism, of delicate or gross eroticism. But notably in the East, male similisexualism acquired early and ever has kept its pederastic tinge. The beautiful boy, the fair-bodied cup-bearer of the wine-shop, the youth just passing into puberty, rather than the mature male, rivalled the woman in the Oriental heart. Thus accented, the sentiment became early so open that half of the mass of Persian and Arabic lyric love-verse makes the lover and the object of passion "He" and "Him," not "She" and "Her," a fact till lately carefully suppressed by English and other translators of Eastern poets. Today, the instinct is as much a part of the Orient as ever. Only nominally is it made an object of unfriendly social sentiment or legislation. The latter deals with the protection of minors and with public decency, where concerned at all.

Enlarged Ideas and More Recent Epochs: Contemporary Ideas and Similisexualism: The Beginnings and Progress of a More Tolerant Legal and Social Consideration of the Instinct.

With the advance of the Sixteenth and the Seventeenth Centuries, we begin to find the philosophers, the legislators and even the clergy beginning to question, in print and otherwise, the real nature and moral weight of similisexual love. 'Is so rooted a human instinct, a natural-moral *sin?*' Broad-minded jurists began to discuss what had been supposed to be out of any argument. The great theorist Beccaria boldly, in the middle of the Eighteenth Century, put himself into a conservative, tolerant attitude toward the passion. So did certain others. The Eighteenth Century, with its many new currents of intellectual and moral thought continued the conservatism. It required courage; but that was shown, in spite of scandalized rebukes by both Protestant and Catholic clergy. Voltaire, so much of whose influence we recognize today as admirably humanitarian, regarded similisexual love as an eccentricity of Nature, originating in deep psychic mystery, and opposed classing it with crimes. Beccaria had desired that the similisexualist should be given opportunity to amend his moral education. Ideas advanced. By the end of the Eighteenth Century, the European laws laying down a death-penalty for sexual intercourse between men were largely a dead letter. There was no direct social toleration of the passion, no religious sufferance of a ground for tolerating it. But it met only imprisonment, loss of civic rights, fines and banishments and so on. Homosexuality was considered abject disgrace, but not felony. Nevertheless, in few European statute-books was its extreme punishment distinctly modified. The penalties were not enforced, the statute was allowed to rust. Even today, this is the fact in some States of first-class importance.

Psychiatric Studies Begin to Influence Social & Legal Views.

About the middle of the century that is just past as this study is completed, the specialists attention of the European medico-psychologists began to look into the problem of similisexual love as a matter primarily in the psychiatric province, in all phases, and requiring new investigations. A large medical literature, and later one of criminology, found place for it, now in one country now another, particularly from German-writing specialists. Important contributions to the topic came presently from

North America. Periodicals gave increasing room to contributions on it. The modifications of the French Code, elicited favourable or other comment. The negative position of Italian and other laws was also discussed with more interest and clearer rationality than had been earlier the tendency in most of Northern Europe. With the analytic study of nervous disease, of sex-problems and sex-instincts calm scientific interest in similisexualism grew firmer in Europe, decade by decade. Of much significance was the fact that the bench and the bar in Germany, France Italy and Austria, especially, began to dissent from legally recognizing intersexual relations and sentiments of the kind, except when forced, or if a menace to the morals of youth or offending by act the public decorum, as proper for legislation. The position of the Code Napoléon was and is such.

Summary of Criminal-Law Attitudes Today.

The following paragraph will sum up for the reader the present relations of Statutory Law in the more important European and other States toward similisexual love: more particularly as to the passion between men. Even today the statutes seem unwilling or indifferent toward the feminine sentiment and its practices, if compared with the masculine.

In Great Britain, where similisexual love is still denounced as a sentiment contrary to all human ethics, it is punished with imprisonment at hard labour for life; and, when only attempted, by imprisonment, also at hard labour, for a term not exceeding ten years; and with loss of civil rights. The offender is a felon, of deepest dye. Legal and popular ideas of more humanely cautious sort are not general. In the British Colonies, not Oriental, similar statutes are enforced, as to the British offender. In the more Oriental British possessions, a modified legislation prevails. But it represents a felony.

In Germany a shifting condition of affairs is noticeable. The public interest in homosexualism is immensely increased within a decade or so, as would be expected in a nation where the proportion of homosexuals of all classes is so large. The topic is no longer regarded as absolutely *tabu* in even social discussions by serious men and women, taking hold intellectually of its grave social problems. Indeed the rights of the respectable homosexual, whether prince or peasant, as a man now under the ban of useless and mediaeval legal provisions are constantly agitated. A strong petitionary movement has twice memorialized the highest German Legislature, endorsed by all professions and callings, in appeal for the suppression of references in the Statutes to homosexual intercourse, except such provisions as shall guard minor youth and preserve public decorum. Eminent German political men have taken part in the effort to repeal the most useless, or worse, paragraphs of the law. This movement has been made part of the platform of the Social Democratic party in Germany. With all respect to that intelligent and powerful body of citizens and agitators, the connection has not yet proved as useful to the repeal of the laws concerned, as would be desired. The Clerical Party have bitterly and successfully fought against any changes. It is to be observed that before the consolidation of the present day German Empire, many of the States showed a humane and reserved aspect toward homosexualism. When the new Imperial Confederation required a more uniform system in the Criminal Codes, intolerance of homosexual liberty became fixed by the laws throughout the Empire; except that there is no reference to penalties for feminine similisexualism. Under the present (1900) Code, and according to Paragraph 175, similisexual intercourse between males is punished by imprisonment for a term of from one day to live years, according to circumstances, and loss of civic rights can be added. A tendency to a liberal construction of offences under the Paragraph mentioned is noticeable, in spite of the foregoing severe attitude. The continual occurence of blackmailing-scandals has made something like a tacit friendliness of judges and jury a plain necessity. But the similisexual is still a felon under German law. An important deduction from its rigours is however to be noticed. In Germany, in spite of Paragraph 175, a merely mutual onanism, *manually performed*, between two adults particularly, uncoerced, under private circumstances, as in an hotel, or in one's own dwelling, is not punishable. This curious construction of the law, which the reader will at once perceive to be ridiculously inconsistent with the express intention of it, holds good, and enables many a similisexual to rout some blackmailer. But the reader must understand that any other manner of homosexual acts between males (such as pen. in anum, pen. in os, coitus inter femora, etc.) is more or less severely punishable. Any sexual acts with any minor, however depraved the minor, are felonious. A more absurd interpretation of a statute is not easily found; but it can be one of service to victimized and respectable similisexuals in Germany.

In Austria-Hungary by the Laws of 1852, including a special paragraph (159), the similisexualist is punished with imprisonment from one year to five years, according to the nature of his offence. But in districts of the Dual Monarchy-as in Germany-is shown a disposition to construe the law favourably toward an offender whose inborn and constitutional homosexualism can be clearly shown by expert examination of him by medical psychologists. Also, the blackmailer, in Austria-Hungary as a rule, is the sufferer in cases where that element appears clearly. A tendency toward milder construction of the statutes is considerably shown in legal proceedings, now and then in Vienna. In Hungary, the penalty for the offense is one year, or more, according to circumstances.

In Switzerland exist curious differences in the legal attitudes according to the different Cantons and their laws. Generally defined, in the German-speaking cantons the homosexual is punished, by a greater or lesser penalty of imprisonment, with here and there loss of his civic rights: whereas in the French-speaking cantons, the homosexual is not recognized as a criminal provided he does not coerce, nor offend public decency, nor debauch minor youth. Briefly, the differences in the Swiss laws are as follows. In Canton Graubunden, no specific age of consent is set nor extenuating circumstances; penalty, imprisonment up to a term of three years. In Waadt (Vaud), the law specifies that "sodomy" shall not be punishable except on formal complaint, more especially if debauchment of minor youth is shown; in which case the penalty is imprisonment for a term of from two months to three years. In the Valais (Wallis) the law regards only public decorum, not even specifically providing against the debauchment of minors. In Schaffhausen, the law punishes debauchment of minors, according to a varying scale of imprisonment, depending on whether the minor is more than fourteen years old but under sixteen, or otherwise, and a penalty of three months imprisonment is fixed for intercourse between adults. In the canton of Oberwalden, there exists a sort of general penalty for all homosexual offences—imprisonment "up to four years." In Luzern, also is a general provision of punishment for all homosexual intercourse, by a term of imprisonment up to five and ten years, according to the special grade of the offence. In Glarus, is a similar general provision for punishment by imprisonment from two years up to ten. In Freiburg, sexual relations with a minor of less than 19 years of age can be punished by imprisonment from two to eight years, and the public decorum is not to be offended; otherwise, the homosexual is relatively free. In Zürich, like Freiburg, only when the offense is with a minor of less than 18 years, or if public decency is in question, can the homosexual be punished. In Basel, homosexual relations with minors apparently if under 18 years, have special penalties of imprisonment, and the circumstances opposed to public propriety are considered. In the Canton of Tessin (Ticino) debauchment of minors over 12 years and under 15 years is punishable by imprisonment. In Geneva (a city where much homosexualism is met) there is no punishment except for the debauchment of minor youths: that is to say imprisonment from one month to one year if the minor be under 21, and for two years up to five years if the youth be less than fourteen; besides regulations as to public decorum. In Neuchâtel the law is similar to Geneva. In Appenzell, the law punishes adults who offend between themselves, or those who debauch minor youth under 15, according to a series of fines and imprisonments, the latter ranging from two to twenty (!) years. In Schwyz, exists a general provision for homosexual offense, with imprisonment for a term of two years. In St Gall, the law regards the matter in relation only to debauchment of minors, or if a public scandal be made; with a term of two years imprisonment. In a large number of these different legistations in Switzerland, according to this or that cantonal sentiment, there also is met a just paragraph which provides special punishment against any homosexual who debauches a minor in the relation to him of pupil, ward, or otherwise committed to the adult offender, in the capacity of protegé. Also is punished all pandering.

In France, the Code Napoléon maintains its wise and humane provisions. There is no legal recognition, no penalty for homosexual intercourse between males or females, in France, unless public decency comes into the consideration of the offence, violence, pandering, scandal, or unless a legal minor be debauched; or unless the offence is committed with the active participation of more than merely *one* youth. In Norway and Sweden, in Denmark, Russia, and in certain Balkan States, in all of which homosexualism is in frequent social demonstration, the penalties are imprisonments for relatively long terms, two to ten years, or with deportation, loss of civil rights and so on. The same penalties exist in modern Greek legislation. It may be noted here that in or out of Greece, the modern Greek is extremely given to homosexual intercourse. Athens is a center of it; especially pederasty.

In Italy, except when the offender is a soldier in military *actual* service, or if violence be used in the acts, or when public decency is outraged or when minor children (under sixteen years old) are debauched, there is no legal opposition to hf similisexual satisfactions. In Holland, in the Grand Duchy of Luxembourg, in Belgium, in Portugal, Spain, the Principality of Monaco, and in Turkey, there is no legal position taken against similisexual passion, except when it is a rape, or is exhibited in a way offensive to public decency, or is corruptive of youthful morals.

It should be noted that the phrase "public decency" is often construed in a general sense by the criminal courts of the countries concerned. Also the age of minors is variable; usually the boundary being fourteen years; but under some conditions twelve years, sixteen years, or even more.

In Mexico, there is no penalty for similisexual relations except when under the conditions of actual rape, publicity, or age, as set forth above. The same rule holds in Latin South-America in general.

In the United States of North America, the punishment of homosexualism is severe, in all the State-Codes. For instance, the laws of New York State against the least manifestations of it, punishing it with heavy imprisonments, are typical. It is a first-class felony. Nor is any other view of it, by jurists, in general and clear consideration in America at present, nor in the general public sentiment or notice.

But each day proves how are powerless all legal provisions to lessen the similisexual impulse in humanity the world over: how vain are ethical or religious positions to put it out of the heart and the life-impulses of mankind in each class. Similisexual love flourishes today, in every phase of finer or deteriorated character and expression; from binding the master-bond of high souls to being the living of sordid male prostitutes of a boulevard. It defies clandestinely all penalties, all social intolerances. With this fact as the more personal material for these pages, we turn now to the practical study of the Intersexual races, the Uranian and the Uraniad.

V

The Uranian, or Urning; His General Physical and Psychical Diagnosis: Types and Biographies

A n Uranian, or Urning, a member of the Intersex previously set apart from the major sexes, may be defined as a human being that is more or less perfectly, even distinctively, masculine in physique; often a virile type of fine intellectual, moral and aesthetic sensibilities; but who, through an inborn or later-developed preference feels sexual passion for the male human species. His vita sexualis reverts, now vaguely, now with vigourous definiteness to the sex to which he seems naturally to belong but does not fully belong, by strict psychological classification. His sexual preference may quite exclude any desire for the female sex; or may exist concurrently with that instinct.

Definition of the Uranian.

The term "Uranian" or "Urning" has been explained as to its classical derivation. It is not a new terminology, at least the use of the word "Urning" is not. "Urning" came into definite psychologic use in the middle of the nineteenth century, through the pamphlets on the topic of similisexualism, by Karl Emil Ulrichs, a homosexual German advocate. Ulrichs's studies of the sexual problem attracted much attention. Though lacking literary method and adequate self-poise, they have been of pionering importance in the topic.

Ulrichs reaffirmed and demanded recognition and freedom for the platonic, Uranian sexual passion, in our modern social life.

Ancient Queries as to the Number Human Sexes.

The existence and characteristics of the Uranian and of his feminine complement, the Uraniad, have already been referred back to the mysterious question of Intersexes between the distinctly male and female ones. This is, no recent query. Plato declares in "The Banquet" that a third sex, hermaphroditic in type, had existed; but had lapsed. Aristotle in his "Ethics" indicates a notion that there was at least one other sex; as part of the premises when Aristotle reasons of sexual manifestations, including love of one man for another. Yet even such comprehensive reasoners, when touching on similisexual love in men, fail to set up an extant, continued Secondary Sex. The early philosophic Latin thinkers on psychology, of the type of Lucretius and the natural philosophers, even the most profound of the classic speculatists of Borne, did not for a long time affirm in so many words the basis of an existing intersex as the explanation of man's intersexual instincts. Later writers hint at its existence. Thus Alexander Severus, in writing of depravities of his cousin, the grotesquely effeminate Heliogabalus, speaks of such men as Heliogabalus as "a third kind of human being." Dion Cassius, also, declared Heliogabalus a blending of man and woman. In the Scriptures there is an allusion that may refer to such an Oriental theory: where in the First Book of Samuel, Chap. XX, v. 30) Saul throws out the

Why the Nature of the Uranian has not been more Freely Distinguished.

scornful allusion to Jonathan (beyond doubt a homosexual young man) as being the "son of the perverse, rebellious woman," a phrase which has a peculiar underlying sexual bearing.

The theory of the Urning, or Uranian, as a third sex, or at least as not being responsible only to masculine sexual instincts for his passions, would undoubtedly have been earlier current, had not the error been made of thinking that sex while it is qualified by intellectual characteristics must be *determined* by the body, and its organs instead of by the sexual instinct. A more correct idea places even an athlete, or a soldier, or a porter, six feet high, built like a Hercules, virile enough in every muscle and nerve, as a creature apart from strictly male human beings, if his sexual desires and admirations incline him to man, not woman. Not fully a man, not fully a woman, he is an Uranian or Urning. In like manner a brilliant jurist, philosopher, physician, ecclesiastic, a prince of finance or of trade, a titanic worker in the literary or aesthetic professions, if strictly-classed, may be semi-male. His sexualism demands completeness of his individuality through a man. His passional admirations, his physical instincts, draw him to men, not to women, and so define him as Uranian, or Urning.

Racial Statistics and Distribution of the Uranian and Uranism.

Of the racial distribution of the-Uranian, in relation to "normal population whether at past epochs of social history, or now, there are conflicting ideas. One is likely to think that in ancient social epochs, with their open showing of

EDWARD IRENAEUS PRIME-STEVENSON

the uranistic nature, especially in Greek and Roman civilizations, there were more similisexual men than nowadays, in proportion to normal. This idea is constantly met as especially an English conventionalism. But the notion cannot be well sustained. The Orient is not more or less similisexual now than of old. The Latin races certainly are now not less Uranistic than long ago, in classic and Renaissance periods, when the impulse was less hid. The concealment of homosexualism, by fear of social disgrace and legal punishment does not mean its being now a whit less common, the world round, as a human instinct, invincible and inevitable; especially in connection with esthetic, military and nervously-sensitive peoples. We cannot make it definitely the cause of national decadences, of a general decline of intellect, morals and virility in a people, though its worser characteristics are likely to coincide with that decadence.

The proportion of Uranians is largest in what can be called the "Philarrenic"—or male-loving—Zone, a belt of several races and populations, topographically reckoned together. The statistical proportion is still largest in the East. In Turkey, Persia, part of Arabia, and so on, there has been set a rate of one Uranid in 60; with this proportion made larger through the Oriental tendency toward bisexualism—or similisexualism in men not distinctly Uranian. In modern Italy, where dionian-uranians are peculiarly a type—in all classes racially, one may say—in Italy, the proportion has been set at one in sixty-five: but in Italy bisexualism of the erotic impulse, an instinctive liking for now the male now the female in the sexual act, is an important aspect. In Germany, it is put at something near to two per cent. In France, it is reckoned at less than one per cent. In England at one in the hundred, or less. In Austria at one in seventy; in Kussia at one in seventy-five to eighty (a low estimate); in Spain and the Spanish-settled countries, at one in sixty-five; and in the United States of North America at one in about eighty-five.

A physician, long busied with practice in neurotic diseases and sexual studies, a Bavarian, tells the writer that he has in his list of clients some "fifteen complete Uranians" that is to say, those who are *wholly* similisexual; also four who though heterosexual for most part of their impulses, nevertheless are "given to sexual relations with men also." An Italian consulting physician, a writer on neuropathology states to me that he has "more than a dozen" thorough Uranians among his clients, two of them married; but has traced bisexualism in constant recurrence. A German doctor who was himself uranistic, mentions knowing of one hundred similisexual men in his city, a town of about twenty-seven thousand inhabitants. The number of Uranians of all shades and characters, from the honoured, aristocratic citizen, to the male prostitute of the lowest type, in such capitals as Paris, Brussels, Berlin, Munich, (where similisexuality is rampant even more openly than in Milan, Lisbon or Naples) in Vienna, Rome, London, New York and so on, can be set, in each place, at thousands. The vulgar and repulsive evidences of this fact are before the eyes of the observant traveller. Contrary to what might be expected, there is a large (Uranistic population in rural life; though part of it is not thoroughly similisexual. In France, Italy, Spain and Austria, the peasantry are strongly homosexual.

As for the similisexual instinct in the more or less barbarous and primitive races of the world today, we have already discussed the inborn tendency to it. A statistical measure can not be established here. A concurrent fact is that three races of the world, constantly in near relations to one or another people and civilization but often little affected by such environments, the Jew, the Gipsey and the North-American Negro, are all excessively similisexual. The Jew, always erotic in temperament, is so frequently Uranian, or uranistio, that there is a sort of psychiatric proverb—"so many Jews, so many similisexualists." The Gipsey makes no distinction as to sex when his passion is excited. He is especially given to pederasty. The North-American negro, whether on the plantations or in the cities, gives way to the impulse freely, although the striking laxity of female morality in the race would appear to counteract such an inborn instinct.

Degrees of Uranianism in Men: The Complete Uranian, Dionian-Uranian, & Uranian-Dionian, Graded.

Between fully Uranian nature and its less perfect phases there are at least two important degrees. A complete, an absolute Uranian feels sexual attraction only to But there also is the type who, while he is strongly similisexual still feels sexual admiration, often most vigorously and romantically, for woman. He seeks, with a greater or less passion and satisfaction, sexual relations with her, even to marrying for love; not to speak of casualities. In such a type, two impulses exist: for the normal man and male sex certainly is approached, yet not fully reached. This type, "uranistic" but not Uranian, has been categorized by psychiatry as the Dionian-Uranian, or "Virilized Uranian." It is a subtly bisexual phase. It is constantly met. The next degree goes further toward a complete manliness of sex. It is represented by the individual almost wholly male in sexual instincts, who as a rule, turns with aversion from relations of the kind with masculine types; but who now and then "lapses" toward the male, surrenders to infrequent similisexualism. These lapses occur either with particular individuals, to whom he is mysteriously attracted, or with others (more impersonally) during special periods—bisexual currents of his life. The thoroughly masculine instinct, the man out of any sort of similisexual tendency, usually is termed Dionian, Dionid, or Dionist. Hence the use of such qualifying phrases in speaking of modified Uranians. The psychiatric literature of the time makes many finer distinctions. In fact it has set forth rather confusing "subdivisions," according to the nature and force of the individual similisexual tendencies. These minuter grades can be dismissed by the average reader as needlessly precise. The complete Uranian, the Dionian-Uranian and the (similar) Uranian-Dionian cover all essential grades between intersex and entire masculinity. They take in all the degrees of similisexual love and its physical expression, in hundreds of instances of complete or partial uranism. Such types are Alexander the Great, Martial, Beethoven, Rafaello, Oscar Wilde. Robespierre, William Rufus, Nero, Lord Byron, Sir Isaac Newton, Gilles de Rais, David, Jonathan, Pope Alexander VI, General Tilly, Prince Eugene of Savoy, Henri III, Shakespeare, Platen, Cellini, Heliogabalus, Jérome Duquesnoy, St. Augustine, Molière, Frederick the Great, Michel-Angelo, Charles XII of Sweden, Peter the Great, Montaigne, Pausanias, Beza, Tschaikovsky, Grillparzer, Erasmus, Bishop Atherton of Waterford, Winkelmann, Servetus, Gonsalvo de Cordova, Socrates, Hölderlin, Abu Nuwas, Hadrian, the Caesars, Alexander I of Russia; innumerable other indisputable instances of the emotion among, especially, notable minds and men; met under all environments, in all professions and social standings. Some have been Uranians *in toto*. Others are but partially uranistic; with the admixtures of Dionism, of normal masculinity, in a firmer or weaker balance, as the countercheck. Thus in Heliogabalus, in Henry III of France, in the gifted poet August von Platen, in the mighty genius of Michel Angelo, in the brilliant intellectuality of Frederick the Great, in Hadrian, we have complete Uranians. Their sexual desire was *only* toward the male. In Lord Byron, Nero, Benvenuto Cellini, Alcibiades, Julius Caesar and Charles XII we have a strongly masculine sexualism, but mixed, illogically, with powerful similisexual instincts. In such cases, the individuality seems to be fairly split into two. Now one sexual instinct comes forward, now the other. In examples of almost complete and normal manliness of sex-instinct (but not wholly so) we have the third, or Uranian-Dionian group. One race, the Italian seems to be particularly impartial in sexual pleasure, inclining to masculine or feminine; uranian without effeminacy, to an idiomatic, a racial, extent.

Analysis of the Typical The Uranian Physique.

Nothing in the Uranistic physique necessarily differs in the least from the normal man. What is more, a magnificently masculine physique often conceals the sex— the intersex—from observation. The Uranian is frequently athletic, robust, virile in powers and movements. A considerable proportion of Uranians whether complete or dionistic, are professional athletes, circus-gymnasts, acrobats, riders, equilibrists and so on. The sexual organs are, as a rule, wnolly normal; often of special virility of aspect. The sexual powers of the Uranian are not to be assumed as in any way less vigorous than in all men of good bodily health. The physical desire for satisfaction of the sexual instinct is strong, often especially if in suppression, it is turbulent. There is no prevalence of bodily hermaphroditism in the Uranian, though that ridiculous idea is a rooted popular one. Your athletic neighbour and friend who bathes with you in the stream, displaying his perfect masculinity of form and of organs may be wholly Uranistic in his sexual life.

Certain Departures From a Quite Masculine Type.

There are, however, certain minor bodily peculiarities that belong in a greater or lesser frequency and number to the Uranian. Some of them meet in one instance, but not in another one; while occasionally an individual presents nearly all to the psychiater's notice. They are not all to be expected, nor do many blend in one type, but they all have been found to coincide with the presence of the instinct. They include delicacy of the osseous structure; breadth of buttocks and pelvis; conical thighs; and a general roundness and softness of the corporeal outlines. Grace rather than strength is noticeable. The breast tends to curve, after the feminine mould; there is often a decided contour to the bosom suggesting female breasts. The fore-arm and the lower arm are cylindrical, even when strong, rather than flat. The hands and feet and ears are small. The skin is fine and frequently less hairy than the normal man's skin. Another rather more frequent skin-idiom is the absence of the masculine odour which characterizes almost any man's skin, especially when a man is nervously or sexually excited, is warm or taking hard exercise. The growth of scalp-hair and beard, or absence, are not significant. The throat is rather round and graceful than massive (a peculiarity that has given rise to the idea that an Uranian neither swallows nor expectorates saliva as easily as the normal man) and the "Adam's-apple" does not project as in the average mature man's throat. The voice of the Uranian is emphatically a trait: being low and full and agreeable, rather than with the metallic, coarser ring of manlier types; not seldom it has a persuasive sweetness. The ability to sing with a soprano quality, or at least higher in the vocal scale than most men, is not infrequent; but this is not a distinctive trait, contrary to another false notion. The uranian head is often small, and the features fine and regular, rather than coarse and square, and it frequently has the quality common to Greek beauty of being transferable to a female figure, with some slight reduction in the size of the features. A particular trait in the Uranian anatomy, though not distinctive to it, is the eye; likely to be remarkably brilliant, full, expressive of softer emotion and aesthetic sensitiveness, rather than sharp and commanding. In the military Uranian this trait is not so striking. The especially penetrating glance of the Uranian is a mysterious "faculty" about which German psychiatry has written a good deal. Undeniable is the fact that one Uranian can often guess at the nature of another Uranian, in any part of the world, by the exchange of a passing look. There is much of this quality in any expressive eye; but there also exists here a constantly verified Uranian trait. The gait of the Uranian is easy and graceful, occasionally too short-stepping, rather than bold, or with a strong stride. The general constitution of the adult uranistic race, by the by, is vigorous, at least not more subject to disease than the normal male one. The Uranian physical and intellectual powers last out their time well, often strikingly long. There is a tendency toward longevity; with strong sexual inclinations, till late in years.

When we examine the intellectual, moral, mental and temperamental, nervous traits of the Uranian, we have further indices. No class of humanity makes a finer intellectual showing, example by example, of one grade or of another.

The Intellectual, Moral, Temperamental and Nervous Individuality of Uranians. High Intellectual and Esthetic Tendency Common.

But we detect a deficiency in robustly originative intellectualism, where the mind must deal with the abstract and practical, rather than with the more concrete, or with the aesthetic and emotional. Many exceptions point out the rule. The Uranian is less likely to be successful in philosophy, in mathematics, *abstract* mechanics, and so on, than in letters, arts, and lighter applications of science. He is often highly appreciative of what goes on in these fields, yet not productive in them. But in the more aesthetic professions his work has been the wonder of the world since it began. The practicing physician, consulted by similisexual clients, hoping to understand their own abnormalisms better, or to be treated for them as for a disease, is continually meeting the man of letters, the artist, the sculptor, the musician, the architect, the actor and singer, or instrumentalist. Numberless are homosexuals whose gifts, business or professions keep them busy in occupations where they deal with practical aesthetics, or with distinctly aesthetic results; not the sterner mind-work. The intellectuality of the uranistic type is brilliant. It has dazzled the world forever with its genius. But it often wants elasticity, and brunt-force in initial conceptions and in hard applications of reason and analysis.

The Uranian's Widely-Graded Moral-Nature.

The nature of the Uranian varies greatly. It ranges from the finest moral and spiritual feelings and practices to the feeblest sense of morals of any kind; much as is the case with the Dionian man. There is no truth in the idea that the similisexual is necessarily morally bad, or feels even the least indifference toward religions. Too many lofty types of all philosophies, all creeds, too many respected officials and model private citizens have lived and died uranistic, for this error to stand. But the fact is proved every day in society, that the more sensuous the Uranian and the more circumscribed his mental horizon, just so weakened or debased is his moral sense. His distinctively similisexual instincts, when his general equipment otherwise is sound, seem to have uncertain bearings on his conduct; while the converse is true of the less fortunate and respectable Uranian. Socrates was similisexual. Not readily can we dismiss the idea that Christ was such—and saints many have been Uranians. But so were Philippe of Orléans, Caligula, de Sade; so is the blackmailing catamite that prostitutes himself for a shilling, incidentally to rob, to murder, to ruin socially some unlucky victim. The reader has seen that he must throw away the unscientific idea that the homosexual, in loving the male with his sexual love, in seeking to satisfy his passion physically, necessarily is committing offence against Nature or an individual morality. He acts absolutely according to Nature, simply working out his fixed, legitimate, sexual sentiment and necessity, exactly as the dionistic man seeks female society to the same end. In the most conclusively Uranian-type homosexuality is inborn; with its concurrent utter *sexual* indifference to women. Frequently there is an utter horror of such intercourse, a distressing nervous inability toward it. Uranianism has its own excuses for existing, the general ethical furnishment of the man often is analyzable much or wholly apart.

The Wonderfully Complex Nerve-Build of the Uranian.

But it is in the nervous fabric of the Uranian that we find more striking data. The uranistic nature, as a German writer has admirably pointed out, is the most sensitive, fine-strung, exquisitely emotional one yet known. We find the homosexual turning emphatically to the aesthetic professions, with alert senses to all that is beautiful. His vivid impressionability, his creative powers are so supreme, that one may say that the world of poetry, the graphic and plastic arts, most especially music (that most neurotic of all arts) and belles-lettres of all sorts are richest by the distinctively similisexual genius. Here he is ever inventive, originative. History, biography, every psychiatric physician, can confirm this. Its chief contrast may be thought, by some, to occur with the fact that the soldier is so notably similisexual; that so many great military men have been Uranians. But the military profession is really one that is highly aesthetic and nervous, as well as one that throws the Uranian into intimate, exclusive, and admiring relations with men. It fosters philarrenism, frequently dignifying it. Aesthetics are to the Uranian the breath of life. No wonder that we find him as authour, painter, sculptor, composer, singer, actor; whatever demands nerves and concentrated idealism, pouring forth his genius from one epoch of the world to the next. Genius and madness are old allies. We need not be surprised to find that the Uranian often confirms that painful mystery.

Characteristic Traits, Types, Tastes, Tempers, etc. of the Uranian.

In part associated with the nervous organization of the Uranian, in part more of his general temperament, are also these matters. The Uranian shows a marked tendency to support illnesses more readily than most other individuals, with a feminine ability to bear physical pain. Mental anguish works with severity on him. Outward surroundings are of importance to him; they affect his nervous status keenly. He is usually orderly, often has feminine tastes more or less developed, such as cookery, needlework, and the like. This fact is curiously combined in military individualities, an odd "inconsistency." The Uranian is likely to be passionately fond of children and animals; they are frequently surprisingly attracted to him, as if by some mystic understanding. But the Uranian is to be counted a creation not far aloof from the eternal World-Child. (As indicated, the best type of Uranian is not typically pederastic.) He is spontaneously benevolent, tender-hearted, and pacific; with a large and philosophic or other tolerance. His instinct for the aesthetic side of paganism is strong. He is often intensely fond of Nature, even to adoration of her most sombre phases; as if in solitary walks and life with her he harks back to some great and elementary sympathy between Nature and his instincts. He is generally, but not typically, a tasteful and even "finicky" dresser. He is fond of jewellery and ornaments, beautiful and valuable or not such, according to his aesthetic education. It is significant in him, that while as a type, he tends to avoid giving pain to anyone, or seeing it, he is (another indication of the feminine texture of the uranistic psychos) often passionately interested in the deliberately brutal sports. He can love the bull-fight, the boxing-ring, the cock-pit, the fierce sort of foot-ball struggles so common in the United States of North America; he is found haunting even guillotinings and hangings: this, along with an almost childish pleasure in simple, trivial, wholesome things. The uranistic temperament is especially mercurial; now wildly gay, now sombre, easily changed. Though great statesmen have been Uranians, in all grades, the quality of patriotic feeling is likely to be lacking. One part of the world, one race, is almost as acceptable as another, even the native one, with great adaptiveness to foreign environment. Ever, too, occurs the tendency to excess of emotion, to unbalanced moods, to sentiments ill-grounded, to effects lacking causes, to traitorous impulses. Manly will is largely absent.

The Sexual Nature of the Uranian.

But when we approach the distinguishing Uranian sex-element of the Uranian, especially of the 'absolute', inborn type—what shall one say that adequately analyses, or at least describes, this profound problem? Its traits have been outlined in a preceding chapter. The psychologic singularities of such temperaments are hard to

EDWARD IRENAEUS PRIME-STEVENSON

put before the average reader in a clarity positive enough, if he be hostile to any such topic. Perhaps the clearest descriptions come when we tell the reader to take any and every phase of admiration, of attraction and sexual love, which a normal, amorous man feels for a woman, and to translate that into the uranistic passion; into sexual love for a man or youth, on the part of a man. There is the same impressionability to the outward beauty. There is the same sense of swimming in a sea of it daily, of letting it play on the eyes, the ideals, the sexual nerves. There is the same falling in love "at sight," vehemently or lightly, worthily or unworthily; the same loving in constancy or in inconstancy. There are the same ripenings of calm interest and vague friendship into vivid passion and physical desire. There are the same struggles, hopes, fears, self-sacrifices, workings for good or ill on the nature of the lover; the same joys, jealousies, despairs; and too often (as we shall see) the same tragedies of slow or of fiercely swift culmination. All, all, are to be "translated" from their normal relations in distinctly masculine natures, into the sexually feminine instincts and experiences of the male-loving Uranian heart.

The "Curse." The Uranian's Necessary Concealment of his "Unnatural" Tastes. The "Mask."

But, alas! between conditions kindly or adverse that meet the normal man in love, and which the Uranian encounters, exists one terribly significant difference; tyrannic during modern eras of faiths, morals and laws. It may be called the curse upon the Uranian. For, the 'normal' man can speak without shame of his passion to the woman who inspires it. Even if she reject it, she is not insulted by it, if it be worthy; spiritual enough and sincere in her eyes. The woman-lover can demand the sympathy of his confidential friend, he can receive such sympathy if he will. He can be the object of sympathy to even the outside world; for his secret can be guessed by it without disgrace on any ground of "unnatural" emotion. But the Uranian must often "go through" the most overwhelming, soul-prostrating of loves, finding his nerves and mind and body beaten down under the passion, his days and nights vivified or poisoned by it, all without his doing anything so persistently as to hide his sentiment forever from the object of it! To hide it from his closest friends, from suspicion by the world! Hide it he must. Accounted a diseased human thing, an outcast from men, a beast, if his secret be probed; hopeless often of its toleration for an instant by the being that, often under the name of friendship, he *loves* with all the fire of intersex; fighting the emotion in himself in bewilderment or shame; perhaps living, side by side with some stranger that is more than any mere friend to him; playing his part like a man, frequently without one human confidant in the wide world, so can pass his social life! Ever the Mask, the shuddering concealment, the anguish of hidden passion that burns his life away! Not always; for sometimes, as if by a Divine grace, the Uranistic love is accepted; or at least its psychical side is pardoned and tolerated by the man to whom it goes out. But this pre-supposes either a peculiarly deep regard and broad-minded nature in the dionian object—if he be decidedly dionistic, as is likely to be the ease in the finer grades of uranian loves; or else he is (most luckily for the Uranian) imbued with an uranistic element himself. Fortunate then is the Uranian, or half-fortunate! He can at least be honest. For he can at least receive sympathy and brotherly pity—human respect and regard. Perhaps he wins more, and so becomes unspeakably blessed. But often he is hopeless as he is helpless, and wears his mask with the smiling hypocrisy of anxious self-protection. He sits in his club and hears similisexualism, not merely in gross and unworthy forms but in manly ideals, mocked as infamy. He listens to the coarsest jests, at the expense of the Uranian nature, when some accident brings a "case" to public notice. He must deny his ability to "understand how a man can fall in love with another man." Particularly, as one invaluable sham, must he take pains to appear sexually interested in women, to be intimate with women, to seem to relish open, and frequently obscene, sexual talk about women. This last is much in his programme for hiding sexual indifference or downright physical aversion to women. The Mask, ever the Mask! It becomes like the natural face of the wearer.

What this "masking" of his real self is to any Uranian temperament naturally expansive, emotional, unfriendly to checks, one can imagine. It is astonishing that it is so successfully worn, sometimes all through life. It begets in the uranistic type that bitter humour, ironic wit, self-mockery, that are often so entertaining to those who do not know what is covered.

The "normal" man is likely to be drawn specially and even tenderly to Uranians of the finer individuality. He is even won to the rather feminine types, as a friend; unaware or the subtle intersexual magnetism. It is very often precisely the hidden femininity of psychos in the Uranian

The Dionian as Attracetd to the Finer type of Uranian: Their Affection Sometimes Stronger than the Dionian's Horror on 'Discovery'.

that wins the virile Dionian. The Dionian friend is unabfe to explain why his feeling for the Uranian is so sentimental, so tender. Deep and lasting dionian friendships with Uranians are many; whether the Dionian "understands" them or not. And although often the dionian friend, when some unguarded moment or false hope betrays the secret, turns in horror and disgust from the Uranian, this is not always the end. Often the friendship survives the psychologic shock. "I cannot understand what you confess to me! I never shall understand it! I shudder at it!" sometimes exclaims the Dionian in such an hour, "but I cannot break our friendship! Let us never speak of *that* again! Help me to forget it. Let us go on as if *that* never had been spoken or known." Occasionally the uranistic love calms into friendship on both sides, at last. So comes a peace enduring. But often the passion grows, and must be borne as best the Uranian can bear it, hidden in silence.

The Uranian by Nature not Constant.

It has often been noted by psychiaters that the uranistic nature is emphatically inconstant. This is most true of the Uranian whose passionate attachments are more physical than spiritual. He loves easily and loves many. He readily recovers from unfortunate episodes. He is feminine in "loving love." But the more idealistic Uranian often abides faithful to one passion through life, to a sentiment borne with him into his tomb.

The Bewildered Question: and Answer.

"Why am I? What am I? Outwardly as a man, inwardly in so much a man! Able to keep my character and sex as a man before the world and yet with this sexual nature of a woman in me. Why am I cursed thus? What ails me? Am I sick, mad?" So cries some 'inborn' Uranian, bewildered and wretched, when he is alone and can throw down the Mask. So demands he of the confidential physician, if he has decided to visit one, hoping to be "cured" of his psychologic disorder. Too frequently the doctor, ignorant but confident, talks to him as were he indeed "diseased," "to be cured"; often advises marriage. But any doctor, really anxious to lead the querist not to feel himself solitary, or morally depraved because of his mysterious sexual nature, can give no better reply in most instances, than—"Friend, you are, what you are—an Uranian, one of the Intersex-race. You cannot be cured. You are not alone. There are thousands, tens of thousands, of you. Fear man, if you must: but fear not to face God who has made your kind as it is. Strive to be the best mortal being that you possibly can be."

Succeeding chapters of this book will offer classified observations or Uranians. Examples of a more general sort are the following. The first is a good instance of complete and inborn uranistic intersexualism. It is furnished from the memoranda of an American physician. The outward social relations with the feminine world are to be noticed.

"B. R—, thirty-one years of age, unmarried, of American and English education, by profession an original designer for a firm of silversmiths, came to consult me with respect to his sexual condition. R—is the son of a father of whose sexual nature R—knows nothing more than that his father was extremely potent, and in early life "very fond of women," and was a nervous, high-strung man, of excellent disposition. R—does not think that he had special nervous weaknesses, though this R—does not know. He died eight years ago. R—'s mother, who still lives, is a sufferer from general nervous weakness, is much confined to her room, spends a good deal of time in health-resorts for the nervous, complains of insomnia, and during the first years of her marriage with R—'s father had hysterical attacks. There were three children; two other sons died early. R—has no pathologic data as to his grandparents. One aunt, on the mother's side, suffered during the early part of her life with paranoia, but R—says that she has entirely outgrown them, being now a (married) woman of about fifty-three. R—has heard it said that his mother was disappointed that he was not born a girl; but his mother has always told him that this feeling "never was the case" In outward aspect R—is thoroughly manly. He is tall, muscular, without being specially athletic; he fences, boxes, shoots and bicycles much. He is fond of outdoor sport in moderation, along with his vivid interest in aesthetics. He is of'course, practically artistic by temperament and profession. Also is musical, plays the violin well, and is member of a prominent singing-club; has a fine baritone voice and a speaking-voice of round, pleasing quality but entirely masculine, like everything else external to the patient. Wears a full moustache, and has worn the so-called "Greek beard" occasionally. The facial hair grows fast, requires daily shaving. Thick hair on head. Skin otherwise, except the pubes, almost hairless. Figure, bearing, general appearance, etc., normally manly. Genitalia entirely normal. Strong potency affirmed.

"Ever since R—was a boy, and much under puberty, he was sexually drawn to boys and men rather than to the other sex. Was fond of girls, and as he grew older always took much pleasure in female society; goes out socially a great deal now. He is much liked by women (R—dances well) and has intimate friendly relations with them, but feels entire disinclination to sexual interest in women, which in the case of those of immoral life and lower intellectualism amounts to great aversion. Has several times, in early life, attempted coitus cum mulieribus, but either could not become sexually excited at all, or with difficulty and with not the least enjoyment accomplished the act. During at least ten years has not tried it again, having an instinctive horror corporis puellae. Dislikes kissing women, even relatives, embraces from them, etc. Otherwise R— feels himself, and is, perfectly normal toward women.

"As a boy, R—admired pictures and statues of men, handsome men, much more than pictures of pretty girls and beautiful women. Fell in love passionately, at nine, with a handsome rather refined young groom in his father's employ; used to be kissed, embraced, etc. by this young man, with "indescribable pleasure"; and was sexually much excited by such contact. The groom himself was heterosexual (a man of twenty-six or twenty-seven years) and was sent away from the place because of his intrigues with a woman-servant, that had lasted months. But nevertheless the groom also was sometimes excited when caressing R—, so that once or twice there was masturb. mut. between them with ejacul. on the part of the older participant. Once, after looking at a photograph of a famous male statue, R—, does not recall which one, he "could not sleep for several nights" on account of thinking of the picture and longing to have it; was affected by his vague sexual ideas of embraces, kisses, etc. from such a type of man. At a little beyond thirteen, R—was sexually potent, he is sure; when fully fourteen was extremely so. Constant excitement as to male beauty, dreams of sexual sort, ejaculatio and the like. Never as to females. At sixteen, when home from hoarding-school one summer, he had another violent flame—for a young physician in attendance on his mother. He could not eat or sleep, haunted the street where the physician lived, and so on. But he had learned by this time to hide carefully his feelings, because he heard such sentiments laughed at, and called "girlish," "perverted" and so on, by schoolmates. At fourteen, R—was sent away to a school, where he stayed three years. It was the same story with him in this school. He had several intense friendships that were first and last strongly sexual.

He was always cold to the talk about girls among his mates, and was constantly brooding rhapsodically over what it would be to have such "friendships" as he learned about from classical books, and miscellaneous reading. He found in this school one friend who was as similisexual a lad as himself, though quite manly otherwise, and had such ideals of masculine "friendships." He formed a close tie with R—including sexual intercourse (masturb. mut. et coit. inter femora, sed non in an. et non irrumatio) R—says that, like most schools, this one was "a regular forcing-house" for early similisexualism. E.g. the "relation" between one of the tutors and one older student was so well known to the pupils that nobody could understand why it was not broken-up by the head-master. After the friend mentioned left school, R—was inconsolable, though he had grown alert as to hiding his feelings. A new pupil came, with whose good-looks, talents and character R—was fascinated, and with whom he was able to form a new, enthusiastic "friendship." He then was "cured" of his sentiment for the first youth. The new friendship however gave R—deep wretchedness; for though it was close and affectionate, young X—was not homosexual "enough," and so R—nearly lost his intimacy by venturing too far in that direction. With difficulty R— removed the impression, and thereafter hid its real passion. He hid it the better because of other similisexual relations with good-looking schoolmates, more or less of his own nature, at same time."

"In the art-school abroad, to which R—was sent for professional study, he became more and more alarmed about his sexual mystery, his utter indifference to women in "that" way, and his "susceptibility" for the male type. He had been troubled, even terrified, at this state of things before, as he realized its abnormality, and had heard what such a feeling was considered by men about him, had learned of the criminality of it in law, and so forth. He heard much more about it in the European city where he now was studying; enough to know that there was a vast deal of it in the world, even if it was spoken of as disgusting and unnatural. It was at this time, that R—made most attempts, by frequenting women, to bring himself into heterosexual order; but with no success. About this time, in deep trouble, he formed a friendship with a fellow-student who was "like himself." The sympathy and the sexual relation between R—and this student (coit. inter femora, and occasionally onan. buccal.) made R—more tranquil physically and mentally for awhile. The friend was perfectly satisfied with his own psychic organization. He told R—that he was "foolish to worry," that "thousands of men were so," and that it was only a question of concealment and custom. R—was, however, morally more and more in unrest, believing himself vicious, criminal, and also dreading the reactions that came: fearful of the mystery of his increasing horror femin. etc. He had intense pleasure, however, in all the sexual acts with his friend. The latter went to Italy some months before R—had finished his art-course, and there W—lives. The friendship is still warm though they only occasionally meet, and it remains also sexual. In all sexual roles, R—is temperamentally rather active than passive. Coit. analis, actively or passively, is usually disgusting to him."

"While abroad, and since returning to the American city where he lives, R—saw more or less of male prostitution, including juvenile, but always was disgusted with it. Only once, since returning to America, has he had relations with such a type; abstaining not only because he dreads scandal, blackmail etc., but in real sexual loathing. Once his physical repression led him to make such a 'connection'; it gave him more sense of shame and physical and moral disgust than relief. In fact, all R—'s impulses so far as one can infer are of the most moral, decent and refined sort. He also says that 'very seldom' in his life has he been able to maintain a sexual passion for any length of time when his intellectual and moral interest in the man has failed."

"On his return, R—became at once very busy and successful. He has a fine mind, and he was always a superior student in other than his art-education. He was quite unhappy sexually, and in constant nervous excitement, till he came into touch with a respectable element of American similisexual life, and made a sexual intimacy with a young jurist of the city. This friend was considerably dionian, though he was sufficiently uranistic also to be on sexual terms with R—, and had some idea of the general temperament of R—'s, kind."

Unfortunately, at this same time, in spite of the relationship mentioned, R—fell into a state of violent similisexual love for another individual whom he met; a young foreign musician visiting the country professionally. This passion has been the most intense and nerve-shattering in its course and consequences of any that R—has ever known. The affair was the cause of his confiding his condition and history to me. He was by this time past his twenty-sixth year. He fell in love "at sight" with the musician, who is really remarkably engaging in person and manner. R—soon could not eat or sleep. He made the acquaintance of the young foreigner and being a good linguist, as also a most attractive companion, R—soon became his most intimate American friend. Unluckily the musician was not morally at all what he should have been. He imposed on R—s kindness, which extended to generous pecuniary and social help, treated R—with systematic insincerity, and (though half-uranistic), being himself not at all homosexual as to R—, he worked on R—s interest in him with gross selfishness. He understood perfectly the nature of the sentiment he had excited. After R—'s disclosing his sentiment, he encouraged R—to believe that it was returned, and that there were merely hesitations of a delicate, romantic sort, till R—would enjoy the fullest sexual relations desired. The unfortunate R—presently found out that the musician's plans were wholly false to any such idea; that he, R—, was not in the least beloved; that the musician was using R—'s money and social aid toward carrying on a sexual intrigue with another man in the city; and also had an intimacy, not free from sexual relations, with a woman. R—'s discovery of the trickery and moral worthlessness of his new friend almost destroyed his reason. Violent scenes and a rupture came, of course. But R—could not "get over" this really *grande passion*. He had hid the undercurrents of the affair, of course, and they were known to only the musician and himself and one friend. R—made efforts to go about his work as usual and to be active in lively society. Pressently he broke down completely in nerves, became sleepless and was ill in bed for weeks, the excuse being prostration from overwork. The matter told on him desperately. He went to a sanitarium. While there he attempted suicide, but failed because a drug was too weak. At last by extreme efforts toward self-control, he pulled himself together, the musician having gone back to Europe, and the sense of the rupture being somewhat dulled. R—resumed his work and social life. He says that, so far as he knows, only one person, that one person being an elderly (married) lady with whom he has always had a specially warm and sympathetic friendship, suspects the nature of his nervous break."

"This affair is relatively recent. R—is not by any means "well" of it. Between hatred of his nature, disgust at life and dread of (as he frankly says) not only the past but the future, as well as through his too uncertain ideas as to his nature, he made up his mind to ascertain what a nervous specialist would make of his "case"; would give as advice, toward getting rid of it—if it could be got rid of at all."

"R—, as intimated, has played perfectly his rôle in outward life as a man. He takes assiduous part in all sexual talk about women, and is in such intimate relations with two or three of them that what is only an intellectual relation is supposed to be sexual. He has been urged to marry; by many friends. He would marry if he were not now certain that there would be no sexual help in the tie. He fears marriage would only be a melancholy error, bringing great disappointment and worse. Several times he has had reason to know that he has been loved by women whom he would have been glad to marry "if marriage were only an intellectual bond" in its duties and expectations. The *horror feminis* is too intense now for him to think of such a step, even with his dearest female friends."

"R—smokes and drinks the milder spirituous liquors very moderately. He has intimate friends whom he values as "merely friends." That is, he feels closely attached to them, but without sexual emotion. He is a member, since early boyhood, of a Protestant church; but he has now no dogmatic religious belief of any sort; the less because he says frankly that he has tried to overcome his sexual nature by religion and has found religion of no help. In fact, R—has lost religious sentiment from the effort. He makes the impression of a perfectly upright, high moral nature, and of strength of character in general."

"I could advise him only against any idea of marriage as an artificial attempt at changing his inborn similisexual nature; against losing faith in himself as to being morally depraved, etc., on account of his misfortune and the secret unhappiness it entailed; against allowing himself time to brood; urging him to as much intellectual and physical distraction as possible, to strong efforts toward sell-control; and suggesting other generalities."

Such is one interesting instance of the uranistic passion. It affords the reader good opportunities of "translating" the abnormal and similisexual love into the workings of the 'normal-sexual' sort; or vice-versa. In the chapter on "The Uranian in Military Life" will be found a case quite as suggestive.

Continuing the examples, may follow four memoranda, of the eminent Austrian psychiater, lately deceased, of the University of Vienna, Dr. Richard von Krafft-Ebing, a man whose work for a juster view of similisexual tendencies has been invaluable; and who probably was consulted previous to his retirement from his labour by more eminent uranistic sufferers than any physician in Europe. The instances are of congenital, complete uranism in highclass natures.

"Mr. N—, unmarried, born of a marriage between blood relations. His parents were sound types, but a brother of his father was in

Instance.

an asylum for the insane. The brother of Herr N—was exceedingly heterosexual. At nine years old, N—felt himself sexually drawn to his boy-friends. At fifteen years and onward, mas. mut. et coitus inter femora with boys. At sixteen, began a regular love-relationship with a young man, which developed just as normal love between a man and a woman develops. Only young men of from twenty to twenty-four years attract him. He feels himself rather in the feminine role in such sexual intimacies. He believes that from earliest childhood he has had a more feminine than masculine nature. Later than childhood he has had no pleasure in masculine sports, nor in drinking, smoking, etc. In his unsettled sort of life occurred one episode in which he was a cook, in service in a foreign country, giving excellent satisfaction as such; he lost his place because of entering into a love-affair with the son of his employer. After 22 years old, N—realized that he was of an abnormal sexual life. He was disturbed by this discovery, sought by forced visits to brothels to correct himself, but had only disgust. (Nulla erectio). One day, in despair as to his sexual situation, and the discovery of his disgrace by his family, he attempted suicide. Cured of his wound got in this attempt, he again travelled in foreign countries, ever feeling unhappiness, at odds with himself, and repudiated by his family. The only hope now left him has been that with his advancing life he will lose his sexual desire toward men. For the sake of "honour and peace," N—begs aid in his case. He declares that he will either go into a cloister, or else castrate himself. I advised a suggestion-treatment. In physique this unfortunate man is thoroughly virile (genitalia normal) in type of the secondary sexual characteristics."

Instance.

"Mr. M—, forty-four years old, a business-man by occupation, believes that his parents were healthful types; but his brother is epileptic and idiotic. His sister, of sound health, is married. From early childhood M—has been intensely attracted toward men and never has felt sexual interest in women. At his puberty, and afterwards, masturb. et irrumat. (passive). His sexual dreams always have been about men. Several times M—has tried coitus cum mulieribus, but has found himself impotent in it and wholly unmoved sexually by women. During some years he has had a lasting sexual intimacy with a (married) man. M—cannot say that in it he is more active or passive, but thinks that he is rather the feminine in such relations. M—has never had any taste for the masculine sports, is no drinker nor smoker. As a youth, he used

EDWARD IRENAEUS PRIME-STEVENSON

to "dress up" in women's clothing, with pleasure. Instance.
Is of the secondary sexual type, psychically and
physically. Genitalia normal.

"Mr. H—, thirty years old, of upper middle-class rank, is a descendant from a neuropathic mother. His sisters are suffering from nervous disorders, and he himself, since his puberty, is constitutionally neurasthenic. Even as a boy, H—felt himself attracted sexually to his schoolmates. When he was fourteen, coitus analis with an older schoolmate. He passive, and allowed it willingly, but afterwards felt great "remorse," and never has given way to such an impulse since then. When grown up, masturb. with others, instead. With his increasing neurasthenic tendencies, it has been enough to make him exclaim sexually when merely embracing another person of his own sex. This remained the method of his sexual satisfaction. He never has felt any sexual attraction toward the female sex. He became conscious of his abnormalism, and after his twentieth year he made energetic efforts to have sexual intercourse with prostitutes, in order to bring his desires into a healthfuller state. Up to that time he had believed his abnormal inclinations were only a youthful confusion of impulses. He tried coit. cum mulier. but felt wholly unsatisfied, by it, and so returned to his relations with men. He inclines to young men, from 18 to 20 years old. Older men are not sympathetic. He finds his social situation painful. He constantly fears the discovery of his perversion, and he asserts that he could not long survive such a shame. Nothing whatever in his aspect or demeanour betrays the contrary-sexualist. Genitalia normal; particularly no signs of degeneration. Mr. H—does not believe that there is any possibility of his changing his sexual abnormality. The female sex has not the slightest interest for him."

"Mr. E—, thirty-one years old, is the son of Instance.
a father exceedingly potent sexually. Otherwise
there is nothing that signifies hereditary traits in
the sexual instincts of the family. Mr. E—grew up in a solitary village. When he was six years old, he felt special pleasure in being with bearded men. After he was eleven, he used to blush when he met handsome men, and did not trust himself to look at them. In the company of women he was wholly unmoved. Till E—was seven years old, he was dressed in girl's clothing. He was unhappy at having to lay it aside. At this time, too, his favorite amusements were helping in the housekeeping-matters, in the kitchen, etc. His school-days passed calmly. Now and then he

had a deep but not lasting sentimental interest in a fellow-pupil. By night, he used to dream rather often of men "with blue clothes, and mustaches." Growing up, Mr. E—went into the gymnastic classes, so as to be with men, and for the same reason he attended balls, not to look at the girls who were wholly a matter of indifference to him, but at the male participants, imagining himself in their arms. He continued to feel that he was lonely, unsatisfied, and little by little he realized himself to be unlike other young men. His whole thought and aim became the finding-out, somewhere, a man that would feel love for him. When he was seventeen, a man induced him to permit masturb. mut. But the reaction for E—was a mixture of pleasure, shame and distress. He knew now the abnormalism of his sexual feelings. He was at first depressed, and thought once of suicide; then he accepted the peculiar situation, continued to long for men, etc., but by his girlish timidity he passed years without such relationships. (Masturb. solit. as a physical resource, but not often, being really not so strongly inclined to physical desire). It has been a pain to him, in the utmost degree, when a girl showed her preference for him, as was not seldom the case. When E—was 26 he came to the capital to live, and therewith he had ample opportunity for homosexual relations. He lives now, since some time back, with a man of like age, the two keeping house together as "man and wife." He is happy in.this, and is rather in the feminine role in it. (Masturb. mut. et coitus inter fern). E—is a valued workman, noted in his calling, in demeanour and aspect thoroughly manly, with normal genitalia, without signs of degeneration. He informed me that his younger brother who is a "woman-hater" is also externally manly and yet feels himself homosexual. It is a striking fact that two sisters of E—who died early were masculine in their tastes, preferring stable work (!) etc., to female occupations.

Instance: Uranistic Dionian Type.

The problem of a nature strongly heterosexual, seeking relations with women eagerly, but intermittently similisexual, has been touchedon. In the following narrative, which is given me by an English medical friend, the type is illustrated.

"H. O—, aged thirty-four, architectural assistant, married, and the father of a son of seven years of age, came to consult me partly on account of his own nervous troubles (insomnia, violent headaches and general neurasthenia) and because of certain signs of nervous and sexual abnormalism in his young son that he lately had remarked. After two or three interviews, Mr. O—became more explicit, with the result of enabling me to make the following notes of his sexual history:—

The father of O—was exceptionally given to sexual relations with women, and was very potent. Otherwise O—knows of no peculiarities of O—senior's vita sexualis, but does not think he was ever in the least similisexual. O—'s mother is a robust, strong-nerved woman of over sixty. The parents married early. They still live, in a German capital. One uncle was homosexual, so O's father once told O—, and was mixed up in a blackmailing affair in Dublin some twenty-five years ago. One aunt suffered from religious excitement and was two or three times in a sanitarium, where she finally died. O—has three sisters and a brother, all married; he cannot give any information as to their sexual traits, but believes them normal. They all have families and live apparently happily. Outwardly O—is of fine and entirely virile aspect, much more than of any secondary type; athletic formerly, takes much exercise now; and smokes, uses liquors, though not to any excess. Wears full close beard, and has handsome features, not in the least feminine. Genitalia normal and large. He speaks of himself as uncommonly potent.

In early boyhood O—was attracted to girls sexually; as early as ten years attempting coitus with them, and (sine ejaculatio, of course) took pleasure in it. At fifteen found opportunity to get into sexual relations with girls older than himself, was potent and remarked by them on account of it. Strong sense of female beauty, and always much libido as he matured. At eighteen, O—nearly got into serious scandal from the pregnancy of a young woman in his city, who claimed that she was enceinte by him, after numerous rendezvous one summer; the case being turned away from O—, on O—'s father's finding proof that O—was not the only youth with whom she had misconducted herself. During his university course, and afterwards O—had frequent relations with prostitutes of good class; also several sexual intrigues of more "exclusive" sort. He believes that he is the father of a child by a woman of superiour social position in the city of X—. He always had great libido in normal sexual conditions. He really has fallen in love two or three times with young women, not very deeply, rather sensually than intellectually; admiring their physical beauty, sexual suggestiveness, and so on. He says that he married his wife during such a frame of mind, she being a very beautiful young actress when he met her, because he "could not possess her otherwise"—as she insisted. They have lived happily, except as to the fact that «occasionally (of late much more frequently) O—has been dull toward his conjugal duties, for the reason following:

O—has always had a most vivid sexual admiration for male beauty, along with all the foregoing normal enthusiasm and libido. When a boy of eight or nine years, took great pleasure in secretly watching men or lads bathe, as an opportunity to observe their genitalia, and was excited strongly. Great susceptibility for photographs, pictures, statuary and so on of handsome males. At the same time that O—was attracted so prematurely to girls, he was in love (at least there was a powerful sentimental and sexual emotion) with a boy-companion. On several occasions, at puberty, he and this friend had relations which he himself sought. They gave O—great satisfaction. (Masturb. mut. et pen. in os). Then when about fifteen, he went to a circus in the town, and became so enamoured of a young rider that he forgot for the time all his normal, if boyish, amours. He managed to get a photograph of the circus-rider, kissed it often, and finally used to masturbate with the portrait in bed with him. During his nineteenth year, O—went to France and Germany with his parents; while there his two-sided sexualism was rather increased than lessened. He met in Munich a painter of similisexual tastes, was sentimentally struck with the man's looks, and became sexually intimate with him. At the same time, he was in normal intrigues at least twice. Leaving his parents in Germany, O—came back to England by way of Italy. In Home he felt for the first time since his early youth a distinctly pederastic passion. He fell in love with a young waiter in the hotel where he was stopping, a lad of about eighteen of uncommon beauty. O—managed to get into sexual relations with him, the waiter coming up to O—'s room "several nights in the week." (Coit. in anum, et inter fern.) On such occasions O—states that he is preferably in the masculine role, only; in fact as to coit. analis he cannot be otherwise. It is noteworthy, that in his sexual intercourse with women, O—has not the least inclination (so he says) to any abnormal methods. O—was so enamored of this Italian youth that he nearly induced the latter to come to England with him as his servant. Returned to London, O—, however, forgot the whole adventure, for he became busy professionally, as an architect's assistant, and also socially. Had now several normal love-affairs with women. In the course of a year or two, he met and married the young actress now his wife, as mentioned, a matter that has made considerable disturbance in O—'s relations with his parents and others in the family. He has been almost wholly normal in his sexualism till within a year. He met in his club a gentleman somewhat older, of attractive personality, and of interesting intellectual character, who fascinated O—in the old "unaccountable and sexual" way. O—finally confessed himself, to discover that the gentleman was homosexual. The result is an intimacy, existing today, which, as has been indicated, has made trouble for O—with his wife, who thinks that O—is intriguing with some other woman. O—and his friend have been convinced that their intimacy must be broken off. They have several times tried to give it up. But O—as yet cannot resign himself to a separation or to a colder relation, and has induced the prolonging of the matter. (Coit. in anuin, with O—again in the active role; also onan. bucc.) Lately O—feels the effect of either over-indulgence in this, along with his efforts toward not wholly neglecting his marital duties to his wife. O—still strongly admires her sexually, though now he is sensible of her intellectual uninterest for him, to a depressing degree. This has made O—extremely neurasthenic. He also has noticed signs of contrary sexual instincts in his son. Affection and solicitude for the boy have troubled him more than any preceding causes. He has never felt any worry over the mystery of his "dual sexualism"; at least, never seriously, for he saw early "how many more people were like him." The matter became soon one of concealment and of "watching opportunities." O—gives one the impression of a man of fully the average moral character, is distingué, refined, distinctly intellectual and aesthetic, etc."

Two further examples of the mixture of contrary and similisexual instincts in the same individual, I take from Dr. Krafft-Ebing's observations:

Instance.

Uranian-dionian Similisexualism. Mr. H—, an official, forty-two years old, dates his contrary sexualism from a rape on him, by a schoolmate, when he was ten. . . He came to feel the greatst enjoyment in sexual relations with a schoolmate two years older, then later kept up the practice with other young men. From his puberty, onward, as a growing youth, H—has felt far too much sexual inclination for young men, especially if waiters (!) When he was twenty he recognized his abnormalism of his vita sexualis; made sexual approaches to young women but felt repelled by the act and was hardly potent iii it. He succeeded in refraining from homosexual relations, along with those with the other sex. At twenty-four he came to know a ballet-dancer, was charmed with her, and in coitus was perfectly potent; had the greatest satisfaction, etc. The same sort of success in the following year with other women. But with the thirtieth year of his life, this normal period of sexual feeling vanished. He continued to lose his normal libido, and since live years he makes no heterosexual approaches. Masturb. mut. with males, from 17 to 20 years old; strong desires, great sexual satisfaction, etc. Became mixed up in a blackmailing affair. Lately his sexual act is expressed in kissing, embracing, etc. Orgasms and exclamation follows. The psychical personality of Mr. H—is abnormal, he is intellectually limited, and trivial. Of his (deceased) parents he knows nothing of importance in his case. He was an only child. Build of body and outward appearance thoroughly virile.

Instance: Uranian-Dionian.

Mr. J—an official by profession descends from a father who was most neuropathic. The four sisters also are very nervous in their type. A cousin seduced him (masturbat, mut.) when J—was hardly seven. At eight years, his greatest enjoyment was opportunities of looking at nude men. He grew up in a country boarding-school, and till he was sixteen had no opportunity to be with the female sex. Had intense passions for his schoolmates. At twenty-six, he was initiated into the mystery of homosexual love. Several sexual relations with men, actively and passively; but in pederasty no enjoyment. His (rare) sexual dreams turned to men. He was not wholly unimpressionable, however, to the other sex; but held back from coitus femin. by his fear of sexual disease, two of his relatives being diseased so. Since his twenty-seventh year, he has grown neurasthenic and has gone about to many sanitary resorts. Since then libido et erectio lost. Three years ago he had a passing heterosexual episode: he became enthusiastically in love with a young lady. But soon after, he was captivated by a male friend, with whom he still remains in sexual intimacy. But he now feels discontented with this. For lately he has become interested in another lady, and is considering the idea of a marriage with her. But his courage fails. He does not believe that he could dispense with homosexual relationships when a husband, but believes that he can keep on with them, when once married, "like so many other of his married acquaintances." He presents the physical and psychical secondary sexual characteristics of manhood. Genitalia normal.

In the "Psychopathia Sexualis," which is rich in personal observations, occur other cases of this dual sexualism; some of them of extreme vehemence and morbidity-to which the reader is referred.

EDWARD IRENAEUS PRIME-STEVENSON

A further example of the uniting of dionism and uranism is the following from an American observer of the phenomena of contrary sexualism. It is striking in the dionistic aspects of the subject.

Instance: Uranian-Dionian.

C. T—thirty five years of age. American by birth, of no profession since giving up commercial interests of active kind. Married several years ago, but no children. Consults me as to his sexual status, which he finds burdensome, though not as a new matter. Main facts are as follows: T—comes of a father of exceptional mental ability, a rich merchant; who became deranged just after retiring from business and passed the time between his fifty-fifth and sixtieth year in a private asylum, was ocasionally violent, and died insane. The father was rather a potator, fond of "good living," and was extremely given to sexuality, prior to his marriage. T—'s mother is a very highly organized woman; aesthetic, and for many years a sufferer from chronic nervous disease. Of the grand-parents, T—has no information that is of bearing on his case. He is a most virile type, full, athletic figure, manly and handsome features, strong blond beard, and strong voice. Skin is fine and, on the body is hairless, apart from the pubes, which are fully haired. Genitalia large and normal. All his demeanour masculine. There is one brother who is a potator and has been till lately, on his marriage, a constant frequenter of women. The only sister is perfectly normal in intellect, and of fine physique, with no traces of neurasthenia, etc. and is married and has four strong, healthful children.

T—was inclined to similisexual feelings as a boy of eight or nine. He used to watch a certain serving-man of the family undress—with vivid pleasure, and (he thinks) with strong erectio. In school, he was led by two older students into the usual sexual practices among lads. (Musturb. mut. et penem in os mut, with intense satisfaction). His puberty was early, and he was potent at thirteen. But when in school, he had frequent sexual relations with a female servant, with thorough enjoyment. Also visited, when he was sixteen and later, a brothel, and had great libido. During his college-course, T—kept a young woman as his mistress, or at least was one of a set of two or three young men who supported the same puella. But T—'s feeling for masculine beauty, and his sexual liking for handsome men, older or younger, did not leave him, in spite of normal instincts and satisfactions. He fell vehemently in love with a fellow-student of athletic beauty, at this same time. The matter came to a disclosure. The result was a strong friendship, instead of a rupture between T—and this college-friend, who was not at first at all similisexual but became so with T—. From then T—lost interest in the puella, and gave over visiting her. Intense pleasure in his sexual intercourse (coit. inter fem. et penem in os, mutually) with his male friend. He and the friend however became troubled as to their instincts, and the friend went to a physician, who warned them of dangers in it; and also held out the certainty of their losing their emotions if they would seek normal satisfactions. They followed the advice; the friend "recovered"; but T—did not. The result was a time of great unhappiness for T—, as his friend was sexually "lost" to him, though their friendship swung back to its old unsexual plane, and so was not broken. After college, T—went into business with his father, conducting soon an important branch-office of it in a distant city, and with great success. He is an excellent organizer, and is very practical, despite aesthetic traits, such as his fondness for music, pleasure in fine-arts in general, in elegant literature, etc. When in the town of Z—, there came about a clandestine normal intimacy for T— with a society-woman, that was of much pleasure to him; again strong normal libido and complete satisfaction. The lady leaving town with her husband, T—for a time frequented brothels, then grew tired of that, and the more as he contracted a gonorrhea that gave him much trouble to cure. He was sent to Europe on business, and met in Brussels a Bavarian physician who was similisexual, and with whom T—travelled for several weeks, in constant similisexual relations that "drove him nearly wild with pleasure." In London, this episode being over, he met the young lady also a traveller and a compatriot, in whom he fell in love, and who became his wife. T—and she have lived happily. But T—is by no means faithful to her as regards avoiding homosexual relationships; as to others he is wholly so. Mrs. T—however is not strongly sexual in temperament, and so T—is freer to indulge his incorrigible desires for males. He has two friends in the city with whom he has such relations; what is more, he often goes to certain baths, saloons, and other localities where homosexuals of various grades congregate, and where there are more or less opportunities for their practices; running risks of blackmail and other trouble from such similisexual adventures. He meets often men with whom he has much delight in the sexual acts (especially penem in os). He has occasionally taken pleasure in distinctively pederastic intercourse (coitus analis) but only with adults, can suffer that only if himself in the active role. He has not the least sexual interest in immature youths, etc. Some weeks ago, T—had a meeting with a young man, a stranger in the city, and now remote from it again, in which he contracted what he has feared was a disease in his mouth, of sexual sort. (It is not such however.) After hesitation, he came to me for treatment. He has become candid as to his case. He would be glad to change it, the more as he sees that it brings him in peril, socially and legally, that his health suffers from his adventurous excesses, and also because he thinks that with an improvement in the health of his wife (to whom he is warmly attached, and with whom he "has great pleasure" in the sexual acts) he may need a thorough recruiting and care of all his sexual forces. He is glad that he has no children, as they would be a worry to him, lest they should display sexual abnormalities. His wife is not supposed to be at all incapable of bearing children. T—guards against the possibility of offspring with her, under various excuses. He has been a father more than once, he is sure, during some preceding irregular sexual intimacies."

In the late Otto de Joux's study of uranianism entitled "Die Enterbten des Liebesglücks," a book which despite its tendency to a romantic accentuation and even to ill-placed levity contains useful matters for lay-reading, the authour gives the following sketch of an Uranian's "love at sight." The narrator is spoken of as a young scion of a noble family of the Continent; and the object of his passion a is German or Austrian army-officer.

"I have absolutely nothing feminine in me as to my looks; my bearing indeed is noted for its genuine masculinity. But, for all that, I have a soul like a woman's. I am a man: but I love another man, burningly, passionately, to death itself. I know too it is a mad hopeless struggle that I have kept up against my all too-tender nature, since my boyhood's years. So I have given up struggling against my fate.

Instance: Typical Case of Uranistic "Love and Sight."

"I was young, free, rich but not happy. . . I fell in love with a man whose name I did not know. It came over me like a flash of lightning when I saw him for the first time. It was in a café; my eye caught sight of a dignified officer. He had an illustrated paper before him, but his glance was far from it; visibly he was sunk in deep thought. My first idea was of what preoccupied him. . . the noble profile with lines so strong and definite; everything about him suggested intellect and will-power. . . Finally he got up and went away; and I followed him, compelled by an irresistible force. How is it possible that one human creature can exert such a violent influence over another of like sex? I had never had any experience like this. The fresh air brought me to my senses: "You are a fool!" I said to myself, and went home. But from that evening he and I met often, in the street, in social life; though the stars went against me, for I could never find any suitable opportunity to get into a nearer relation with the man—even if I did get his photograph. . . I believed that he was an Uranian-sufferer, as was I. We greeted one another at times. By my way of looking at him, he must soon have known that he was unspeakably dear to my heart."

"At last we were at a brilliant ball, and in the same quadrille. . . We came to the figure "Trenis," where the men, so to say, embrace; in order to turn about in a circle, while the ladies on their side do the same. I would have said something different to him; instead, I could only murmur.—"This is the best moment of the dance"! He answered, "Be still, be still, dear fellow!—we will get away from here at once! "I could hardly wait till the quadrille ended. Ceremoniously I left my glittering partner. What was Hecuba to me? I hurried to the dressing-rooms, for my fur-coat. He came upon my heels and put on his cloak. We left the vestibule, got into the same carriage, and fell into each other's arms. Neither of us could utter a word. At last God had given me a friend to my soul! . . . He and I have lived together now more than three years, like a married pair. We have never had one quarrel. Rudolf is somewhat jealous, but is kindness and thoughtfulness itself. When he goes to the annual military maneuvers, I follow him; if he should be stationed elsewhere I shall go with him to the end of the world—to the Esquimaux! . . . We are happy without misgivings or remorse. There is a happiness that knows no end."

The Strength of the Tie of Dionistic Friendship with Uranians.

The warmth of feeling for the Uranian on the part of his unsuspecting dionistic friend has been mentioned. "Jack, I could not care for you more if you were a woman!" lightly exclaims some affectionate Dionian—"though, thank God, you are not one!" He wrings the hand of the silent Jack, whose heart is pierced by the bitter irony of that "Thank God, you are not one!" from the lips of the man he loves with a woman's heart, under the mask of a male friendship. Another painful aspect of an "undeclared" intimacy between two friends can long-continue with a double concealment. This phase is treated in the English novelette, "Imre: A Memorandum." A virile urano-dionistic type sometimes struggles with an uranistic sentiment which he detests, cannot understand, fights down fiercely. A striking study of this sort of psychologic tragedy is made in a French novel by Mme. Alfred Valette, whose pen-name is "Rachilde"; the story "Les HorsNature" being originally published in the well-known Paris periodical, "Le Mercure de France," a magazine in which French uranistic fiction has long been a feature, including stories by Eckhoud and others. Aside from disclosures or suppressions of a romance, many broken intimacies between men occur when the Dionian after he has become more or less uranistic in his emotion for his friend, is led back to his normal sexual interests by falling in love with a woman, and decides on marriage; realizing that it must mean a break with the too-sensitive Uranian. Miserable indeed is the Uranian then, unless he can rise to a less sexual plane of sentiment. He is abandoned, his dream is over! He cannot blame anyone. He can, he should, simply submit. But what shall console him? How can he surrender the man he loves, even when it is for the other's happiness? In a later chapter, "The Uranian in Relation to Marriage," one or two instances of this struggle are given.

Uranians as Valued Friends of Women.

Not able to love a woman sexually, the Uranian not a woman-hater, and who is in fact fond of the society of charming and interesting women, is frequently precisely their most valued, useful and beloved friend. The Uranian can be the "model" friend of the other sex. To them he is dispassionate yet cordial, perceptive and sensitive to their emotions, as is no Dionian. Many are the speculations in social circles, why some attractive, superior man does not choose himself a wife, become plighted to some girl whose preference for him is as marked, as is his admiration for her. So warm an intimacy, but to no clear result! Is there a secret bar? Does she not love him enough? Does he not love her?

The Tragic or Comic Results of the Uranian Attitude of Defense.

Often indeed the woman herself, as well as her friends cannot understand why man's affection stays where it does, no disclosure of warmer feeling upon her admirer's lips. Unfortunately, sometimes it crosses hers; to meet his deepest regret and embarassment. Now and then, tragic, or tragic-comic, results of the silence of the Uranian, are heard of; more dramatic if the recalcitrant male is suspected to be cynically too indifferent. In such cases feminine revenge can go crudely far. The mystery of the death of Monaldeschi, the secretary of Queen Christina of Sweden, whom she ordered be beheaded with scandalous precipitation one night, during her famous visit to Prance, lately has been partly attributed to this cause. Similar stories are told of the abrupt and cruel strokes of pseudo state-justice by Catherine II of Russia, not to mention other romantic sovereigns of more ardour than patience. A few seasons ago, in Lisbon, took place such an affair, that made much scandal at the time. Among the brilliant literary men of the city, was one L—, renowned for his beauty and charming manners, but outspoken in his aversion to any sexual relations with women, and equally frank in similisexual intimacies. One of the most beautiful of the Lisbon *cocotterie* was a young woman whose services as model to a well-known French painter have made her face and figure the common property of Europe. She made repeated advances to L—with no success. As her interest warmed, came his plainer avoidance of her. At last occurred her ardent offer; and his cold refusal. One summer evening, toward midnight, L—was returning from his club. A close carriage overtook him. Two strong negroes stepped down from the box, and one of them asked L—if he would speak to a lady in the carriage. The unwary L— advanced. He was gagged, tied, thrown into the vehicle and driven away with its occupants—two ladies. One of them was the slighted Venus, the other a lady-friend who also felt aggrieved against the uranistic gentleman. L—was taken to the residence of the friend. There he was literally ravished to exhaustion! Towards morning he was conveyed to one of the remoter spots of the Campolide, and left, still bound and gagged, on a bench, where he was found by a watchman and taken home. The affair was the talk of the Portuguese clubs for weeks. The heroine left Lisbon, with her establishment and friend, the same day.

The Complete Uranian's "Horror Corporis Feminae."

The antipathy of a completely uranistic man to bodily contact with a woman, not merely his physical insensibility, or his aesthetic coldness cannot be "explained" or "reasoned away." Not more can we explain many primary instincts in human nature, by argument. But one element of the sub-conscious kind in this aversion, in multitudes of cases is the Uranian's sense of a woman as physically a sort of *unclean* thing. She seems to the Uranian far less wholesome, than a man. Her embrace and reception seems to him full of secret impurity; even if he knows her to be most attentive to all manner of toilette-processes; absolutely free of disease. He feels, too, a disgust at the sexual periods of women. Her pregnancy is a repulsion. There is the dread of venereal diseases. Not inappropriately may here be mentioned the theory of many Uranians that their intercourse is a valuable check against the over-population of the globe. The uranian sexualism has thus a theoretic connection with the malthusian doctrines. Many homosexuals claim that for this end similisexual relations should be encouraged; just as we have seen that under the Mosaic Code, and facing the problem of the increase of the Jews against the Canaanites, it was a felony because more or less a hindrance to the desired census.

How is the Uranian Physically Satisfied.

As to what brings to the Uranian his physical gratification and appeasement absurd popular notions are plentiful enough, including those grounded on the ideas of bodily hermaphroditism. There is a general ignorance of this matter among otherwise educated people. The law confuses physical expressions of similisexualism, both active and passive. There cannot, of course, be precisely the same bodily conjunction, even when coitus analis or buccal coition are the processes, as when the opposite sexes unite. But the Uranian is satisfied without such perfect physical union. Nude embracements and close contacts genitally as a rule suffice for all the pleasurable sensations of normal sexual intercourse. Mere close embraces, or a coit. inter fern, is usually adequate toward complete orgasm by him. Often less than that is needed. For, one must remember that the Uranian passion is informed much by a sort of idealism, far more vivid and nervous than the sensation of normalists. The Uranian's instinct demands less of the actual physique. Usual as are buccal onanism, mutual masturbation and so on, they are not invariably instinctive to Uranian. In his more refined class he is intensely sensitive to a spiritual possession of his friend, his psychic conquest of the beauty of the male. Imagination has a powerful share in even the physical pleasure of all superior similisexualism. The bodily aspects of similisexual loves and their harm or good as compared with effects of normal sexual gratifications by Dionians, will be treated in an Appendix to this study.

Of "Active" and "Passive" Uranianism.

There are two salient phases and temperaments in similisexualism, often not indicated by exterior detail; as has been noted. In one, the similisexualist always inclines to give himself up; instinctively makes the surrender, psychical and physical as does a woman, avoids exertion. He leaves most to his partner, even while he has strong desires and enjoyments. Here is the "passive" temperament, of course. The "active" type in which the individual feels inclined always to be the aggressor, physically to dominate, has been somewhat specially illustrated in the foregoing examples. In the following group we can observe this more feminine temperament. There is no rule of preliminary judgment on the psychiater's part, though in delicate physiques and weak morale generally is met a more passive than active temperament. On the other hand, a vigorously masculine physique, a bearded pasha or some athletic warrior or bronzed sailor, may always have the desire to be passive, rather than active, in homosexual intercourse. The differences, divergences from a fully virile type, even to physical effeminization, are important in the passivist. Especially by passive uranians, when physical rapports are in question, is anal coition desired. I cite here an example from "Psychopathia Sexualis."

Instance: Passive Uranism.

"Mr. C—, not in public life, comes from a neuropathic father and a very nervous mother. One brother suffered from paranoia, and another one is physically degenerate. Three sisters, younger, are wholly normal. Mr. C—is neuropathic, has a slight 'tic.' C—was talented in music, poetry, and interested himself in the theater. Toward scientific studies, especially mathematics he was not at all talented, and with trouble got past his school-examinations. As far back as he can remember, he felt himself attracted to masculine individuals. In the beginning he had "passionate enthusiasms" for older schoolmates. With entry into puberty, he fell in love with a male teacher, a guest of his parents. His feeling was toward the feminine role. His sexual dreams, etc. directed themselves only to male persons and passively. C—declares that he feels himself physically like a woman. As a boy he played exclusively with dolls, and later was interested in women's affairs, felt an aversion to male interests. He most liked the company of young girls, because they were "sympathetic," etc. He dislikes smoking and drinking spirituous liquors. He has specially cared for cooking and embroidery. Never has had strong libido. Seldom had sexual relations with men while growing up. His "ideal" was such a relationship, himself in the female role. The idea of coit. cum mulier. repelled him with horror. Since reading "Psychopathia Sexualis," he has been terrified about himself, at the chances of legal punishment (if caught in intercourse with males) and has succeeded in keeping clear of sexual intercourse with men. This abstinence has induced pollutions and neurasthenia. On this account, C—has sought medical aid. C—has a vigorous beard, and except for delicate features and a remarkably fine skin, he shows no signs of departure from the virile type. Genitalia normal, except the want of due descent of scrotum. In his deportment, on the street, walk and general bearing, there is nothing striking, though he is tormented with dread of his sexual peculiarity being remarked. On this account he is shy of people. If he hears coarse conversation he blushes like a girl. Once when somebody was talking of contrary sexualism, he fainted. Music puts him into a nervous perspiration. On close inspection, Mr. C—appears psychically feminine; quite too timid, in a girlish way, and wanting independence of character. The nervous restlessness, 'tic', and moderate neurasthenic indications, betray the really constitutional neuropathic type."

The Uranian Impulse Respects no Class: Pervades All Social, Moral, Mental, Grades.

The similisexual sentiment is no respecter or station in life, and interesting exhibitions of it occur in humbler as well Grades as exalted ranks. I select here such a case, from the psycho-pathologist last mentioned: condensing somewhat the memorandum:

"B—a waiter by occupation, single, was sent to me by his family-physician; with whom B— had fallen in love, as suffering from contrary-

Instance.

sexualism. B—willingly and with decency described his vita ante acta et sexualis, specially; glad at last to obtain an authoritative opinion as to his sexual condition, which has seemed to himself diseased. B—cannot give any information as to his grandparents, His father was a quick-tempered, excitable man, a potator, and much given to sexuality. After this father had had twenty-four children by the same wife, he separated from her, and then three times made his housekeeper pregnant! The mother of B—is a healthy woman. Of many sisters, six are alive, several are ill with nervous maladies, but none is abnormal sexually, except one sister who has a sexual aversion to men. B—was a sickly child. His sexual life began at eight years. . . At twelve years, he began falling in love with men, mostly those in the thirties and with mustaches. At that early time, erectio et pollutio. From that date, daily masturb. in thinking about some man with whom he was in love. Most special satisfaction if penem viri in os arrigere: at this ejaculatio, with extreme enjoyment. Only twelve times till now this satisfaction. He has never felt any disgust for the private parts of another man, but quite the contrary. Pederasty (coitus analis) is disgusting to him, in the highest degree, and he has never allowed it. But he feels inclined always to the passive role in his perverted sexuality. His love for a sympathetic man is unlimited. He is willing to do anything for such. He shivers with excitement and delight if he merely sees such a man. When B—was nineteen he allowed himself rather often to be induced by his comrades to visit brothels of women. He had no pleasure in such coitus and only in the actual moment of exclamation was he sexually relieved. . . But he has twice been a father. The last child, a girl, of eight begins to show perverse sexualism, which much troubles him. He wonder if there is no help again it. C—declares that he always has the feelings of a woman when in the sexual role with men. In order to attain erectio when with a woman he was always forced to call up the image of some man that he loved. He has always believed that his sexual perversion rose in the wish of his father to have him born a girl. . . Drinking, smoking, masculine occupations and amusements he has never had any taste tor; on the contrary he likes sewing and cookery and whenever he could do so, he used to dress-up as a girl, and he was often ridiculed because of his liking for dolls when a child. His interest in circuses is for the male performers. . . He has never had any sense of feminine charms. . . The patient is graceful in build, has slight growths of hair on the cheeks, and slight mustache (which did not come till he was twenty-eight). Except as to a slightly wavering walk nothing betrays his womanish nature. . . His demeanour in the highest degree is decent. Genitalia large, well-developed, normally hirsute; posteriori masculine, etc.

Male Prostitution Generally Passive.

In two later chapters of this book will be illustrated the uranianism which while debased ideally and effeminized physically is associated with irresponsable social life, an absolute vagabondage included, and is largely passive. As may be inferred, the male prostitute is much of this class, whether he be completely similisexual or not. He has the "professional" disadvantage of being obliged to avoid the open publicity of solicitation, etc. of the female prostitutes. How readily he overcomes that set-back, and utilizes his chances toward blackmailing-schemes, we shall soon see in examining homosexual prostitution.

Can the Uranian Be "Cured."

We have thus glanced at various phases of the second Intersex, without making special classifications such as will be the subject of our further studies. Accepting generalities of the sort are we to conclude that Uranian mankind is "curable"? The word presupposes something too much. The question of change in the Uranian depends on how far his nature is completely inborn; how far it may be bred in temperament and nerve; how far absolute intersex; in what degree there has been prenatal condition. How much of the manifestation is a cultivation, by the individual, how much is a psychic process associated even with physiologic traits?—though, as we have pointed out a typical physique is not essential. Can we "cure" Nature? Can we make the leopard change his spots?

The Primary Errors in Diagnostis Pathological.

We must here, particularly meet here a series of fundamental errors of not only the popular notion, but of even the scientific mind, time and again; viz, that the Uranian suffers from a nervous disease; that his status is indisputably "pathological;" that his outward type determines his sex; and that in consequence of being intersexual he is morally vicious, degenerate, and criminal. We have seen how modern law, in many parts of the world, still makes him the latter type. We see how statute-books visit on him the penalty of his "contrary" intersexual condition, with truculent severity. But this all is acting toward a man much as if the man were to be punished because he has a leg or arm shorter than his next-door neighbour, or prefers vegetable diet to fleshmeats. Of "moral cure" often there should be no question, because no need. Complete, inborn, intersexual uranianism cannot be "cured." The shame of a gross blunder falls to the psychiater who promises a "cure" of what is not a disease. Too many a doctor, otherwise intelligent and honest, advises marriage as a "remedy"; or experimentally commits his patient to courses of useless "normal" sexuality. In vain does the real, innate Uranian seek to feel as to woman the absorbingly aesthetic, the intellectual, the sexual drawing awakened in him by a male. The male is the only natural completion of his Ego. In vain does such an Uranian seek to overcome his *horror corporis feminae*, even if as to women he have intellectual interests, close friendships, kind affections. In vain is made by him the experiment of marriage. Complete, natural similisexualism is no real abnormality, no disease. It is unchangeably intersexualistic Nature. Undoubtedly a well-gratified, skilful, virile psychiater should strive to "cure" an imperfect, fanciful and superficial similisexualism; to correct minds and bodies really morbid. Acquired and surface diversions of sexual instinct, frequently can be so corrected. But to the inbred Uranian coming to a physician for help, a psychiater can best give sympathy, enlightenment, moral encouragements to self-respect, counsels against anything obviously degenerative to soul or body, in such mystic, disturbing, tyrannic instincts. The intersexual type must be stimulated toward an elevated intellectual and ideal plane, in his sexualism. He must be helped to make the most of himself, before God and man. He must be warned from cowardly wishes for death; urged to carry his burden bravely, till death shall seek him and (let us try to believe) lay it aside for him. This—with due aid to the physique of a "patient" is all that most psychiaters can do. Ignorantly unjust sentiments of society against legitimate satisfaction of similisexual instincts, the want of equable laws for man, woman and intersex, will slowly be bettered. Meantime must the man who is homosexual be taught that he is not more criminal or monstrous than the "normalist." Common-sense, science und humanity together demand this sort of medical-psychiatric sentiment; and in time social ideas and laws, the world around, will endorse such logical, humane acceptances.

When only is the Uranian Capable of "Unnatural" Sexualism?

In fact only in one way can the real Uranian be guilty of "unnatural" acts of sexualism; for we are of course putting aside such obvious offences against nature and humanity as bestiality or the debauchment or physical injury to minors, a forcible sexual intercourse, and so on. Unnatural condition for an Uranian comes when involuntarily he attempts "normal" intercourse, with a woman; with the sex that by nature's decree repels him, that often he loathes in any corporeal relationship. Prostitute, mistress or wife—then is he indeed guilty of a sin against Nature, violates his sexual Ego, as does the normalist, the completely masculine man, sin against his nature in sexual relations with other than a woman.

The Highest Type of Uranian often Does not Wish to be "Cured."

The fact is much in evidence that the best type of Uranian often does not wish nor seek a "Cure" when once enlightened as to himself, and is clear about his moral position. Such intersexuals in a large proportion have no desire to change psychology or lot, unless perhaps such wishes come in hours of bitterness, under social persecution and injustice, or when some unhappy passion overflows. But often not even then would the Uranian be other than he is! He suffers. For his own sake, and for the sake of others he wishes that their lot were better. But there is likely to be firm in his soul the conviction that the impulse in him is pure, is perhaps the truest and highest sort of love; that in the Scriptural phrase, it is a "thing of God." Races, laws, society long may persist in repudiating or punishing it. But the world will progress slowly to wider sexual insights. Coming generations will redeem a present-day and ignorant intolerance of similisexual impulses, when united to sound ethical concepts, to superiour intelligences and to respectable lives.

VI

The Uraniad, or Feminine Complement of the Uranian: Her General Physical and Psychological Diagnosis: Types and Biographies

I n reaching the second of the intersexes, sometimes termed the Third Sex, our first inquiry is for its clear general definition, as in the case of the Uranian. Such definition follows closely the phraseology of the description of the Uranian. For the Uraniad

The Uranian Defined.

is a human being more or less perfectly, even distinctively, feminine as to physique, and often of superior sensibilities, intellectual, moral and aesthetic, and psychically most feminine in a long series of aspects'; but who by either an inborn or an acquired preference feels the passion of sexual love only for the female type. She desires sexually that sex to which she seems to belong by so many aspects, but to which she does not absolutely belong.

Such is the outline of this mysterious and third Intersex; one presenting, in its turn, strange problems; being feminine, yet not adequately woman, according to the great determinative of sex, the instincts of sexual love. The more we study this curious product of human nature, we realize more amazedly into what a further demesne of intersexual singularities we have entered.

The present book is not intended as so full a study of Uraniadism as of Uranian humanity. Outside of this chapter, what will be said of the Uraniad, must be restricted, under various classified headings, to supplements to the chapters that deal with male similisexualism. By

The Uraniad Physically, etc.

other works in psychiatry of Uraniadism the reader easily can gain a completer intimacy with the problems and types involved in feminine similisexualism.

As is the Uranian continually in externals "perfect man," so also is the Uraniad, incessantly a "perfect woman," in her physical appearance, her manner, and all that is not intimately sexual.

There is no necessary question of hermaphroditism, or of imperfect sexual organic developments. Often a perfect Uraniad is a veritable Venus, realizing the fullest feminine loveliness and grace. But there is to be admitted in the Uraniad class a tendency toward imperfect sexual organization and functions; to divergences from the delicacy of the female anatomy. The Uranian is likely to have nothing saliently feminine as to his general physique and personality, and to possess most perfectly male organs. On the contrary, the Uraniad is often obviously "boyish" when a girl, has unfeminine proportions, bizarre muscular strength, and activity; and shows preference for boy-companions and for a boy's sports. Also as she matures she frequently coarsens in body. When this occurs (not at all necessarily the case) we have the heavy-set, "mannish" woman, with a masculine walk and carriage, with a male timbre of voice; not seldom a woman-type who is malely athletic by instinct and practice. The Uraniad's features can be in due female proportion, but often of hirsute tendency, even to her showing a beard or mustache. Almost all "bearded women" are more or less Uraniad, and of "contrary" sexualism. Such also are those rather repellant musical artists, the "female tenors," "female baritones" and "woman-basses," such as are occasionally heard. But although the Uraniad is likely to enter upon what may be her troubled life with outward sex-signs of it, still she may be born, may live and may die by one's side, friend and neighbour, without showing these outward hints. We must especially beware of confusing with the Uraniad a woman of strong physique and of manly intellectuality, but who is sexually quite normal. In fact, within a few decades, the strong-minded and strong-bodied woman has gained such social emancipations that she is a confusing product for the psychiater.

Classes of Uraniads. Geographical Distribution.

The Uraniad differs in her similisexualism from the Uranian in other traits. She is less likely to revert to normal sexual passion, and her interest in aesthetic masculine externals is less. The Uranian as we have seen, is frequently bisexual in impulses; now heterosexual and now similisexual. The Uraniad temperament tends to strict exclusion of the male. When accepting him, she is likely to be attracted to rather a weaker, less vibrant even effeminate sort of man, who frequently lives in complete subordination as her husband or lover. There is a marked proportion of the Uraniad sex in the Philarrenic Zone, following the general topographic distribution of the Uranian. But the Uraniad is not so diffused as a distinctive type in the North-West of Europe. Apparently, too, she is not so numerous in North America; she comes less often under direct psychiatric study in Anglo-Saxon civilizations. In France, Italy, Germany and Russia, she is common, with a tendency to be more numerous in less aristocratic life. In Spain and Portugal the Uraniad sex is in considerable proportion, by imperfect statistics, as she is in all the Latin South America. In the East the proportion is large, by all accounts.

Classic, Biblical and Historic Uraniadism.

Feminine "contrary sexualism" is as natural a tendency as male homosexuality. It is ever lurking in barbaric races. The Mosaic Code does not speak of it, though that code has particular injunctions against a woman's committing bestiality. One can infer that female similisexuality was among "all those things" which Jehovah declares as common among the Egyptian and Caananitish peoples, vices to be avoided by the Hebrew fugitives. In ancient Greece, where the impulse appears to have been widely distributed, though our data is relatively obscure when contrasted with that for Uranism, one brilliant woman of genius mysteriously connected with it has given two familiar terms to it—the poetess Sappho and her Lesbos. Sappho while she was of normal sexual emotions, even to a tragic passion for the youth Phaon, was also similisexual; and "sapphism" and "lesbianism" have passed into psychiatric language. Confused in use with male similisexualism, the expression "Greek love" also pertains to Uraniad-love. In Rome, under the Empire, it flourished. But of it less was spoken, less written, than masculine relationships. Juvenal speaks of the "infamous complaisances" for each other of "Taedia, Cluvia, Flora and Catulla." The Apostle Paul refers to it as a Roman vice. In classic days, as now, it was not taken so seriously as a moral or immoral problem. It was counted a feminine peccadillo, a faute de mieux that could easily be forgiven in a woman. We have already seen how largely it has been and is yet overlooked, by modern criminal law.

General Psychology of the Uraniad.

Under successive chapters of this study, we shall present the Uraniad's temperamental, social and professional relations to life and history. The following are general observation.

The Uraniad is met in almost all social situations that show superiour moral, intellectual and social traits. She can be highly receptive as to aesthetics. Under the latter type, let us remark her intense susceptibility to music,, which susceptibility can be blent into merely high nervosity, without any intellectual sense of the art. The Uraniad frequently enters with absorbing earnestness into severe professions of the masculine order. She exhibits more success in meeting their abstract sides than the Uranian does. The Uraniad also is likely to be rather undomestic, and to care relatively little for the personal concerns, for the minutiae of feminine dress, ornament, and so on. She does not seek to attract the man as a lover, but as a comrade and friend. She shrinks from maternity, often with intense repulsion. Many Uraniads are incapable of maternity when the sexual organs otherwise seem wholly normal. Altruism, courage, perseverance, judgment, belong to her moral or intellectual furniture; just as are met rugged male attributes, relish for man's work, man's dress, male amusements, in peasant Uraniads, and other crude types. The Uraniad is unlikely to be a good diplomate; not even of the degree of the normal woman. Her mannish bluntness of speech and of plan disaccord. She lacks intuitions. The Uraniad shows her vaguer, inherent femininity by interesting minor traits, such as the fact that she is not distinguished in inventive processes more than is her normal sister. In literature she is constantly successful. She is a good executive, especially when she has at her side, as in royal and official instances, the physical aid of man. If we pass to the Uraniad who is of the lowest grade of social humanity, whether we meet her in a brothel or prison, she is depravity in the abstract; an *épave* complete, if fallen into the uttermost social pits.

General Aspects of the Uraniad's Sexualism.

To depict Uraniad love, we can best employ the process by which the student of male similisexuality advances to understanding it; viz., a "translation," taking phases of normal love and contrasting the similisexual emotions. In the Uraniad-love we meet again sudden passions, excited by the mere beauty of another woman; or the more gradual growth of desire. We find the blending of intellectual and moral admirations. We observe the amorous wish for physical possession, with the instinct for the surrender of self, as the only possible completion of the Ego. We find the indifference to male beauty as a sexual feeling, and a coldness or horror as to the man's sexual embraces. There are the jealousies, the struggles, the despairs, the vengeances, the emotional nuances, social dramas of every kind. The physical rapports of Uraniadism, as contrasted with male similisexual relations, do not allow the bodily satisfactions of the

Uraniad to be organically so vivid as the man's. Man's seminal system and its exclamative process make his pleasure more acutely physical. Again, the Uranian embraces are not necessarily at all dangerous to his nervous system. But the nervous demands on the Uraniad frequently make the gratification of her desires pernicious; disturbing gravely her intellectual and nervous poise.

The Uraniad Mask: Neither so Elaborate nor Necessary as the Uranian One.

As the law and society, concern themselves so much less, hardly at all, with feminine similisexualism than with the masculine, the Uraniad need not be so solicitous about the hiding of her nature. Men are not curious. Normal women are not aware or keen. Even daily undercurrents of such a sexual instinct escape observation, far more than Can the Uranian's predicaments and practices. Indeed, similisexuality is the unseen basis of hundreds of close friendships among women around us. Marriage often intervenes to end it. The Uraniad shows here a distinction of her nature. For unless "inborn" to her unfortunate instinct, she is much more likely to lose it with maturity and marriage than is the Uranian to lose his. Her abnormalism often declines, even if it has been extremely vehement, after she marries. She ceases to be of the Third Sex. The man is her best physician, in such fortunate cases of "cure." But there must not be the too-confident notion that she can be so transformed and normalized. For her marriage can be as dark a tragedy, as melancholy a failure, as for her brother in misfortune, the Uranian. For the Uraniad of high nature and pure life, not given to professional sexuality, it can be often a perfect renovator.

The Uraniad Intersex inferior to the Uranian One as a Secondary Sex, when Both are Contrasted.

We are led to the conclusion, however unwillingly, as we contemplate the Uraniad closely, that she is by no means so finely-endowed, so ethereal, so interesting an intersex as is the Uranian. Her inherently feminine shortcomings are pronounced. The Uranian stands above her as a secondary sex, when both "races" are compared at their best. He refers back more eloquently to a vigorous, well-balanced human type; not to speak of higher suggestions. The Uraniad, while she often excites admiration and enthusiasm, leaves a more unsatisfactory physical, moral, intellectual and social impression on us.

The following are some general examples of this curious between-sex. They are from the memoranda of various pathologists. The first one is given by an American physician, from his personal acquaintance.

Instance of Inborn Uraniadism Fine Moral, Intellectual and Æsthetic Type, but no Outward Evidences.

"Miss A—an American, thirty years of age, by profession teacher of the pianoforte, but not now in active professional life, was referred to me by her family-physician in M—where she resides most of the year, when not traveling, visiting etc. Miss A—in type is a blonde, of middle height, figure wholly feminine, has much elegance of form and movements, and a beautiful face. Nothing suggests masculinity' unless it be a certain rapid firmness of her walk, a long step, and her rather heavy timbre of voice in speaking. She sings a contralto, not specially deep. Anatomical examination of more particular sort betrays nothing abnormal. Full bust and feminine contours of limbs, genitalia normal; rather unusual development of clitoris. But Miss A— is much disturbed as to her vita sexualis, and so seeks medical advice."

"She has no knowledge of abnormality of temperament in her family except that one uncle was mixed-up, directly or indirectly, in a blackmailing affair in Paris, many years ago, which matter Miss A— now indicates as of a pederastic sort. Miss A—was however often told by her mother that before she was born the mother "had prayed and hoped from morning till night that she would have a boy"; as two girls had already been born. Both these sisters died in infancy. The parents still live. Miss A—was a quick-minded child. She has had excellent educational advantages, of which she has made the most. Was a good scholar, except as to mathematics and chemistry, developed early fine musical gifts, took special courses and prizes. As a little girl, was highly sensitive to female beauty, and cared little or nothing about a boy's looks, or a man's. Remembers strong sexual feelings as to theatrical posters giving portraits of a beautiful actress. When about nine, she stole the picture of a lady, personally unknown to her, from a photographer's shop, and slept with it "on her bosom often," with indistinct sexual feelings for it. At dances, and so on among young people, she felt either indifference or repugnance to dancing with a youth, to being kissed by him, etc; while to dance with a girl, and to be embraced by one whom she admired gave her pleasure, "making her quiver all over with delight." Her dreams of embracing other girls were frequent. She had many strong sentimental attachments, and was often morbidly jealous, as to her own sex. Between 12 and 13 her sexual maturity was emphatic. She used to masturbate with either an "ideal" female image in mind, or looking at the portrait of one special friend, her senior. Her emotions now centered on women older than herself, At seventeen, she began a regular sexual relation with a schoolmate, who was like herself. (Masturb. mut.) Another affair came about this date, as the preceding one cooled, and the former friend, then about eighteen, fell in love with the son of a neighbour. The second relation lasted about a year and a half, when the young woman confessed to Miss A—that she had a similar sentiment for a female cousin, and so wished to maintain much less intimate relations with Miss. A—This declaration cost Miss A—grief, jealous despair, morbid sense of injury and loss, and affected her nervous organization seriously. At this same time, she became the object of a strong sentiment on the part of a young man, who was much admired by all her girl-friends. She discouraged him entirely. Miss A— never was coquettish nor vain; in the case of several discarded lovers she has continued to retain their friendship and even intimacy."

"When about twenty years old, Miss A—fell deeply in love with a well-known young actress, who had a similar passion for her. So began an affair of more intense similisexualism than anything preceding (Masturb. mut., sapphism, mut.) This lasted several months, till the actress went on a professional tour. But the two friends have never lost sight of each other, and occasionally meet in one or another European city, and on the former terms. Miss A—has several times been the object of similisexual "addresses" from other women, sometimes favourably received sometimes not. Her professional work has been successful, not merely as to teaching, but in connection with private musicales, and as accompanist in public concerts. But she has suffered much when in active career as a teacher from her tendency to sexual interest in attractive female pupils. This she has always earnestly "fought-off," for she feels, most conscientiously, her personal responsability to her pupils and also has a strong regard for the innocence of youth. She slowly became aware of her abnormality but has never had clear idea of the matter, and has thought only of hiding it from those not likely to understand it. She went out into social life much in past years, but chiefly to see other women. Miss A—has never had any desire to wear male attire, her own beauty is a pleasure to her, in so far as it attracts to her women whom she admires. She dresses handsomely and takes pleasure in her toilettes, though she does not study them as do many of her friends. She is a fine dancer, and a brilliant conversationalist.

She has always attracted men, and has declined three offers of marriage. Her continuing in single life has perplexed her relatives and made "family trouble." When she was twenty-five, one offer of marriage, specially persistent, was from a young physician, of attractive personality, successful, etc. Miss A—admired him, and valued him as a friend. She was held back from accepting him simply by horror of sexual intercourse with a man. "If he had been a woman, I would have been the happiest being in the world." After much reflection, she decided to confess her secret to him. Naturally, he begged her to try their marriage as a remedy, and promised all degrees of sexual reserve with her, "till she should become more normal in sentiments." But he knew something of homosexualism, and he "could not promise" Miss. A—that her instincts would disapear. She therefore broke off the intimacy. The episode enlightened her somewhat as to her psychologic status. She was frightened and bewildered and again thought of suicide. At this time, a death in the family made Miss A—independent of her profession. She laid it aside, and though ardently fond of it, she now rather avoids music as a recreation. In course of last year, Miss A— has been in homosexual relations with a lady of high social standing, some years her senior, married but living in platonic relations only, with her husband, who is believed to be homosexual. Miss A—lately has become despairing of a normal vita sexualis. She dreads especially the increase, or non-decrease, of her feelings as she grows older, and (as she frankly remarked) becomes less attractive. Insomnia, hysterical tendencies and so on, are becoming more pronounced. She has again turned to the idea of marriage, the more as an excellent offer has been repeated. But even in thinking seriously of this her horror corporis as to a man is extreme."

"Miss A—takes interest in belles-lettres, is a great novel-reader, but of good fiction only. She likes the theater and says that she is fond of fancying herself as the heroine, oftener however as the hero, of a drama. She is frequently excited sexually by descriptions of female loveliness, by depictions of how a man feels in sexual excitement, and the like, as it offers "just what she feels" when with a woman that she sexually loves. Miss A—impresses me as having a fine moral nature, as a person who instinctively loves truth, unselfishness, modesty, refinement, dignity of character in general. She does not know exactly how far she is wanting in domestic tastes, for though she has orderly habits, is practical in various affairs and sometimes assists her relatives or friends in domestic duties, still she has lived chiefly in boardinghouses and hotels, and has not much experience of routine feminine work. But she dislikes all sewing and fancywork, knows little of cookery, and does not like to make use of what little she knows."

"Miss A—thinks that during sexual intercourse with women she feels herself wholly "active," and "quite as if she were the man," and she "usually gives that impression" to a partner."

Another instance of adult uraniadism that is appropriate is the following, which I cite from Dr. Krafft-Ebing, with some condensation. The subject is not of the "amazonian" type at all, and is of an intellectual and social class that may be called superior.

Instance.

"S. J—, thirty-eight years old, a governess, seeks medical advice on account of nervous disorder. Her father was mentally unsound and died of a brain disease. The patient was an only child, and suffered in her early years from headaches, painful emotions, excess of conscience, morbid interest in death, etc. In her earliest years the patient was sexually excitable. By instinct, masturb. till nine years old. She has never felt any sexual inclinations toward a person of the other sex. If she ever has thought at all of marriage, it has been in view of practical life. On the other hand she feels powerful sexual inclinations toward young women. She supposed that such inclination was only warm friendship, but came to learn the nature of the feeling; by an excited "longing" in it felt that it was more than mere friendship. . . The patient finds it incomprehensible that a girl can love a man, but well "understands how" it is that a man loves a girl. For beautiful women and girls she has always had a lively interest, and constantly has been sexually excited by the sight of them. Her longing has always been toward kissing and embracing them. She has never dreamed sexually of men, but only of girls. Her delight has been giving up herself to the sight of such. Partings from such friends made her "desperate." The patient whose outward appearance is thoroughly womanly and in the highest degree decent, has no special sense of her being "active" or "passive," even in her dreams. No traces of a masculine physique."

Instance: Physique Not Quite Normal: Ethical-Mental Grade Not High.

The following example, supplied to me by a French physician and neuropathologist is of use in presenting the type of Uraniad who is of relatively low grade as to ethical and intellectual nature, while not a criminal.

"R. E—, thirty-two years old, French parents and ancestry on all sides, profession (nominal) has been advised by another patient to consult me. She resides in Paris. Miss E. suffers from general nervousness and from what seems to be the milder epilepsy, attacking her but very occasionally. Parents (living) have some marked nervous disorders; one brother insane at S—, is semi-violent at times. Miss E—, from extreme youth, has always felt herself sexually interested in beautiful women, and has wished to embrace them, concumbere eis, etcetera; but on the contrary has never had any desire for masculine caresses, or the least interest in masculine beauty, male personal charms, etc., except of a calm, platonic sort. Her antipathy to corporeal intimacy with a man amounts to horror corpor. hominis, in fact. The patient says she feels it the more intelligently, compared with her pleasure in embracing, kissing, masturb. mut. and occasional sapphism with women, because she was the victim of a kind of rape some years ago. She insists that she then experienced ample proofs of her being congenitally unsympathetic to male relationships. During a walk with a young man whom she admired as a friend, and who was of distinguished personal beauty, he ravished her, or rather he succeeded partly by force and partly by what she vaguely calls "very vehement persuasions," in having sexual intercourse with her. She was not in any way conscious of the least sexual sympathy, but is sure that fear or moral aversion had nothing to do with her antipathy. E—now has two sexual intimacies with women; a middle-aged married woman being the more intimate friend, the other one, a young lady employed in a banking-establishment. (Sapph. mut. et masturb.) R. E—shows emphatically signs of secondary mental and, to some extent, moral individuality. She "has no religious convictions" and calls herself an agnostic. She had good educational advantages in youth, but disliked study and was never proficient in even ordinary matters, such as reading, simple mathematics, geography and history. She writes a clear but unformed hand, and spells uncertainly. She has never cared to read anything except the newspapers, and novels by Xavier de Montépin, Gyp, Eugène Sue and Paul de Kock. She likes the kind of theatrical pieces that are given at such theaters as the Palais-Royal, and, so far as I infer, the broader the humour the more acceptable. She often goes to the Folies-Bergères, with a male friend, and even to the Moulin-Rouge now and then. In the latter place, she sat down one evening, near to a young, pretty prostitute of similisexual tastes. In the absence of the gentleman who accompanied her, she made enough of an acquaintance with this person to give her male escort the slip, and went for the night to the apartment of the woman; but only, as she insists, in a mad sort of freak, "just as a man would do." Of such women as a class, she has what is apparently a proper aversion. She is exceedingly fond of dress and jewellery, and I learn that she has a poor sense of the moral obligation of a debt. At least, she has not hesitated to open accounts with tradesmen, to order costly articles of dress, etc., that she could not pay for, and did not expect to pay for; in one or two cases suits having been brought. She confesses to being almost devoid of jealousy, in her relations with women; "if she is not loved in return or if her friends are untrue," she seeks others, and is "as well satisfied with one pleasant person as with another." She appears to lack any constancy in her emotional life, and professes that she has no sympathetic feeling toward her relatives, "though they are a very good sort of people." From certain incidents, not directly of her vita sexualis, I am inclined to think that R. E—has small respect for truth, when subterfuges, not to say falsehoods, are convenient. She told me, on her second consultation with me, an incident involving her deliberate theft of a private journal of a friend, to learn how the pecuniary affairs of the lady stood, and also to try to discover a detail in regard to a Bourse speculation. R. E—says that she is passionately fond of all games of chance, and has visited Ostend and the Riviera for the purpose of gambling there."

"R. E—is a fine-looking blonde, in type. She has no signs of masculine physique externally that the ordinary observer would note, except that of a slight growth of hair on the lips and chin, for which she has taken an electrical treatment with partial success. Manner and voice wholly feminine. Hips normal size. The genitalia, however, are abnormal; the patient having a pseudo-penis which is almost of the dimensions of the organ of a boy of ten years, with a nearly complete glans; vagina is imperfectly developed, etc. The breast-development of the patient is not normal. She has always had very irregular periods, and lately they have ceased entirely."

Instance: complete Uranianism but with unusual Feminine Temperament, Tastes, etc.

From a distinguished Hungarian specialist in neuropathic disorders, the authour receives the following memorandum of interest as illustrating the Uraniad whose feminine nature is in many respects perfectly normal; only the decisive factor, her sexual instinct, setting her apart from women.

EDWARD IRENAEUS PRIME-STEVENSON

"Mrs. K—, twenty-seven years of age, Hungarian by birth and of both Hungarian and Russian descent, has been under my care at the Baths of X—this summer, for the sake of a recently developed tendency to insomnia. Otherwise the patient is in excellent health, accompanying her husband to the Baths, he being rheumatic. The confidence of the patient was sufficient to disclose gradually to me the following facts. Mrs. K—was from childhood perfectly indifferent to the other sex, but strongly susceptible to female beauty. It has always acted upon her sexually. She has never had anything except "complete indifference" or aversion to male beauty of person, to physical contact with men; and kissing, embracing, etc., by youths and men have been repugnant to her in the extreme. On the other hand, passionate pleasure in contact with female beauty; warm friendships, always tending to be "like love affairs," and in some cases such, (masturb. mut. et cunniling.) She was "in sickening terror" at the idea of marriage to her husband, which event family-circumstances made necessary. Her husband, however, soon made her understand that he was not disposed to insist on conjugal rights; having no mind to give up a mistress in the same city. Mrs. K—was glad to be so released; has never made any dissent from the other ménage that her husband continues. She had no pleasure in the rare coitus, that her husband soon gave up entirely; though she managed to subdue her horror hominis enough to deceive him as to her real instincts. These he has never known. She has lived in a constant homosexual relationship with one or another friend, during many years; and takes intense pleasure in the sexual acts. (Mast, mut., cunniling. and so on.) The most intimate of these intimacies, that with a cousin, has been broken, within some months, by death. The shock and the physical deprivation together have worked severely on the patient's nervous system. Hence the insomnia. Her husband has not suspected the sexual abnormalism of his wife; at least he has never intimated such a suspicion, the less because he is an army-officer, obliged to be a great deal of the year absent from the city; and when there he passes his nights with his mistress. Hence he is always glad if his wife has one or another relative or friend with her. He has never shown jealousy, having perfect confidence in Mrs. K—s integrity and "coldness." Mrs. K— goes much into society."

"Respecting her outward and other physique, Mrs. K—has nothing unfeminine. She is a woman of elegant female figure; full bosom, and hips; posteriors female in size and contours. She has a charming face (very expressive) and the grace of a woman of the world. She dresses handsomely, and tells me that she "takes great interest in the matter." She is also interested in housekeeping; fond of the finer sorts of cookery. She has much pleasure in sewing and embroiders beautifully; has lately presented a handsome piece of such work to a church. She is fond of light reading and of the theater; a brilliant pianist, and sings very well, with rather a high soprano voice. She seems to he of sincere and superiour character. She once worried much, and suffered greatly on account of her sexual abnormality, as to which a friend early informed her. Little by little, she has given up thinking it morally or physically wrong, being so innate and complete. The patient has no abnormality of the genitalia that I could discover; certain details of minor importance are plainly the result of her homosexual intercourse. She has never been a mother, probably could not be; though my examination as to this was not conclusive. . . She speaks of herself as having great libido when with a woman that she loves. She also thinks that her "rôle" is by natural instinct decidedly the "active" one in such intercourse, and says that she "knows she feels exactly as a man does." Menstruation irregular, and very scanty at times."

The "Amazonian" Uraniad.

Of the "amazonian" or "viraginous" Uraniad, the really man-like type, at its farthest physical advance, will occur examples elsewhere in this book. But aside from the Uraniad who has a physique robust enough for rudely muscular labours, who becomes mechanic, sailor, soldier, or what else, let us glance here at a grade so decided that living as a man among men, and even marriage with a woman have been a part of the vita sexualis and social life. A particularly large sequence of these cases is set forthin the "Jahrbuch für Sexuelle Zwischenstufen," annually published in Leipzig (Max Spohr) and in the studies of Moll, Krafft-Ebing and others. The last-named psychiater can be cited as to the following:

Instance of Viraginous Uraniad.

"Miss X—thirty-eight old, came to me in the autumn of 1881, on account of serious spinal irritation and obstinate sleeplessness, in struggling with which she had become a morphinist and also took chloral. The mother and a sister in the family were nervous invalids, the rest normal. . . With the very first meeting, the patient impressed me as striking, by her peculiarities of dress, her features, etc. She wore a man's hat, had her hair cut short, wore a man's eyeglasses, a man's cravat, a frock cut like a long, wide masculine coat, and men's boots. She had a set of harsh, mannish features, a rough and rather low voice, and made the impression of a man in woman's petticoats, rather than of a lady, (unless one observed her female contour of bosom and feminine breadth of hips. The patient offered no signs of erotism in a long diagnosis. When asked about her clothing, she answered that such wear was better for her than another sort. Gradually she stated that as a little girl, she had preferred horses and masculine occupation, and had never been interested in feminine work. She had, later, taken to reading with much pleasure, and had become a teacher. She has never liked to dance, and has thought it "nonsense." She has never been interested in ballets. The circus, however, has always been her greatest enjoyment. Until her sickness in the year 1872, she had felt no sexual inclination, either for man or woman. But from that time on, strong friendships with female persons, especially young women, and also the wish felt and gratified to wear clothes of masculine cut." (The physician here states that the patient's sexual instincts for women alluded to, though mostly psychic, in one instance had not been wholly platonic. The patient later entered an institution for the cure of mental ailments, and died there. The fact is noted that there was no hermaphroditism, but that there were indications of abnormalism as to the genitalia).

Instance: Semi-Viraginous Uraniad, Good Social Grade; Complete Concealment.

An advanced type of the "viraginous" Uraniad, in no particular professional life, but of good social standing, occurs m this example, from a Chicago physician:

"Some two months ago, I was called to a hotel of this city to treat (for peritonitis) a guest registered in the house, and known as Mr. L. Z—, of Boston. I found the patient in bed. The patient was of rather undersize, somewhat more delicate of extremities and generally frailer in osseous structure (as far a passing glance would indicate this) than is the average man, but not really markedly so; a smooth face, plain features not distinctively feminine; short greyish hair abundant. Various articles of exclusively masculine clothing were lying about the room. There were cigarettes and liqueurs on a table. The patient was seriously ill, and spoke asthmatically in a low, masculine voice. As I began to make some examinations, I was requested, perfectly calmly, "Not to be surprised at anything." I was however a good deal disconcerted to become convinced in a few minutes that my patient was not a man, but a woman. This concealment of sex the supposed "Mr. Z—" promptly admitted, at the same time requesting me to observe the closest secrecy as to the matter. The patient's attack of peritonitis was warded off, so that "Mr. Z—" soon was able to proceed on *her* journey to New Orleans; but not till she had reposed enough confidence in me to gratify my curiosity as to such a masquerade and to allow me some professional examination of as singular a type, which advanced far toward full masculinity."

"The facts in the case are as follows. "Mr. Z—" who is really Mrs. X—, a widow (after a married life of only five months) is of American-Scandinavian birth. The family has several times included members of weak, or worse, nervous constitution. One grandfather died insane, and an aunt was of such masculine traits, and so eccentric that she was "the talk" of the community. Afterwards this aunt died in an asylum. The parents died in the patient's infancy, and "Mr. Z—" was brought up by other relatives and educated in a convent in a Southern city. She has always disliked female work, female society, female clothing; preferring the life and society, of boys and men in every way. She has always wished that she were "really a man," the more as her physique has become increasingly masculine with her maturing. In the convent she was much the object of remarks on account of her mannish features and figure, and because of strongly expressed desires to be as unfeminine as possible. She made up her mind that as soon at she could do so, she would "try to be a man." She took great pains to observe carefully the ways of masculinity in general and even has taken lessons in manly deportment from an actor, under a pretext of turning to the stage. She grew up, aside from school and the convent, much alone; has few relatives, and so has always been rather on a free footing toward society. She came into a considerable fortune from her parents, on her majority; and during visits to friends, at hotels, in the summers, and so on, she became set on the idea of completely transforming her outward life to that of a man. A friend of hers had done this same thing with perfect success, and now lives in an English city as a man, not suspected to be anything else. But just when "Mr. Z—" was preparing to make such a change, including a residence abroad, she met a gentleman whom she very greatly admired intellectually; and as to his moral character, and who was also of considerable wealth. He fell in love with her, and she decided to marry. But she frankly told me that she not had the least physical attraction to her betrothed though she could not say that she had had distinct horror corporis. She was in fact rather curious of what, would be her physical emotionality toward married life. Of her vita sexualis I will make some further note, presently as it is of importance in so strange a case. She accordingly married Mr. K—, and though herself indifferent (she found herself quite unmoved by sexual intercourse, such as it was, between them) their relations in this respect were "happy and satisfactory" to her husband. He was always travelling commercially; they had no settled home; she was wholly free from domestic life. For some time—during her first weeks of marriage—she lost much of her masculinity of tastes, and, forgot that she would rather be of the other sex. But this retrogression in feeling was wholly apart from the sexual effect on her of her new relationship; so she insists. Also the feelings of repugnance were returning, just when her husband suddenly died while they were in a Mexican city. This left her again to herself. She decided that she "would be a man now, for all and for good." Her relatives were so situated that she need not fear any obstacle or even interest from them. She assumed male attire. From the first, she has wholly deceived everybody, has travelled and lived in the United States, England and the Continent with perfect freedom, and never with detection; the more readily as she passes for a man of invalid constitution and suffers from asthma. She smokes, drinks light liquors temperately, plays billiards, rides horseback, fences, and goes into considerable general society all as a man, and undetected. She has a confidential lawyer who manages her property, which is considerable, and who does not disclose what he knows of her transformation. She went to Boston, and (rather nominally) resides there, because she had no acquaintances there to betray her sex, and there could start out in a new life as a man." She passes much time in England, with the man-woman friend indicated. I have not mentioned that the patient is forty-seven years old, though looking younger; an only child."

The vita sexualis of "Mr. Z—," is completely homosexual, the marriage-episode having made no change in it. As a young child, she was passionately interested in exclusively female beauty, dreamed of sleeping with women, sexually, at an early age, and had no sense of the opposite sex. When in school, she had intense friendships, and was always "falling in love" with other girls. One such friendship in the convent-school became sexual; but (despite the confessional) it was a secret never betrayed by her or by the other party to it, a young nun, who calmed any scruples of conscience. She has often had, later, sexual relations with young women, and once or twice she has kept a regular mistress! She has now a young friend in such a relation. They often travel together, at "Mr. Z—'s" expense, as man and wife. The English friend, by the by, is also from birth wholly homosexual, and has an intense horror hominis as to sexual matters. After some hesitation, one day, Mr. Z—permitted me to make a close anatomical examination, with the following results. . .

The memorandum (which I here condense) established a quite abnormal development of the patient's clitoris and the presence of a more than rudimentary scrotum, with one testicle plainly to be felt, though there was.no seminal secretion, nor related system; along with a normal vagina, etc. In short, a near approach to actual hermaphroditism of the genitalia. There was hardly any feminine development of the bosom, the hips were narrow, the thighs concave, the general muscular development was masculine in externals. Other particularities of the sexual system are given. It is of interest to notice that the patient had no clear ideas that she was organically abnormal until her husband explained the fact. There was no complaint on the part of the husband as to any obstacles to coitus, nor as to indifference etc. on the part of patient: but there seems ground for supposing certain organic defects on the husband's part.

Instance: Virile Disguise, Male Externals, Strength, etc. in Uraniad of Humble Class.

Lately in a London police-court, was arraigned a defendant that proved to be an interesting case of masculine, viraginous, external uraniadism, lower middle-class life. Brought before the Marylebone police-justice, was a certain Catherine Coome, aged sixty-six, dressed as a man. She was charged with obtaining money on false pretenses, in various small sums, from a woman in the same house where she was lodging. She had shared a room with a person of the other sex, without detection. For forty years, as it transpired, Catherine Coome aggressively had personated a man, with entire success; even to marrying a young woman in England. The defendant had been first married (as a woman) at about fifteen years of age. She well enough educated to take a post as a schoolmistress. When in Birmingham, she decided that she would personate a man henceforth, as she could "get on better so." She took up the trade of a painter and decorator, on board the Peninsular and Oriental Line steamers, and also was employed in London by several excellent West-

EDWARD IRENAEUS PRIME-STEVENSON

End firms as a skilled decorator. She was also for two years at sea, in service as a head-cook, always in male disguise, on a steamer of the Line named. She gave that up, and after returning to England married a female servant in the family of Lady Campbell, at Hampton Court; and so lived for not less than fourteen years at Huddersfield. After this, circumstances brought her to London. Here she fell into poverty, had accidents, illnesses etc., and so was obliged to lead a precarious sort of life, even to being in a workhouse as a male pauper. The prisoner looked thoroughly masculine, and in voice and manner was so manlike that there was no wonder in her identity being unguessed. She was shrewd in her dishonesty, and availed herself of her education in such deceptions; but did not seem to be really of criminal preferences or lacking conscience. She had lived honestly as long as she could do so, it appeared.

Unfortunately the medical analysis of this case has not reached the writer, nor does he know how far there was organic abnormalism. But the wife in Huddersfield "had never suspected" that her partner was not sexually masculine.

Typic is the history of a well-known Austrian Uraniad, Johanna Buchbinder. Of relatively low-class family, she was born in Vienna, and from youth was masculine in her physical type, even to being vigorously muscular. She decided early to personate a man, from reasons of convenience and innate masculinity of feeling; her vita sexualis included. She secured the legitimation-documents of a brother who had died, and she became a mechanic. She was of great bodily strength, and of a coarse temperament. She smoked, drank freely, was obliged to shave herself daily, and rode restive horses like a man. She entered into politics, having a talent for speaking and a male voice, and became active in the Social Democratic party. She was sexually interested only in women. Her sexual system was somewhat abnormal, but not hermaphroditic. In consequence of a quarrel with a woman with whom she had lived maritally, the "wife" being perfectly deceived, Johanna was involved in a stabbing-affair, and in a hospital her sex was disclosed. The remainder of her history seems lost.

In London, 1901, occurred an aristocratic suicide, that of Countess V—, a foreigner by birth, but long identified with English social life. Her death had some connection, sedulously

Instance: Johanma Buchbinder: Strong Viraginity. Entire Concealment.

Instance: Countess V—.

concealed, with the uranistic nature of the deceased. Countess V—an Hungarian lady of high family, well-known in political and social affairs in its time, had been from first youth an Uraniad. She was also robust to virility, though not amazonian or coarse. She had been allowed in childhood an almost boyish liberty of tastes, amusements, dress, and so on. She was a hunter of large game and an expert boxer and fencer, when other young women are thinking of dances, toilettes and domestic duties, and was passionately fond of horses. She was obliged to marry from reasons of family-convenience: but though she became a mother, her vita sexualis was totally averse to such a normal union, and presently the marriage was dissolved. Countess V—therewith settled in England. She became much engrossed in sporting life, and was a steady patron of the turf, was constantly at racing-meetings, and so on.

It was a near collateral member of the family of this lady who is the hero of an Uranian tragedy, given in another chapter of this study.

Unwholesomeness of College Theatricals & Athletics for Young Women.

The Remark may be made here, that exactly as certain forms of college-theatricals for young men develop their similisexual instincts, and much as react, if in less direct degree, athletics in university life for men, so comes with the theatrical and athletic interests of women's colleges a tendency to abnormal sexualism of young women. It sometimes confirms the instinct in the "born" Uraniad. The question of athletic work and sport for young women is too little regarded by parents and by physicians, in its relations to sexual life. Further consideration of this topic will be met in the next chapter.

Three Instances of Viraginous and Concealed Uraniadism.

In Riga, some time age occurred one of those distinctive cases of concealed uraniadism that are so constantly spoken of as being "unique," and "unexampled" and the like, when really not such at all. The widow of a man of standing in Riga presented a petition to the authorities to be allowed to resume her maiden-name; the more justifiably as her deceased husband had been a woman. With the latter she had lived happily, and as it appeared with satisfactory sexual relations between them (the deceased partner being in the masculine rôle) during about nineteen years. On being asked why she had not disclosed the matter earlier, she said that she had been "afraid and ashamed" to do so.

Another case of simulation of a man, recorded in Vienna, is that of a certain Anna Drexelberger, middle-aged, and dressed as a man during about thirty years, ever since girlhood; detected as being feminine through a charge in a police-court of falsifying facts. Her case excited sympathy, as it was made clear that she had played the part of a man so long because of the difficulty of finding feminine employment. She had even been a house-porter and general man-of-work. She was exonerated of the charge of perverting her identification, etc., and was presently offered a position of companion, by an elderly lady; which post she accepted. There was every reason to suppose that Anna Drexelberger was sexually more or less abnormal, from various facts in her career. She went to England, and died soon after in London, leaving a estate of considerable value in cash to a young woman in Vienna with whom she had lived sexually and most happily, and who "had never known" that Anna was not a man. The will, by the by, was contested, but was fully sustained.

A pertinent case occurred lately in the city of St. Louis, in the United States of North America. Through the statement of a local physician, a type-setter in the town was taken into custody, when employed in the office of a local journal, on a charge of abduction and as being a woman, though known as "Johann Bürger." The facts soon were clear. Anna Mattersteig was her real name. She was thirty years old. She was living matrimonially with another young woman, Martha Gammater, the daughter of a Leipzig jeweller, and had so lived before they came from Germany. Then, but apparently not earlier, Martha Gammater had discovered that she was the partner of a woman, not of a veritable man. The shock had made the wife insane. At the time of the arrest, she was in an asylum. Anna Mattersteig appeared in court in full male attire, and looked like a fine-appearing man. She disclaimed any intention of contravening the law, in respect of her impersonation and of the abdication (for such it had been) of her companion. She declared that she had assumed the role simply because she "felt herself wholly like a man" and was sure that only by a mistake of Nature had she come into the world at all otherwise. She "would suffer any penalty" rather than wear women's apparel.

To an astonishing case of successful imposture of masculinity by an uraniad, that of Margaret Erb, known as "Prince Egon," which came before the courts of Vienna in March 1908, reference will be made in the tenth chapter of this study, where the morally degenerate type is particularized.

A noteworthy example of extreme masculinism, coincident with the merely feminine physique as being otherwise almost lost, came to notice in a hospital in Buffalo, in the United States, in 1903. A certain "Harry Gorman," an employé of the New York Central Railway, a robust, athletic, heavily built "man-cook" of about forty, was discovered to be a woman, so far as sexual organization committed one to the conclusion. Nothing else in Gorman could bear out such a sexual classification. For more than twenty years she had concealed her sex, with perfect ease. All the atmosphere of femininity was not only unsympathetic but impossible to her. She did heavy work, drank liquors moderately, and not as an alcoholic, smoked strong cigars, frequented saloons and dance-houses every night, and was untrammelled by any feminine conditions of existence. She swore that "nothing would hire" her to wear women's habiliments. When in the hospital (on account of a broken limb) a clergyman, with pressing views of decorum—if less psychologic sense—came to visit the patient. The visitor wished to argue ä relapse toward female apparel and demeanour. "Harry Gorman" refused to grant the well-meaning gentleman any more interviews. She had voted as a man in several elections—of course illegally. More than this. "Harry Gorman" (the real name was not published in notices of the case) declared that she knew of "at least ten other women," who dressed as men, appeared wholly manlike, and were never suspected of being otherwise, also employed in the same railway-company; some of these being porters, train-agents, switchmen and so on. They often met together and made themselves not a little merry over the success of their transference from one class of humanity to another. The medical examination of Gorman in anatomical detail, is not at the writer's hand: nor did "Harry Gorman" communicate anything as to the similsexual intercourse between the members of this curious confraternity—or sorosis. But that most of the group were similisexual is to be inferred, probably with some organic abnormalities, in one case or another.

The proportion of German Uraniads of virile physique is considerable. In some German cities, Berlin especially, where the "Emancipation" of feminine interests has obtained certain balls and assemblies have illustrated the undercurrents and the uppercurrents of similisexual instincts in women. An entertaining account of an artist-ball, so called, in which only women-workers in the fine arts, literature, and so on were permitted attendance on the dancing-floor, to the exclusion of male guests, is given in the "Jahrbuch für Sexuelle Zwischenstufen," for 1901; copied from a Berlin newspaper, with the descriptive title, "Ein Fest Ohne Männer." The best element of female esthetic life in the German capital, and male costumes were much affected, especially by the large contingent of similisexual women present. This ball is an annual affair at present. With "The Uraniad in Æsthetic Professions" we shall refer to such matters more appropriately than in the present chapter of general study of types.

VII

The Uranian and Uraniad in Their Earliest Youth: The Inborn Similisexual as Boy and as Girl: Types and Biographies

The Uranian and the Uraniad, especially of the higher grades, constantly seem reflexes of pre-natal influences. Their instinct is inborn. The mother's imagination and wish, quite likely sub-conscious, during her pregnancy here can come into plain coincidence with the vita sexualis of her offspring. The similisexualism of the father is repeated in the child. Or, sometimes over passing a generation, referring the boy or girl back to a remoter ancestor, the mystery of atavism is before us. The organic sex of unborn infants we know as not determined for a considerable period of gestation. Nature herself seems to hesitate, to postpone. The boy comes into the world not obviously affected in his sex as to any virile trait, born with a boy's body and a boy's mind; but unluckily for him endowed with the sexual impulses of a girl. Or the girl, blamelessly feminine in her physique, must go through life yearning for sexual union with a woman. Victims of pre-natal obsession, they may too easily mature, burdened with the intersexual Ego, bewildered as to themselves, at cross-purposes with their environments, occupations, society, moral sentiments, religious notions, with the laws, and all chances of relief.

The practical warning to married people is strong in such a history. No effort should ever be made to "influence" by any mental processes the sex of the coming child. How far this is practical is still an uncertainty, in spite of the theories of the learned or of the charlatan. But there is no disputing recurrent heredity in similisexualism. One of the first duties of a woman especially is to avoid any strenuous thought as to the sex of her unborn offspring. Her refraining may save it unspeakable misery, shame, and failure in life.

Not less imperative, while frequently involving a melancholy sacrifice, is the caution

Parental Desires and Pre-Natal Uranianism.

The Warning to the Married.

Transmitted Similisexualism.

to the Uranian who wishes to marry, be it for one reason or another. The chances of his transmission of similisexualism are many. If the similisexual impulses are inborn, it is safest (if often a most unwilling conclusion) to regard them as ineradicable, more or less, even when early taken in care by the watchful parent. If a man believes that in "the blood, the bone, the soul of his breed," even if not obviously in himself, the similisexual instinct has been active, he should question his right to marry. His son or daughter may suffer what he has escaped. If he do not forego marriage, then he may wisely avoid offspring. Or, as the least of compromises, the parents must double their vigilance in the nursery and schoolroom. The maternal opportunities for watchfulness and for counteraction are less lasting. Of this topic more will be said in other chapters of this book. A striking study of inherited similisexualism in a young lad, occurs in the "Psychopathia Sexualis" of Krafft-Ebing (eleventh edition, p. 266) too long to quote here.

Difficulty of Detecting Youthful Uranianism.

Unless the Parent has clear ideas of similisexual traits and habits, the sharpest eye can fail to notice them in the child. A boy or girl assumes "the mask" with curious precocity. Children are loyal to each other, as they are secretive, in sex-secrets. Similisexual practices among little boys and girls, to say nothing of larger ones, are concealed, by instinct. Fathers and mothers should not wish to be spies and martinets. As for the parent's deputy, the school-teacher, governess, tutor or housemaster, whether in the family or at a boarding-school, he or she is even more hampered. One of the most mischievous skeletons in the family-closet and boarding-school dormitory, is the similisexual one. The pederastic tutor himself may be the enemy in the camp.

A vast proportion of active and passive onanism and masturbation both in schools and at home, is due to inborn similisexualism, not to merely a temporary and ignorant instinct. Sometimes the fraternal home-life of two lads, or of two sisters, fosters the sentiment and practices, from day to day. In Hungary a special paragraph of the law recognizes this fact.

Of course, the uranistic instinct often cannot be traced to hereditary sources. Its origin is too remote or too obscure. Perhaps some other current of nature has deflected the juvenile psychos. The instinct is communicated

Uranianism when not Obviously Inherited, is often Early Developed.

swiftly, not seldom ineradicably, from boy to boy, from girl to girl. But the question recurs if complete, rooted similisexuality is ever quite extraneously implanted in a man or woman.

Instance of Strong Youthful Uranianism with Early Sexual Potency.

The following example of early Uranianism is from the letter of an English professional man, written to the authour.

"It was not until I was past thirty, and had met some German literature on the topic, that I knew how early my homosexual nature had declared itself. The first matter that I recall was that as a very little boy I was never sensitive to the caresses of women, nor liked to be with them. On the other hand, I do not remember when I had not a sort of sexual interest in handsome boys and men, and in pictures of them; liked to be caressed by men. Once, when I was about eight, my nurse and a female friend and myself one afternoon were passing a photographer's shop. We stopped and looked at the likenesses. I was struck by that of a handsome man, and spoke of it. My nurse said, "Oh, but a little gentleman should never waste his time admiring another gentleman. He must always admire the ladies." I answered with much decision, and I know feeling what I said—"But I think that a gentleman is always a great deal handsomer than any kind of a lady!" I proceeded to argue my statement out from the pictures, much to the amusement of the young women. My nurse had a lover, a line looking young butcher. His caresses, when we met, used to excite me sexually very much. All this before puberty. In school, I felt great admirations for certain handsome fellow-scholars. Their type was invariably blond, with a rather large (but not coarse) body, and with very clear, white skins. One such lad, from Surrey, exercised a remarkable influence on me, though I was careful not to let him or any one else notice it. I used to follow him with my eyes, for quarter-hours at a time. His least signs of friendliness put me into an intense nervous happiness. Often I could not sleep till late at night, just for thinking of this C—. At the parties for lads and girls, to which I was asked, the girls seemed to me of no mortal interest, while I used to note eagerly every trait and type of good looks or enhancement—a becoming cravat, a well fitted suit in my boy-friends. A thirteen, I decided that I would cut out of any illustrated journals and books that I could discover, the pictures of every handsome man, or boy, that they contained. This resolution I carried out with great secrecy, hiding my collection as if it had been so much counterfeit coin! It was a pleasure that increased very swiftly. In fact, this "gallery" not only was an outcome of early homosexualism but added fuel to the fire. For, with advancing puberty, such illustrations became powerfully stimulative to sexual feelings. Especially as I began to add pictures of male statues to it, having procured some fine old Exhibition catalogues, by a boyish thievery that might have got me into trouble! I remember one afternoon, looking at this remarkable assemblage of "types," and being then stimulated for the first time to solitary masturbation, by a sort of irresistible impulse. Hitherto when alone I had not had done this. I may add that though I could have collected feminine types quite as easily and numerously, I never had any interest in them. I always let them pass, or tore them up disdainfully. There was in our neighborhood a certain remarkably good-looking young Hebrew merchant, who came into a business-post there. His good looks took deep hold on me. I used to haunt the large shop where he was employed. One day, I walked after him along the street. He happened to notice it, and presently spoke good-naturedly to me. The chat upset me with pleasure and sexual excitement for the next few days. It led to the young Hebrew's taking a decided interest in me, the more as I was a robust, handsome, eager lad, and as he must have seen how I-was sentimentally drawn to him. He asked me to call at his lodgings. I hid this invitation from the members of my family, and did not tell friends of it. I went to my new acquaintance's home (he lived in an attractive lodging near my father's house) and what did I do, the very first time of so going, but take with me my picture-gallery of male subjects of all sorts—from criminals to classic marbles! My new friend looked over them with me, saying that he too "was interested" in such pictures. He questioned me cleverly, to see how far he could rely on my discretion. After we had finished looking at the pictures, he gradually "led the situation up" to our beginning, then and there, sexual relations of the most passionate sort. I was fully potent at fourteen. This affair I have always regarded as the turning point (though if I could have turned in the other direction at all, I doubt) that made me homosexual forever. With my friend I continued "relations," meeting him at least once a fortnight, for a full year, without any damage to my health. I loved him intensely. He was an "active" type, and I was at that time passive; for matter of that am still quite such. Nobody ever suspected us, even after my family had noticed that I knew the young man well. . . When I was nearly sixteen, after several other episodes, I fell into a violent sexual passion for a young sea-captain that used to visit some neighbours, when on his leave. This sentiment did me real mischief for a year. It was not suspected by its object, nor could it have been in the least relished by him. . . , I will add that the physical type I have defined always has remained "the" one most appealing to me. . . At twenty, when I was at X—University, I had an awkward experience by being sexually attractive to a pretty young married woman, the relative of a friend. She once lost control of herself, enough vainly to attempt my seduction, But I had by this time a complete hatred of the idea of having to do with any woman in that way. I was engaged in regular sexual intimacy with a college-mate, and also with a young coachman, employed in a family some miles distant. . . I had never been able to think of a woman as a sexual partner, except with a vague dread. But at this time I did not realize that such a feeling of horror would be an obstacle to my marrying, a plan that I did not give up till some years later; at least not completely and knowing why. . . I have not mentioned that in school 1 used to fall into queer "states" of what I think now was a sort of premature sexualism, when I was reading of the manly beauty of warriors, or when close male friendships were talked about, or if I read a book that turned on such a relation. I have mentioned my affair with my young Jewish friend as my first really "serious" incident of the sort. It was such only in a relative sense; there had been two or three mates of mine at school that, if homosexual permanently or not so, were then on the usual "schoolboy" terms of physical intimacy with me. With one of them, a brother of the handsome G—mentioned, I was accustomed to masturbate chiefly because he looked so much like his relative. He could stir up all sort of romantic thoughts in me. This was my real reason for caring for it with him, rather than some others. . . I have forgotten to mention an incident when I was not more than seven or eight, that has always appeared to me striking, as hinting that "we are born so Several older people were once talking, in my presence about a neighbour's young son who had committed suicide because of his rejection by a young lady of the vicinity. There was a pause, and I, whom nobody had thought of as attending, exclaimed. "What a fool! To kill himself for love of a girl!" There was a general burst of surprise and annoyance at my being so near. But soon somebody asked—"For what sort of other love, T—, do you think a young man should kill himself?" Without an instant's hesitation I answered, "Because he loved some man who hated him! *That* would be good reason, I think!"

At this notion the company smiled, and made some fun of its romantic suggestion. The observation passed, without reflections as to what sort of a nature might be shaping in my stout little frame. . . I remember to have had no other "sexual convictions" in my life. The instinct was inborn—I could never have got it from any outside source, so rooted it was it in me from my first youth. . .

Two Leading Types of Uranian Youth.

Two types of Uranian boyhood prevail. The child being in this the father of the man, as in other foreshadowings. One is the physically delicate youth, graceful, spiritual, and dreamy, highly impressionable. To this type also belong often detail of uncertain health, of shunning the ruder sports of lads, of indifference or dislike to the society of noisy male playmates; along with a proportionate relish for playing with girls, dressing in girls' clothing, and a natural ease of comporting oneself in it. A boy should never be permitted to "dress up" in female apparel, nor a girl allowed to travesty herself as a boy. To such a delicate boy-type, pertains, the love of quiet, of solitude, tastes tor reading and for arts, admiration of what is beautiful rather than what is rudely grand and heroic, and of intellect, not action. Above all, in such young Uranians occurs vivid appreciation of adult male beauty, the charm of mature male society, when the man concerned is gentle of temperament and gifted. These latter traits are more or less recurrent in heterosexual youths. But they arrive at a proper proportion in normal lads as virile maturity advances and they do not have that sentimental tinge in normal boys that they possess in the young Uranian. This Uranian frequently matures to "passive" sexuality.

The second type of young Uranian has nothing feminine in his tastes. He is, on the contrary, averse to girlish interests in life. He, indeed, passionately attaches himself to friends. He perhaps is wholly careless of other relationships. Often he is noticed as concentrating his sentimental nature, so far as it is revealed, on one or another intimacy with a boy, no matter what be the masculinity of his general equipment. At least, this is frequently a trait in him. But in his case, as in that of the relatively feminine youth, there is the superseding sense of the beauty of the male physique and male character, indifference to girlish charms, and inner responsiveness to what is manly attractiveness. Perhaps it is all hid; reserved by the lad with great pains. Naturally, this type is far less easy to separate from the normal-natured lad growing up into a quite dionistic nature. But often it is strong "active" Uranianism, under a vigorously boyish veil.

Instance: from
Ulrichs.
Some years ago, appeared m England a little tale "Tim" (anonymous) gracefully written, giving subtly a minute study of psychic Uranianism between two school-lads of these diverse types.

An Austrian Uranian wrote to Karl Emil Ulrichs as follows, concerning his boyish similisexualism, as an inborn instinct.

"I was fourteen years old when I first felt love. My brother was a cadet in the hussars. Once upon a time, I had to go to get a leave of absence for him from the Rittmeister, an officer that I did not know. He proved to be a handsome, rather sombre-looking man of remarkable physique; about thirty years old, with a moustache and with blond hair. As he talked with me, it seemed to me that his voice had the ring of metal. He asked me in a friendly way to sit down, and sat beside me. While he talked with me so kindly, I began to find him less sombre in expression. But that look of his "went through" me. I could not stand it. As he touched my hand, my whole body began to tremble, and when he sat closer by me, my teeth fairly began to chatter—from a sort of delight and terror together. At last he kissed me, and asked.me why I was so frightened. Then it came over me! I threw myself upon his breast, weeping. Each kiss that he gave me went like a shot through bone and marrow. From that instant my heart was full of him, as my divinity. My only thought was of him. With him the joy of love flowered-out for me. That was the hour of my "Rosenliebe." . . .

Instance: Very Strong
Juvenile Uranianism,
Psychic and Psychical.

A pertinent example of boyish uranianism is this, which is furnished me by a French physician: the subject of the memorandum being however, an American sculptor, a distinguished member of the profession on the Continent.

"I doubt if many homosexual "victims" have come more directly than I have by their instincts in that direction, or have more plainly felt them from early boyhood. My father was of German-English blood. I once overheard him conversing with a friend on the general subject of homosexuality, in a confidential interview. He was of a plainness of speech in the talk that has made me certain that not only he, but my grandfather also, were homosexual, to a considerable degree, notwithstanding their pleasant married lives. . . But this conviction did not come to my ears till long after my own tendency was clear."

"I often wonder if more *precocious* "examples" of homosexualism occur. I was really precocious in many matters. For one detail, nobody ever "taught" me to read, nor could say how I had, even learned my letters. I could and did read any ordinary English book easily and correctly for most part, when I was less than six years old. When I was eight, I was as far advanced in general information as most boys of fifteen. I was fully prepared for college at seventeen, having also then a vast amount of general knowledge not common to boys of such age. But my sexual feelings, which were exclusively homosexual from the first moment that I remember anything in the way of admiration were remarkably developed, when I was in first youth. I hid them from the first. I remember how when I was about six years old, I used to feel drawn with an intense interest to handsome men in our family-circle, or to handsome lads; to one especially, who was much at our house with my older brother. At the same time, I did not like to be "petted" by women, nor at all welcomed their society, however pretty and friendly. I also took strong pleasure in looking at pictures in which men were the subject. I was a very nervous, high-strong youngster; used to fall into violent tempers, etc."

"The first incident that I remember in which my premature homosexualism was unmistakably shown, came when I was less than seven years old. It is curious enough to be specially mentioned. I usually slept by myself, in a little room ajoining my brother S—'s room; that is to say, after I was no longer in the nursery, with a female attendant. One day there came to visit my brother S—(who was about fifteen) a schoolmate from the same boarding-school that S—attended. This guest, young A—, was a very handsome boy, about seventeen. (He grew up to be a particularly good-looking young man of twenty-four, at which age he was drowned in the Hudson.) This lad occupied my brother S—'s room during his week's stay. S—slept in another part of the house. From the first moment that I saw G—, he had what I now see was a most extraordinary "sexual attraction" for my little self. I fairly "fell in love" with him. For the first time, I began to take definite interest in the idea of seeing a nude male body. For, A—became the special object of this *instinctively* homosexual passion. I had to go to bed considerably earlier than A—, or my brother; the two often did not come to A—'s room till I was asleep, or should have been so. Also my brother's presence hindered my curiosity, night and morning. But I soon became adroit, and was nervously wakeful enough to get the better of such difficulties. The sight of A—as he undressed, even before I first saw him quite naked (in the way I shall describe) made me violently "excited" in my mind; though I do not at this time remember how far, at so early an age, there was a physical effect of the kind. (I was capable of strong erectio at eleven.) One morning, very early, I woke up, and just as if I had thought of nothing else all night, almost at once I slipped out of my bed, and stole into the room where A—was sleeping. Trembling I approached his bedside, and looked at him. A—did not wake, being a sound sleeper. For some time I gazed in an indescribable interest, pleasure and excitement at his face and his exposed bust and outstretched sturdy, long legs; for he had partly thrown off the coverlets in his sleep. Becoming bolder, as A—did not wake, I yielded to an irresistible wish, even at risk of arousing him. I gently turned down the sheet, and for the first time looked, with a perfect fever of interest and desire too, at A—'s well-developed genitals. For the first time I really could see, and "study," if so I may speak, such organs, and especially the admired A—'s. With this came a boldness, a sexual fire to my young nature that I well recall, and which led me to a sheer audacity, a strange evidence of my inborn feeling. I saw that A—slept like a log, and that he was not likely to be disturbed if I touched him. So I slipped into bed by his side. Without caring for consequences, too excited with sexual desire (at seven years!) to "mind" much the situation if I should waken A—by accident, dexterously I came nearer and nearer to a contact with him, laid my head against him, and then I began gently with' him pen. in os, without disturbing him. This continued several minutes. A—did not waken, but gradually was excited. I do not know what would have ended the situation, had not a sudden noise in the hallway terrified me, and sent me flying back to my own little bed. As it happened, A—was obliged to leave my brother that day. He did so, to my profound regret. I remember how I kissed him and, as he had taken a fancy to me, how he embraced and kissed me, at leave-taking. I did not see him for many months. But when next A—came to our house, the situation was for me far more explicit. I had grown older, and was considerably more mature in my precocious homosexualism. This time, A—slept in the same room. My brother, was also there, but in another bed. I slept now with one of the two, now with the other, as my room was wanted for my cousin. A—at this time disclosed himself to me as a homosexual boy, of strong maturity in the trait. He made his advances early, when we were sleeping together. I gave myself up in delight to his passion which, as you may guess, was fully exclamative, as he was so old a lad; and we were mutually intimate sexually, then, and often later in his short life. His death deeply affected me."

EDWARD IRENAEUS PRIME-STEVENSON

"I will add that I am sure that my brother was homosexual. But I do not know how far so as to his friend A—. I never had opportunity to determine this, though I remember how I tried to do so. But my brother was in homosexual relations with many other friends, in his school-days and later, as I came to know when going through his letters and other memoranda by him, found after his death, when I was about twenty-five."

"So much for my earliest episodes of this sort. I come now to an incident of another bearing, when I was at Brussels, in 18. . ."

The remainder of the instance is not appropriate to the present chapter.

Instance from Ulrichs: Psychic (Youthful) Uranianism.

An interesting delineation of boyish uranianism occurs in the little work "Memnon" of Ulrichs. It is, in part, as follows:

"The first pure and true longing for love awoke in me when I was not yet ten. The object of it was one Eduard d'H—, a schoolmate two or three years older than I, when at the Aurich Gymnasium. He was a class higher than I; he being in the fourth form, and I in the fifth. Our parents were strangers to each other. I was not thrown with him. His beauty of person charmed me. He was not athletic in his type, but in the bloom of youth, almost pale in face, with fine-cut, beautiful features all that, there was absolutely nothing girlish about him. . . A certain longing, never felt before, drew me to him, not however with a trace of sensual feeling. My tenth birthday came, and I took the notion to ask him to spend it with me. But four days before it, my father died, and so that invitation never was given. It was, in fact, only thus that Eduard and I remained separated. Once he accompanied me from Aurich to my home in the country near by, at Westerfeld. When I left East-Friesland, a year later, he wrote a page in my album. I cared more for that page than for all the others. After our parting, I liked well merely to think of him. When I had exercises in "letter-writing" in school, I preferred to begin them. "Dear Eduard!" I could not find any other name so beautiful."

"Why was all this? I did not know. A feeling that I had never known before had come over me. Later this sort of sentiment grew to passion, but not more inwardly such. Eduard d' H—'s very features, only little weakened by time, still unforgotten, are ever in my mind. I shall never forget him" . . .

Another Instance: Ulrichs.

Of a further development of his uranianistie sentiment, the same homosexual autobiographist writes thus:

"I was fifteen years, ten-and-a-half months old, when the first nocturnal signs announced my entrance into manhood. There had never been any sexual occurence, either uranistic or other, till then. The incident mentioned was quite normal. But much earlier had awakened in me certain gentle longings, partly indefinite, an objectless glow. At this same period however, such feelings were separated, never aroused by one and the same young man. These sensuous though "objectless" flashes of feeling often had troubled me in my lonely hours. There was no use in fighting them. They first became changed to the following actual aspects when I was past fourteen, and was a student in Detmold. An architectonic supplement to the plates in Normand's "Orders of Architectural Columns" wakened me, through the figure of a Greek god, or hero—in the nude. The image, a hundred times banished from my soul, came back a hundred times. My sub-conscious uranianism was roused" . . .

"And next this came. If I studied in my little room, or if I was going to bed, there would recur, suddenly and often, the idea—"If a soldier would only suddenly clamber into my room, by that window there." And then my fancy would picture a handsome soldier, of twenty-two or twenty-three years; and then something would burn within me like a fire. But even then such a fancy was without; definite sexual object. Somewhat later, only, it tended toward special satisfaction. I had never had had any relation with any soldier. . . had never spoken to a soldier. While in the case of the architectural picture, the sight of the unclad male sexuality had excited me greatly, the idea of nudity in this soldier-fantasy was remote. It was a condition of mind which. . . existed without an exterior effect. I had never read of man-to-man sexual love, nor ever heard of such a thing. I did not know that it existed. It was a state of demand for sensual love and for the pain of love, but attached to no definite object. I was not in the same situation as had been my more fortunate friend in Vienna, who was of my age, for his story of the Hussar officer had proved more kindly; whereas in mine mere imagination juggled with me. If my soldier-fancy had become life, and had met me in flesh and blood, I would also, have "trembled with delight."

"Not till two or three years later did I come really into touch with a soldier. On a journey, I was alone in the vehicle with the driver. The driver permitted a young soldier to ride part of the way with us. I accordingly sat alone with the young man in the carriage, very close to him. The nearness of physical touch roused strong sensual emotions in me. But there was no special, final goal for them in my mind. It was merely a matter of vague wishing that I could lay my hand on his thigh. I felt the pains of Tantalus because this desire was not gratified."

Another Instance.

An Hungarian Uranian, thirty-two years of age, in an official position, and of entirely masculine type outwardly, wrote this of his own boyish predisposition:

"From first youth my sexual inclination for the male was felt. I had an unlimited horror of normal relations, with women. I have often made vain attempts at it. But with the merest sexual touch of a male physique I have complete satisfaction. My night-dreams, from earliest youth, have depicted only male shapes to me. O, had I only known of Uranianism sooner! I have suffered for seventeen years unspeakably" . . .

The "Byron" Description of Boyish Uranianism

Although Lord Byron is little known as one among the world's vast array of homosexual men, and has passed into social history for a normal—or abnormal—Don Juan of Don Juans, the inner life of the great romantic poet was strongly tinged by homosexual relations with several special male friends. This is shown early and late in his career. Both psychically and physically, the history of it is conclusive; but it is considerably reserved. Many of the chapters of it never have been even near to publicity, probably never are to be so. Of the prose references to Byron's boyish "friendships that were passions," as he styles them in his letters, diaries, etc., we need not here speak. But a curious versified allusion to the topic has been at least ascribed to the poet. In 1866, appeared in London the poem "Don Leon," as being an authentic fragment of Byronic verse, but not published till that date. The lines have not the young Byron's diction, fire or fancy. But if they be at all from his hand, it is not impossible to ascribe them to his hesitant muse, and to place their composition as among those miscellaneous first poems (several of them homosexual) which Byron put together as a collection for the year 1811, out of which series the young poet withdrew certain pieces either by his own or by other counsel. The title given the lines. "Don Leon" suggests *per se* some indifferent imitator; they have the quality of an immature or second-rate verse-writer, on a stereotyped model. Nevertheless, the allusion contained in them is in key with Byron's childish days at

Newstead Abbey; and the poet's intimate biographers have alluded to it. Byron met, soon after his mother had removed with him to Newstead, a young village lad, and became almost inseparable from this humble friend, day by day. Byron continued the intimacy even after he had less opportunity, by being sent to Harrow. The poetical description tallies with this juvenile acquaintance that in its time filled such a place in Byron's lonely boyish life at home, and in his precociously sensitive—if then so immature—heart: they even convey with some elegance the quality of one boy's homosexual love for another;

"Then say, was I or Nature in the wrong?
If, yet a boy, one inclination strong
In wayward fancies, domineered my soul,
And bade complete defiance to control?
Among the yeomen's sons on my estate,
A gentle boy would on my mansion wait. . .
Full well I know, though decency forbad
The same caresses to a rustic lad,
Love, love it was that made my eyes delight
To have his person ever in my sight. . .
Of humble birth was he, patrician I,
And yet this youth was my idolatry!
Oh, how I loved to press his cheek to min!
How fondly would my arms his waist entwine!
'Twas like a philter poured into my veins. . .
. . . .

. . . . What lights this fire?
Maids, and not boys, are wont to move desire,
Else 'twere illicit love! O sad mishap!
But what prompts Nature then to set the trap?
Why night and day does his sweet image float
Before my eyes? Or wherefore do I dote
On that dear face, with ardour so intense?
Why truckles reason to concupiscence?
Though Law cries "Hold!" yet Passion onward draws.
'Twas Nature gave us passions, Reason laws.
Whence spring these inclinations, rank and strong,

EDWARD IRENAEUS PRIME-STEVENSON

> *And harming no one? Wherefore call them wrong?*
> *How many captains, famed for deeds of arms,*
> *Have found their solace in a minion's arms?*
> *Say why, when great Epaminondas died,*
> *Was Cephidorus buried by his side?*
> *Or why should Plutarch with eulogiums cite*
> *That chieftain's love for his young catamite,*
> *And we be forced his doctrine to decry,*
> *Or drink the bitter cup of infamy?"* . . .

Many a mature man not suspected, by friend or foe, of such a sexual emotion as that in the foregoing lines, Byronic or not, can echo their confession, looking back on past boyhood.

School-life, even when not in a boarding-school, frequently is highly developing to similisexual sentiments. There is no easy method of counteracting this tendency. To work against it too directly means the injury of the free, childish companionship, damage of wholesome, juvenile confidentiality and loyalty, and a check on the expansion of a lad's character by intimacy with his mates. The sexual danger must remain side by side with the good, in our educational systems. Naturally the kind of school-life that is led by the boy at home is not so provocative of the similisexual instincts. The English public-school, the French *lycée*, the German '*Gymnasium*,' the monastic school for young lads, offer genial atmospheres for it. But even the school-life which throws young lads together for only stated daytime hours is a lively factor.

School-life and Uranianism.

Indeed the general categories of schools for lads of all ages, including impressionable æsthetic natures of tender years, are the seedling-houses of uranistic impulses. The types of young Uranians mentioned above concentrate themselves on the school-friendships of this time. These become real passions. The sexual relations that spring out of them are not merely misdirected boyish impulses, as one is so often told. They are unities rooted in the elementary temperaments of many of the lads. As the boy grows up, the instinct may keep him a pederastic homosexualist for all his life, or he may experience its mutations toward mere idealism. But, first and last, it is likely to be the same aesthetic passion for masculine

Most Boarding-Schools Unavoidably the Forcing-Houses of Boyish Uranianism.

beauty of body, in preference over the feminine; a sense of the psychic superiority of the male, a "drawing" toward him, as the expression of sexual desirableness; of personal charm, trustworthiness, and "completeness." From the first days that the lad looks into the world, distinguishes a man from a woman, a boy from a girl, the youthful Uranian makes his choice instinctively. He knows where his heart leads. Professor Kuno

Fischer gives a striking reference to this quality of school-friendships in his allusion to the famous Karlschule, at Stuttgart. Many Englishmen could duplicate such reminiscences.

Dionian-Uranians
Common Among
Schoolbys, as Among
Adults.

Sometimes the sexual relation of young lads is not mutually uranistic, but (as in riper years) a dionistic lad is drawn to an uranistic mate. He grows bound to him; is sexually intimate with him, while puzzled or ashamed. Such young Dionians when maturer, often lose all taste for similisexual intercourse, look back on it with consternation and disgust. Unfortunately the really uranistic partner undergoes no such change.

The first abandonments to a male love, the first physical expressions of it will have been subtly educative. The *gout* of it is forever fixed.

A Sign of Early
Uranianistic Nature:
Friendships of
Too Sentimental a
Warmth.

Indications of passional, abnormal friendships ships between boys as boys, and girls as are worth precautions. Friendships which seem to take a strong nervous hold of the boy's character, to dominate his psychic life, to possess a distinctively sentimental colouring, are to be discouraged by the parents and guardians, however sympathetic they may be to such intimacies on general grounds. Diversion, separation, diplomatic obstacles, should be utilized. Especially so, when the lads are of the weaker, more idealistic classes described. There is small use in explicitly reasoning on the topic with a boy; not more than there is use in such a course with the adult Uranian. One meets only denials and evasions of all sorts; a deeper self-inclusiveness. The curious and painful topic of juvenile suicide is by no means unconnected with precocious similisexual instincts. In a German city, a year ago, a lad of fourteen hanged himself. It was found that he had committed the act, not on account of a failure in his school-examinations (as was mentioned) but because he had lost the intimacy of another lad, homosexual as himself, and was "too miserable" without it. A young English boy, not fifteen, attempted suicide at a summer-resort recently, leaving behind him a note for a mate, which said that the death of a young tutor in his school with whom, as was presently discovered, he had had sexual relations, "made life a blank" to him. "I loved him and he loved me and, I cannot live without him."

I cite from a comunication that is made to me by a friend, whose term was long in an English public school, of the first class, in fact, till his University matriculation:

Further instances; Boarding-School Practices.

"Of homosexualism at X—, I can say that it was never failing, on all sides. While in many instances, especially between older boys with younger ones, there may have been the only mere temporary substitution of such intercourse for the more normal kind, still I know plenty of examples where the sentiment never has been lost by the parties as they grew older. I can count now a dozen such that we all knew of. . . We laughed among ourselves, never taking them as a real disgrace, no matter what we said or would have said, "outside." We had two regular marriages, between well-grown boys, partly in fun, as caricatures of a Roman wedding-ceremony, partly in earnest. One of those "matches" has never been interrupted, both the men being homosexual and living in together in X—. (Of course no suspicions of their relation being what it is.) Our Latin tutor, Mr. Z—was homosexual. He had no conscience about it, no responsibility. He seduced several lads during my stay at X—. As to one of his later intimacies, with the present Lord S—, who was then a remarkably beautiful boy of seventeen or eighteen, we all had a regular, tolerant sort of understanding. . . At the time of the Cleveland Street Scandal in London, you will remember how prominently the name of T—occurred. Nobody who had ever been at our School with him would ever be surprised at his share in such an affair."

Instance of Permanency of the Instinct.

The foregoing writer alludes to tracing in the matured mend the schoolboy-similisexual. The following extract is in the same connection, the writer being a dionistic pederast. . . "Since the days of my youth, I have had to carry about with me—my secret. How often has my heart been so heavy and troubled!—but I dared not trust anybody. I find my highest, purest pleasure in sight of a beautiful boy. Sexual connection with a young man, on the other hand, gives me a shudder. I cannot understand how anybody can tolerate the mere idea of that. Nevertheless, something ever impels me toward a blooming lad, far more than to a girl, although I also feel sexual desire for the latter. For girls I have now and then been in a state of enthusiasm, but never so sensitively as for a boy. I grow indifferent in course of time to the girls I may have loved. I seldom think of them later, and then without any special interest. On the other hand, a boy that I have loved is unforgettable. Women find me good-looking. I have received many a love-letter. . . I never dance, and I have not the least desire to marry. The only thing that disturbs my illusion is when the the handsome boy grows older, so that the beard develops; then my passion lessens. . . I am fascinated only by quite young, graceful, girlish lads, not muscular or robust, and only if of clean and pure mind. How often would I like to press such a boy to my heart, to cover his pure eyes with hot kisses. But I cannot!" . . .

The Tutor an Uranistic Influence.

An appreciable influence in developing Uranism is the fact that the tutor to whom the boy is committed may be an Uranian of pederastic inclinations. With all sympathy for his nature, there is too often a conscienceless failure to his trust. But the tutor's situation can be terribly trying to self-control. Sensitive to boyish beauty of mind and body, a twentieth-century instructor of lads can fall in love with them as ardently as any Greek academician. But in these days such an "unnatural" sentiment easily can be social ruin. Not only does the unhappy Uranian nourish the instinct in similisexual youth; he undoes himself by the surrender to it. Particularly in monastic gymnasiums and boarding-schools, directed by a celibate clergy, many of them young priests, is the atmosphere of uranism latent, whether in type delicately esthetic or rankly gross. The school-study of classic literature has a close connection with boyish similisexualism. To explain honestly many episodes in the best poets and historians of Grece and Rome is to teach homosexuality, unavoidably. Close companionships out of the classroom between impressionable lads and their tutors; sociable hours in the teacher's apartments; quiet excursions with lads into the country, beget many romantically pédérastie ties. Painful tragedies occasionally spring out of them. Criminal statistics annually are filled with the stories of educators, secular aud clerical, guilty of debauching of boys; by no means always in satisfaction of brutal and vulgar sexualism, but carried along by aesthetic uranianism; sometimes with despairing moral contest. When an intimacy is not known to the outer world, but takes a calm mutual course between lad and guardian, the latter may change colour in the

EDWARD IRENAEUS PRIME-STEVENSON

boy's nature and in his concepts of sexual love, as he outgrows his "derived" uranistic tendencies; or it can bring grave consequences if he remains homosexual.

I have following from a teacher in a Continental institution for lads, a secular one. "No words can tell what I have suffered, morally and physically, through my passion for generous-minded, high-natured and beautiful

Instance of Uranistic Struggle on the Part of a Tutor.

lads. I was in continual warfare with the sense that I must not betray myself; not only because at that time I did not understand homosexual love and natural right to the emotion, but because of feeling strongly, as a sexual and moral duty, that I must avoid encouraging such ideas in any boy's nature. I was very often greatly troubled. I had two or three such passions. One, for a lad named D—nearly drove me insane. . . My position in a large public-school, a homosexual and boy-loving teacher, attractive to his charge, sometimes is terrible now. . . During the latter part of my stay in W—, I gave up the moral contest several times, detesting myself for my weakness, overcome by love, But I allowed myself what relations came from the surrender only when I was sure that the boy was plainly of the same temperament, was eager to be the object of my passion, and would be perfectly secretive. Even this qualified liberty led to several intimacies. . . I call God to witness that always, then as now, it is the spiritual traits of the youth that mostly draw me to him. . . The most violent affair of this sort, my love for L—K—led me to consider suicide, and for a time interrupted my whole life. . . Even now, when the physical passion for beautiful and noble boys has passed from my nature, so that my interest and admiration is intellectual, I shudder to think of those six years in W—. The nervous cost to my life was permanent."

Instance: School-boy Impression-ability—Dionistic and Helpful Tutor.

The ensuing is from a correspondent, now a man of mature years.

"Among first influences to strengthen my uranistic instincts, were four years at the E— school. I was a handsome lad, full of all sorts of romantic notions. My Greek tutor was one of the most winning men that I have ever met. At about thirty years of age, he was of unusual attractiveness; athletic, robust, elegant, with beautiful features. I simply fell in love with him! The sentiment was a real misery. I did not dare to let Mr. Z—see it.

I was tormented with hopes, fears, and bitter jealousy also of one other schoolmate for whom Mr. Z—appeared to care specially. This "rival" was much more clever than I. . . In my second school-year when I was fourteen, to my great joy two things occurred. My rival (who never knew himself such, I am sure) went away. At the same time, I found that Mr. Z—was disposed to become more interested in me. At length, the passion on my side came to my open confession. It was made in a burst of angry feeling, because of Mr. Z—'s stirring, up my jealousy of the boy who had gone away. It happened one afternoon as we were alone, and Mr. Z—was giving me help in a lesson. To this day I remember with gratitude the tact, the careful preservation of my self-respect and innocence of mind, with which Mr. Z—(who was not at all homosexual, though perfectly intelligent in the tendency) met my confession. He calmed me, and managed to give the sentiment at once a less disturbing course for me. We became close friends. There was never any further real unhappiness for me. I overcame the sexual element in my feeling for him, without loss of warm affection or intellectual drawing to him. Unfortunately such a change was exceptional. It did not lessen the passionate sexual colour of episodes in which other men were the objects of my regard" . . .

A French fiction (wholly such?) "Les Pervertis," by a precocious young French authour, Ferri-Pisani, is so special and doubtless true, a picture of homosexualism in a great Paris *lycée* that it may well become a classic in its type.

A mysterious attempt at murder, and therewith a suicide, on the part of a trusted servant, under circumstance pointing to homosexual relations with his young master, occurred in a well-known New-York family, in the autumn of 1907. It is mentioned more at length in another connection of this study.

Instance: Homicidal Jealousy.

The uranistic youth is prone to sentimental passions for men on the stage. In a study already cited, "Hellenische Liebe in der Gegenwart," by the late Otto de Joux, the authour tells the story of a boy of thirteen, the son of a high official, who fell violently in love with a certain operatic barytone, a man of distinguished beauty when on the stage. The boy contrived to begin and to keep up a most eloquent love-correspondence with the singer, under a female name. He wrote in

Similisexual Lads given to Concealed Sentimental Passions for Actors, Singers, etc.

his diary. "Only once, once, to be kissed by those cherry red lips, to be clasped in those strong arms, to be allowed to rest on that marble-hard bosom! what unspeakable bliss it must be. . . He sings heroic roles and he is himself a hero. Oh, my Conte di Luna! why are you so unattainable, as far out of my reach as your name-sake? Have you no idea that I love you,—you, my only beloved until death?" The reader perhaps may fancy that one meets here the sentimentalism of a feeble-framed, morbid-natured lad. Not so, for the diarist was a rugged young Uranian, who grew up to be a marine-officer of distinction and is to day a virile type of humanity. But his inborn uranianism is intense, under the mask.

University Life and Uranianism.

Though the Uranian busy in college-life is not in earliest youth, yet he is not mature enough to make consideration of his temperament impertinent to this chapter. Universities, the world around, are centers of similisexual attraction and of 'relations' between fine-natured young college-men. Under such sexual circumstances often begin those absorbing and exclusive intimacies for life, not much understood as more than long and remarkable "friendships." The influence of hellenic and Latin literature and classic social aspects, the virile daily ambient, athletics as a great element of modern university life,—all promote the sentiment, are an element of the problem. Oxford and Cambridge, Heidelberg and Jena, Harvard and Princeton, Vienna and Berlin, Bologna and Padua, the chronicles of their homosexualism between the young men populating them give much significance to this phase.

College-Theatricals and Youthful Similisexuality: Instance.

The homosexual influences of certain kinds of university theatricals, nowadays so popular and artistic, are not trivial, especially because of the present tendency to neglect dignified drama in favour of burlesques, operettas, musical farces, parodies, and so. These demand that young men play trivial female roles, in female costume, as imitatively as they possibly can. The more perfectly a young undergraduate, beardless and graceful, can assume a womanish personality as a "chorus-girl," or soubrette, in public, so much the more is he praised. "You cannot tell him from a girl, when he is on the stage" . . . "I am the prettiest ballet-girl that ever you saw in a theater!" . . . These are common sayings when talk is of the college-performance in rehearsal, or just given in some town-theater, to smart audiences. Stage-dancing by young men in female dress, has been made a "feature" by promoters and patrons of "college-shows." Undergraduates have acquired national reputations for grace in short skirts, and for female softness of contours highly attractive to audiences. Curious bits of inner college-history hinge on the admirations that result. Here is one such confession:

"I had never felt any clear sexual emotion for another man till one Spring, when we rehearsed and gave in X—a musical farce, under fashionable patronage, for the benefit of our University boat-club. I had always been athletic, and had not thought much of my looks; certainly not as being femininely attractive. I had the part of "a beautiful princess" in this piece. What with the talk of the "régisseur" and the dresser and of my chums, and the constant fuss made over my dancing, I took the rôle more and more seriously. There was a great deal in the papers about my "wonderful female beauty" in the costume, my producing the "perfect illusion of a lovely girl," and such stuff. We had several costume-rehearsals, and we gave the piece six or seven times. Soon after the rehearsals in dress came, I began to notice how some of my classmates, even the most masculine, began to "fall in love" with me when *en scène* Some of them showed the same sentiment afterward. I found it amusing. One evening the feeling of "bisexuality" was strong in me; the half-womanish instinct was roused. I saw a certain H—plainly in a state of suppressed sexual excitement. So I deliberately seduced him. From that night, we had frequent intercourse of the kind. It was partly under a veil of fun, but it was not mere jest—no! really I was for the time a woman, in my sexual nature, and H—was my victim. The relation lasted long after all the play-giving was past. Nor was A—the only instance of my giving way to the same feeling. To tell the truth I became demoralized by my own adaptability to appear feminine! Another homosexual student became quite mad about me. I had a long sexual intrigue with him. An older (senior class) chum became sexually my slave. . . It passed out of my life, after I left the University. Now we all are married, except the homosexual friend last referred to. But I learned a lesson from it. I have never allowed my young son, now at X—College, to take part in theatricals; whether plays by Plautus or operas by Sullivan."

In the columns of the "New York Tribune" some ten years ago appeared a strong American communication on this same topic, intimating the homosexual side of it. There is also an article in the "North American Review" of the same time, discussing such questionable aspects of smart college histrionics, that have no connection with a really literary element of university life.

Another Instance.

An Uranian of a distinguished American family, a man of line intellectual and moral attributes, at one time married but separated from his wife (on discovering how vain was a marriage-relation to effect his "cure") narrates thus his experience as an undergraduate, with a chum engaged in amateur-theatricals:

"My first irresistible love-affair of a homosexual kind was the outgrowth of a friendship with a chum in the University. J—was wonderfully clever at different "female roles" in our college farces and operettas. I had not appreciated his "bisexual" sort of beauty, till he was made a "flower-girl" in a burlesque, richly staged, that we gave in the B—Theater. J—'s photographs were sold all over the town, everybody talked of him. Then I realized how like a lovely, if rather robust, girl he was; and the feeling of sexual desire began to mount. I began to make more of our intimacy, and soon I found that the emotion I speak of continued when we were in ordinary conditions of life together. J— was a dionistic type, but I may as well confess I succeeded in bringing him to my wish. The effects of that sexual passion and its continuance for a year between us have been a part of my whole after-life as a homosexual! I think J—outgrew it. But I did not. J—was my idol for a long time. There was no other bond between us; intellectually we had not much in common. I know of a dozen other undergraduates, and of one professor, who were all more or less in love with J—, some of them to any degree of "success" with him, One such intimacy gave me miserable hours. . . In the same dramatic society were half a dozen homosexual intimacies. The fact that the men concerned were some of them splendidly athletic did not count; unless (as I sometimes think) it assisted the sentiment."

Artistic and Aesthetic Sensitiveness of the Young Uranian.

The youthful "aesthetic temperament" is generally one that must be peculiarly watched and guided. The possession of much musical susceptibility should be a danger-signal. Not painting nor sculpture nor literature can act on a young similisexual Ego as does its musicality. Also should be observed the tendency to admire only male performers in the circus, when the admiration seems specially physical; and the passionate interest in handsome actors, singers and soldiers, etc.

Superior Scholarship by Young Uranians.

The young Uranian's mind in school or other educational training is likely to be brilliant, though his quickness of intelligence does not generally extend to more abstract tasks, such as mathematics—not to formulas and intangibilities, rather than concrete topics. He is frequently a quick linguist, a good geographer, and a precocious literary worker. On the other hand, his equipment sometimes is annulled by an indolence that no rod will cure; all the more irritating because it is a mysterious failure of will, not of wish.

Precocity in what is Unmoral or Vicious.

In all grades of Uranian youth; in school or not, including boys not necessarily of decadent type and origin, a propensity toward general moral weakness is met with painful frequency; if along with many redeeming traits. This class contrast, sharply with the high-natured type. A large proportion of brilliant and well-born young Uranians are innate liars, cowards cheats, mischief-makers and shifty young characters. The Uranian lad of really undergrade social tissue is especially often a thorough *mauvais sujet*. The boy-murderer, expert thief in his teens, and so on, are likely to be similisexual lads. This sort, side by side, with the finest instances of noble and pure characters in the young uranian sex, in its manliest, most sensitive morality.

Feminine similisexulism in Early Youth; the Youthful Uraniad.

This study, as has been said, concentrates itself on male aspects of similisexualism. Only secondarily can it set forth aspects of the Uraniad's sexual life and nature. So much of them are mere translations of the masculine into feminine terminology that separate discussions of the two intersexes seem superfluous. The present chapter is a particular example of this. Almost every phase of the boy-uranian, whether at home or in school, and college, finds its parallel in the Uraniad, in her early environment. Like the Uranian, the Uraniad is constantly an inborn, precociously intersexual existence. Her nature as a little girl, at home, in the nursery and schoolroom or away at school, often pulsates with an irresistible directness. The present tendency to educate young women in colleges for "girls only," promotes feminine similisexuality. American and English girl-colleges are famous cultivators of the passions that belong to the Uraniad. Often a mature Uraniad looks back over a long life, in which not for one moment since her first friendships, her earliest "teens," her college intimacies, has she been other than a woman-loving woman. Possibly she finds that a long life has been saddened by the possession of precocious sexual impulses which she has neither dared to disclose, nor even now has begun to understand; in which her university-life, with its encouragements to masculine ways of thought, feeling, dress and sentimentalisms, has been a potent factor.

Inborn Uranianism in a youth, and real and inborn Uraniadism in a girl (the latter's outlook less decisively) cannot be "cured." If genuine, it defies "remedial" processes. Acquired similisexualism of a superficial quality frequently passes away in women under matrimonial influences, maternal emotions and other alterants. The parent, the tutor, the mature friend of an Uranian boy can help the lad to grow up with his similisexual instincts in reasonable physical and moral restraint. Intelligence and tact can define the course to prevent the boy from becoming as a homosexual man, what so many grow up to be—degenerates, criminals and victims. But beyond such solicitous, tactful help to a lad no results can be achieved, in nine cases in ten,—except illusions and failures.

Is Early Uranism "Curable"?

And interesting and unconventional aspect of the parental problem as to a homosexual boy (and, to some extent, to the youthful Uraniad) is the fact that fathers and mothers sometimes express themselves as much preferring that their son should be, and should grow up, homosexual; provided that the 'relations' consequent be happy, tranquillizing, elevating and idealistic; concentrating the lad on special; 'love-friendships' of the kind; and acting as an outlet of his juvenile sexualism that protects him from being the victim of those debasements, diseases and other mischiefs that are so largely part of a boy's early heterosexual experiences. Several well-known psychiaters have met this conviction. Its results obviously depend too much on the individual cases to be easy of brief consideration and résumé here.

Parents Approving Juvenile Uranianism.

VIII

THE URANIAN AND THE URANIAD IN THE
MILITARY AND NAVAL CAREERS; IN THE
ATHLETIC PROFESSIONS: AND IN ROYAL,
POLITICAL AND ARISTOCRATIC SOCIAL LIFE:
TYPES AND BIOGRAPHIES

E specially contrary to the notion that the man-loving man is always effeminate in body and temper, stands the fact that in scarcely any other profession—in no other walk of practical life—has the full sexualism of Uranistic passion been more general than in the ranks of soldiers and

The Military Homosexual: in No other Profession is the Uranian More Frequent.

sailors. We might say that in no other one is it so large. In the army and the marine we find the Uranian in enormous proportion. Here, too, he is met in the full display of his bodily vigour, his force of character, his activity of mind, his virile courage, pugnacity, indifference to troublesome luxury, and his generous comradeship. In short the "race" is here seen being and doing "all that

may become a man," save preferring womanly embraces to those of some brother-in-arms, or comrade of the watch. The fire of similisexualism nowhere smoulders, or burns up, more ardently than in casernes and forecastles, in the officer's mess or on the quarterdeck. From the first days of armies and argosies, uranian comrades have marched and sailed and fought together as friends and—lovers.

How Far a Result of Environments?

With the instance of the sailor his homosexualism seems in a considerable degree, a cultivated—, unconsciously cultivated— condition. In the course of sea-life come the long voyages, where men are continually in companionship only with men; where solitudes, duty and the battles of the elements emphasize masculine nearness. There is the necessary abstinence from women, the bachelor-state common to the sailor, the tendency to idealize in the finer-natured seaman; the sense of living in a mysterious elemental relation to Nature herself, of being only vaguely bound by conventional human notions—if bound at all. These conditions may not create the emotion of man-love; but they stimulate it. It has been said that "every sailor in two or three" is more or less homosexual. Certainly sailors criticize lightly the homosexual ties in constant existence round them. It is a sort of sea-secret. And it can level even rank. Incidents of uranianism point out the naval officer and the common sailor, as Uranian or Dionian-Uranian in "friendships." The theory that a sailor's sexuality turns him toward having 'a wife in every port' is notably wrong. It would sometimes be better to say 'a wife in every—ship'.

Distinguished navigators and sea-warriors, daring pirates, storm-defying Wikings, bronzed captains in the merchant-services of the world, have been also uranian lovers. Some names are historic. We find one such Dionian-Uranian in Yasco da Gama. Another, according to accusation, was Cornelis van Tromp, the son of Martin van Tromp. Such too was Magellan (Fernâo de Magalhaes, one of whose descendants not long dead, the Brazilian diplomat and litterateur Domingo Magalhaes (1811–1882) was professedly Uranian, and the authour of the sometime famous "Urania" poem (Vienna, 1862). One of the most eminent of English naval commanders of the century just closed was prominent in an homosexual scandal, suppressed vigorously on account of the high personages involved, but disconcertingly general at its date.

That the British navy long ago was remarked for homosexual cultures, a classic English novel hints. A curious sea-incident occurs in Smollet's Roderick Random," where the hero of the novel is stationed on a ship commanded, for a time, by an effeminate uranistic officer, living in open sexual intimacy with his doctor. Also is to be cited the other passage in the same story, where a homosexual nobleman, enamoured of the young surgeon, tries to broaden Random's views as to intercourse between males, by the praise and perusal of Petronius. (See chapters XXXIV and LI, of the novel).

In illustration of what has been said, the following extract from a letter from a naval-officer, in the English service, is offered:

Letter from a Naval Officer.

"I have been stationed, as you know, on two or three ships, and I think they have been thoroughly representative of the best sort of British seamen. On the D—, homosexuality was rife, and one could see with his own eyes how it was going on, even between officers, i have been told that in some services (the Austrian and French, for instance), nobody ever remarks about it, taking such a thing as a natural proceeding. That may be so or not; but in any case nobody was "shocked" on board either the A—or the B—. There were half a dozen "ties' that we knew about. To my knowledge, sodomy is a regular thing on ships that go on long cruises. In the war-ships, I should say that the sailor often pereferred it. . . In the instances that I have described, the intimacy was spoken of—slyly. The friendships between men, in all grades of service at sea, tend to be much closer, more sentimental than when ashore, Everything makes for confidentiality, one is shut away from the world, and so much in pairs with his friends, during watches and so on. . . Of course when the forecastle men come ashore they are keen after the girls, but sometimes that interest quite disappears, I am told. . .

That it does in the case of many sea-friendships between homosexual officers, I know. . ."

Instance.

An example of homosexualism in a greatnaval milieu occurred in the summer of 1908, at Brest, France; with a grave scandal, caused by the rape of a voung sailor one night by a drunken-ship-master, in the same caserne, who also forcibly outraged (the same night) two other young sailors, in the same barracks. A series of homosexual "rivettes" (cliques) were disclosed; and matters were kept with difficulty from wider notice. The affair was made more agitating because of the confusion in it of the identity of the amorous *patron-pilote* responsible, between whom and a certain other officer a remarkable likeness unluckily existed; leading to a violent but rather comic rectification.

Something of the influence elemental to sailor-homosexuality is admirably expressed in the novels of "Pierre Loti," already referred to; the authour being a captain in the French marine. "My Brother Yves," for instance, is manifestly uranistic, the passional affection for young Yves on the part of the narrator going beyond mere friendship; a strong note of sexual relationship at times sounded in the tale.

The Army-Envirouillent and Uranianism.

The army-environment does not so shut in the soldier from general external influences, and from contact with women. Yet the soldier, whether a general or of the file, in numberless examples is instinctively indifferent toward feminine beauty. Day-by-day comradeship, the night-life of an army-corps, in peace or war, are pervaded with a vague similisexual ambient. It would seem that, being himself so robustly male, there is no place in a soldier's heart, or sexual impulse, for anything not vehemently manly. Here advances the theory of the Uranian as a super-virile, not sub-virile, sex.

The Direct and Indirect Aesthetics in Naval and Military Life.

The naval and military atmosphere are highly aesthetic. They are full of colour, romance, life, grace, symmetry. They possess an outward and inward beauty, and dignity in their beauty. Severe practicalities do not deduct from it. In fact many such details expressly add to it. Courage and an aether charged with virile force fuse in the social atmosphere. Beauty of body, the effective uniforms that enhance the physique in constant appeal to the eye as well as to temperaments sensitive to masculine good-looks, the free and often tender intercourse, intimacies of specially fine psychic fibre between men, all make part of the aesthetic attraction.

Historic Examples of Soldier-Uranians.

The Biblical warrior meets us early with his uranistic personality. We find his type in the swift, passionate love, not to be construed as mere friendship, (if any one knows the Oriental) between David the beautiful boy-warrior—a mere shepherd-lad—and Jonathan; whose mutual attraction and tie is distinctly uranistic. One may surmise from the respective ages of the two, and from the accentuation of Jonathan's share, that it was pederastic on the part of Jonathan, who seems to have fallen in love at sight with the humble peasant-boy. The story is highly suggestive sexually, as we read it in the First and Second Books of Samuel, with its development of a sudden passion which. . . "knit the soul of Jonathan with the soul of David; and Jonathan loved him as his own soul" The lament of David after the tragedy of Mount Gilboa is in no common strain of even oriental bereavements, with its cry for the love "passing the love of women," a phrase which also suggests the character of Jonathan's sentiment. The story might be a page from Firdausi or from "Antar." Its dionian-uranian colouring is strong. A hint that Jonathan had inherited some traces of similisexualism occours in the Hebrew of the insult of the angry Saul to his heir—"Thou son of a perverse, rebellious woman, do I not know that thou hast chosen the son of Jesse to thine own shame, and to the same of thy mother's nakednes."

Classic Greek and Roman Warriors.

We have early some examples of classic homosexuality among soldiers. Going back to the more shadowy epochs and types begin the numerous instances. Achilles and

Patroclus, and the legendary Nisus and Euryalus will be remembered. In mythology we have the boy-ravishing Jove, with his rape of the beautiful young Ganymede; Apollo as the lover of Hyacinth; Hercules loving the lad Hylas, and undertaking the famous Twelve Labours because of a passion for Eurystheus. But we meed not enphasize the uranianism of classic fable or of the beginnings of national history. As hellenic civilization grows more definite, the similisexual soldier is a frequent study. In Athenaeus we learn that Agamemnon loved Argynus sexually, the naked beauty of the latter having caught the king's eye irresistibly; and that Antigonus, another royal uranian, was in love with his handsome lute-player, Aristocles. We have Charitonus and Melippus in a sexual relation. The patriotic assassination that so glorified Harmodios and Aristogeiton was in a vengeance for what was a homosexual marriage, we may say, between the two youths—whose uranic love was so virilized. As for Alexander the Great, he is mentioned as intermittently pederastic, by the account of Athenaeus, especially with respect to Bagoas, and to Hephaestion, whose sudden death plunged Alexander into an agony of grief "that exceeded all reason." Pausanias, also Epaminondas (with Kephidorus and Asophicus); Alcibiades—who was at every period of his career an irresistible seducer of men—are other examples. Julius Caesar was not only notoriously the lover of the young King Nicomedes of Bythinia, and of the youthful hostages of Gallic tribes, but of his nephew Octavianus, who later became the homosexual Emperor Augustus. The first great Caesar indeed was so well-known for some of his male amours that the coarse personal taunts which they stimulated under public circumstances, and such attacks as the ribaldry of Catullus, appear never to have been challenged. Julius Caesar presents also the type of a soldier who was passively homosexual, as plain allusions indicate; and the peculiar gentleness of his temperament is significant. That he was dionistic to strong bisexuality of the impulses is pointed out by the historic charge that he was "every man's woman and every woman's man." The subjection of Pompey to homosexual (apparently quite pederastic) favourites is depicted in the account of the great warrior's passion for the young freedman Demetrius—"the person who had most influence with Pompey, a youth not without understanding, but who abused his good-fortune"—although Pompey himself often made young Demetrius less an object of odium "because he submitted without complaint to the caprices of Demetrius," allowing to the

EDWARD IRENAEUS PRIME-STEVENSON

petted boy all sorts of uncivil liberties, even with formal guests.

Ancient Teutonic Gothic, Slavonian, Turanian, etc., Armies.

The German and Gothic nations were not lacking in warrior uranians. The phrases of Tacitus in speaking of the Germanic tribes are familiar. The fierce regiments of the Turanian hordes that invaded the Danubian basin were homosexual; as notably the Magyar is today, especially as a passivist. Slavonian regiments sometimes carried about with them groups of male prostitutes, as did the ancient Scythians. The Arab, the Ottoman, the Moor and the Persian soldiery have always been male-loving. The Janissary and Mameluke regiments were distinctively pederastic. Today the Turkish soldier rapes a handsome boy even more instinctively than he does a terrified girl, when raiding some helpless village of Macedonia or Bulgaria.

The Crusaders; The Fighting Orders; the Paladins and Arthurian Chivalry.

The Crusading Epoch brought subtle influences toward a male-loving soldiery in Europe. The Christian cavalier transferred to the East soon became pederastic. Especially is it curious to discover how the vowed Orders of knighthood circumvented the letter of their pledge to be chaste sexually, by their permitting coition with males. Several great military orders tacitly decided that pederasty was materially a lesser sin than to break the vow of continence as to women. Hence the sombre Templar fraternity gradually became riddled with homosexualism, noble and ignoble. The downfall of the Templars indeed was intimately united to that fact. Not less similisexual was the tremendous military Deutscher Orden. Its warlike social story, in Venice and Poland, is filled with uranianism. The Order of Malta has always been a chosen retreat for the uranian aristocrat.

Suggestions of more than merely spiritual bonds between the famous Paladin confraternity can be discerned in the pages of its chroniclers. The same observation applies to some of the passionate intimacies between the Arthurian Knights of the Round Table. Indeed, at this period of chivalry, love for women was continually a mere idealism, expecting and receiving no sexual return. Often it could not, by any stretch of honour, receive such return. Knightly woman-worship was much a matter of lute and lay, a spiritual pose. Malory sounds notes of passion that vaguely make similisexual melody. Later, incontestable representatives of soldier-uranians thicken. It may startle many a reader to know that

Gonsalvo de Cordova, General Tilly, Prince Eugène of Savoy, certain princes of Orange, Duke Charles of Burgundy (1433–1477) that great soldier-prince Henri de Condé, the Duc de Vendome, Pietro Duke of Parma, the youthful and brave Conradin of Hohenstaufen and his kinsman Friedrich of Baden, the "blameless" paragon of chivalry, Sir Philip Sidney, Charles XII of Sweden, Gustavus III of Sweden, Peter the Great of Russia, Paul I of Russia, Amadeus of Savoy (who became Pope Felix-Amadeus VIII)—not to mention a wide circle of typical Italian and Spanish "fighting princes" such as Cesare Borgia and great war-making Umbrian and Tuscan and Lombardian chieftains, indubitably were homosexual. The luckless warrior of the Pfalz, Richard Puller von Hohenburg ended his career in a trial and at the stake, as a confessed sodomite, along with his last young paramour, Anton Schärer. The fine soldier Filippo Maria Anglo Visconti, duke of Milan, conspicuous in the early part of the Fifteenth Century was uranistic; one of his special favourites being Scaramuzza, who had been a good-looking young palace-cook.

Modern Soldier-Uranians.

Of the modern soldier-uranians, without bringing us quite to contemporary army-lists, two high names stand out with special clearness; Frederick the Great, and Alexander I of Russia. Frederick was not only a declared woman-hater, but an undeclared sexual adorer of men, from his youth up. The sentiment coloured all Frederick's life, military or civil. Among such episodes were his relations to Baron Trenck and the ill fated Lieutenant Katte, intimacies with young Count Keyserlingk and other. Their nature—suspected or proved—entered into the furious outbreaks of his father against him, that in Frederick's unhappy youth nearly cost his life. In the dramatic affair of Baron Trenck, the fierce jealousy of Frederick played a more cruel role than his anger at Trenck's intrigue with Princess Amalia. It was partly a homosexual tragedy. Von Katte lost his life through the bond with his Prince. The intimacy with Keyserlingk is an episode of the same kind. Another is that of Count Görz. What Voltaire said of his royal friend's foible was not simply ill-humored irony. Frederick's list of male amours extended even to stalwart members of the famous body-guard of young soldier-giants. At the examinations for admission to the robust regiment, the King made notes that he was given to consulting on—other occasions. Frederick was indeed, precisely the princely Hohenzollern to be homosexual. The trait is special, along with the diversified talents, in the famous royal line. It has offered later examples; including exalted—

not to say august—ones, of very contemporary Hohenzollern family-history.

Alexander I of Russia was unequivocally homosexual. Of great physical beauty, adored by the women, he was in youth, and he remained, as glacial to love of their sex as Frederick the Great, or more so. The many similisexual episodes in Alexander's life, in campaign or court, justified the pointed remark of Napoleon that the statuesque Emperor of Russia was "the slyest and handsomest of all the *Greeks*." The reader can consult such memoirs as the Potocka series for items. Alexander's mysticism of temperament, as he grew older, is not inconsistent with his similisexualism.

Was Napoleon himself ever tinged with uranianism?—he, that continual amateur of women, that brutally sexual Dionian, when in mature soldierly individuality! One can hardly entertain such a suspicion at first thought. Or is one again confronted with the eternal, inconsistent uranistic throb of dionistic natures? It has been affirmed that Napoleon in his humbler soldier-days, when Lieutenant (or Captain) Buonaparte, had a homosexual intimacy with a young officer of his regiment. Probably the truth or falsity of this vague charge will never be determined. But certainly Napoleon had no strong moral theories against the homosexual instinct. He was a Latin, as well as a man of wide philosophic horizons. His Napoleonic Code avoids carefully any punishment of sexual intercourse between men, except where violence, public decency, or debauchment of minors, are concerned. Probably Napoleon's attitude to the topic was similar to his mocking remark when told of the habits of bestiality (with a mare) on the part of a certain gallant officer of the army; "So? And what, pray, have I to do with his—love-affairs?"

The hero of Khartoum, General Gordon, a soldier-like type, if ever one was, and a devout almost superstitious, Christian, was Uranian. Incidents of this inner life of Gordon used to be narrated in his Chinese days and later. His bond with Lord Arthur Hamilton was of the truly hellenic colour. An Uranian-nature has long been attributed to another contemporary English soldier whose name is linked popularly with Egyptian campaigning; along with his exceptionally persistent "woman-hating."

Within a few weeks of the time when these pages are written, England, and Continental Europe were shocked by a notable loss to the British army, and by a melancholy social tragedy—the death in

Paris of Major-General Sir Hector Macdonald, who died a suicide in consequence of uranistic intimacies, while commanding officer of the British forces stationed in Ceylon. Personal friends of Macdonald long had been aware of his homosexualism. In course of his long service, there had been relationships that were open secrets. But in Afghanistan, India, the Sudan and South Africa alike, Macdonald had fought with great distinction. Clandestinely pederastic, after being stationed in Ceylon, occured incidents in connection with native youths that invited official investigation. The affair might nevertheless have escaped further consideration had not a member of the legislative council in Ceylon brought charges. The governor of Ceylon judiciously attempted to suppress them, but the effort was vain. Summoned to London to answer accusations against his private character at the War Office, Macdonald made a hurried and secret journey to England. He had interviews with a few friends, including Lord Roberts. Macdonald was urged to face the accusations; "they would be dismissed Certain unfortunate aspects impaired his courage, whatever might have been his best course. During the last days of March, 1903, in incognito, he took up his quarters in a Paris hotel. One morning he was found dead in his room, having shot himself. The episode excited much grief in Great Britain. Indeed, British hypocrisy in speaking or writing of homosexualism, on this occasion was considerably laid aside. The public and the press paid high tribute to the deceased soldier. Some of the English and Scotch journals spoke of him as the victim of unnecessary official scrutiny uinto personal affairs." A public monument to the dead warrior has been erected in Scotland. There was much more temperate allusion to the trait which had brought Macdonald to death than in any previous affair of the sort in England.

A curious case of uranianism, coincidental with a soldier's profession and temperament, occured in Commandant J—R—, in charge of an important army-station in the western part of the United States. Commandant R—in no sense neglected his military responsibilities. But he had homosexual intimacies with younger or older soldiers, according to lively report. He also was fond of attiring himself like a woman, when in his officer's quarters, yet would have none of womankind round about him. A small literature of his eccentricities has appeared. The diffusion of uranism in the officer's life today, points out the hellenic fact of the soldier-

In Modern Military Life "Love" levels Ranks.

nature as still "man-loving physically as well as spiritually. An uranian Mars seeks union with the male not perhaps because he is effeminate, but because too virile to tolerate what is womanish. Certainly Uranianism is enormously prevalent in the armies of Germany, Austria, Russia and France, as well as in the East. Certain military romancists, such as Pierre Loti and Georges Eckhoud, have expressed this in their stories, and many works on military service on the Continent have referred to it. The English, French, German, Italian and other regiments in Africa and Asia, on foreign duty, have aided in cultivating the taste. Occasionally grave scandals have occurred, through some sudden discovery of homosexualism in a garrison or caserne. In France and Germany and Austria several such dramas may he fresh in the minds of reader of this study. The English army has had its share, whereat an aghast British public has gasped in horror and disbelief. The British tongue can hardly stammer its disgust as to such "unnatural offenses," in mess or plebeian circles, pretending to know nothing of what is tolerated, right and left. A famous old-time scandal, dragged into glaring publicity,—serving as type of such regimental and garrison uranism among officers—was the Augustus Cornwall *esclandre*, in Dublin. The "De Cobain Affair" was notable in the annals of such explosions. Ruined careers and accounts of self-destroyed existences usually follow their publicity. Of military prostitution in the ranks, as a vastly broadened practice in England and on the Continent, a regular institution, will be said something presently.

German army-centers fairly reek with pederasty, in all regimental grades. A melancholy proportion of "unexplained suicides," unaccountable disappearings, and so on, in military life, are to be traced to homosexual undercurrents; exactly as runs the dark story in civil life. Within a few years, the phrases "severe nervous illness," or "suffering from incurable headaches" have passed.into the cant of the journals when a young officer's suicide is reported. Sometimes the words mean the end of a dire struggle to explain Nature—to excuse it. Sometimes they mean the need of excusing closest associates, with a scandal hanging over many heads. Sometimes the cause is blackmail. More common than one would expect, is the fact that the young officer, overloaded with debts, has agreed to a marrriage as arranged by his friends. His bride's dowry is to set him free from creditors. He accepts the project, but presently is unable to face the physical union. His horror feminae is not

The Tragic Side Here, as in Civil Life.

to be fought off, he takes his life. Another element of such suicides in the brotherhood of arms, is the sense of broken ties of the garrison-life henceforth to be solitary, for some regimental "friend" of the benedick. There are many shades and degrees of the uranistic sentiment in such "unsoldierly" mysteries.

Often one meets with a newspaper-reference similar to this one, translated from a journal of the very week in which the authour is writing this chapter:

"No further light can be thrown as yet on the suicide of Lieutenant R—B—last Sunday. The personal and professional affairs of the deceased young man were in good order, and no family matters exist that explain his want of interest in life. The letter to his brother K—B—, in F—, in which Lieutenant B—spoke of himself as the victim of "an incurable nervous disease from which he had long suffered," is contradicted by the dead man's having been examined about four weeks ago for a life-insurance policy, with an excellent report. No one has heard him speak of any sort of nervous or other ill-health. The letter which Lieutenant B—left, addressed to his friend Captain O—, the latter declines to make known. Captain O—wishes it understood that there is no ground for the report that affairs with the other sex are complicated in Lieutenant B—'s death. Lieutenant B—was of most regular habits; did not frequent the society of the opposite sex except under ordinary social conditions. He had many warm friends. The deliberation of the suicide, makes the affair mysterious."

Or take the following:

"Captain F. N. of the O—Regiment,—now at G—, after a visit to the Franciscan Church last Sunday returned to his lodgings in—Strasse, and after sitting at his writing-desk, put a revolver to his breast and was found by his orderly, lying by the desk, dead, some hours, later. . . A letter to a fellow-officer declared his intention of making away with himself. The suicide was evidently quite clear-minded. Captain N—was a young man, of regular habits, and retiring in manner. He was often called the "woman-hater" in view of his avoidance of "gay" society in G—. His health was good; his family affairs and money-matters were entirely in order. There is, in short, no accounting for his act. The friend to whom the letter mentioned was delivered declines to give information as to its contents."

In a garrison-town in Italy, two or three winters ago, occurred the suicide of a high officer of the Italian Service; an incident which awakened regret and surprise in Italian army-circles, owing to the high character and distinction of the deceased. He had fine social qualities; there was a want of motive to explain his act. V—had been in his usual spirits, had mixed freely with his friends on the preceding days of the same week, and was just promoted. He blew out his brains in his room, one afternoon, leaving on the table a four-line letter saying—"The disease which afflicts me prevents my dragging out this life of mine any longer. Please notify my brother, with due caution." No "disease" existed. The fact that the dead man had been homosexual, and the victim of a melancholy long-concealed from human scrutiny, was afterwards known. He had given up existence in a fit of neurasthenic despair.

Before the close of the thirties, in the nineteenth century, occurred in Vienna, a chain of episodes in army-life, based almost wholly on uranistic facts. How much so was known to few persons outside of a trio directly involved. Among the Magyar Imperial Life-Guards in Vienna, was a certain young Count U—, a member of an excellent family as well as of an aristocratic circle. Count U—was of a physical beauty which made him the object of feminine admiration in half the drawingrooms of Vienna. Complaisant proposals were lavished on this Apollo of one of the most picturesque regiments in Europe. He was a Don Juan as to the women. Nevertheless, Count U—was a Dionian-Uranian. He maintained a sexual relation with a young brother-officer in Budapest, a famous swordsman and rider, of notable attractiveness. Between the two young men came a difference. The *fidus Achates* of Count U—was a declared woman-hater, entirely homosexual. But in course of time, Count H—, apparently reverting to the normal, fell in love with a young and beautiful girl. It became a question of his marriage. The Count offered his hand and name. Fraulein X—accepted him. Unhappily one obstacle to the marriage existed. The young lady was of Jewish stock, the daughter of a wealthy financier. At that time the local prejudice against such marriages, on the part of aristocratic Vienna, was more sharp than it is today. The engagement might however have been acceptable to the U—family, but for a direct intervention, made by the friend of Count U—. He had been willing to tolerate Count U—'s passing flames, but the idea of the marriage was unendurable. Whatever he could do to strengthen the opposition of the family of Count U—he did. But he maneuvered this so adroitly that Count U—had no idea of any such intrigue. The jealous soldier played his rôle with the finesse of an actor. He could not succeed in bringing the parents of Count U—to a definite refusal to receive the young lady into their intimacy, should the marriage occur, until about a week prior to its date. Some of the members of the U—family had declared their willingness to be present, but others had not. The night before the date set for the marriage, Count U—visited his parents, having every reason to suppose that displeasure as any obstruction was past. He found the situation changed. His father nor mother would neither be present at the ceremony, nor under any circumstances would receive the bride socially. A violent scene ensued. There was no mistaking the obstinacy of the family. Count U—went to his rooms, and shot himself dead. The young officer who had been the real agency of the resolution of the U—family, was overwhelmed at a result which he had not foreseen. In remorse and grief he followed his friend to the grave, by putting a bullet through his own heart on the evening after the funeral of Count U—. He left a note to a well-known officer, in which he confessed the sexual history. The young lady, by the by, survived the tragedy, and presently married—into her own faith. The U—family, it is of interest to note, included more than one abnormal member. Another member, Countess U—was always believed to be an Uraniad, so masculine was her individuality, in spite of the fact that she married and had children. Her separation from her husband was supposed to refer to this element. She also, when in middle life, without any obvious reason, committed suicide suddenly in a foreign land where, as a sort of interesting amazon, she long had resided.

Uranianism in the French "Lost Legion."

Strange tales of Uranianism are met in the gloomy annals of humble service in foreign countries by Asiatic and African regiments, with European recruits of unknown but oviously good antecedents. We encounter in such records the Uranian who has fled from recognition at home, outlawed by some homosexual experiences. The rank-and-file of such a Foreign Legion as that of the French service in North Africa contains soldiers of aristocratic social station, whose lives have been ruined by homosexualism. Such riddlesome "men without a country" suddenly appear, and enlist themselves in wearisome, dangerous services. Frequently they are well-educated, brave, unable to "hide the gentleman" in them. Their lips are sealed to explanation of why they have expatriated themselves. Such books as Georges d'Esparbès studies of the Franco-Algerian

EDWARD IRENAEUS PRIME-STEVENSON

service touch on this aspect. Many such volunteers gladly fling away not only names and social grades but their lonely lives, without a word to anyone. The sands of the desert or the grass of a jungle cover the bones of many social *cidevants* who have danced in Court balls in London or Wien, or who have headed the hunt across the Campagna on a Spring day, in the pride of fashion, wealth and blue-blood.

A sanguinary little drama, based on uranism in the ranks was played in a Galizian barracks one night, a few years ago. A young infantry soldier had during many months maintained homosexual intercourse with another recruit. The friend took a fancy to another soldier, and avoided his former comrade. The latter discovered the situation. A fierce quarrel ensued, Finally the deserted man threatened to kill the deserter and anybody else concerned. In the middle of the night came a shot, then a scene of terror. The soldier had crept stealthily out of bed, had taken his carbine, and had slipped over to where his "false" comrade lay. He fired at him in the dark. As the roomful of sleeping recruits was roused by the report, they leaped up, striking lights. The lad saw that he had missed his mark. He began firing right and left wildly— twice aimed at the rival soldier. In the flickering light he merely grazed him. The youth was secured by his half-naked comrades, and was shut up, out of his senses, till morning should come. During the few hours of that imprisonment he contrived nearly to make way with himself. He was tried for attempt at murder, but refused to explain his motives, till he was put under medical examination. Then he confessed the affair.

Belles-lettres have not been silent as to the homosexual soldier. The French novelist "Pierre Loti" mentioned, introduces such an element in his tales and sketches, though Loti conveys more homosexuality in his sea-stories. Short episodes, in various familiar fictions, are uranian enough to merit attention. One such occurs in Tolstoi's "Anna Karénina," when the hero of Anna's unfortunate romance, Wronsky, notices the entrance of two Russian fellow-officers, into a restaurant, one older, the other a young type; who are indicated as notorious for a pederastic relationship so much so that Wronsky avoids their society. But another Continental authour, now many years dead and almost forgotten, Alexander (von Ungern) Sternberg (d. 1868) rises par excellence among- portraitists of some of the most sympathetic aspects of soldierly uranianism. He has presented many phases of

A Romancist of Military Uranianism: Alexander von Sternberg.

it. Particularly is this the mainspring of psychologic study in one of Sternberg's novels of the Napoleonic era, entitled "Jena and Leipzig." We find there the homosexual tie that unites two young officers, who begin their friendship-love with their confinement in a hospital after the Battle of Jena, and die together in the struggle at Leipzig. Along with this military novel may be mentioned von Stenberg's story, "Die Beiden Schützen," which has also a soldier-uranic atmosphere; the narrative of a tragic sexual love between two young Berlin recruits at the time of the so-called "Berlin Revolution" in 1848.

A brief résumé of these two military stories by Sternberg is timely here, as being typical. In "Jena and Leipzig." Franz von Selbitz of aristocratic birth, loves passionately but in troublous secrecy, his companion-in-arms. Andreas Walt, of humbler social station, but who is a sort of Antinous in his classic beauty. Unluckily Walt has not been at all attracted to von Selbitz—not even as a friend. The sense of jealousy has worked bitterly on von Selbitz. Precisely on the night before the battle of Jena, von Selbitz challenges Walt to a duel, in sheer nervous irritation. But the duel cannot be fought; duty to their country postpones any private quarrels in the army. Next day both young men are dangerously wounded. They are left on the field, near each other. Franz von Selbitz crawls over to the side of the man whom he loves more than his own life, and at the risk of his chances of surviving his own wounds, he binds up those of Walt. He is carried to an hospital, along with von Selbitz, each of them quite unconscious from exhaustion. Arrived at the hospital, Andreas is presently brought out of danger: but Franz is thought to be beyond hope, though he has been brought to a certain degree of improvement. He is perfectly rational, and has still the relics of former strength. Aware of his critical state, he begs that, no matter at what risk, he may be allowed to speak once with Andreas Walt. Bandaged and weak, Andreas consents. He makes his way to the bedside of von Selbitz. The following scene occurs:

Andreas heard Franz's weak voice, and undecided what to do, whether to enter the room or to withdraw, he stood in the door.

"Andreas Walt?" called the sick man.

"It is I," replied Andreas, without coming nearer the couch. Not till the other had stretched out his hand to him did Andreas Walt sit down on the bed. Lying there, Franz pulled aside the paper screen which muffled the light; and the rays fell full on the face and figure of Walt. Franz fastened his gaze on Walt, and did not turn his eyes away even on meeting the still unfriendly, almost hostile, look of Walt.

"In what can I serve you, Herr von Selbitz?," asked Walt coldly.

"I am a dying man" replied Selbitz, in a low voice. Then he paused. Again Walt said nothing, and a long silence ensued. Then suddenly Franz seized the hand of Andreas Walt in his own; covered it with tears and kisses; and cried "Andreas! Can you forgive me?" "Oh, comrade!" answered Andreas, flushing a blood-red, and drawing away his hand in his surprise and embarrassment. But Franz, lifiting himself up, continued. "If to night is to be my last, Andreas, so much the more reason for you to know that—l love you." "You—you speak so in your fever," replied his late antagonist, bewildered.

"No, Andreas! By God and by His Eternal Grace, I tell you the truth! Be cold—be proud if so you must be, after I humiliate myself before you. Yes, Andreas only a glowing love, hidden from all the world, not understood by even myself—this has made me treat you as I did. Know now that in my bosom lives a quite other heart; as long ago you would have known—found out under other circumstances. I tormented you, I insulted you, only because I loved you! I could not endure it any longer—that you were so cold to me, made no more of me than of other comrades. Yes—I have felt as if I would kill you, rather than find you so cold to me!"

"I cannot understand—"

"Listen, Andreas! When I saw you for the first time—when you first came into my room, as I sat alone and dull-hearted on my bed that day, a ray of sunshine fell through the old torn curtain. It fell on your face, on your breast and shoulder; and something cried out in me, "*That man belongs to you!* He is your brother your friend! Without him you ought not to live, you cannot live! . . ." Only because I could not throw myself upon your neck and kiss you, did I treat you so ill then and afterward. . . Oh, if you could have known that though I have mocked you in the presence of others, I have crept in the night to the door of your room, only just to hear the sound of your breathing while you were sleeping!—my heart tortured with dreams that perhaps you might die suddenly! that so I might be left alone, in cruel misery, without you! What a folly mine has been! . . . Point out to me, Andreas, any other such heart as mine! And so at last in my mad torment, ever more wreched, did I cry out, "This must come to an end! either by his bullet to my heart, or by mine to his! When he or I are dying, then, then, I can tell him all! Death shall unite us, since Life cannot! And so now you know all: forgive me, if you can."

Franz had turned his face to the wall, the agony of his wound overcoming him. But Andreas Walt knelt down beside him, and said in a tone that showed how much he was moved at this strange confession, "Herr von Selbitz all this seems to me so very strange. I beg you to feel sure that I have never had the least idea of—what you tell me!"

"Oh, call me "Thou," not "You"! exclaimed Franz, "you can do that now—for am I not dying!"

"I will get the surgeon—"

"No, no! Stay *thou* with me! Be *thou* my physician! See, see, Andreas! I am quitting this mortal life, and never have I known what is its highest joy. I am twenty years old; and yet never have I come into touch with what men call love for woman! God has kept my heart open only for—friendship! Thou, thou, art mine all! my life—my love! Here, now, on the edge of my grave, I throw off the unnatural mask, for now I shall have dared to clasp thee with the arms of love—I can go Home satisfied."

Andreas felt something like a well-stream flowing to his breast from the heart of this dying comrade. All other emotions had fled; bending over Franz von Selbitz he exclaimed "My friend! My brother! For, so do I greet thee!"

"—In death and in life!" whispered Franz.

Von Selbitz fell back on his bed, and lay there still, in a swoon of exhaustion. Andreas summoned help, forgetting his own perrilous condition, living only for the friend who had given his very soul up to him, as so unexpected an offering. . .

That little attic-room, where Franz had been lying, must needs now shelter both these friends. The Angel of Death hovered over first one of the pair, then the other; he touched their young foreheads, but his cold finger was not laid upon their hearts. They grew well of their wounds slowly—slowly. But by the coming of the Spring, they could leave their sick-room. . .
Their comrades greeted them gladly, once more of their old circle. Often, often did talk busy itself with the strange change—two men once such bitter enemies now such affectionate friends."

The remainder of the novel deals with the sacrifices of Franz von Selbitz as he finds that Andreas Walt, who is a Dionian-Uranian at most, loves a young girl and wishes to marry. The torments of wounded hopes, of jealousy, of separation, all are of course inevitable to this situation. Yet Franz, who is the superiour nature, realizes that respect for the more normal temperament of Andreas, and regard for his happiness, alike demand that the marriage must come. "I have suffered frightfully, Andreas," he writes. . . "I have battled with my heart, I have won. Go, love this woman, marry her! Sooner or later that would have to be. I have seen the girl, and though she does not seem to me worthy thee (for when could any woman be worthy of a man?)—still, she is not unsuited to thee, Andreas. So—farewell forever! I cannot live near thee, knowing that I now have only *half* thy heart. Nothing on earth is there more wretched than a half-heart! I want either all my heaven; or else all hell" . . . The separation however is maintained with difficulty. One meeting between the pair of friends is particularly moving. The military course of the story is resumed. The two men are ordered to Leipzig. In that great battle they are both severely wounded. Franz von Selbitz dies in the arms of Walt, just as he has long desired to do; while Walt survives Franz only during a few hours.

In Sternberg's other tale, "Die Beiden Schützen" ("The Two Shots") are again two protagonists, both young men; the brown-eyed Tony Wickye, a Neuchatellois, and Friedrich Forst, from far-away Pomerania. The deep affection between these two, and their solemn pledge that it shall never fail of *anything* in life and in death, are sketched in a succession of manly and graceful incidents, during their soldier-service. Once, when Tony overstays his furlough, his alert friend contrives to transfer the punishment to himself, and so willingly suffers arrest for Tony. Friedrich Forst is, in fact, ever the more unselfish nature of the pair—more perfectly uranistic, intersexual. A feminine pleasure in self-sacrifice marks his sentiment. Forst has, too, a portent that he is to die early. One night, while possessed by a sort of revery, when on watch-duty, he counts the grated bars of a cemeterygate near him, and finding them to be eighteen and a half, he feels strongly the conviction that he will not reach his nineteenth year. More than ever, in that sad fantasy, does his soul go out toward his beloved Tony Wickye. A few days later, Friedrich is mortally wounded—horribly—in a skirmish. Every second is torture. In his agony he implores Tony Wickye to take his musket, and to shoot him, then and there, simply to end such sufferings. He knows that he cannot be healed. He would fain die by the beloved hand of Wickye. After a direful moral and sentimental battle with himself, and refusals to his friend, the tragic vow of their friendship conquers Tony. He obeys; the shot from his hand puts Friedrich Forst, out of misery.

Such are some of von Sternberg's military stories in the intersexual key. Reference to those of other sort will occur elsewhere in this volume.

In the "Autobiography" of Edmondo De Amicis, where that charming Italian writer is describing his boyhood with its vivid sentimental undercurrents, he depicts his intense admiration for a comely young *bersagliere*, an episode not free from suggestions that the soldier had uranistic instincts. The narrative, however, may be read simply as a charming study of how a temperamental admiration for soldiers, and a sort of innocent boyish "flirtation" with one, can influence a sensitive lad's inner life for a time, and be more or less reciprocated by the friend of maturer age. De Amicis writes:

A Citation from De Amicis.

"My mind was forcibly diverted from Latin grammar by a passion which had a distinct effect on my whole life, finding vent fourteen years later in a book which marked the first stage of a journey that may end, perchance, with these pages. I refer to my passion for soldiers; or, to speak more accurately, for the *bersaglieri* who formed the only garrison of our city. If they had been infantry of the line, I am certain that my enthusiasm would have been less; since my devotion, though due in part to the warlike spirit of the time and my own ardent nature, was also partly due to the beauty of the uniform, the agility of the manœuvres and the personal prestige of these "Children of Alessandro La Marmora." Never I am sure did lad of my years entertain a more ardent passion; though many have been much more strongly inclined than I towards a military career. It was a real monomania, not to be cured by exhortation, reproof or punishment. On every holiday, and on other days too, both before and after school, I ran away from home at all hours in order to follow the cocks' plumes to the training held, to the rifle-practice, to the "athletics." Among my many likings, I made one friendship, which remains among the dearest recollections of my childhood. There was a trumpet-corporal—a native of Mortara if I am not mistaken—a young fellow of medium height, lithe and robust, a typical *bersagliere*.

His features were strong and wore a serious expression, but he was full of kindness; his manners were simple and pleasant; his name was Martinotti. He took a fancy to me through having seen me plunging along to the sound of his trumpet, with my tongue lolling from my mouth. We scraped acquaintance on the training-field; then we began taking walks together during my leisure hours in the neighborhood of my home. He treated me like a man, which flattered my vanity and enhanced my affectionate gratitude. He spoke to me of his family, his career, his superior officers; told me all the garrison-gossip, giving me all particulars with greatest gravity, while I listened with the most devoted attention. At home, my one, theme of conversation was Corporal Martinotti, whom my brothers to tease me dubbed "the General," He wanted me to say "*tu*" when I spoke to him, but I never got up sufficient courage. To be seen on the street at his side was my pride, and when he took me to the *café* to drink soda-water, I felt a halo settle round my head: I should not have been more set up had Count Cavour himself invited me. He called me by my Christian name, but abbreviated it because it seemed to him too long as it was, and hard to pronounce. He turned it into "Mondo" or "Mondino" . . .

My adoration for him reached such a pitch, that I imitated his walk and accent, and whistled from morning to night the marches which he most frequently called upon his trumpeters to play. I do not remember how long this happiness of mine endured; I know that I expected it to last forever—as if Martinotti were likely to live his life out in our city because it would hurt my feelings to have him go! But the end came suddenly.

One night toward dusk, at the hour of "retreat," meeting me on the ramparts, he said:—

"Did you know that I am off tomorrow, with tho battalion, Mondino?" And seeing that I did not understand, he added— "Off for the Crimea."

People had been talking about the Crimean War for some time, but somehow it had never occurred to me that he might be ordered there. I could not find my voice. He smiled at my emotion, bis eyes full of compassion, then tried to console me by saying—

"I've good hopes of escaping the Russians. They won't want to kill us all. And if I get off, it's quite likely that I shall come back here. Courage, Mondino! We shall meet again some day."

I could not keep back my tears. He looked at me for a little time—earnestly, gravely,—then turned and ran away, as though he had heard the sudden call of one of his superior officers. I went home sad at heart, and had hardly crossed the threshold when I told my mother the mournful tidings, broken by a sob, "Corporal Martinotti. . . is going to the war."

"Poor fellow!" she exclaimed; then added, to console me, that I would better go and wave him a farewell at the station.

Next evening I rushed to the station; but it was empty. The battalion had left in the morning!

I stood there awhile, gazing with tearful eyes at the shining rails along which my friend had been borne away, following him in my fancy to that far-distant country, full of terror and mystery, from which I did not believe that he would ever return. . .

What I do remember is that I often thought about my corporal, so far away; and that after bis departure I ceased to have anything to do with the few *bersaglieri* who still remained, as if he had taken with him all the poetry of his corps and all the enthusiasm of my heart."

The account of how by-and-by Martinotti came back, lively, well and gay, to renew the intimacy with "Mondino" is equally suggestive.

A recent American book entitled "The Spirit of Old West Point," presents the military souvenirs of General Morris Schaff, of the United States army, in a volume remarkable for grace of literary style and sympathie sentiment In its authour's pen-portraits of early friends in the famous Military Academy (the Woolwich, or Saint-Cyr, of the United States) are to be noted many delicate suggestions of the uranian emotion in young and soldierly comrades. Indeed the accent of a manly similisexualism of psychic quality pervades the record. To many Anglo-Saxons it will make a peculiarly subtle appeal, even if its sub-uranistic accent may not be intelligently appreciated. Especially in its elegiac passages, it is eloquent of the homosexual thrill in young hearts that beneath uniforms can beat so passionally for each other.

————————
Two Other Literary References.
————————

In the novelette "Imre: A Memorandum," by the present writer, a homosexual romance that has something of a military atmosphere—the hero of the little tale being a young Hungarian officer who is an inborn Uranian—there occur several references to the struggles of a soldier nature, unclear as to just what may be the troublous sexual quality of its regard for other comrades-in-arms, dreading detection of the mysterious feeling, hiding all its promptings day by day in regimental life; and finally tormented by an almost insupportable struggle with a passion for a brother-officer who never suspects the character of the younger man's regard for him. Hourly terror lest his homosexuality should be guessed, makes Lieutenant Imre von N—seem unemotional, reserved and unappreciative. The following passage is near the close of the story, where is reviewed Lieutenant Imre's difficult social policy toward warm friendships:

"Twice Imre had been on the point of suicide. And though there had been experiences in the Military Academy, and certain much later ones, to teach him that he was not unique in Austria-Hungary, or elsewhere in the world, still Imre unluckily had got from them (as is too often the hap of the Uranian) chiefly the sense of how widely despised, mocked, and loathed is the Uranian Race. Also how sordid and debasing are the average associations of the homosexual kind; how likely to be wanting in idealism, in exclusiveness, in those pure and manly influences which ought to be bound up in them and to radiate from them! He had grown to have a horror of similisexual types, of all contacts with them. And yet, until lately, they could not he torn entirely nut of his life. Most Uranists know why!"

"Still, they had been so expelled, finally. The turning-point had come with Karvaly. It meant the story of the development of a swift, admiring friendship from the younger soldier toward the older. But alas! this had gradually become a fierce, despairing homosexual love. This, at its height, had been as destructive of Imre's peace as it was hopeless. Of course, it was impossible of confession to its object. Karvaly was no narrow intellect; his affection for Imre was warm. But he would never have understood, not even as some sort of a diseased illusion, this sentiment in Imre. Much less would he have tolerated it for an instant. The inevitable rupture of their whole intimacy would have come with Imre's betrayal of his passion. So he had done wisely to hide every throb from Karvaly. How sharply Karvaly had on one occasion expressed himself on masculine homosexuality, Imre cited to me with other remembrances. At the time of the vague scandal about the ex-officer Clement, whom Imre and I had met, Imre had asked Karvaly, with a fine carelessness,— 'Whether he; believed that there was any scientific excuse for such a sentiment?' Karvaly answered, with the harsh conviction of a dionistic temperament that has never so much as paused to think of the matter as a question in psychology. . ." If I found that you cared for another man that way, youngster, I should give you my best revolver, and tell you to but a bullet through your brains within an hour! Why, if I found that you thought of me *so*, I should brand you in the Officer's Casino tonight, and shoot you myself, at ten paces, tomorrow morning! . . . Men are not to live when they turn beasts. . . Oh, damn your doctors and scientists! A man's a man, and a woman's a woman! You can't mix up their emotions like *that*."

"The dread of Karvaly's detection, the struggle with himself to subdue passion, not merely to hide it, and along with these nerve-wearing solicitudes, the sense of what the suspicion of the world about him would inevitably bring on his head, had put Imre, little by little, into a sort of panic. He maintained an exaggerated attitude of safety that had wrought on him unluckily, in many a valuable social relation. He wore his mask each and every instant, resolving to make it his natural face before himself! Having, discovered, through intimacy with Karvaly, how a warm friendship on the part of the homosexual temperament, over and over takes to itself the complexion of homosexual love—the one emotion constantly likely to rise in the other and to blend itself inextricably into its alchemy—Imre had simply sworn to make no intimate regimental friendship again! This, without showing himself in the least unfriendly; indeed with his being more hail-fellow-well-met than otherwise with his comrades in the A— Infantry."

"But there Imre stopped! He bound his warm heart in a chain, the vowed tepid fraternity to the whole world, he assisted no advances of warm, particular regard from any comrade. In his soldier-life gradually he became that friend of everybody in general who is the friend of nobody in particular! He lived in a state of perpetual defence in his regiment, as in whatever else was social to him at Szent-Istvánhely. So surely as he admired another man—would gladly have won his generous and virile affection—Imre turned away from that man! He covered this morbid state of self-inclusion, this solitary life (such it was, apart from the relatively short intimacy with Karvaly) with laughter and a most artistic semblance of brusqueness; of manly preoccupation with private affairs. Above all with the skilful cultivation of his repute as a Lothario who was nothing if not sentimental and absorbed in—woman! This is possibly the most common device, as it is the securest, on the part of an Uranian. Circumstances favoured Imre in it; and he gave it its full mystery. Its cruel irony was often almost humorous to Imre."

To the important topic of male prostitution in general an extended reference will occur in this book presently. But at this point must be noticed specifically military prostitution: particularly by young soldiers in large cities and garrisons.

Military Prostitution.

This phase of "the social evil" has become enormously diffused and obvious in Europe, as in the Orient. The common soldier, likewise the soldier of better than humble grade, in almost every country, every military administration and garrison town, exercises largely clandestine prostitution. The motives are various.

In some cases the young soldier is more or less constitutionally homosexual. He likes coition only with a male, and would seek that, even could he not expect to be paid for it, like any other harlot. In a proportion of examples he is bi-sexual. Perhaps he is too poor to give himself heterosexual relief through a brothel; or else is afraid of disease. In another proportion, the soldier is not at all homosexual. He sells his body to a stranger, or regular patron, simply as an easy though rather irksome avocation. A mercenary motive is probably the most common. In those countries where the standing armies are large, compulsory service long, and the soldier in the ranks has but meagre pay, he takes to prostitution to increase his narrow exchequer. He finds that he does not get enough to satisfy his proverbially good appetite; unless he in an orderly or has won over a sympathetic cook-maid. He cannot keep in his pocket the few extra coppers for such trivial luxuries as his cigarettes, his glass of beer, his little stake at a game of cards, his evening in a cheap seat in a theater; not to speak of possessing cash for female society of an easy no-virtue sort. Sometimes he cannot without economy even keep his uniform and appointments in smart order, or pay for his postage-stamps to write to his people or his sweetheart, unless his family allows him a modest fund. That aid is not usual from humble households. He cannot make a penny for himself, so long as his military "time" lasts. Even as an officer's servant, he has but derisory wages. Soldier-life, the duties of barracks and drill are tedious or hateful to him. He wants diversion when the day is over; but many a time he cannot allow himself anything more amusing than a walk, or a free seat in a public park, till he returns to his caserne. On holidays, he often does not know what to do with himself, to kill the idle time.

But the stratophilic civilian is always near, to prevent a wholly unprofitable use of some of the recruit's hours of freedom. We will suppose the lad tall, well-built, robust and from eighteen to twenty years old. He is probably not sexually "innocent." If he be so, and hears what is said among his fellows in the barracks, he soon loses in moral sensitiveness. As was said, he may not be—often he is not—a born homosexual. But he allows himself to drift into the practice of sitting in public resorts where strangers come; in the parks and restaurant-gardens, well-known for equivocal usefulness. He goes to certain baths, to cheap cafés and theaters, of like repute; letting friendly gentlemen scrape acquaintance with him. In a park or suburb, comes the classic aid of a cigarette. Complaisantly he "takes walks" into secluded corners of the place with affectionate strangers, or gets into the way of accompanying them to their lodgings, for an hour or so. The price of giving his physical beauty and sexual vigor, even if with no good-will for the act, to the embraces of some casual homosexual client brings him more money in half an hour than he is likely to receive as his whole week's pay, even at the low *quid pro quo* of two or three marks, a couple of florins, three or four lire, or a couple of half crowns, for his amiabilities. The "Trade" aspect of it grows on him.— "Why not?" he asks himself. The commerce in a large town becomes easy, successful, and it is practically undetected. He soon discovers that whatever is suspected among his companions of him or of each other, little is said. So many of his fellows engage in the same by-trade of an evening! And as indicated, while soldier-prostitutes may vastly prefer sexual intercourse with women, and may make homosexual complaisances pay for normal gratifications, still, they are likely to lose repugnance to homosexual coitions. Many a young soldier grows into preferring it; he literally first "endures then embraces" it. Lasting intimacies are formed between soldier-prostitutes and civilians, when a particular regiment is stationed long in the same city. It is a curious fact that, while all sorts of soldiery are given to homosexualism, and furnish amateur prostitutes for the pleasure of the civilian, the cavalry, the artillery and the hussar regiments offer the majority. Various explanations of this are given.

The danger to the morale of a young soldier is obvious. He is not so likely to impair his vigour for duty, as to become morally inert

Mischief to the Soldier-Prostitute.

and unambitious. Mercenary, cynical by such a resource, he degrades himself, to degrade others. He laughs at the shy complaints of new boy-recruits in want of money, and tells them how to "make something" by a twilight stroll in Hyde Park or the Prater; by an half-hour in the promenade of a music-hall in London or Rome or Berlin; in a bath-house, or wherever else. But, far worse, such circumstances readily put the soldier-prostitute into associations with the directly criminal classes of a metropolis. When his military-term is over, he has developed toward a professional prostitute of the lowest civilian-class; toward thief, housebreaker, forger, blackmailer and what not else. With degraded uranistic feelings, not inborn but cultivated, he loses an idea of marriage, of raising a family. Thus his country's census is the poorer. Many a young soldier-prostitute of the famous Stadt-Park alleys in Vienna, of the Thiergarten in Berlin, of the boulevard of an Italian town, thinks that he will forget all such sexual chapters of garrison-days when he is mustered out, and at home.—"It is just a part of one's life now, for me as for thousands of others!" But the consequences may be deplorable. He may not "forget"—anything so potent toward his ruin.

The Uranian patron in a vast array prefers the soldier's "services"; is what we have termed "philostratic"—or specifically soldier-loving—in his sexual impulses.

Why the Uranian Affects the Soldier-Prostitute.

There are practical reasons, even when the patron is of far superior social grade. The young artillerist, cavalryman, or what else, is soldierly, well-dressed, and generally gains a fine physique. Often he has distinct beauty of face and figure. In Italy where lower classes are strikingly beautiful, to which attraction is to be added the refinement of the Italian proletariat and the pleasure that many a young Italian soldier takes in homosexual intercourse, the military prostitute is specially engaging. He is a marked contrast to the dingy, chlorotic male prostitute of civilist kind, who is hanging about the homosexual's steps. The soldier is physically magnetic. He is a logical complement to the average Uranian. He is often attractive by his boyish candour, or what passes for it, by a pleasant manner and companion ability. Even sophistication does not always destroy these traits; the young soldier realizes that to assume them is an alluring part of his evening-profession. Again, he is not a pickpocket or thief, as a rule; he can be brought into the lodging of his hirer without danger of petty losses. The soldier, too, is usually satisfied with a small sum for an hour's surrender of himself,—"for any thing you like to do"; while even more decent civilian male-prostitutes are as greedy of money as their female concurrents. The soldier is clean in person, as part of his military education, if not of his instincts. When he is emphatically homosexual himself, then he is almost certain to be free from sexual diseases. Thus the specters of syphilis and its like do not haunt the philostratic patron.

But above all reasons, at least in a large part of Europe, why the Uranian chooses a soldier-prostitute are the facts that the soldier is likely not to be brutal, and not a blackmailer. (See a succeeding chapter.) The soldier has the wholesome fear of military disgrace if he compromises himself. True, he may wish that he could get "something extra," little or much, by threatening his client with scandal; and he does sometimes attempt it. But such a disagreeable surprise is not usual. The soldier knows that he has as much to lose by "a row" as has his patron. So he is discretion itself, as a rule; makes himself useful; is paid his few marks or kronen or lire; and goes his way, with a friendly shake of the hand and his smiling—"Till next time!."

Military Prostitution in Central Europe and Elsewhere: Its wide Diffusion.

The assertion is often met that military prostitution in Europe, is less in the French and British armies than in any others; and more in the German, Austrian, Hungarian, Russian and Italian services than elsewhere. There seems to be fact in the statement that the French soldier in the ranks is less often a prostitute than is his colleague in other territory. This is part of the racial sentiment against homosexualism in France—of the Gaul in general. Perhaps the same is true of some Scandinavian armies, though prostitute-soldiers are plentifully met in Sweden, Norway,

Denmark and so on. The Russian armies are full of prostitution. Any open-eyed visitor to Russian posts soon satisfies himself as to this fact. In Germany everwhere soldier-prostitution is particularly rampant and extended. Here too is the racial instinct. Whole regiments, garrisons, acquire notoriety for it. In some centers, such as Potsdam, the military authorities, after having long winked solemnly at it, have sometimes been unable to ignore its publicity any longer, and have gone so far as to forbid the soldiery certain details of their uniform which have become a sort of smart advertisement that the wearers are to be "had." Any quiet part of a public promenade has its group of young warriors strolling about or sitting in im-modest obscurity, waiting for "business." The shady parks of Potsdam, Dresden, Berlin, Hamburg, Cologne, Munich, Breslau, Wiesbaden, Karlsruhe, offer this suggestive spectacle nightly.[1]

Copenhagen, Christiania and—especially—Helsingfors, are also notable posts for typical soldier prostitution.

In Austria-Hungary, soldier-harlotry is universal. Such parks as the Stadtpark of Vienna, or the Erzsébet-tér in Budapest, or almost any square or promenade of Linz, Innsbruck, Prag, Debreczin, Temesvár, and so on, are notable markets of an evening for any type of military youth that may be preferred. The Uranian has only to stroll, or to seat himself in a tranquil corner, to have unmistakeable opportunities. Usually the soldier-prostitute detaches himself from any companions; and even if several of the same regiment are *en vedette* for custom, they carefully leave each other alone. Comparing of notes, if any, will come later—at the beer-hall or the caserne. Sometimes however two soldiers have an understanding; they hunt in couples only, or intermittently, and keep a sort of silent partnership; a practice neither so "safe" nor so agreable for the client. In Vienna, some years ago, there were two young Hungarian troopers of exceptional beauty of physique who, always advertised their attractions in company; walking arm-in-arm about certain

---

1. The testimony elicited during the very recent homosexual scandals known as the Harden, Schulenburg, Eulenburg, Lynar, and concurrent processes in 1907–8, have thrown some interesting side-lights on German military, prostitution, as on German homosexualism in general, especially in high life: though such data are in no way novel, and although every method possible to suppress such matter from publicity was used by the legal and military courts concerned. The press-work of this book being fcfar advanced at the time of these remarkable processes—some of them being not yet ended as the writer makes this hasty reference to them—it is unfortunately not possible to cite them at any length in course of this study.

haunts, in their smartest uniforms, and often declining absolutely to be bargained-for—separately!

The reader must not suppose that military prostitution is confined to merely the lowest rank of the army. In Germany and in Austria-Hungary a considerable proportion of non-commissioned officers are committed to it, though naturally more cautiously, and at a "professional" tariff perceptibly high, but not always sexually quite logical. In England, France, Spain, Russia, Italy, South-Eastern and Oriental Europe, a good number of impecunious petty officers, and others not such—lieutenants, second-lieutenants, captains—maintain sexual relations with uranian friends of wealth, to add to their pay. The "tariff" is, we will say, from twenty shillings upward, per "rendezvous," or else a special (often largo) subsidy carries them past tailor's-bills, mess-expenses and so on. There is, of course, an element in officer-prostitution due to the officer's real homosexuality. But if he can make money by the secret, he is quite likely to do so. In Vienna, several young officers of elegant appearance, and of distinguished but impoverished stock, have recently become known as "accessible." The "relations" of sundry military-men, removed members of a reigning house, awhile ago were commented satirically. One officer of a great royal Guard carries his cynicism so far that ho systematically haunts baths and public resorts where rich foreign clients are to be met. In Berlin, there is much of the same thing. Under-officers to be "had" abound. To give only one instance, a certain young Bavarian officer in Munich is said to have met paid almost his living expenses and debts, by "cultivation" of homosexual foreigners of wealth. He travelled some months, a few years ago, on this sort of basis with a wealthy Englishman. In another capital lives a certain gallant Hauptmann Z—, whose lavishness, always an object of wonder to his unsuspecting comrades, is explicable by the relation he sustains to Prince X—, a well-known figure in local aristocratic and military life. In Florence, a young officer of distinguished family and looks was long known as an *entretenu*, and was a topic of frequent gossip, until his suicide a few seasons ago.

Britishi Military Prostitution.

The hypocrisy, or the ignorance—or the pride—of Englishmen, whichever it may be, frequently asserts if so recondite a topic is touched, that—"British soldiers, thank God, never do *that* sort of thing! *That's* a vice they leave to the Continent, sir!" Such an illusion is admirably English. The skeptic

EDWARD IRENAEUS PRIME-STEVENSON

has only to walk around London, around any English garrison-center, to stroll about Portsmouth, Aldershot, Southampton, Woolwich, large cities of North-Britain or of Ireland, to find the soldier-prostitute in almost open selfmarketing. Certain private resorts of British homosexuals "deal" in such an element. It holds its ground against the cheap and dangerous civilian-pederasty of England, which is so common. On any evening, the street-corners, or the promenades of the big music-halls and cheap theaters of London and other cities show one the fine flower of the British soldier-prostitute, dressed in his best uniform, clean-shaven, well-groomed and handsome with his Anglo-Saxon pulchritude and vigour—smilingly expectant. He is sure to be approached by some admiring stranger or regular "friend," and asked to take a drink or offered a cigar; and so is brought delicately to a bargain, at a tariff from the modest five shillings to three-and-six, or a sovereign. Sometimes a criminal-trial will point out especially London's soldier-prostitution. Thus in the mysterious "Studio-Murder" affair, in London, a few years ago, the victim, a young homosexual painter named W—, had relations only with young soldier-prostitutes, such as he picked up continually in Hyde Park and at such resorts as the "Alhambra," or on the streets. The most important witness was one such soldier, who was not otherwise connected with the bloody tragedy. His evidence was admirably illustrative of London's homosexual soldiery, and there was a prospect of such unpleasant military scandal if the crime were cleared up that there is little doubt why it was allowed to remain "unexplained," and the soldier-murderer not traced. A further reference to this "Studio Murder" occurs in this book in the chapter on distinctively criminal aspects of homosexuality.

In the United States, and South America.

In Canadian garrison-towns there are to be met quite the same aspects of wide-spread, everyday British soldier-prostitution. In the foreign Colonies of Great Britain, not only does the British soldier sell; he becomes a client and buyer of pederastic favours from young natives, as in the Orient.

In the United States of America where only a relatively small standing-army is part of the military-system, it is an army well-paid, and distributed widely. Its regiments are so dispersed, in fact, that the soldier is hardly an appreciable social element in the largest cities. . . Distinctively military prostitution is not discernible as in Europe. The Anglo-Saxon American is certainly highly homosexual, and when he is a soldier he does not lose that quality. But he has no reason to use it in a mercenary manner. He lives well, without being obliged to trade on his person. His home-subsidy is considerable. He is largely stationed where he has a constant sense of practical duty, in his Western posts or other responsabilises. He shows his philarrenism more as a buyer of the foreign-born male prostitute, for his own satisfaction, than offering himself to clients. In the Sandwich Islands, Cuba, Porto Rico, the Philippines and so on, he is not a prostitute of obvious rivalry to the native youth. Not even when he is of Latin or Teutonic or Keltic or what other race, by near blood; as is so much the case in a country not yet racially formed and consolidated. But the philostratic uranian who is near an army-post in the United States often finds an ample *curée*. For instance, a garrison noted for its homosexual contingent has been that of San Francisco, California, where especially during the time of the sudden Spanish-American War excitement (1898) soldier-prostitution was so active that the "Presidio" quarter was the regular goal of the philostrats of San Francisco. In fact, amiable young soldiers were to be "had" so plentifully that their tariffs fell to nominal prices, and the lodgings of popular amateurs were fairly invaded. This in a country where homosexual intimacies are severely punishable! Conditions more or less similar every now and then obtain in other United States posts, particularly if the soldiers are largely recruits of latin, teutonic or Scandinavian blood.

The Greek army (like that of Finland—an instance of *les extrêmes se touchent*) has long had the reputation of being one in which soldier-prostitution along with all phases of military similisexualism are excessively diffused. The prevalence of homosexual relationships between Greek officers and the rank-and-file, and the "acessibility" of all troops of the Greek service, from philostratic civilians, have been almost notorious. Recently an unpleasant little international incident occured between Greece and Italy, in consequence of an article exposing homosexuality in the Greek army, written for a Roman journal by Professor Spiro Ladikos, of Rome; which led to a request for his expulsion from Italian territory, on the representations of the Greek Government—which was rather disturbed by the indiscretion of the statements so published.

In the French army, scandals of similisexual kind are far from being unknown, though they are not so often manifested as in the German service. A serious affair of the sort occurred recently (in July, 1908) at Angers, in which eight or ten soldiers were implicated, and a rape on a young comrade was disclosed as an incident.

A significant aspect of military prostitution, perhaps more particularly in Germany, Austria-Hungary and Scandinavia, occurs in the way of every-day homosexual relations between officers and their soldiers in the ranks. This is far from being uncommon in spite of what would seem to be strong reasons of refinement, personal dignity, prudence, or discipline. Young recruits, as orderlies and otherwise, are discreetly brought, now by money, now by terrorizing, and often enough by tastes, to accepting such sexual relations with either their immediately superiour officers or with remoter ones. Scandals, blackmailing and so on, do not often take shape in consequence, even when there would seem to be so dangerously strong a personal leverage for the soldier to use against his superiours. In fact, a variety of sentiments can restrain him from that line of conduct. Often a passionate affection matures, so that the last thing in a lad's heart would be to betray either his superiour or himself. Young recruits are diplomatically "broken in" to this sort of harness, and often come to accept it as part of their duty. It is sometimes made worth their while. Little saturnalia are held, to which the most discreet are invited; such as those lately sketched in course of the testimony at the Eulenburg Trial. Stettin, Stralsund and some other garrisons have had scandalous explosions of this colouring within the past year; but the majority of regimental amours of so venal and undignified a type do not become known to the uninitiated.

An appendage to military prostitution in Continental Europe is the class of more or less ill-paid, minor Government officials, employed in one or another Civil-Service Department. Such young men are in railway, postal, financial, and like routine capacities,

particularly in Germany, France, Austria, Spain and Italy. The young man is not salaried enough to live as he wishes. His tasks are monotonous. He cannot gratify his normal sexual desires, for want of money. So he, too, cultivates a clandestine and secondary profession. This class is a combined result of immature years, moral contagion, starvation-wages, and lively racial instinct. It is largely homosexual by really individual taste. Some curious bureaucratic scandals have some times indicated its undercurrents.

Prostitution in the
Naval Services: its
Relatively Small
Proportion as a
"Profession" and as
Systematized.

The topic of military prostitution will recur in the tenth chapter of this survey, when we shall have under special consideration the most openly criminal aspects of homosexualism—the uranian delinquent as blackmailer, homicide, *souteneur* and so on, or as the victim of such dangerously degenerate types.

The common sailor is not averse to sell his person, to gratify his homosexual taste. He has relatively less opportunity however, unless some long stay in one port occur. But he is not mercenary by instinct or education, in the degree that the soldier is. As a "class," the sailor-prostitute is restricted. In some sea-services he can almost be said not to exist. Still, when on shore, in certain ports especially, he is always "to be had"—Russian, German, English, Italian, Spanish. He has his regular rendezvous in many such localities, where homosexuals, who like the sailor as a "type," can be met: and some procurers "specialize" sailors among their professional *étalage*. Of course, such tendencies practically are much a matter of a sailor's race.

Turning to the varied types of homosexuals not in distinctively military or naval profession, but of superiour bodily virility, let us note that similisexualism is widely manifested in the professionally athletic occupations. It is common to circus-riders, tumblers, acrobats, to men who are devoted to sports and professions of high physical dexterity. The "super-virile" theory may be recognized here, the male so emphatically masculine as to repudiate instinctively the feminine. Among "ring" gymnasts often. exist lasting intimacies of this sort. In athletic circles of all social grades, there is more or less uranianism. The Uranian who is not athletic is almost always attracted to the manly symmetry and masterful strength of the circus-acrobat. Sometimes this in inverted. In the professional pairings of acrobatic associates a vivid psychic interdependence is common. The reader will recall its study in the pair of brothers, united by a passionate affection, in the de Goncourts' "Les Frères Zemganno." A homosexual circus-performer who had also a career of transient literary brilliancy, was the lively Viennese novelist, Emil Mario Vacano. His fictions are now three or four decades old, and the personality of their extraordinary authiour is only a memory to a few admirers; but his sparkling and audacious pages offer some examples of truth stranger than fiction. A clear depiction of homosexual intimacy between two young men, one of them an Eastern acrobat, occurs in a novelette by Vacano, entitled "Humbug." But we need not turn to novels. One of the most distinguished of "strong men" and wonder-athletes of the day, whose physique is famed the world over, is similisexual, almost to complete indifference to women. Another great "physical culturist," as also a renowned professional wrestler and athlete, are uranian in their sexual life. In athletic-clubs, scandals of the homosexual kind are not rare. In London, Paris and Berlin, especially, some such have made social convulsions. In "Turnverein" organizations, for gymnastics and social intercourse, that are so much an institution of German and Austrian town-life, there have been many such episodes.

In the "Jahrbuch für Sexuelle Zwischenstufen" for the year 1900, is a reference to the prevalence of homosexual relations between Oriental athletes, ring-performers, and the like; the text being the famous Arabic troupe known as the "Uled Sidi" one; communicated by Herr M. Gudenfeldt. An eminent "bare-back rider," an Englishman by birth, well-known as one of the international artists in the Circus X—, (a man to be esteemed for refinement and serious character) stated to the present writer, some four or five years ago, that in his judgment "one male circus-athlete ring-rider, gymnast, etc., in ten was homosexual"; whether as a complete Uranian or vacillating between uranianism and dionianism. Some highly passional "homosexual affairs" have had, as protagonists, the aristocratic lovers of riders in the ring, or of statuesque trapeze-artists.

From the camp to the Court is a short step, though a sovereign is not always a leader of battles. Earlier paragraphs of this chapter concern princes not alone theoretically but really Soldier-Uranians; fighters and chieftains, by career and temperament. Turning from such, let us glance at royal, noble, and otherwise

The Uranian in Royal, Aristocratic and Political Life: Various Instances, Ancient & Modern.

eminent personages, (occasionally military withal) for the list of homosexuals in high-life. They are not always aristocratic Uranians to honour the philarrenic intersex and "cause." Often they are princes typically decadent in morals as in intellect; weak, cruel or puppet-like kings; tyrannous or unprincipled statesmen; disgraces to high, or to any other, society. But it is to be said in apology for some such exalted homosexuals that they were men who by birth, by social or political or other responsabilises, stood in false relations to life. We can believe that many such careers would be more edifying reading had such Uranians been born in private station, or could they have turned their backs on courts, cabinets and crowns. The destiny of being " born in the purple" has often warped and ruined character, besides exposing a man to every temptation that lofty station invites.

Rome.

We have spoken of Cæsars who were distinctively soldier-emperors,—ever with sword in hand. Numerous Cæsars not military except by proxy present examples of homosexualism. The reader can refer to the chronicles of Suetonius, Tacitus, Lampridius, Dion Cassius, or to modern studies of the Roman Empire socially, to compare the shades of homosexual instincts and practices of Augustus, Tiberius, Caius ('Caligula'), Claudius, Nero, Galba, Otho, Vitellius, Titus, Hadrian, Heliogabalus, Commodus, and so on. Of Augustus as homosexual in youth and in maturity, we have ample testimony. Hadrian's pederastic loves for the young Antinoüs and others have passed into art forever. It is however to be noted as quite impossible that Tiberius ever was a sexual satyr, a monster of brutal cruelty, as Suetonius and others depict him; the moral and personal character of Tiberius nowadays is justly retrieved. But Nero, Caligula and Heliogabalus are repulsive types. In the amazing story of Nero occurs a minutely clear example of a gifted, intensely receptive but superficial aesthete. We remark a young man unlucky enough to be obliged to reign as an emperor instead of struggling to live as a second-rate actor, or stage-singer. Nero, if divested of his royal atmosphere, if imagined as powerless to command human lives and fortunes, becomes almost wholly an object of pity. He even wins our sympathy. The aesthetic temperament was fundamentally the undoing of Nero, exactly as of thousands of less exalted decadents. A considerable likeness exists between Nero and an impressionable, aesthetic, out-of-place Uranian of modern days—Ludwig II of Bavaria. In each story we see the struggles to be free from political responsibilities that stood in the way of a life of art, of a super-aestheticized existence. Each case points gradually a moral tragedy. Nero became, beyond doubt, the prey of homicidal mania. That same madness is latent in the blood of the erratic Wittelsbachs, just as are their intensely artistic enthusiasms.

William Rufus of England seems homosexual, by natural temperament and habits. The mystery of the death of William, in New Forest, can easily have had some uranistic cause, though historians have ever differed as to whether William may not have been slain by accident. Guillaume de Nangis, Eadmer and other early chroniclers state that the sons of William the Conqueror were "man-loving men"; and the course of life of William II of England was much in consonance with such an idea. In fact, the great Conqueror, William I, was himself not clearly only dionistic. His relations, marital or other, with women had little accord with his natural sexual temperament.

England.

The uranianism of the gentle—but femininely obstinate—Edward II of England was the ruin of his career. Only a homosexual prince would make so much of worthless male favourites. Edward's indiscretion, doggedness and evasiveness on their behalf were so extreme that we do not wonder at the social scandals and bloody political dramas that were part of his reign, ending in his own assassination. The king's idolatry for the handsome Piers Gaveston, on whom he conferred dignities never more unluckily bestowed, has often been told in history and romance; including that striking English drama which German critics still assign to Shakespeare—not to Marlowe. Hardly less vehement and equally homosexual in the relationship was Edward's passion for Hugh Ledespenser, or De Spenser, who became Gaveston's successor sentimentally, after the latter had met his fate. The method in which Edwards murderers performed their horrible regicide, was perhaps chosen not only to avoid immediate suspicion that the King had met a violent death, but as brutally allusive to his passive sexual habits. In "Edward II," Marlowe, has indicated the King's doting passion for his "minion," in several scenes; including one in which the English nobility in their anger and solicitude, with the Duke of Lancaster, the truculent Mortimers and one of the high clergy at their head, compel the sovereign to sign a decree of banishment against Gaveston. In part, it is as follows; couched in Marlowe's extravagantly theatrical diction, which however does not spoil its psychical realism:

Edward II.

KING EDW.: Meet you for this, proud, overbearing peers?
　　Ere my sweet Gaveston shall part from me,
　　This isle shall fleet upon the ocèan,

And wander to the unfrequented Ind.
.... I will not yield!
Curse me, depose me, do the worst you can!

....

Make several kingdoms of this monarchy,

And share it equally amongst you all,
So I may have some nook or corner left
To frolic with my dearest Gaveston.
ARCHBISH: Nothing will alter us, we are resolved.
LANCAST: Come, come, subscribe!
YOUNG MORT.: Why should you love him whom the world so hates?
KING EDW.: Because he loves me more than all the world.
  All, none but rude and savage-minded men
  Would seek the ruin of my Gaveston.
  You that be noble-born should pity him.
ARCHBISH: Are you content to banish him the realm?
KING EDW.: I see I must, and therefore am content.
  Instead of ink, I'll write it with my tears.
(*He subscribes*)

YOUNG MORT: The King is love-sick for bis minion.

KING EDW.: 'Tis done! And now, accursed hand, fall off!

Several French kings possess historic distinctness as Uränians. Henri III was a Valois homosexual, and a type in general of the unprincipled, vicious, effeminate prince. Three of Henri's so-called "mignons" (a word that turned into the English "minion" now has lost its full offense) were François Maugiron (Duc de Bellegarde); the Duc d'Epernon; and the even more celebrated Quélus. To all of them Henri was attached by passions that bordered on erotic manias; to none so much as to Quélus. The assassination of Quélus brought Henri to a morbid climax of grief, like that of Alexander the Great for Hephaestion. Another royal French homosexual was Louis XIII, a

French Sovereigns.

somewhat more tolerable uranian, but not much more so in the weakness, fatuity, faithlessness and selfish egotism that gave full play to the statecraft of Richelieu. The most impassioned uranistic love of Louis XIII was that for Henri d'Effiat, better known as the Marquis de Cinq-Mars. Not only a private and political vengeance made Richelieu inflexible in demanding the death-penalty for this young nobleman, when Cinq-Mars was detected in his famous conspiracy; for the great Minister was resolved to break forever the sentimental influence of Cinq-Mars on Louis. Cinq-Mars seems romantically homosexual also in his relation to his nearest friend, François-Auguste de Thou, the son of the historian. De Thou was a quite different type from Cinq-Mars. Highly intellectual, profoundly moral and religious, the latter trait was emphasized even to pietism in de Thou. But his passion for young Cinq-Mars—considerably his junior—was intense. De Thou not only joined in the ill-starred plot in devotion to d'Effiat, but may be said to have deliberately thrown away his life, rather than survive his friend. Both ascended the scaffold at Lyons.

Another French sovereign, one of wholly different stamp from the two just named, the marvellously politic tyrannical, superstitious, cruel Louis XI, impresses one as an innately uranistic nature; uniting it with a cold-blooded homicidal mania worthy of Caligula. One of Louis's special favourites (see Comines's annals) was Cressol, Governor of Dauphiné (1473). A woman-despiser, turning to sexuality furtively when cynical passion moved him, Louis XI is a dark shape in the gallery of vaguer royal homosexuals.

Philippe d'Orléans, the Regent of France, a prince of fine natural qualities but corrupt to the marrow early in his manhood, casts a particular shadow across the line of kingly homosexuals. His orgies, in the Palais-Royal and elsewhere, have been given sufficiently in detail for many generations of readers of French backstairs scandal. One such "affair" between Philippe and a certain much petted companion, the Abbé de Choisy, is distinguished. The same Abbé de Choisy furnishes possibly the most brilliantly demoralizing, cynical type of an uranian courtier to be met in French print. The caustic private correspondence of the Regent's German mother, Elizabeth-Charlotte, Princess Palatine, by her marriage, Duchess of Orléans (1652–1721), throws fugitive light on aristocratic uranianism in Paris under the Regency—anything but to its respectability. Numerous other records, even more graphic and at first-hand as depictions, are at the service of the curious.

The period of the Regency, as also that of Louis XY, developed aristocratic French uranianism so much that really scandalized remark on it was not over-common. The Bachaumont Memoirs, the secret "Journal" of the Police Inspectors under Sartine, the Cheverney, d'Argenson, Barbier and similar records, offer interesting witness to this. About 1760, for instance, we are told quite casually that the Italian ambassador Erizzo,—"has just given to young Fleury, an actor in the Montensier troupe a cabriolet and horse, so that Fleury can come offener to Paris. . . The Ambassador keeps Fleury, just as he would a pretty woman. . . Some days ago, coming from a supper with the Duc d'Aiguillon, the Ambassador went to bed with Fleury; and gave him a ring worth fifty louis d'or and twenty-five louis dor in cash. . . They say positively that the Ambassador has just settled an income of eight thousand livres on Fleury, over and above thirty louis d'or a month. . ." Under the Regency and during all of the reign of Louis XV, the garden and arcades of the Palais-Royal were notoriously (and practically without any hindrance) evening by evening, the grand pederastic resort and market for homosexual prostitution in Paris. Very distinguished personages were not above resorting thither. Handsome boys, frequently of tender age, were openly bargained-for, between their parents or other keepers, and Parisian gentleman of wealth and rank: while adult types of the profession, or amateurs, intrigued in unabashed gayety and assurance.

Scandinavia, Russia, etc.

The Duc de Vermandois, is an addition to the list of aristocratic French Uranians. Whether the mysterious Chevalier d'Eon was one or not—at most, in part—Is to be questioned. His memoirs do not determine him nor do the many records from others, as to his being wholly free from uranianism. Of him, more in another chapter, as of some others we have mentioned.

Gustavus III of Sweden, the son of the great Vasa, brilliantly endowed and fascinating, full of soldierly quality, was philarrenic to his heart's core. The assassination of Gustavus at a court-ball, in consequence of the Ankerström Conspiracy referred itself to an under-welter of homosexual circumstances and relations, known to Ankerström, to Axel Fersen, to Ribbing and to others of the King's favorites.

Several royal Muscovite homosexuals have reigned. One was Paul I. The other was no less than Peter the Great. Peter is a further instance of dionism and uranianism, blended in one individual. Vehemently erotic as a young man, he was given to homosexual intimacies while a frequenter of women. The dualism 'of taste did not disappear as Peter grew older.

In view of his relations with both sexes, and of his wonderful energy of character, there appears much of the Oriental in Peter's complex, ungovernably animal tendencies. A special uranian favorite of Peter was the celebrated parvenu Mentschnikoff. The notorious uranianism of Alexander I of Russia, has already been mentioned. But Alexander was not the last of Russian princes to be known as an Uranian. Two conspicuous scions in our own day have been actors in "affairs" that excited brisk comments in other cities than St. Petersburg.

We turn again to the history of English sovereigns. James I, an eccentric mixture of the kingly and unkingly—of the well-balanced and the "just not mad"—was, first and last, a consistent Uranian. His court became aware of it, even to its use by state-intriguers. James never could resist a handsome young man. Once in love with him, James was almost incredibly indifferent to moral un-worth behind mere beauty of body, exactly as dionistic princes have been mischievously bewitched by mistresses. The histories of James's chief favourites are good illustrations of the dangers of becoming a royal pet. Unluckily, James was incompetent to protect the young objects of his passion from the consequences of their elevation to his favour, or from the results of their own follies and crimes. His liking, too, was a shifting equation. Not simply a pederast, that quality distinguished fractionally James's sentimental intimacies with beautiful youths. Good-looking lads were deliberately put in the way of the royal Uranian to make use of his passion, either for themselves or others. James was always eager to teach an ephebus Greek or Latin—and Greek and Latin morals. Two or three of these favourites played pernicious roles, even to disturbing the English throne. Prominent was Robert Carr, a mere groom of the stables, but of unusual beauty, brought into the eye of the king by what was not just an accident—a fall during a pageant. Of young Carr James became dotingly fond. The boy was so swiftly the recipient of estates, titles, privileges and so on, especially as Earl of Somerset, that scandal and hatred could not well have failed soon to attach to him. Carr was a thorough-going young reprobate, devoid of heart or conscience, boasting of his sovereign's very weakness him; and in time instigated the murder of Sir Thomas Overbury. Carr was essentially a dionian; his relations to James were of the most mercenary sort *au fond*. With some difficulty, he was saved from the death that he deserved. But the

England's James Stuart.

rest of his life passed in obscurity and want; for James had turned to a new favourite, George Villiers, a remarkably handsome young student at Cambridge. Villiers ultimately was made Duke of Buckingham; the famous "Steenie," for his royal lover. The reader need not be reminded that Buckingham was however à man of other and better traits than the fair-faced predecessor, Carr. In Buckingham's hands rested, now and then, much of the statesmanship of two successive reigns; and his murder in 1628 was rather more than a merely sentimental incident. It was à-propos of this favourite of James I that the royal Uranian himself one day declared—"I am neither a god nor an angel—and I confess to loving those dear to me more than other men. You may be sure that I love the Earl of Buckingham more than any one else. Christ had his John, and I have my George!"

In the reign of Charles I, occurred the famous divorce case of Lord Audley on similisexual grounds of explicit detail, a celebrated scandal of its epoch.

The English Commonwealth by its iron-bound, Hebraic, code of social and political life, made a profession of turning England into a second Canaan, with a Pentateuchal conscience as to thought and word and deed. Did it banish homosexualism? Could such a super-abomination of fleshly sins, according to Christian ideas, find any nourishment, while Cromwell was at the head of the nation?—with every parson and hedge-preacher, Leviticus in hand, a censor and a judge over his neighbour? We may be certain that not a thousand Cromwells, not the most sharp-seeing religious tyranny of even Protestant sort, could root it out; any more than could the confessionals of the Roman Church or the harshness of civil laws. Natural instinctive in Anglo-Saxons, it would defy the cant of pietism, the rule of Moses and the Prophets. One brilliant leader of the Cavalier party, Montrose, is said to have been dionian-uranian. We may observe here, by the by, that in the Scotch temperament, as in the Irish, there is a vivid, racial element of homosexualism.

With the Restoration period came quite another aspect of English social ethics. That most scandalously immoral, that most crudely licentious of royal courts, which centered on Charles II and his crew of familiars, male and female, was by no means wholly heterosexual,

The English Commonwealth Epoch.

The English Restoration, Georgian etc., Periods.

in spite of its putting a premium on feminine harlotry. Homosexual intimacies, often of repulsively gross sort, were a social jest. The curious can study this state of affairs in the secret diarists, the prurient back-stairs chroniclers of the time; can trace it also in the grosser satirical poets and dramatists of the date. Pepys has hints of it, though Pepys is chiefly preoccupied with heterosexual gossip as to the frail ladies of Whitehall. There is a curious pathos in one of Pepys serious anecdotes, vaguely uranian of motif—the foolish quarrel between "Sir H. Bellasis" and his best friend, "Tom Porter," in 1667, which led to their fatal duel; of which affair all London talked with wonder and pity.

In the reign of Queen Anne and of the first Georgian sovereigns there were enough suggestions of homosexual intimacies between personages in high society and politics to receive cutting allusions of poets and other satirical writers. Lampoons and squibs of such kind flew about the clubs and coffee-houses. Pope has biting references to such Court-favourites as Lord Hervey—"*Sporus*, that mere white curd of asses'-milk."

In the Guelphic blood have been remarkable, from time to time, traces of reaction from a notorious heterosexualism to a notorious homosexuality. The Hanoverian dynasty has shown it. George III, when a young man, was charged by common report with sexual intimacy with his personal and political favourite, Lord Bute. The caricaturists of the time are prodigal of allusions to this accusation. Bute, when prime-minister, was the subject of countless pasquinades not omitting it. It is to this sort of gossip that Byron refers in his poem "The Vision of Judgement" when he declares that the annals of George III show—"How to a minion first he gave the helm." George the Fourth seems to have been consistently heterosexual. But his brother, Ernest, Duke of Cumberland, who in his younger days had the family-beauty, early was marked out in English society for uranian amours; and eventually had to appear in a court of justice because of the murder of his valet Sellis—an affair about which floated a thick cloud of homosexualism. Between the Duke and certain members of his household there had been criminal intimacies. The trial mentioned was the sensation of the hour. Sellis was supposed to have had a connection with the Duke, and to have been supplanted by another servant, Neale. According to another theory, Sellis (who was found dead in his room, with his throat cut, in circumstances that precluded ideas of suicide) was murdered by the Duke, because Sellis had threatened the latter with exposure of his intimacy with Neale. The Duke got out of the affair with great difficulty. He became presently King of Hanover, and was the center of a German court plentiful in homosexual interests. Within the present generation of English royalty, another princely personage (since deceased) was supposed to be among an aristocratic clique implicated in a famous London homosexual *esclandre*. It is, in fact, believed that this affair was hushed up "so expeditiously, because it came so near to the throne; certain other high-born participants gaining time to "leave their country for their country's good."

Various Historic Uranians.

The wide prevalence of Uranian relationships in British "high society" today is too well-attested, too familiar the world around by more or less noted scandals and malodourous legal processes, to require extensive reference here. Several phases of it must be cited in other sections of this study, in appropriate connections. Mayfair's sensational divorce-proceedings have added evidence to the aggregate. Of the similisexual tastes of Englishmen of "our finest social circles" at home, a tacit evidence is their persistent residence abroad in countries where they can feel safer from suspicion and from blackmailing scandals. One eminent personage in British political life, who once reached the highest honours in a career that has appeared to be taken up or thrown by with curious capriciousness or hesitancy, is a constant absentee in his beautiful home in Southern Europe, whence only gentle rumours of his racial homosexuality reach his birth-land.

In fact, every period of social history has an interminable catalogue of homosexuals of quality. We have already encountered them in course of observations in preceding chapters, when speaking of classic Greece and Rome. They multiply as we review the Middle-Ages, the Renaissance courts, castles, palaces and camps. It is an aristocracy of all ages of life. Gallant young Conradin of Hohenstaufen and his beloved and not less gallant cousin, Frederick of Baden, those two brave boys only in their teens, united (1268) in perhaps the most pathetic tragedy of political murder in history; Prince Eugene of Savoy; the famous Ban of Kroatia, Joseph Jellachich (1801–1859); Count Wenzel-Anton von Kaunitz (1711–1794), the colossally active, efficient, cultured chief-minister under Maria-Theresia; Prince Heinrich of Prussia, (1726–1802) the brother of Frederick the Great,—as superiour a general, as accomplished a man of letters and arts as was the great Frederick himself; Baron Von Pollnitz; the philanthropic Count von Zinzendorf; Cambacérès, patriot and statesman, Count Khevenhüller, the Austrian soldier and statesman under the Maria-Theresian regime, and the victor over Turkey, Russia, France and Germany; the terrible Robespierre, whose homosexual relations with young Duplay, during his most sanguinary Revolutionary days seem to indicate his temperament as one of maniacal bloodlust and erotism.[2] Prince Kolowrat-Liebkinsky (1778–1861), distinguished as minister of Austrian affairs, as patriotic Bohemian, and as a true Maecenas in the development of Viennese art and letters—all these men, so diverse in types have shown more or less unequivocally their intersexual impulses. The royal portrait-gallery (which will be considered more in detail presently) also offers the eccentric Prince Adolph-Friedrich of Mecklenberg (1766–1794) among curiously femininized uranians; Leopold-August, Duke of Saxe-Coburg, (1772–1822: see later); and King Frederick-Charles of Württembtirg, who was noted for his homosexual relationships, little concealed. One of his favourites, von Dillenburg, had been a groom, Dillen; who rose to the nobility by his complaisances. The same royal Court, at Stuttgart, in the earlier eighties of the last century, was the scene, of a complicated political and homosexual drama, reminding one of the dilemmas of King Edward II of England; in the ascendency, notoriously homosexual, gained over King Charles by two American favourites, neither of them much passed his teens, both of humble origins. They fairly exploited the enamoured king—for their common benefit—instead of being rivals (a truly Yankee stroke of cynical practicality) until they were expelled the city, by a

---

2. During Robespierre's long sojourn in the Duplay family, his intimacy with the handsome young son—eighteen years old—was increasingly a topic of scandal and satire behind the back of the dreaded Incorruptible. For the persistent legend of any romantic tie with Eléonore Duplay, one of the daughters of the family, a girl who seems to have cultivated a sentiment for Robespierre, there is no foundation of fact—Robespierre maintaining a fraternal and rather bored attitude toward her. Of Robespierre's taking sexual interest in any woman no evidence sustains sifting. As to the lad Jacques-Michel Duplay, an indication of the scandal occurs in the fact that when the boy was hustled into the Prison of Sainte-Pélagie, on the 9-10-th Thermidor, somewhat after Robespierre had been brought thither, one of the prison-crowd called out—"Ladies and gentlemen, I beg to annonnce to you the arrival of Robespierre's *ganymède*—along with his Prime-Minister!" (The latter reference was to young Duplay's father).

ministerial coalition against them; ending thus the famous "Jackson-Woodcock Affair" of 1884. One of the most esteemed and admired of the Austrian arch-dukes of the present line, whose striking soldierly personality is seen towering above most other conspicuous assistants at high and fashionable functions; his relative, of the older arch-ducal circle; also a young scion of the same great gens, the hero of a serious homosexual.scandal in London,, at the time of the last Coronation, to which he had been sent among other representatives of the Imperial Court; Prince A—of A—, recently divorced under circumstances of homosexuality; an enormous list of teutonic homosexuals of blue-blood—all could lengthen the procession. The painstaking and never too-rash Wissenschaftlich-Humanitäre Komitee, in Berlin, has lately put in its table of statistical estimates, an average of five per cent of the German aristocracy as being homosexuals; two persons in each forty. The army-percentage must also be considered. (See other chapters.)

Particularizing Germany, the newest "Berlin Scandals" as they have been called (for which there is room for only a few lines in this book) are showing how German homosexualism wears the broad-striped toga; approaches the throne now as ever; is perhaps even more contemporaneously born in the purple than might prudently be admitted. The "Harden Cases," and their immediate successors, which have not spared even an Imperial Chancellor (though in his instance there was no obvious personal foundation for the suggestion—repudiated as a libel) have been of indirect as well as direct bearings. There can be little doubt that the Schulenburg, Moltke, Eulenburg, Hohenau and Lynar cases, as others, have been got out of nervous public attention as quickly as possible, to avoid compromising hundreds of aristocratic similisexuals in Germanic territory. The notorious scandals before Berlin aristocracy, in 1903 known as the "Affair of the Lakes," in which a clique of young scions and old ones, mostly rich and titled residents along the beautiful shores of the Müggelsee, were in the habit of quitting their villas at night, and sailing around the lake, naked but not at all ashamed, their boats wreathed in garlands, lighted with torches and lanterns—amid orgies of the sort described by Tacitus, more or less imitated—were distinguished for nobly-born participators. The need of interrupting these proceedings without making too great an aristocratic scandal gave the Berlin courts much trouble. Matters were compromised after the most unavoidable arrests, and by fines and hints to self-exile.

The social and political history of the Italian Renaissance is incidentally a history of uranianism in high-life, so diffused that the emotion was a concurrent of patrician æstheticism, in all major

centers of Italy's awakened culture. Such families as the Baglioni, the Medici, the Borgia, the Sforza, the Visconti, offer numerous contrasted examples. Savonarola's sermons in Florence vehemently dealt with such instincts. Its aristocratic tolerance was considered, by the Italian Church particularly, as the principal cause of scourges of the epoch—the plague, famines, invasions of the Turkish hosts, earthquakes and inundations. The jurist Carpzovius, as late as 1645, advocated the burning alive of all homosexuals, for the reason last mentioned! That homosexuality should flourish in the Renaissance in Italy, was natural, as a part of the return to Greek cults of the Beautiful. But it did not decline as that sentiment calmed: and it has not done so in Italy today, nor will it do so, especially in Central and South-Italy. The Italian is perennially heterosexual and homosexual, in a degree sometimes puzzling. He has by race-inheritance an intense sexual feeling for male beauty, along with his sensuous-sexual appreciation of feminine charms. In Italian high life, especially where not strongly parisianized, the Italian aristocrat as uranian or dionian never is rare.

One of the most melancholy and picturresque figures in recent royal homosexualism was King Ludwig II of Bavaria. King Ludwig is another example of the gifted Uranian inextricably "out

of place', by being born to a throne. He was a true Wittelsbach in his vividly intellectual and aesthetic sensibilities; with the concurrent Wittelsbach taint of madness in his blood. Aversion to Ludwig II as a careless ruler, as a vast spendthrift, through show-castles and Wagnerism, of his country's revenues, as imitator of Louis XIV of France in banality, not dignity, becomes less as we sift the story of his life. From his betrothal with the Princess Sophie of Bavaria Ludwig broke away, only because he could not enter into marriage-relations with any woman. He could love only the male; and he loved many. The list of his favourites is long; men distinguished for not only their personal attractiveness, but for high mental or artistic individualities, whether writers, actors, composers, singers,—artists in every branch of aesthetics; His *protégés* in the military-calling, the youths in humblest life—it is a remarkable catalogue. A literature exists on this topic, enlarged since the end of the King's career in the Lake of Starnberg. Whether that fate was accident, suicide or murder is not yet quite clear. The tone of some of King Ludwig's letters to Wagner is nothing if not uranistic, as in this example: "My innermost Beloved! I have just heard that you are once more entirely recovered. Oh, with what an outburst of joy did I greet this news! How I burn with longing for those tranquil, sacred, hours, which shall vouchsafe to me once more the long-missed sight of the being dearest to me of all on earth! To death itself—your true Ludwig." The present King of Bavaria (Otto) never has been more than a nominal ruler, because of his insanity, and is slowly closing his life in complete seclusion as a patient; but Otto, when entirely sane was also homosexual, and he has shown this sort of erotism since his madness deepened.

'There is no need in lengthening this list. Obviously into the demesne of contemporary aristocratic life there is both delicacy and difficulty in entering too frankly. In the next chapter, we shall see how incessantly is homosexual the man professionally of literary and aesthetic callings. He is often aristocratic of position; is often also of finer fibre than many kings and princes.

Differences in Sexual Choice: the "Phylosyrphetic" Uranian of High Class.

À-propos of the universality of philarrenic nature, we may observe in aristocratie Uranians two distinct expressions of personal tastes marked out as to homosexual connections. There is the sort of Uranian, himself a gentleman, who is attracted only to individuals of his own grade; desiring intercourse sexually only with a man of refinement of physique and of superior psychic individuality. The other class, however aristocratic, seeks always lower social types for partners; demands coarser physiques and uneducated and unrefined natures; this choice along with particular aversion to sexual intercourse with equals or superiors. Such aristocratic similisexuals may be called "philosyrphetics," or lovers of "the man of the mob," the *voyou* from the slum; and the preference often turns out a dangerous one—as we shall see later. But it is an idiom quite as marked as sexual dislike of women. We find the prince who would rather be embraced by a dragoon, the peer who prefers a butcher or a blacksmith, the cultivated leader of a social circle to whom only a common waiter, or a rough mechanic, appeal sexually. In such "philosyrphetic" Uranians— extremely numerous—just as among heterosexuals, we have a psychic problem illustrating the fact that like seeks unlike, and that sexual love is

EDWARD IRENAEUS PRIME-STEVENSON

often an unity out of dissimilarity. But constant sexual association with lower intellectual or social homosexuals impairs the manly idealism, coarsens the nature, and destroys the original refinement of its victim. In homosexual love, as in heterosexual love and friendship, the man easily becomes what his company is; especially under circumstances so potent on the psychic essence.

A distinction is not always easily made between the sort of woman in high and responsible station—a queen, warrior or political leader—who is notably masculine in her intellect, her tastes, her habits, and with little or no amorous bias through her career; and the really similisexual woman the Uraniad. Types of female sovereigns showing, minds and dispositions male rather than female, are presented familiarly to us in Elizabeth of England, in Catherine de' Medici, in Christina of Sweden, and so on. But many are indistinctly uraniad, if at all so. Elizabeth of England was certainly a normal woman in the unchaste private life of a nominally "Virgin Queen"—about whom there mdst be talked "no scandal." Catherine of Russia is said to have become uraniadistic as she grew old. In the royal house of Wittelsbach there has been a strain of female contra-sexualism, along with the excessive heterosexuality and uranianism of the males. Three princesses, two of them becoming sovereigns, are recent illustrations; in each case with tragic circumstances in their histories and one of them ended recently in an abominable assassination that shocked the civilized world.

The Royal Uraniad.

Many presumptive examples of the intersexual female, the virile uraniad, occur with the veritable woman-at-arms; queen or peasant. In her mannish temperament are to be added the unfeminine traits of physical and moral courage, and her masculine muscularity. The woman-warrior has been a picturesque interloper in camp and battlefield, ever since wars were waged. The old legends of the Amazon race and of the Centaurs are deviations from realities, the woman who much preferred to wield a spear rather than bear a child, and the man who so dominated his horse that he seemed a part of it.

The Soldier-Uraniad.

Classic types of amazonians are plentiful. Among early ones we have the Biblical Deborah, seeress, judge and captain over Israel—all at once. We have Bonduca, Boadicea, Tomyris, Zenobia, Jeanne Dare, Margaret of England, the terrible women-warriors of the houses of Flanders and Penthièvre—every school-girl knows thorn. The pages of mythology and romance furnish a long array of soldierly ideals; Semiramis, Penthesilea, Thalestris, Camilla, Bradamante, Brindomart, Hippolyta, the screaming Valkyrs the resplendently divine Minerva—that noblest conception of female divinity ever evolved by human imagination in any religion—and the mystic, cruel Bellona. Diana is un-feminine. Even Venus enters the battlefield, in Homer and Vergil. Apart from myths, the military spirit seems almost supreme in such uraniad types as Samura, the heroine of the defence of Ancona, the American Moll Pitcher, the valiant Anna Liihring, of Bremen; or the Hungarian heroines of Erlau's siege, who fought like the strongest and bravest of men. In many savage tribes to day women are as expert fighters as the men. But despite outward virility in such types, we cannot classify them as true Uraniads: for their amorous instincts are either too unclear, or else are more or less conclusively heterosexual. We say—"But yet a woman."

Sudden political upheavals create the soldiering amazonian. Sometimes she is fiercer and more sanguinary than most men. In the French Revolution period, the Vendée campaigns elicited squads of women, fighting in the ranks. Remarkable examples of feminine soldiering enter into the savage Chouan chronicles; But we may note that the French Revolution, though in the Vendée productive of notable heroines of camp and battle, does not afford us so many examples of women-soldiers, who were drawn to combat- by patriotism and natural firmness of nature, as it does instances of women who were *détraquées;* unheroic in their blood-thirstiness and in sheer passion for excitement; lower-class amazons particularly. One realizes such a strain of sanguinary unfeminity in Latins, at a Spanish bull-fight or a French guillotining. Such were the terrible *tricoteuses* at the guillotine, in 1792–93–94.

The sporadic courage of a-woman-duellist, with rapier, broadsword and pistol, is essentially of the military kind. The French Communal struggles in 1870–71, developed many amazingly courageous women-soldiers, who defended barricades and fought like tigresses. But such amazons were of doubtful moral courage; often killing and burning for the mere frantic nervous pleasure of such a debauch of blood. Many of these unsexed women were similisexual—sapphistic prostitutes, or similar, in instincts and habits. On the other hand, many were entirely normal sexually.

In fact, the woman-soldier whose type and history night be taken as presupposing her being an Uraniad, but whose similisexualism should not be affirmed without conclusive knowledge, is of constant recurrence. Captain Rosa Castellanos, a heroine of the recent Spanish-American War in Cuba, was a conspicuous example of the woman-warrior. One of the recently-deceased *pensionnaires* of the Hôtel des Invalides in Paris, Madame D—, had fought with great distinction in the Napoleonic campaigns, had received formal right to wear male clothing (of course including her uniform) and died at a great age, in the national institution named. Very recently came to newspaper notice quite as striking a military woman. One of the magistrates presiding in the chief criminal court of Toulon summoned as witness in a robbery-affair Madame I—, mentioned as a widow, employed at La Verriere. The justice was rather surprised when a gentleman presented "himself," correctly attired as such, in frock-coat and overcoat, and so on. But Madame I—, for she it was, explained that during thirty-seven years she had worn only male clothing, by special permission from the French Government, because of her notable service in the Franco-Prussian War, in which she had taken part with honour and danger, as a spy and in the ranks. Madame I—gave no other than a masculine impression of herself; she smoked and drank moderately. She declared her age as about sixty-four. She had been a witness in the trial of Marshal Bazaine.

The annals of all military nations are full of examples of women-soldiers. They have marched in the ranks with common soldiery, they have commanded with skill as officers; this, in a great proportion of instances, without detection of sex, till wounded or dead on the field or in the hospital. They have defended trench and bastion against the Ottoman in Hungary, the Spaniards in Holland, the Moor in Spain, the invader in Italy, and to a particular extent have served Poland. The hundred wars of Germany and Austria have found women fighting shoulder to shoulder by their brothers, with pike or musket, serving the cannon instead of rooking children to sleep or sweeping kitchens. The latest frontier-fighting in Albanian, Macedonian and Turkish localities has striking examples of female soldiering, several officers being women,

The career of Catalina de Erauso, a noted Spanish soldier-uraniad, is a story of curious interest in Spanish warfare in the Sixteenth and Seventeenth Centuries. Catalina de Erauso, called the "Monja Alferez"—"The Fighting Nun"—was born in San-Sebastian in 1585. There appears to be nothing in her origin or earliest life to influence toward her becoming the man-woman that she

A Fighting Uraniad:
Catalina de Erauso.

grew up to be. In her childhood she was committed to a relative, the abbess of a convent, for her bringing-up; and till she was about fifteen Catalina wore a nun's habit. She was expected to adopt a religious vocation, the last one that circumstances suggest as natural to her. Catalina was an unruly little novice; slapped and fought with the sisters; and finally decided to escape the convent for a purely secular life, and to be incidentally as wholly masculine as possible. She hid in a wood several days, having a page's dress at hand. When she emerged from this forest-intermezzo, Catalina de Erauso had disappeared; she was the page "Francisco Loyola." She was daring enough to go at once toward San-Sebastian, and to take a place as servant in the family of a citizen of distinction. Unrecognized as to indentity or sex, Catalina remained in this post, till one day her father came to make a visit to her master, with the particular object of talking over the long-discussed disappearance of his daughter. She was not recognized when she met her parent in the hallway. But no sooner was he closeted with his host, than Catalina though it prudent to disappear from the house and San-Sebastian; first taking a handsome sum of money (not hers) as provision for the way. She became a cabin-boy on a large gallion, owned by an uncle, Captain Estevan Eguino, who had scarcely ever seen her, and so did not recognize her as a relative or a girl. He became extremely fond of Catalina—or "Francisco"—and made her his personal servant. Catalina remained with him as such, till she grew tired of him. Therewith she decamped without warning; again with a considerable forced-loan, from her affectionate kinsman and master. She took ship for South-America and arrived in Panama, The rest of her life was mostly to be passed in the Western World. By this time Catalina was a fine, manly personage indeed, in every external. She was servant, house-porter and other things, for different masters. She was much liked, though continually fighting with fellow-employés. She was the object of several love-affairs, and of marriage-proposals which she declined. She continued to conceal her sex. After a while she went to Lima. In the city of Concepcion, Catalina had a brother, engaged as a secretary to the Governor. Here begins a queerly romantic part of Catalina's career. The brother did not know her. Apparently homosexual, he quite speedily fell in love with the good-looking "boy"—whom he met at some entertainment. He made the "boy" his companion. Catalina, undoubtedly was physically feminosexual to some extent, more or lest abnormal enough to deceive women as to her masculinity of body, but one doubts that she was able to "explain herself," to her brother as being fully male. A war with one of the native tribes broke out, and Catalina enlisted. She fought with distinction, and captured a lost standard. She was made an ensign. Her brother was in the army with her, and their intimacy was still close; but he did not yet know of their kinship. For five years, Catalina remained in active service as an ensign. In every way she demeaned herself, in camp and mess, as a man of bold spirit. She was a fine swordswoman. After taking part in several duels, she fought one of peculiar savagery, with "seconds" on both sides taking their share. It, occurred in total darkness. She left her enemy dead. When her brother came to help her to recover from her wounds, she disclosed her secret; and that she was his sister, Catalina de Erauso. Such a success in male travesty surpasses many improbabilities of the stage. After this duel and consequent disclosure, Catalina—deserted. She went to Tucuman, in the Argentine territory. She suffered much hardship, and yet managed to keep well, and was attractive enough for the daughter of a wealthy native land-owner to fall in love with her. But, unfortunately, just then a high ecclesiastic in the country to which she had fled chose Catalina as a model husband for his niece. Catalina was not willing to be married, though certainly she could have played the husband well, and had duped many female friends before this date. There must have been something incorrigibly opposed to "settling down" in her temperament. So, on this occasion, Catalina affianced herself to both young ladies; received rich presents; and then as the weddings drew near, she—fled. This episode ended in the first confession of Catalina that she was a woman; except the admission made to her brother. In course of further adventures, of a new term of military-service, and associations with robbers and rascals of all grades (twice she was sentenced to death, once being reprieved when at the very gallows) she was involved in a fierce night-quarrel in a gaming-house in Guamanga. She was demanded by the police, but fought the officers like a tigress. The Bishop of the place protected her, and when in his care, a fugitive from justice, she confessed her story to him. He was thrown into such consternation and admiration as few ecclesiastics experience. He begged Catalina to resume her womanly station in life. She consented, and entered a cloister. Her kind adviser dying while she was in this humour, she passed to another convent, in Lima. After two years of this retirement, she decided to return to Spain. During the voyage, she wrote her autobiography. There is no reason to suppose its details much exaggerated; many of even the most extraordinary facts have been verified. In Spain, she became a sort of wonder. Her story was noised abroad all Europe. Still, she does not seem to have been as notorious a visitor as she expected to find herself. She went to Rome, and was received by the Pope. She entertained him with her autobiography, was forgiven her sins, and received papal license to wear male attire, a permission that she had not much troubled herself about, till then. After Rome, she went to Naples. She managed to get into a scandalous street-fight, with ready blade, as usual. From that time, her history is wholly unknown. It is not clear whether she returned to South America, nor where so restless a mortal died. Her appearance during her Roman visit was described in a letter from the noted Italian traveller, Pietro Delle Valle. He speaks of her as a tall, strong, dark, and "eunuch-like" person of some thirty-five or forty years, "in no wise suggesting a woman."

An Heroic Soldieress: Franziska Skanagatta.

A masculine soul in feminine physique is found in the famous Franziska Skanagatta, one of the heroines of modern Austrian history She was educated in the Military Academy at Wiener-Neustadt, in Austria, without being detected as a girl; as she managed to be enrolled in the name of a brother who was dead. Maturing into a fine, athletic young soldier, Franziska was made an officer. She entered then upon a completely military career. She was a superb horsewoman, swordswoman, shot, and all else, and had a commanding presence. She went into regular and hard service, and took part in the Austrian portion of the anti-Napoleonic struggle—with high honour. Her most intimate friend was a young officer, passionately attached to her, but unaware of her sex. The officer was mystified as to his profound feeling for Franziska, and she felt a deep reluctance to expose the fact which would have relieved him. At length, after being severely wounded she told the secret to him. She therewith left the army, allowing her sex to be known generally. With ovations to her courage and career, she went to Vienna, where the Emperor decorated her, and confirmed her military honours. She married her friend of the camp, in what proved to be happy wedlock. She was married in full uniform, but after the ceremony she never, resumed male attire. She became gradually feminized, had several children, and her family is represented today in Austria. A portrait and memorial to Franziska

Skanagatta are always shown to visitors to the great Wiener-Neustadt Military Academy.

No nobler type of the woman-soldier occurs than the famous Angela Postovoitow, a participant in the latest of the Polish insurrections. Of excellent family, patriotic and strong-natured, of deep religious feeling, she took part in field, in council and in camp, as soldier and officer in the uprising—with splendid enthusiasm—a sort of contemporary Jeanne Dare. Of great personal beauty, in her uniform she was one of the handsomest and most romantic figures in the Polish army. If she was feminosexual in her nature is not clear. She appears indeed rather as a sexless creature, rapt in work for her unfortunate country, when sons failed in Poland and daughters took their places. She was adored by her companion-in-arms, General Langiewicz, but "could not give him more than warm and uninterrupted friendship." In the battles of Chrobrze and of Busk, in which Angela was one of the glories of those days, she was severely wounded, leading her troop of young Polish patriots. Very presently she was forced to fly, with so many other refugees. She died some years later, an exile in Switzerland, in the arms of General Langiewicz. A virgin-warrior, indeed, her memory is imperishable in Poland. There were several female-officers of equal virility and heroism, in the same melancholy campaign.

Angela Postovoitow, the Heroine of Poland.

In the Russian Departement of Wiatka, at the town of Jelabuga, recently was unveiled a memorial erected to the honour of the heroic soldier-maiden Nadeschda Andreievna Durowa, She died in 1866, at an advanced age. She served with great distinction in the anti-Napoleonic campaigns, especially in 1812, under the name of "Alexandroff." She was advanced to the colonelcy of a Lithuanian regiment, won numerous attentions from her superiors on account of her brave and skilful leadership, and was decorated with many orders. She did not withdraw from her profession till her services were not needed. She then betook herself to active literary work. Her sketches, historical studies and personal reminiscences of periods of her service and other observations were widely popular. She lived to be eightythree years of age, and died with general respect. The unveiling of the monument to "Colonel Durowa" was accompanied by a full military-mass, and the Russian army was represented by special delegates.

A Female Cavalry-Colonel.

These warrior-uraniads remind us, verily, of Schiller's lines, in his "Jungfrau von Orleans" where the heroic Maid exclaims:

> *"Nicht mein Geschlecht beschwöre! Nenne mich nicht Weib!*
> *Gleich wie die Körperlosen Geister, die nicht freien,*
> *Auf irdische Weise, schliess ich mich an kein*
> *Geschlecht der Menschen an!"* . . .

An English classic poet has written an amusing bit of verse on "The Lady at Sea." Experiences of marine travel discourage first ideas that feminine sailorship could ever be of much practical use. As a matter

The Uraniad as A Sailor.

of fact, a considerable proportion of sailors have been curiously like Uraniads, in merchant-marines, and even war-service. In some countries industrious in coast-fisheries, women take a liberal share of the regular work of navigating craft; often on voyages of duration and hard weather. In Brittany, Normandy, Norway, Denmark and Sweden, in Finland and along the North Sea, and in several Eastern ports, the ships are womened, as well as manned. About forty certificates now are held by Frenchwomen, as being "able seamen," folly experienced in their calling. On the Brittany coast nearly three-thousand women are officially certified as competent seamen, with no concealment of their sex, but under the restriction from the French government, against promotion to any command. One steamer in the Turkish coast-service, is wholly "manned" by women-sailors, though not entirely so officered. In Denmark, the occupation of a pilot is followed by numerous women, under due legal certificates. On the Greek island of Himla, near Rhodes, the majority of the women are sailors for a livelihood, *pari passu* with the men of the place; and rival the latter as divers. In this Greek island prevails too the curious custom that a girl is not quite marriagable till she has made three voyages, and has attested her skill in sponge-fishery. In Santa-Barbara, another community abundant in female sailors, an appropriate fact has been the care of the lighthouse by the old mother of a family of thirteen women, each one a sailor! In Japan and China, many women are well-trained professional hands on the native coast-ships. Some Chinese ports have a large fleet of women-manned boats. Lately in Bristol an excellent seaman disclosed her sex as feminine to a hospital-doctor, as a secret for many years undetected. The second officer of an American ship, personally known to a friend of the writer of this study, is a woman; which fact seems not even suspected by her ship-mates, after years of service.

Many of these examples are undoubtedly not so much those of the Uraniad completely, amatively such, as either of "asexuals"; or of women more or less masculinized in body, temperament, nerves and intellects. But they illustrate departurer from the feminine toward an Intersex of manifest individuality, and of characteristically similisexual impulses in love-desire.

Female acrobats, women-riders in circuses and so on, are feminosexual in a considerable proportion. Communications that the writer has received from a physician with a considerable clientage of acrobatic women, indicate several who prefer peculiarly feminine women as object of sexual intercourse. The most intimate friend of a female royal personage of great beauty, much spoken of as feminosexual, was a "star" of the Continental ring; a magnificent equestrienne, she was said to-be also of abnormal physical development. The intimacy was close enough to add to the gossip about one of the most gifted and unhappy of sovereigns who ever mounted, not horses, which she loved, but a throne that she hated. The severer athletic and acrobatic professions are however emphatically those in which sexual impulses of any sort must be most carefully controlled; eveu to severe repression of their physical gratifications.

Women-Acrobats.

IX

THE URANIAN AND URANIAD IN THE DISTINCTIVELY ETHICAL, RELIGIOUS AND INTELLECTUAL LIFE: AND IN THE DISTINCTIVELY ÆSTHETIC PROFESSIONS AND ENVIRONMENTS: TYPES AND BIOGRAPHIES

In intellectual developments of civilization, through letters, science, philosophy, religion, in the liberal arts, in all phases of aesthetics, we find the Uranian to be either worker or amateur. Turning to homosexuals classically famous in such careers, as philosophers, religious teachers, scientists, poets, romancists, dramatists, musicians, painters sculptors, actors, architects, they are bewilderingly numerous. Readers who know only the more conventional sorts of biography, where all the *vita sexualis* of a man can be "edited away"—especially if abnormal—easily become skeptical when told that such and such a personage has been Uranian.

Socrates and Plato.

But sooner or later one can satisfy himself that countless such statements are true.

In philosophy and ethics, clarifying the profoundest principles of social and aesthetic life, Plato remains foremost; forever incorporated with Socrates. It is hardly needful to point out the Greek homosexuality pervading the Platonic-Socratic attitude toward love. An exalted pederasty, but manifestly pederasty; the physical passion for a beautiful youth, as well as the love for what in him wins intellectual and moral admiration—these are fundamental to the Socratic system. Platonism is anything but "platonic," as exhaled from the "Phædrus," the Lysis and the analytical "Banquet." Corresponding indifference to heterosexual love, the sense of its triviality compared with the man-to-man passion, are marked in Plato. The reader has only to take one of the complete, "unbowdlerized" editions of Plato, to be convinced. Nothing can explain away homosexualism, pederastic love, in Platonism. Sensitive-minded and dishonest "schools" of Platonists have tried to do this, ever since the beginnings of our Hebraic Christianity. Socrates himself was unquestionably homosexual. He idealized the physical as well as the intellectual, in social relationships to a young man. We realize as we study his personality and teaching, how justifiably Socrates himself could be called "a corruptor of youth." There is constant evidence of his practical homosexualism. It meets us off-hand in dialogue between Socrates and beautiful youths; such as that occurring in the "Phædrus." Or, one can cite what we find Plato setting forth in the way of Socratic concepts, in the "Lysis," the "Charmides" and the highly suggestive "Banquet." The first questions of the "Protagoras" are not merely ironical or idealizing ones—"Whence come you, Socrates? Can there be any doubt that you come from the chase after Alcibiades? And indeed when I saw him lately, he appeared still beautiful; though, between ourselves, Socrates, he is now a man, he is growing a pretty strong beard. . . Surely, though, you have not met with any one more beautiful in this city, at least?" In the "Lysis," we have approving reference to the homosexual love between young Hippothales and the lad Lysis, as to the one-sided passion of Hippothales for Lysis, inasmuch as a young Athenian, Menexenos, is beloved by Lysis. Hippothales declares himself "delirious," and "mad" with his passion. In the first third of the "Phædrus," we meet with a considerable analysis of homosexual sentiment. In "The Banquet" we find carefully stated the Platonic statement as to the "two Venuses," the nobler or man-to-man love, a product of the Uranian Venus; and the commoner, grosser sort—love for woman. Here occurs the beautiful theory that the German Grillparzer has woven into verse; the creation of a protosex, a bisexual human type which has been divided. Each of the moieties is ever seeking thro the world his missing fellow; each when met is immediately drawn to the other, no matter what the outward, organic sex. In the "Banquet," Plato speaks also with definiteness enough of the theory of a composite sex, a third sex, an intersex, as having existed, but k no longer in the scheme of creation and reproduction. All these and other matters enter into the Socratic-Platonic systems of love; a structure that essentially was made up of a certain amount of philosophic rhetoric and idealism, with a large modicum of physical homosexualism. The fire of bodily desire smoulders through the most important Platonic references to the topic, and complex Socratic love-philosophizings amount chiefly to an agreeably simple—pederasty.

The importance of the classic Greek belles-lettres in the history and study of homosexual Hellas will be further touched upon presently; especially as to lyric and dramatic poets.

Romanian Philosophy and Uranianism.

The classic Latin philosophy, social or other, adds nothing to our knowledge of Roman analysts of uranianism—personally or otherwise. The Roman philosophic mind occupied itself with other explorations. We have no Latin Socrates. Lucretius, Seneca, Cicero, are not engrossed with it. We know of no important Latin philosopher who was himself uranian, though doubtless many were such. One of the obscurer sophists, whose attitude toward similisexual instincts can be causally queried, was Favorinus of Arles (A.D. 135) the tutor of Aulus Gellius; who was a physical hermaphrodite.

Apostolic and Primitive Christianity.

We have seen in the earlier portion of our study that Christianity, from its organized ecclesiastical start, opposed homosexuality as the vice of vices; and that especially as mariolatry and hagiology matured, the Church was hostile to all philarrenism as tending to undermine idealism of the Virgin Mary, and of woman-saints. As such cults, especially of the Virgin, became of the first importance in Latin Greek and Oriental Christianity, similisexual intercourse was blasted with the blackest curses. It tended to diminish marriages, and the rearing of Christian families. Yet the really Apostolic attitude toward uranianism is not particularly severe in the Canon. St. Paul rebukes it, as part of the social paganism which he would root out. Yet what Paul, a. Jew by birth and education, says against it is not stronger than his injunctions against irregular heterosexual relations, fornication, adultery. When he declares that "abusers of themselves with men" are not to inherit the Kingdom of God, and when he speaks of the topic in the often-cited passages in his Epistles, the apostle seems to animadvert against bestiality, vicious prostitutes of either sex, hired catamites and degraded lesbians, as much as against homosexuality. The other apostles are even more casual in their references, reprimanding particularly the gross and venal aspects of heathen similisexuality. But the Post-Apostolic Christianity developed and fortified denunciations of the homosexual as the almost nameless sinner of sinners.

Christ and Uranianism.

Christ himself so far as any records that we possess inform us, never rebuked homosexuality. We can believe that Christ's silence was of intention; its origin being finest moral perspectives, profoundest intuitions into Nature's ethics. Adultery, a foe to social order (though to be pardoned) is denounced, with other carnal sins. But of homosexualism, so common about him, in all classes of Hebrew, Syrian, or Roman social life, Christ says not a word.

Indeed, as we study Gospel narratives and familiarize ourselves with Christ's emotional personality, have we not cause to believe that Christ was an Uranian?—the highest type of Uranian that the world could see. There is nothing ignoble, nothing at all lowering in this theory. The ideal Christ in omniscient sympathy must be profoundly acquainted with all human love, the Uranian's emotions included. We cannot separate from Christ such intimacy with mortal nature, with the innermost soul? Again, no negative trait in Christ is so clearly indicated as his reserved interest in women. Christ is unmoved by warmer sentiment for women than friendship. He is affectionate and interested toward them as only their brother, Mend, teacher. On the contrary, his sentiment for Lazarus is openly passional; he loves, he laments in tears, he restores the dead young man to life, Christ's love for John is spoken of as jealously observed; explicit with even the physical demonstrativeness of the picture of so young a Disciple leaning on his Master's heart; as nearest and dearest, even at Golgotha. The type presented by painters from the first has always depicted a young, fair, femininely boyish John. In fact, references to "love" in connection with Christ's life occur only when young men, not when women, are spoken of; notably the "young man" whom Jesus "loved"—again an intentional phrase. Christ's personality and career; his vivid attraction to total strangers; the immediate spell that, right and left, he exercised on all men, so that they left everything for his sake; his magnetic charm over each human Creature, young or old, who came within personal contact with him, are all traits of the mysterious powers of a noble and beautiful Uranian. Such a type casts its spell inevitably over woman also, though unmoved sexually by womanly beauty. One may even ask whether the treason of Judas was the madness of a jealous homosexual passion, on the part of the betrayer; in a hatred of John, or of whomsoever else. We may also remember that Christ was a Jew, and that his apostles were of an Oriental race inclined to homosexual passions.[1]

1. Not only adultery but fornication, and many another long-recognized offense, according to Jewish theology and daily life, were particularized by Christ, some of them more than once. But as'to what might have been thought one of the chief immoralities and vices under the Law, he is silent; no matter how near his discourses might bring him to a direct allusion.

To many an Uranian not only the conviction that his homosexual instinct is worthy, but also the thought of Christ as an Uranian, as understanding the gamut of the homosexual's joys and sorrows, are consoling and elevating. An English similisexual wrote to the authour of this study "—The idea of Christ as possibly an Urning has saved me from loneliness, from solitude, from loss of self-respect and of faith, as to this world and the next!"

Concidentally we find St. John, the supremely Beloved of Christ, eminently the herald of the widest gospel of human love. This message runs through the Johannean Epistles like a passionate leading-theme in some celestial symphony. "Love one another"—"Little children, love one another—" "There is no fear in love, for perfect love casteth out fear"—"That we should love one another." Is such an insistance of the gentle Apostle addressed exclusively to a sexless life of the spirit?

St. Augustine.

The primitive Church did not lack the note of homosexual feeling, in the case of saintly men. St. Augustine is an example. The history of Augustine's relation to his passionately-loved young friend in Thageste, his retrospects of its influence over him, afford one of many human passages in his famous "Confessions." Thus writes Saint-Augustine:

"About this time, as I began to teach in my birthplace, I made a friendship with a young man between whom and myself was such a conformity of inclinations and of sentiments as to make me love him above anything that one can express. We were both of an age, in the flower of our youth; we had been at school together. But that former degree of friendship between us did not approach that which now followed, if in fact one can call it friendship; for there is only one true friendship, the tie of that love with which our hearts are filled by the Holy Spirit."

"Nevertheless, between myself and this young man there was a tenderness that is incredible. It was founded, as I have said, on a perfect conformity of inclinations and sentiments. He would have brought to me all that holy and healthful doctrine in which he had been brought up (though in them he had, for all that, but mediocre practical instruction) while I would have thrown him back toward those, fancies and pernicious suggestions which so afflicted my mother, and made her shed so many tears on my account. But we understood each other, even in error; and this perfect union of our hearts made it impossible for me to live without him. But thou O God! who art at the same time the God of chastisements and of pity, thou didst serve us two as a master serves runaway slaves; since scarce had I enjoyed one year the sweetness of this friendship, which was the greatest joy of my life, than Thou didst remove from the world him whom I loved. The young man sickened of a violent fever, and therewith fell into such a sweating, all at once, that they thought it was of death; and he remained a long time unconscious. As there seemed no more hope of him, they baptized him, though he did not know of it. I made nothing of this, convinced that what.had taken place, merely a thing done to him corporeally, would not affect our relationship. But not so went the matter. I waited eagerly till he could speak with me of what had occurred; for I did not quit him, our attachment for one another not suffering me to leave his side for a moment. So as soon as he was better, I began to rally him, on that baptism which had been given him while he had been so unaware of it. . . never dreaming that he would not join in my mockery. But he showed a horror of me now, as if I had been his worst enemy, and with a firmness that astonished me, so unexpected was all this, declaring that if I wished him to keep to our friendship I must avoid such discoursing. I was much amazed to hear him speak so strongly, but I restrained myself and waited till he should become well and strong enough to talk with me as to what was in my mind: when Thou, O Lord! didst take him away from my seductions and madness, and by one stroke (that was to be, by and by, my consolation) Thou didst set him safely in Thine own bosom. For, a few days after, when I was absent, he relapsed to the same fever, which therewith ended his life."

"The grief of that loss made a strange impression on me; who had from thence onward only trouble and darkness in my soul. I saw Death everywhere; my country became as a land of exile, my own dwelling grew intolerable; and all that had been such a joy when I could partake of it with him became torture, having him no more. Mine eyes sought him everywhere, and found him nowhere; what I beheld instead filled me with loathing, because I saw him in no place, and because each spot which when he was alive had always seemed to say to me "Look, he is coming! You will soon meet him!" now was silent. I did not know myself. . . I found solace only in my tears, and they became now for me what had been my friend."

"Behold to what a state of soul was I brought, O my God! Thou my only hope, who dost purify my heart from the stains of these too-passionate friendships, Thou who now keepest mine eyes fixed on Thee, and who forbiddest me to fall into the pitfalls which surround me! . . . While my friend lived, it seemed to me that his soul and mine were almost one spirit in two bodies. And so when he was dead, life became a horrible thing to me, inasmuch as I could not grow wonted to life without the other half of my soul. . . What madness it is not to know how to love mankind as we should love all that must die! My heart was utterly torn, bleeding; I knew not what to do. The cool shades of the woods, sports and music, perfumes, good cheer, whatever in the commerce of love is most potent to impress our senses, books or poetry, in short all that had been life to me, without him now became hateful and as naught save something for sighs and tears."[2]

This is the language of pagan homosexualism, of pagan-philosophy, much more than the utterance of ascetic, Christian self-rebuke. Augustine reverts to this early passion as if its human sweetness suddenly exhaled into the air of his cell; as if for a moment he was again the young uranian man of the world, not a Christian saint. His outcry as to why we cannot better regulate our hearts has its eternal echo in the Uranian soul.

A bibliography of references to similisexualism in the early ecclesiastical fathers and commentators presents many works of importance in considering the cloistered homosexual, the uranian who was also an anchorite; and the solicitude that he caused the Church and the laity. Johannes Cassianus, Peter Damiani and many more are attentive to him. Sometimes the sexual casuistry is curious, as when we find Dolcino, in his famous "Instructions," of the opinion that "conjuger ventrem ut cesset tentation non est peccatum"—between cloistered *religieux*.

---

2. Transl. X. M.

Modern philosophy offers the names of Erasmus of Rotterdam, of Spinoza, of Sir Isaac Newton, of Bonfadio, of Hegel, of Schopenhauer and Nietsche, as among those who either were homosexual, personally, or who contemplated

Modern Moral Philosophers and Uranianism.

the instinct from a liberal standpoint. Almost in our own day, the great nature-student Virchow wrote to Ulrichs in acceptance of the Intersexual theory, Virchow expressing a conviction that the Uranian should be free in making the relationships it invited. Schopenhauer terms homosexuality a passion so "universal and ineradicable" that it must be a part of our inborn human nature, and self-justified ethically. Also the naturalist and explorer, Gustav Jaeger, considered homosexuality a principle "inborn in the individual," through which he originates in an unalterable "disharmony" with woman, and can be in sexual key with only a masculine type; in many instances impossible of alteration as a natural expression.

Among the greater philosophers, perhaps the profoundest humanist of the Renaissance epoch, was Erasmus of Rotterdam. That Erasmus was homosexual is one of the many interesting studies in circumstantial evidence of biography. Again, the eccentricities of life and of *vita sexualis* on the part of the great English philosopher Sir Isaac Newton, his hatred of women sexually, have cast a colour of uranianism over the personality of the elaborator of the theory of gravitation. There is some ground to infer that Spinoza, gentle natured and noble-hearted, an Italian Jew by race, and as cold to women sexually as he was warm in friendship (especially with one intimate) was similisexual. Among quite modern philosophers whose biography and teaching have uranian currents was Friedrich Nietsche. There can be little doubt that Nietsche's passionate hero-worship of Richard Wagner was homosexual, at its most climatic stage, and that Nietsche's bitter disappointment in Wagner's sordid personality, as he came to know it better, and Nietsche's feeling that an idol had been shattered—the glory of which had been largely in the worshipper—were factors in the advance of Nietsche's mental distresses and overthrow. We are warned by Coleridge that "to be wroth with one we love doth work like madness in the brain The writings of Nietsche have various references to homosexual love, including the epigrammatic counsel—"Sondern physisch; und wenn möglich dionysisch," in "Zarathustra."

Servetus.

The accent of homosexualism occurs in the personality of Michael Servetus, the Spanish physician and theologian, who during the fierce civil-wars of Calvinism, became so special an object of Calvin's intolerance that his doom to be burned alive at Geneva, in 1553, is constantly charged to Calvin. Servetus was an Aragonese. At first a physician and engrossed in secular life and social concerns, he went in 1530 to Strassburg. The first of his series of Theological polemics attracted so much attention that Servetus gave himself wholly up to disputations in the fields of religion and philosophy. One of the most learned and argumentative minds in dogmatic cross-currents, he was not long permitted to escape the controversial anger of Calvin. His book "Christianismi Restitutio," published at Lyons in 1540, especially drew on Servetus the bitterest denunciations of intolerant Calvinists, and of their chief. Servetus imprudently put himself in the power of his fanatical spiritual adversaries. In Geneva, he was arrested as a dangerous heretic; and after a vainly heroic defence, he was burned to death (with peculiarly cruel torment) at Champel, on October 26, 1553. A noble homosexualism characterized Servetus. Intellectually he was a sort of universal genius, far beyond his theological dialectics. His medical learning was immense for his time; his discovery of the circulation of the blood (an honour to him far in advance of later claimants) gives him ever a high place. He-was also a brilliant geographer, physicist, astrologer, mathematician, botanist, and much else; all before his middle years.

Beza.

Another brilliant religious light in the early history of Calvinism, the much prized Beza, is accused circumstantially of being Urananian; as by his own confession withal. Beza (1510–1105) was born Théodore de Béze, at Vézelay, in Burgundy. After lively secular years in Paris, having decided on the profession of religion, he passed from Catholicism to a strongly Calvinistic theology; becoming a distinguished factor of the Reformation. Two intimate friendships, one with a certain "Pomponius" and another with a remarkably beautiful youth named Audebert, were of so passional a nature, according to Beza's descriptions in his Latin poems (the indiscreet "Juvenilia") that classic language need not be much more confessional. Much was made of this when Beza apostatized. Fierce and many were the attacks on his sexual morals. Franz Balduin, F. Claudius de Xaintes, Jerome Bolsec, Coccius, Bisselius, Maimbourg, Baillet, in the course of the XVII Century, and in the XVIII the polemist Daniel, virulently proclaimed Beza not only a vile heretic, but a sodomite. One cannot get help admitting the basis of uranian accusations when we glance at Beza's verse. The fact that in later life he was twice married of course does not negative his early memoranda as to "the beautiful Audebert, and the beloved Pomponius." The lament for Pomponius included in the "Juvenilia" says, for instance:

> *"Tevirum mihi sustulere fata!*
> *Quod unum licet his quo quotannis*
> *Pares inferias dabo sepulchro,*
> *Ut meo Pyladi, meo Achati.*
> *Sic qui finis erit mihi loquendi,*
> *Deflendi mihi finis est futurus*
> *Te meum Pyladem, meumque Achatem!"*

One of Beza's longer Latin poems, entitled "Theodorus Beza de Sua in Candidam et Audebertum Benevolentia," deals with feeza's young friend, the lad Audebert, and with a young woman named Candide; depicting Beza's conflict in loving the young man as much as he loves the lady, and his inability to lessen his passion for Audebert, even though Candide jealously demands that he shall do so. One passage beginning "Sed utrum rogo proferam decorum? Utrum invisere me decet priorum?"—may be translated thus: "But which of these two, I ask myself, is most to me? Which one should I first seek to see again? Who could be dearer to me than, art thou, Candide? But whom could I ever place in my heart before thee, Audebert? Yes, if I should cut myself into two parts, one part would be Candide's but the other would be Audebert's." There are several such episodes. Beza's fierce Catholic enemy, Bolsec, in one of his attacks on the historian, in the lines "Spintria nunc fueras" etc., declares—"Awhile ago you were a passive sodomite and a filthy poet; now all at once you have turned yourself into a man learned in the Holy Scriptures!" Also Laingeaus exclaims, in an arraignment of Beza—"He was tortured by burning lust for his young Audebert, a remarkably handsome boy, with whom he was united in a sodomistic love." Beza was even accused of being ill, owing to certain sexual excesses, in Paris. Says Xaintes (de Sanctis) "Instead of your Audebert, now you have embraced Calvin, and so have substituted a spiritual male-whore for a carnal one; thus being still what you were,—a sodomist." All which may be called rather plain talking between holy conversationalists!

The topic of uranian clergy especially in the history of the Catholic and Orthodox priests, bishops cardinals and popes, in every degree of moral and intellectual endowment, would make easily a volume by itself. From the hermits of the Thebaid, whose orisons and mortifications of the flesh could not purge them of sexual desire, up to the occupants of the Chair of Peter, the Romish hierarchy have been uranianistic. The debaucheries of homosexual pontiffs, such as Alexander VI, Sixtus IV, John XXII, Julius III, and others exhibited especially pederastic passion in the higher priesthood. The Monastic Orders, century by century of their existence, have been sorely troubled (or else practically have not been *troubled* at all) by invincible homosexuality in the cloister. The austerities of the Carthusians and Trappists, the intellectualism of the Jesuits and Benedictines, the fervid piety Of Dominicans, Franciscans and any others, have never eradicated it; and in some chapters of Church-history we find that they thought best to tolerate it. Today it flourishes in the Catholic seminary and the parish-rectory, We must not argue that its existence implies the unspirituality of the Church, and a dismissal of moral conduct. Where it is not inborn, it has much to do with the celibate life of the Catholic ecclesiastic, the attitude of personal reserve toward woman that he must cultivate. One can even trace an antiquated spiritual-sexual casuistry in it. It is contagious in the novitiate. Many a dionistic priest becomes perceptibly homosexual before he has received his tonsure. The theory of a strictly celibate clergy is untenable in natural and social morality. It rests on no divine authority. It is a human abnormalism, except when invited by a distinct frigidity of temperament, a weakly frame, or advanced years. Unfortunately, a young priest usually has vigour of bodily constitution, and often has quite as strong, or even stronger, impulses to sexual intercourse than the average. A sedentary life increases his emotion. A proportion of such clergy are born uranians. Strange dramas are played in their clerical surroundings. In religious schools for the laity, under ecclesiastical care pederasty is a common weakness of the cassocked tutors. Of this, another chapter of the present study speaks.

It is of interest to notice that, *nolens*, an attitude of philosophical and scientific toleration of similisexuality is to be observed in the Roman clergy today; quite another matter, of course, than mere complaisance toward vice. A priest, whose confidential opinion of the prevalence of uranian instincts in superior moral natures was asked some years ago, by means of a species of circular-letter addressed to the Catholic pastorate, issued by the Natur Wissenchaft Komittee, in Berlin, wrote: "The best and most learned and most pious men have frequently the homosexual instinct. I am convinced that just because -of this fact, many men enter into a monastic life, fleeing solely from the homosexual desires, ignorant of inclinations to the other sex. I am also convinced that the homosexual man has a far harder battle with himself than has the heterosexual. I have even advised penitents to go away' to oriental countries to live, where such unfortunate natures are not punished by laws as criminals. Particularly do I recall the suicide of one popular man, on account of being blackmailed by a studio-assistant, with whom he had been culpable."

Another Catholic pastor stated that his experience in his profession, and his opinions, had convinced him that if female prostitution is to be tolerated, then there should be no penalty for male sexual intercourse; and that having known many such individuals he believed that the general excellence or unworth of a character has no connection with the homosexual impulse. He wrote,—"I have known two individuals, formerly young parishioners of mine, who are each homosexual, but always patterns of Christian morality, whether of old or of today."

In the same confidential symposium of ideas of present-day Catholic priesthood in Germany concerning uranianism some twenty-five replies to the circular-letter mentioned were received, such replies being, of course, anonymous as to publication. Some of the writers alluded to the theory, not new, that Saint Paul was not free from homosexual instincts, if indications in the Epistles be accepted.

The reader is referred to the interesting correspondence mentioned, as it appears in the "Jahrbuch für Sexuelle Zwischenstufen" (Max Spohr, Leipzig) edited by Dr. Magnus Hirschfeld; Volume II, pp. 161–203. Also as an instance of minute study of the Biblical attitude toward similisexuality, may be remarked a contribution made by a Catholic clergyman (anonymous) in the fourth volume of the same "Jahrbuch." In that study, the commentator reviews practically every pertinent passage of the Scriptures; and, as a scholarly priest, he reaches the conclusion that there is no authority for holding decent homosexual love as a sin in the eyes of God, or of society. Instead he finds every reason to think uranians the victims of a warping of social common sense, by mere dogmatic influences.

Removals of the Catholic clergy for similisexual scandals are incessant. The Continental newspapers especially show this, each year. Several grave affairs of the sort are current in the press, as these pages are written; one of them involving a priest distinguished for high attainments and for social and ecclesiastical respect. The murder in 1857 of the saintly and almost adored Archbishop Sibour of Paris, which tragedy occurred while the Archbishop was at the altar, came through the uranistic frenzy of the murderer, himself a priest. It was an episode that cast all Paris, not to say all France, into mourning.

As may be supposed, in Italy and Spain crimes connecting Catholic clergy with uranian habits are not rare. The recent murder of a priest in Naples (which case is before the court as these lines are written) by another ecclesiastic has proved, by the confession of the survivor to have had a homosexual *liaison* between the two men, and a scene of jealousy as the source of the affair, known as the Adorni-Costantini assassination.

The College of Cardinals, in very recent days, has had several members of whose philarrenic tastes gossip has been eloquent; including one distinguished politician of the *cappa magna*, some years deceased. Another membee of the Sacred College, a contemporary of high birth, with a distinguished career at—apparently—his back, long has had attached to his name the rumours of invincible uranianism; and a sobriquet that his political enemies have lately lent him, because of his present policy toward his church, is frequently uttered with a sarcastic accent, to mark its double meaning.

À-propos, of the Uranian clergy of the Continent, there lately appeared in the sedate and calvinistic "Journal de Genève" a cryptic little advertisement—literary?—which the present writer has not yet explained quite to his satisfaction; and so will leave to the queries of his readers: "L. Prètres Homos-Sexuels du Noviciat de Jersey 2, V. Lesin-Viersère, avec documents bien détaillés, 1898–1899."

In the Greek Church, the permission to the clergy to marry lessens homosexual scandals, as it does heterosexual Ones. But such episodes are not unusual.

The Established Church of England, and the ranks of an innumerable and sectarian Protestant clergy, the world over, are far less often scandalized by homosexual episodes than the Roman priesthood. There is certainly a considerable proportion of more or less distinctly uranian pastors in Protestantism. Occasionally some individual case in manifested. One such has been recently before both the English and the American public. But the Protestant clergyman is freer to square his homosexuality, if he have it, with his general moral convictions, education, and religious ideas, without reference to a rule of eclesiastical celibacy, built up against the force of Nature, such as adds to the problem of sex for the Catholic priest.

Bishop Atherton.

Remarkable homosexual personalities and dramas are met in the history of the English Church. One painful instance in that of the distinguished Bishop John Atherton (1598–1670) of Waterford, Ireland, and later also associated with Dublin. Pew British churchmen have been more conspicuous for their intellect, their lofty spirituality of life, their social influences, and for a passionate philanthropy of the most practical sort. The downfall of Bishop Atherton, because of a homosexual scandal, in which he was hopelessly involved, and for which he suffered death, was almost'an incredible religious tragedy, according to English notions at the time. Great efforts to save his life were made; but in vain—the more so as he had admitted the charge, and said that he desired to expiate it. A curious detail of Atherton's case was his preparation, while in prison, of a long and learned study and defence of homosexual instincts, which document he nevertheless refused to utilize, and burned, before his appearing in court. He met his fate, in fact, in a state of abject contrition that much edified the religious world about him.

Even more dramatic is the history of another great Irish churchman, Bishop Jocelyn, of the See of Clogher, in the early part of the nineteenth

Bishop Jocelyn.

century. Relatively a young man, though already advanced in dignity, Bishop Jocelyn was also an inborn uranian. After having had several homosexual relationships without detection, Jocelyn fell in love with a strikingly handsome young soldier, in the Life-Guards, stationed in the diocese, a trooper named John Moverly, who was also uranistic. The Bishop was handsome, genial, and a man of the world, though he filled his religious station becomingly. In 1822 the intimacy came to light. A great scandal ensued. Bishop Jocelyn fled to the Continent, and escaped punishment. The unlucky young Moverly was condemned to a long term of imprisonment. In fact his life was technically in danger, owing to the penalty then statutory in Ireland.

Pagan Religions and Intersexualism.

The topic of intersexualism as a part of ancient or modern paganism and mythologies, is one of much material in detail, as may be supposed; which wide subject the writer is obliged at this time to pass over with only a reference, on account of changes in the plan of this work. A large proportion of antique religions, ecclesiastical societies, priesthoods, temple-confraternities, ceremonies and fêtes, more or less integrally have had to do with male-to-male, or with female-to-female sexualism, symbols and licenses of intercourse. Forms of worship among the Assyrians, the Phænicians, in several Asiatic, African, Oceanian, American cults have accepted such an element. The deification of Antinöus was developed—appropriately—toward pederastic practices, as part of the ritual. Buddhism in Japan and China has admitted homosexualism along with its covert phallic symbolism; and not until 1838 did the Japanese Government put a stop to the astonishing licenses of phallic and homosexualfeminosexual orgies, that used to take place at the temples of U-ji and Saidai-ji. Lamaism in Thibet has occult uranianism widely diffused through its organization, and lamaseries are noted centers for debauchment of boys and for general homosexualism.

Let us turn again from the distinctively religious life to secular intellectuality. A wonderfully gifted Uranian occurs in Johannes von Müller, the famous German-Swiss historian (1752–1809). Müller's monumental works in history, particularly as to mediæval Germany, Switzerland, Italy, and other parts of Europe, gave him in the prime of his career the sobriquet of "a monster of learning," and his labours are not yet unconsidered. His general scholarship was profound, even in his youth. His life was passed in an unbroken literary activity, at successively Göttingen, Geneva, Bern, Mainz, Vienna, Berlin and Kassel. The eyes of the learned world were fixed on him wherever he was, with respect and wonder. Müller was absolutely homosexual. He was capable of sexual passion only for one or another of his friends, pupils or others; and he was highly idealistic in such emotions. Toward women, Müller was either entirely indifferent or an agreeable friend. Especially singled out by Müller in his uranian biography we find Baron Karl von Bonstetten, another eminent Swiss authour, early associated with Muller. In physical aspects, Müller was perceptibly feminine, conveying no, idea of his strong intellect; and his conversation suggested a brilliant, humorous, amiable but rather satirical—woman.

During Müller's life time, he was frequently spoken of as homosexual—pederastic—by more or less tolerant friends, or by literary enemies. His return to Switzerland, and his continued residence there, were said to be his escape from serious scandals, and because he wished to live out of the legal jurisdiction of Germany. The letters of the historian to Bonstetten were published (by Cotta, Stuttgart) under the editing of Brun. Another collection, of miscellaneous sort, was issued by Orel in Zürich, edited by Füssli. The Bonstetten correspondence mentioned ("Briefe Eines Jungen Gelehrten an Seinen Freund") stirred up much comment, when in print. They mumber about one hundred and fifty, often being long. Nearly every page, each paragraph, speaks the heart of an Uranian lover before his beloved. In citing them one hardly knows where to begin. A few passages only are the following:

"Without you I can never be happy; with you all my misfortunes find their alleviation. . . You letters are my eye-salve, since what heals my heart is my body's health. . . You love me as I love you. . . I shall love you till my death. . . Good God! How far I am from you, my own Bonstetten! Among such ordinary mortals! And yet, my God! Bonstetten is mine! . . . Remember ever, my Bonstetten that you are my friend. No matter where I may live, still my greatest bliss is only you. Bethink you, too, that every idea, every principle of wisdom I have learned and possess, my whole individuality, belong to you. Yes, dispose of my person as you choose. . . My dearest of all! I find our friendship indeed extraordinary, because no other feeling has any comparison with it. I love you even more than even when in Habsburg. All that I have would I give if at this moment I could embrace you! I feel what the unity of our two hearts would fain speak out. . . Yes, my B—, I am yours and you are mine. I love you as no other man in this world of ours today can love another. I love other men just in the measure that they are like you. I hold it as the priceless bliss of life that in the twenty-first year of my age, by a chance, I found you out, among a group of forty-two other mortals; you who have been my brother throughout the many changes of my life, and who will be my companion until my death and whose heart is worthy to be the object of the whole overflowing stream of my friendship; you, the only single human being, among all others, who is noble enough and of a soul sensitive enough to love me as I love him!" . . . "The only thing that gives me anxiety is my fear that my friendship for you is not warm enough! My dearest, my friend! My heart is oppressed when I think of that four-days-long dream from the Gods that has been ours! . . . I count the hours and the instant until the post shall bring me news of my B—. Believe not that ever another human being was loved as are you. . . Tell me why it is that I love you always more and more? You are always within me, round about me. My dearest friend! How much better is it for me be alone, to give my thoughts to you, than to be going about with others! How is it possible to desecrate that heart which is consecrated to you? No friendship is like ours. We two are Athenians, not Swiss. . . And if you and I know what it is to love each other according to our sort of love, why, then not allow to others to love after their sort?."[2]

There are many such epistles in this curious collection. Not often does the personal correspondence between two extremely learned men (for Bonstetten was also a savant of high qualities) keep such an unliterary and passionally personal accent. In other letters we find Müller calling Bonstetten his Apollo, whose godlike beauty and grace have inspired Muller's heart. He names Bonstetten his "Cory don." He writes to Bonstetten in a fever of longing, for a letter from his "friend" and in feminine anxiety for his welfare. He narrates his dreams of Bonstetten. Bonstetten himself was an older man, and a calmer personality, though equally homosexual. His reciprocation of Muller's extravagant affection was more contained and dignified. Muller in his correspondence with another friend Kinloch, writes with similarly homosexual emotions; and there are interesting traces of rivalries and jealousies in the intimacy. In even the historical writings of Muller a delicate colouring of uranian feeling is to be remarked, when he is dealing with biography which admits of it.

Winckelmann.

The German archeologist and critic, Winckelman, (1717–1768) not only was all his life an Uranian, and in sexual relations with friends or acquaintances of the same nature; but lost his life by uranistic intimacy. Whether Winckelman was an "inborn" Uranian, or if his strong homosexualism was largely the result of aesthetic studies in Italy, where his life and labours long continued, need not be analyzed here. He had love-affairs with several young men in Rome that have long been historic, including

---

2. Transl. X. M.

the ungrateful Lambrecht, his acquaintance with von Stosch, Berendis, and so on. His friendship with the homosexual painter Raphael Mengs was apparently not of such character. The ultimate chapter of his sexual history brought tragedy. In 1767, Winckelman left Rome to visit some German friends, and travelled North as far as Regensburg. At that place, he abruptly decided to return to Italy, by way of Vienna. In Vienna he was made much of by the learned world, and by the Empress Maria-Theresia, who presented him with a quantity of curious ancient money, mostly in gold, that she knew would gratify his archéologie taste. He reached Triest, to sail. There, Winckelman fell into the society of an extremely handsome young Italian (mis-named Arcangeli) a café-waiter, in poverty, and a dangerous character. Arcangeli was homosexual, ingratiating and a thorough rascal. His beauty charmed the idealistic savant. For some days, Winckelmann kept Arcangeli with him, and the two men passed each night together. Winckelman however did not disclose his identity; but he was imprudent enough to inform Arcangeli of the money! A day or so before Winckelmann was to have left Triest, Arcangeli began to be insistant on Winckelmann's real name and so on, and demanded a sight of the gold. Winckelmann refused. A quarrel came. Winckelmann, thinking to end it, sat down at his desk to write. The murderous Italian glided behind Winckelmann, with a cord in his hand; and first garrotted and then stabbed the unfortunate savant. Arcangeli was tried, convicted and executed, the facts in his intimacy with Winckelmann being elicited during the trial. Apart from the regular biographies of Winckelmann, where the affair is presented with much reserve, they are embodied, with some romancing, in one of the narratives in Alex, von Sternberg's volume "Künstlerbilder." (See a later reference).

The fact that a man is engrossed in severely scientific professions does not always mean a quiet or virile *vita sexualis*—as often has been pointed out. At the bar, on the bench, in the laboratory, in most abstruse and austere branches

Uranianism and the Professions of Applied Science.

of intellectual labour, among inventors, perfecters of scientific principles and processes; in chemistry, in metallurgy, in everything—we come face to face with the Intersexual. Such types are likely to be homosexuals without vivid idealism. The same remark applies to the industrialist. A striking case of this last type was Alfred Krupp, the millionaire German manufacturer. Krupp was much a man of pleasure. The island of Capri and a fine yacht were his homosexual homes. He was pederastic. The tragic end of his career, for which scandal the indiscretion and the persecution of others were mainly responsible, were closely related to Krupp's "philosyrphetic" nature and crude sexual tastes.

Recently the alert "Committee" in Berlin, already mentioned, succeded in making a remarkable "census" of the students in the great Technical School, in Charlottenburg, as to the proportion of homosexual young men in that institution. The showing was between one and two percent, a result closely conforming to other statistics of Germanic uranianism.

Professional Medicine and Uranianism.

A remarkable proportion of physicians and surgeons are homosexual; fully (Iranians, or Dionysian-Uranians. The contingent "census" of any city points this out. Life in the medical-schools is not hostile to the instinct. The doctor often loses all sense of sexual charm in the feminine psychos, and a woman's physique ceases to rouse his sexual excitement. This is especially true of doctors devoted to women's diseases. The physician appreciates peculiarly the weakness, the limitations, of feminine psychology. He turns reactively to the richer s nature, the masculine. Usually, such a physician must wear his 'mask', like the rest of the uranistic fraternity. Sometimes when he finds that he cannot do this, he quits his profession, or even quits the world.

A distinguished French surgeon writes thus: "Always homosexual, my marriage did not alter this, nor do any of the intellectual and professional currents of my life. I have a large practice, and I am much in social demand. I have intimate friendships with women, and I have never had reason to think them indifferent to me. . . But I have always found in the homosexual embrace infinitely more satisfaction than in intercourse of the normal sort. . . When I find my homosexual desires overpowering, I go to B—where I have a colleague, a former student with me in the B—University, who is "like myself," and I pass some time with him. I have also a similar relation with a student here. My wife seems to have never suspected the nature of my sexual coldness, she herself being rather frigid. . . My colleague, Doctor X—is another homosexual member of the profession. I know of his intimacy with a certain patient (a member of the Chamber of Deputies) and with others. They, however, are fortunate in being unmarried. My marriage was absolutely a necessity, for family-reasons. I am aware of numerous such instances as mine. . . You probably know that the eminent German surgeon Z. . . is homosexual; and that his intimacy with the young son of a noble patron menaced him with scandal a few years ago, the matter being hushed up by the intervention of—I might write—one of the royal family." . . .

A minute autobiographical study of a German physician, typically Uranian, occurs in Dr. von Krafft-Ebing's treatise "Psychopathia Sexualis" in the eleventh (German) edition of that work, under the reference, "Observation No. 148."

The most expressive outlet for the Uranian's temperament is that of belles-lettres. He cannot always be philosophic, nor an analyst in the colder forms of literature. Ho is likely to lack courage to preach to the uncomprehending public. But his capacity for feeling, his faculty for romance, find vivid expression in elegant literature. Often his pen and paper have been his only confidants; and sometimes in fiction or verse of genius he has taken the world into his secret.

The Uranian in Belles-lettres.

The homosexual's literary communicativeness varies widely in dignity; varies as widely as the clearly personal homosexualism of writers. Beauty, refinement, power, idealism are shifting qualities. The uranian library ranges from the classic elegance of Greek and Latin idylls and elegies, from sonnets by Shakespeare, Buonarroti or August von Platen, from exquisitely oriental ghazels of Hafiz and other Persian and Arabic classics, from the novels of Alexander von Sternberg, Wilbrandt, "Rachilde," Essebac, Pernhaum, Loti or Georges Eckhoud, to the pornographic prose and verse that flooded the East and the West of old, just as it does London or Berlin or Paris today. But a literature of high quality, in all languages, is of uranian authourship, and wide suggestiveness to its readers; a real literature, so diffused and accessible that we can forgive many pages of vulgarly homosexual eroticism. It is very largely a serious, deeply emotional literature. Humourous modern literature owes less to the Uranian than does any other class of writings. The Uranian's temperament, and his problematic social life have checked his mirth.' His gayety tends to irony, or is of that artificial good-humour often characteristic of him.

It is Imminently a sincere and personal literature, this homosexual library. "Look into thy heart and write!" is a long-heard counsel. The Uranian has obeyed it with clarity and courage. His page has mirrored his soul. But he has not always been allowed such liberty. Not only does prejudice in society and religion

Falsifying Editors, Biographers, Apologists, etc.

obstruct his press. Exasperating are the comments of critics, editors, translators and so on, to conceal or to ignore altogether, the personal homosexuality of such or such a writer and of his literary intentions. The conventional modern biographer avoids recognizing the homosexual nature, in his subject. The editor is equally timid. The publisher not less so.

Classic Greek Belles-lettres; the Lyrists.

Happy or unhappy, idealistic or sensual, with his muse either of first-rank or inferior accents, the uranianistic Greek wrote himself into letters with all the ardent, pagan candour of his passion. The question of homosexual love in Homer has already, been noted, in connection with general aspects of the sentiment in antiquity. We have also indicated relations, both literary and personal, to hellenic homosexualism, of Socrates, Plato and the philosophic schools radiating from Platonism or of other colouring. Their almost incomparable aspects in the light of belles-lettres need no comment here.

According to the late John Addington Symonds, who his life through was extremely interested in the subject of homosexualism in letters and art, and made minute studies of the topic, the homosexual influence in the Greek "lyrist-age" was Dorian. It was largely pederastic, like the Platonic references to homosexualism. We have Theognis, Ibycus, Theocritus, Anacreon, Pindar, Meleager, Alkman, the fairest singers of Greek lyrics, all pederastic to a greater or less degree. Ibycus has been called "the male Sappho," in fact. Theocritus is passionally homosexual. Pindar, whose feeling for beauty in a youth is profound, has made the lad Theoxenos immortal among the group of beautiful boys loved by classic verse-makers. The Greek Anthologies are almost wholly pederastic. A large literature now lost to us, except by fragments, and a proportion tolerably extant, have offered examples of greater or lesser interest and elegance as to hellenic similisexual writers.

The Hellenic Dramatists, etc.

The Greek stage, too, became uranistic as hellenic drama took its most human phases. Lost plays of Eupolis, Eubolus, Antiphanes, Diphilos, Lycidas, Aelian, Lucian, Kratinos, either made it a special theme, or touched on it in episodes. It was a motive in dramas by Aeschylos (such as his lost "Achilles' Lovers." and "Niobe") and by Euripides. Euripides' "Hippolytus" is a subtly homosexual drama. We have no direct information as to the sexual inclinations of Aeschylos, as a man. Euripides was characterized by a special *gout* for women. Aristophanes makes, *passim*, characteristically sly allusions to a sort of morals inevitably under the eye of the great Athenian satirist. As to Sophocles, in Athenæus's "The Banqueters" Book XIII, occur anecdotes of plain sort as to his pederastic nature. Considerable information as to Greek literary homosexuals is found in "The Banqueters," the erotic memorabilia and gossip of which made Mr. W. H. Lecky term it "a book of painful interest" for those studying the theme. Lights and shadows on personalities, myths, incidents, in various periods of Grecian literary development, all tinged with uranianism are also met in Plutarch, in Xenophon, in many historians and biographists, as we have seen. Xenophon in his double, dignity of a great military leader and an authour, we know conclusively to have been personally pederastic. His vehement passion for the beautiful boy, KliniaS is eloquently recorded by the authour of the "Anabasis" and "The Symposion," in such a self-confession as "—Now is the mere sight' of Klinias more to me than all the other beautiful things in the world of men! Might I but become blind for everything else, keeping my eyes only for beholding Klinias! Night and sleep irritate me, because in them I cannot see Klinias; while beyond all measure do I give thanks for the sun, for the day, which show Klinias to me again!"

Greek writers were rarely gross, even when personal. The Hellene, at home or in his colonial environment seldom approached vulgarity in æsthetics. One can linger over the examples of his pederastic loves; so refined the speech, and in such sympathy with Nature; ever sounding the psychic note, even when explicitly uttering the praise of physical loveliness in male youth. For the Roman, a descent to the literary obscene was easy. We have no Latin Pindar or Meleager. Even Hierocles and Philagre were not Martialesque.

Lucian of Samosata in many of the "Dialogues of the Dead" touches gaily and gracefully, ironically and slyly,, on the homosexual loves of the gods and heroes. It is to the last-named authour, so prolific, brilliant and charming, that we owe the- most important and interesting of all classic discussions of male-to-male love, when to be considered apart from philosophical theorizings. This is Lucian's long dialogue (which is also occasionally attributed to Aristhetenes) "Love": an-argument between Charicles a handsome heterosexual of Corinth, and Kallicratides the Athenian homosexual, as to which of "the two kinds" of sexual love is the most honourable and æsthetic. The discussion closes with the victory given by the umpire to the boy-lover. In this disquisition we find Lucian citing two lines by an unknown poet, suggesting that the tie between Achilles and Patroclus was sexual as well as less ardently psychical:

> *"Formosum tuorum sanctæ consuetudinis,*
> *Quid pulchrior!"*

Roman Belleslettres. We have already spoken of important Latin belles-lettres, of the Imperial age. This finest period of literary Rome is highly eloquent of Uranian love; sometimes—largely—pederastic, sometimes of more dignified sort. The muse of Ovid sings of the diverse sexual loves, with Greek charm in uranian suggestions. The similisexual vignettes that occur in Vergil's Eclogues, imitations of Hellenic models in hoy-love, lyrics are doubtless personal to his own heart. The pederastic note, the voice of the poet in his own individuality, is unmistakeable. We find Vergil even more eloquent as to an heroic pair of young soldier-lovers, when he tells us the dramatic story of the friends, Nisus and Euryalus, in the Ninth Book of the Æneid:—

> *"Nisus. . . acerrimus armis*
> *Hyrtacides. . .*
> *Et juxta comes Euryalus, quo pulchrior alter*
> *Non fuit Aeneadum, Troiana neque induit arma,*
> *Cum puer prima signans intonsa juventa.*
> *Hic amor unus erat, pariter in bella ruebant."*

It is the uranian elegist that we hear in Vergil's splendid and skilfully patriotic eulogy of their affection and bravery:

> *"Fortunati ambo! Si quid mea carmina possunt,*
> *Nulla dies upquam memori vos eximet aevo,*
> *Dum domus Aenae Capitoli immobile saxum*
> *Accolet, imperiumque pater Romanus habebit."*

The Great Latin Erotists, Elegists, Satirists, etc. But more vehement is the language of personal homosexualism met, the Uranian heard as a singer of his own love or lust, of his own bliss his own sorrow, or else as the mocking commentator on homosexualism in others, when we review such poets as Catullus, Propertius, Horace, Tibullus, Juvenal, Persius and Martial; the great social lyrists, elegists and satirists. Now refined, now grossly realistic, (even to being indecent as is no Hellenic poet) the whole kaleidescope of Roman uranianism is to be seen here. Catullus seems to have been a Dionysian-Uranian, as so many Latins always have been and are now—bisexual in their sensibilities. (An English example among poets is Byron, as we shall again see.) Catullus at first is met in his homosexual references as a coarse lampoonist; as in the famous scurrility directed toward two fellow-citizens who had been talking about his verses and his morals:

"Pedicabo ego vos, et irrumabo,
Aureli pathice, et cinaede Furi—"

There are many such flights of the catullian *blague;* especially toward "passives," including Julius Cæsar and Mamurra, and in vulgar flouts at Mentula, Gretlius, G-allus, and others of the lewd "smart set" in Rome. But Catullus is plainly concerned in his private and pederastic personality, when attacking angrily sly Aurelius, who is trying to rob the poet the affections of a boy about town:

"Aurel, pater esuritionum,
Non harum modo, sed quot aut fuerunt,
Aut sunt, aut aliis erunt in annis!
Pedicare cupis meos amores?
Nec clam, nam simules, jocaris una:
Haeres ad latus, omnia experiris," etc.

Catullus is not converted by Lesbia nor by any other mistress, from uranian boy-loves, no matter how femininity may have attracted his capricious heart. He addresses the beautiful lad Juventius, telling him that of his kisses he can never have enough (quite as he declared of the better-known osculations of Lesbia) and rhapsodizes over the boy's eyes as "sweeter than the golden honey of the bee"—those eyes which Catullus would fain "coyer with a thousand kisses." To this same boy, Juventius, are those lines that call him "the floweret of the youth" of all Rome. Catullus angrily and jealously sneers at Juventius on account of a flirtation with another lover, so poor that he has "neither a purse nor a valet." Bitterly too does Catullus complain of another youth, Alphenus, as "without faith, insensible, and forgetful of Catullus, the constant and the tender one";

describing Alphenus as a boy "whose seductions have carried me out of my senses, by ties of whose potency you have been boasting."

Tibullus, despite the charms of Delia, of Nemesis, of Neara, and so on, was personally and poetically a pederastic homosexual; with verses that can be painfully modern to uranians. In the Fourth Elegy of the First Book, Tibullus addresses an old terminal Priapus in a garden-alley, begging the stone god to tell him how a man as he grows older still can be attractive to boys—a problem perennially eloquent and difficult to many homosexuals. The grey statue replies with a store of good counsels—tact, shrewdness, patience, devotion, and so on; but emphasizing the common sense of one's not falling in love at all after youth ends.[3] Tibullus is incidentally told that in loving a boy one "must seek to win him by everything that thou canst do to please him—soon he will come under the yoke of thy love." We have warnings and encouragements, in Tibullian hendekasyllabics:

> *"Avoid thou the throng of such beautiful lads,*
> *For theirs is the reason and right to know love.*
> *Lo, that one shall win thee in reining his horse*
> *Or that one when, shining, his form cleaves the wave;*
> *By boyish assurance yon youth gains thy heart;*
> *Another with cheeks that are soft as a girl's.*
> *But though he be shy to thee, standing aloof,*
> *Anon wilt thou find how he yields to thy love.*
> *By the patience of men even lions are tamed,*
> *The dropping of water will soften the rock,*
> *The sun ripens slowly cold grapes, on the hills;*
> *Nay the very stars fall. . .*
>
> *But beware of delaying too long! See, the year*
> *Passes swiftly—" etc. etc.*[2]

---

3. The same sort of wise counsel—but to heterosexuals—is met many centuries later in Racine; where the great French dramatist of the human heart makes his grizzled Mithridates exclaim, in self-rebuke and anger:

> *"Ah, qu'il eût mieux valu, plus sage et plus heureux,*
> *Et repoussant les traits d'un amour dangereux,*
> *Ne pas laisser remplir d'ardeurs empoisonnées,*
> *Un cœur déjà glacé par le froid des années!"*

2. Transl. X. M.

EDWARD IRENAEUS PRIME-STEVENSON

In two others of the Elegies of Tibullus, the Eighth and Ninth of the same Book, mingled into the addresses to the unworthy Delia, are the verses of Tibullus to yet another boy, Marathus. The poet's comments on his really *grande passion* for that youth, who seems to have given Tibullus a great deal of unhappiness. In the Eighth Elegy we find the poet in somewhat the same situation as was Shakespeare. The inconstant Marathus has fallen in love with a mercenary girl, Pholoe, who is cold to Marathus; making the boy wretched with desire. The jealous Tibullus is altruistic enough to reproach Pholoe, and to wish the ungrateful lad success; reminding Pholoe of what a treasure of sexual delight she is scorning:

> *"A boy more precious is than gold! On his soft lips*
> *No rough beard wounds thee, as he clasps thee close.*
> *It should be more to thee to press thy arm,*
> *Around a neck so white, than to possess*
> *The wealth of kings."*[2]

But soon Tibullus is not so philosophical as to being neglected by Marathus. A storm of passion breaks out. The poet appeals to the justice of heaven since

> —*"Marathus has scorned my ill-starred love,*
> *Not thinking on the vengeance of the Gods!"*[2]

Worse follows; for, in the long Ninth Elegy we learn that young Marathus has sold his favours to a rich man—a married homosexual—casting aside Tibullus, forgetting him. This extraordinary Elegy pours out a volcano of love, grief, of dolorous retrospect, of bitter reproach to Marathus; and even warns the rival whose gold has won the lad, that the dionysian Marathus easily may debauch the young wife in the family. The apostrophe to Marathus ends angrily:

> *"Kisses once mine thou givest to others, fool!*
> *Weep when some other lad shall be my love!"*[2]

---

2. Transl. X. M.

—and declaring that when cured of this passion the elegist will dedicate a golden *ex voto* to Venus, in her temple.

As for Propertius, whose muse is consderably in a higher and more varied strain (except where Propertius is recording his passion for Cynthia) we find a touch of sensibility to pederastic love, more or less personal, in the charming address to his friend Gallus, who was in torment by a certain beautiful youth named Hylas. Propertius reminds Gallus that the name "Hylas" is classically an ominous one that Gallus must not let the nymphs of Rome ravish the boy from his lover; the poet proceeding to tell the story of loss of Hylas, the beloved of Hercules. Propertius also reminds a jealous friend, Demophöon, in the Twenty-Second Elegy of, the Second Book, that although he, Propertius, is so susceptible to women, still he cannot resist the charms of some handsome and sweet-voiced male actor in the theater; declaring truly that Nature makes each man with some weakness:

> *"Unicuique dedit vitium natura creato,*
> *Mi fortuna aliquid semper amare dedit."*

—a confession, not to say a predicament, that many an Uranian will echo, joyfully or ruefully, a long life through.

Uranians in Latin Drama.

Of the *vita sexualis* of the Latin comedy writers, Plautus, Terence, we have no data. Even in their pieces, allusions to homosexualism are relatively brief, vague or insignificant. But of what very plain things of such sort were said on the Roman stage, we can judge by references; such as the odd anecdote of the free behaviour of the audience toward no less a person than Augustus (who seems to have taken the episode in the best of good humour, with that curious democracy of attitude often met in the Imperial times) when upon an actor's reciting a line describing an obscene act by a male prostitute, all the theater "burst out laughing" and "applied the verse to the Emperor, with great applause."

Of Latin tragedians we have only imperfect data, as also only imperfect fragments, except as to Seneca, who has always descended to posterity as a rigid stoical moralist in theory at lease, and whose sober plays are not in touch with homosexual themes.

Juvenal and Persius the great social satirists, Juvenal: Persius. of Imperial Rome, are plentiful in similisexual allusions. We have nothing to warrant our supposing that their rebukes of such aspects of Latin fashionable life were not entirely sincere. But they do not repudiate it as any more repehensible than venal, shameful heterosexuality in the City. Juvenal (who pointedly refers to intersexualism in high life) writes one amusing satire on a young town-catamite, a kept-youth; under the title, "The Sorrows of Nævolus"; a most explicit and amusing complaint of his badly-paid and exausting *métier*.

Horace, in spite of his dionysian sexuality was pederastic, not only by what he indicates but from allusions of various members of his dissolute "set." His relations with the youth Lysicus are a topic of raillery from Martial. Martial also accuses Horace of carefully hiding away a certain handsome boy in his employ, lest visitors should desire him.

In considering the many apostrophes by Martial to his pederastic loves, Telesphorus, Alexis, Diadumenos, Earinus, Dion, and Hyllus, the homosexualism of Martial has little that is

Martial; Sentimentalist, Satirist and Pornographist

idealistic. Only in a few such tributes to boyish loveliness is the poet refined and hellenic. The same explicit animalism informs his Epigrams concerning female light o'-loves. Martial was a kettle that called every other pot black. Virulently obscene is the ridicule poured out against the homosexuality of acquaintances, Mends and enemies. He attacks Gallus (ever a special object, of mockery) Sextillius, Charinus, Nævolus, Bassus, Sabellus, and a dozen more, with the frankest *signalements* as to "technique" and—anatomy. The Epigrams incidentally constitute a sort of encyclopedia of Roman homosexualism. As has been said of recovering all the art of harmony should only the works of Johann Sebastian Bach survive, so had we nothing except Martial we could restore all the arts and methods of decadent Roman Uranianism. Let us cite only a few of the "Epigrams."

> "Mentula cum doleat puero tibis, Naevole, culus:
> Non sum divinus sed scio quid facias.
>
> Artemidorus habet puerum sed vendidit agrum;
> Agrum pro puero Calliodorus habet.

Die uter istis melius rem gesserit, Aucte,
Artimedorus amat, Calliodorus arat.

Mollia quod nivei duro teris ore Galaesi
Basia quod nudo cum Ganymede jaces,
Quis negat? hoc nimiumst. Sed sit satis! inguina saltem
Parce fututrici sollicitare manu.
Levibus in pueris plus haec quam mentula peccat
Et faciunt digiti precipitantque virum:
Inde tragus celeresque pili mirandaque matri
Barba nec in clara balnea luce placent.
Divisit natura marem, pars una puellis
Una viris genitum est. Utere parte tua.

Illa salax nimium nec paucis nota puellis
Stare Lino desit mentula. Lingua, cave!

Invasit medici Nasica phreniticus Eucti
Et percidit Hylan. Hie puto sanus erat.

Multis jam, Lupe, posse se diebus
Pedicare negat Charisianus.
Causam cum modo quaererunt sodales,
Ventrem dixit habere so solutum.

Addixisti, Labiene, tres agellos:

Emisti, Labienus, tres cinaedos:
Pedicas, Labiene, tres agellos!

Ut pueros emeret Labienus vendidit hortos.
Nil nisi ficetum nunc Labienus habet.

Triginta tibi sunt pueri, totidemque puellae:
Una est nec surgit mentula. Quid facies?

Rideto multum qui te, Sextille, cinaedum
Dixerit et digitum porrigito medium.
Sed nec pedico es nec tu, Sextille: fututor,

Calda Vetustinae nec tibi bucca placet.
Ex istis nihil es fateor Sextille: quid ergo es?
Nescio, sed tu scis res superesse duas.

Dormis cum pueris mutuniatis,
Et non stat tibi, Galle, quod stat illis?
Quid vis me, rogo Phoebe, suspicari?
Mollem credere te virum volebam,
Sed rumor negat esse te cinaedum.

Stare, Luperce, tibi pridem mentula desit
Luctaris demens tu tamen arrigere.
Sed nihil erucae faciunt bul bique salaces
Improba nec prosunt jam satureia tibi.
Cepisti puras opibus corrumpere buccas:
Sic quoque non vivit sollicitata Venus.
Mirari satis hoc quisquam vel credere possit
Quod non stat, magno stare, Luperce tibi?

Secti podicis usque ad umbilicum.
Nullas reliquias habet Charinus,
Et prurit tamen usque ad umbilicum.
O quanta scabie miser laborat!
Culum non habet, est tarnen cinaedus.

Sit culus tibi quam macer, requiris?
Paedicare potes, Sabene, culo."

Was Petronius, voluptuary, critic and literary dilettante—Petronius the brilliant "Arbiter" of the Neronian court-circle—personally

Petronius Apuleius.

homosexual? There is good cause to argue it, by indirect conclusions, as well as from the first great pederastic novel that we know of, the "Satyricon." Along with all the satire and heterosexualism and *fougue* of that remarkable social study, we discern a subtle sympathy, an earnest concept of love for the boy Giton. The story's real action condenses in the furious jealousy of the hero Encolpius and his companion Ascyltos, for the favours of Giton. The passing-over of the lad, now to one rival now to another, with a hint of his boyish constancy of heart for Encolpius, is the theme that holds the loose texture of the tale together. Giton rather wins us, spite of his effeminateness, and his want of moral fibre. The lively story is Greek, rather than Latin, in this quality.

In a finer instance of Latin novel-writing, "The Metamorphoses; or The golden Ass" of Apuleius, occur passages referring us to pederastic uranism, hellenic in suggestion. We know no more of Apuleius sexually than of Petronius; but we are informed that he gave over a wild life to marry for money, unsuccessfully—in which sacrifice he was not in the end more fortunate than are many men, homosexual or dionysian!

Nothing in the recitals of such historians or philosophers as Livy, Tacitus, Suetonius, Lampridius, Dion Cassius, Ammianus Marcellinus, Sallust and so, gives us indication that they were uranistic. They rebuke its sentiment as coarsened, venalized. But they are nowhere strong moralists against it. Suetonius depicts imperial homosexualism in decadent Rome with only capricious austerity.

Under the Byzantire Empire homosexualism pervaded more or less decadent Greek or Latin literature, to an almost unlimited degree; as did every shade of uranianism—especially pederasty, boy-love, and the sexual interest in the ephebus—pervade the Eastern Empire. Byzantium was saturated with uraniastic verse-writers and prose authours, as frankly homosexual in their lives as in their writings. A vast majority of these late-classic or other *littérateurs* have come downto us only in names; the destruction of libraries having been so general in consequence of either carelessness or—more often—of religious fanaticisms. Few cities of the world today are more distinctively pederastic than Constantinople, the successor of the social center of Theodosius, Justinian and the Constantines; whose courts were turbulent with the cult of the Venus Urania, however ardent the zeal for Galilean mysticism.

The Byzantine Epoch.

Oriental Belles-lettres.

Oriental literature, is continually uranistic. Like the Greek, we find it a pederastic uranism. One becomes somewhat weary of its accent of amorousness toward the beautiful boy-cupbearer, with cheeks just showing the bloom of puberty; as also weary of comparisons, hyperboles, allusions to wine, roses, lilies and so on, handed down from one Persian, or Arabic rhapsodist to another. We begin to wonder if no Oriental boy-lover ever was also a man-lover, capable of firmer sentiment, desiring the mature friend. Of course there is a large and important body of Oriental love-verse with the female sex as its inspiration—the 'normal' love. But the amours of Megnoun and Leila, are not more firmly a part of the Arab and Persian muse-erotic than the frenzy or melancholy of the pederastic Hafiz, Abu-Nuwas, Nizami, Djâmi, Ferid-ed-din-Attar, the world-famed Firdausi, Chakani-Haikaiki, Saadi, or the famous El Nefzaweh, the authour of the classic "Perfumed Garden"—which Sir Richard Burton translated—to have it destroyed by Lady Burton after her husband's decease. Omar Khayam has enough of the same sentiment to include that Anacreon of Nishapur in the same category. Many English readers of Persian and Arabic love-verse, through the "established" translations," must be reminded that in the largest body of such amatory poetry as the "Ghazels" etc., the personal pronouns invariably are masculine—"he," "him" and "his"; and refer us directly to a youth, not to any maiden, as the object of the poet's flame. A large proportion of English, French, German and other translators invariably changed to the feminine, line by line, the masculine pronominal and other references. Only lately has this misleading squeamishness been abandoned. The same sexual falsification has been the practice in translations of Michel Angelo's intensely personal sonnets, including those addressed to Cavalieri and to others of Buonarroti's homosexual loves. Prudish editors and commentators also have solicitously obscured the homosexual tenor of many of Shakespeare's sonnets.

To return to the East—we must not forget how openly (often grossly) uranistic are many episodes in "The Book of the Thousand Nights and A Night"; nor pass by suggestions in that other nobler and more virile work, "Antar." In "The Thousand and One Nights," the homosexual sentiment is occasionally not wholly pederastic. But it is so in the majority of examples; sometimes with the coarsest sexual accents. Examples are "The Tale of the Third Saluk" (Kalendar); "The Story of Bedreddin-Hassan" (which occasionally is a sheer rhapsody of oriental admiration for a beautiful young man; "The Story of Kemmerezzaman," to which a climax and explanation of mysteries comes by way of a scene of homosexual passion; the narrative of the host who wished to prove another man's sexual morals by the advances of of an homosexual boy, on a terrace at night; and in several other tales, formal discussions and many lyrics. The complete English translations of the "Nights,," by

Burton or Payne exhibit this matter faithfully: earlier English translations do not. The French version by Mardrus is even more illustrative, *passim*. In the "Thousand and One Nights" we are given liberal extracts from Eastern pederastic poets, classic and popular; especially from one famous bard, Abu-Nuwas, an incorrigible boy-adorer; whose stanzas waver between line idealism and—none whatever; including sundry particularly outspoken passages as to boy-prostitutes, a class to which Abu-Nuwas was incorrigibly partial.

Japanese Literature.

Homosexuality, especially pederasty, is met in a vast mass of classic and modern Japanese romance and poetry. No class of novel has beenmore popular in Japan; none more grotesquely and obscenely supplied. Few of these books have found their way to European acquaintance. They are sold in great quantities all over Japan. A limited proportion only are better than pornographic.

Early Italian, German and French Belles-lettres.

The scanty belles-lettres of the very early Christian epochs of Europe, do not long detain us. In Dante, we find references enough to his renascent Italy as a land filled with uranianism. The "Divina Commedia" consigns certain personages to infernal fires on account of sodomy, sometimes with plain language from the virulent Alighieri. We know nothing of Dante himself as being homosexual. Beatrice represented largely a symbolic, disembodied sort of love; but Dante had sexual intimacies with several women. Advancing to the Renaissance in Italy, and to the *novellieri* (whose tales, more or less were derived from social facts)—Bandello, Firenzuola and countless others, we have frequent references to homosexual intrigues and to homosexual men, of many callings. Bandello has several such stories—all of them coarsely comic, rather ridiculing the sentiment than blaming it. The famous "Ermafrodito" by Beccadelli,—a collection of epigrams composed in Latin, resembling those by Martial—indicates that its writer drew on his own early history liberally, for this or that theme of his obscene verses, offered to Lorenzo de' Medici and much esteemed by him.

We have already spoken of Michel-Angelo Buonarroti, and of Cellini. Fuller allusion to the uranianism of those remarkable men will occur when we shall consider the Uranian in other than literary aesthetics.

Homosexuality in the German Minnesingers has been discussed recently in considerable special literature; the types of minstrels exemplified in Wolfram von Eschenbach, Walther von der Vogelweide and Heinrich von Morungen, etc., etc. Their piety, as mediaeval

German Belles-letal tres—the Minesingers—the later Teutonic poets:

Catholics informed by a pagan-sensual temperament, rather drew them toward homosexualism than away from it. The tendency to glorify and idealize the feminine did not expel the aesthetic masculine from the poet-heart. Friendship by them was extremely sentimentalized; was made a cult. Mediaeval-Teutonic Europe rather substituted pederastic homosexualism by love of a man for a man, not for a mere lad. The Germanic race insisted on the psychic spell, the virile element enforced. It was uranistic love elevated in instinct and voice.

This progression has continued in modern Germany and Austria, in their belles-lettres; by the poets, the romancists, the dramatists. Typical Germans who were not only similisexual in their writings, but personally uranians have been Hölderlin, Platen, Iffland, Hebbel and von Kleist; the sombre Lenau—that Hungaro-Austrian Shelly; Mosenthal; Alfred Meissner (the latter's life being concluded under an homosexual penumbra) and Alexander von Sternberg. But much of what was uranistically significant in the histories of these men was scarcely understood till they had long passed out of the world. Only with full publication of diaries, letters, and so on, held back for a greater or longer period (by accident or by dread of publicity) have such homosexual individualities became incontestable. A special chapter, of this study is given to the brilliant poet and dramatist August von Platen, whose remarkable diary has only lately been accessible.

It is a salient fact that in no other language is annually published so much distinctive literature of the similisexual instincts—novels, essays, poems, dramas—as in German. No other presses are as occupied with the topic as are those of Germany and Austria-Hungary. This belleslettres element is to be distinguished from the wide output of scientific publications, which are of first importance to an up-to-date knowledge of the subject. Leipzig, Berlin, Munich, Stuttgart, are centers for such books and reviews. The Germanic belles-lettres publication in a homosexual key, while often anonymous or under pseudonyms, and of qualified merit, have always included, and still include, the names of authours of first distinction; the classics not absent.

To both Goethe and Schiller tinges of uranianism attach themselves. An incident in "Wilhelm Meister" suggests Goethe's literary willingness to recognize homosexualism, and a personal incident in Goethe's later years (to which his verse bears witness) his mysterious feeling for a young Italian ephebus who crossed his path, caused his moral compatriots some uneasiness. Such an impulse would be part of Goethe's hellenism, Schiller was somewhat more distinctly an intersexual. Always cold to women, he was an enthusiast in his friendships with men. In the Marquis Posa, the chief figure of one of his best dramas, "Don Carlos," he has fairly embodied homosexual devotion and altruism. It is also significant, that among the unfinished works of Schiller was a drama intended to be based essentially on homosexualism, "The Knights of Malta"; while a novel, "The Game of Destiny," was another such project.

With Friedrich Hölderlin (1770–1843) we meet a sort of *revenant* from the Greek Academy, embodied in a German.[4] Hölderlin through his melancholy life (prolonged while in dementia) was wholly homosexual, save in a short and superficial episode—his sentiment for the brilliant wife of Gontard. Hölderlin's chief tie, that with his faithful Eduard Sinclair, was of passionate uranianism, a quality obvious in his writings, both of verse and prose.

Hölderlin.

The following extract from Hölderlin's novel "Hyperion" illustrates the quality of hellenic similisexuality in that book. The scene and time of the tale are modern Greece, and the hero Hyperion is a young Greek who has been educated under German culture, only to reject it rapidly and scornfully. He has returned to his native land shortly before a Greco-Turkish struggle in 1770. He is hyperæsthetic, patriotic, quite pagan in his temperament. He wanders for awhile in unfrequented rural districts, meditating and yearning romantically—to which phase are devoted the first chapters of the story—at most a slender matter. When alone in Asia Minor, he happens upon another mysterious rover, named Alabanda, somewhat his senior, who is a neo-hellenic kind of Childe Harold. With Alabanda is cemented an uranian bond. In spite of the sentimentality of the style, the episode has some graphic quality:

---

4. A considerable study of Hölderlin, published some years ago, by the present writer, deals somewhat minutely with Hölderlin's hellenism.

"The summer was nearly over; I had now the gloomy days of rain, and the whistling of the wind and the swollen rush of the mountain torrents about me: and Nature which had been like a foaming spring, leaping in the forest-plants and trees, now was in a melancholy mood, shutting herself into herself—as did I.

I would fain have carried about within me for the coming time whatever I could of all the vanishing life about me: I would have stored up all that out there, in the forests, I cared so much for: inasmuch as I knew that another year would not find me here, among these trees and hills: hence, I daily walked or rode more than usual, in the neighbourhood of Smyrna.

But what also particularly led me to be out and about so, was a secret longing to see again a certain stranger, whom, during a short time, I had met every day, under the trees, outside the gates of Smyrna.

"Like a youthful Titan stalking among dwarfs, so had this magnificent young apparition seemed to me; even the crowd covertly regarding with eager eyes his beauty, his height, his vigour, the warm, sunburned head, that were a refreshment to see: and it had been a thrilling moment for myself when the stranger's eye (for which even the free air seemed too contracted an aether) cast about with a careless pride, had met my own glance, when we had blushed at so noticing one another and had turned away.

"One evening I had been riding deep into the forest, and was coming homeward late. I had dismounted, and was leading my horse down a steep, lonely path, over tree-roots and stones. Then, as I picked my way along through the bushes that opened before me, suddenly a couple of common highwaymen attacked me. During the first instants, I had some trouble to ward off the two swords drawn upon me; but the men were already wearied out with earlier activities, and I was soon out of any danger from them. I mounted, and rode on.

At the foot of the mountain, between the woods and the rocks, stretched a little meadow. It was a bright night. The moon had just risen above the trees. At some distance I saw a horse stretched out dead on the greensward; some men were lying motionless around the horse.

"Who are you?" I cried out.

"You are Hyperion!" called to me in return, a fine round voice, as if its owner were pleasantly surprised. He continued "—You know me, too; for I meet you each day under the trees, at the town-gate,"

My horse and I flew to him like an arrow. I knew him, and I leaped from my saddle.

"A good evening to you!" exclaimed this winning Unknown, looking at me with a kind of wild tenderness, and pressing my hand in his sinewy ones-a contact that I felt in my innermost being.

Ah, now I knew that the emptiness of life was over for me!

Alabanda, for so was the stranger named, proceeded to tell me his story: how he and his servant had been attacked by the robbers of the neighbourhood, as had I; how he had put them to flight before meeting me; had lost his way; and so had been waiting alone in this spot. He pointed to his dead steed, adding sadly:

"The affair has cost me a friend, you see."

I gave my own horse to his servant, and we walked onward together.

"All this has served us both quite right," I said, as we went along, arm in arm. "Why have we two been so tardy to know one another?—always delaying, until accident itself brings us to each other?"

"As to that matter," responded Alabanda, "you have been the colder one; the blame is yours. I have been riding after you, this very day."

"Friend," I exclaimed, "you shall never be my forerunner in our love!"

Ever more and more joyful, and deeper within the natures of each other, did we feel ourselves growing, now that we had met. Coming near to the city, and passing a good khan that stood amid plashing fountains and scent laden-fruit trees, we resolved to pass the night there. Long did we sit together in the open window. A deep spiritual hush had come ever us. Earth and sea were silent as the stars that looked down on us. Scarcely a breeze from the waters came into our room, to play with the lights and shadows; scarcely the strongest notes of some distant music reached to us The occasional thunder in the highest aether overhead sounded from afar in the stillness, like the breathing of a giant in his terrifying dream.

Our souls came together all the more vehemently, because so involuntarily had come at last their joining. We met like two brooks that rush down from the hills, breaking past the weight of earth and stone and rotten wood and all that first burdensome chaos, to make a wayto each other; until, with the same strength of current, they go onward in one majestic stream, to the open sea.

He, on his side, driven hither and thither among strangers, sent forth from his home by destiny and the cruelty of man; embittered and grown ruder and ruder since earliest youth, though with a heart in his breast ever full of love and of yearning, struggling forth from the rough outer shell of his personality toward a kindlier element: I, on my part, already so set aside, so lonely and strange among the men about me and, yet so full of hope, so full of expectation of some future existence.

What should two such young men do, except clasp each other to the heart, with the glad swiftness of the storm-winds. . .?"[2]

The personal and patriotic relationship between Hyperion and Alabanda deepens after their first night thus together. Hyperion describes their enthusiastic companionship, and the sudden transfer of his own individuality to the more dominant Ego of Alabanda. Unluckily the course of their intimacy, after what Hyperion calls their "bride and bridegroom days in Arcadia," does not run smoothly, the friends being separated for a considerable time. Hyperion is wretched under this; but he cannot early see his way to their reunion. Later in the tale, on one occasion Hyperion and the rather vague heroine of the story—a young Greek girl, classically named Diotima, who gives a dionystic touch in the book are sitting in a garden, with some other enthusiasts. The homosexual friendship between Harmodios and Aristogeiton is alluded to, by one of the youths:

"When Harmodios and Aristogeiton lived," said he, "then there was friendship in the world!"

"We ought to plait you a laurel-wreath, just for saying that!" I exclaimed to him. "Have you then really an idea, a concept in

2. Transl. X. M.

your mind of just what was such a friendship as that between Harmodios and Aeistogeiton? Forgive me but, by—the very aether itself! I think one would have to be Aristogeiton to comprehend how Aristogeiton could love; and a man certainly would not fear a lightning's bolt who was loved with the love of Harmodius; for I am deceived by every thing in this world if that terrible youth did not feel a love vehement as Minos. . . There is nothing grander on earth than such a pair."[2]

With the revolt in Greece against the Turks, Hyperion and Alabanda are restored to their former unity, which is strengthened to an evenmore heroic character, in the key of antique warrior-love—by battles and vigils and camp-life together. In the naval conflict at Tschesme, Hyperion is dangerously wounded. He lies several days in unconsciousness, until he opens his eyes to find Alabanda caring for him:

"With tears of joy he stood there before me, so grand a figure to me. I held out my hand, and he, that stately being, kissed it with all the transports of love. "He lives!" he exclaimed,—"O Nature thou saviour! thou kind and all healing one! Wandering pair that we two are, now without even a fatherland, thou dost not desert us!"[2]

But the two friends must part for good and all, presently. Alabanda is subject to the orders of a mysterious political society, such as abounded in Greece at the time. He is already in peril of death, as a punishment for his love for young Hyperion, which has more or less drawn him aside from certain political services. The story concludes with Hyperion returning to Germany; lingering there alone henceforth, ever rancorous in his hatred of Teutonism in temperament and social culture. Hölderlin expresses constantly his ideals and personality during the story; especially when he sums up the German race as "—barbarians through all the ages, made only more barbarous by their diligence their and science and even their religion; wholly incapable of any high emotions, spoiled to the marrow for any felicitous sense of what the Graces bestow; insulting every refined nature by their exaggerations and their

---

2. Transl. X. M.

deficiences; dull and tuneless as castaway barrel-staves! A hard judgment, and yet I write—for it is true!"

A special study in this book concerns August von Platen-Hallermund, the lyric poet and satirical dramatist, whose heart-story is a long series of homosexual loves. For the most part

August von Platen.

unhappy in their courses, the poet has chronicled them in his verse, with a feverish courage such as has no parallel in European poetry. Some hundred sonnets of a personal and poetic eloquence; the imitations of Persian "ghazel" lyrics, penned with fantastic elegance, sprightliness and passion unsurpassed even from Orientals; his masterly Odes; the poets "Epistles," to "Cardenio" and others, besides a large number of poems under varied classifications: all record Platen's male-loving history with minute faithfulness. His personal "Diary," however voluminous, should be read by every Uranian that desires a mirror of the homosexual nature, as well as the "key" to those persons and circumstances that inspired Platen as a poet. There would be an embarrasment of uranistic literary riches in making extracts here from Platen's verse, The Ghazels and Sonnets of Platen constitute a sort of thesaurus, a Canon, of uranistic emotions; as well as the portrait of a noble-minded and brilliantly intellectual man of letters.

In the short Autobiography of the Austrian dramatist Franz Grillparzer, written late in the life of one of the most deeply *human* writers for the poetical stage since Shakespeare, Grillparzer

Grillparzer.

says, at one point of his narrative: "—It seemed to me at this time as if I would never write anything more again. Into this burdened mood entered certain affairs of the heart. I concluded to bring this condition in me to an end, by a journey. (This the poet made—to England, etc.) Of what these affairs of the heart were, I shall not give any account, either now or at any future date, although such have played a great—alas, not useful!—rôle in my development. I am master of my part of the secret: but not free as to what part belongs to others." This reference became better understood upon the publication of the fragmentary pages of the dramatist's Diary and Correspondence, with other documents. Intensely had Grillparzer suffered from love. But the warm affection for this or that female friend—(including his relations to Katherine Fröhlich) had but a vague sexualism, or none at all. Grillparzer's sexualpsychic experiences of any real depth—dignity—were uranistic.

From youth, until his sombre character had matured and aged, he was first and last, an Uranian, if now and then superficially "normal." Those interested in his type should not omit to peruse especially the record of how so proud, so secretive a heart could glow with uranistic fire, and how he repudiates by implication as foreign to him any other tender sentiment. Take one of his letters to his chiefest friend, to whom he was united by a classically uranistic bond, till the latter's death,—George Altmütter: where Grillparzer's troubled and unclear self-analysis is met:

"—You beg that I should describe to you '*her*' whom I love? '*Her*,' whom I love, you put it? Would to God that my being were capable of that complete surrender, that self-forgetfulness, that attachment, that sinking of one's self in a beloved object! But—I do not know whether I must call it a highest grade of Egoism, or if it be the consequence of an unlimited striving after Art, and what to Art belongs, putting out of my vision all other matters which I momentarily grasp—in a word, I am not capable of love. However near a precious other existence may attract me, still there is always a certain *Something* that stands higher before me; and this Something's influence so works on all other feelings that after a Today full of glowing tenderness, readily—without interval, without any particular cause—comes a Tomorrow of the most removed coldness, of forgetfulness, I might say of enmity. I think I have already said that in 'the feminine Beloved' I love merely the image which my fancy has made out of her, so that the Actual becomes an artificial creation which, has charmed me by my making a sort of compact with just my intellectual side; only to be so much the more strongly cast back on the least decline of my mood. Can one call that 'Love'? Lament me, and lament any *her* who may deserve really, for her own sake, to be— loved." "The consciousness of this unfortunate peculiarity of my nature has so worked that I have always as possible kept myself out of all relations with women; to whom my physique makes me rather inclined. Everywhere that I have allowed myself to yield, have come melancholy experiences; so much the oftener as a matter of course, because I feel myself attracted mostly or exclusively toward the type that is least suitable for me."[2]

2. Transl. X. M.

Grillparzer's relations to Altmütter were not always smooth. One early storm came at the time of closest intimacy, with a quite concrete similisexuality in the emotions. Grillparzer found that Altmütter was maintaining a clandestine intimacy with another young man, whom Grillparzer considered quite unworthy of Altmütter's regard, and much inferior to himself. He discovered that Altmütter even used the sacramental "*thou*," of German Mendships of closest sort. The entry in the poet's diary is on June 16:

"I went today to Altmütter; and while waiting I picked up some of his books and written things, as he was not at home. As I was glancing through the last-named matters, I came on a section of his diary, in which were some letters from him to Karl N—(I do not yet know his last name) and some observations on his relationship to this Karl. Certainty I have never felt the strength of my own friendship for Altmütter so deeply as in that instant; but at the same moment came, into play my strange vanity, which I so often have cursed. For—his letters referred to me. I read eagerly on, and kept hoping to come on some expression which made for my honour; but alas! I had made a mistake, I hit on nothing that was to my praise, and so came my pride into revolt: but more painful than that was the 'impression that Altmütter gave me of feeling himself disappointed constantly in the friendship between us. I hardly remember anything which has made so severe an impression on me. Wounded egotism, shame, and jealousy threw me into a state of mind which was only increased when Altmütter came into the room. I was undecided what I would do; but I could not hold back. I reproached him for his falsity, and then instead of giving him any explanation—which, by God, was simply impossible for me, as I was so angry!—I threw the diary down on the table before him. He did not excuse himself for having addressed his dear Karl with '*Du*!' How often has he told me that he himself, was jealous of my intimacy with Maillern, for which he has never had any reason—and now! The thought of my being supplanted by that young man is unendurable to me, from any point of view!"

"Since some time I have begun to notice that the force of my emotions grows less, decidedly—a condition of which I unwillingly convince myself—but which, for all that, is irresistibly clear to me. Like a dream, do I remember the time when in the moonlight nights I could forget the whole world; could elevate myself to a degree of emotional enthusiasm, to think of which nowadays makes me feel fairly dizzy. I am no longer in a state to turn out even a mediocre poem. . . In a word, I am an unlucky mortal, and if destiny does not soon pull me out of this torturing condition, I shall put a bullet into my head But fie! I am ashamed of such a contemptible picture of myself! Am I he who was once so full of courage and strength, ready to accept the course of destiny!—am I the fiery, the deep-feeling creature who fairly swam in all that was poetical, a part of the domain of measureless, vast fancy? I can endure anything except despising myself. That must be got rid of, come what may! One way or another! If no old road out of it all appears to my view, then I will make one for myself, even if the path out of my labyrinth be also that out of my life—I must break one, cost what it will. Another such a day as this one, and—!

"It is not possible for me—I cannot get the damned thought of it out of my head! This relationship (to Altmütter) that I have so long regarded as a part of my happiness! . . . Parted, parted from him who has betrayed me through every word that is more confidential with another *this* could make coldness into deep melancholy. *I*, sacrificed to a new-coming, unknown young fellow! of whose want of sound character his recent obtruding of himself has so plainly given evidence! And Altmütter, who cannot change in me my frequently ill-considered and repellant demeanour, he seeks now in the bosom of this. . . creature, the Friendship that he cannot find with me! Till now, he feels himself "always deceived in what is friendship"!—and therefore he flies to this other person! So then has happened what I have always thought impossible to happen, and Wohlgemuth is quite right; but the break is not through my inconstancy (with which Altmütter has always so reproached me) but through his own But where have been my eyes? Why have I not seen, this long time, his indifference to me? He in whose arms I lay in that holy hour; he who alone, out of all humanity, saw into the innermost of my neart; he is it who began first awhile ago to interest himself in that Arabian pedant! and he is it who again gets to knowing this common fellow—he can write to him, can call him "*thou*!"

Oh, that evening, so unforgettable for me, when for the first time I called Altmütter "*thou*," and set the seal forever on my friendship, with that word!—and now what misuse he makes of it!—And then, to make the thing complete, he borrows twenty gulden of him! That, just that too, has taken the worst hold on me! What a degree of confidentiality that stands for! Or else— Oh, how much have I been mistaken in thee, or how much hast thou deceived me!

"I must go to him again, I must have some sort of a clearing-up of the affair—I cannot endure to remain long in this mood. Still—what use in clearing up what already is clear enough? Well, the clock strikes—I shall go to bed, and find forgetfulness for at least some hours."

June 17, seven o'clock, evening.

I have been with him. He is innocent! The letters which I read are not meant for any real correspondent, and our friendship remains as firm as ever! Another man, in my position, would have still doubted him; yes, Altmütter himself certainly would do so: but no! no suspicion of the truth of what he has told me enters my soul! He is my friend, and by God! there is no shadow of mistrust in me! I feel cheered—easier in mind; but still melancholy has not yet disappeared."

The "explanation" which Altmütter elaborated to his friend in this curious episode of uranian love and jealousy, is apparently open to much more suspicion that his wounded Pythias thought proper to—formulate. Grillparzer seems to have been too miserable in the situation to be exacting.

Grillparzer during, his London visit took a strong sentimental interest in a young Londoner of foreign parentage, who was the poet's daily guide in the city—a youth named Figdor.

In the dramas of Grillparzer occur some striking passages that touch on the homosexual sentiment, the force of destiny in it, its power, and so on: He has also finely,paraphrased the ancient platonic theory of the original 'unisexuality' of man; of divided existences that have supervened. In the famous passage in "The Golden Fleece" cyclus, says Jason:

> "In my fair home a fair belief is held.
> That doubled, by the Gods, each human soul

Created is, and once so shaped—divided!
So shall the half its missing fellow seek
O'er land, o'er sea—till, when the lost is found,
Those parted halves unite, and forthwith blend,
Are one, at last! Feel'st thou, then, this half-heart?
Beats it with pain, divided, in thy breast?[2]
O, come!—"

Another vibrant instance, in "Well Dem Der Lügt" expresses well the immediate personal attraction between two men, and the subjection of one to the other, often part of the chemistry of their first intimacy:

"Only to see him walking through our streets.
Within me cried a voice—"Him must thou serve!
Him!—yea, though 'twere but as stall-boy!"

The same mystery of immediate, unreasoning sympathy between two human souls, before acquaintance knits their attachment, is admirably put by Grillparzer in these lines:

"Like flash to metal, magnet sped to iron,
A Something goes, a Current mystic, strange,
From man to man—from human breast to breast!
Yet 'tis not Beauty, Grace, not Virtue, Right,
That bind or shall unbind, the magic thread:
Unseen is Inclination's charmed bridge—
The more we point it out, the less 'tis shown."[2]

A. von Sternberg's Miscellaneous Uranian Novels.

Allusion to the military romances of Alexander von Sternberg has been made in an earlier chapter. But the homosexual soldier was only one type treated by Sternberg. He was a voluminous writer in his field, and what with his imagination and his use of historical personages he made a sort of portraitgallery of homosexualism. He was born at Reval, in Esthonia, far up to the North-East, on the Baltic; and passed his days

2. Transl. X. M.

in many German and other cities, especially at St. Petersburg, Dorpat, Mannheim, Weimar and Dresden. His life was wandering; full of the nervous restlessness of so many of his type. He lost this trait with riper years. He married when about fifty—a marriage of convenience, without obvious sexual impulse. He died in 1868, on his estate at Granzow, not far from Stralsund. To his natural interest in Pommern, may be attributed that element of personal or local colour in some of his tales, as we have seen.

Von Sternberg's stories, are a curious study. They have not been republished in German within many years. What English translations of them ever appeared (the present writer has not been able to find any) seem to have become lost. The most characteristic stories would not be admissable in England, though not a phrase that is not in good literary taste appears in their authour's pages. Their mixture of fanciful and real personages individualizes them. Thus in "Molière" we discover, as the mainspring of action, the passion which the great French actor and dramatist (when past middle life) felt for a beautiful youth in his theater-company, named Baron. Molière so loves young Baron that he considers renouncing his career; retiring to some lonely, rural spot with Baron, as his greatest happiness. But a tragedy develops, in which Sternberg also utilizes the rash marriage which Molière made, when fifty years old; young Baron becoming the betrayer of his patron's bed. In "Galathée," Sternberg gives us the reminiscences of an extremely sensual love by an old and eccentric ээрроуéзэ, Prince Favourite, for a marvellously beautiful boy, the Chevalier Hernsdorf. . . "I burned for him, I swore that I would possess him, cost what it might. Ah, what delight, could I but see those dark eyes bent on mine with love!—to banquet on those fresh lips and cheeks—so softly and sensually moulded!—which had not yet been desecrated by any sinful caresses!" . . . A quarrel leads to a duel, but not to a favourable outcome for the too-inflammable Prince Favourite; though his advances are not wholly declined by Hernsdorf. In yet another novel, "Saint-Sylvain," the action is of the time of Frederick the Great. One hero is Dionys, son of a Saxon country-parson, and bound by a homosexual passion to Count Floras von Saint-Sylvain, a, young nobleman, the more prominent figure in the plot. The narrative by Saint-Sylvain of his early love for young Dionys is closely analytic in passages. This story develops a situation of some dramatic strength, as other persons take part in it; including the father of Dionys, who is turned out of his parish on account of a charge of heresy—with a painful suspicion of betrayal between the friends. Next follows the imprisonment of Dionys on a accusation of treason; and so the tale attains a climax. In another book "Kallenfels," comes the history of Julian von Kallenfels, an Antinoüs, who becomes not only the protégé of his uncle, the President Clemens, but is loved homosexually to adoration by this elderly relative on account of Julian's wonderful beauty. Unluckily, Julian has a heterosexual nature, and he falls in love with Leontine, the daughter of a village-pastor. In anguish and jealousy, Uncle Clemens separates the youthful pair. Julian looses all trace of the girl, until he discovers her too late, only to have her die in his arms.

Of "Jena and Leipzig" and of "The Two Shots" sufficient has been, said elsewhere in this study. A longer story in the Sternberg collection, the "Memoirs Of A German Gil Bias," where the lively imagination and irony have Voltairean accents. The earlier reminiscences offer several homosexual figures and episodes, particularly where the hero, an officer named Xavier von Violet, describes his life as a page at the court of a certain eccentric Prince Heinrich. In the "Rittter von Marienburg" is introduced the secret uranianism of the Germanic Order, in its grim stronghold. Several scenes are notable, such as the "initiation" of the handsome Goswin von Wedenburg (seventeen years old) into obedience; the Grand Master of the Order, Ulrich von Jungingen having fallen madly in love with the boy, and being determined to enjoy him by any pretext. In this tale, sexual flagellation has a share. In "Winckelmann," Sternberg had no need to go far outside of biography, especially in ending the novel with the murder of the great archaeologist by a male prostitute. A graceful episode is developed, more or less fanciful, but quite in key with the character of Winckelman; where he falls in love, on the street of a village near Dresden, with a Saxon peasant-boy of marvellous loveliness. Young Arlo comes to Winckelmann's lodgings; an accident makes it necessary for him to pass the nigh! there. But Arlo is so perfectly innocent of all sexuality, so untroubled in emotions, his psychic purity is so exquisite, that Winckelmann cannot bring himself to lay a hand on the lad—who is docility itself. He guards Arlo in his sleep, all the night, seated by him, contemplating his loveliness, but resolute against violating it; fights off the sexual temptations that trouble the vigil involuntarily, and sends the boy away next morning as virgin in mind and body as when he came. This tale is managed with much delicacy and taste, while peculiarly homosexual in essence. The

Sternberg collection does not end here. It includes, "Claudia," "Iffland," "Kombat," and many others, shorter or longer.

Rather more than twenty years ago, the brilliant playwright and romancist, Adolf Wiibrandt, stirred up a brisk sensation in German reading circles by the publication of his uranistie

Wilbrandt.

novelette "Fridolin's Heimliche Ehe—" "Fridolin's Secret Marriage"—a cleverly symbolic title. In this story is sketched admirably the common problem for the Dionysian-Uranian—his divided inclination, now toward the male, now toward the female, if with the sentiment stronger for the male type. The brisk humour of the book skilfully alternates, with its graver notes. When dramatized for Vienna, as "Die Reise nach Riva," its performance created scandal, though nowhere does it too overtly condone homosexualism. A typical instance is a serious scene in the third chapter of the tale; Professor Fridolin's "confession" to his former "flame" (but ever fast friend), young Leopold—in the moonlight, in the park, after a lively studio-supper; describing how he is swayed so troublesomely by what electricians call 'alternating currents' of his dual sexualism—how he cannot marry, as he sometimes would like to do, because he lives already in a sort of "secret marriage"—with himself. His male psychos is wedded to his feminine one, both disputing his individuality, though neither of them suffices to each other; so that Fridolin is continually falling in love with now a youth now a maiden. This bit of self-study, in the mouth of Professor Fridolin, is a masterpiece of dexterous, swift, witty, analysis.

More suggestive even is an episode toward the conclusion of the story. The bisexual Fridolin after being fairly engaged to a charming girl, with whom he fancied himself "really and permanently" in love— all his boy-loves forever relinquishing his heart—is humiliated to find that uranianism reasserts its power. He fairly deserts the field, in a sort of panic, under circumstances—unknown to him—that make grave complications in the chaperonage and protection of the slighted young lady. They bring Fridolin face to face for the first time, with Ferdinand, the brother of the deserted *fiancée*; a handsome, manly boy of about eighteen, who has indignantly come to hunt out the fugitive Fridolin, to call the latter to strict account for his conduct to Fraülein Ottilie. But Ferdinand is even more beautiful in his anger than when in amiable humour. The susceptible Professor falls in love at sight with the boy! The lad's sister vanishes from his heart, a dream in which he no longer has any interest. The boy-loving moiety of his nature reacts. Little by little, he succeeds in explaining to young Ferdinand the outward tangle of coincidences that has so excited and angered the lad. The Professor's charm of manner, his evident sincerity, captivate Ferdinand, as they have done so many other youth. From suspicion and wrath Ferdinand's frank, impressionable heart is caught; a fervent peace is sworn. The story ends with their expecting to settle down together as tutor and pupil, for the fair Ottilie marries Leopold. Professor Fridolin is more than consoled for his superficial "loss";—with his Ferdinand in his arms. The story is extremely amusing, farcically droll in places, but subtly philosophic—a small *chef d'œuvre* in its kind. Here is the conclusion of the meeting between Fridolin and Ferdinand, with Fridolin's running fire of soliloquy, comment and tactful open-heartedness with the lad who stands before him in subsiding wrath:

". . . (Ottilie as a boy!—the most interesting boy that I ever saw in my life!) . . . Have a little patience, for once, please. . . (how becoming his bad temper is to him!) . . . and be so kind as to tell me in a couple of words just what has really happened. . . (Yes, he has just exactly the same nose as hers!—how captivating such a *male* Ottilie is—that saucy way of speaking to me! When he looks in that way at me, he has just such eyes as his sister's—*such* brown eyes!) . . . Where I have been to blame, my dear young man, why of all that later; the business now is to discover this lost sister of yours. . . (He smiles a little—he smiles like her, too! Oh, *what* a smile he has! Yes, he smiles more charmingly than his sister.) . . . You really won't have anything to eat? Well then, we must at least drink together, and out of this green glass here, Mr. Ferdinand. You allow me, an old professor (Fridolin was in his thirties!) to call you by your first name? (He nods, he smiles again! That fine-bred expression of his face!) . . . There—the sound of the wine in this glass in my notion belongs to the most charming sounds in all Nature—just like the lingering, caressing sigh of a first kiss—"

Fridolin stopped. All at once he thought again of Fraüiein Ottilie. But what a transformation had come to him! The thought of Ottilie now gave him no pain! He was himself again—the bachelor Fridolin, who neither should nor would marry. He was no longer the handsome "Count Egmont" type of man, sighing for a girl, but the "Professor Socrates" individuality, whose whole being could sink only into the soul of some youth. He collected himself, and thensmiled. For, it seemed to him that Nature, behind her veil, bent her calm eyes on him, and whispered, "See, my son! So do I sport with thee! So do I tempt thee back again, from the girl to the boy—and therewith do I lead thee back to *thyself*, and rocking thy spirit thus to and fro, so do I hold thee fast in a compact between thyself and thyself, as—Two. What wouldst *thou* from Ottilie? Here she stands, in another shape! Look on this gentle-natured, innocent youth here!—beautiful and noble-natured as thyself, Vivify his soul, educate it, All it, *win* it for thyself—why, it is indeed already thine! Was Socrates happy with Xantippe? No! Good, noble youths, to whom to be teacher, master, father, *friend*—there was his joy. And that is thine. It faces thee here again. Fulfil thy vocation!"

"The wine is capital. Herr Professor," said young Ferdinand gently, breaking the deep silence between them, but you are not drinking any of it."

Professor Fridolin came to outward things of life again: then he fixed his pleesant, gentle eyes on the boy—"You have called me "Herr Professor" for the first time. Be it the last, Ferdinand— for it sounds to me too unnatural—too inhuman—from your lips. "Herr Professor" indeed! How fortunate were those old 'Greeks who knew no use of titles!—who were just man and man, when together. Ah, call me from this moment "Fridolin"—and nothing else! All my young friends call me so—and I regard you already as my friend! Speak to me so, I pray you! Only as "Fridolin."

"Fridolin" cried young Ferdinand springing up in his exciteent, "what kind of mortal being are you? Can it be possible—ah, if it only were possible!—that you could ever really—care for me?"[2]

Whereupon the two new Mends, in this hellenic mood, throw themselves into one another's arms—as master and pupil, friend and lover, the older spirit and the younger mutually seeking and surrendering. The episode, like all the story, is of charming psychologic vivacity and grace.

---

2. Transl. X. M.

E. M. Vacano
("Mario Valmariaco").

When speaking of the professional acrobat as uranian, the name of Emil Mario Vacano (1841–1892) was mentioned. In the extraordinary career of Yacano, who in course of a life not very long,, and even if we allow for uncertainty of this or that episode in so complex a chronicle, was certainly acrobat, circus-rider, actor, nun, monk, ecclesiastic (to some degree of initiation) journalist, camp-follower, and successful *littérateur*, his avatar as a novelist is almost a mere detail. But it is a detail of importance. Of Yacano himself one can only wish, in vain, that he did not leave behind him the sort of autobiography which he planned. Such facts toward it as are available bewilder one by their fantastic, kaleidescopic incoherence. But as the career so was the man. In Otto de Joux's "Enterbten des Liebesglücks" occurs a considerable reference to Yacano. In Peter Rosegger's kindly and discreet volume of literary reminiscences "Gute Kamarade" is an interesting sketch of Vacano, if more particularly of Vacano's later and *quasi* literary personality, when the mysteries of his wild and wonderful youth were quite past, and he was ending his days in philosophic obscurity and poverty, in Vienna, or at St. Pölten. A more recent newspaper reference to him appeared in the "Wiener Journal" of March 27, 1894—some reminiscences signed "S. S." But the almost phantasmagoric Yacano is not yet clearly of record. Undoubtedly some of his books have much of autobiographic colour. He was ever the sport of his own incorrigible vagabondage, his brilliant but undisciplined gifts, his mixture of temperaments which wavered between deep religious sentiment, pagan philosophy and the impulses of a rococo voluptuary. Of splendid physique, which in early life was so bi-sexual in beauty that he could readily passed for a woman or a man (during his later and soberer years he wore a full blond beard and an aureole of hair) his stature not to great to be womanish. One of Yacano's long escapades was being celebrated (during years) all over the fashionable circus-going world, as "Miss Corinna" ("Mademoiselle Corinne") one of the most artistic and beautiful of female equestrians—engaged right and left by the Barnums and Wolffs and Busches of *her* time. As an equestrien*ne*, his adorers were numberless; but the secret of his virility was rarely disclosed. During the Italian war of 1859, when in travesty as a woman, and not suspected to be other than an attractive *vivandière*, Vacano conceived a passion for a young officer, and this relationship was so much more elevating than certain of his other *béguins* that ho decided to be a man for the future. But new escapades and changes, now to one sex now to other, followed. He passed months in a convent as a nun, giving himself seriously to religious life—for the time. His literary career was brilliant as brief; but his best books—"Die Gottosmorder" and "Die Heiligen"—and some shorter stories have not only unflagging verve but a superiour philosophic suggestiveness, and deserve to be remembered. With all Vacano's levity, cynism, capriciousness, in much he was a nature of fine ethical quality; generous, affectionate, a devoted son to his mother (whom he adored) charging himself with the care of the children of a relative when he was in his least prosperous days; and always a severe critic of himself. He craved affection and friendship with the accent of femininity which is part of the uranian ego. He died June 19, 1892, in Karlsruhe, at fifty-one; died not unwillingly. In one of his letters to Koseggor, not long before his death, he sounded a note that many uranians can echo. . . "Well—I shall close here today my little letter of chatter to you. My table is full of sheets, my portfolio looks just as if had the dropsy, so many unanswered letters are yet stuffed into it—I must clear things away, and I am so tired to death that no human words can express it—yearn so for *rest!* I feel just as if I were ending a long pilgrimage to some holy resort—but where one finds the church-doors all fast-shut! How I wish I could just feel 'slept-out' for once! But can one expect that anywhere down in this world of ours?"

In one of Macano's novels, occurs the subjoined episode. The hero of the tale, young Count Alexander Althoff, of remarkable good-looks, is roving about America (in the famous "Forty-Nine" period) in incognito, as "Bosco" as a circus-artist. Althoff is a dionysian-uranian. One night, when in poor spirits, he finds that a young Arab, an athlete in the troupe, Kassad, whose person and strength make him the admiration of the town, is similarly depressed. Different members of the show have received invitations from their feminine public to be guests at suppers, after the performance ends. But neither young man wishes for *demi-mondaine* or other female society; they are indifferent to all billets-doux. Kassad, like Bosco, is a dionysian-uranian; Kassad being described as "the pearl of the Beduin troupe, a youth of the build of Hercules, a creature as if cast out of bronze, with his ravenblack hair and his eyes like those of a gazelle." . . .

"Bosco and his new acquaintance were standing under the street-lamp. They read their "invitations.""

"Do you care to accept; dear Kassad?" asked Bosco. The athletic Bedouin shook his head. "No—no," said he in his deep yet soft voice. "And you, Bosco?"

Bosco crumpled up contemptuously the note that had been given him.

"Not I, any more than you."

Then the two looked at one another—a long keen look. And they had—*understood* each other.

Each of them had been invited by a young and pretty woman to a—tete-a-tete; and yet each one declined, and had sent away the two maid-servants who had brought them the messages.

Then each young man held out his hand to the other, with a strong, lingering clasp, knowing what each meant; and then they gave one another the kiss of Brotherhood. From now on they would be inseparable—united for life—for they *understood*. With them it was as Wilhelm Müller, the poet of the "Schöne Müllerin" cycle, sings in his verses "Quick Friendship," where the two travellers in a moment are brothers in heart.

"Come with me," said Bosco, throwing his arm over the Beduin's neck.

"Yes—come!" exclaimed Kassad.

And so they went along together. In the hotel, Bosco had his own little room. A little one only it was indeed—plain, poor, with only one bed. But they ate something together, and drank something together; and then they put out the light and lay down together, on that hard little bed, each with his arms about the other, with heart next heart. The gas-lamp out in the street cast a narrow, shimmering light on the ceiling.

"Brother," said Bosco, "awhile ago, when thou wast reading the note from the woman who desired thee—from the way thou didst so, also from the tone of that "No!," I knew that it is with thee as with me; that thou too art suffering as am I. That thou too art in pain, because of a real, a true love, which will not away from the heart, let one do what he will!"

"Thou hast thought aright," said Kassad; and he pressed his dark head upon his new brother's breast, and wept there—half for sorrow and half in joy that he could weep with a Brother. And Bosco stroked gently the tossed, black locks, and murmured soothing words; and at last he said—"*Now* tell me thy story" . . .

The narrative of the young Bedouin is of his early and only real love with a woman—an affair however wholly psychic.

> . . . "And then Kassad pressed himself ever tighter to his new Brother whom he had thus found this night; and he wept himself out, like a child—he, this strong-muscled, brown-skinned, barefooted athlete of the desert—poor fellow!
>
> And then, in turn, did Bosco relate to Kassad his own heart-history. A sad, a heart-breaking one. . .
>
> Long talked they thus together; and then they slept there together, no longer without consolation; for each true and feeling heart rested on just such another heart! . . .

While they were sitting together on the bed, in the early morning, with yet many matters in each others' lives to tell of, Kassad said to his new brother:

> "Bosco, thou seekest curiosities. I have one for thee." And therewith Kassad drew from the quiver, which he wore in the circusring along with his white burnus, an arrow, rusted with time. . ."[2]

After the young Beduin has told the story of this arrow, which is a family-relic, (connected with the murder of the young Prince Louis Napoléon, in Zululand, in 1879) Bosco hesitates to accept the gift, as too preciously personal to Kassad. But Kassad says:

> "No, I would not sell it; but I will give it to thee, O, my Brother! Does not my life itself now belong to thee, shouldst thou ask it? Art thou not my second Self?—another Kassad, just as I am another Bosco? Have I not given thee much more than any arrow—my *whole* self!" . . .

Such is this curious and touching little scene, in which homosexual-physical love is traced between the lines. Another episode is that in which Bosco—after whom all his female spectators and acquaintances sigh in vain—refuses the advances of a fair Mexican girl; thereby nearly

---

2. Transl. X. M.

drawing upon himself a peculiarly treacherous and horrible death. The story is a singular mixture of the serious and the humourous, the dramatic and the satiric, thrown into an extravagant plot; but is certainly artistic and picturesque.

Contemporary Ferman Fiction and Homosexualism.

A considerable contemporary series of novels, more or less openly and distinctively homosexual, more or less to be classed as real literature, is noticeable in German. This element grows larger annually. It is usually under pseudonyms, or is anonymous; and a portion of it is privately printed, or nominally so. Of course, the merits of such tales, their vigour of emotional concepts, ideality, refinement, truth to life literary art, sincerity of accent and originality are extremely variable factors. Many representatives of this class of novel make their way into the more "specialistic" German bookshops; being from publishers who particularize the literature of uranianism, scientific and popular. None of such recent stories are to be met in English translations, no matter if irreproachable in their aspects as belles-lettres. The present writer would be glad to cite passages from several of these newer romances—some evidently not merely romances—if space allowed. A few only can be briefly characterized:—

A recent story of the sort, with, a classical hellenic background and Greek types, is the "Eros" of Wilhelm Walloth, in which is depicted the tragic passion of the young sculptor Gorgias for Lykon, a trivial youth of great beauty, the sculptor's model. The boy, becomes entangled in a passing dionistic love for a woman-sculptor; partly in trying to do his friend a service of bad professional morality. But Lykon's uranian instinct returns; he repents his treason, and he commits suicide with Gorgias, the two casting themselves down from the roof of the Akropolis. This tale is typical of a special group in German.

Pernhaum, Kupffer, Kleist, Heyse, Dilsner, Langer, Kitir, Brand, Evers, Friedrich, Bahr, etc.

A story entirely homosexual in *Leitmotif*, and of considerable literary eloquence, artistic construction and taste, is the "Ercole Tomei" of Fritz Pernhaum. Like the majority of its congeners, it is tragic. Two uranian schoolmates begin life in a close physical and psychic bond, Tomei and his friend Buchner; the former a dionysian-uranian type, in some degree. They grow to manhood, and Tomei marries. Buchner's love for Tomei is disinterested enough to accept a situation acutely painful for him, though his adoration for Ercole is unchangeable.

He frequents his friend's home; but now only as a friend, repressing any demonstrative sentiment which can disturb the happiness of Tomei. This quite usual permutation of the relationship might continue permanently, if fate would not bring into acquaintance with Tomei, a homosexual musician, Büllman, who succeeds in carrying off Tomei, in a professional *tournée*. Suddenly stirred to pain beyond endurance, Buchner seeks out Tomei, and throws himself upon the pity of the latter, in a scene of strong emotionality. Buchner conquers. Not only is the rivalry of the musician overcome, but Tomei's Italian bisexualism, his old-time love for Buchner, resumes its authority, Tomei is willing to sacrifice his marriage to his friend. Unfortunately Tomei dies, through a revolver-shot. The re-uniting of the two uranians is not long for this world.

A group of other immediately contemporary romances of similisexualism includes "Anders als Andern," a book that in psychologic study, serious purpose and literary quality in general is among the best on the topic; in its basis suggesting the remarkable Diary of August von Platen, and conducted with, firmness of delineation, and taste; Schumann-Arndt's "Wir Vom Dritten Geschlecht" (a novel that includes a study of uranian degeneracy); Elise Kupffer's "Sein Räthsel der Liebe," with the contest of the bisexual type in a lover; "Der Junge Kurt," where the dormant homosexualism in the lover of a woman is vivified by her young son, so that the one emotion in the uranian Ego gives place to the other. We have also "Die Wahre Liebe" by Norbert Langer: tales and verses by Joseph Kitir, the Viennese poet and journalist; novelettes and collections of verses by Hans Heinz Evers, Adolf Brand and others.

Certain novels by the well-known romancist Sacher-Masoch deal with homosexualism, though this writer's stories of psychiatric sort concern themselves more with "fetichism" etc., in sexual instincts.

Apart from certain plays that indirectly, at most episodically—"atmospherically"—are touched with homosexualism, such as the beautiful "Prinz von Homburg" of Kleist, (1777–1811) who was himself homosexual; the "Hadrian" of Paul Heyse; and several others, occurs the drama "Jasminblüthe" by Ludwig Dilsner, in which is presented the struggle between two theorists in homosexualism. One man believes the emotion a perfectly natural, in fact, a bisexual manifestation, such as is the double sexuality of the jasmin-blossom; the other (both men are physicians) holds it

The German Uranian Drama.

as a perversion. The young son of the austerer scientist is an inborn homosexual. He becomes involved in a disgraceful blackmailing affair, concocted by another homosexual. His confession is made to his father; the latter is about to banish the youth from home and country, as an expiation. But the more humane and liberal-minded colleague intervenes, in an argument to spare the boy such an exile. The old dispute thus has "come home" terribly to one theorist! Why not try the boasted experiment, test the father's ideas of homosexuality—try the "cure" by a normal marriage? The son consents to the alternative. He becomes engaged—only to take his own life, rather than give himself sexually to any woman.

Another intersexual study *via* a psychic drama, is "In Eigener Sache," by August Adolf Friedrich. We meet a brilliant homosexual and parliamentarian, Doctor Auer, who loves a boy, a minor of fifteen years, of extreme beauty. Auer wishes to escape from the sentiment, yet without losing sight of the youth. He betroths himself to the boy's sister, who resembles the brother, and who loves the Doctor. Among unsuccessful suitors of the young lady, is a journalist and publicist, who learns of the intimacy between Auer and the boy. In revenge he denounces the unfortunate doctor legally, as a criminal under the famous "Paragraph 175" of the German Code against homosexuals. The doctor succeeds in defending himself. He is acquitted. His *fiancée* has never believed him criminal; she remains true to her love for him. In the curious last act of the piece, the German Parliament, in a debate on the Paragraph mentioned, is before us. Deputy Auer speaks in support of the suppression of the harsh law, and ends by saying that he takes such a view in the interest of personal and family life. A letter is brought to him; his *fiancée* has learned that he has been guilty of the offense of which he was legally acquitted. She has committed suicide. The champion of tolerance becomes all at once indeed a suppliant—with anguish and disgrace before him. In this piece, occurs the expression of opinion—or rather the non-expression— "I do not dare to say whether homosexuality be a crime, a madness, or the results of the maximum of intellectual culture"—a striking *pose* of the question.

The comedy "Die Reise nach Riva," August Wilbrandt's dramatization of his brilliant novel "Fridolin's Heimliche Ehe," has been mentioned here already. It will long hold its place as a sort of little classic in the homosexual theater of the finest literary class. But its production before the Viennese public excited a lively hostility at once; and the play has not seen the footlights since its tumultuous first presentations, nor is likely to do so.

Another drama of superior literary quality is the one act piece "Narkissos," by Elise Kupffer, the romancist and essayist mentioned above. It is of fine emotional currents, and occasionally rises to lyric elegance of diction, being at once a sort of ode to the beauty of the male and a deprecation of female loveliness.

To the poet and dramatist Mosenthal is due the libretto of at least one German opera which is often called "the homosexual opera"—"Die Königin von Saba"; that richly melodious and sumptuously instrumentated score, by the Hungarian-German Karl Goldmark. In the relationship in its text-book, between King Solomon and his adored favourite, the young Assad, who falls under the spell of the hypocritical Queen, there is a delicate but certainly not unintentional *Hauch* of homosexualism. Mosenthal himself was wholly homosexual; and died in the arms of a male friend—"the being he loved best in the world."[5]

Apart from quite medico-psychiatric studies of all sorts, now so innumerable in German, the Germanic essayist of belles-lettres class is not silent on the topic. A striking instance, which may or may not have been intended as homosexual literature, but which reads as a highly idealized kind, of plaidoyer—is that by Hermann Bahr, the distinguished Viennese psychic-dramatist, novelist, essayist, and critic in so many branches of æsthetics. In his charming little fantasy. "Die Hauptstadt von Europa," which appeared some years ago, in the Vienna "Neue Freie Presse," are subtle suggestions of hellenic homosexualism, on classical lines.

There are also numerous German fictions and other matters of belles-lettres by no means to be characterized as "homosexual novels," or approaching closely that category as to their emotional contents, plots, salient individualities and so on; which tales nevertheless contain brief episodes, types, or allusions that make them quite pertinent to notice

---

5. The "Harden Case," the "Eulenburg Affair" and other homosexual scandals in Germany in 1908 insinuated a good many allusions to homosexualism into German burlesques and so on, as well as into even more pretentious pieces. For instance, a perfectly direct reference was introduced into Eisler's comic opera "Schütz-enlise" (at least as that piece was given *à l'étranger*) where a bit of dialogue in the second act and some lively "business" made no doubtful matter of it—sometimes received with laughter in the audiences, sometimes with manifest disapproval.

in more minute studies of how far the uranian sentiment intrudes itself into the heterosexual romance in Germany.

Also in Germany has been published at least one periodical of belles-lettres kind, distinctively for homosexual readers; the little "Der Eigene" of Adolf Brand. Its career was troubled, and it is no longer issued.

As previously pointed out in another connection, the activity of scientific German writers in the way of studies—social, legal, psychologic, psychiatric—of similisexual instincts is very large each year. At present it is attaining by itself the proportions of a vast Bibliography; much in excess of that in any other language, and by far the most exhaustive, intelligent and progressive. In many cases the writers are well-known as uranians. In quite as numerous and authoritative instances not such, and impersonal in their relation to the topic. Both in the graver literature or in lighter presentations, the subject of the similisexual is now freely before German readers and thinkers, with an insistance and a variety of perceptions such as nowhere else.

————————————— The brilliant German-Hungarian lyric
Lenau: Madness and   poet, and poetical dramatist, Nicholas., Lenau
the Literary Uranian.   (Niembsch von Strehlenau) belonging to the
—————————————   classic galaxy of the first half of the nineteenth
century, has become to biographers a clearer and more, complex homosexual personality, as the dolorous story of his life has been unfolded from its mysteries. Few men of genius have had so stormy and tragic a history. Much of it has come to light only reluctantly, in fragments. The poet's lyric drama "Faust," his "Savonarola," and "The Albigenses" (in the first-named fantastic poem occurs an uranian accent) will preserve his literary fame; while the dark drama of his own life might well be a subject for a Baudelaire or a Poe, not to speak of Lenau himself. It has been well said of Lenau that in his career we find mounting ever higher, step by step with his intense idealism, and in spite of his poetical enthusiasms and successes, a painful antagonism with his *sexual* being; as with his intellectual existence. His incessant wanderings about the world bred a melancholy more and more emphasized in his verse, as well as in his own private records; and they never pacified the contrarieties of a secret Ego that terrified himself. His struggles culminated in Lenau's sudden, unexpected betrothal, in 1844; with the shattering by him of the engagement, almost as soon as it was undertaken; in the angonized scene with his betrothed, finished in the poet's frantic rushing from her presence with the cry, "One of two

must go mad!"—as Lenau very soon did. After six years in an asylum, he died; the glooming-over of his career suggesting the fates of Hölderlin, Nietsche and Schopenhauer.

As a classic English poet has reminded us, "Great wits to madness surely are allied." The literary, imaginative and aesthetic similisexual all too easily gravitates across the border of unreason. His brilliancy is too frequently the precursor of shattered nerves, especially if an ignorant anxiety and the intellectual sense of his strange predicament increase his life-secret. The feverishly tense sense of physical beauty, vain desire for it, efforts to realize it in at least word and page, invite perilous agitations of the poetical temper in finer types of homosexuals. The longing for an unattainable companion, for the real friend not merely a romance of his own creation, who may be passing him undeclared in the crowd—the dread of social obloquy, the moral struggles!—one should not be much surprised when the intellectual homosexual throws aside his pen to take up a pistol or a flask of poison; or becomes the subject for a madhouse.

French Homosexuality and French Belles-lettres.

Among the antique Latin romancists of similisexual land was at least one Haul. Homosexual literature of the imagination is to day abundant in France, though mostly ephemeral. An unpleasing trait of it is the tendency to depict the trivial, the effeminate, the decadent, the vicious phases; rather than those which are virile, wholesome and of finer psychic quality. Here the French man of letters, and French woman of letters, are,in key with the French homosexualism, which turns toward neurotisms, perversities, effeminacy, to the grossly sexual—to the decadent in general. In France the pederastic passion for the very youthful minor is strong. In no other European country are small hoys so much in demand by debauched elders, or by 'clients' by no means elderly. To a large contingent of Frenchmen who write 'eccentric' literature, or what passes for literature, homosexuality means merely a vitiating eroticism—hermaphroditism, orgies of jaded men with chlorotic youths, womanish in psychos and body. In other nationalities (as for example the teutonic) poets and novelists present, as a rule, a more wholesome uranianism; seldom laying stress on debauched febrilisms of Parisian kind. But the French novel-writer in the intersexual field delights in tableaux of obscene *détraqués*. Unnatural homosexuality, masochism, bestiality, flagellation, erotic manias, are incessant ingredients. The French Uranian seems hag-ridden by debased fancies and phases. This is typified in the romances of the infamous Marquis de Sade (1740–1814) whose stories "Justine," "Julie" etc., minutely pourtray almost everything that is repulsive in a diseased uranian psychos. The sex-emotions of de Sade himself, were maniacal vagaries, and he ended in madness. Of him something more will be said in a succeeding chapter. The problem of urnindism, of feminine similisexualism so widely prevalent in France, enter into many stories of the day. Lesbianism is the staple subject of a school of Parisian tale-tellers, who deal with it in the crudest way that anything like literary diction allows.

In French heterosexualism there appears also far less of the ideal, of dignified and virile qualities, than in any other society in Europe. France indeed is the land of an apotheosis of—vulvolatry. Of course one must remember that Paris is not France, and that Parisian story-writers should not be considered as wholly representative of French racial aspects. But even so admitting, there is an inherent racialism in the repellant materials and atmosphere of some of the worst 'sexualistic' French fiction.

Among what we may call classic French literary Uranians, sometimes expressers of its emotions in letters, have been, for example, Molière, Montaigne, Michelet, Diderot and Voltaire. The relations between Molière and the young actor Michel Baron, indicate the great dramatist as having developed into a dionian-uranian, as his maturity advanced. Many allusions to Molière's homosexualism were current in social literary and theatrical circles of Paris, during Moliere's lifetime. Boileau suppressed a series of ironical lines as to this delicate topic, and they are to be met only in certain rare editions of Boileau. Montaigne's closest intimacy of sentimental sort, with his adored friend Etienne de la Boétie, was uranistic; the noble and richly-endowed Boétie seems to have been completely homosexual. The story of Michelet and his *fidus Achates*, Paul Poinsot (the eminent geometer) includes the relation of Poinsot as an outspoken homosexual. Voltaire, whether ever physically and sincerely uranian or not, was one of the early unprejudiced and tolerant recognizers of the homosexual instinct; an accepter of Greek love as a legitimate passion, however mysterious and contrary to modern moral concepts. When Voltaire was writing for the "Encyclopédie" he attested this attitude.

In the catalogue of nineteenth century and contemporary French novelists and poets, who have concerned themselves distinctly with uranianism in its various *nuances*—authours who have in many cases more or less identified themselves personally with it—we have Balzac, Huysmans, Pierre Loti, Verlaine, André Gride, Mendès, de Souillac, Henri d'Argis, Eckhoud, "Rachilde," Péladan, Adelswärd-Fersen: while the subject has also been at least *abordé*, incidentally but explicitly, by Zola, Paul Adam, Oscar Meténier, Abel Hermant, Willy, Colette Willy, Edmond Fazy, Achille Essebac, Norvèze, Nozière, Raymond Laurent, J.-A. Raimbaud, Pierre Louys, Lucien Descaves, and a long succession. This study cannot be an anthology of them, nor even an index. Two of Balzac's novelettes.deal with, respectively, the masculine and the feminine similisexuality—"La Dernière Incarnation de Vautrin," and "La Fille aux Yeux d'Or"; and we remember how explicitly the dark and dingy "Maison Vauquer" was a "Pension Bourgeoise des Deux Sexes—et Autres." Joris Huysmans left "A Rebours," and a study (more such than story, so slight is that texture of the book) in his "Là-Bas," where we have not only an incidental "Black Mass" (not accurate however, in its details) but a sort of monograph on the career of the young Breton pederast, boy-murderer, and sorcerer, the Marquis Gilles de Rais (1404–40) to whom we shall refer under the topic of typical decadents. Pierre Loti's military and naval tales have already been touched upon; "Mon Frère Yves" and "Le Roman d'un Spahi" being typical. The voluminous fictionist and poet Catulle Mendès has written numerous homosexual sketches, almost invariably dealing with perversities. In the "Sodome" of Henri d'Argis is depicted a neurasthenic young uranian who after an agitating adventure with a physical hermaphrodite, falls in love with a beautiful youth named Henri Laus; has a stormy episode of his *vita sexualis* with him; and finally goes insane—the reader's last vista of him being a tableau of Laus watching his former protector "delivering himself up to a furious onanism," in the asylum-garden! These sorts of *agrémens* are typic of a large selection of French homosexual belles-lettres.

From the Belgian novelist Georges Écklioud came some years ago "Le Comte de la Digue" ("Escal Vigor") a story of tragic colouring, entirely pederastic in sentiment; the action taking place in a Flemish village. The aristocratic protagonist, is a homosexual of middle years. Intensely susceptible to the physical beauty of boys, ho falls in love at sight with a comely peasant-lad, whom he sees dancing in the firelight, at a rural festival. The boy becomes his; adoring his master and patron with an equally frank sexual surrender, regardless of consequences. The youth is torn to pieces by the furious villagers, whose morality is outraged to the point of madness. This book is perhaps Eckhoud's most representative one in its key.

The most elaborate, thoughtful French study in a novel of homosexualism, which the present writer has happened to meet— one not new—is "Les Hors-Nature" by "Rachilde" (Mme. Alfred Valette, one of the editors of "Le Mercure de France") which novel has been noted in another connection. "Les Hors-Nature," in fact, stands quite apart from other uranian tales in French belles-lettres, in its dignity, and in general individuality. In spite of a certain nervous roughness, and over-condensation of style, it has emphatic literary excellence; and in its psychology it has been carefully worked-up. It paints in nearly four hundred, pages, with much movement, the violent moral struggle of a mature man, highly intellectual, strong-natured, altruistic, austere (once meditating the priesthood but now agnostic) the Baron Jacques-Routier de Fertzen. He is indomitably proud, self-contained; is far from attractive in his herculean person. The object of his love is his young brother, Paul-Eric de Fertzen—a type as unlike Reutler as can well be, in his decadent and effeminized temperament. This young Parisian, Paul-Eric, about twenty years old, is a complex creation, but undeniably time to nature. His beauty is girlish, he has an hundred temperamental lapses toward womanishness; but he is yet indistinctly homosexual and has held aloof in indifference from such rapports. He has no end of vivacity, of wit, of a curiously conflicting, lively—virility, one may say. His disposition is utterly selfish, frivolous, and *taquinante* enough to take pleasure in tormenting the affection of Reutler, without appreciating its sexual force. Reutler's struggle is emphatically an ethical struggle. He believes himself alone in the world under such sexual torment. He will never let Paul-Eric know! He will even accept the cruel comedy of seeming to despise, to hate Paul, of humiliating and alienating the petted boy utterly—rather than confess himself unable to conquer himself. He will maintain the strictly psychic limits. One episode is that in which Reutler loses control of his temper, through Eric's own outrageously bad behaviour. He insults the spoiled youth so practically that Eric shuts himself up in a fury, in his own apartments in the chateau, refusing to meet Reutler. When Reutler begs him, for the sake of his health, at least to go down sometimes to the garden, the youth sends a curt note that he will go into the garden when the garden comes up to his rooms! Reutler therewith has a superb staircase, corridor and garden-terrasse built—as his tacit expiation.

Heterosexualism is made a complication of the story by several women; especially through a pretty waif, Marie, brought into the chateau. The final scenes bring not only Reutler's disclosures, and Eric's assent, but a voluntary death to the two brothers, as their chateau burns.

Two brief incidents only in this curious romance can be cited here—in part; the extracts being the first English translations of any portions of the story. The first is the soliloquy, the prayer, of Reutler, as he watches Eric asleep, still dressed in an extravagantly costly female costume, that of a Byzantine princess, which the lad has worn to a public masquerade-ball; where he has unfortunately disgraced himself and the family-name, by being recognized and insulted. In consequence of this incident, a duel is impending for Reutler:

> ... "Under the dais of florentine velvet, the "Byzantine Princess" was sleeping, and sleeping ill; for Eric's livery of infamy had not been yet laid aside. He was smothering in his double girdles; what heavy ornaments were left on his costume were bruising his flesh. The pearls of the dalmatic, the rosaries of amethysts, the rings, the Greek crosses, were in a tangle together along the charming form, pressing little by little into the skin; and even the fine threads of gold-lace were printing strange letters in violet on one of the "Princess's" cheeks. On her neck showed a tiny red fleck, like the bite of a vampire; her diadem was sliding off; her head, thrown far back as she lay there, seemed the head of some one dead, crowned so, with only the hair turned up in two bizarre crescent-shaped masses. The sleeper's mouth was parted; the teeth—of such dazzling whiteness—clenched a little; their setting rosy as if with blood. Her long robe fell in chaste folds; one did not see the legs, but only the shoeless feet, made more delicate to the eyes by the fineness of white silken fleshings— feet stretched out there, like those of a statue on a tomb. Still smothering, the "Princess" made an abrupt movement, putting one arm above her head.
>
> Reutler knelt down before the bed. Tomorrow the beautiful Princess of Byzance would awaken dishonored. At three o'clock in the afternoon she would get up, laughing still at the merriment of the evening; she would ring for her valet, she would take her bath, her douche, she would ask for piquant dishes—and not seeing anywhere her elder brother, she would strike her hand

upon her brow in despair—remembering—and calling herself a coward!

The elder brother!—he so necessary as the unhappy witness of all Paul-Eric's follies, the sad-hearted spectator, participant, in all those caprices!—Reutler hoped indeed that the Princess would not see him coming back again. . . Reutler had regulated everything as to the function before him, the new task that was now ahead. No, he must not come back, he *must* not live any longer—that would be too much for him!

Paul-Eric murmured an indistinct word—"Reutler"—very softly. Out of his sleep, the sleep of a spoiled child who still is amused at some excellent farce, the boy was calling Reutler, to show him Madame de Croissac, there in the box at the theatre, in all her rumpled disorder. It all seemed simply fun to Paul-Eric; he wanted to laugh at it with his friend—with Reutler, his only real friend. . . Reutler buried his face in his shaking hands.

"Lord," he began, thinking—praying—almost audibly, "I have denied you"—he did not say "Thee"—"and you have cruelly punished me. Perhaps it is just that which proves your real existence; yet if you do not exist any more within me, then I *recreate* you, O Lord God! I summon you to be existent, I call you; and my Will ought to be enough here to make you come down to me. Where is even the atheist, who when he has reached the very paroxysm of his despair, does not vomit out your name, as if from the very depths of his entrails?—does not tear out of himself the confession of your power, in the realization of his own weakness? If it be you who have brought me here, Lord, is it not because now you are willing to reveal yourself unto me? to hold out your right hand to me? Yes, Lord, I stand on that, now; I need you, once more. It is shameful! Oh, I know that well—you did not hearken at all to Him who cried out to you, "Father, if thou wilt, let this cup pass from me!" But your Son, he was a god—so it seems—and I, I am only a man. I do not want the divine mission of suffering which you have entrusted to me. Listen, Lord—it is not going to be allowed to you—understand that—to assault my honour without my being allowed to defend myself, because you have put me face to face with something unknown to man. You have set before my eyes a fiery Cross—one that is not met in your every-day problems for humanity. Really, really, Lord, you are carrying things too far!" Here a terrible sort of smile came across Reutler's face; he raised his head. "You, you are responsible for this new crime of mine. If I am not your Only Son among all mankind, I am for all that at least—quite alone. You know well that the shame of my soul is the very greatest of all shames; that nothing can go beyond such ignominy as that in me.—Take care, Lord! When I came near to being a priest, I missed holding you in my two hands; I missed the power of creating you, for the consolation of other men; of distributing out your body, sacred to poor human creatures who hunger for—illusions! Take care, then, lest to console me—me, the inconsolable!—I do not terrify you some day with my blasphemies; . . . crucify you with my finger-nails. Yes, I say it again to you, this is too much! You must come down here, to know what is going on! Come!—I will have it so! I am not mad; until this very night I have not to reproach myself with the least crazy action. But I know now that the fixity of thoughts can carry me whither I have resolved that I would never go— without you." . . .

"The only kindly choice that you have left for us is, I think, that we should be enemies: but I see that that kindness is not genuine—for you stoop now to take it back. Speak—at last! *Must* I kill him? Is *that* what you wish? Tomorrow, it can be too late; I shall not be here—the boy will be alone—and then"—Reutler burst into a strangled sobbing, "My life will no longer protect his, if I die tomorrow; nothing, nothing will protect this creature beside me." Reutler went on, as if now not quite sure of what he was saying, very softly, almost as if fearfully: "Lord, you are not a physician, no, for it is you have created all the diseases, all the nervous ills of humanity. You cannot know what things prowl around this being so dear to me, who has no other defender than the slave that I have made myself." Reutler clenched his fists. "Speak then!—come!—manifest yourself to me Lord! I swear that ten years of torture such as I have undergone, without complaint, they ought perhaps to be reason enough for such a miracle!—Lord, I do not quite know any longer what I am saying; and that means that I am sure to be saying what is true! Yes—yes—you *are* a doctor! Just think of it. For, you sent an angel, once on a time, to one of your servants—to an imbecile, *he* was!—to let him know that the gall of a fish was a sovereign cure for an inflammation of the eyelids. Don't you remember it? I am an intelligent man, worth the, trouble of your sending some sort of a messenger who will show me how I can preserve my eyes from the horrible vision of my brother here, my child, alone in the world, at the mercy of—brutes! Lord, my Will was strong enough for matters yesterday; but—but—tomorrow, escaped from the bullet-hole in my breast, whither is to go my Will? Can you promise me that if I am not here my soul, my breath, will envelop by their protection this human creature beside me? My Will! Why, it is strong enough to sot before your face the most monstrous of men, the most dreadful of enemies for you, another Satan—one who will end by honouring himself just because he is a Satan—one that shall find himself more God than are you! Are you daring to make so much of a plaything out of me that you will even turn me into your accomplice? Lord, I am crying out to you because my very pride is so great that it can turn for help only to God! Since you have dazzled, blinded me, by a superhuman temptation, make me your equal, Lord!—if you mean that I am to resist!

On his knees, Reutler pressed nearer to the bed on which the Byzantine Princess still lay, stretched out, as if on a monument. She had just let her left arm slip downward; and her hand shone near to the very lips of the unhappy Reutler. It was an extremely beautiful hand, that hand of a boy; long, narrow, tapering at the extremities; so much the hand of a woman, as Paul -Eric lay there, in that heavy sleep after the fatigues of the night-long ball. Reutler looked at the hand, in dread.

"No," said he, "that is not the hand of my brother! I do not recognize that hand—"

But he took it, and drew gently from it a ring, chosen from the others by chance—an opal, set in dull gold, which had come from Jane Monvel, the actress. Reutler slipped it quickly on his own ring-finger; hut it was too small for him after the first joint, and stopped.

Paul began speaking again—still fancying that he was talking to Geneviève, trying to calm her nervous crisis—his voice warming as he spoke; decidedly Reutler had not appeared to him in the vision of the ball, to see the disorder of the unlucky victim.

"I—have never—felt as much love for you," Paul was murmuring to Jane.

"Oh, my God," tried Reutler, "trembling in every limb now, is that the sign? Must I kill him? Must I spare him? Must I try to go back, to retreat? Ah, Beloved!—Beloved!" he repeated, as if echoing his brother's voice.

Paul-Eric did not awaken.

The elder brother rose now. Softly he went into the boudoir with its huge mirrors, which had always been Paul's dressing-room? even when he was a little fellow; and where still were standing two costly playthings of his infancy, ironical phantoms of his youngest life; two huge mannikin figures, in their gaudy costumes. One was a Punch, half in rose and half in yellow; the other a tall diver, the gloomy eyes in his water-tight helmet staring out like those of a corpse into space. Reutler bent down, and detached from the diver's side a small hatchet that hung'there. It was the same hatchet that Paul-Eric had used when he was breaking the pearl shirt-stud.

"I—I too," said Reutler, "am going to know now how one crushes a pearl—a fine pearl! I shall strike him on the temple—only one blow it must be—so that he shall not suffer. I shall shut all the doors tight—I will give my orders—nobody will come up to see anything, until my crime shall have met with its—recompense. Hurrah for the Shades—! We shall meet again, if our Wills are really our only vital forces—our all! Yes—now to set about it—it is simple, after all—and I wish it."

He returned to Paul's bedroom.

The Byzantine Princess was sitting up there, on her bed, awake now. But she was so tired that she could not unclasp the metal claws of her girdle.

"Reutler—what a torment"—said Paul, yawning, in an accent all the softer for the champagne and sleepiness. "Come here—help me, big brother, to get out of this—I am simply choking. . ."

Reutler stood there, motionless, letting fall the hatchet.

"Oh, my soul! Oh, my Beloved!" he answered very softly. "I shall try not to go back—to retreat—"

Then he fled the room, locking the doors behind him, not daring to look back; as if pursued by ironical phantoms—the diver, with enormous glaring eyes, and the Punch, in his costume of rose and yellow. . ."[2]

The final episode brings not only the confession—rather to be called surrender—of Reutler, and Paul-Eric's reversion to homosexual conformity to meet it, but also the inevitable tragedy. Reutler here has quite crossed the bounds of sanity. His servants in terror have mutinied, and he is to be sent to a madhouse. The chateau is set on fire. Reutler flies to his lonely astronomical observatory and study, far up in a tower; where Paul-Eric is sleeping—towards dawn, unconscious of the revolt of the domestics and of the fire. Reutler bars out all aid, and with Paul-Eric in his arms, half-cynical, half passional in his consent to their death, they meet it. But even to the last, Reutler's homosexuality is restrained to a passion more psychical than physical.

"The night-wind was storming into the building, blowing the flames after the very heels of the lost Reutler. The pack was finding the track! Reutler tore away the coat which still was smouldering on his shoulder; and halted, to listen and to look. "They are following me—we shall not go over this road again! Eric—up there—what if he be lying dead, overcome with his despairing terror not *waiting* for me! . . . What if I am not to find him?"

He was at the last landing; above him were glittering the tranquil stars. He made himself certain that the flames down below were checking themselves somewhat—to devour poor Jorgon. He reached the trap-door; the bolt had been adjusted as he had ordered. He entered the observatory, . . .

Paul-Eric was sleeping; half-naked in his draperies of a flowery Japanese silk; despoiled of all his virile ornaments, of all manly masking, his cheek, the cheek of a beautiful woman, once more resting on the gold bracelet that he wore on his left arm.

Reutler shut the trap-door behind him.

"God exists!" he murmured, looking down at that peaceful tableau.

Before Paul-Eric had gone to sleep there; he had drawn the great shade across the dome of the observatory, not wishing to

2. Transl. X. M.

be awakened too early by daylight. Around him was already the beginning of the reddening dawn, a tender rosy, light soon to be that of the sun. The ambergris with which was saturated the idol in its niche filled the cell of the learned Reutler, which was in fact completely turned upside down. The books pulled out of the open bookcases were scattered about in a sea; on the edge of the alchemist's furnace sparkled a glass of champagne, with its bubbles; a page of figures, Reutler's metereological calculations, was spread out in the middle of a desk; a fan thrown across it, had its margins covered with wonderful little drawings—obscene ones. Evidently the boy had been entertaining himself!

Reutler went to a closet, took out a slender flask, and poured, its contents into the champagne.

"There will be enough for two," he said to himself—"I hope we shall not have time to suffer. . ."

Once more, he listened sharply.

A dull roaring came up; under his feet it was beginning to grow warm. He caressed Paul-Eric's hair gently, and awakened him.

"What! Really day again!" exclaimed the young man, ill-humouredly, rubbing his eyelids.

"Yes—it is dawn!" answered Reutler, smiling.

Paul looked sharply at Reutler, and smiled in his turn. "You're awfully good to come up to—but what's happened to you?" Reutler had forgotten that he was in his shirt-sleeves; he, always so punctilious in his dress when with Paul-Eric.

"If only he does not guess anything!" he said to himself; then gently adding, catching up the champagne; "Aren't you thirsty, Eric?"

"There you are again!" cried Eric pettishly, "the traditional moral lecture is going to begin! They've been telling you that I was tipsy last night, and so you are going to talk hygiene to me?" His voice became that of a plaintive child. "You are always putting me into penitence, for something—you treat me like a schoolboy! So I've had to find out some amusements. I have been making love-philters here. Reutler, my big brother! your medical books have given me some perfectly extraordinary recipes! Ah, I haven't lost my time up here!" He made a face." And what about your *fiancée*, Marie? Is she running around the countryside, still?"

A dull sound could be heard, like that of distant artillery, or a storm.

"Yes—I have found her," replied Reutler with an ironical gesture; "she is down below. She is well—very well, too. And she has released me from my promise. So I shall never marry."

Paul-Eric stretched himself out voluptuously, and draped himself in the Japanese silk-stuff, taking care however to uncover his breast as he did so.

"Hand me the rest of my philter there, so that I can clear my brains" he said. "You look queerly yourself, Reutler," he murmured.

Reutler, holding the glass, was trembling.

"Will you allow me to taste it?" he asked.

"What, you? In my glass? Really you are scandalous this morning!" He burst out laughing. "If you do that, I warn you that you'll do a stupid thing, my big brother! One of my wonderful little powders is in there—and—and—between ourselves, Reutler, *do* you need it?"

Reutler, with one spring, was at the dormer of the room, and threw the cup out into space. "No!" Paul exclaimed angrily,—"It is disgusting! I've done well to trust your-loyalty! Have you any right to concern yourself with my dreams—? Good God, no more champagne for me then, no more of my aphrodisiac; and you will propose to me cold baths or a gallop in the forest?" Paul-Eric interrupted himself, to spring up in his turn—with a cry; he had just perceived the large red patch under his brother's shirt-sleeve. "Reutler, what is *that*—on your shoulder?"

"Nothing," replied Reutler hesitatingly. "I did not care to tell you—but I've been in a fight. . . the servants have been behaving like mutineers—they seem to think that I am going crazy—they have wanted to shut me up—like you here—me! Nothing but that. My beloved, do not be disturbed. They have been putting leeches on me, before the last douche—I've escaped from their claws, though—escaped to take refuge up here with you, you see. Don't be afraid—I'm not mad!"

Paul shook his fists in the air.

"Oh, the dogs! The brutes! The vile beasts! Now I'm not surprised at your melancholy looks. All this has been hatching itself out in the house, for a good while! They want to shut you up, do they? Well—they'll pay for it to me, Reutler, when I go down stairs! To dare to lay a hand on my big brother Reutler!—and—just *because he is in love with me!* What idiots!"

He threw his arms now around Reutler, and hid his face in Reutler's bosom. Reutler began to think that it would be very difficult to kill him, now. He had no longer at hand that revolver that Eric had thrown away; and the poisons left in the laboratory were all slow. " There will be other way left for me but to strangle him!—to realize indeed all the *impossible!*" he thought.

But he smiled still, even in so thinking; caressing Paul's hair; while Paul began lamenting softly to him:

"What—*is* going—to become of us?"

"I do not know," murmured Reutler.

The boy had not yet marked the Are below them, confined, but gaining fast. "If they talk about.madness—if they only might shut us up in the same cell—God, Reutler! What sound is that! That noise under our feet here? Listen, listen, Reutler!"

The elder brother pressed the lad frantically to himself. "Dearest—the time has come to be brave!" he said.

"Oh, I know that" cried Paul-Eric, in a sudden revolt. "It's Corneille, with his *'Rodrigue, as tu du cœur?'*—and so on! But no-no! Not this morning! Above all, not with such a dawn about us as this—a light that makes your face green! No, no—I don't want to die—to go down *there*—Reutler, when I'm only twenty—! But I wont have them shutting you up for a madman, for I won't live without you, Reutler—my big brother, my great Hercules! Suppose they come up stairs—they will kill us—"

"*Eric—do you love me—very much?*"

"How your heart beats, Reutler! You aren't a marble man any longer!" . . .

"And if I ask of the Princess of Byzantium that just for me, her adorer, she would be such a superhuman creature in courage as never there was yet? If I ask her—to look death in the face—and to smile at it? Are we two going to lie to each other, to cheat each other,even to our last minutes?" Reutler gasped the words, kneelling down now in front of the idol.

Paul-Eric stood straight up, a figure for the theater; wonderful in his blue robe, with its flowers and chimæras. He held up his joined hands high above his head, around which now began to glow the rose of the dawn.

"I should answer then 'I am ready!' And I should never speak a falsehood again!"

The elder brother opened the trap-door.

"Come and look" he said, "it is an odd sight."

The young man leaned over the furnace far below.

The first landing of the great stair was blazing. The flames had encircled in graceful volutes the acanthus leaves of the little pillars of the staircase. The carpet, devoured step by step of the stair, boiled like a purple wine; a rosy smoke wound in a spiral, up, up along the balustrade, carried along by the air through the dormer-windows in the dome. The whole donjon was nothing more than a colossal chimney. Little sparks rose to the nostrils of Paul-Eric. He drew back, choking. Reutler shut the trapdoor.

"You understand now?" said the elder brother.

"I should say I did!" returned Paul-Eric carelessly. He added, in his plaintive *other* voice. "It will teach us, big brother, to set up the kitchen-fireplace in the drawing-room! Hand me my fan— it's going to be warm here!"

He had become transparently pale, his young lips were trembling;, his quivering fingers, shaking like those of old age, brushed convulsively the stuff of his robe. But there was no cowardice in his eyes.

"Ah, Princess," exclaimed Reutler, "you are really worthy of all this apotheosis!"

But Paul-Eric was staggering now, and had fallen on the divan. Reutler fell down before those bared feet, contracted in terror.

"They cannot save us, no! We are up far too high for that! The joke goes pretty far!" faltered Paul-Eric, fanning himself mechanically. "And nobody down there who can climb up to us, either by outside or in! Your apotheosis, as you call it, is a pretty business! Nobody at all to admire it!" He hid himself in Reutler's arms. "When I think how you have come across all *that*—! You are a god! Only you must do one thing more—keep me from being burned *alive*. Where is your revolver?"

"I haven't it any longer. And to think it was you that made me throw away, just now, my very best poison—such a sweet one, that would have given you such dreams. A nice state of affairs!

"Big brother, I. . . That racket stuns me. Listen, listen—!"

The roaring of the fire was growing stronger. One could hear the wood-work cracking in the coridors. A thin smoke began to fill the room, the perfume in the idol grew ranker, with a sulphurous smell; little jets of flame filtered through the strong trap-door.

"I—I have confidence in Jorgon" stammered Paul-Eric naively.

"Jorgon is dead—at least I hope so, for his sake," replied the elder brother, rocking the lad to and fro in his arms, against his broad chest. "Burns, dearest, are not really very painful—just press your nails here and there along my shoulder, and I shall not feel any thing that hurts. Why, it's enough only to think of something else—of my love."

Reutler did not cease smiling; he was perfectly happy.

"Oh, you seem to be very well entertained" cried Paul, starting up in terror. "But take care to eittertain me, or I shall call for help! Oh, I—I—am choking—I am going to be afraid—I am going to be afraid! Reutler, do something to make me lose my reason! *I am afraid of being afraid*—don't you understand?"

With a vehement gesture, the young man tore away the silk from his bosom. The white skin—those two points of rose—they piqued the eyes of the tall Hercules who, looked down at them, with a strange look.

"That is what Marie did!" he murmured, with a sigh. ". . . Look here, Eric, you are not behaving well. Real beauty, real, isn't—that!" Reutler held up the robe around the young man's haunches, that it might not slip downward; then he carefully drew up the folds of what was to be so elegant a winding-sheet, draped it about the lad's bosom; and finally put his hands about that slender throat. Eric's face turned away from his own. "Yes—I love you! Don't call anyone, for it is useless! Dont think of anything now, except of the happiness it is that we are together—*free*. Put your head closer to mine. My agony will be much more terrible than yours—but I shall be looking all, the longer at you, and I shall not feel *the other burning*. Do you remember, Eric, my boy, the words 'I have made Nature herself the scene for my Will?' Look me straight in the face! Open your eyes wider—kiss me, for I want to drink-in your very soul. Yes—we are gods. . . !"

Only the first pressure of those powerful hands!—Reutler had strangled him.

The mad force of the flames forced up the trap-door; one single, enormous red flame mounted up, as if to devour the very sky.

"Too late, my little sister!" cried out Reutler proudly, to the fire, "I am still master in my own house!" And his calm face was bathed in a purple-red glow, as if splashed over with the blood of wars."[2]

Fersen.

A distinctly homosexual quality, chiefly pederastic and referring to very youthful ephebi, recurs in the novels, and verse of Count Jacques Adelswärd-Fersen—a sonnet by whom will be cited in course of this chapter. The most artistic of Fersen's tales is met in "Une Jeunesse." It is a simple and graceful sketch of the passion of Robert Jélaine, a young French painter—sensual and prematurely disillusioned but not wholly embittered—for a Sicilian youth, Nino, with a head "like that of the David of Verocchio." The boy is living with his grandmother, at Taormina. Nino has inherited homosexuality, though he does not know it. But the instinct, and consequent incidents, bring his sudden separation from Jélaine. The lad is led to undertake in Verona, a noviciate which is to lead him to the priesthood; for which he has obviously no vocation. He is expelled from the seminary, partly because of an intercepted letter from Jélaine (the character of which is too explicit for doubt) and partly because of the lad's suddenly awakened heterosexuality, his love for a young girl in whose society he has been thrown in his holiday-hours. The end of the talc is not a conclusion. Jélaine finds Nino, in his disgrace, sitting alone at night, in the half-ruined Amphitheater in Verona. His friend implores him, now that he is free and so utterly alone in the world, to return to him. But Nino refuses; be it in sexual bewilderment, fear, conviction that it would be an error,—or vaguer prescience?—and the two part. This final scene is as follows:

> . . . "At last after a long and slow climb, arriving at the top of the ancient tabellium,—like some gigantic cup turned upside down into which stars were raining—Nino distinguished a circle relatively light. . . Then suddenly the moon leaped out from the torn robe of the wet sky. The whole circus appeared, magnified

---

2. Transl. X. M.

by the pale light. At the same moment, came a sudden squall of wind, so strong that Nino just escaped being blown over. He gripped fast; and as he wished to take in, at one look, both the night and the city, he must needs clamber onward up to the last rows of seats. There he sat down, and looked on at the festival; For it was really a festival, worthy the caprice of an emperor,— the wild night playing on the ruin. The clouds, like resuscitated heroes, rushed along endless avenues, broad as the sea, or as their processions. Defiles that by turn were sumptuous or fragmentary, as marked out on the hard sky or softened by the moonlight, passed onward with the wind, before the imaginary stage-box of some Caesar! Then circling above the city's campanili and palaces, reflected in the curve of the Adige, sweeping across the flat country, they went on to be lost to sight in the south—where the flowers warm to life. . .

Nino felt clearly these things, though without force, without volition, as he sat up there. He saw himself, too, as some stranger would have seen him; the tears slowly came into his eyes. But a groan, at his side, made him tremble. Was that, too, a dream? He looked about him. Someone had just fallen down at his very feet, a lamentable human shape, shaken by sobs. . . Not till there came again a trembling blue ray from the moon did the lad bend his head, only to raise it suddenly with the cry—"Jélaine!"

"I have been following you for hours, for days, for months, for years—Nino!" the man murmured—"all my life was waiting for you! I could not stay away from you. I am willing to do whatever you wish. Insult me—strike me—hate me—revenge yourself. The only strength that I have, like the only weakness, is to breathe the same air that you breathe!—I have suffered, I have been dragging my life around with me as a drunkard drags his feet in the gutter! I have stooped to all cowardly things—I can be ready to endure all shames—only with one condition—that I see you, Nino!—only that I shall be near enough to you to hear your whisper if you speak to me, to inhale the faint warm odour of your body. You are in my blood!"

"Do you know what you have done for me with that letter of yours?" interrupted the boy with a hiss in his voice. "I have lost my road in life forever! Do you understand that?—in spite of your fine phrases? The Seminary? I'm driven out of it! Family?

Don't speak of that! Anything left me anywhere? Ah, yes,—for what is left me? An unhappy little girl, whom I have abused, ill-treated, like a coward; abused, yes! since only that line from you was lacking to make it clear that I was unworthy of her. See what you have done!"

"Are you then dreaming of that girl,—that Micaela, whom they have been telling me about?"

"Yes—for I loved her!"

"Ah,—and now?"

"Now I feel something else, more violent still."

"What?"

"Hate."

"For, whom?"

"For you."

"Bah! Hate is all the same a desire—!"

"Also a vengeance."

"Perhaps so, but one—remembers."

"Those remembrances are odious to me!"

"No" cried Jélaine, "you cannot have forgotten! You are not willing to confess that just those things were so beautiful. But your will cannot go so far that you can recall, without a thrill going through you, those kisses at Taormina! Ah," continued Jélaine, as if half-drunken with his own memories and words, "I should always have expected to And you once more, on such a night and in solitude! Look, I am here, in that desert-pathway of which you know nothing. I know all, Nino—your flight, your ruin, your scene with the old Chevalier, your leaving the house there. And so is it that with a last fearful hope moving me, I have been able to come to you. For, now, as it was of old it is my duty, Nino. In yielding to our embraces—in your looks when I speak, to you—in your dreams, in your actions, in your attitudes, in your beauty above all which is the divinest form of human art—since it is life breathed into a masterpiece—in all this I have recognized the ineffaceable print of my *initiation*. That, you will not deny!—When you think of engaging yourself to any girl—in your evoking any girl to your help -you go against Nature and against your future. It means only unhappiness for you and for her. One does not contradict Nature and go unpunished, Nino. The future is something that we make within ourselves, as something that is only Self, blindly Self. Nino—we two should do such great things together! Two hearts that throb with the same enthusiasms, Who are trying to look out toward the same ideal—they are made to understand each other, or to die!—"

"But what if the struggle is not worth while—for *me?*" asked the boy, thrown into sudden trouble, already hesitant.

"Ah, that cry is the sort which comes from people who last out their lives, but do not live them! There is a difference between enduring,—living on—and living! One must fight the fight, down here below. Do you understand that? It is truth, all the same. How you deceive yourself!—allow yourself illusions—"

"Be that so; but I have suffered!"

"Not enough; since you still believe in the kindness of this world. Have you not found out the masques, the puppets, the buffoons which are all about us, who sneer and snivel in mockery? For my part, I know of only one school where one can learn them better—the madhouse. There, in their cells, they show what they are. . ."

"Father Serafino used to tell me that. But, there was Micaela—she believed in me. . ."

"Nonsense! Has not a single phrase thrown at you, only one vain accusation, been enough to make her fall down in a fainting-fit!—to desert you! I thought you had more sense, my dear fellow! Except when women are mothers—which is their sanctification though not always 'except'—women are nothing but so many skirts with emotions under them! Look at yourself. You are their rival! How do you wish women to love you?"

"I—I do not know them. . ."

Jélaine was silent. Then after a moment, "Come—come with me." he faltered, while the wind seemed to snatch away the voice from his lips.

"It would have been better to leave all," answered Nino, looking over the town, where the lights were already extinguished. . . "better to say 'Never more!'" . . .

"Come—come with me!" repeated Jélaine beseechingly. . .

But Nino stood up, very pale, his lips half-parted but silent. In that instant, God knows what prayers, what remorses were sobbing about the world, without echo.

"Nino—come—!"

Nino turned away, with no reply. The sky was clearer now. The Milky Way already shimmered over Verona. Above the gray-black level of the roofs, dominating the marble balustrades and blanch terraces, rose the many campanili, slender, as if chiseled out with.their crosses. One would have said that he was in an immense cemetery. Crosses! Oh, there must indeed have been some part of the divine in those things, that whole generations of men should have lived, slept, wept, around that symbol of torment! Why not take it as after all emblem of the evil of a world?—the sign of our own disenchanted hearts? Imagination creates a large part of truth; perhaps the most charming part of truth since, it just hesitates on the side of error. To 'believe', has been enough to put Death above Love, to throw beside the tomb of a Juliette the grimacing munmy of a saint!

'Become a priest'! Facing troubled or disordered existences, the cloister or the chapel opens itself, in the kindly penumbra of renunciations. . . 'Become a priest'? The thought was to him—a mere lad, wounded and still wild—like that of those crumbling houses with no windows to look out on the horizon, with no gardens for letting in the light, but which, in tempest, shelter the poor who have no other hearths. The boy looked at Jélaine, who seemed in the night to be dressed, like himself, in a soutane of shadow. Once, at least, before now their lots had been separated. But then, a gleam of hope had subsisted after they had parted at the desert-pathway, like those red fires which shine down in the plains at night. Now those beacons were only ashes—it was all too late.

"Farewell," murmured Nino with trembling lips.

Jélaine remained inert for some seconds, crushed.

He understood that the word meant the boy's final choice. With a dull mockery, echoed in his head some words that he himself had uttered one evening—"We have the right to be free."

"What are you going to do, Nino?"

"My duty."

"You have not anybody—?"

"No."

"Take care, Nino! We are weak. You are going to suffer—"

—"For victory—"

—"And perhaps you will keep only the feeling of having deceived yourself; of having caused pain and evil about you. Some day you will know remorse—desertion—restlessness—"

"Which is—life!"[2]

A large anthology of contemporary French verse could be compiled, reflecting uranianism—especially if pederastic—in, or by, many types of lyrists. As the founder of a "school" of elegantly (or other) decadent verse, the uranian Paul Verlaine has described lyrically a pederastic amour with an ecclesiastical background, in a narrative-poem of some length. An episode in this particular Parnassus, was the recent suicide, in Venice, of Raymond Laurent, a young Parisian homosexual and *litteratéur*, just fairly started on his career; the authour of some poems dealing with uranian emotions. His tragic end is stated to have been the direct consequence of an homosexual passion, inspired by a young anglo-saxon acquaintance.

The numerous fictions of Achille Essebac merit by their individuality in recent French literature of homosexualism, a longer notice than this volume can give them. Of the

Essebac.

series, "Dédé" is of special quality; being a sort of romantic elegy—retrospect describing the instinctively passional love between two schoolmates. Their sentiment is unequivocally intersexual, though rather subconsciously such, and free from the least tinge of physical grossness. Essebac's other tales, including "Partenza" and "Luc" are in much the same vein, though more elaborated in episodes. The Essebac group is distinctively pederastic, in relation to love for young boys—the very juvenile ephebus; which sentiment has been pointed out as rather particular to French homosexuals of aesthetic tempers and education. Essebac's stories suffer from their authour's style; a manneristic, *recherchée* diction, frequently so affected and self-conscious as to be tiresome reading, and his key of elegy soon grows monotonous. Never theless, he has pages when (as if forgetting to write "for a style") he shows real eloquence of emotion and of phrase.

The French stage now and then is directly concerned with uranian drama. (To the personal connections of, Parisian theaters with similisexualism will be made a later allusion in this study.) For

---

2. Transl. X. M.

example, at the Nouveau Théâtre de l'Art, in 1908, was produced Amory's "Le Monsieur aux Chrysanthèmès"; a symbolic little piece, to which a well-known group of actors gave a brief vitality—only brief, in spite of considerable elegance and skill in construction and literary aspects.

The well-known review "Le Mercure de France," though its range is wider than any merely special currents of belles-lettres, devotes much notice to similisexual literature. Certain of its serials—by Georges Eekhoud and others—have been of such category. In this trait, though always subordinating it to literary aspects of a production, this important French review is unique.

Homosexualism in English Literature, and in English Literary Circles.

The Anglo-Saxon uranian presents himself to us less frequently as a man of letters than does his Continental colleague. He dares not. Social ostracism and criminal prosecutions, can easily follow. He may write books having homosexuality as an ingredient, whether in them he expresses himself, or is only an observer: but he cannot readily find a publisher who will risk their printing, and risk the legal proceedings likely to ensue; no matter how truly the work be one of literature, or how discreet and decorous the management of its uranian elements. Not all authours can afford to print at their own expense. The most offensively erotic stories, poems and social studies, with heterosexual passion in them, can be sold freely in English bookshops, are circulated in the lending-libraries all over Great Britain, and are reviewed in the British press. In contrast, a homosexual tale of the most reservedly careful diction and sensitive good taste in treatment, informed with high idealism or spirituality, and which might be "read aloud in a lady's drawing-room by an archbishop" will not be permitted British publication.

Yet the Englishman, ever belonging to one of the most homosexual of races and societies, never has failed to contribute to the world's uranian literature; in large part the authours themselves being similisexual. The Renaissance unlocked the lips of the English Intersexual, in prose and in verse. Warmed by that Italian sunshine, he has sometimes written out his personal message, with a genius of universal recognition.

Shakespeare: the Sonnets.

Beyond doubt Shakespeare was, for at least a part of his life, dionysian-uranian; alternating between passion for a beautiful young man, and amorous sentiment for a woman. No other commonsense conclusion is possible, in view of the Sonnets. Who was that youth whom the poet styles their "onlie begetter"? The mysterious "Mr. W. H—" maybe long disputed, and is probably unlikely ever to be known—whether he was the Earl of Southampton, or some other ephebus. But that Shakespeare loved the lad with a perfectly pagan, sexual passion, is not to be questioned. Those other sonnets that have a feminine *motif* (the word "onlie" in the dedication of the Sonnets is significant) often read like foils to those of the male love. It is as silly to try to reduce the sexualism of the Shakespearean personality in the Sonnets to mere romantic idealism and fantasy, as it would be to try to construe Hafiz and Sadi into spiritual lyrists and elegant allegorists. Men do not write, as did Shakespeare write, of their consuming love for a young man, of adoration of his fair body, of consequent jealousies, hopes, doubts, despairs, slavery, in such verses as those of the Sonnets from, we will say, the first to the twentieth or the twenty-fourth, (with the rhapsodic "What is your substance, whereof are you made?") unless such poets are, or would be, pederasts. It is either hypocrisy or idiocy on the part of a commentator on Shakespeare to misconstrue such addresses as "A woman's face, with Nature's own hand painted," or "Lord of my love, to whom in vassallage," or "Against my love shall be as I am now," or "What's in the brain that ink may character," or "O thou my lovely boy," or "That thou hast her, it is not all my grief"—the last-mentioned among the dionysian-uranian group. We know little of the personal Shakespeare. We know little of his life. But we know enough of the poet's matrimonial infelicity, and of his charm of personality for his own sex to support the evidential theory of his uranianism; even had he not made it into his poetical autobiography.

That the plays of Shakespeare contain so extremely few references of any sort to homosexual love is not more than remarkable, in view of the general uncertainty of just how much

Shakespeare's Plays.

of the text of any dramas that we ascribe to Shakespeare ever was from the authour of the Sonnets. There are many references to the beauty of boys; to the physical and spiritual charm of male youthfulness. We meet such in the dialogue about the supposed Fidele between the sons of Leonatus, in "Cymbeline." There is a flavour of sentimental homosexualism in the comedy that Orlando consents to play with the mysterious Ganymede. So too in the fascination which Viola, as a boy, exerts over the Duke of Illyria. But these and other passages are of elusive intent. One of the few outspoken remarks in the Plays comes in "Troilus and Cressida," where the railing Thersites calls Patroclus a "minion"; and adds explainingly, "male whore"—of Achilles. The portraits of Shakespeare himself have that curious mixture of intellectuality and sexualism met in many men of genius. But the Shakespeare of the Plays is yet a vague individual; an editorial, managerial and personal *ignis fatuus*.

The Boy-Actor and English Pederastic Tendencies.

On the English stage at the Shakespeare epoch, and much later, the custom of committing female rôles to boys of physical grace and beauty, must have exerted homosexual influences on impressionable Englishmen. "Behold divineness no elder than a boy!" found its echo in many a pederastic heart, after some performance of "Cymbeline," or of "As you Like It," or of "Twelfth Night." Samuel Pepys—not at all homosexual—speaks of seeing the famous young actor of female rôles, Kynaston, in a part that made the youth seem even to Pepys "the loveliest lady I ever saw in my life"; and Pepys was a most experienced connaisseur of female charms. There must have been many English "stage-boys," quite able when in their women's robes to excite other than tearful passions of uranian spectators, seated in "The Globe" or "The Swan" or at "The Duke's House"; even if Shakespeare has made his Egyptian Queen repudiate the idea of having "some squeaking Cleopatra *boy* my greatness."

The English Drama of the Shakespearean Era in General: Marlowe

Apart from Shakespeare himself, dramas and other matters from his contemporaries allude to male-to-male love and to male beauty, especially boyish, with a Greek-Italian quality. Presumptively, it often expressed the real personality of the writers—reflexes of the individual. Occasionally the subject of a stage-play or poem overtly brought such atmosphere into the printed page, the acted scene. To Christopher Marlowe's "The Troublesome Reign and Lamentable Death of King Edward II" we have referred. But even in that piece there is no crude accusation that Edward's passionate tenderness for Piers Gaveston or Hugh Ledispenser is more concrete than of psychic sort. Such a *motif* is somewhat enhanced in clearness by the dialogues between the King and Gaveston, as by the jealousies of Queen Isabella, who complains that her caresses are despised for those of Gaveston. Noteworthy is the bold word on the royal tie to Piers which the Elder

Mortimer speaks when leaving England; cautioning his nephew not to intrigue rashly against Gaveston:

> *"Nephew, I must to Scotland; thou stayest here.*
> *Leave now to oppose thyself against the King.*
> *Thou seest, by nature he is mild and calm;*
> *And, seeing his mind so dotes on Gaveston,*
> *Let him without controulment have his will.*
> *The mightiest kings have had their minions:*
> *Great Alexander loved Hephaestion;*
> *The conquering Hercules for Hylas wept;*
> *And for Patroelus stern Achilles drooped.*
>
> *And not kings only, but the wisest men:*
> *The Roman Tully loved Octavius,*
> *Grave Socrates wild Alcibiades.*
> *Then let his Grace, whose youth is flexible,*
> *Freely enjoy that vain, light-headed earl,*
> *Fer riper years will wean him from such toys."*

Marlowe's genius, unpruned and rugged, was part of a personality licentious, unrestrained and intemperate. His death, as we know, came in a vulgar brawl. Was he homosexual? Suggestive is not only his choice of subject in "Edward II"; but such descriptions of a beautiful young man as occur in his poem, "Hero and Leander"; and in the opening scene of his "Dido." Young Leander is thus painted:

> *"His body was as straight as Circe's Wand,*
> *Jove might have sipped out nectar from his hand.*
> *Even as delicious meat is to the taste,*
> *So was his neck in touching, and surpast*
> *The white of Pelops shoulder: I could tell ye*
> *How smooth his breast was, and how white his belly,*
> *And whose immortal fingers did imprint*
> *That heavenly path, with many a curious dint,*
> *That ran along his back. But my rude pen*
> *Can hardly blazon forth the loves of men,*
> *Much less of powerful gods: let it suffice*
> *That my slack muse sings of Leander's eyes.—*

Those orient cheeks and lips, exceeding his
That leaped into the water for a kiss
Of his own shadow, and despising many
Died ere he could enjoy the love of any.
Had wild Hippolytus Leander seen,
Enamoured of his beauty he had been.
His presence made the rudest peasant melt,
That in that vast, uplandish country dwelt.
The barbarous Thracian soldier, moved with naught,
Was moved with him, and for his favour sought.
Some swore he was a maid in man's attire,
For in his looks were all that men desire—
A pleasant-smiling cheek, a speaking eye,
A brow for love to banquet royally;
And such as knew he was a man would say,

"Leander, thou art made for amorous play:
"Why art thou not in love, and loved of all?
"Though thou be fair, yet be not thine own thrall."

Openly pederastic, in the same poem by Marlowe, is the passion of Neptune to possess the swimming Leander. Neptune supposes that so beautiful a mortal must be Ganymede, and determines to "enjoy him." The-god swims beside Leander, eager to rape the lad in the very waters:

"He watched his arms, and as they opened wide
At every stroke between them he would slide
And steal a kiss, and then run out and dance,
And, as he turned steal many a lustful glance,
And throw him gaudy toys to please his eye,
And dive into the water, and there pry
Upon his breast, his thighs, and every limb,
And up again, and close beside him swim,
And talk of love."

The opening of Marlowe's tragedy "Dido," presents to us "Jupiter dandling Ganymede upon his knee, and Hermes lying asleep," with the exclamation from Jupiter:

EDWARD IRENAEUS PRIME-STEVENSON

"Come, gentle Ganymede, and play with me:
I love thee well, say Juno what she will"!

—continued by a dialogue in which the boy bargains his favours to Jove like a knavish young harlot; his final demand being—

"A jewel for mine ear,

And a fine brooch to put into my hat,
And then I'll hug with you an hundred times."

In the English drama of the Elizabethan quality and epoch, occur certain catch-words and sobriquets, some of them of Anglo-Saxon, some of other derivation, that refer to homosexual characters and passions. Such are however more intelligible to philologists than to less erudite readers, being largely obsolete in the language today.

We do not arrive at any conclusion of Milton as uranian in examining not over-clear details of his personality and history, in England or when

Milton.

he lived abroad. There are however indirect, vague suggestions; his domestic life, his social theories, his passion for Italianism, and Hellenism, and the accents of his most lyric verse, which seem not merely imitative notes. Never was an Anglo-Saxon—albeit a Roundhead in so many affiliations—tuned finer to the harp of Greek pederasty, than was the authour of "Lycidas" (Milton's threnody on his dead friend Edward King so intensely beloved), of "Hylas" or of episodes in "Comus." One can half-forget in reading them, the luridly epic Milton, the Michel-Angelo of Christian themes in verse.

With the Restoration, and the gross sexual-sensualism of the Court and epoch of Charles II, uranistic passions came into removed public notice. Private "friendships" were full of the quality. It was the same sort of "platonic"

The Restoration Dramatists; and Other Men of Letters

atmosphere that pervaded the French Regency. But even debauched French conceptions became more vulgar in the English air. We have only to look into memoirs and correspondence of the time, into yet unprinted pages of Pepys, the letters of Rochester and Sedley, to know what was male to male love in the Restoration, exactly as love for woman had become lust. In all countries, in all lands, the homosexual passion takes colours of refinement or crudity, its aesthetic or grossly opposite, according to the social civilization about it. It does not degrade or elevate social morals, so much as become degraded or elevated by social morals. In the licentious dramas of the English Restoration epoch, though we do not find them plotted on the passions of the Uranian, are plain references. Perhaps the most outrageously open allusion to homosexuality in any theater, since the days of Greek and Roman comedy, even to presenting a homosexual in a state of excitement on the stage, occurs in Vanbrugh's famous play, "The Relapse," where an uranian bawd is sexually inflamed by the manly beauty of his complaisant client, during a visit at the latter's lodging. The episode, extraordinary in its crude suggestion of homosexualism is as follows. We may well remember that the play was one highly popular with the most aristocratic society of England, not to speak of the lower social orders in London, at the time:

COUPLER: Let me put my hand into your—bosom.

FASHION: Stand off, old Sodom!

COUP.: Nay, prithee now, don't be so—coy.

FASH.: Keep your hands to yourself, you old dog you, or I'll wring your nose off!

COUP.: Hast thou been a year in Italy, and brought home a fool at last? By my conscience, the young fellows of this age profit no more by their going abroad than they do by their going to church! . . . But come, I'm still a friend to thy person though I've a contempt of thy understanding, and I would willingly know thy condition that I may see whether thou standest in need of my assistance: for widows swarm, my boy—the town's infected with' em. Egad, sirrah, I could help thee!

FASH.: Sayest thou so, old Satan? Show me but *that*, and my soul is thine.

COUP.: Pox o' thy soul! Give me thy warm body instead, sirrah! I shall have a substantial title to't when I shall tell thee my project.

FASH.: Out with thee, dear dad!—and take possession as soon as thou wilt!

COUP.: Sayest thou so, my Hephestion? . . . The lady is a great heiress. . . If therefore you will be a generous young dog, and secure me five thousand pounds, I'll be a covetous old rogue and help you to the lady.

FASH.: Egad, if thou canst bring this about, I'll have thy statue cast in-brass! But don't you dote, you old pander you, when you talk at this rate?

COUP.: That your youthful parts shall judge of... When the fatigue of the wedding-night's over, you shall send me a swingeing purse of gold, you dog you!

FASH.: Egad, old dad. I'll put my hand in thy bosom, now!

COUP.: Ah, you young, hot, lusty thief I Let me muzzle you! (*Kisses him*) Sirrah, let me muzzle you!

FASH.: Pshaw! The old lecher...!

COUP.: Well, sirrah—be at my lodgings in half an Hour, and I'll see what may be done. We'll sign and seal and eat a pullet together; and when I have given thee some farther *instructions*, thou shalt hoist sail and be gone. (*Kisses him*.) T'other buss!—and so—adieu!

FASH.: Um! Pshaw!

COUP.: Ah, you young—warm—dog! What a delicious night the bride will have with you! (*Exit*)

As noted, Smollett's "Roderick Random" contains two episodes that show acquaintance with the prevalence of uranianism in England, in his day. In Chapter XXIV, an effeminate young commander, Captain Whiffle, comes aboard ship, presently followed by the Captain's equally effeminate friend, Surgeon Simper. With Simper, the Captain is accused of "maintaining a correspondence not fit to be named." Another passage is the long and audacious narrative in Chapter LI,where the homosexual Earl Strutwell (one of the authour's political caricatures) after hugging and kissing the good-looking young hero, presented to him by a pimp, tries to seduce Roderick by way of Petronius; entering upon a long panegyric of uranianism as being the most healthful and *fashionable* kind of sexual intercourse.

We are likely to repel the idea that the delightful cynic Horace Walpole could experience either heterosexual or homosexual affection. No woman ever more than stirred the heart of Horace Walpole. He had only intellectual and aesthetic interest in the sex. But homosexualism was in his blood. The quality of his friendship with Conway did not always remain passionless. In the Letters, one now and then comes on a passage warm enough to show that Walpole had a heart, given to

Conway with an ardour hid from gossips about him. We are almost equally likely to doubt if the philosophic and often acid Pope could so betray himself, in spite of Pope's artificial gallantry to Lady Mary Wortley-Montague. The great satirist and social philosopher was outlawed from love,by disposition and bodily defects. Yet underneath Pope's cold cynicism smouldered the fires of sexual desire. Once the flame broke into life, for a young and beautiful man, who despised the poet, being indeed incapable of understanding him. Pope was perceptibly a dionysian-uranian; for his misfortune.

Lord Byron: a Uranian. Dionysian.

Lord Byron is a striking example of the literary Dionian-Uranian. During all his life, the great English poet was more or less temperamentally homosexual; an idealistic, hellenic, romantic homosexual. In Byron's boyhood and in his university-days, his homosexuality was the most really passional emotion of love which he knew. In maturity, it retained its psychic hold. To many readers will seem incredible the statement,—one nevertheless well based—that it is to be doubted if Byron really ever loved any woman, save in that superficial sense which he himself despised. He did not believe that he ever fully surrendered himself, could surrender himself, to any woman. Even as important and durable a *liaison* as that which was his final one, with the young, beautiful, intellectual and devoted Countess Guiccioli, became presently a burden of which he was tired, socially and sexually. Under that entanglement, Byron chafed, and was scheming how he could bring it to an end, "like a gentleman," with decency and honour, when the Greco-Turkish War gave him an an excuse, apart from his philhellenic enthusiasms. He would never have resumed the intimacy had he lived. His marriage with Miss Milbank had no passion in it. In nearly all his affairs with his mistresses, in Venice and everywhere else, a sort of sexual contempt pervades the memoranda. Byron despised women, first and last; despised the sexualism of his epoch, while he made it so much a part of his outer, animal life. His own words as to the feeble hold that women had over him are conclusive.

On the other hand, how enduring and explicit were Byron's numerous friendships!—ties that were, to use his phrase, "friendships that were passions!" His journals and letters tell us not only of Lord Clare—that Clare so immeasureably loved by Byron,—Clare, whose name Byron could not hear spoken his life through without nervous excitement overmastering him, and whom to meet, even for a few moments, long years after their early life, was unmanning to him; but of Wingfield, Long, and the choir-boy Eddleston. There were many others. These were *loved*, as he defines it, with a vehemence not felt in even his deep affection for such friends as Hobhouse, Moore, Shelley, and so on. In previously alluding to Byron's boyhood, we have mentioned his passionate intimacy with a village-lad. But Eddleston has a clearer history. Eddleston was a handsome young chorister, who caught Byron's fancy and heart at the University. Byron writes of him, later:—"His voice first attracted my attention, his countenance fixed it, and his manners attached him to me forever. I certainly love him more than any human being, and neither time nor distance have had the least effect on my (in general) changeable disposition. In short we shall put Lady E. Butler and Miss Ponsonby to the blush, Pylades and Orestes out of countenance, and want nothing but a catastrophe, like Nisus and Euryalus to give Jonathan and David the go-by. He certainly is perhaps more attached to me than even I am in return. During the whole of my residence at Cambridge we met every day, summer and winter, without passing one tiresome moment, and separated each hour with increasing reluctance" . . . This is no ordinary college-friendship from Byron, who already had little to learn in discriminating the colours of sexual emotions. Never did Byron write of d woman in such a tone, in all his letters. His using the names of two women—the celebrated "Ladies of Llangollen"—is suggestive. Eddleston was far below Byron in social grade; of no particular intellectual gifts; and of highly musical temperament. He died untimely in 1811, in his twenty-second year, to Byron's unspeakable grief. The letter which Byron wrote to a lady, at the time, asking her to send back a certain little souvenir of Eddleston in her possession, refers to the same theme; as does a poem on "The Token." Another friend of Byron's young manhood, for whom a peculiar sentiment hovers between uranistic and dionistic attachment, was Lord Dorset. "At school," writes Byron, "I was passionately attached to him;" and he adds that although years had cooled the ardour "there was a time in my life when this event would have broken my heart." The account that Byron set down of his emotion in his last hasty meeting with Lord Clare, unexpectedly, (on a journey), is a witness to the enduring nature of their bond. Another passionate sentiment for a youth, in which homosexualism is even clearer suggested, occurred in Greece, in 1811. Byron's mood invited such an affair. The object was a young French-Greek boy, of great beauty, named Nicolo Giraud. Giraud was a model for the Italian painter Lusieri. Not only for the moment was Byron wholly free from any feminine preoccupation, but his heart was reactive against the sex. He saw young Giraud, found him "the most beautiful being I have ever beheld," and took possession of the youth with characteristic impetuosness. Moore makes a nervous allusion to the affair, as expressing interest an in Giraud "similar to those which had inspired Byron's early attachment to the cottage-boy near Newstead, and to the young chorister (Eddleston) at Cambridge;" Young Giraud completely dominated the poet. Byron made a testament at this date, leaving practically his whole fortune to Giraud—the first article of the document! In the poet's affection for one of his young body-servants, the lad Robert, are other *refléts* of no common regard. That Greece, and everything Hellenic appealed to Byron from the first, is appropriate. Greek in his intellectual and sexual nature, he was Englishman by birth but Athenian by heart.

Is there no uranianism in the mature Byron's verse? The writer of these pages has received, from a source that claims strong private authority in discussing Byron's homosexualism, a pertinent comment on "Manfred." Among all Byron's dramatic poems, none remains more a subject of speculation. What exactly is the mysterious burden on Manfred's conscience? that unspeakable sin, to bind him and the dead Astarte together?—a sin inseparable from passion. That it was sexual is indicated. It is the expression of a feeling out of key with ethical and social toleration, yet with a fearful beauty, and in near relation to some strange, resistless under-current of our mortal natures. Are Manfred and Astarte brother and sister?—or what else? Is incest their crime? Manfred's moral horizon is not circumscribed by any Church or theologies. He is in revolt against all. An exceptional deflection burdens this exceptional type.

From a letter before the writer he quotes the followin: ". . . When my grandfather had finished his account, which you can imagine was done with great embarassment, Byron said after a moment—"Pooh, I don't think any the worse of you for such an affair. . . Why, let me tell you I expected awhile ago to write a drama on Greek Love—not less—modernizing the atmosphere—glooming it over—to throw the whole subject back into nature, where it belongs now as always—to paint the struggle of the finer moral type of mind against it—or rather remorse for it, when it seems to be chastized. . . But I made up my mind that

British philosophy is not far enough on for swallowing such a thing neat. So I turned much of it into "Manfred" . . . Lord Byron then went on to give my grandfather some other observations on the abandoning of his original plan for the poem mentioned. My grandfather alluded to L. . . , and to the M. . . affairs. . . The conversation was interrupted, and before my grandfather had an opportunity to meet Byron again (though Byron expressed himself most cordially anxious to do so) Byron had left Venice."

We may then argue "Manfred" as, in a sense, an uranian drama, according to the foregoing; a sexual love between Manfred and a youth, or some more mature friend, as the burden on the conscience of Manfred—or rather the loss that oppresses him. Astarte thus becomes a psychic allegory; under her feminine personality is hidden a male relationship, which (startling as is the idea of incest) was thought by Byron too audacious a motive for the British public. The structure and even the diction of the play require little changing to meet the idea of homosexual passion, on which, has descended a divine Nemesis; a vengeance on Manfred for what he still feels—however against his will—as a defiance to earthly existence, to religion, to God, to human Being; all this, while he so adores the memory of it. He and that Other have been carried away, by their mystic and criminal mutuality. What part Manfred has in it can be expiated, forgotten, in only death. Perhaps not the transgression but some circumstances in it, of Manfred's fault, make him feel such remorse and longing for release. If this interpretation be correct, even in part, "Manfred's" vagueness as homosexual literature is a loss. In any case, the study is curious.

In the celebrated oriental novel, "Anastasius: or Memoirs of a modern Greek," by Hope, a work that maintains a respectable place in English classics, the authour has depicted his hero's hellenic relationships with two male friends. The first is pederastic in its colouring. It is the swift, passional intimacy between Anastasius and Anagnosti, a handsome effeminate youth—a male dancer. This boy induces Anastasius to seal their intimacy by going through a formal secret marriage, celebrated by a priest in a church; thus reviving a disused ancient custom—a plain relic of paganism. This intense friendship ends in a tragedy. The young dancer bitterly rebukes Anastasius for faithlessness to their bond, when Anastasius, for selfish reasons, is afraid to acknowledge Anagnosti before some political enemies. Anagnosti falls against a dagger drawn in the

Hope's "Anastasius."

angry Anastasius's hand; and dies. The second episode in the same novel is longer, and suggests the higher offices of Grecian homosexualism—through the ardent friendship of Anastasius with young Spiridion, his protégé and junior. Spiridion, saved from death in boyhood by Anastasius, acquires a supreme influence over the latter. He undertakes the moral reformation of Anastasius. Their mutual affection, for a time transcendent, is broken off in a foreign city, by a misunderstanding which Anastasius is too proud to set right. Spiridion quits him suddenly, when they are estranged, and returns to his home, and to months of unhappiness, before he dismisses Anastasius from his mind. Anastasius learns, in time, that Spiridion is married and has a family of lovely children. Anastasius, on his side, feels intense anguish and solitude at the separation; and bitterly reproaches himself for it always—as he may justly do. Lord Byron said this novel made him weep—for two reasons—first, 'the beauty of the story; second, that he 'had not written it.'

Both to Leigh Hunt and to Shelley attach episodes of their sentimental lives, earlier or mature, that have a similisexual accent.

Oscar Wilde.

The history of the gifted Irish novelist, essayist and dramatist, Oscar Wilde is a literary tragedy remembered by many contemporaries with grief. Wilde was in early life dionistic-uranistic. As he grew older, he became more and more conclusively uranian, notwithstanding the fact that he was happily married. Wilde's first literary successes were his poems, including the noble "Ave Imperatrix!" His dramatic, novelistic and critical work followed, including the dramas "The Importance of Being in Earnest," "Lady Windermere's Fan," "Salome," etc., and a novel of vague homosexual suggestiveness, "The Picture of Dorian Gray." At the height of his career, Wilde was attacked by a virulent personal enemy, the notorious Marquis of Q—. For a good while, Wilde's eccentric intimacies with young men of far inferior station and even of notoriously venal pederasty, had been whispered around London. Among a set of Wilde's more aristocratic literary friends was Lord Alfred D—, the younger son of the Marquis of Q—mentioned. Of this young man much gossip was current. Presently the Marquis of Q—, in a grotesquely vulgar fashion, publicly charged Wilde with homosexualism. Wilde felt obliged to bring the accusation into a court (April, 1895), as a libel; a step anything but well-taken. The case was not made out, and sentiment went wholly against him. A second criminal charge, from the Crown, was laid and tried. Put into the position of a felon under the English laws relating to homosexuality, Wilde was convicted, and sentenced to a two-years term of imprisonment, at hard labour. The evidence in the case was anything but a credit to the poet's æstheticism, or idealism of male-love. After his release, his wife having divorced him, his career broken, Wilde lived for a time in obscurity in Paris, and there died suddenly, within a year or so after his enlargement. For a considerable time the super-hostile public sentiment of Great Britain ostracised his plays and other writings: but British popular feeling has grown more tolerant of Wilde's name. Indeed, he may be said to have assumed, even to English dionysians something of the aspect of a judicial martyr. An exaggerated personal cult for Wilde (considerably due to imperfect knowledge of his individuality) and a correspondingly exaggerated estimate of his intellectualism have become noticeable in circles of English homosexuals. In France, the same curious error of perspective is common. The brilliancy of Wilde, at its brightest, did not reach the level of genius. His originality of thought, and even of expression in his writings, his suggestiveness as an aesthetic theorist, his epigrammatic independence in conversation and print, all are highly discutable traits. Again, Wilde's type of uranianism was in no sense classic. It was far below the level of idealism which his intellectuality would lead one to expect. His sexual instincts were concentrated on vulgar boy-prostitutes of the town. His receiving the halo of a "martyr" to homosexualism is also the less well-bestowed, since he repudiated in his last writings (though perhaps with his constitutional insincerity) the morality of the homosexual instinct, and so died "repentant." That Wilde was a victim of British social intolerance and hypocrisy, and of the need of new and intelligent English legislation as to similisexual instincts is perfectly true; but Wilde himself was not a little a shrewd and superficial poseur, to the very last.

The name of Lord Alfred D—is perhaps indissolubly linked to that of Oscar Wilde, as being the latter's literary protégé, in some sort; apart from any other relationship. Much Wilde's junior, and possessed of considerably literary ability, he early identified himself with uranian literature in such verses as the sonnet with "I am the Love that Dares not Speak its Name" and others, in the extinct periodical "The Chameleon"; in the sketch "Priest and Acolyte" (attributed also to Wilde at one time) in some well-written articles, analytic of Wilde, in London literary print; and in various other contributions. The sketch mentioned "Priest and Acolyte," depicts the passion ot a young homosexual priest and a lad, and ends in their drinking poison together at the altar. It is an immature trifle, not distinguished for good taste in concept or elaboration. Its authour has since its date advanced far beyond such productions, and seems progressing to a position of some distinction in English belles-lettres.

When first was published Tennyson's memorial to his dead friend Arthur Hallam, the

Tennyson.

passionally sentimental elegy, "In Memoriam," exhaling elègiacally so much psychological uranism, it met a storm of British rebuke. The young poet's glorification of his unity with "my loved Arthur," his feminine lamentations and apostrophes, were called worse than merely "maudlin" sentimentalizings. Tennyson and his friends, were compelled to defend the poem ethically. Certainly "In Memoriam" is open to the charge of being a homosexual threnody. It offers, despite its reserves, aspects of a panegyric of the uranian-psychological bond between two idealistic young men. Of "In Memoriam," when it appeared (anonymously) one English reviewer said that the poem was certainly the work of a woman—"the widow of a military officer!" Hallam, who died suddenly in Vienna, was perceptibly of homosexual type.

Italianistic influences of uranian effect, in the

English
"Pre-Raphaelites."

Pre-Raphaelitish "school" of English verse have not been distinctly studied. They are not vivid. In the Pre-Raphaelists femininism was pronounced; idealized, neuroticized, Catholicized. They affected a mediaeval or early Renaissance pose toward woman, sexually, socially and spiritually. The label of personal homosexuality hardly attaches to any of the high-priests of the "Fleshly School" or to the studios of its epoch. They cultivated a pictorial feminism. To Rosetti's youth a vague episode of homosexuality—bisexuality?—attaches; and in the verse of Swinburne are pagan suggestions, but of a deeadently French, colouring, rather than even hellenic.

The atmosphere of uranianism hangs around

Burton: Palgrave.

the personality, and some of the literary work, of two eminent British orientalists—Captain Sir Richard Burton and W. G. Palgrave. Was it the excursions toward—into? homosexuality that were bruited about in Burton's life, and his attention to the topic so exhaustively in his oriental studies and translations, which stood in the way of the political advancement of one of the most remarkable men in similar service, in all the contemporary history of English oriental workers? Only the Foreign Office can answer that query.

W. G. Palgrave, that subtly-gifted and adventurous traveller (of Hebrew blood) also a man of letters of fine individuality, was frequently spoken of as sufficiently "easternized" to "accept the homosexual." His curious and beautiful oriental novel, "Hermann Agha," with its scenes in the wild country about Diarbekir in the end of the eighteenth century, is a book far superiour to anything of its type yet public from English hands and eyes; a perfect mirror of life and character. Cast into a heterosexual romance, occurs the incident of an Arabian uranian friendship, better to be called love, in the bond between the hero of the tale, Hermann Agha, and young Moharib; a tie first sealed in blood, then ended in blood. One of the many exquisite lyrics in this story occurs in Hermann's agnostic lament for the boy—

> *"Could the Resurrection be,*
> *I had wished it but for thee;*
> *For, though changed all else, and new,*
> *Thou unchanged wouldst rise—and trug!*

From a contemporary English novelist Robert Hichens, a writer of superior literary traits and often of penetrant psychology came early in his career a brilliant little satirical story (or rather portrait-gallery) of London uranianism, "smart-set" cynicism and aristocratic decadence, entitled "The Green Carnation." In this were introduced, with more or less fidelity or exaggeration,

Hichens; Juvenile Stories; M. E. Coleridge; Dickens, and Passional "Friendship" in English Fiction.

personalities like Oscar Wilde, Lord Alfred D—, and sundry others of "the set" about the city. While nowhere being veristic as to word or deed of homosexualism, aesthetic pederasty is an obvious suggestion in the relationships of the two chief personages in the story—the effeminate young Lord Reggie Hastings and the epigrammatic decadent Esmé Amarinth. From the same authour recently has appeared a novel of quite other atmosphere and of more subtle philarrrenic *nuances*, in its sincerity of character-painting and delicate art, "The Call of the Blood." Here occurs throughout (in tact as a psychic mainspring of the action), the impulse of hereditary bisexualism, in Maurice Delarey; an artist suggesting a dionysian-uranian—of Sicilian blood though English birth. Between him and a Taormina youth, Gasparo (a type admirably presented) springs into being at once a vibrantly passional tie; though the artist is newly wedded. The background is Taormina; and the local colour and Ionian-Sicilian psychology are truthful. The scene in which Delarey watches the boy Gasparo dancing the tarantella is unique in recent English romance, for spiritual and pictorial management. The absorption of the lad's nature by his passional relation to his patron is conveyed unmistakeably, to the end of the tragedy in which they are involved. Whether the average British reader at all 'understands' the story is another matter, so artistically is it conducted, in diction and incident.

Fiction for young people that has uranian hints naturally is thought the last sort for circulating among British boys, and girls. A pathetic story "Tim" (mentioned in the seventh chapter of this book) a direct and specialistic study of 'psychic homosexuality' in two school-lads—one of them wholly intersexual in type—is nevertheless to be classed in the library for young Britons. The authorship of this little tale remains anonymous. Another juvenile, "The French Prisoners" by Edward Bertz, better-known by his active career in German belles-lettres, has a subtle note of the psychologic kind in question, in its emotional development. A recent story of Harrow school-life, "The Hill," by Horace Vachell (a book exceptional in its crowded field, for its vividness of characterizations, manly moral uplift and charm of style) offers even more than "Tim" the ingredient of an absolutely absorbing "passion of friendship," a self-forgetting devotion and intense admiration on the part of one lad for another—the 'god of his idolatry." A kind of mystic struggle, of which jealousy is a factor, against the evil charm of a third scholmate—the beautiful and conscienceless "Demon," as he is nick-named—enters into the the story. It has no hint (in fact a passing incident is particularly to the contrary) of physical emotionalism. But almost first and last it is suggestive of the key of sub-conscious youthful uranianism. No other emotional factor in the book is on the same plane of elaboration and import. Also in "White Cockades" a little tale of the flight of the Younger Pretender, by E. I. Stevenson, issued in Edinburgh some years ago, passionate devotion from a rustic youth toward the Prince, and its recognition are half-hinted as homosexual in essence. The sentiment of uranian adolescence is more distinguishable in another book for lads, "Philip-and Gerald," by the same hand; a romantic story in which a youth in his latter teens is irresistibly attracted to a much younger lad: and becomes, *con amore*, responsible for the latter's personal safety, in a series of unexpected events that throw them together—for life. From this writer are also to be noted in various periodicals a considerable series of dramatic studies of passional friendships between adults—in accent chiefly tragic.

A noteworthy historical novel, "The King With Two Faces," by the late Miss M. E. Coleridge, deals with the personality of Gustavus Third of Sweden. It is based on his strongly emotional intimacies, his favouritism, and the conspiracy of Ankerström, in which were intrigued against their unfortunate and impolitic sovereign many of the comely young noblemen, who played such mystic roles in his psychic life. The authour discerns in her studies the "abnormal" currents of the King's nature. Throughout the story, there are such phases—as to Fersen, Ribbing, and so on—that are faithful to historical analysis. Almost the final scene (a strange one, in which Fersen and his dying king look into each other's eyes confessionally, for the last time) is to be 'noted. The introduction of such an ingredient in the story is as reserved as one would expect in an English romance; but its authour's literary manner in general inclines to the merely suggestive, elliptical and over-terse.

The commentator on homosexualism in belles-lettres is often criticized for supposing such an ingredient to be latent where it does not at all conclusively appear. Indeed, one recent German psychiater makes the foolish observation that uranians are so predisposed that they are incapable of seeing, either in letters, arts or life, the difference between ardent friendship and homosexual love. This accusation is anything but well-based. The first duty of the sexual psychiater is to keep clear two such currents of emotion. When however the sentiment of friendship, so-called, is invested with a distinctly *passional* quality, such a tale merits recognition as perhaps more or less of uranian tendency—verging perceptibly, but not committedly, to uranian love. There is here some interest in noticing how frequently certain British novelists have made "passional friendship" a vehement factor in their stories, even to its being the most vital trait of a book. Thus Dickens, in a series of his stories and their characters: David Copperfield and the handsome Steerforth—Eugene Wrayburn and Mortimer Lightwood in "Our Mutual Friend"—and Sydney Carton in the tragic "A Tale of

Two Cities." There is a touch of the same "passional" inspiration in Reade's "The Cloister and the Hearth." A more recent British novelist, the-late David Christie Murray, in his fine tale "Val Strange," practically builds all the story on an intensive sentiment of the sort, and utilizes it perceptibly in others of his novels.

A Caution.

Those who enter into the study of uranianism in literature and in arts, whether as to Anglo-Saxons or other races naturally must be solicitous in guarding against the idea (and not less so against the statement) that because such or such an authour deals with intersexual love in a story, poem, or what else, the authour himself is uranian. Many instances which will recur to the mind of the reader of this book as pertinent to be categorized in it in one way or another, do not have clearly any association of personal homosexuality, despite more or less merely literary suggestiveness.

Mayne: "Imre."

A few years ago appeared a distinctively homosexual story in English; referred to in the eighth chapter of this book, and from the same hand. In this is depicted, with more serious purpose than entertainment, the homosexual sentiment in two highly virilized uranians, one of them a young Hungarian officer. The story takes its course against a background of Magyar soldier-life. Both the young men are of strong moral and intellectual fibre; and their respect for each other, their dread of being repudiated, of losing the first friendship which each feels for the other, make them wear the mask, day by day, until finally it is thrown away, first by one, then by the other. From this tale, are appropriate in this literary connection two excerpts. The first summarizes the quality of the immediate and close friendship between the two young men; which presently pulsates inevitably to a warmer and more physical sentiment:

"Now of what did two men thus insistent on one another's companionship, one of them some twenty-five years of age, the other past thirty, neither of them vaporous with the vague enthusiasms of first manhood, nor fluent with the mere sentimentalities of idealism. . . of what did we talk, hour in and hour out, that our company was so welcome to each other, even to the point of our being indifferent to all the rest of our friends roundabout? . . . centering ourselves on the time *together* as the best thing in the world for us Such a question repeats a common mistake, to begin with. For it presupposes that companionship is a sort of endless conversazione, a State-Council ever in session. Instead, the *silences* in intimacy stand for the most perfect mutuality. And, besides, no man or woman has yet ciphered out the real secret of the finest quality, clearest sense, pf human companionability—a thing that often grows up, flower and fruit, so swiftly as to be like the oriental juggler's magic mango-plant. We are likely to set ourselves to analyzing, over and over, the externals and accidence... the mere inflections of friendships, as it were. But the real secret evades us. It ever will evade. We are drawn together because we are drawn. We are content to abide together just because we are content. We feel that we have reached a certain harbour, after much or little drifting, just because it is for *that* haven, after all, that we have been moving on and on; with all the irresistible pilotry of the wide ocean-wash friendly to us. It is as foolish to make too much of the definite in friendship as it is in love—which is the highest expression of companionship. Friendship?—love? what are they, if real on both sides, but the great Findings? ...

As a fact, my new friend and I had an interesting range of commonplace and practical topics, on! which to exchange ideas. Sentimentalities were quite in abeyance. We were both interested in art, as well as in sundry of the less popular branches of literature, and in what scientifically underlies practical life. Moreover, I had been longtime enthusiastic as to Hungary and the Hungarians, the land, the race, the magnificent military history, the complicated, troublous aspects of the present and future of the Magyar Kingdom. And though I cannot deny that I have met with more ardent Magyar patriots than Imre von N—(for somehow he took a conservative view of his birth-land and fellow-citizens) still, he was always interested in clarifying my ideas. Again, contrary-wise, Lieutenant Imre was zealous in informing himself on matters and things pertaining to my own country and to its system of social and military life, as well as concerning a great deal more; even to my native language, of which he could speak precisely seven words, four of them too forcible for use in general society. . .

And besides more general matters, there was. . . for so is it in friendship as in love. . . ever that quiet undercurrent of inexhaustible curiosity about each other as an Ego, as psychic facts not yet mutually explained. Therewith comes-in that kindly seeking to know better and better the Other, as a being not yet fully outlined, as one whom we would understand even from the farthest-away time when neither friend suspected the other's existence, when each was meeting the world *alone*—as one now looks back on those days. . . and was absorbed in so much else in life, before Time had been willing to say. "Now meet, you two! Have I not been preparing you for each other?" So met, the simple personal retrospect is an ever-new affair of detail for them, with its queries, its confessions, its comparisons. I thought that, but now I think this. Once on a time I believed that, now I believe this. I did so and so, in those old days; but now, not so. I have desired, hoped, feared purposed such or such a matter then; now no longer. Such manner of man have I been, whereas nowadays my indentity before myself is thus and so. Or, it is the presenting of what has been enduringly a part of ourselves, and is likely ever to abide such. Ah, these are the moods and tenses of the heart and the soul in friendship! more and more willingly uttered and listened-to as intimacy and confidence thrive. Two natures are seeking to blend. Each is glad to be its own directory for the new comer; to treat him as an expected and welcomed guest to the Castle of Self, while yet something of a stranger to it; opening to him any doors and windows that will throw light on the labyrinth of rooms and corridors, wishing to keep none shut. . . perhaps not even some specially haunted, remote and even black-hung chamber. Guest? No, more than that; for is it not the tenant of all others, the Master, who at last, has arrived!

The ensuing second fragment is from the dialogue between Oswald and Lieutenant Imre, when both are in a strong nervous tension from their mutual reserves. It occurs just before Oswald reaches the point of a narration of his tragic life-story, and confession to Imre, under stress of an expected parting which suddenly seems inevitable by Oswald's summons to England; a self-revelation which, however, the timorousness of Imre does not reward by equal frankness until the story's end.

"We had made a detour around the lonelier portion of the park. The sun was fairly setting as we came out before the open lawn, wide, and uncropped, save by two cows and a couple of farm-horses. There were trees on either border. At farther range, was the long, low mansion, three stories high, with countless white-painted *croisées*, and lime-blanched chimneys; an odd Austro-Magyar style of dwelling, of a long-past fashion, standing up solid and sharp against that silver-saffron sky. Not a sign of life, save those slow-moving beasts, far off in the middle of the lawn. No smoke from the yet more removed old homestead. Not a sound, except a gentle wind. . . melancholy and fitful. We two might been remote, near a village in the Siebenbürgen; not within twenty minutes of a great commercial city.

Instead of going on toward the avenue which led to the exit— the hour being yet early—we sat down on a stone bench, much beaten by weather. A few steps away, rose the monument I have mentioned. . . "To the Unforgettable Memory" of Lorand and Egon Z. . .

Neither Imre nor I spoke immediately. Each of us was a trifle leg-weary. I once more was sad and. . . angry. As we sat there, I read over for yet another time. . . the last time? . . . those carved words which reminded a reader, whether to his gladness of soul or dolour, that love, a love indeed strong as death, between two manly souls was no mere ideal; but instead, a possible crown of existence, a glory of life, a realizable unity that certain fortunate sons of men attained! A jewel that others must yearn for, in disappointment and folly, and with the taste of aloes, and the white of the egg, for the pomegranate and the honeycomb! I sighed.

"Oh, courage, courage, my well-beloved friend!" exclaimed Imre, hearing the sigh and apparently quite misreading my innermost thoughts. "Don't be down-hearted again as to leaving Szent-Istvànhely tomorrow; not to speak of being cheerful even if you must part from your most obedient servant. Such is life! . . . unless we are born sultans and kaisers. . . and if we are that, we must die to slow music in the course of time."

I vouchsafed no comment. Could this be Imre von N—? Certainly I had made the acquaintance of a new and extremely uncongenial Imre; in exactly the least appropriate circumstances to lose sight of the sympathetic, gentler-natured friend, whom

I had begun to consider as one well understood, and had found responsive to a word, a look. Did all his closer friends meet, sooner or later, with this under-half of his temperament—this brusqueness which I had hitherto seen in his bearing with only his outside associates? Did they admire it. . . if caring for him? Bitterness came over me in a wave, it rose to my lips in a burst:

"It is just as well that one of us should show some feeling. . . a trifle. . . when our parting is so near."

A pause. Then Imre:

"The 'one of us', that is to say the only one who has any 'feeling', being yourself, my dear Oswald?"

"Apparently."

"Don't you think that perhaps you rather take things for granted? Or that, perhaps, you feel too much? That is, in supposing that I feel too little"?

My reply was quick and and acid enough:

"Have you any sentiments in the matter worth calling by such a name, at all? I've not remarked them so far! Are friends that love you and value you only worth their day with you? . . . have they no real, lasting individuality for you? Your heart is not difficult to occupy."

Again a brief interval. Imre was beating a tattoo on his braided cap, and examining the top of that article with much attention. The sky was less light now. The long, melancholy house had grown pallid against the foliage. Still the same fitful breeze. One of the cows lowed.

Presently he looked up, and began speaking gravely—kindly—not so much as if seeking his words for their exactness, but rather as if he were fearful of commiting himself outwardly to some innermost process of thought. Afraid, more than unwilling.

"Listen, my dear friend. We must not expect too much of one another in this world—must we? Do not be foolish. You know well that one of the last things that I regard as 'of a day' is *our* friendship—however suddenly grown. No matter what you think now. . . for just these few moments—when something disturbs us both—*that* you know. Why, dear friend! did I not believe it myself, had I not believed it so soon after our meeting—do you think I would have shown you so much of my real self, happy or unhappy, for better or worse? Sides of my nature unknown to others? Traits that you like, along with traits that I see you do not like? Why, Oswald, you understand *me*—the real *me!*—better than anybody else that I have ever met. Because I wished it—I hoped it. Because I could not help it. Just that. But you see the trouble is that, in spite of all—you do not *wholly* understand me. And the worst of the reason is that I am the one most to blame for it! And I—I cannot better it now."

"When do we understand one another in this life of half-truths—of half-intimacies?"

"Yes, all too-often half. . . or less! And I am not easy (ah, howI have had to learn the way to keep myself so, to study it till it is a second nature to me!) I am not easy to know! But, Oswald, Oswald, *ich kann nicht anders! nein, nein ich kann nicht anders!*" And then, in his own language, dull and doggedly he added to himself—"*Mit használ, mit használ az én nekem?* (What matters it to *me*?)"

He took my hand now, that was lying on the settle beside his own, and held it while he spoke; unconsciously clasping it tighten, and tighter till it was in pain, or would have been so, had it not been, like his own, cold from sheer nervousness. He continued:

"One thing more. You seem to forget sometimes that I am a man, and that you too are a man. Not either of us a—woman. Forgive me—I speak frankly. We are both of us, you and I, a bit over-sensitive—high-strung—in type. Isn't that so? You often suggest a—a regard so—what shall I call it?—so romantic—heroic—passionate—a *love* indeed (and here his voice was suddenly broken) something that I cannot accept from anybody without warning him back, back! I mean back if coming to me from any *man*. Sometimes you have troubled me—frightened me. I cannot, I will not, try to tell you why this is so. But so it is. Our friendship must be friendship as the world of today accepts friendship! Yes, as the world of our day does. God! What else could it be today. Friendship? What else—*today*?"

"Not the friendship which is love, the love which is friendship?" I said in a low voice; indeed, as I now remember more than half to myself.

Imre was looking at the darkened sky, the gray lawn—into the vague distance—at whatsoever was visible save myself. Then his glance was caught by the ghostly marble of the monument to the young Z. . . heroes, at which I too was staring. A tone of appeal came as he continued:

"Once more, I beg, I implore you, not to make the mistake of—of thinking me cold-natured. I, cold-natured? Ah, ah! If you knew me better, you'd not pack that notion into your trunks for London! Instead, believe that I value unspeakably all your friendship for me, dear Oswald. Time will prove that. I have had no friend like you, I believe. But though friendship can be a passion—can cast a spell over us that we cannot comprehend nor unbind"—here he withdrew his hand and pointed to the memorial-stone set up for those two human hearts that after so ardently beating for each other, were now but dust—"it must be only a spiritual, manlike regard! The world thought otherwise once. The world thinks—as it thinks—now. And the world, today's world, must decide for us! Friendship now—now—must stay as the, man of our day understands it, Oswald. That is, if the man deserves the name, and is not to be not classed as some sort of an incomprehensible—womanish—outcast—counterfeit—a miserable puzzle—born to be every genuine man's contempt!"

We had come, once more, suddenly, fully, and because of me, on the topic which we had touched on, that night of our Lánczhíd walk! But this time I faced it, in a sense of fatality and finality; in a rash, desperate desire to tear a secret out of myself, to breathe free, to be true to myself, to speak out the past and the present, so strangely united in these last few weeks; to reserve nothing, cost what it might. My hour had come!

"You have asked me to listen to you!" I cried. Even now I feel the despair, I think I hear the accent of it, with which I spoke. "I have heard you! Now I want you to listen to me! I wish to tell you a story. It is out of one man's deepest yet daily life—my own life. Most of what I wish to tell happened long before I knew you. It was far away, it was in what used to be my own country. After I tell it, you will be one of very few people in all the world who have known, who have even suspected what happened to me. In telling you, I trust you with my social honour—with all that is outwardly and inwardly myself. And I shall probably pay a penalty, just because *you* hear the wretched history, Imre— *you*! For before it ends, it has to do with you; as well as with something that you have just spoken of, so fiercely! I mean—how far a man, deserving to be called a man, refusing, as surely as God lives and has made him, to believe that he is—what did you call him?—'a miserable, womanish counterfeit—outcast'—even if he be incomprehensible to himself—how such a being can suffer and be ruined in- his innermost life and peace, by a soul-tragedy which he neverthless can hide—*must* hide! I could have told you all on the night that we talked, as we crossed the Lánczhíd. No, that is not true! I could not then. But I can now. For I may never see you again. You talk of our 'knowing' each other! I wish you to know me. And I could never write you this, never! Will you hear me, Imre?—patiently?"

"I will hear you patiently—yes, Oswald—if you think it best to tell me. Of *that* pray think, carefully."

"It is best! I am tired of thinking of it. It is time you knew."

"And I am really concerned in it?"

"You are immediately concerned. That is to say, before it ends. You will see how."

"Then you would better go on—of course."

He consented thus, in the constrained but decided tone which I have indicated as so often recurring during the evening, adding—"I am ready, Oswald."

The North-Aunerican (by such term indicating particularly the United States) with his nervosity, his impressionability, his complex fusion of bloods and of racial traits, even when of directly British stocks, is usually far more "temperamental" than the English. He has offered interesting excursions at least towards, if not always into, the homosexual library. His novels, verses and essays have pointed out a racial uranianism. In the United States and adjacent British possessions, the prejudices and restrictions as to literature philarrhenic in accent, are quite as positive as in Great Britain. The authour or publisher of a homosexual book, even if scientific, not to speak of a belles-lettres work, will not readily escape troublesome consequences. Even psychiatric works from medical publishers are hedged about with conditions as to their publication and sale. Nevertheless, similisexualism is far from being an unknown note in American belles-lettres, and has even achieved its classics.

American Philarrhenic Literature.

Walt Whitman. An American poet, who has assumed an international significance and cult—well-deserved—Walt Whitman, can be regarded through a large proportion of his most characteristic verse, as one of the prophets and priests of homosexuality. Its atmosphere pervades Whitman's poems; being indeed an almost inevitable concurrent of the neo-hellenic, platonic democracy of Whitman's philosophic muse. One series of Whitman's earlier poetic utterances, at once psychologic and lyric, the famous "Calamus" group in "Leaves of Grass," out of dispute stands as among the most openly homosexual matters of the sort, by idealizing (but sensually idealizing) man-to-man love, psychic and physical, that modern literature knows; in virility far beyond the verse of Platen; while Whitman much exceeds Platen in giving physical expressiveness to what he sings. Of Whitman's own personal homosexualism there can be no question, if anyone be acquainted with the intimate story of the "good gray poet's long life." Episodes in his reminiscences called "Hospital Sketches" (many others were never put into print) are personally significant enough. Whitman's choice of intimates, too was significant. The tie with the young Irish tram-driver, Peter Doyle,was only one of the Whitmanian divagations of the kind. To women, Whitman was sexually quite indifferent; philosophically contemptuous of them. In physical type the magnificent manly beauty of Whitman, and its endurance, even late in his life, are in key with his philarrhenic nature. To cite more than a few of Whitman's expressions of uranianism, from his poetry only, is impossible here, and perhaps not necessary. For the sake of illustrating to readers who do not know him at all in such guise, are here appended passing instances from "Leaves of Grass"—including of course, some in the "Calamus" section;

"A glimpse through an interstice caught,
Of a crowd of workmen and drivers in a bar-room, around the stove,
late of a winter-night, and I unremarked seated in a corner.
Of a youth who loves me, and whom I love, silently approaching and
seating himself near me, that he may hold me by the hand
A long while; amid the noises of coming and going of drinking
and oath and smutty jest.
There we two—content, happy in being together, speaking little,
perhaps not a word."

". . . Whichever the sex, whatever the season or place, he may go
freshly and gently and safely, by day or by night;
He has the pass-key of all hearts, to him the responses of the prying
of hands on the knobs;
Pis welcome is universal—the flow of beauty is not more welcome or
universal than he;
The person he favours by day, or sleeps with at night is blessed."

"O tan-faced prairie-boy!
Before you came into camp came many a welcome gift;
Praises and presents came, and nourishing food, till at last
among the recruits
You came—taciturn, with nothing to give. We but looked on each other,
When, lo, more than all the gifts of the world you gave me!"

". . . Behold me, well-clothed, going gaily or returning in the
afternoon, my brood of tough boys accompanying me,
My brood of grown and part-grown boys, who love to be with no
one else so well as to be with me;
By day to work with me, and by night to sleep with me."

"I too knitted the old knot of contrariety,
Was one with the rest, the days and haps of the rest,
Was called by my nighest name, by clear loud voices of young men, as
they saw me approaching or passing;
Felt their arms on my neck as I stood, or the negligent leaning of
their flesh against me as I sat;
Saw many I loved, in the street or ferry-boat, or public assembly, but
never told them a word. . . . . .
Sound out, voices of young men I loudly and musically call me by my
nighest name!',

". . . The beauty of all adventurous and daring persons,
The beauty of wood-boys and wood-men, with their clear untrimmed

faces."

". . . I sit by the restless all the dark night; some are so young,
Some suffer so much? I recall the experiences sweet and sad.

Many a soldier's loving arms about this neck have crossed and rested,
Many a soldier's kiss dwells on these bearded lips."

". . . One turns to me his appealing eyes—poor boy, I never knew you,
Yet I think I could not refuse this moment to die for you, if that

would save you."

"Armed regiments arrive everyday, pass through the city, and embark
from the wharves.
How good they look as they tramp down to the river, sweaty, with
their guns on their shoulders!
How I love them! How I could hug them!—with their brown faces,
and their clothes and knapsacks covered with dust."

"Whoever you are, now I place my hand upon you,
that you be my poet.
I whisper with my lips close to your ear,
"I have loved many women and men—but I love none better than you."

"What is it I interchange so suddenly with strangers?
What with some driver, as I ride on the seat by his side?
What with some fisherman, drawing his seine by the shore, as I

walk by and pause?"

"Are you the new person drawn toward me? . . .
Do you suppose you will find in me your ideal?
"Do you think it so easy to have me become your lover?"

"I saw in Louisiana a live-oak growing.
All alone it stood, and the moss hung down from its branches.
Without any companion it stood there, uttering joyous leaves of green.
But I wondered how it could utter joyous leaves, standing alone there,
Without its friend near; for I know I could not.
And I broke off a twig. . . and brought it away. . .
Yet it remains to me, a curious token, it makes me think of manly love:
For all that, and though the live-oak glistens there in Louisiana,
solitary, in a wide, flat space,

Uttering joyous leaves all its life—without a friend, a lover near—
I know very well I could not!

In a large succession of Whitman's philosophico-political poems he accents the idea of the importance of masculine ties on lines of the old hellenic sort—the Sacred Band—as vital to the State, in the restoration of the true democracy. As in the following:

"I will sing the song of companionship
I believe these are to found their own ideals of manly love.
I will let flame forth from me the burning fires that were
threatening to consume me.
I will lift what has too long kept down these smouldering fires,
I will give them complete abandonment:
I will write the evangel-poem of comrades and of love.
For who but I should understand love, with all its sorrow and joy?
And who but I should be the poet of comrades?"

"I dreamed in a dream I saw a city, invincible to the attacks
of the whole earth.
I dreamed that that was the new city of Friends.
Nothing was greater there than the quality of robust love—it
led the rest.
It was seen every hour in the actions of men,
And in all their looks and words."

". . . I believe the main purport of these States is to found a superb
friendship, exaltée, previously unknown;
Because I perceive it waits, and always has been waiting, latent in
all men."

". . . Come, I will make the continent indissoluble,
I will make the most splendid race the sun ever shone upon,
I will make divine, magnetic lands,
With the love of comrades,
With the life-long love of comrades!"

". . . Far, far in the forest, or sauntering later in summer, before I
think where I go—

O, here I last saw him that tenderly loves me, and returns again,
never to separate from me."

"Ah, lover and perfect equal!
I meant that you should discover me so by faint indirections;
And I, when I meet you, mean to discover you by the like in you."

"O you, to whom I often and silently come where you are,
that I may be with you
As I walk by your side, or sit near, or remain in the same
room with you,
Little you know the subtle electric fire that, for your sake,
is playing within me!"

. . . I ascend, I float in the regions of your love, O man!
O sharer of my roving life!

There are dozens of such passages in Whitman. They culminate in certain outspoken idyls of psychic and physical homosexuality; as the impassioned nocturne, "When I heard at the close of the day"; the threnody "Vigil strange I kept on the field one night"! in many lines of "The Song of the Open Road"—which ends with its manly, joyful acclaim of the comrade-lover "Camarado, I will give you my hand in the retrospective "As I lay with my head in your lap, Camerado"; and in the lines ending "Paumanok" that are like an orgasm—"O, Camarado, close! O you and me at last, and only!" In numerous utterances Whitman, proclaims his socratic mission; admits the accusation of immorality that is cast at him; retorts with his intention to he frightened by no modern conventionalities; hints his recognition of the uranian nature of Christ; affirms the profound and antique concept of male love, which modern religions and ethics obscure. In the most solemnly, widely purposeful, as in the most lyrically personal Whitman, whom we meet throughout "Leaves of Grass," is to be heard a new voice, if with an accent classically old, in its philosophic message of conviction as to the purity, the naturalness of true uranian love and its high mission to the individual and toward nations.

By a coincidence, perhaps not quite unintentional, an American poet of the immediate day, W. E. Davenport, who follows the verse-structure (or no-structure) of Whitman, lately published in a leading New York magazine an hellenic vignette "The Parting" that might have been written by the youth-adoring Whitman himself. It seems to be an Italian reminiscence:

> *"After so much of, art, pictures, statues, rich and towering churches,*
> *And nature's infinite splendid sights, my South-Italian mountain-*
> *towns—Agnone, Sala, Acri and Cosenza—*
> *Sticks in my mind one simple scene, of cheerful, fond intent—*
> *befitting not the expense of many lines:*
> *A teacher scarcely old, a traveler, seer of sights and observer of men*
> *and their ways,*
> *By a group of youths at eve in the open street surrounded.*
> *Of these—their pleased looks, their manners, easy, free, full of*
> *cheerful resolve;*
> *Their wit, brightness, mirth, courtesy, confidence, outstreched hands,*
> *with or without words—*
> *And he, the elder, pleased just as much, easy and confident as they—*
> *Toward dusk in the street, before the hotel, bidding good-by;*
> *Saying only, "Good-night, good-night, we shall see each other again."*

Several contemporary poets of the United states, older and younger, have interjected the accent of at least psychic uranianism in their verses, though none known to the present writer

American Verse of the Day.

approach Whitman in loftiness, directness and clarity. Professor George E. Woodberry, of Columbia University, is the authour of a long elegy, giving title to a volume, "The North-Shore Watch;" a retrospect and lament inspired by the death of a lad—a poem hellenically passional, and of superiour poetic quality. Noticeable, *passim*, is also the poetry frequently tending to the sort of psychology here in question (though unequal in inspiration) by the Canadian-American, Bliss Carman.

In prose, as in verse, of American origin, the connection between the addresses of ardent and absorbing friendship and a stronger emotion is not one to be taken for granted, any more than in belles-lettres not in English. In Emerson's

Suggestions in American Prose.

neo-grecian attitude to friendship, in his essays and his poetry, there is no clear uranian suggestion. To read uranianism between even such Emersonian lines as those that say that only through the friend is the sky blue, the rose red, the fountains of hidden life fair, is not by warrant. The same reserve applies to numerous contemporaries, including many in minor letters. Here and there, however, in current American periodicals, occur tales or poems of at least a two-coloured psychic suggestion. In the chapter on military uranianism, was mentioned a recent volume, "The Spirit of Old West-Point" a charming series of reminiscences of cadet-days, by General Morris Schaf. In certain sketches of the late H. C. Bunner something of the uranian strain occasionally echoes. An openly homosexual novelette, apparently unique in such an explicit category in America, came many years ago from a New York journalist— "A Marriage Below Zero," signed with the pen-name "Alan Dale." The story, not one of any artistic development, narrates (in the person of a neglected wife) her marriage with an uranian, apparently a passivist, who cannot shake off his sexual bondage to an older and coarser man, an officer. The story ends in the young husband's suicide in Paris, after an homosexual scandal has ostracised him.

In the charming "South-Sea Idyls" of Charles Warren Stoddard, a Californian writer, and university-professor, occur episodes and suggestions of uranian complexion; though in case of a book so light-heartedly fantastic it is difficult to say where the personal and absolutely reminiscent are to be understood. Kána-Aná, Niga, Zebra, Joe, are eloquent as personalities. For example, can be cited here a fragment of the narration of one of the authour's predilections—the beautiful lad Kána-Aná, to whom is devoted the chapter "Chumming with a Savage:"

". . . I knew I was to have an experience with this young scion of a race of chiefs. Sure enough I have had it. He continued to regard me steadily, without embarrasment. He seated himself before me; I felt myself at the mercy of those questioning eyes. This sage inquirer was perhaps sixteen years of age I saw a round, full, rather girlish face; lips ripe and expressive, not quite so sensual as those of most of his race; not a bad nose, by any means; eyes perfectly glorious,—regular almonds—with the mythical "lashes that sweep," etc., etc. The smile which presently'transfigured his face, was of the nature that flatters you into submission against your will."

"Having weighed me in his balance—and you may be sure his instincts didn't cheat him—they don't do that sort of thing—he placed his two hands on my knees and declared, "I was his best friend, as he was mine; I must come at once to his house, and there live, always, with him." What could I do but go? . . . This was our little plan—an entirely private arrangement between Kána-Aná and myself. I was to leave, with the Doctor, in an hour; but at the expiration of a week, we should return hither; then I would stop with Kána-Aná, and the Doctor would go his ways."

"There was an immense amount of secrecy and many vows, and I was almost crying, when the Doctor hurried me up that terrible precipice, and we lost sight of the beautiful valley. Kána-Aná swore he would watch continually for my return, and I vowed I'd hurry back, and so we parted. Looking down from the heights, I thought, I could distinguish his white garment; at any rate I knew the little fellow was somewhere about, feeling as miserably as I felt—and nobody has any business to feel worse. How many times I thought of him through that week! I was always wondering if he still thought of me. I had found those natives to be impulsive, demonstrative, and—I feared—inconstant. Yet why should he forget me,—having so little to remember in his idle life, while I could still think of him, and put aside a hundred pleasant memories for his sake? I often wondered if I should ever again behold such a series of valleys, hills, and highlands, in so small a compass. That land is a world in minature, the dearest spot of which to me was that secluded valley, for there was a young soul watching for my return."

"That was rather a slow week for me; but it ended finally. And just at sunset, on the day appointed, the Doctor and I found ourselves back on the edge of the valley. . . I heard the approach of a swift horseman, I turned; and at that moment there was a collision of two constitutions that were just fitted for one another; and all the doubts and apprehensions of the week just over were dismissed; for Kána Aná and I were one and inseparable-which was perfectly satisfactory to both parties."

"The plot which had been thickening all the week, culminated then, much to the disgust of the Doctor, who had kept his watchful eye upon me all three days—to my advantage, as he supposed. There was no disguising the project any longer; so I came out with it, as mildly as posible—"There was a dear fellow here" I said, "who loved me, and wanted me to live with him. Also all his people wanted me to stop—his mother and his grandmother had specially desired it. . . I needed rest; his mother and his grandmother assured me that I needed rest. Now, why not let me rest here awhile?" The Doctor looked very grave. He tried to talk me over to the paths of virtue and propriety; but I wouldn't be talked over. . . The Doctor never spoke again but to abuse me; and off he rode, in high dudgeon, and the sun kept going down on his wrath. I resolved to be a barbarian, and perhaps to dwell forever and ever in this secluded spot."

"Over the sand we went, and through the river to Kána Aná's hut, where I was taken in, fed and petted in every possible way; and finally put to bed, where Kána Aná monopolized me—growling in true savage fashion if anyone came near me. I didn't sleep much after all. I think I must have been excited. I though how strangely I was situated—alone, in a wilderness, among barbarians; my bosom-friend, who was hugging me like a young bear, not able to speak one syllable of English, and I very shaky on a few bad phrases in his tongue. We two lay upon an enormous, old-fashioned bed with high posts—very high they seemed to me in the dim rush-light. The natives always burn a small light after dark; some superstition or other prompts it. The bed, well stocked with pillows or cushions, of various sizes, covered with bright-colored chintz, was hung about with numerous shawls, so that I might be dreadfully modest behind them. . . I found our bedposts festooned with flowers in the morning .. Oh, that bed! It might have come from England, in the Elizabethan era, and have been wrecked off the coast—hence the mystery of its presence. It was big enough for a Mormon."

"There was a little opening in the room, opposite our bed; you might call it a window, I suppose. The sun shining through it, made our tent of shawls perfectly gorgeous in crimson light, barred and starred with gold. I lifted our bed-curtain and watched the rocks through this window—the shining rocks, with the sea leaping above them in the sum I wondered what more I could ask for to delight my eye. Kána-Aná was still aslep, but he never let loose his hold on me, as though he feared his pale-faced friend would fade away from him. He lay close beside me. His sleek, figure, supple and graceful in repose, was the embodiment of free, untrammeled youth. . . I dropped of into one of those delicious morning naps. I awoke, again presently; my companion-in-arms was the occasion, this time. He had awakened, stolen softly away, resumed his single garment—said garment, and all others, he considered superfluous after dark—and had prepared for me, with his own hands, a breakfast; which he now declared to me, in violent and suggestive pantomime, was all ready to be eaten. . .

"If it is a question how long a man can withstand the seductions of nature, and the consolations and conveniences of the state of nature, I had solved it in one case; for I was as natural as possible, in about three days."

The relation between Kána-Aná and the narrator ends in the death of the lad, after the latter has visited America with his friend, and has returned to his island, but not to happiness; his young spirit out of poise by his experiences in civilization, miserable without his friend, and ever pining away, untill he is drowned in the sea—by accident or intention. The sketch ends:

"I can see you, my beloved—sleeping naked, in the twilight of the west. The winds kiss your pure and fragrant lips. The sensuous waves invite you to their embrace. Earth offers you her varied store. Partake of the offering and be satisfied. Return, O troubled soul, to your first and natural joys; they were given you by the Divine hand that can do no ill. . . Dear comrade, pardon and absolve your spiritual adviser for seeking to remould so delicate a soul as yours; and though neither prophet nor priest, I yet give you the kiss of peace at parting, and the benediction of unceasing love."

In Italian fiction (notably a crudely physical sketch, of slight literary quality, by Giorgio Cattelani, entitled "Ermafrodito," in that writer's "Turpi Amori') are contributions to the topic that are more or less explicit. In Italian verse we have also the promptings of that uranian muse, who is nevertheless not Urania.

In Scandinavian literature of the day names of several writers of greater or lesser note suggest themselves—including some of the Strindberg school. The pederastic homosexuality of that charming fabulist and mystic. Hans Christian Andersen was recently the subject of a close and affirmative German study.

As one acquaints himself with the personalities of many a distinctly uranian man of letters, and realizes the unrest, the solitude, the disappointments, the agonies of soul which have entered into lives, if not always into printed pages, he realizes the truth of a sonnet by a French uranian already cited, Jacques Adelswärd-Fersen:

> *"Vous qui lisez nos vers au clair de votre lampe*
> *Et feuilletez nos cœurs avec un doigt distrait,*
> *O vous, les inconnus, qui, sachant nos secrets,*
> *Ecoutez le sang battre aux veines de nos tempes.*
>
> *Vous qui, l'esprit tranquille et les sens apaisés,*
> *Demandez à nos cris l'émotion divine,*
> *Et sous votre douleur voulez que l'on devine*
> *Les agonies du Rêve et l'espoir écrasé,*
>
> *O vous, qui froidement, désirez la torture*
> *Et dépecez à vif nos cruelles amours,*
> *Qui cherchez dans un livre l'éphémère toujours*
> *En oubliant nos noms, nos vies et nos blessures,*
>
> *Pensez à ces instants de sauvages douleurs*
> *Où notre enthousiasme au désespoir se brise,*
> *Et pour que votre esprit trouve notre âme exquise,*
> *A ce qu'un de nos vers doit contenir de pleurs!*[6]

---

6. In making the foregoing references to belles-lettres that in colouring are more or less immediate to the topic of this book, its authour is well aware of how incomplete and arbitrary they may seem. Many names and titles inevitably must be absent that are of much interest and importance. The reader in fact is asked to accept what is offered as only a small contribution to a suitably general survey. Especially from the field of essays, philosophic studies and so on, there has been no room here, at the date when these pages go to press, to include several recent allusions of value. For a single English instance a special word is due to Mr. Edward Carpenter's new little volume "The Intermediate Sex: A Study of Some Transitional Types of Men and Women" (London, Swan, Sonnenschein & Co.; Manchester, S. Clarke, & Co.) The essayistic and anthologie work of the distinguished English social philosopher named mark him as a pioneer in the path of British enlightenment on philarrhenic questions. "The Intermediate Sex" is a study that all thoughtful Anglo-Saxons should take pains to read.

As has been said here, the Uranian meets us in no other career and life so plainly and so often as in the directly æsthetic atmosphere. He turns toward the even more spontaneously and successfully than to letters; for literature requires a far firmer Intellectuality than is demanded in painting, sculpture or music. Indeed, the Intersexual, though a long way from being (in

Similisexuals in Distinctively Aesthetic Professions and Environments: Painting, Sculpture, Music, etc.

the scornful phrase of the of the philistine) "good for nothing else" except art, seems often to us not *as* "good for anything else. He is aesthetically receptive, because of his natural predilection for what is concretely beautiful. He is productive in them because the finer uranian nature inclines to produce and to diffuse, even subsconsciously, what is beautiful. Again, in creating out of marble or on canvas the beauty of the male physique, the uranian utters his sexual creed. Generally he cannot publish it to the world any more plainly, and not more sympathetically. He turns to his chisel, to his palette, to his score, to his pianoforte, as a refuge. His physique is often adapted to only such a life. The relative unintellectuality and emotionality of several of the arts are consonant with his type, be what inspires him valuable or trivial, a jewel or paste.

Fortunate is that æsthetic homosexual who can really live a life of art, professionally and completely. A thousand traits of his type are accepted in such a situation as being intelligible, interesting, appropriate, excusable, even laudable;

Aesthetic Careers and Environments as a Refuge for Uranians.

in many cases as matters of course; all of which, were he not of a distinctively artist-profession, would be remarked, questioned, satirized, or suspected of being "vicious." Uranian effeminacies and degeneracies are passed lightly by, as being mere artistic "eccentricities." Hazy scandals are smiled at, if not too frequent. Even scandals not hazy are dismissed by the public in amiable indifference, as part of the aesthetic privilege. "Artist are *all* such children—sometimes such naughty children!"—"Oh these musical people!—these painting people!—these sculptors! They are not like the rest of us I They really must not be judged like common mortals!" Such tolerant dicta are not misapplied to similisexuals in art-life; for, we may repeat it, the uranian in much is the Eternal Child.

Not only does absorption in the arts hide the homosexual nature from friends and from the public, not only do necessities of this or that branch of aesthetic work screen the sexual interests in the male, on the part of the homosexual man. They do more. When the homosexual is not clear as to his own nature, and cannot reconcile—with his moral conscience or religious training—his intense sensitiveness to masculine beauty, cannot analyze the dominance of the male over his emotions, then his professional art can obstruct his growing wiser as to himself—whether to his advantage or to his loss. For many intersexual men, art is a sort of psychic outlet, not necessarily enlightening. A surging idealism, whole currents of philarrhenic sexuality, spend themselves in the studio and concert. The very body is sometimes (by no means always) "kept down," by a kindlier *régime* than that of a cloister—by enthusiastic art-work.

Good morals have no necessary relations to aesthetic genius. To produce the very beautiful does not mean that the producer is very good. We discover, in studying the æsthetic uranian, that repulsive, effeminate, grossly sensual, despicable men have demostrated superbly their superbly artistic natures. In this, the uranian presents a contrast to similisexuals in the military, intellectual, and otherwise robust life. Still, the dionysian chronicle'of art is far longer in the same unsatisfactory tenor. The biography of art is convincing proof that art does not *per se* ennoble, does *not* refine, does *not* strengthen, does *not* ethically uplift the moral or intellectual man; a vast amount of sentimental theorizing to the contrary.

It is easy to see why many painters and sculptors have been similisexuals. They turn to it instinctively, in admiration of male forms. Such are nude in the studio by prescription. The delight in reproducing them is perennial to artists. Joy in their study is part of the homosexual's sense of the superiority of masculine beauty to feminine. Often the comely model becomes the Beloved.

Painters and Sculptors in Ancient Greece and Italy, and in Modern Epochs.

We need not wonder at tales of the uranistic passions of classic Greek and Roman sculptors, during the far-away epochs of Hellas. As sculpture advanced in idealism, and as a preferential sense of the beauty of a youth intensified, as Greek social culture, Greek athletics, the Greek religion (with the very gods as homosexualists and pederasts) progressed, also developed philarrhenism. So was it in Rome. The Renaissance brought into the studio of marble-carver or painter, at the potency of the uranian impulses, all the plastic beauty of the naked male. In Italy especially, the Renaissance art took pederastic tinges; and a beautiful, budding youth became even more sensitively admired and desired than a virile young man. In vain did Savonarola cry out against pederasty, sodomy in Florence; a city notably homosexual in its proletariat today.

We have seen that Michelangiolo's best verses were inspired by homosexual and pederastic-uranistic love. In his social and artistic life and career, Buonarroti never is interested clearly by a woman sexually. He was incapable psychically of such desire. But one or another young man was continually and successively taking the place of such "normal love" in the soul of the great sculptor and painter and architect. A pederastic emotion of the sort was his feeling for a beautiful boy of seventeen named Cecchino dei Bracchi. Cecchino was already the beloved of another noble Florentine. Luigi dei Ricci, of Buonarroti's social circle. But there was no rivalry between Michelangiolo and Ricci. One letter from Michelangiolo to Ricci, accompanying an ardent madrigal to Cecchino by the poet-sculptor, Michel Angelo tells Ricci could be "thrown into the fire—that is to say into that thing which consumes me." At the same time, Buonarroti recounts a strange dream of young Cecchino which has come to him. When Cecchino died suddenly, Buonarroti wrote a set of elegiac quatrains to his memory. (A sonnet penned after this grief is often cited.) The sentiment in Buonarroti for his handsome friend Tommaso Cavalieri, is recorded in several other Sonnets, including that which terminates with a play on the Italian word for "Knight"; a declaration that the writer "abides the captive of an armed knight." The colour of this intimacy with Cavalieri becomes more definite by their correspondence. Unfortunately representatives of the Buonarroti family have thought proper to suppress many of these letters, along with others, because of their homosexual tinge. Also uranistic was Michelangiolo's passion for Febo di Poggi, to whom he wrote many eloquent love-letters. Buonarroti never married. His sexual insensibility to woman influenced his want of artistic expressiveness as to the female figure and the female face. Buonarroti's feminine types are amazonian, androgynous beings; more like athletes than women, in their heavy contours. In one sonnet—numbered usually as "LIII," Buonarroti deprecates the love of man for a woman, as compared with man's love for a male. It is not be forgotten that Michelangiolo's poetry and correspondence, especially in the English translations, has long been

Michelangiolo.

edited and adapted, by timorous Anglo-Saxons, so as to give the reader the impression that their passional quality was ever inspired by feminine loves. This dexterous travesty has only lately been discontinued. There are now faithful English versions obtainable, especially that superior one by J. A. Symonds. Symonds particularly clears away the old idea (on which have been written volumes of mis-statements) that Buonarroti's admiration and friendship with that elderly, learned lady, Vittoria Golonna was of a warmer hue; and that some of Buonarroti's sonnets were addressed to her, instead of to masculine objects. The sentiment from Buonarroti to the gifted Vittoria was unsexual—intellectual. The sculptor who carved the Young David, or the Torso in the Accademia in Florence, the famous Christ of the Santa Maria in Minerva at Rome, or he who painted the robustly naked males crowding the frescos of the Sistine Chapel, could not conceive of a Venus on canvas or in marble worthy of his immortality!

Buonarroti was not alone in his epoch in Italy as uranistic in nature. Raphael was a dionysian-uranian, turning psychically now to the male, now the female. Bazzi the Sienese, one of the most individualized of all the Renaissance painters, derived his nickname, "Sodoma" and sanctioned its use in public—at Siena—from his tastes and practices; being withal a superior and respected man, in spite of his eccentric life. Correggio, Bronzino and Guercino were uranistic. Benvenuto Cellini, in his famous "Autobiography," gives us many hints at his pederastic homosexualism; such as the episode of Cellini's sudden flight to Venice when accused of sodomy with his handsome studio-aid, Cencio; later, his being flatly taxed with the habit, by a spiteful rival, in presence of the Pope; and the fact that Cellini was imprisoned on direct charges of the sort, by a cabal, in 1556.

Other Distinguished Types.

One of the renowned sculptors in the Seventeenth Century, the Fleming Jérôme Duquesnoy, was not only homosexual but came to his tragic death by a pederastic charge. Jérôme's great brother François (commonly mentioned in Flemish art as "Le Flameng," or "Le Flamand") has somewhat overshadowed Jérôme in fame, but was of no finer talent. In fact in Flemish art, Jérôme Duquesnoy is without superior. He lived and studied in Rome, at the same time that his brother François, with Antony Van Dyck and many other brilliant young artists of the North were students in Italy. Jérôme

Jérôme Duquesnoy.

and François were not harmonious in temperaments, and their quarrels have led biographers even to accuse Jérôme of having tried to poison François—a groundless charge. Some time earlier, Van Dyck also had come to Rome, to reside for a time. The two brothers Duquesnoy awhile were wholly separated; though Van Dyck maintained a close intimacy with both. In fact, Italian pederasty was strongly influential on the Northern colony in Rome at this time—as ever; for not only Jérôme Duquesnoy but François and Van Dyck became sensibly affected by its æsthetie elements. Jérôme Duquesnoy left Italy and went to Spain for a time; and after halts in Italian and French cities, he set out for Flanders along with his brother, who died suddenly at Leghorn. A brilliant professional career in Flanders began for the sculptor, once back in his own land. He executed commissions for the most important art-patronage of Belgium, and became official Court-sculptor. He went to Ghent, to complete the magnificent tomb of the Bishop of St. Bavon. In Ghent, ruin overtook the unfortunate Uranian. He was accused of sodomy with two young lads, acolytes of St. Bavon's Church, who had been his models. He was condemned. Every effort to save his life was frustrated, because of vehement clerical hostility. His magnificent private collections were confiscated; and he was strangled and burned in September, 1654.

The accent of similisexualism, "not distinctly of pederasty, attaches to Van Dyck, that most "cavalier" of portraitists, whose sense of physical beauty and distinction in both men and women was so fine. Van Dyck's psychos seems to have been dionysian-uranian, in many aesthetic aspects. There is a strain of uranianism in the personality and work of Raphael Mengs (1728–1779) the once much-admired painter—an intimate Mend of the archeologist Winckelman; although Mengs was considerably "a married man," in his attitude toward domestic and social life. Anecdotes more amusing than edifying are in key with Mengs's bisexuality.[7]

---

7. There is a striking element of the plastically uraniah quality in the paintings of a group of French classicists, i.e. David, Giron, Girodet (particularly the second-named artist), which the visitor to various representative collections, including the Louvre, will remark. The suggestion applies to artists whose youth or maturity subjected them to influences—social or intellectual—of the French Revolution, with its vehement sentimentalities for everything that was Greek and Roman, from the political diction in the Convention, or at the Jacobins, Cordeliers and other clubs, down to names, emblems, bandeaux, sandals and phrygian bonnets. In fact, a curious study has yet to be written on the Revolution's influences toward homosexuality in France, as a result of the revival of a pseudo-"classic"

It is not in the province of this study to catalogue, contemporary painters and sculptors to be counted as uranistic; now in one degree and phase, now another. The studios of London, Paris, Munich, Vienna, Rome, Naples, New York and anywhere else acquaint one with names of homosexual artists of the first importance in art of today The list is not limited to the less practical of aesthetic arts. Architecture, that almost uniquely virile and intellectual of aesthetic professions; designing applied in commercial connections; the finer industries, where the intimate sense of the beautiful has essentially a large part—these callings offer the practical uranian abundant fields for his gifts.

Music and Drama and Uranianism.

Reviewing all artistic temperaments and genetic classes, we find that music and the dramatic stage present the greatest census of uranians. Singers, players, composers, amateurs "passionately fond of music," actors of all ranks— they seem genetically homosexual. A crude saying among the observers of uranianism is—"Show me a Jew and you show me an—Uranian." A like statement might run "Show me a musician and show show me a homosexual." Doubtless music is preeminently the Uranian's art. His emotional nature goes out to it and in it, as in no other. This occurs though his understanding of music as an art may be most limited.

The Neurotic Nature of Music.

Not superficially is music among finer aesthetics; it is the most neurotic, the most "essential," the most subtly nerve-disturbing of arts. Music, as a mystery in aesthetics, unites logically with uranianism as a deep problem in psychology. Precisely what music "says," when we think it "says" something, and has such or such a "message" to us, we really do not in the least know. The dog who howls during a symphony or a waltz, in what we call his canine "nervousness" perhaps *understands* music far better than the greatest composer that has ever lived. The more complex music has become, the less appears its beneficence; originally doubtful. The neurotic character of music reaches its contemporary height in Wagner and Richard Strauss. Nerve-exciting as are the scores of many other operatic giants, none have quite so concrete an action on the nervous system, affecting both musical and unmusical auditors. Here

and greco-roman colouring of life and ideas, and of the Revolutionary abrogation of Christianity.

clearly cultivated tastes or quite the contrary are in question. Hence the popularity of Wagner, himself a homosexual nature, and of Richard Strauss. If we turn from the formalized neurotism of such great composers we may say that no music seems as directly *sexual* as the Magyar; wonderfully beautiful in its rhythms, melodies and harmonies. And the Magyar is a distinctively 'sexual' racial type.

It can be theorized further, that music has an articulate significance, seemingly dangerous. Is it not possibly a language, the broken diction of intenser existences, of which we catch troublous

Music an Eternal Sphynx of Art.

accents?—a speech which if—or *because*?—misunderstood cannot be for the good of mankind? Is the eternally music-loving, music-making, intersexual Uranian verily a sort of creature from another sphere?—still in touch with it?—an "Overman," an "Over-Soul?"—one ever sharply sensitive to the language of his early Somewhere Else, and alert to the chief medium for its communications, however little he or we may now *understand* it?

Composers present homosexual types; during either all their lives, or portion of them. The supreme secret of the noble-natured and moral Beethoven seems to have been an idealized homosexualism. In Beethoven's sad latest days, can be traced a real passion for that unworthy nephew Carl; who, it is said, once sought to extort money from Beethoven, on threats to disclose an homosexual relationship! Beethoven's beautiful sonata, Opus 111, in often called among German and Austrian Uranians, "The Uranian Sonata," from some legendary "in-reading" of the work. The death of the brilliant and unhappy Russian composer Tschaikowsky has been affirmed (if denied with equal conviction) as a suicide, not a sudden illness, in consequence of terror of a scandal that hung over him—a relative being spoken of as the persecutor. Some homosexual hearers of Tschaikowsky's last (and most elegiac) symphony, known as the "Pathetic" claim to find in it such revelations of a sentimental-sexual kind that they have nicknamed the work the "Pathic" Symphony. Brahms and the colossal Bruckner have been characterized as "the ultimate voices in a homosexual message by symphonic music"; even if one sub-consciously uttered.

Gustav Naumann lately has Written a brochure on the theory that art is living, interesting and alluring solely because of its sexual power and sexual quality; *solely* because of

Considerations of Music and Sexualism.

direct working on the sexual instincts of men and women. This influence may exist, even when they are not aware of it, by inseparably sensuo-sexual aspects of the artistic product or performance which they admire. Naumann lays stress on modern dramatic music (especially Wagner's) as "disturbing." our natural sexual harmony and wholesome repose of being; as acting on it unfavourably and excitingly. He claims that chaster and more classic forms of music have a tranquilizing operation; are in better sexual accord with the healthful man. The argument is interesting certainly. Most, if not all all, music seems indissolubly connected with the nervous-generative systems, in men and beasts. If some finer, forms, styles and schools of it do not seem at all sexuo-nervously irritant they are those that are palely elementary, or to which humanity is now accustomed—much as it grows wonted to dubious airs, evil waters or harmful chemical beverages. Unless in simple, familiar ambients, our contemporary human race does not receive music in sexual calm. A pastoral melody on a flute, a ballad on a mandoline may soothe us, as we think; so minute is the unwholesome effect on us. As music's dramatic force and complexity thicken, we ourselves are much as beasts whose nerves quiver when a pianoforte is played, or when a sonorous is march sounded on a military band.

Wagner's music-dramas can be directly an agent of seduction; of loss of sexual control and self-poise. A noted European physician, a dionysian-uranian, once told the writer that a performance of "Tristan and Isolde" was always sufficient to excite him sexually, and that he knew many individuals on whom Wagner acted as an aphrodisiac. A distinguished French student of psychiatrics has stated that the Bayreuth Wagner Festivals represent a kind of homosexual forcing-house. This topic has been treated by the philosophic art-writer Kufferath. Wagner himself, with adroit audacity, chose a covertly homosexual subject for his ripest and most sensuous music-drama, "Parsifal." A fine study of this matter has been written by the well-known American critic, James G. Huneker, in an American periodical, in course of a "Parsifal" analysis, unfortunately not printed entire in the authour's studies as collected in book-form.

The Aesthetic Usually Not "Philosyrphetic." The æsthetic Uranian, absorbed in belles-lettres, in the graphic arts, in sculpture, in music or what else, is more likely to maintain many ideals, to be sexually "consistent with himself," to achieve union with superiour types, than is the unæsthetic. However well-born, well-bred, educated, and whatever his own personal, intellectual or social grade, the Uranian (as we have seen) often wishes nothing of "the gentleman," when he seeks sexual satisfactions. Nevertheless a sensitive artist sometimes selects a clumsy, able-bodied workman, or a common soldier, rather than more refined types. The law of physical and psychic completion makes this logical. Walt Whitman alludes to such a relish for "powerful, uneducated persons"—an inconsistent selection unless we analyze its psychology of complements.

Composition is a relatively intellectual phase of musically. But if we descend to lower uranistic musical levels, the proportion of musical artists, vocal or instrumental, professional or amateur, is enormous. In this trait, music is a huge sexual republic. Conductors, accompanyists, singers, pianists, violinists, cellists, organists, associates of the orchestras of the world, now here, now there, are well-known (at least in confidential circles of uranism) for homosexual lives. Their adventures are the subjects of a thousand and one *racontars*. Not long ago, a homosexual singer was seated one evening with a dionian friend in a leading lyric theater, and pointed the attention of his companion to the fact that the composer of the opera, the conductor, the tenor, the baritone, the assistant stage-manager of the performance, and the secretary of the establishment were "all Uranians." The singers in question were the objects of unlimited female admirations and aspirations. Just then, there entered a box near by a distinguished pianist of the day and a violinist famed in two hemispheres. "Those two also!" exclaimed the companion; and then in a burst of *naive* confidence—quite unsolicited—he added "And—and—so am I!"

In amateur musical life, the cultivated and aesthetic classes constantly present the homosexual male. The type inclines to effeminacy of at least psychic sort; but the exceptions, as to that are legion, and disprove most rules.

The dramatic stage would yield almost an equal census, especially in particular nationalities and localities. It has always done so from the days of Nero, of Paris and of Mnester till now. It always will do so. The fact is interesting that many actors who are most the subjects of sentimental admiration from women, on account of manly beauty, are uranistic. They cultivate a wide female-worship, for advertising or social convenience. Homosexual prostitution, the actor as *entretenu*, are by no means rare among the more mercenary adonises of the theater. Young actors often profit by the passions of rich male adorers. A

The Actor.

notable scandal in a large European city, a few years ago, came from the sudden discovery by an elderly amateur of the play, amateur also of the handsome *jeune premier*—that the young'; man was false to him, despite a large subsidy. Four young Parisian actors of distinction are notoriously uranian. Another *artiste* on the French stage who has been called "the handsomest actor in France" is homosexual. One of the most distinguished of the protagonists in classic-romantic productions; also his colleague who just now is perhaps the most notable young comedian of Paris; another comedian adored by the smartest sets—all are homosexual. The most distinguished romantic actor on the German stage is uranian. The same may be said of a world-famous Austrian romantic actor, and of a dozen stars of the English stage—including one of an unusual popularity and beauty. But these are only types. Their like are legion. The late Viennese singer Theodore Reichmann had a long and successful life and career that was a tissue of homosexualism—either as to its romance or—crude materialism. Reichman left a long and minute diary, not likely to be published complete, so much would it displease Austrian censorship, and interest social Vienna.

Far less mysterious (indeed hardly any mystery) is the neurotic power of the spoken dramatic stage, compared with musical drama—music. But sexual excitement is often the essence of greater or lesser theatrism. Obviously plastic in the every-day theater, as on the operatic stage (but to more variety) the physical beauty of men, as of women, is minutely enhanced. The physique must be part of the attractive thrill. All the senses of sexual enjoyment and of a vague or vivid physical desire can be stirred, for the Uranian as he sits in his stall—in silence.

The Intellectual, Aesthetic and Artistic Uraniad.

The philosopher may question whether a woman of robust, aggressive, fairly masculine mentality be not always contrary to true femininism. Certainly the student of the Uraniad-problem will often class personalities about him with the Intersexuals. Independent intellectual careers exert an "asexual" effect. "Learned women" have been happy wives and mothers, but these types are in the minority. Women of abnormal intellectualism are likely by temperament to be averse to marriage, or indifferent to it. From that attitude to an absolute similisexualism the degrees are few, particularly if intimacies of school-life and college-days have given women ideas of uranian relationships. When woman muscularizes her mind beyond the harmonious vigor to make her man's companion, without her being his rival, her natural quality of sexual sentiment often suffers. There is small sensibility in her toward the normal, passional love which attracts man and surrenders to him, in the highest type of intellectual-masculine women. She is less a heart than a brain,—a sexless mind.

The types, biographies and psychology of the intellectual and aesthetic Uraniad suggest a volume, not yet written; a capital study for some Uraniad. Distinguished and royal women have been mentioned in an earlier chapter; types whose masculinity sets them apart from their apparent sex, whether they are as warriors, sovereigns and stateswomen. The less aristocratic, and robustly male Uraniad is a wide study, impossible in this work.

A striking example is met in Anna Maria Schurmann, the Hollander, who attracted world-wide notice during the middle of the Seventeenth Century. She was a precocious girl, with an intellectual maturity early famed in Cologne, where she was born in 1607. A brother being a student at the University of Utrecht, Anna became his fellow-student, and graduated with high distinction. Her first literary successes were in the way of Latin poems; but soon such diversions were left behind. She continued her scientific, classical and artistic education, partly to assist her brother in his career (he was a remarkable scholar) partly in zeal of learning; and her abilities presently became universally applauded. She read, spoke and wrote some fourteen languages, with ease and precision, including Greek, Latin, most of the current European tongues and several Oriental ones. She compiled a grammar of the Ethiopic language simply as part of her study of it. She mastered philosophy, theology, and was "a library of scientific knowledge." She wrote forceful treatises; advanced important theories, being one of the; earliest women-writers of Germany to discuss the wider relations of women to intellectual and moral life; like the famous Italian *savantes* Lucretia Marinelli, Novella d'Andrea and the celebrated Frenchwoman, Marie de Jars-Courtenay. Anna Maria Schurmann also travelled widely, everywhere received by learned and distinguished men of science and literature. She became the object of pilgrimages of respect and curiosity on the part of the wise, the noble and the eminent. Christina of Sweden made her visit to Anna Maria a particular object. With her severer pursuits, Anna had pleasure and

Anna Maria Schurmann.

facility in the arts. She drew and painted, especially portraits, with superiour skill, carved in wood and stone, and embroidered elegantly. This last was one of her few specially feminine occupations; she was averse to the toilette, to cooking and household cares. In her later life she maintained close friendship with Labadie, the Calvinist theologian. (Its course was wholly intellectual.) With her mental distinction, Anna Maria Schumann possessed high moral qualities, and generously sacrificed herself for others. She never married. No heart-romance appears in her history. She was of strikingly masculine exterior, and had the air, the voice and tastes of men. She had friendships only with men; or—significant trait—with gentle, feminine and unintellectual women. She died in 1678, at an advanced age, with the wide recognition of learned Europe. If we cannot include her among among Uraniads, she is apart from true womankind; a neighbour of the second Intersex.

In the Intellectual Uraniad class, we can include many keenly professional women who quit the sphere of private and domestic life for practical science, higher educational work, or for solider departments of literature; as womenpoets, women-critics, women-novelists, editors, preachers, musicians, painters, architects. A proportion of specially serious-minded women, administrative in commerce and finance are Uraniads in temperament rather than "real" women. Frequently their sexual life accords. Many such women live together, where no other family-ties bind them to a less emancipated life. The intellectual Uraniad faces boldly the clamorous struggles in great literary and commercial commercial capitals of the world. She resorts to the great artistic and educational centers, for aesthetics and for a free life. London, Paris, New York, Berlin, Vienna and Munich are familiar with her. The Bourses and Wall Street and Capel Court often take note of her. In the bustling United States, many an Uraniad is "the right hand *man*" of the private-office, counting-room, shop and factory.

In social studies, essays, verse, and fiction the women-writers whose works have unfeminine aspects are endless. They occur especially in Anglo-Saxon, French, German and Scandinavian literatures. The personal or literary type of George Sand has little that is graciously womanish in it, though no feminosexual legend whatever attaches to

Uraniads in Earnest Professional Activities.

Literary Uraniads.

the authour of "Consuelo." The English novelist George Eliot, though her sexual intimacy with Lewes contradicts her 'unfeminism,' was intellectually more intersexual than really womanly. Her long *liaison* with Lewes was not robustly sexual-passional on her side: and her marriage to another man (much her junior) later in her life was considerably a step of intellectual and social policy. On the other hand, no one can properly include the famous Mary Somerville as at all uraniad, save by her vigorous mind for the abstract.

Suggestive friendships of uraniad force and constancy are many among women of the intersexual type. In numerous cases their literary records are striking. Thus we remember from youth, the history of the famous "Two Ladies of Langollen," whose romantic retreat to a rural life, in the end of the eighteenth century, was so remarked. A biographical record of a long relationship, that seems to have has a strongly psychic uranianism, an an intersexual quality in it, came a few years ago from an American lady, Miss A. C. Wood, in a volume "The Story Of A Friendship"; sketching the personality and life of Miss Irene Leache, a Virginian lady with whom Miss Wood had been intimately associated for more than thirty years. Their companionship was of exceptional closeness, excluding approach of any counter-sentiment to interrupt its, passional quality. Miss Leache had a nature of classic breadth and depth in its acceptances; was mystic, perceptive by intuition and virile; was, in fact, one of those magnetic types whose educative currents of mind impress themselves on even casual acquaintances. Her outward type—judging from her portrait—was equally of classic suggestiveness in the gentle gravity of the countenance, the philosophic repose of features, and the profound eyes.

The literature of Uraniadism, whether due to uraniad authours or quite impersonal as a study, including a large number of books by male writers, is a large aggregate. Much of it (indeed most of it) is in French, and by Frenchmen or Frenchwomen. By far the greater part of it depicts whatever is vitiating, grossly sexual, neurotic, "realistically physical and repulsive. Hundreds of novels have the feminosexual instinct as their theme, but to call them "literature" is a politeness. Two studies—so to say—presenting typical aspects, with more or less decency, are "Madame Adonis" by "Kachilde" and "Zéboïm" by Souillac. The story "Deux Amies" is also— conspicuous. Pierre Louys touches on the theme in his "Aphrodite " with delicate art. But there is not space or utility in entering here into the bibliography of uraniadism. The German literary catalogue is growing annually longer and of more acceptable traits in this curious field of fancy or fact. In English, there is chiefly pornography—of crudest kind.

The French Theater and Uraniadism.

It is not likely that tho acting-stage will ever allow to uraniadism as openly suggestive doings—not merely hints of the feminine intersex—as are permitted to Uranianism; at least not such as some Paris theaters and music-halls have tolerated. In the autumn of 1908, was played at a well-known house, a piece called "L'Après-Midi Byzantine," by tho well-known Parisian authour and critic, Nozière. An openly sexual suggestiveness of the kind in question was an essential episode (as well as hinted homosexuality) which two actresses played as if—*con amore*. In the same season, came before a Paris police-court the cases of the proprietor of the "Little Palace" Theater, and of some others concerned in the affair (including four or five actresses) for "outrages to the public decency," by a far too realistic pantomime named "Griserie d'Ether," In this spectacle, Mademoiselle Bouzon and Mademoiselle Lepelly. . . "interprétaient une scène d'ivresse et de passion lesbienne. . . renversées sur un fauteuil" . . . in a semi-nude condition, and "se pressent contre elles, en caressant les seins, et en laissant les mains s'égarer plus bas. . ." The manager of the theater was fined and imprisoned—not heavily—for this scandalously uraniad audacity. The actresses were not punished.

The Uraniad and Aesthetics.

Quite as the Uranian turns himself instinctively to the arts, so do we find the refined Uraniad in a grateful atmosphere when she is painter, sculptor, musician, actress, or busied in some one of the callings that are practical but aesthetic. Certain commercial ocupations gratify her sense of the beautiful and give her opportunity to be creative in it. They also keep her in close contact with lovely femininity. Of course, this type is widely removed from the unidealistic sorts in feminine intersexualism.

An interesting suggestion of the intersexual painter is met in the famous Madame Elizabeth Vigée-Lebrun (1750–1842) not only lauded as a portraitist, but of notable intellectuality in many branches of letters and science. Mme. Lebrun married; but for reasons explicitly apart from sexual interests. As to their entire dismissal of them she had a solemn understanding with her elderly husband, before and after the ceremony. Dargenville remarks of her slyly—"I could well say of her, as of Madame Dacier, that under their traits as two illustrious women one saw two great—men."

An interesting recent example in aesthetics—productively—was Rosa Bonheur; a man in appearance, with not a little of the male in her vigorous artistic personality. Numerous such artists will recur to those who are familiar with the *salons* of today.

In music, we find often (as in the foregoing study of the Uranian) that the aesthetic Uraniad is passionately musical. Uraniad passions are met often in those female musicians conspicuous for bodily abnormality, and masculinity. They occur in the instances of female tenors, female baritones, female basses, such as are heard in "freak" concerts, or as artistic "curios" under more diginified conditions. A Berlin physician, who has a particular clientage among musical professionals, says that experience has led him to the conclusion that the contralto voice in a woman indicates an abnormal sexualism more than does a higher vocal *timbre*; that the deeper the female voice, the more to be suspected is intersexualism.

On the stage occur types of the masculine-feminine; presumptive or known Uraniads. Sometimes theatrical life offers a type of woman, who in spite of a normally sexual past seems more a man than many men, in her force of intellect, in her dismissal to the secondary plane most sentimental feminine interests. Such is Sarah Bernhardt; who has, with advancing years identified herself more and more with male roles, masculinizing her life, and uniting in her many-sided personality aspects of the intellectual and the physical of two sexes. In fact, this great actress's real sexual history is considerably uraniad; more than is well-known. A strongly uraniadistic actress (psychically) was the noted American tragedian, Charlotte Cushman. Like Sarah Bernhardt she was acceptable in male roles; at her best only in the severer and almost unfeminine characters, her bodily personality being rather virile than female. The French and Italian theatrical stage has a large contingent of uraniads of mark. One distinguished actress of Italy; also a South-Italian dramatic contralto; also a distinguished vocal instructress; a great German dramatic teacher; three female painters; a Scandinavian sculptress—all recur to the writer of these pages as being identified more or less as Uraniads. A noted female sculptor who died about a decade ago in Rome, was not only of masculine nature and physique, but carried far enough her sexual indifference to- everything male to embarrass occasionally her friends. Sometimes she admitted visitors to her atelier while working from nude male models. On one such occasions her calmness was amusing. A distinguished sculptor, a man, was present, though the model was nude. The model, a robust young Trastevere lad of some fourteen years, became sexually excited. Somehow timid of a change of pose or expecting his agitation to subside, he remained conspicuously—priapian. Miss X—, without interrupting her chat, walked to the other side of the room, caught up a large jug of cold water, poured it gently and slowly over the youth, talking away gaily all the time, and sat down to continue her study of his oustretched thigh when he was in—repose!

The Uraniad and
Artistic "Trades."

In the ornamental trades and callings, such as dressmakers, milliners, dealers in fine underwear and hosiery, costume-designers and so on, the Uraniad has a large field. Here she can come unsuspected into intimate bodily contact with beautiful women. *Jeune filles appétissantes* innocently can titillate daily her sexualism. Professional acquaintances second it. The professions of mantua-making, millinery, corset-ateliers and so on are recognized as screens for the Lesbian bawd in many great cities, especially Paris. The smart "hat-parlours," the rooms of *corsetières*, the establishments of discreet màsseurs, etc. are made useful for similisexualism between women; even to being recognized as rendezvous. Scandals of a sort imaginable have often darkened such establishments, not suspected save by the inner circles of *initiées;* thus emphasizing to us the fact that what the poet calls the "eternal womanly" often is anything but such in the beckonings—on of the mysterious intersexual passions.

X

The Uranian and Uraniad as Degenerates, as Criminals and as Social and Legal Victims: Types and Biographies

W ithin a few years, particularly through printed "disclosures" of similisexualism, in London New York and Paris, in club-life and other social fraternities, we have seen the word "degenerate" in frequent employ. So used, it has

Misleading Uses
of the Word
"Degenerate."

acquired a meaning inexact for close students of similisexual problems. The American and the English newspapers especially have aided in misusing "degenerate" as a common vocable. The work of psychiatric specialists, should teach thoughtful men and women that the similisexual instincts—Uranianism, homosexualism, even feminosexualism and Uraniadism—do not necessarily mean clear physical, intellectual or moral degeneracy.

The similisexual passion is a sex-determinant,—without the stigma of sex-decadence as its necessary consequence. It is a concurrent quality in all sorts and conditions of human beings, good and bad, moral and immoral, superior or inferior, as to physiques and minds. As we have seen, Uranians and Uraniads may be (in a great proportion are) perfectly developed and normal; they often are striking examples of "model" humanity in many traits. The intersexual instinct mixes in temperaments of the more or less perfect or imperfect, of the noble or ignoble. It can appear in types richly endowed with bodily vigour and sexual force, possessed of an aggressive mental, physical and ethical superiority. Or else it can be blended with effeminacy and a shameful un-virility. It can join to a perfect external womanliness and unwomanliness. It characterizes the high and debased. It is an ingredient that often unites to no determinative externals. It is not strictly, psychologically, a definitely "contra-sexual" impulse. It refers to no hard-and-fast logic of individualisais, in innumerable instances. It has no necessary and inevitable relationship to any disease, to any distortion of the intellectual aesthetic, ethical or physical types. It is a product and an impulse by itself, the nature-right of distinct, or of indistinct and medial sexes; the semi-tones of the psychic and sexual gamut. Each intersex sounds the melody of its own string, in the mysterious human instrument of which it is arbitrarily made a part. It completes, as an indispensable, Nature's calm cycles. In fact, as to the term "degenerate" one of the very first principles in studying homosexualism is to remember that a similisexual man is not necessarily demonstrable as a decadent man or woman.

"Not Necessarily."

"Not necessarily," has been written. Nevertheless, it is not remarkable that decadence has been so placarded on the homosexual, that to the mass of educated people not uranistic, and even to the Uranian himself, the terms have become synonymous. For—unfortunately—there are obviously large elements of debasement in the legion of Uranians and Uraniads. They depress the observer by salient degeneracy of mind, soul, heart, and body. To analyze such phases is our least agreeable task. But the true Nature-student has no right to shirk Nature's problems, nor must he be deflected by what is ugly, grotesque, unclean or vile.

Correct Use of the Term "Degenerate."

Compared with some other aspects of Uranian degeneracy, we find that downright bodily effeminacy, corporeal imperfections or abnormalities do not play a peculiarly large role in homosexualism, even when linked with weakness, disgrace, vice and crime. Often the "worst" type of homosexual differs physically from the normal man by merely the less obvious details of structure; or by none. It is in his temperamental, in his mental and moral making-up that we remark vicious divergences. By the Intersexual Theory, much that is called degeneracy is divergence from relatively a few male sexual attributes only.

The examples of Uranianism joined to such decadence are varied, just as are instances of Uranianism when conjoined with fine moral and intellectual fibre. We can pass from the Uranian who exhibits merely a refined weakness of character, or a 'secondary' physique, to the Uranian that is a prostitute, blackmailer, thief, child-ravisher, murderer; or perhaps a type physically deficient, plainly abnormal and even monstrous.

Moral Degeneracy Often Less Noticeable than Intellectual; or Other Sorts.

This degeneracy of the Uranian often appears only intellectually. It is true that disgracefully debased, degenerate Uranians are frequently simply shrewd. The applied intellectualism of such types is usually not remarkable. On the other hand, a vast number of quite homosexual men, Uranians of widely diverse social educations, show little loss of moral sensibilities. In social, life and in family and business relations they are not ethical "degenerates"; while details of mental shortcoming may be noted. Again, wholesomeness or unwholesomeness of the soil from which the human plant springs, youthful environments, later associations, all share in the growth or the checking of real degeneracy in the homosexual world, just as they affect so much else in humanity.

Two types of Uranians we constantly find morally and intellectually deficient. First, the non-mercenary but passive sodomist in general, Two Special Classes. without regard to his class or to his social station. Second, the Uranian prostitute, who is professionally quite of the mercenary class, active or passive. Sexual passivists, offer a considerable proportion of types, with even a degeneracy of the sexual organs, as of some other physical traits. To this topic an Appendix to this study will refer. Passive similisexualism seems to work toward bodily and intellectual degeneracy, far more frequently than does "active" homosexualism. There is some intersexual logic here. The passivist (*cinædus*) is more feminine than the activist; and his deficiencies and degeneracies often logically are in key with distinctively womanish deficiencies.

An example of degenerated mentality though not perceptibly linked to degeneracy of the moral nature (and scarcely such as to the, physique) occured to the notice of Taylor. The physician was called in to determine, by exploration, the sex of a certain Elise Edwards, an actress" by profession. So came the Instances of Degenerately Psychic Kind; but not Physically nor Morally Such. disclosure that the patient had a manly body of normal structure and appearance, in all essentials; which the "actress" had long concealed in womanly attire. Since the fourteenth year of the patient (whose real name was Z—) he had always worn woman's dress. He had been every where received professionally as an actress. He wore his hair long; had cultivated a female pitch of voice, and so on. The facial type was sufficently feminine to support the role with ease; but the body was male, from head to foot. The generative organs were vigorously male: There were indications of passive sodomy; distention of the anus, etc. In this case, the degeneration seemed merely temperamental and mental. The patient was morally, normal, so far as an impressions suggested. In an earlier chapter of this book, a converse of this case was cited.

A striking example was that of the young German, known in certain circles of Munich homosexualism as well as in many other cities, by the title of "The Pompadour." His autobiography has appeared in part, by the editorial aid of Johannes Guttzeit, in a recently-printed brochure. (Leipsig: W. Besser.) Well-born, of a Dionian-Uranian father and of a perfectly normal mother, fairly educated, and of manly exterior (including, when he wished it, a full beard) this subject achieved wide South-German notoriety. He was the hero of countless adventures, with the military and the civil, with the Church and the world. Incorrigibly bohemian, "The Pompadour"—for so he came to be nicknamed—threw away efforts at keeping any fixed social station. He became now a confidential servant, now a mere waiter, now a secretary; uniting the complaisances of a passivist with one or another occupation. "The Pompadour" travelled about Europe much. Speaking two or three languages besides German, he became international. The moral nature in him did not degenerate toward criminality, in fact his ethical personality was rather firm. But mental application, a serious view of life and depth of feeling, wholly failed. The muscular organization gradually became degenerated; and the practice of anal coitus had debilitating local effects.

A singular case comes from across the Atlantic. A few years ago there was a popular woman-barber, who also kept a confectioner's shop, in the town of North Haven, Maine (United States). Women-barbers are not altogether rare in Yankeedom—where so many odd customs are met by the European visitor. Lilian Carver, as she was known, seemed a local fixture, and was a respected member of the small community. For many years, the shop was patronized by the men of the town. Miss Carver also was an expert *coiffeuse* for— one much demanded. The Carver family had come to North Haven very quietly, and were members of a Baptist Church there. Miss Lilian was their only daughter. She was a plump, fine-skinned, handsome brunette. A circle of admirers hung about her, and some of them were on at least vague sentimental terms with her. One day, Lilian Carver went to Boston. A few days later appeared the published statement in the newspapers of the county, to the following startling purport; sworn-to by "Lilian," by her parents, and by the pastor of her church-society, the Rev. Lyman W. Sweet. The latter had been taken into a secret that stirred the town to lively amazement and wrath:

"Having been known in North Haven, Me., (my birthplace and home for thirty years,) as a female, by the name of Lilian G. Carver, I do hereby publicly declare that I have been masquerading, and for more than ten years against my wishes. Force of habit, filial regard, and dread of the necessary sensation attendant upon such a step have prevented me from doing my duty; which now, as a Christian I undertake to do. My real name is Arthur Leslie Carver. I am a man, and since September this year, (1901) have dressed and have been known as such."

"Lilian's" Carver's degenerative traits were exclusively physical. They were invisible to the layman's notice, as departing much from a plump male type. There was no moral degeneracy whatever in question. The sexual organs were large and perfectly masculine. The sexual tendency was "passive." As Arthur L. Carver, the subject entered business life in Boston, as an employé, and is still in that occupation and city.

A similar case occurred also in the State of Maine about the same date as the "Lilian Carver" one. After having been dressed, employed and known only as a woman during a respectable life, Sylvester Cole, a servant in a family in Vassalboro, had fallen in love with a fellow-servant, Georgiana Bernard. Therewith he disclosed his real sex, ceased to be "Maggie Cole," and was duly married to the young woman of his choice. Cole claimed that the secret of his sex was necessary for reasons of pecuniary kind; but that advantage was not cleared up, although a relative of wealth was named in the riddle. The young man, an Irishman by blood, was not deficient in moral or physical qualifications; although his personal aspect, as to face and figure, degenerated from a truly male type to womanish contours. Also, Cole's mind was not of a robust male sort, and he showed that general temperamental degeneracy toward feminine tastes that comes with the wish to sustain such a masquerade. The sexual organs were stated, by a physician who saw them, to be masculine in all respects, except that of size. The *vita sexualis* of the subject before his marriage could not be distinctly ascertained. A rumour (not originating in Vassalboro) asserted him to be of "passivist" impulses.

Instance.

Similar instances are many. There is a departure from the truly male, temperament and intellect. The bodily "secondariness" is noticeable by comparisons with fully virile models. The contrasts apply to such structural matters as the form and weight of the skeleton, the contours

Degrees of the Physical Departure: Real Hermaphroditism, Monstrosity, etc.

of the fleshy parts of the frame, the muscular strength, the proportions of the features, the voice, movements, gait, etc. A tabulation of these is included in an Appendix, for the reader desirous of finding whether his own type or some other approach at all the uranian Intersex, or toward Uraniadism.

Nevertheless, a limited, obscure proportion of homosexuals, Uranian and Uraniads, are marked by actual hermaphroditism,—plain and unequivocal. That any are so has strengthened the rooted vulgar idea that the Uranian and Uraniad *must* be hermaphrodite. This antiquated notion is strong in America and England. The reader will find in the closer medical studies of the homosexual problem, as well as in other connections, full information as to bodily hermaproditism. It includes male, genitals in a type otherwise female (or vice versa); male and female genitals and hybrid organs in the *same* individual; atrophied organizations; and so on. An interesting series of observations of this anatomical side of homosexualism appears in the "Jahrbuch für Sexuelle Zwischenstufen" for 1902. The present writer examined lately a striking instance, in an Italian city.

The absurd idea of an hermaphroditic body as *necessary* to Uranianism belongs with an old notion in Catholic canon-laws (and others)—that the hermaphrodite must be made a sort of outlaw, as a human being divinely accursed. One «celebrated hermaphrodite has left a published study of this predicament; a kind of desperate appeal and defense. A notable hermaphrodite of the time of Trajan and Hadrian was the distinguished philosopher Favorinus, the friend of Plutarch and the instructor of Aulus Gellius. Whether the famous Chevalier d'Eon, who appeared before the world during his long and amazingly adventurous life (1728–1810) now as woman, now as man, with perfect success was hermaphroditic, and homosexual or not at all so, has never become perfectly clear. Some recent studies of his career are to the contrary. Indeed, one can-hardly class the plucky and gifted Chevalier among degenerates. He seems more an incorrigible eccentric and "mystifier;" a type in many traits vigorously—agressively—virile, as his friends and enemies soon learned to their dismay. The Abbé François de Choisy (1644–1724) offers, on somewhat similar lines to d'Eon, a temperament far more saliently degenerate and devirilized: but here again nothing classes the type as an hermaphrodite, in any exact sense of the term; and during de Choisy's bisexual career, with all its effeminacies, orgies, profligacies, *aventures galantes* and so on—now of masculine and now of feminine colouring—there is no question of mental degeneracy. His culture, wit, critical acuteness and general intellectual vigour are attested by his contemporaries, and by his voluminous writings on philosophy, history and religion. He seems to have assumed so much the woman because "to be a woman" delighted him naturally, and licensed the perversities and fantasies of his curious intersexualism. To Emil Mario Vacano, the famous "Miss Corinna" of the circus-rings of Europe, in the middle of the last century (to whom we have referred in citing from his novel "Humbug") something of the same capital and capacity for sexual mystification were notably developed, in course of Yacano's amazing *Wanderjähre*.

We should not forget, although the dictum is opposed by sentimental and popular theories, that the aesthetic life demonstrably does not stand for moral good, nor *per se* for healthfulness of mind or body to the individual or race. We

Relation Between Aesthetic Life and Degeneracy.

may say that there is no demonstrable bond between the Good and the Beautiful, as we accept them. A profound psychic paradox faces us here. Pretty theorizings and a world-old lyrism on this topic are out of tune with daily facts. As we review dispassionately the history of nations, or study individuals, we are led to the conviction that in proportion as we find men and women arriving at a certain—or uncertain—degree of higher aesthetic sensibility they tend to become morally, intellectually and temperamentally decadent. Beauty thus stands before the thoughtful mind as not friend but enemy. Certain authorities in the study of homosexualism, including some who are not disposed to tolerances of its philosophic justifications, have gone so far as to consider the similisexual instincts as a distinctive trait of highly intellectual races; the tokens of advanced mentality in the individual. Germany and Italy here are much in evidence—so far as such argument is tenable.

In keeping with aesthetic sensitiveness in uranianism, we find that luxury, elegances, refinements, afford salient types of degenerate mankind. We have seen some already, under other headings of this study. The sensual, cruel or merely effeminized Roman patricians; a dozen well-known princes in the Cæsarian lines;

Degenerate Similisexualism in Aristocratic Life, with High Aesthetic Sensitiveness.

the debauched Greeks; the Italians and Frenchmen and Teutons of the Middle Ages; the long chain of Egyptian, Turkish, Persian voluptuaries;

a Continental and Anglo-Saxon aristocracy today—furnish examples. We will not say that these types are morally or otherwise degenerates absolutely on account of their aesthetic or other cultivation. But the coincidence with it seems close. The passive sodomist in "high life" is notoriously degenerate, intellectually and morally, as has been noted above.

The complex degeneracy of Nero is extreme. How far Nero s moral abasement sprung out of his riddlesome dionid-uranian nature—was product of his original sexual instincts—is not clear. Nero's æstheticism had not enough higher intellectual counterbalances; a factor which has saved many an artist from decadence. Nero's increasing blood-lust, his indifference to murder, his use of the executioner and the assassin, of the royal command to suicide, all to get rid of inconvenient people; his slaughters of his nearest relatives and closest friends,—all these have no obvious, logical relation with Nero as a homosexual type. Enormously developed cruelty in Nero does not appear to have been essential to his sexual enjoyments. His tendency towards it seems merely a Roman liking for cruel sanguinary spectacles; a trait in many types of women, the Spanish, for instance—who adore millinery, lace, music and bull-fights. The beautiful *madrilena* or French *méridionale*, who cheers the agile "torero," who shudders with delight at bleeding men and disembowelled horses, is much the same type as the Roman lady criticizing with enthusiasm the gladiator in the arena hacking the arms and head from his adversary. Many men of the southern races which offer bisexual aspects, or are only indistinctly homosexual, are similarly feminine.

[sidebar: Elagabalus; Nero; Gilles de Rais, Philippe d'Orléans; the Marquis de Sade, etc.]

In the case of that amazing oriental, one by no means wholly homosexual, the Emperor Elagabalus (or Heliogabalus) we have an Uranian monumental in even juvenile degeneracy. His effeminate beauty of person was so remarkable that he seems to have deserved his adopted name of the Sun-God; a suitable priest to such a deity in his bisexual loveliness. The growth of his delusions and degeneracies was swift, reaching their highest point when he succeeded Macrinus as Emperor, for his short reign of mania and folly. The "marriage" of Elagabalus' to the Moon, his insane expenditures, his sexual debauches as "man and woman," his caprices, fêtes and follies have become history. They lacked almost every element of dignity, elegance or common-sense; being mostly grotesquely-mad efforts to enjoy the impossible in every form. Cruelty however is not a distinguishing trait in Elagabalus, as it was in many predecessors on the Roman Imperial throne. He had rather the weaknesses of a girl, including a girl's aversion to seeing' what is truculently painful.

Prince Eugene of Savoy, had a side to his nature that was indisputably degenerate,—especially from the military-uranian's typic point of view. He was not only known as a pederast, but was given to prostituting himself (he was a passivist) for money, disguised, like a sort of soldier-Messalina. The letters of Elizabeth-Charlotte, the shrewd Duchess of Orléans, have odd references to these disgraceful proclivities of the bold hero of Oudenarde and Malplaquet. Philippe d'Orléans (1640–1701) the womanish, depraved and homosexual brother of Louis XIV, is a remarkable instance of degeneracy not marked by cruelty, in a man not a poltron and not intellectually deficient.[1]

Gilles de Rais: A Fifteenth Cenrury Aesthete. Murderer and Pederast.

A remarkable combination of moral and temperamental degeneracy, intellectuality not being impaired in it to any appreciable degree, occurs in Gilles de Rais. This young Bretagne nobleman was executed, along with certain accomplices, at Nantes, in the year 1440, after an amazing career of erotomania, with the gradual increase of a blood-lust sentiment in it. De Rais was born of a noble and wealthy stock. At an early age he became master of a revenue, for the time enormous. He fought bravely as a patriotic soldier at the side of Jeanne Dare, becoming sufficiently distinguished to be made one of her marshals. Abruptly closing his military career, he retired to his estates, especially to that of Tiffauges, near Nantes. Here Gilles de Rais devoted himself to a life of intense, passionate intellectualism and aesthetics. Collecting a notable library, he also maintained a large retinue of singers, comedians, poets and painters, with whom he passed all his time. Such luxury made deep inroads on his fortune. Accordingly Gilles de Rais undertook alchemy, and anon conjurations and magic, to maintain his splendour of living. These processes soon brought him to the next step—the murder of young children, partly for the use of their blood in diabolical rites, but soon as a regular element of sexual

---

1. The writer take this opportunity to note the loss of some lines in the first paragraph of the eighth chapter of this study (p. 231) by which error, not observed till too late for correction, there is a confusion in referring to Philippe d'Orléans senior and the Regent.

excitement. He had a staff of envoys who kidnapped handsome young lads, and frequently little children. They were brought to certain secret rooms of Tiffauges; where de Rais and his companions in diabolism violated their victims and then cut them to pieces. Often they first slaughtered the unfortunate youths, and then undertook coition in various ways, with the corpses. Hundreds of such murders were consummated before the proofs of their commission were sufficiently established and the timid legal arm was strong enough to act against so powerful a local lord. De Rais was arrested finally, with François Prelati, the famous necromancer—who was his companion and tutor—was duly arraigned and tried, with one or two others implicated; and (deeply penitent, by all accounts) lie suffered the penalty for his hideous crimes in Nantes, in the autumn of 1440. He was only some thirty-six years old. Apart from the growth in him of his passion for pederasty, in connection with death and blood de Rais was a man of singularly sensitive aesthetic nature and culture, as well as of high intellectuality.

_____

Blood-Lust and Similisexualism.

_____

Blood-lust is frequently the inseparable accompaniment of the sexual instinct. If so, to gratify the sexual passion stirs up at once the wish to see suffering, to shed blood, even to murder. We meet this fearful instinct, in many individuals, both heterosexual and homosexual. The sentiment put vice-versa—blood-lust breeding sex-lust—is met often. This fact enters into many assassinations and mysterious murders. Thus acts the passion well-known in sexual parlance as 'sadism,' a word derived from the famous French eroto-maniac, the Marquis de Sade, whose instincts were particularly of the kind. The maniacal instinct to dismember and to disfigure the body of some victim, either before or after sexual use of it, is not at all rare, either in heterosexual or homosexual erotism. The constantly recurring cases of murder with mutilation, the "Jack the Ripper" types of assassination, are almost invariably so explained. It is often associated with the instinct of fiendish cruelty to children, and with their murder, as in the classic (but not at all unique) case of Grilles de Rais. A noteworthy sadistic case occurred some years ago in France—the arrest and execution of a vagrant named Vacher, who had ravished dozens of young country-lads and then killed them, or vice-versa, before he was apprehended. The Paris *apache* has often been observed to possess the sadistic quality.

The shocking "Dippold Case," before the Baireuth assises in October 1903, was a typical instance of homosexuality and lust of cruelty.

The "Dippold Case," in 1903.

In that example they were united in a young man, a private tutor named Dippold, of superiour intellectual qualities and careful education, who made two lads (committed to his care "by negligent parents) lead such lives of martyrdom as only an unnatural monster would do. Beatings, exposure to weather, brutalities of all kinds, with sexual abuse of the two helpless little fellows, left in a lonely country-home, ended in the death of one of the boys—Heinz Koch, aged thirteen. Dippold was arrested for murder, and his sex-relations to the boys were elicited. The story horrified a wide European public. Dippold was sentenced to eight years of severe imprisonment.

Pederastic affairs in boys' schools often take the colour of such brutal crimes. The robbery of newly-made graves, and the outrages on corpses also are due to this same hideous instinct. The topic is somewhat foreign to the purposes of the present study. It can be pursued by the reader in numerous studies of sadism, masochism, and so on, by psychiatric specialists.

The name of the Marquis de Sade (1740–1814), a Parisian and a member of aristocratic society in the latter years of the eighteenth century, and in the first part of the Napoleonic period, has

De Sade.

passed into such psychiatric literature for degeneracy connected with erotic monomania. De Sade strongly suggests Grilles de Rais. In his case, maniacal heterosexualism and maniacal homosexualism are more fairly in balance. De Sade was perceptibly a Dionian-Uranian. From a career of early military distinction he passed swiftly to such an existence of debauch, to so prolonged an orgy of erotism, that madness was inevitable. The reader can review for himself the perversities of this man (a graceful, quiet-mannered type even when maniac) with masochistic passions for flagellation, torture, blood and aphrodisiacs, as part of the sexual act. His novels "Justine" and "Julie" have no literary vigour; interesting only by their atmosphere of delirious lust, the marvel is that they ever were put on paper. De Sade's extraordinary career is the subject of a considerable psychiatric literature, and need not be detailed here.

Fetichism, or the growth of certain fantastic appetites, in connection with homosexual (as with heterosexual) emotion, and as its stimulus, is

Fetichism, and Other Phases of Degenerate Homosexualism.

fully reviewed in treatises by Moll, Krafft-Ebing, Ellis, Hirschfeld, and others. Masochistic flagellation, fetichistic sexual excitements awakened by objects not naturally suggestive, the cutting-off of hair, the shoe-fetich, etc., are in this category. But fetichism, like cruelty to children and lust-murder, seems less an attribute of homosexual depravation than of heterosexualism.

Uranianism and Degeneracy in the Aristocracy and Middle Classes.

As the readers of large daily newspapers well know, the world over, one need not revert to cases of degeneracy similisexualism in past civilizations and centuries. The data that contemporary law-courts, police-blotters and so on can offer, including the reserved "features" of divorce suits, furnish liberal studies. Great capitals, such as London, Paris, New York, Berlin, all large cities and many small ones of the world present (more or less to scandal and wonderment) the Uranian of diseased appetites, and of proportionately contemptible, brutal, vitiated and obscene practices. The "Cleveland Street" Scandal in London, and like affairs, in which distinguished professional men, high members of the aristocratic circles and eminent financiers figured as the debauchers of innocent lads, have born witness to undercurrents of English sexualism. In New York, only a few years ago, a similar scandal (in a popular club) cast the city into a quiver of nervous distress. This affair with difficulty was kept from full publicity, by the general flight of many persons involved.

In Modern Anglo-Saxon Aristocracy: An English Decadent.

Within a year or so, the bankruptcy of an enormously wealthy young British nobleman and peer drew new attention to his eccentricities. Of a degenerately æsthetic kind, they long had been in popular comment. This young man, the wearer of several high titles, owed (at last accounts) nearly six hundred thousand pounds, although his yearly income had been continously about a hundred thousand pounds! His life as a boy was effeminate enough to justify rumours as to his homosexualism, further bruited through his own love of notoriety. His passion for art, for the theater, for dressing in female clothing, for the most expensive costumes, (including those feminine) his almost unparallelled extravagance as to rare jewels—all made him famous. His health was at no time robust, and curious tales were therewith linked. To the amazement of his acquaintance presently he abruptly married. A young relative, of suitable wealth was his bride. Naturally the marriage was not felicitous; but nobody was prepared to find the bridegroom soon bringing suit for the annullment of the marriage, on the claim that he was physically unable to fulfil his marital duties. A Court accepted the medical verdict to this interesting effect; and the marriage was declared void. Six months later, the divorced young gentleman, demanded a second medical examination, so that he could remarry the same lady. Medical inspection having again justified the noble lord, he became for a second time this young relative's spouse, apparently with her hearty consent and satisfaction. A fanatic on all theatrical entertainments, this young peer organized a traveling and residential theater-troupe, and rambled about England with it; or else he acted in his own magnificent private theater, playing almost exclusively female roles. His jewels were valued at half a million pounds, the rubies, cats-eyes, alexandrites, emeralds and diamonds vying with those of any princess or opera-queen. He was the victim of a huge robbery, by a highly confidential companion, of such jewellery, but recovered most of the stolen ornaments, those also valued at a great sum. When in masculine dress, he was accustomed to change his clothes at least three or four times daily, in each case with appropriate jewellery to the amount of thousands of pounds. Before the latest crash in his affairs, he had paid sixty per cent usury. One of his intimacies, that had nothing if not uranian aspects, was the topic of much London and Paris gossip, awhile ago. Not long afterwards he died.

In beginning this chapter, attention was drawn to the error of supposing that the homosexual is necessarily a degenerate in body or in mind, in any such sense of the term as is so common: and the extremely important relation between homosexuality and taste, talent and genius in aesthetics has been shown. But it is not amiss to note here a curious phase that has often been pointed out as to artistic or literary homosexuals of anglo-saxon, teutonic or other northern—non-latin—races who escape timely from social and legal perils plentiful in their own countries, and so betake themselves to Italy, to Spain, and so on—especially to Italy. Their sexual liberty when there seems remarkably often to have the effect of destroying their intellectual or artistic activity and ambition. They become professional drifters and 'dawdlers', degenerate in will, in purpose, and even intersexual virility. They do nothing, accomplish nothing, while constantly talking about doing and accomplishing; and anon having lapsed gently to idleness complete, the capital of talent seems to evaporate wholly away. Their liberty really gained, its relief undoes them. The relation of these aspects to the American, the English, the German homosexuals who become *émigrés* to the treacherous South is particular. Latins and Gauls, born in genial airs, seem to make compatible inborn uranianism with activity of talent much more as a normal condition than do immigrants new to the sunshine and philarrenic security of the South.

Masculine Civilian Prostitution.

In the eighth chapter of this book was considered military prostitution. Let us now glance at non-military prostitution. The place may be Berlin, Vienna, New York, London, Munich, Rome, Florence, Naples, Palermo, Cairo, Athens—any capital, any large city; for no large city exists in the world where the male prostitute is not now to be met and bought as readily as is the female harlot. Along some boulevard, or in a quiet park-alley, walks the uranian 'patron' as evening draws on. He may be rich, he may be poor, of noble rank or humble, educated or ignorant, robustly male in his aspect or delicate in physique, moral or immoral, religious or irreligious. In spite of anything else, along with anything else, he is an Intersexual. He is perhaps among those innumerable Uranians of the better social world who lead solitary lives in their sexualism, no matter what warm friendships they enjoy. He has thus given up seeking any social complement and ideal sex-companion; whose embraces could complete not only his physical but intellectual individuality. Or it may be that' his similisexualism seeks physical relief always "out of his class." Not a philosopher, he knows that he must needs physically satisfy himself in only "that way." Not an idealist, he prefers vulgarized *amours de passage*.

"In that way." In no case, with a woman. As he passes (perhaps a handsome, manly figure) the street-walker tries to attract him. But the Uranian does not give a thought to her ogling. She even angers and bores him. Every throb of his intersexual being is pulsating for a male. As social companions, as artistic creations for the eye, many women may have his admiration and intimacy, especially if "good women." For his sexual relief, woman is an irony. Could the female harlot serve him sexually as she serves so many millions of men, easy would be his choice. But occidental Europe in general does not permit brothels of males, nor allow the boy-harlot too openly and scandalously to *racoler*.

Yet now and then, as the sexually-excited Uranian continues his stroll, he meets a furtive, keen look from a man or a youth who passes. It is the mysterious *Anblick* of the Uranian fraternity; that psychic-sexual interrogation, that signal and challenge ever where current and understood among homosexuals. It is true that homosexuality of an Uranian is not met in his glance unless he means it to be so met. Many homosexuals sedulously avoid it. Part of the protective "Mask" is the watch *against* such eloquence of a mere exchange of looks. True also is it that the "Look" in part is explained by the fact that the Uranian eye, especially in the higher type, is almost always singularly luminous, and that its penetrating gaze can be disturbingly direct. But the 'homosexual glance' is not mere fiction.

Before a shop-window, or perhaps at a bench in a park, halts the Uranian. Soon another stroller, loitering in professional alertness, walks toward him—catches his eye expressively and stands or sits near him. The newcomer may be a boy of sixteen or eighteen, or much more an adult good-looking or plain; likely not really well-dressed; and artificial aids improve (?) his physique. He may have a certain *fausse élégance*—cheap jewellery and a gaudy cravat. A conversation is begun. Little by little, it slips on toward confidentialities—the discomforts of living and of travelling alone, the effects of the evening air, the quiet of the place, the amusements of the town. The talk grows indistinctly erotic as the other man becomes surer that he has here one of the—profession. Presently the Uranian, certain of his ground and well-enough suited with his interlocutor's physical type, proposes that they take a walk together; or go to some near restaurant. During the promenade, or at the café, there is the necessary bargaining, good-humoredly, and as with a woman-harlot. The two men also are pretty sure to pause at the nearest latrine, by common consent, if the patron be especially disposed to estimate the physical capital of the other. If satisfied with the *étalage*, he accompanies the vendor to the nearest safe locality—a corner of a deserted thicket in the park—an open field; to an equivocal hotel, to the quarters of his new friend; perhaps to his own lodging:

"Allons, retirons-nous, ne troublons point leur joie."

The client pays the tariff agreed or disputed—five or ten shillings, five or ten marks, two or three florins, ten to twenty francs—local and personal prices differ. Anon he says good-evening to his acquaintance, whom he may or may not care ever to meet again. The incident is closed: leaving the Uranian sexually pacified, precisely as is the Dionian by the functions of a female harlot.

The foregoing is a typical incident. The army of such male prostitutes in large cities is of thousands. Boys of precocious debauchery, either in the pay of mature male procurers and patrons, or "working" by themselves, idle and corrupt youths in their later teens, young men in twenties and thirties, older types (often of repulsive maturity) catamites of all ages, complexions, physiques, grades of cleanliness and decency. As a rule, those who begin with health and robustness of body and pretentions to good-looks become feeble, pallid wrecks. Sexual debilities, the precarious, nerve-shattering life, misery, late hours, weather, careless habits of person, drink—all sap away physical attractiveness. The concurrence of the female harlot is not troublesome. But the civilian prostitute suffers much in his 'business' in those many cities where soldiers and sailors are his rivals. A large proportion of the clientage much prefer a soldier-prostitute; for reasons we have mentioned in a former chapter.

The homosexual—or *de facto* homosexual—prostitute who if older or younger, solicits publicly in a female costume, is a frequent phase; as we have seen in foregoing instances. Such types haunt the parks, public thoroughfares and so on, after nightfall; or are met in the lowest of *café-chantants*, balls and bars. But to make a practice of such a *travesti* requires a style of physique, an age, and a natural effeminacy not so general as is supposed. The trick is not always useful, either; for the imitation may be so perfect that a homosexual client looking for a male pathic is deceived, and pays no heed to the maneuvers and charms of what he supposes to be a woman street-walker. Again, if he recognizes the under-sex, he is perhaps repelled by any masculine type that appears so womanish, and so will have nothing to do with it. He is seeking for virility; a robust, coarse soldier, or even unclean but manly *voyou*, is vastly more to his taste. An additional reason against such masquerading is that it is an immediate offense against police regulations, and makes the male prostitute liable to arrest, even if, he is not caught in soliciting. Hence it is not favoured by much the largest proportion of prostitutes, whether they can adapt themselves well to it or not.

A general custom in the world of homosexual prostitution, though perhaps more one that is observed in its "smarter" grades, is the changing of the masculine names to its female equivalent, especially when correspondence or conversation concerning the subject is in question; or assuming some female name of independent source; or taking some nick-name—vulgar or aristocratic, delicate or crude—belonging to the feminine category. Thus Henry becomes "Henrietta," Charles signs himself "Charlotte," Paul is known as "Pauline," Jules as Juliette, and so on. Such *noms de guerre* as "La Belle Hortense," "Cleopatra," "La Marquise" "Die Schöne Salome" and "Petite Fleur" are attached to youths or men, perhaps with moustaches that a trooper would envy, and of blamelessly male sexual qualifications—according to what popularly would seem to decide that matter. The fantasies in these sobriquets are endless, descending to the most obscene picturesqueness, But merely feminized male names are most in favour, perhaps because this practice is so usual among homosexuals distinctly effeminate, but of thoroughly good social station and wholly apart from any venal or proletarian classes. As to the latter, an amusing caricature appeared lately in a Paris humorous journal, in which a severe old valet is projecting his head from out of the door of his master's bedroom, saying to an elegantly dressed young man, on the landing—"The Baron don't receive to day—he's abed!"—to which the youth smilingly replies, "Ah yes—but he expects *me*. Please just tell him it's *Lucy*."

Such is homosexual street-prostitution of usual sort. It differs from female prostitution in that it is not so observable by the uninitiated. Nothing is more common than to hear heterosexuals, all their lives in some noted center of male prostitution, deny, angrily or serenely, that it flourishes in their town. Any much-frequented, street music-hall, ball, theater witness the contrary.

Define Resorts for Male Prostitution.

In a large radius of Europe the male prostitute can "labour in his vocation" with impudent frankness. In Madrid, Belgrad, Constantinople, Naples, Florence, Paris, New York, Palermo, Milan, Marseilles, and so on, while homosexual brothels are not encouraged by statutes or police, there are houses for—sometimes exclusively—male rendezvous. The police always deny their existence. But they contrive to exist, sometimes exist a considerable length of time, on a greater or smaller footing. The police, particularly as many policemen are homosexual, know when to know a thing—or not. An amusing example of this fact occured to an Austrian homosexual, a year or so ago. Solemnly assured by a comely young police-official in -Milan that there was no *maison de rendezvous* for male prostitution in the Lombardian capital (!) about a week later he was offered the policeman in a well-conducted establishment, not ten minutes from the officer's station—the whole personnel and custom being masculine, his former acquaintance always at service of the house! In Paris, such clandestine resorts are many. In Asiatic and African cities, similar houses are plentiful. In Egypt, English military-rule has practically overlooked their existence, and the English patronage in Cairo, Alexandria and Port-Said justifies such myopia. The farther East, the more open and numerous are facilities of male prostitution. Regular 'boy-houses', as they are sometimes styled, are maintained in Farther-India, Japan, China, etc. In the baths at St. Petersburg, (generally speaking, in all large baths in Russia, the male-prostitute has a curious degree of tolerance and opportunity. In Italy, France and Germany, more or less orderly and clean assignation-houses are common. A resident contingent of vendable men and boys enables the proprietor to have a supply that can at any moment be summoned for a patron's choice—all types. But in a large part of Europe the law is fairly vigilant to root out and to punish such rendezvous and their frequenters.

Clubs of Uranians; Private Homosexual Resorts Numerous in All Countries.

When effort is made to maintain such establishments in cities where homosexual intercourse is severly punished—New York, London, Berlin, Munich, etc.,—the resort is masked in many different ways. If it is to be rather exclusive and aristocratic, it passes as a literary-club, an athletic society, sometimes as a dramatic-society, a chess-club, and so on. No outsider easily suspects what really goes on. Every precaution is taken against allowing unsympathetic visitors to invade it, and to fend-off spies; all manner of devices are used if by some mistake such a wolf in sheep's clothing has managed entrance, or if the law is alert. The precautions are just like those in political secret-societies, when suspicions are to be warded-off, guests regarded with lynx-eyed suspicion, and subterfuges kept well-oiled before danger comes. These, homosexual clubs are of all grades of aristocracy or democracy. They are not always *locales* for homosexualism between their members; though many such clubs are that. But they give the opportunity for social acquaintances, for personal soundings, for practical similisexualism elsewhere, for international correspondence, oral information between internationals, and the like. Now and then dire scandals come from them, and with more or less social horrifies they suddenly disintegrate. In spite of all pains in

The Uranian of Better Type Averse to Boyish Pederasty.

concealments, the homosexuality of the members and the procedings in such fraternities have a bad trick of leaking-out. Official and personal jealousies, lax management, incautious admissions to the penetralia, bring gossip. So come quarrels,

EDWARD IRENAEUS PRIME-STEVENSON

explosions, and flights, right and left. But new societies of the sort take the places of the old ones, disclosures are forgotten. All goes well with those peaceable organizations—till their turn comes. The suppression of private homosexual clubs, in big capitals, is like the cutting-off the heads of an Hydra—but without searing the severed arteries.

The boy-prostitute of tender years does not monopolize the homosexual marts of at least Western and Northern Europe. Many Uranians prefer a decidedly mature youth, and will rather embrace and be caressed sexually by a vigorous man from twenty-two to thirty-five, than by a boy in his early teens. A robust-natured Urning is repelled by too-feminine suggestions in boyish types, however graceful and winning. "I might as well expect to find enjoyment with a pretty young woman!" he exclaims. He must have virile contacts, the mature embrace, male magnetism, the sense of physical lust which a man imparts; this even when the innocence of youth does not deter him. If of strong characteristics he is also likely to detest the company of effeminate, flaccid homosexuals; to which types the male prostitute constantly affiliates. Many Uranians suffer sexual torments, live in sexual solitudes, rather than visit any Uranian club, or have to do with male prostitutes. This is particularly an attitude of the virile Uranian, of high-grade idealism. His body is the sufferer by his idealism. He will accept nothing less worthy, less psychically his own complement; he will not tolerate the ugly and degenerate and unclean.

"Why, then," asks the reader, "does any Uranian, of refinement, dignity and superiour station, descend to physical *rapports* with a street-catamite? Why does he make such acquaintances? Why does he ever enter a miscellaneous, vulgarized homosexual club? Why associate momentarily, not to speak of long-time, with coarse or sordid types?" Explanations are easy. In innumerable cases, the Uranian of higher nature is not so lucky as to have among his friends even one to be *loved*, physically and psychically; with such a sentiment returned, and with circumstances favouring the intimacy. His ideal, is never thus realized. He must lead his life sexually alone. But his sexual physique demands its relief, craves its pacification. Nerves and brain alike suffer, to torment. He feels often the need of being able to be himself with any other human being sexually *at all* like himself. As a parallel— the heterosexual man who would gladly keep a mistress of a refined type—socially, physically or psychically—or would joyfully marry the

"Why, Then At All—?"

wife worthy respect as well as love, must often content himself with the embraces of female prostitutes or by trivial *liaisons*. Exactly such is the case with thousands of Uranians. The sexual physique claims appeasement. What dangers are run, personally, socially and legally, by intimacies with low-grade homosexual acquaintances, we will presently see. But when a starving man cannot get appetizing viands, he will eat moulded bread; if he cannot find clean water for his long thirst, he drinks of a brackish, fetid springs. The superiour Uranian, tormented in body, turns to vulgar and utterly unæsthetic elements, buys the street-pederast, surrenders to the obscene; and therewith mixes in the strangest, (often the most dangerous) cross-currents of the democracy of Uranianism.

The proportion of homosexual prostitution in many capitals is notably large. In London, Paris, Berlin, Naples, New York it is an *armée de vice*. Berlin's male prostitution is calculated at 20 per-cent of the whole prostitution of the city. In 1909, an official Commission in Paris reported a startling percentage of habitual prostitution by minor youths under eighteen years, including a vast proportion of small boys—eleven, twelve and thirteen years old, or even younger. The adult male prostitutes were stated to be thousands; a formidable rivalry to the female battalions. The Eighth Chamber of the Paris Police Tribunal, in the Palais de Justice, deals with dozens of flagrant cases each week, such offenders being the special charge of the tribunal named. According to such students of the topic in France as MM. Berenger, Joly, Prévost, Meunier, Bourdon and Brun, male prostitution, especially by minor youth—younger or older—"is alarmingly increasing in Paris."

Really Contra-Sexual Prostitution by Dionian Types.

It is to be observed that not all similisexual prostitutes, including thousands of young men who habitually sell their bodies to all passions of the Uranian patron, are homosexual. Often they are thoroughly dionistic; dislike and even detest, by natural repugnance, such relations; and have strong preferences for sexual intercourse with women. They violate their natures, turn prostitutes, because too idle to work; frequently only to get money to spend on women-harlots. Many younger or older male-prostitutes have other occupations; earning honestly their real daily bread, they are not homosexual by temperament. By prostituting themselves similisexually,—clandestinely—they make considerable additions to their modest wages. However repugnant be the embraces and *attouchements* of the Uranians, they accept them complaisantly, and even play with verve at homosexual harlotry. But in a large part of Europe, as we shall see, they aim toward the confidential bond with any Uranian, because of the opportunities to blackmail, to rob, to victimize their unlucky homosexual client.

This is a potent inducement to the simulated catamite; exactly as it is so terrible a weapon pecuniarily in the case of the prostituting rascal who is really homosexual.

Every shade and grade of the venal homosexualism occurs, exactly as occurs every shade and grade of feminine whoredom. We find the ill-clad, graceful, dirty lad, of an Italian or Spanish or French city, who sells an hour of his person in a shabby hotel, for a few francs. We encounter the type who is: ready to oblige a client by the most expeditious technique—almost publicly—in some near latrine or deserted by-place, for a handful of cigarettes. We have the quasi-respectable and middle-class pathic, who fulfills his functions under more formal, decent conditions. We encounter the male-harlot that is well-dressed, well-fed, perhaps still young; and not so compromising in looks, or not so personally dangerous, that he cannot be taken to his respectable client's bachelor-lodgings, or saluted in a café of good grade. In due professional ascent of scale, comes the aristocracy of homosexual love-making—the young man, or lad of attractive manners and good-breeding enough, who is kept by some rich Uranian; or the mature, high grade *élégant* who "receives" in his own apartments a list of regular clients—a true male *cocotte*. Frequently the real sources of support, the real vocation or avocation—of this type, is not discerned by many friends outside the secret. In pederastic homosexualism there is met often the boy of fifteen to seventeen, of the beauty that has Sodoma's Saint Sebastian; who is ostensibly even legally adopted and put on a filial or nepotal footing by a well-to.do bachelor Uranian, or by a married one. This sort of "adoption" occurs often, even when Uranians must marry for such practical reasons as money, or for achieving a lawful heir—while thoroughly averse to sexual connection with the wife. We encounter other degrees social or intellectual, as among *demoiselles galantes*. Such are the handsome actor, the stage-singer, the studio-model, the poet, journalist, student and good-looking clerk; each simply a kept male-mistress, or clandestinely an *homme de joie*. Wealthy Jews and countless opulent non-semites, are mainstays of such well-conducted he-hetairas. The sexual nature of the intimacy can be kept below the surface of ordinary social notice. Such *entretenu* youth can readily be seen in the Bois de Boulogne, the Prater, the Pincio, Hyde Park, or Riverside Drive in their own automobiles. Their handsome apartments can be a luxurious rendezvous of dionysian society, as well as of Uranians known or not known as such.

In this regiment of masculine harlotry of course are met all dramas of faithfulness or unfaithfulness, disinterestedness or venality, comedies and tragedies, jealousies, rivalries, ruptures and reconcilements. "*Tout comme dies nous!*" might the female concurrence exclaim. Women-prostitutes well understand what a rivalry in the profession the masculine concurrent has set up, to lessen receipts and patronage; low street-walker, prosperous woman-prostitute, or high-class kept-woman, she hates her male competitor as a mystery and abnormality, a sexual insult as well as a commercial rival. Both sexes of the underclass nevertheless are met in alliance; tolerating each other, even living together, for common profit. Many of these partnerships—immediately, dangerously criminal—are prolific in incidents where the Uranian is a helpless victim. The police of all large cities know well the disorders and crimes by this armed truce between the two prostitutions.

The Vocabulary and Technique of Male Harlotry.

There is a large technical vocabalary for the different kinds, ages and methods of masculine prostitution, just as for the heterosexual sort. What is more this "dictionary of the trade" has become curiously international; many terms being much the same in all tongues, like the idiom of the sporting-world. However homosexual terminology, its slang included, inclines to follow French vocables. Thus an elderly male prostitute, or homosexual lover, is known as a "*tante*," especially if he act as the protector and agent for younger and more active catamites than himself. A handsome young man who is available is classed as a "*jésus*,"—long a classic term: while a young boy is "*un petit jésus*." The German-spealdng countries much employ the general term "*Pousserant*" for such homosexuals. The present writer will not undertake to transcribe even a small fraction of the enormous lexicon of the slang of homosexualism: for even in an assortment, it would take many pages. The old Roman and Greek *argot* for every type and *pratique* was not larger nor more descriptive—which is saying much. In Carlier's valuable study "Les Deux Prostitutions" this topic is presented in its French aspects very fully; as in many dictionaries of slang, of *argot français*, etc., are French terms the most universal of use. There is a large and cryptically crude English stock.

Below the high aristocracy-professed of this curious half-world, are the recruits already indicated as still in touch with their legitimate occupations; waiters in restaurants and clubs, petty officials, domestics in private families, robust young mechanics, youthful shopmen on small wages, students, and so on. Valets more or

The Middle Ground of Male Prostitution: Share of the Amateur in It.

less homosexual or complaisant, for the sake of place and money, are plentiful. From these upper ranks secede some of the most dangerous types of prostitutes for a respectable Uranian's intimacies. In all large cities certain restaurants and cafés are known as places where the homosexual visitor can meet with friendly social circles, or find types to suit his taste. The whole personnel is sometimes made up of homosexual servants, the patrons are almost wholly philarrhenic. Particularly Russian and Turkish baths everywhere are a rendezvous for homosexuals. At least fifty baths, in fifteen or twenty capitals, have established, widely-circulated reputations, as being homosexual meeting-places, among Uranians who live in the cities in question or travel about the world.

One such bath; in a large Central European capital, has achieved international renown, as not only the great local market for homosexual

A Bath-Resort.

prostitution, but also for its amazingly mixed and democratic clientage; being of its kind rather unique. It is a very large establishment, in one of the best quarters of the city," adjoining the chief public park. It was opened many years ago, with no obvious intention of development into a homosexual rendezvous; but it soon acquired that colour, and has maintained it ever since. The entire service, from the management to the chiropodists, is by homosexuals, be it more or less so. On entrance, the first detail of striking suggestiveness, is the huge piscina full of tepid water. On special days of the week, such as Sundays and holidays, it is also full of a most mixed multitude of homosexuals, all naked (the ironical towel being made into an equation of nothing) and all immersed in the water up to their shoulders,—decorously enough. All are promenading together, in a sort of friendly *cotillon;* their hands kept under water, not for swiming, but for—mutual investigations, which are to be expected when one enters the pool. They are of course well-taken, unless some heterosexual, a stranger to the ways of the place, creates a scene, by being surprised, coy and insulted. Boys and men, youths and elders, tradesmen's clerks and archdukes, actors and musicians, officers of the army and common soldiers, hundreds of male prostitutes of all grades—these all meet in this amazing *mélange*. Various steam and hot-air rooms afford other, but less direct, opportunities for cultivating acquaintances. Friends meet known friends; new intimacies are ever in the air. The dressing-rooms, all private, have vague surveillance—by express absence of guardians. Each bather has his cabin; for the afternoon' or evening it is his castle. He can take whom he pleases to it, and he can do what he pleases in it; always provided thereb be no open indecorum, no *tapage*. There seldom is such. The partitions of many of the rooms are of groundglass, in part, but do not interfere much with freedom of proceedings; besides which most occupants are too busy to attend in curiosity to their neighbours. A prostitute—boy or man—is always to be had for a couple of florins. But if such a youth attempt extortion with any approach to disturbance, the bath-attendants at once are aware of it with surprising quickness, and come to the spot. The indiscreet party is ejected, and is told not to come again—a privilege that most of his profession in the city do not care to lose. So he usually accepts—one cannot say 'pockets'—his couple of florins, or his three crowns, without any *"Krawall."* The respectable client is always protected thus, by the bath's personnel. The reputation of the house must not be compromised. Scandals connected with it always have been hushed up. The place is a local institution. The local police are of course perfectly well-acquainted with its character, its sexual, offices as a mart and brothel, day by day in each week; and in no city are the laws more explicit against homosexuality, and against any places of its proxenetism. But nothing seems likely to be done to close this temple; first, because it seems an absolutely necessary outlet for the vast homosexual life of the city; second, because it is managed with outward decorum; and especially because its clientage is so much of the best citizens in the place, along with the rabble of the town, that it has a sort of inherent and general protection. There is not anything else of its class so notorious, and on such a scale, in Continental Europe. For all of its freedom, per the bath-ticket price, the bather pays about two shillings.[2]

---

2. Since writing the foregoing paragraph, this bath has been subject to a surveillance that, according to information at hand, has perceptibly changed its aspects as a *practical* rendezvous.

In Paris, are at least a dozen baths that are homosexual rendezvous. Five or six are of wide popularity. In London, is a small group well-recognized. New York has several. But these, as most others, cannot be utilized, then and there, for homosexual practices. They are merely establishments for—anatomic inspections; for making appointments to meet elsewhere—some near hotel, for example. Berlin has a considerable list of such baths, with an homosexual *personnel* of impeccable discretion. In Italy there, are almost none; other rendezvous are efficient substitutes, and in Italy there are few vapour-baths of the kinds and sizes so common in other parts of Europe. The vapour-baths of Constantinople, Smyrna and so on have notoriously homosexual aspects.

Nothing is more curious in metropolitan aspects of homosexuality, when its democracy is studied, than the formal entertainments which in cities of size are organized by, Uranians, patronized by Uranians, are for Uranians only; but given under relatively private conditions. They include balls, soirees, masquerades, marriage-ceremonies and the like. In France, Germany, Italy and Austria, before the license of the Carnival's gayeties had declined as now, the homosexual, balls in Berlin and Vienna were sometimes saturnalia of the Intersex-Masculine. They recur as such occasionally. Eccentric, mischievous, or merely effeminate homosexuals, who delight to dress as women, are sometimes of remarkable beauty when in female costume, and sustain the rôle of a coquettish *fille de joie* with vast success. Hence such assemblies are, or were, natural occasions for most deceptively feminine aspects. Such balls, attended by all grades of homosexuals, were condoned by the police-authorities, as belonging to the season of masquerades; though too many of them became pandemoniums, by "high-jinks" not at all moral, as the hours advanced, they were not until recently so much suppressed. Aside from these large affairs, in Berlin, Munich, Paris and Vienna, each winter there still are notable dances and social gatherings, in which all the guests are homosexual, with a large part of the younger or older guests in female evening-dress. The aristocratic kept-mistress is escorted by "her" lover, or the less favoured male-harlot comes, errant as to luck, but equally elaborate in *travesti*. In the "Jahrbuch für Sexuelle Zwischenstufen" appear accounts of such reunions. Dr. von Krafft-Ebing's work "Psychopathia Sexualis" cites a ball that occurred in Berlin, in what Berlin homosexuals sometimes style "the good old days" of such gallimaufries, back in February, 1884. The

Uranian Balls Soirées, and Social Meetings.

report of a ball given October, 1889, in the Hotel "König von Portugal" Berlin, is extant as follows (in part) in the Berlin "Morgen-Post."

The gentlemen who take the place of ladles are mostly young men, from twenty to twenty-five years old. They poise themselves with feminine, grace on their hips, in walking about; scatter their, coquettish glances right and left; and when fatigued with dancing fan themselves with their lace-handkerchiefs. But an hour, later the company has quite another aspect, because of the advent of its—"ladies" is here written but "gentlemen" is meant,—in ladies costumes, duly accompanied by male escorts in evening-dress. These newcomers conduct themselves exactly as would their really feminine colleagues at a dance—with decorum, style, and the effort at being "charming." The so-called "Baby" (really a young fellow) halts in embarrassment at the door of the hall, in spite of the encouragement of his escort, an elderly gentleman of distinguished appearance, whom one easily recognizes as an ex-officer of the army. . . Tripping in with downcast eyes, quite as a young girl going to her first, ball, comes forward the "belle" of the evening, at once surrounded by an assortment of cavaliers who pay "her" the most flattering compliments. Much more self-conscious is yonder elegant, almost queenly, apparition in black silk *décolletée*, with a Rembrandt hat on "her" curling blond wig. "That is the "Baroness," remarked a gentleman sitting at my table. Under that name, in fact, is styled a well-known young actor of the city, who as—lover—on the stage fascinates all girl-patrons of the theater employing him. In a simple but "Parisian-*chic*" style are arrayed two other "ladies." They understand also how to keep their admirers at a distance. . . A Paris' like coquette, but tall as a grenadier, enters the dance, amid a general acclaim from the guests. This is the so-called "Handsome Emily" (in real life a barber of Berlin named Emil F.) who throws himself, smiling into the arms of a graceful young partner; and so begins a bacchanal galop through the hall. . ."

The same reporter described how, toward two o'clock in the morning, this remarkable exhibition of uranianism reached its climax, with the advent to the ball of representatives of the real feminine demi-monde, in a high state of curiosity and rivalry. ("Jahrbuch für Sexuelle-Zwischenstufen," for 1900, page 470.)

The preference for dressing like a woman, even to feeling oneself at ease only in woman's dress, has been a perennial trait of effeminate Uranians; sometimes of "Uranians not otherwise effeminate. Heliogabalus, Philippe d'Orléans and Henri III, are aristocratic examples. It is a common artifice of male prostitutes, and of the homosexual who finds fun in adventures in such costume. Here is an English example in prostitution from a contemporary London police-blotter:—

"Much attention was stirred up today we are informed, in the Clerkenwell Criminal Court, over, the examination of a young man

Instance.

who appeared in the dock as an elegantly attired—lady. He wore an irreproachably-fitting black walking-costume of the newest fashion, made to order, a gray feather 'boa', and a coquettish sailor-hat of fine felt. His hands were covered with ladies's gloves in pearl-grey, and he carried a handsome muff. According to his responses to, the Court, the defendant had been until recently a domestic servant in a family of distinction in G—street. Having been discharged he had appeared in Euston Road in this array, and had attracted the notice of the passers-by. A member of the detective-police of the city has been for some time "looking after" the fellow, and on the evening in question the latter approached him and accosted him. To his disagreable surprise, he was promptly arrested for a misdemeanour. He resisted the arrest, in great indignation, declaring to the officer "You wretch! I am a lady!" As the officer did not regard this statement, the complainant gave him a violent blow in the face; and a fierce battle began at once, in which the "lady" bit the officer's finger! With the assistance of other policemen, he was overpowered and brought, struggling, biting, scratching, and spitting, to the police-station. He was sentenced to three months imprisonment for wearing female attire, and to three months more for "resisting arrest."

The following item from a Paris journal, of December 9, 1908, is of the same category; the device being invariable among a certain category of French and German male prostitutes whose physique admits of such a trick:

"During some weeks the police of the flying squadron in charge of the Champs-Elysées quarter have been interested in the odd behaviour of an elegant young street-walker, in costly clothing and ornaments, who has been seen each evening strolling around the approaches to the Grand Palais des Beaux Arts, a quarter where overt *racolage* is not favoured. The young woman seemed very willing to be conducted by belated men into deserted thickets and alleys. Yesterday morning an officer happened to see her going into a house in the Rue Geoffry-Angevin. On inquiry, they learned, to their surprise, that the "lady" was a young man named Frederic B—, thirty years old, a German by nationality and of effeminate type, who more or less as 'professional' always went about at night in female dress,' and thus satisfied— equivocal passions. He was arrested last night when in a most compromising situation with a 'client', and was locked up with his partner, for scandalous behavious in a public place. Some of the most worst of our dangerous class of criminals are caught disguised in the same way."

The reader will find elsewhere references to this sort of masquerade by the *bas-fonds* of homosexuality in many cities. There are numerous instances in Berlin and London police-records each year.

Such renegade intersexuals remind one of the reply of a tall, bronzed valet to an American lady, awhile ago in a Cairo hotel, where there were no female servants. "But I rang for a chambermaid," she said in some embarrassment. The young man bowed respectfully and gravely answered, "Madame, I am she."

Other Instances.

Here is another example of the "womens'-clothing" passion, in a homosexual of rather superior social grade. A German newspaper offers it:

"Baron Friedrich-Wilhelm de C—, a resident of this city, was arrested at the railway-station yesterday, on a charge of a criminal act, set forth on a requisition from Dresden. Among his 'peculiarities,' Baron C—is accustomed, when at his home, to wear female clothing almost exclusively. For rich gems, jewellery, perfumes, etc., he has been for a long time a lavish spender of money. His family-connection is an old and very aristocratic one in France, and the Baron himself is a person of superior education and breeding."

An amusing case, similar to the "Lillian Carver" one cited, occurred not long ago, where a young man disguised himself with perfect success as a young woman; for some six weeks filling a position as book-keeper in a factory in Allenstein, Germany. It originated in a bet. The young gentleman soon was surrounded by male adorers, being of exceptional elegance and beauty in his *travesti*. The surprise of his employer can be imagined when, on entering the bedroom of "Fräulein Louise" one morning, he found there, only a wonderfully good-looking, rosy youth of faultless masculinity, clad in a top-hat and handsome morning suit, pipe in hand, who smilingly greeted his employer—"Awfully sorry to give you inconvenience, but from today I am a man—again!" With which adieu "Fräulein Louise" betook herself to the railway-station, leaving half-a-dozen wounded hearts.

Two curious cases of the passion for women-attire, on the part of adult homosexuals, appear in Augustus of Saxe-Gotha (1772–1822) who lived much of his private life in gowns, laces, and jewels; received guests in them; had himself painted as a woman by portraitists of his capital and by foreign artists (the Duke's feminine beauty quite justifying such records) and on his death left millions of money in debts—and enormous masses of women's habiliments, women's jewellery and women's wigs. This sovereign, a wit and satirist, was perhaps the first of aristocratic German homosexual authours in belles-lettres; by his novels "The Kyllenion: or A Year in Arcadia" and the "Emilienne Lettres." In his correspondence he wrote that he "never felt so strong, so well, as when he could get rid of all his masculine vestments of a forced virility." Napoleon found him brilliantly clever. Goethe spoke—though without criticism—of the Duke's open effeminacies. To a quite similar type, Adolphe-Friedrich, Duke of Mecklenburg (1753–1794) who also constantly affected feminine gear and ways, reference was made earlier here.

In the first volume of the series "Vieilles Maisons, Vieux Papiers" by Georges Lenotre (the eminent chronicler of so many little-known personalities of the French Revolutionary period) occurs a careful study of the pretended "Mademoiselle Jenny Savalette de Langes," who

Curious Historical Example of Travesty of Sex: "Jenny Savalette."

was really of male physique, and who had an eventful and discreditable history at her back before "she" began an extraordinary imposition of feminism, upon a wide circle of distinguished and humble friends; until "her" death (in 1858) at Versailles. "She" received large pensions and was greatly esteemed, during a long career, as the "daughter" of a noted émigré, who had served the Artois family before the Revolution. One odd explanation of such proceedings makes "Mademoiselle Savalette de Langes," a certain "B—," who forced a lady of high title to aid in such a long concealment of sex. The affair is, however, not at all clear today, and is not likely to be so. A colouring of homosexualism seems part of it, in view of "Mademoiselle Jenny's" love-affairs with an official of the Assistance Publique; as also_with an officer named Lacipière. "B—" (if such the man was) sustained his rôle with absolute success. Not until his death was his sex disclosed; a revelation that was at first discredited everywhere he had lived.

An American example of such masquerade, a military officer in active service, came several years ago in the person of Commander James R—, of Missouri. In 'hours of ease' he dressed as a lady, and at large expense. His feminine wardrobe was complete and fashionable. The writer of these pages knows an English colonel (a capital soldier, a firm disciplinarian and drill-master withal) who has the same eccentricity, and in most private circumstances can be seen as a majestic—dowager! A peculiarly noteworthy instance of this sartorial weakness, can be read in the "Jahrbuch für Sexuelle Zwischenstufen" Vol. II; p. 332; an autobiographic statement written with queer *naïveté*. In that case the similisexual impulse is not apparent.

A young Uranian's adaptability to female dress jg sometimes wonderfully complete. In course or Ulrich's rambling but valuable diagnostics of Uranian types he gives the following autobiographic account of two such young homosexuals of Vienna. They belonged to thoroughly respectable social life, and were dissociated from venal similisexuality:

Degenerate Tendencies in Youthful Homosexuals: Disguising as Girls at Dances, etc.

"When I was seventeen, I had a friend of twenty, like myself a distinctively feminine Urning. We two used to help my sisters for hours at a time, in making their finery. Since we both had good taste in such toilette-matters, we were welcomed. If the girls' new clothes were very successful in their working-out, we two used to ask to try them on ourselves, which doings were the pleasure of everybody. But I knew better than anybody could suppose how to deport myself in such feminine costumes. I knew how to wear a train with such majesty and grace, and so to wield my umbrella or fan, that often my mother was sorry that I was not a daughter!

"But the desire awoke in my friend and me to show ourselves publicly in woman's dresses and to attract notice of men, as girls. So we decided to make a visit to one of the regular "Universum" dance-evenings; in company with a couple of our lovers; our escorts of course in male attire. We thought out how to manage the trick, and knew how to arrange it so that an old aunt in the family invited our parents and sisters, one Sunday, to drink coffee. We took our sister's maid into our confidence, and she promised to adjust our coiffures for us. . .

At last the family-party went off, and we could "get ready" undisturbed. We locked every door, opened every wardrobe. Gowns, underwear, shawls, shoes, garters—we rummaged till we had picked out the very handsomest. Ah, what delight it was to make ourselves so fine! What a pleasure when the very maid herself was perfectly fascinated with our looks! Then we heard the carriage. Our escorts had come to take us. They were simply amazed at our brilliant exteriors, but still more at the ease and elegance with which we wore our costumes. We stepped into that carriage like a regular pair of princesses."

"We arrived at the "Universum" dance. The music sounded out towards our approaching feet. We jumped out like two young roes. We made our progress through the ranks of the ball-guests, on the arms of our cavaliers. (As a fact, our toilettes were much too fine for any "Universum" ball.) We took our seats. Therewith up came a robust, handsome man to me, and asked me with a questioning look "May I have the pleasure, Fräulein?" Scarcely had one such dancer broken the ice, than two or three others put their names down. We simply revelled in our delight at the success of our scheme. Meantime we had lost both of our escorts! But instead of them, we had two capital partners, who asked us to supper, and as both were handsome fellows, we consented.

"The two of them took us for young *demi-mondaines*. Our conversations with them gradually became more confidential; and we grew very coquettish, of course, when they asked us to go to a hotel with them—for the night. We did everything possible to get out of that scrape, but nothing was effective: We had to get into a carriage with them! Almost fainting in terror, we fairly got to the hotel. Now, now, must our secret be unmasked! We were swindlers, and had played our parts with a most thorough intention. When finally, we were really in a room in that hotel, my friend began to cry,—I threw myself on my knees before our new acquaintances. I begged forgiveness for our naughty joke. I confessed that we were not girls, at all! I begged the gentlemen to let us go home. Confounded, the two men looked at each other. Then, at last, they declared, up and down, that—it was all the same thing to them—stay We simply must. And we did so—and we went back to my home the next morning, a where regular "scene" of course was waiting for us!"

The same amazingly enterprising young specimens of Uranian effeminacy in course of their shining careers in Vienna, used to seek diversion in much lower planes of non-Uranistic society. Here is another chapter:

". . . After this, we two used to frequent the smartest balls, and that without a man ever recognizing our sex, in our rich costumes. . . But once on a time there was a Coachman's Ball, in one of the Viennese suburbs. Among the Viennese hack-drivers are good-looking, lively fellows. They like to have a jolly girl at supper with them. Now the laundry-girls also go to those coachmen's balls, absurdly dressed-up, though frequently such girls are real beauties. So we put on four to six rows of underskirts. . . red-flowered gowns, tight satin bodices to make our waists small, dressed our hair in the correct scalloppy sort of way, tied on screaming orange-yellow head-kerchiefs, painted our faces with rouge and white—and you had in us a pair of laundry-maids handsome enough for an artist's eye! Into the ball we marched, two laundry-girls without escorts! The women present all pulled us to bits with their eyes, angrily. But the men broke out into a general buzz of admiration. They got up on the, tables while wo sat down—just to get a good look at the 'two pretty washers.' They stared as if we had been wild animals, at a show. The real girls grew angrier and angrier. Then a couple of handsomely dressed young men came to our table, and began to chaff with us. (Such fellows of better sort often appear in these popular balls as spectators.) This provoked the hackmen. A lively, handsome black-eyed chap drew near. 'Well, my yellow-kerchiefed darling!' he said to me, 'would you favour *me*?' So up I got to dance, gave my skirts a shake, and put my hand in his. I noticed that everybody was again getting up on the tables to watch. The band played a polka-mazurka, at that time a dance in which few were practised. My young man and I hardly had danced down that hall once, when a regular storm of applause came, just as in a theater. So the ice was really broken. The young women ground their teeth, in their jealous anger. But the young fellows just swarmed after us! "We were victors! And my friend and I knew how to chaff the men in a way not to be beaten. When, toward midnight, we and our two hackmen began to sing 'Jodel' songs, with a zither-accompaniment, in our artificial soprano and alto, there was no end of a jollification. The fellows kissed us to their very heart's content, treated us to refreshments, were delighted if we would sit in their laps. One wished to buy me a splendid shawl. . . another made me a serious proposal. I do not understand now how we could carry the affair so far, in some details. For instance, as the better sort of the male guests and the hackmen pressed around us, we called out, 'Well—who sets up the champagne for us?'—at which the gentlemen and the commoner guests fairly scuffled over us! We were indeed just in our element! And we often repeated this sort of "an adventure, and not only we two but many of the 'sisters' . . ."

To find a more predisposed instance of sexualism and effeminacy in a Uranian type would be hard, outside of the regiment of venal homosexual prostitution.

Formal uranian marriage-ceremonies are not Uncommon among Uranian lovers. Nor are many such marriages at all foreign to psychology of homosexual passion. Among Uranians is likely to be sought a serious quality in some of their connections. Fortunate enough to possess bodily, as well as psychically, the man they love, the youth that they desire—so comes the wish to make the tie solemn. Such earnestly-meant ceremonies are offset by others for the sake of mere eccentricity, sensation, caricature, costly homage, and notoriety. Intersexual marriages vary in their felicity as do normal marriages. Sometimes they appear to be merely deep friendships between two men, living together in city or country;'but really represent formal homosexual matrimony, ceremonial union, with or without witnesses. Especially are such relations of interest (and frequently most happy, at least for a time) when some young Dionysian-Uranian is the "wife" of an older Uranian, both being refined natures and constant—the latter trait being rare.

The celebration of Uranian marriages, whether lightly or seriously made, are sometimes luxuriously 'smart,' with a considerable company of guests. In Carlier's work "Les Deux Prostitutions" (a book of value to those interested in the underworld of French homosexualism, though written with no reference to a correct scientific theory of homosexualism) will be found some anecdotes of these homosexual uranian weddings. Here is such a matter, a Berlin affair, from a German newspaper, some years ago:

"A young and wealthy American named R—W—was lately arrested here in Berlin. As to the grounds of this arrest the following. In the middle of last December, appeared in a well-known hotel in the Moabit quarter, three gentlemen, who asked the proprietor of the house if he could hire-out his assembly-rooms for a wedding on the 20th of this month. Receiving an assent, they hired the rooms, and by the 18th had prepared a regular chapel out of the hall, with elegant furniture, a portable altar and numerous expensive floral decorations. But on the evening of the day for the "wedding," when the guests were due, the police informed the horrified proprietor that the "bride" was to be the aforesaid young man, R—W—, masquerading as a young woman. The police however did not prohibit the proceedings, there being then no formal ground for that step. In course of the evening, carriages began to roll up to the rooms; setting down, especially, numerous handsomely dressed "ladies" (who proved later to be all of male sex) in rich feminine costumes, worn with perfect ease and deceptiveness. Other carriages presently brought the "clergyman" who was to perform the ceremony (he is a certain Dr. S—) and the "bridegroom," who is an ex-Uhlan officer named D—L—, and his "bride," the above-mentioned R—W—. The latter was a strikingly handsome young partner indeed, in full white satin toilette, with wreath, veil and bouquet of orange-blossoms. Unluckily the complete progress of the programme—an actual parody of a religious service which would be a criminal offence—could not occur, as the presence of the detectives was gradually known; and so the evening offered merely a dance and a costly supper. These festivities were prolonged till a late hour, whereupon the company of gentlemen and "ladies" and the fair "bride" and her groom dispersed with much gayety, but with entire decorum. Nevertheless it has been found needful to enter special charges against the American originator of the proceedings; who, by the by, looks completely a handsome, manly young fellow in his male attire, and has worn a fine moustache, which he sacrificed to the solemn occasion described."

Possibly the famous marriages of the Emperor Nero with his favourites Sporus and Doryphorus, extravagantly costly solemnities that scandalized Rome, meant not so much a sacrilegious orgie as Nero's vivid idealism and his intersexual enthusiasm. Toward Sporus, Nero appears to have been, the "activist"—the husband; to Doryphorus the Emperor was obviously "passivist," considering himself the wife. The femininized boy, Sporus, loved Nero to his last hour. The late Ludwig II of Bavaria, in the long line of his homosexual escapades, was with difficulty prevented, toward the end of his melancholy career, from solemnizing a marriage with another similisexual. He planned a sumptuous private ceremony, in the seclusion of one of his costly retreats. The certainty of such proceedings being known checked them abruptly.

In the foregoing summary of marriages and Uranianism, of course we are not touching on normal wedlock for homosexual men who are seeking sexual relief, if possible a "cure" for their nature. Another chapter of our study presents that grave subject by itself. Some unfavourable aspects of it have already been indicated.

IN REVIEWING SO FAR HOMOSEXUAL prostitution, uranian decadents, the similisexual as *déclassé*, we have not yet descended to the many strata of its robust criminality. Just as in the feminine harlotry, we mnst penetrate to darker, profounder levels; to a brutally vicious male similisexuality. We have traversed only those clearer avenues out of which open truly infernal alleys.

In prisons occurs much similisexual prostitution, difficult as may appear the opportunities. Such intercourse is however relatively facile, especially if two men must be confined in one cell. A warder of an Italian prison, and a high official in a large French prison, alike admitted to the writer that homosexual intercourse between male prisoners is taken for granted, and even accepted as a *necessity*. Of course external

Penal Servitude, Jail-life and Homosexualism.

decencies of prison-discipline must not be affronted. In the maritime prison of Cherbourg occurred in August, 1908, a great scandal because of homosexualism rampant among the prisoners and jailers. According to an official conclusion published in the daily papers. . . "Homosexualism goes on every hour of the day in the prison, not only with the knowledge but full connivance of the guardians, and in a most open manner. Men and boys are to be observed mutually practising pederasty—with scarcely any concealment. All new-comers are subjected to an examination as to their physique and tastes, and young sailors are forcibly violated." One young man named Brisset, from the "Valmy" was obliged to submit his person to the embraces of a roomful of men, and was also *épilé* by singeing his sexual parts.

In centers of Convict-life in colonies—New Guiana, Siberia, Algeria and other stations, the same undercurrent is incessant. Criminal psychologists have written of this penal inconsistency. Terrible dramas of sexual love and jealousy are met in the criminal settlements of Bussia and France. In the certain of the British penal colonies, now abolished, the story was similar.

Topographical Distribution of Homosexual Prostitution.

The non-military male-prostitute (still differentiating him from the soldier-prostitute) is as legion in countries of South America, Eastern Asia, Africa, and Central and Southern Europe, whether there exists or not special legislation against man-to-man sexualism. The larger the city, of course the more the profession is overt. An evening walk in the streets near large hotels, a stroll in frequented arcades, parks, plazas, is prodigal in all familiar aspects. St. Petersburg, Moskow, London, Amsterdam, Brussels, Paris, Marseilles, Bordeaux, Toulouse, Stockholm, Hamburg, Berlin, Breslau, Munich, Madrid, Vienna, Lisbon, Budapest, Belgrad, Sofia, Constantinople, Florence, Rome, Naples, Palermo, Milan, Turin, Venice, Geneva, Zurich—are notably such *foyers*. So are scores of *Kurorte*; of other summer or winter places of fashionable resort. Dozens of large commercial towns (particularly in Germany and Austria) not national capitals but places of large movement, frequented by foreigners, are in the category. Particularly wherever on the Continent the English and American travellers converge, the prostitute finds it to his account to go. Since the English occupation of Egypt, Cairo and some other tourist-centers have a representation of male prostitutes of all races. In Lisbon, until within a few years, male "houses" were *quasi* tolerated as a local expedient. In Italy, the German is recognizedly a special patron of boy-prostitutes, at all rendezvous.

Uranianism in the Moral Degenerate as united to the Thief, Bully, Decoy, Murderer, etc.

The league is eternal between female prostitution and worse criminality; including crimes of personal violence. Just so is it a part of male harlotry, though it has not such wide opportunity. It makes up in quality for what it lacks in quantity. It is always, inevitably, in touch with the thief, pickpocket swindler, bully, blackmailer, and murderer, according to chance and individual. The uranian prostitute is often debilitated in body and timorous, compared with the heterosexual. But frequently he wrangles, hectors, blusters, maltreats, murders, if a fit subject be in his power; in his anger or cupidity. A vast proportion of Uranians who patronize masculine prostitutes are not athletic and not stout-hearted. They are aware that they are contravening the laws, in many countries where similisexuals are enormously numerous, with male whoredom a vast social class. Uranian strangers, in a town where they are looking for sexual adventures, are likely to carry considerable sums. Such travellers are often foolish in confidences, unprepared for being victimized. Even if the treacherous catamite be timid, or a weakling, he is likely to have close at hand a robust partner to use immediate violence, as a wind-up to a sexual episode. In Berlin, Paris, Naples, and so on, effeminately attractive he-prostitutes often have their "ponces," their *souteneurs*, in call; as do she-prostitutes. This muscular aid de-camp is quick to make the most of a "row." The small-boy prostitute, in Germany or France, almost always "works" under the protection of a stout exploiter, who does not baulk at knocking down, or plundering, or killing—or all three. Mysterious crimes, unexplained disappearances, are part of this record. Of such extremes another word, presently. Before it, let us consider that redoubtable phase of debased and criminal-minded homosexualism, known as the "*chanteur*," the "*Preller*" the "*Erpresser*," and by many other terms summed up in the formidable English one—"blackmailer."

Blackmailer!—the blackmailed!—tyrant and writhing victim! In all sorts of relations where human rashness, passion, folly, weakness, carelessness, sordid mercenariness or vengeance attack the individual, we meet this dark process. | The Blackmailer, and Blackmail.

But nowhere else does blackmail operate with such terrible alertness as in the uranian world. We have reserved it as the concluding portion of this survey of homosexual decadence and criminality, because of its all-important bearings on the social and legal status of the uranian intersex in so many contemporary civilizations.

When the Code-Napoléon was evolved by France, with the Revolutionary instincts strong as to each question of individual rights, the French opposition to including references to homosexuality, if not in outrage against | Prevision of Blackmailer under Some Extane of Ethics in Uranians.

public good morals and innocent youth, was especially because of the dangers of increasing crime by such a paragraph; of causing scandals of uselessly humiliating social sort; of prompting espionage in private life—all recognized evils. The Napoleonic and the Post-Revolutionary legal mind stood, out against it; along with other deterrents. Before the consolidation of the present General Code for Imperial Germany, crimes, menaces and scandals referring to homosexual incidents were met mostly in those parts of Germany where the older law-systems existed. One might almost say that compared with the shocking frequency of blackmailings and murders today in the Reich, they "did not exist," until the present "Paragraph 175" became the law of the land. When this same paragraph was discussed, with the unification of German laws, such eminent jurists, working at the Code, as Virchow, Hofmann and Langenbeck most positively opposed such a law as a mischievous, socially pernicious paragraph. The sentiment of distinguished criminalists, of police-judges, of Councils of Public Hygiene and Safety, have since then urged its removal, as in every interest a law desirable to be dropped. But, so far, such opinions, not to mention the general petitionary movements against the paragraph in Germany, have been vain.

Blackmail is of course of the essence of espionage; of vicious leverage against the individual's peace, against his social protection. It is often the most impudent of attacks. For success it requires some cleverness, some moral (or immoral) boldness, and not seldom physical courage; especially if the blackmailer must arrive at not only extortion but at robbery and murder, as finale. It is the constant resource—the sharp Sword of Damocles that the average homosexual prostitute points against his client, wherever the country's laws invite it. No arm is so powerful—so silent, so safe. No female blackmailer, however audacious and cruel, ever has shown herself quite so torturing in shattering nerves, happiness, fortune, courage, social quietude and life as has the methodical, homosexual, blackmailing demon proved himself, time and again, the world round.

Homosexual Blackmail Social Mysteries.

The police-annals of all countries witness these melancholy episodes. Broken careers, shipwrecked lives, disappearances, interrupted marriages, inexplicable money-embarrassments, murders, suicides by hundreds are to be so explained. The incessant examples of "unaccountable affairs" too often mean that some intersexual victim, persecuted by a grasping enemy, threatened with exposure as an Uranian, can hold out no longer. Perhaps early in the attack he has seen no way out. Suicide especially will cheat the blackmailer of his blood-tax, or hide from the world the motive to drive the unfortunate into the tomb. Or else murder will be a deliverance, and flight a hope.

In blackmailing homosexuality at present, and Law-Codes the blackmailer, in too many countries, has not only social disgrace as his basis of attack on some victim whose, secret is known to the rascal. To a certain extent this powerful *appui* is at his service, without regard to actual legislation. He uses then the arm of only social scandal. But very widely in Europe, the blackmailer has now in his power not merely a man that will be thought disgraced, depraved; for in Great Britain and its Colonies, in Germany, in the United States of America, in the Austria-Hungary States, in the Scandinavian Monarchies, in some parts of the Swiss Confederation, and under certain circumstances or pretexts even in France, Italy, Russia, Spain, Portugal, Belgium Holland, Luxemburg and other tolerant lands, the victim—as shown early in this book—is a felon. Subject to more or less severe State-laws, he is amenable to penitentiary and jail, liable sometimes to terms of long imprisonment for even such least, nominal offense. We have indicated (in the Fourth Chapter of this book) details of most of the Statutory Codes as to homosexual offenses. Legislation is blameless in protecting innocent youth from debauchery, in punishing homosexual rape, in opposing public indecencies. But the law under the present ignorant, unscientific, Jewish-Christian basis, is too often a lamentable injury and menace to the best elements of society. The blackmailer has only to make a victim believe that a charge of "unnatural vice" will be his inevitable public infamy; as too often it really is. The homosexual so blackmailed melts like wax, in his terror of disgrace or a prison-cell.

Occasionally the blackmailer has hot been the direct *particeps criminis*, but, has merely got second-hand possession of facts. Occasionally there has been no felony committed. The ignorant, trembling victim is made to think so. In any case, either by the cynical prostitute himself or by an accomplice, the screw is turned. Much male prostitution is solely for an opening for blackmail. By demands for greater or smaller sums of money, threats, terrorizing letters or visits, week by week, month by month, year

Social Prejudice in Law-Codes as the Great Props of Blackmailing.

by year, can be applied the outrageous art of "bleeding" the victim. Sometimes the extortioner is skilful enough to avoid disclosing in his procedures exactly what was the fact to give him such a hold on the victim. The latter knows it; that is enough. Generally the extortioner has some sort of evidence in hand; a note, personal possessions stolen from the victim; or has ready the assertions of third parties, with true or false witness.

Prevalence of Homosexual Blackmail.

Aspects of such blackmail, whether by some single enemy or a league of rascals, whether successful for a week or a lifetime, are continually functional in social life. Of course they are undercurrents of misery frequently masked, first and last. Many intersexuals thus victimized are Uranians of blameless moral, social and religious life and instincts. They can be royal princes or humble citizens. We realize how general a population of the homosexual world in Europe are such social and legal victims, by incessant episodes that find outlets to publicity.

The Technique of Blackmail.

As to the technique of blackmail, its systems are much alike the world over. Differences in legal Codes and in social sentiments of different countries have much to do with it. In North America and in Great Britain any sort of sexual intimacy between men, or between men and youth, is severely punished, and socially is a horror; without much regard to circumstances, age, innocence or *un*-innocence of either party. Hence the blackmailer has an especially fine field. In France, Holland, Italy, Spain and various other countries; law-questions (as we have seen) dull the blackmailer's sword, unless his victim is ignorant or weak-spirited. But even in Codes that do not recognize mature, voluntary and private homosexuality as a *crime*, a rascal can bleed and fleece many a trembling lamb. In Germany and Austria-Hungary, the activities of the blackmailer are vigorous and tragic. The Germanic races are especially homosexual; and their General Codes and religious-social feelings are formidable against any homosexualism. Judges and juries must do their legal duty. True, enlightened sentiment in Germany and Austria-Hungary strongly favours dismissing punishment for homosexualism, except under circumstances similar to provisions of adverse Napoleonic Codes. But meantime Germanic Europe is a prolific territory for the blackmailer.

Terminology in blackmailing is so large that it needs a dictionary. In France the blackmailer is called a "*chanteur*," his methods "*chantage*"—

now international words—and a melancholy tune it is that the victim "sings"! In Italian, the same terms are translated, or called *"estorsione,"* though Italy happily knows little of them very cruelest art. In German-speaking countries blackmail is "Rupferei," "Erpressung" and so on, in common nonprofessional comment.

In cities like Hamburg, Berlin, Paris, Vienna, sometimes operate regularly organized cliques of rascals; either similisexual prostitutes, or in touch with such. These lay traps for the homosexual, concoct plans for terrifying him, and live by such industry. The demands on the victim are large or small, repeated or not, according to his social station, to his estate, to skill in keeping him in postal-distance or interview-distance; and to success in frightening him into continued yielding. It may seem incredible, but instances are not rare in which bank-accounts of large size, fortunes and estates, have dribbled away by "bleeding" a victim. Thousands of pounds,francs, marks, florins, dollars, have passed into a blackmailer's pockets, when a fly of the right sort is in this spiderweb. The victim sometimes can escape soon, by luck or pluck. But this is not the rule, one fears. Over and over, too, we hear that a secret which destroys a victim's estate or life has been disposed of to some "pal" of the original *"Erpresser,"* and is to be "worked" further; with new devices of villainy.

The Audacity and Success of Blackmailers: Large and Successful Demands Frequent.

What can the average victim *do* to escape? Despairing, fearing social disgrace and a prison's cell, perhaps already mulcted for more money than he can afford and dreading the next demand—how can he win out? Possibly a single hour, nay, a few minutes of homosexual passion, or even no approach to it at all, will cost his peace of mind, his income, his home, his future! The blackmailer, who seemed so friendly an uranian type, has plundered him; has exiled him, if the unfortunate man is able to fly; or flight has been impossible or a vain expedient. Few Uranians, in the hundred can afford to fly from the legal or social zone of their persecutor. The blackmailed may be married, a father of a family, at the head of a business that is his all; or otherwise not free-footed.

What Can the Victim Do to Escape?

The attacked can (and he *should*) courageously seek the police-authorities, to reveal the situation. At the price of more or less suspicion on himself, perhaps of his semi-confession, he can have his tormentor arrested and nearly always fully punished. Blackmailing is *per se*, an offence of which modern Codes take severe notice. That is the best rescue, the safest escape, the only legal method, *coûte que coûte!* Unluckily the victim has not always the knowledge, the courage, or evidence enough for this heroic stand. So he submits. Sometimes he resolves to kill the blackmailer. He often has done so, and has suffered death for it. But, as last and too-usual resort of the victim in half of Europe (particularly in Germanic Europe and often in America) he "gets out of it all" by—suicide. The motive of his self-murder may transpire; but usually it does not. At least, it escapes general notice. Like Sir Peter Teazle, he must go away leaving his character behind him. But the blackmailer's visits, or letters, cannot often follow him into the tomb.

Instance of Systematic Blackmail.

Some examples of this dastardly art and of the misery it causes, follow here. They are only a few of such.

The following details, in a long autobiographic narrative from a German victim, are given in the "Jahrbuch für Sexuelle Zwischenstufen," for the year 1900, under the signature "Max Kalte"—a pseudonym. It shows the effects of a blackmailer's operations on a man of high education and excellent social position, but of timid temper—betrayed by sexual accident. After describing how he had been obliged to break off an intimacy with a friend of his own class and type, because the latter could not satisfy high psychic ideals, the history continues thus:

". . . I was again orphaned. And yet, after all the deceptions which I had passed through, my heart demanded love ever more ardently, wished to be surrendered to some noble-minded human being, who would understand me—my psychical side as well as my intellectual aspirations. But before I found any such person, I had an experience worse than any one before it. For—I fell into the hands of a blackmailer of a type that I had never known anything about, and who could hardly have been more abominable and dangerous than lie was."

"At a social gathering, in the organization which I have mentioned, one evening when a theatrical performance was given, I met a young assistant in a friseur's shop, with whom I arranged a "meeting" for the following day. I admit that it was not the right sort of thing to do. But what do the heterosexual men do? Do they not often make acquaintances with girls with whom they are willing to keep up very intimate relations without being willing to marry them? My inner self was solitary and lonely, and sought some mere substitute for the sort of love really longed-for. . . When next day we were together, I recognized by all the outward traits of my new companion that he was not suited for me. He was trivial and lacking in conscience, as was plain from what he himself told me of his former relations, with a tailor whom he had known. We talked of another meeting, but I wrote him and broke the appointment. Thereupon the young man tried to find out my name, condition in life, and place of residence, Which I had not given to him; a thing however he could easily do, by applying to the direction of the social club above mentioned. After that, he came to my rooms, in company with another young man whom he called his brother, but who was not so; and asked me to help him with money, as he had lost his employment. I replied that I could not do so. He answered that he did not intend to be put off in that sort of way: and made a reference to our previous rendezvous. Just at that moment my charwoman came into my room to put it in order, and further dispute was an unpleasing idea to me, so under the pretext that I had to go forth, I left my lodgings; but accompanied by my two companions, with whom I strolled along several streets. I asked the friseur once more what just exactly he wanted; and when I declined again to give him the assistance he desired on any ground of our previous relations, then he declared that if I would not accord him his wishes, he would attack my character socially, and also denounce me to the police as having been guilty of a criminal offence. Therewith I demanded that the companion of the friseur (who up to that minute had not quitted us) should leave us, in as much as I had in any case nothing to do with him and did not know him. He accordingly left us, for awhile—but soon he came back. The friseur then plainly said to me that unless I would give him some money, he would "make a circus" for me, then and there—in the public street. Finally, on my further request, the third party to this dialogue left us again: and then I told the friseur that he had not any right to demand money from me and that his conduct was blackmail. He replied that it might be so or not, that was all one to him: I would be punished as a criminal, if he made revelations, or even if not (since I insisted that what had passed between us, mutual onanism only, was not criminal)[3] then at least I would be disgraced socially though *he* could manage to slip out of the affair. So after he had further threatened me thus, I gave him, to get rid of him, five Marks. He said that he must have more, and he followed me along the street, I trying to hurry off, till at last I gave him two Marks more. Then he left me."

"With what emotions I went home, who can guess? It was not the money, but the consciousness of having fallen plump into the hands of a shameless and abandoned creature, and of having had anything to do with him—if only once! Gloomy portents and fears coursed through my mind, and for weeks I went about depressed and dreading to meet my enemy again. And in fact he did not wait two months. The second time, he came with another companion who behaved with unexampled impudence and vulgarity. I shall speak of him as the "Cologner"; for by his accent he was from Cologne. They rang my bell, I opened the door, they fairly squeezed themselves in, with the "Cologner" first. On my asking what they wanted, the friseur answered "Money!" On my replying that I was not in circumstances to give him any, just as I had told him before, then the "Cologner" spoke up: "Oh, that is just all rubbish!" and added a very vulgar accusation. When I repudiated this, earnestly yet calmly, then the friseur remarked that "For all that, it was true!" With this the "Cologner," who from this point monopolized the conversation, declared that it would "be much better for me not to refuse—the friseur wanted to go to Cologne to hunt up a job,—I ought to give him money for the journey—and that then I would not be "bothered" any more. When I continued to refuse, the "Cologner" threatened me with denunciation to the police, through the friseur, and with public disgrace. I returned that they were both guilty of blackmailing, to which the Cologner retorted that while it was true that in case of the denunciation the friseur would be imprisoned, nevertheless the burden of blame would come on me. Would I not therefore better be sensible, and just pay out the money for the journey—twenty-seven-and-a-half Marks?—

---

3. See preceding reference to Germanic Law, Chapt. IV, p. 67.

and that then they would both promise, in writing, to give me no further trouble. The written memorandum was laid readly. Thereupon the "Cologner" demanded *fifty* Marks, in view of the friseur's living expenses "in the meantime." I consented. With the written promise, which the "Cologner" refused to sign, I paid over the sum mentioned. With that the "Cologner" demanded twenty Marks more, just on his own account! I replied that I owed him nothing; he said that was nonsense, and threatened to make a regular uproar in the house if I would not give him the twenty Marks. So in order to keep such an ugly episode out of the house, I yielded. But as I held my purse in my hand, the "Cologner" said that he "wanted to see how much money there was inside it—he would give me his word of honour not to take anything from it." That I refused, goes unsaid. But he seized it; I held fast. I was now furious; I struggled, with the resolution to make an end of the whole shameful and nerve-shattering business for me. But I hesitated—fear of public disgrace kept me back. The "Cologner" and I had already begun to pull the purse in two between us, and with the second observation from the "Cologner" that he 'would only look inside it', which I did not believe—I let it go. The "Cologner" took out all that was left of larger money—forty Marks. I had been to the bank that day, and had taken out one hundred Marks, for my living expenses, as I keep very little money in my lodgings, living alone as I do. I let the money go. They took themselves off after that. The "Cologner" assured me that that he would never come again, but at the same time he remarked that if I told the police what had happened "something" would "happen" to me!"

"When they were gone, I sank into a chair and burst into tears. Must I have dealings with such base creatures?—I who still felt my heart a-glow with youthful ideals, who felt the breath of that same great love of humanity which Christ so purely and perfectly has embodied? But I collected myself; I hurried in my despair to a confidential heterosexual friend whom I have mentioned, that he might give me sympathy, and calm me. From another quarter, however, that later I decided.to turn to, came the advice to enable me to get rid of the two blackmailers by going to the police and a law-court; or otherwise I would have been simply a permanent victim."

"I took that advice: but not till after two whole months, when the "Cologner," and this time quite by himself, came to my lodgings. Before he opened the door, I had put on the chain. But he put his foot forward so that I could not shut the door after I had recognized him. He also tried to force the door open by throwing himself against it, which he could not succeed in doing as I held myself against it. Three times I ordered him away—he refused, and struck me with his cane as I pushed off his hand—wounding me on the cheek and using the most vulgar language, and uttering fresh threats. As I warned him that I would call the police, he answered that he would rather be arrested than go away. I stepped back from the door quickly, seized a garden-stick, and struck him, through the open door. He sprang back, I shut the door. But he threw himself against it several times, so that I had to press steadily against it to hold it in place. He rang the bell again, demanding entrance, used more abusive language, and finally when he saw that he was not able to succeed in his attack, then he asked for "one Mark,"—to go home" . . . if he did not get that, then he "would charge me before the police with bodily injuries to him." So in order to finish the scene, I threw him the money through the post-slit in the door: and then he really went away." . . .

After describing his agitation and despair, now meditating suicide as his only relief from above disgrace, the narrator did at last what he ought to have done first. He went to police, disclosed himself as the subject of extortion under threats, and demanded aid. His tormentors were arrested and tried. The "Friseur" received six months imprisonment at hard labour, and the "Cologner" two years. The victim's charge was so managed by the authorities, that he did not incriminate himself. In fact, this accent is manageable in such processes, if the police-justice and jury are intelligent as to the philosophy of homosexualism. Many high germanic authorities, both medical and legal, are so. But this cannot always be depended on. In the foregoing, one must confess that the victim seems very) weak-nerved and feeble-hearted. He should have promptly withstood the impudent *friseur*. Such rascals are nearly always routed, the moment they meet bold negatives and counter-threats. But many homosexuals are not good at such "bluff."

Let us review a series of every-day blackmailing histories, drawn from printed reports in various Continental newspapers, especially those of Austria and Germany. The

procession is edifying in human suffering. These instances are cited largely from the admirable "Jahrbuch für Sexuelle Zwischenstufen," so carefully edited by Dr. Magnus Hirschfeld, the eminent consulting psychiater of Berlin:

"A waiter named N—was arrested in Berlin yesterday on account of attempt at blackmail. He beongs to that dangerous class of persons who attach themselves to gentlemen that walk in the Thiergarten, to extort money from such strollers. This particular affair became known to the city-police because of said N—'s conduct in a well-known resort for criminals, where he spoke of having "come into a big legacy" on the night before, A friend of his was "with" an American gentleman in the park named. N— thereupon came to them, declared himself to be a policeman in plain clothes, and threatened to arrest the American gentleman. The American was willing to give over 500 Marks, to get away; but N—and his accomplice were not satisfied, and demanded more. N—wore a badge like that of the criminal police. The victim of the attempt proved to be travelling from Warsaw, and a guest in one of the best hotels in town. N—declared that the stranger had "given him the money," which included Russian and English pieces. He also made the gentleman hand over his ring, etc."

This blackmailer, too, received six months imprisonment. The American accuser was not asked too many pressing questions, luckily for his own case. Again, *seriatim:*

"By trial before the Criminal Commission, with closed doors, were sentenced yesterday eight young men, on account of an in instance of their habitual blackmailing of strangers in this city, by accusations of offences against the all too-famous law known as "Paragraph 175," of our present Code. The defendants were of various callings, mostly humble ones, and also mostly nominal; for such mischievous rascals can thrive quite too well, by the fear of their victims, to be forced to work for bread. The group included a certain Kubicky, Gebers (a notary's clerk), Gleisberg (a binder) Staupe (a goldbeater)—Hanck, Krall and Paul (waiters in a café) and Schuckhardt, (a cabman). A ninth member of the clique managed to be acquitted for lack of direct evidence. Those named however received sentences ranging from nine months to two years of imprisonment. The matter came to head on the charge of a well-known professor in the University, and of an officer in command of a regiment here. One result only of their proceedings terrified their victim into turning over to them 1000 Marks—at once! Our city is quite too full just now of this class of banditti, who hang about the streets, parks and cafés, well-dressed and friendly, making themselves agreeable to strangers, luring them into "compromising situations" and then—turning on the thumbscrew."

"The case of Captain D. v. Tz—, who is accused of an unnatural offense, under Paragraph 175 of the Criminal Code, in company with a certain young barber of the town, was tried yesterday in a private session of the Criminal Court. The only witness against Captain Tz—was the plaintiff, sixteen years of age, who asserted that the defendant had twice misconducted himself with him when alone in the Captain's rooms, where he came to shave him. The Criminal Court acquitted the Captain. The story told seemed to the judges too strongly as a made-up narrative, carefully learned by heart, and in too close likeness to the filed complaint of the young barber. There appeared to be grounds for supposing that the complaint wps all a scheme of blackmail, aided by some outside parties, using the young man as a catspaw."

"A raid on blackmailing gentry of this city was made last night, in the Thiergarten (Berlin) alleys and copses, near the railway-station, on the part of the local police of Charlottenburg. Repeatedly has it been stated lately that unknown persons attack masculine visitors to the gardens with accusations of immoral offences of a special sort, and have done so by pretending themselves to be secret-police on duty, who will let the victims off—if money be forthcoming! In once instance lately, a large sum was handed over. Three individuals were captured on this kind of charge They were the brothers G—of Charlottenburg, and they are now in the hands of the authorities."

"As we reported yesterday, two non-commissioned officers of the—Cuirassier Guards, named Ebert and Rother, have been put under arrest on account of what seems to be a disgraceful case of conspiracy toward blackmail; both being also, it is thought, concerned in a previous case of the same sort. The facts as to the present charge are these. The accused, on April 14, made their appearance in the apartments of a very distinguished gentleman of this city, a member; of the higher aristocracy, and after charging him with an unnatural offence according to the text of Paragraph 175, they demanded several hundred marks as hush-money. The victim, much terrified, yielded to the demand; but having less than the sum exacted at hand, he asked the two rascals to wait till he could obtain it from a friend. In his absence, the two accused parties drank his liqueurs, became very noisy and violent, smashed mirrors, glass and porcelain in his dining-room, cut pictures out of the frames, and otherwise played the ruffian. Their victim returned and gave them the sum agreed on. A week later they wrote him, demanding a larger amount, and saying that if it were not forthcoming he would receive "another call" which "would not leave a chair on its legs." The intervention of the police being asked, the matter is now in the hands of the military court concerned."

These audacious rascals were imprisoned and degraded from their military service. Their case is interesting (and admonitory) to stratophilic homosexuals, as an example of blackmailing by soldiers. Within a few years, this sort of trouble, once uncommon, for civilians has perceptibly increased in frequency.

Here is an example of how can be utilized a bit of family-history; or its counterfeit:

"A bold attempt at extortion of money by blackmail was made lately against Herr G—a merchant, over in K—strasse. A young man came into his shop and handed over a letter, the contents of of which made Herr G—not a little angry. The writer (who feigned himself 'N. N.') informed Herr G—that his father-in-law had committed a certain sort of criminal act. Unless Herr G—would send at once 300 Marks, then the writer of the letter would immediately communicate the affair to a newspaper, with the full name of the gentleman, and all details needed to bring the affair to publicity. But Herr G—did not fall into so clumsy a plot. As 'N. N.' was to wait near by, in the street, for a reply to the letter, Herr G—accompanied the bearer of this precious communication out to K—strasse, to meet 'N. N.'. The latter was not to be found. But tho next day the same sort of demand was made in sharper language. This time, Herr G—succeeded in meeting his enemy, and also in having the fellow, a certain Emil W—, taken into custody as a blackmailer. Emil W—is in fact a well-known "operator" of this sort. He was given six months imprisonment, with two years loss of civil rights."

The examples so far selected are taken especially from Germany, because they multiply there and are carefully reported. In England and America there are plenty of current cases, more or less of the same stamp. But in England and America the publication of legal or other proceedings that bear on so-called "unnatural offences" is not encouraged by the press, nor often detailed as in Continental Europe. The squeamishness of the Anglo-Saxon mind as to *speaking* of homosexuality, the British ignorance of how homosexualism should be regarded and is regarded in other countries, considerably suppress such matter from print; or disguise its nature.

Blackmail Often of Audacity rather than Substance: Perils of Urinals: Instances.

The vulgar blackmailer is not always choice in trying to got hold of compromising facts. Sometimes standing in a public urinal, on an entirely innocent errand, some unlucky visitor is seized by a strong hand—just where he is most open to attack. A rough voice hisses—"Twenty francs, or I call the police!—charge you with indecent conduct in a public latrine! Put the money in my *other* hand!" The intruder often will have 'adjusted'—or disarranged,—his own apparel in such a way as to suggest that an attack on his person really has been made. The terror-struck stranger pays the tax and flies, glad to escape. This impudent trick is mot especially in France, Italy and Spain, because it implies an action criminal under publicity. In Germanic and English cities it is yet more dangerous. Common, too, is the advent of a *feigned* policeman, to take the two parties into arrest unless a round bribe be paid over. Foreign loiterers, especially if homosexuals, should avoid public urinals and retired parts of public gardens, when the hour is favourable to this highway-blackmail. (The motto must *not* be "Siste viator!") Exactly this sort of attack, made on a gentleman in Paris—where it is far from rare—is described in a Paris newspaper, as the writer ends this page. In Germany and Austria-Hungary it is much in vogue among the dregs of male prostitutes and pseudo-prostitutes. In one of Dr. Magnus Hirschfeld's many and valuable local studies, "Berlins Drittes Geschlecht," he cites such a case, in a letter from a provincial official; an elderly man, not in the least homosexual. He was followed in the street one evening, by a young prostitute, demanding money. The inexperienced stranger did the most unwise thing; he turned presently into an urinal, thinking that his whining persecutor would respect privacy, and would quit him. Instead the rascal followed him into the retreat, and stood in the door. When the official was about to come out, the blackmailer—with his dress disordered—stood in front of him, and said If you do not give me sixteen Marks at once, I will have you arested, and get you into prison, for an outrage to public morals in this place with me! So be quick! Out with the money!" The terrified stranger managed to hurry to a cab, in the middle of an increasing street-scandal; fortunately before a policeman appeared to make inquiries. By throwing a piece of gold at the rogue, and by having the coachman start oft at a gallop he succeed in getting away. A similar example was communicated some weeks ago to the present writer. In Rome, in the spring of 1907, a young Englishman, who was homosexual, coming home one evening to his hotel from a music-hall, stopped in a latrine, off the Corso. He was at once followed by a young boy-prostitute, who at once began pestering and disgusting the Englishman by exhibiting himself. Finding that there would not result any tangible consequences, the young rascal accused the Englishman of violating public decency—and with a minor. He would not be shaken off. He ran after the carriage, sprang into it, and only at the door of the traveller's hotel leaped down, and ran away, not daring to face the *concierge*. The Englishman (who could not speak a word of Italian) was greatly disturbed at the prospect of a scandal. Fortunately there was none.

Another specimen of this kind of vulgar night-assault is as follows. The instance is reported in the Vienna "Neue Freie Presse," for June 14, 1901. It was much talked of in the capital at the time, as can be supposed.

"The secretary of a distinguished person here—the latter being an Archduke—on the night of May 15th, after a late supper, happened to stroll along the edge of the Rathhaus Park. He had been taking considerable beer at the Spatenbrau and in the Café Scheidl. Ho is a man in the thirties. He had wanted a little fresh air, and had been also taking a turn in a cab. At the place named, he alighted and walked along, till he reached a certain urinal. He entered it, and found two young men there, the defendants Karl Horak and Karl Mildner, The statement of the gentleman was this: "When I was leaving the latrine mentioned, one of the two defendants came to me and asked for some money. I would not give him any. Then he accused me of an offense. I said that that was not the fact. He repeated his demands, with the remark that if I would not give him money, then I "could not get away from there so easily." I wished to put an end to the situation; so I put my hand in my pocket and gave him a couple of *Kronen*.—"You'll have to give us more than that, or we dont let you off! We want a 'Tenner'—then we will let you go." I wanted to stop such a scene, so I took out my purse. He seized it out of my hand, (it had some thirty florins in it) and ran off. I wished to pursue him, when the second fellow came up and demanded my watch. Just to get rid of him, I gave it him. I had to borrow money of a café-waiter to get home." . . .

But this was not the end. Decidedly serious consequences that brought victim and blackmailers in court, were to ensue. These developed as follows:

"In the purse, or card-case, was the visiting-card of the victim, with his name and address, also the coat-of-arms of his royal employer, a photograph of the children of the latter, and other personalia. The two blackmailers actually dared to come to the palace the next day, and asked to speak with the secretary. They were admitted, and demanded two hundred florins hush-money. If they got it, no further "fuss;" if not—a great deal. The noble secretary wisely had them arrested, though he had every reason to dislike any public notice of the adventure. The young men were well-dressed, had a certain degree of education, and one of them was decidedly good-looking. Both were quite of the regular Vienna male prostitute sort—and investigations showed that Horak already had a similar charge of blackmailing, referring to the same locality, against him. The Secretary mentioned that when they threatened him with public proceedings for an offense, he had said "But *you* will be punished too, if I am;" to which young Horak had coolly replied "That's so! But you will be *ruined*, and we haven't anything much to lose." Each offender was given eighteen months imprisonment, at hard labour."

The Court conducted the complainant's case carefully. He was not incriminated.

In Italy, as in France or Germany, the conditions of publicity are useful to such crude blackmailers. About two years ago, an American

Instance.

officer of the army, while in Naples, happened into the *vespasienne* close by the San Carlo Opera. That latrine is notorious for the number of men, more or less homosexual, who turn into it, not so much for urination as for those exhibitions which make it locally quite unique. Two young reprobates were also there. After liberally exposing their persons to what seemed to be his interest '(an interest not admitted by the foreigner) they followed him, and threatened him with blackmail because of improper behaviour "in a public place"! One of the two declared himself a minor; a statement that would have made him a circus-marvel—had it been true. The foreigner had much trouble to get rid of them, not knowing that a resistance on his part would probably put them to flight. Finally, the stranger, in round language, declared he would call an officer patrolling near. They fled.

The reader probably has made up bis mind that in some cases foregoing (as he may make it up in regard to some that will follow) there was more or less ground for a charge against the unlucky victim; even if the blackmailer deserves no less our execration. We can well admit that

Groundless Blackmailing, Arrests, etc.

when a blackmailer tries such a game, usually there is a basis of fact for it. But this does not alter the aspect of the need of suppressing the oppressor. Furthermore, the blackmailer is not rare who has not a shred of reason for his'attack, especially in large cities. Some years ago, a distinguished musical artist, the violinist B—, was arrested and imprisoned in Brunswick, on the charge of having violated a young tailor's apprentice. The affair made a great scandal. But on examination, it proved to be made out of, not whole cloth from the shop of the young tailor's employer but—entirely from a romance in print; with some sexual and other changes. Awhile ago, two tourists were arrested by a blackmailer's impudence, and were confined in a Berlin prison nearly a fortnight, until the fact was clear that the rascal had invented the case, with clumsy impudence.

Be it observed here—with regret—as to Germany that during the earlier years of the existence of the Paragraph 175, of the German Code, there was much blackmailing by arresting, etc., from the city-police, as trumpers-up of charges, for the sake of seeming to be vigilant, or for money. This was one of the reasons why the late Herr Meerscheidt-Hüllesem, of the Berlin Police, so strongly urged the removal of the Paragraph mentioned. He found it encouraged crime and roguery in men of his squads, not all of whom were proof against such despicable but infectious temptation.

Other Examples.

To blackmail is instinctive in those parts of Europe where the law is severe, where the homosexual, (especially of means) is widely met, and where the avocation of prostitution is a side-industry among young fellows of humble life. They form such associations with cynical designs of fleecing all clients unlucky enough to give them the least leverage. Here is a Vienna affair; along with two Munich incidents:

"The butcher's assistant, Maximilian Strauss, a very good-looking young fellow, was brought to the bar today, on a charge of, blackmail. Lately Strauss sent to Herr-Theodore Reichmann, the eminent baritone of our Opera, a most impertinent letter, accusing the distinguished singer of a certain offence coming under Paragraph 129 of our Statue Book, and threatening Herr Reichmann with publicity if a considerable sum of hush-money was not to be forthcoming. The letter was not signed, but Herr Reichmann knew whence it came, and at once put the matter into the hands of the police. In spite of the defence from Dr. Chersch, the young blackmailer was sentenced to four months, with hard labour. Such cases are constantly increasing in our city."

"Georg P—, calling himself a baker by trade, lately became a dangerous sort of character for the artist, Herr X—, of our city, for whom said Georg P—had posed as a studio-model. Systematic attempt at blackmail resulted. The said P—appeared one day at the painter's residence in company with a certain Ludwig A—and Albert A—, bakers, and Albert M—a pork-shop clerk, and conducted themselves so impudently that the painter gave them, first, twenty Marks and then fifty, as hush-money. That however was not sufficient for presently the artist, received the usual threatening letter, demanding 100 Marks, stating that otherwise the accusation would be made in a police-court. It is worth noting that the three companions in rascality did not accuse *themselves* of being partakers in the offence, but spoke of a *fourth* person, who was in a hospital, on account of the "physical injury" he had "suffered" from the relations with the artist (!). The painter paid over the 100 Marks more, but as the demand for a like sum was repeated, he did what he should have done in the first place—went to the police with the correspondence."

These blackmailers were sentenced to various terms of imprisonment that ranged between two years and one-and a-half years, at hard labour. The complainant suffered no legal inconvenience. The second Munich item runs:

"On account of an offence against the public morality, as well as an attempt at blackmail, the case involving Johann Erhard, of Bayreuth, 23 years old, and also Albert Schneider, of Nürnberg, 20 years old, was brought before the Court. According to the complaint, Herr August F—thirty-seven years old, a merchant of Wertheim, was involved, the said F—being charged with conducting himself improperly, under Paragraph 175 of the Code, with young Erhard, in the Hofbräuhaus, one evening: also taking Erhard to his lodging, to pass the night—for similar practices. Erhard confided these matters to his friend Schneider, and prompted Schneider to write Herr F—a threatening letter, demanding GO Marks if there was to be no more "trouble" about the story. The merchant sought aid from the police. But neither he nor Erhard appeared in Court. The proceedings turned on Schneider, and the evidence determined his share. He was sentenced to five months."

Notable Examples of Systematic Blackmail; the "The "Bürkl-Wölfl Case."

Inattentive have little idea to what heights of success blackmailing mounts; of how rapacious and successful are blackmailers who systematize their terrorizing. What large sums are "bled away" by them are shown somewhat in such instances as the famous case of an official of the Kehrmann Bank, Berlin; and a similar recent one—of a distinguished European professor. Both of these were heavily mulcted. But in January, 1908, there came before the Assises of Munich, a case known as the "Bürkl-Wölfl Case" which is almost unparallelled in the records of its class. It is also interesting as -an example of what may be called blackmail by second-hand mechanicism—a frequent device. In outline it is as follows. As far back as 1886, an attorney of Munich named August Bürkl, had an intimacy of equivocal colouring with a youth named Götz—beginning when Götz was about fifteen or sixteen years old. Bürkl denied this explicitly—of course—on his oath, during his testimony, and it was tactfully kept from incriminating him. It lasted some years. Bürkl (unmarried) was very rich and very timid. He dreaded any sort of scandal, because of his profession, his social station, and his great affection for his aged, mother and his other family-connections. Young Götz easily blackmailed Burkl out of many small sums, during several years. Then Götz died. But unfortunately the intimacy had been known, or strongly suspected, by a barber named Wölfl. After Götz was dead, Wölfl and his wife began the most elaborate, audacious and prolonged series of extortions which can be conceived, against the unlucky and frightened Bürkl. First, Wölfl claimed to have letters from Bürkl to the dead boy, Götz. He claimed that a whole set of his—Wölfl's—acquaintances "knew all about" what had passed between Bürkl and young Götz, and meant to make trouble. These parties Wölfl kindly undertook to "keep quiet," to "buy off," and so on—at the plundered Burkl's-expense. Such persons were fictions—the "Mrs. Harris" sort of creations of Wölfl and wife. The parties were said to live in America and elsewhere; to be on the point of coming to Munich to prosecute

Bürkl. Their letters were concocted by Wölfl and his wife, and the timorous Bürkl never saw any post-marked envelopes for these precious communications. The Wölfls grew rich. Their uneducated wastefulness was talked of, in their quarter of Munich. Their wealth was all at the cost of the miserable Bürkl! Automobiles, jewels and tine clothes, bank-interests, prodigal and foolish squanderings, transatlantic journeys,—all entered into the mystery of the *parvenu* Wölfl ménage. The sums demanded and received from Bürkl ranged upward and upward; from first a few dozen Marks, to hundreds—and to thousands and tens of thousands. Josephine Sarvi, a pseud'o-betrothed for the dead Götz, was presented. She also received a large sum, as hush-money for "what Götz had told her"—a complete fiction. At last the despairing Bürkl who—in spite of his large wealth—saw ruin facing him if the matter did not end, with a belated courage put it before the court. The two Wölfl were arrested and tried. (See, the "Münchener Nachrichten" and other journals, for January 23, *et seq.*, 1908.) The amount that the blackmailers had "got out of" of Bürkl approximated the almost incredible sum of five hundred and forty-five thousand Marks; all between the time when young Götz died (1893) and the date of the weak-hearted Bürkl's final recourse to law-protection. Wölfl and his wife were sentenced (after preposterously impudent efforts to maintain a defense) to the maximum penalties for such doings, under German law—long terms of imprisonment at hard-labour, and to fines as heavy as could he set—though trivial in comparison with what sums the pair had extorted from Bürkl. The latter was not incriminated homosexually before the law, by his case.

In like category, may be mentioned the Schultz Case, in Hamburg, in January, 1909; the "Gensler Case" before the Elbing Criminal Court, in the same month of 1909; and several other cases, (in which greater or lesser sums were systematically obtained by the accused) brought to trial in Germany in 1907, 1908, 1909. They were typical. A few pages later here, will be found notes of a recent French blackmailing case, as of an Italian one, each involving a large extortion from the victim.

The Parisian male prostitutes, of attractive externals, such as haunt the boulevards, are nowadays extremely dangerous as blackmailers on social and criminal leverages, according to circumstances. These French-speaking pests invade in their annual overflow the smart summer-resorts and Riviera centers, according to season. Rich guests of hotels there often suffer from them.

As another example of systematic extortion, in which affair we again meet with soldiers as blackmailers, here is an instance that occurred in Oldenburg, as cited from a local journal:

"A notable blackmailing affair, which has victimized several persons a good while, has at last been brought before our criminal Court. The matter in question as to its operations has "bled" the victim for as high a sum as 28,000 Marks, and has been carried along against a well-to-do citizen in private life here, viz. Herr von Seggern, on the charge of unnatural offences (Parag. 175, RSB). Two of the seven blackmailers (chimney-sweeps in Oldenburg) were the first arrested; but the main conspirator against Herr von S—, also a chimney-sweep, unluckily was not easy to catch. He was prudent enough to go over to England, and sent thence his threatening letters to his victim, demanding the money; or else wrote his comrades, directing the 'campaign' against Herr von S—through these agents. The active participants extorted sums that varied between 700 Marks and 40. The sentences ranged from one year and six months, to six months. Two soldiers have been found to be of this same conspiracy, and have been tried in the Military Court, and sentenced to degradation from service. Since the proceedings began, the absent leader in the affair, Kirchhoff, has comitted suicide, to avoid extradition."

The blackmailer is often right, in spite of all the law's judiciousness, when he warns his writhing victim that even if he, the blackmailer, will be punished as an offender—or co-offender—so will the victim be punished. The law cannot always distinguish. Sometimes it will not do so—whether failing intolerantly or stupidly. The famous Hasse Case, in 1905 is an example. In December, 1905, Herr Hasse, a high-standing jurist of Breslau—in fact, the president of one of the most important of the Breslau tribunals—one day in Berlin, shot at and wounded a young blackmailer who long had mulcted Herr Hasse of money through their having had homosexual relationships. The sums extorted reached to the thousands. The unlucky Herr Hasse went to the nearest police-court, laid down his revolver, surrendered himself, and was duly tried for attempt at murder. He had wounded the blackmailer only slightly. The affair made a great local sensation. Hasse was highly respected. But in this case, when the matter was raised of a reason for the shooting, the court regarded both the blackmailer (a youth named Lechel) and blackmailed as duly to be punished for homosexuality. Hasse, as well as Lechel, was sentenced to several months of prison. Such an outcome raised a violent outcry against judges and law. But the sexual case was clear as to both parties; and it was not handled so as to favour the unlucky Herr Hasse.

In the current year, a bold German blackmailer named Otto Schlanger made attempts against no lower grade of victims than Prince Heinrich of Prussia (the son of the late Prince Albrecht); and by means of letters demanded five-hundred Marks, under threats to inform the Emperor of sexual facts in the life of Prince Heinrich that would gravely compromise him in the ramified and interminable Eulenburg, Hohenau and Lynar scandals. This blackmailer, also threatened Prince Joachim-Albrecht of Prussia with, exposure as an habitual homosexual. The affair was brought to trial, and Schlanger was given a sentence of two years penal servitude.

The notable "W—and Jirgl Case," occurring in Munich, in the latter years of the nineties just past, presented on its surface an outcome that was perhaps too severe for the blackmailer; not a common aspect. The plaintiff had recourse, most unwillingly, to the law; dreading a scandal. He was of the aristocracy, and a member of the royal household. The defendant was a young man named Jirgl, who was trying to extort money. The facts were that Herr von W—had met the young man in the Pinakothek; had fallen in love with him; and presently Jirgl (who was exceptionally good-looking) though he was a pious youth and a theological student, had become the "mistress" of the rich admirer. They lived together, travelled together, and so on. But Jirgl's health and beauty declined. He grew ill. His protector tired of him, and cast him aside. Jirgl for revenge, and in full appreciation of his hold, blackmailed the deserter. The aristocrat won his case. The ruined Jirgl was sentenced to eighteen months of imprisonment. The high-born complainant was not incriminated legally (the latter adjective is important) in the case, being considered guiltless of technically homosexual rapports with his deserted ephebus. This decision was loudly commented on as personally biased, and influenced by Court intrigues against impartiality of justice. W—had undoubtedly been guilty not only of pederasty but of seduction, and of ruining a youth's whole life.

Manifestly the blackmailer relies primarily upon fear on the part of the victim. To terrorize is the first necessity. A man otherwise brave too often cannot cow such an assailant by bold demeanour or by calm ridicule. He fears more than the attack the "talk" over the remedy! True is it that a good kicking from one's doors is generally enough to send a common type of *Erpresser* flying, for good. But (Iranians are too often not muscular nor valorous. The victim's ignorance of the legal dispositions for his aid is general in the countries where he needs most such aid. Physical strength, moral resolution, legal knowledge, are defences not too universally practised in any troublesome affairs. The victim is likely to be unaware that he has the good-will of law and police-court, rather than has the rascal. Unless he be examined by pedants of morality, the victim has enough chances to avoid direct compromises by his own recital: at least that is now a tendency, in many countries. But the social whispers that will inevitably fly about hold the victim back. People will comment; they will believe more or less, will be scandalized, even if the Uranian predicament be all a tissue of persecution. Hence the struggle against some vampire, or pack of vampires, can go on for years! Immediate recourse to legal help, to betake oneself to the nearest police-court—to call the nearest police-officer, to face down the blackmailer with rudest or calmest contempt and with counter-threats and action—these are not only the first defenses but often perfectly efficient ones.

Here is an example of English blackmail; cited from the London press:

"Behind closed doors yesterday in the Court last named, before Sir James Smith, was tried the blackmailing case against William Belton, nominally an agent for a patent-medicine, but of no present occupation; the suit brought by Mr. Albert H—of Birmingham. Mr. H- charged that one evening, six months ago (April), while walking in a secluded part of Hyde Park the defendant accosted him, and walked some distance with him chatting. He finally asked the complainant for some pecuniary help, which the complainant gave him—a mere trifle at the time. The defendant managed however to ascertain the name, residence and position in society of the defendant. He presently wrote plaintiff threatening letters, and also twice visited him, against the will of the complainant, at his London lodgings; demanding money, and continuing to threaten the defendant with loss of character and with a felonious charge. He declared that the offence in question had occurred on the evening mentioned. Mr. H—wholly denied the charge, but was however timorous enough to give the defendant considerable sum as hush-money, to avoid any chances of public defamation. The defendant has continued his demands and his visits, and has greatly annoyed and terrified Mr. H—by Ids threats and exactions. He has received from Mr. H—not less than sixty pounds, on one occasion, on another thirty, on another fifty, and so on. The whole amount that Mr. H—has paid over, in a mistaken course toward such scandalous extortion, amounts to four hundred and eleven pounds; and the complainant's estate is seriously injured as well as his peace of mind much impaired. The defendant told a circumstantial story, which the Court concluded was manufactured out of few real incidents. The defendant was sentenced to one year's imprisonment; taking his sentence with a burst of obscenity against the complainant."

In such instance, the victim seems to have succeeded in keeping clear of incriminating himself sexually, while proving the blackmail; an important, troublesome—often impossible—aspect of such a case in England, where the plaintiff in the blackmailing suit may be visited by the law for homosexual offenses. In libel-suits, divorce-suits and the like, this point is grave. It was, as we have seen earlier in this book, the ruin of Oscar Wilde.

"Evidently," remarks the thoughtful reader, "to be courageous against the blackmailer *is* obviously the first policy! But one also sees that the victim may get himself into great trouble; coming out of the court a blacker kettle than seems the pot, or fully as black! In cases like one of the foregoing, "The sword of justice cuts the hand that grasps it!"

Discomforts and Risks of Legal Resistance: Legal Tendency to Help the Victim.

Blackmailing cases do take that turn. The victim can suffer shameful imprisonment, as well as can his.enemy. But the sound principle of legal resort is not invalidated by this fact. The tendency now, in many

Continental courts is tactfully to "manage" the victim's case so that he does not incriminate himself. What is yet more significant, in the French, the German, the Austro-Hungarian and other Courts of law, in some Continental countries where most homosexualism acts still are a felony and an obloquy,[4] there has come within a few years an important detail of procedure and sentiment. If the person necessarily incriminating himself in the complaint against his blackmailer, when arrested and on trial on homosexual charges, can prove medically psychiatrically, that he is homosexual by inborn, ineradicable nature, then his case is often materially made light or even dismissed. This is especially helpful when a respectable homosexual has to combat a charge against him begun not by extortion but made in the "interests of public morality." Of course there should not be offenses to public-decorum, nor rape, nor corruption of minors impairing the force of this defence. It it be accepted, the homosexual is turned over to a specialistic physician, who decides (in course of some weeks), whether his "patient" is to be reported to the Court as homosexual by incurably natural propensities or not. Sometimes this examination obliges the defendant to pass months in prison, till the doctor be ready to pronounce on his "nature." But if his status be so settled, he finally is absolved from felony, and is free.

In such cases, sometimes previous psychomedical data are already at hand. The term of examination usually in subtracted from the term of imprisonment under sentence, for a homosexual patient. This attitude of law of course is not shown to homosexual *blackmailers;* but simply to those respectable homosexuals under arrest for sexual misconduct. Sometimes comes no further penalty. But in Germanic territories, be it noted that when a homosexual offender of good moral character, has been pronounced naturally, "incurably" homosexual, and is discharged (having his detention for examination as his only punishment) it is decidedly advisable that he leave the place where his case has occurred; as soon as possible should arrange to live out of Germany or Austria. He will—naturally—nearly always do this, but sometimes it is inconvenient enough. He is lucky to escape with only exile. A few years ago, as a similisexual he would not have "got off" so lightly. Continental law had not then endured, even vaguely and unwillingly as now, the idea that something quite other

Inborn Homosexualism as Defense.

---

4. See Chapt. IV.

than vice underlies much homosexualism; that the uranian Intersex has excuses, has demands, even has rights, however.abnormal they have seemed. Medicopsychic research herein.has affected the jurisprudence of Continental Europe importantly; though much is yet to do.

The reader may observe that while in Europe (even apart the tolerance of Latin races) scientific excuse for homosexualism is making way, old standards hold in English and North American law-courts. Ignorance and indeed vehement hostility against any excuses for homosexualism obtain in England and the United States. Outside of the most reflective and learned class of lawyers, nothing is heeded of recent Continental theories as to similisexuality by medical-legal specialists even of first rank. Indeed little is known of them. They are yet much outside of Anglo-Saxon medico-psychologic jurisprudence.

An Improved Legal Sentiment Especial to Germany and Austria; not in Great Britain or America.

The unlucky fact been observed that legal proceedings necessary for the rescue of some victim of blackmail on homosexual grounds (even cases in which blackmailers are punished) seem to do more harm than good toward obstructing the vile 'business.' They suggest to the mob the ease with which timid victims can be bled, and they teach the technique of blackmail. It has been well said that "one blackmail-suit creates a dozen blackmailers." Rascals are willing to take their chances. Immediately in consequence of this fact, as well as in view of the agonizing histories of victims, and of the inducements to robbery and murder, has come—with questions of moral aspects of homosexualism—the movement in Germany and Austria-Hungary toward the abolition of *any* penalty for private and adult similisexual relations, if voluntary. To tolerate "decent homosexualism" as in Italy, France, Spain, Portugal, Holland, Belgium, parts of Switzerland and so on, puts the blackmailer out of combat to a great and wholly beneficent extent.

Public Proceedings Against Blackmailers as Mischievous, however Necessary.

In France, Italy, Belgium, Spain and so on, where is no legislation punishing homosexualism (except when coercion or offences to public decency, or innocent minors are considered) the crude, vulgar blackmailer can frighten a stranger by pointing out that to commit sexual acts in a

Blackmailing not Unknown in France, Italy, etc., though Exceptional: Instances.

latrine or in a park, or an inn's more public premises, however retired and deserted, makes the victim a statutory offender. We have seen above how he sometimes will dog the traveller to his hotel, threatening his disclosures to the nearest policeman. Where the Latin blackmailer has not the leverage of law or of public decorum, he will threaten public social opinion; especially if the stranger be English or American. The victim's name will be printed—will be telegraphed to his native town. In all such cases, the victim's stout personal resistance, or threats of calling up the nearest policeman, will nearly always get rid promptly of the blackmailer. A favourite trick of this blackmailer is an accusation to the victim of pederasty with an "innocent" *minor* youth. This is not always easy to rout off-hand.

In France and Italy, be it noted, if on a charge of debauching a minor the minor can be proved an *habitual* offender, the case breaks up. To scandals, whether with or without blackmailing aspects (usually with such) in in countries where the liberal Code-Napoléon is the basis of legislation as to similisexuality, many criminal cases are based oh the perversion of minor youth. To these processes belong the famous and tragic Krupp Affair (already referred-to here), along with the "Allers Case," which it rather eclised, in Capri and Germany, in 1902. Its actual legal territory was Italian. The "Krupp Case," in which the victim was accused of pederastic offences with innocent minor lads, ultimately resolved itself, in essential aspects, to a carefully-planned scheme for extortion; the matter of "innocence" being more than vague when the youth typically concerned came into question. In the concurrent "Allers Case," the plan of concerted blackmail was discernible. The distinguished Munich painter was warned by one of his young models— it is said, by the son of the Capriote who brought the attack into form; and the artist fled Capri, in time to escape arrest. He was sentenced (as an absent defendant) in the Naples court, to imprisonment and a fine.

The same leverage against homosexuals has lately shown itself in the affair, in Home, of the well-known photographer P—, charged with habitual proxenetism and corruption of minors; a case involving a large number of persons of high station and of all nationalities, professions and social distinctions. This affair was not brought to trial until many months after the arrest of P—and the assistants in his studio; which arrest, by the by, was made when a noted German concert-singer was discovered in the photographer's premises, in compromising circumstances as to his relations with a youthful *civus romanus*. The unlucky photographer was shut up in durance all the long delay between his arrest and his trial; it was said, because the Italian authorities wished to give to as many, persons as possible their time to escape from Rome and appearances in court. A large and extremely compromising correspondence, between P—and clients all over the world, was seized. The photographer had long specialized nude male "studies," and did a large business in such portraits of *tipi midi e ben membruti*, as do several Italian photographers, including a near relative of P—, resident in Taormina. The painter was sentenced to some eight months of imprisonment and to a large fine. The affair was as much as possible kept out of the local journals, to which satisfaction, for all concerned, a general "strike" of the printers of the daily newspapers in Rome most opportunely contributed. At last accounts, P—had been duly enlarged from prison, and had resumed in Rome all his specialities of business. Another noted Roman photographer of *modelli nudi*, G—was arrested and punished for "injury to public morality" at about the same date, on account of too-audacious "studies" in photography for general sale— even in Rome.

As blackmail in France—but not as to England, Germany, America, etc.—the law is so adjusted that the question of the relations of the blackmailed to the blackmailer are not of obligation to be defined clearly in the trial of a blackmailer, no matter how clear; nor later need they recur, *obbligato*. They are often not part of the evidence. This simplifies and protects. But social disgrace of course may be resultant. In 1896, occurred in Paris the curious case of the pretended police-agent Sourdville, who played the comedy of accepting, as if against his duty, a bribe to let some unlucky stranger go—free of scandal. This rascal however went on to thievery by the aid of chloroform; and was trapped and sentenced.

French Law Discreet; French Instances: the Leverage of Scandal Only.

A recent remarkable case of blackmail came into the Ninth Correctional Chamber, in Paris, in the first, week of February, 1908. A gymnastics-professor of Dijon, named G—, a highly respectable and esteemed man, met on the boulevards in Paris a young maleprostitute named Eugene-Georges Peyrin, twenty years old. G—made the acquaintance; Peyrin accompanied him to his hotel, though without entering—on that occasion. An appointment

Instance; Paris.

was made for next day. But even on this opportunity Peyrin asked for money, and received twenty francs. After the theater, next evening, about midnight, Peyrin designated an hotel where "male-guests" were particularly received—one of the many such *bouges* in Paris. Once in the room together, Peyrin allowed himself to be embraced and kissed and generally *attouché*, for a few moments—in smiling consent. Then he said "—Come, let us undress!" G—complied with haste, stripped, and sat on the bed. As soon as Peyrin saw G—quite naked (Peyrin having not taken off more than his coat and waistcoat) he turned on G—menacingly. He seized the unfortunate man by the throat. "Now we'll change our tune!" he exclaimed, "—I want money, a lot of money! He demanded three thousand francs; or else "he would make a scandal." This would ruin the Dijon victim socially and professionally. So G—then and there gave up to Peyrin, his watch and all the money he had about him—a thousand francs—and signed a promissory note for two thousand! These amounts were supplemented by others, sent presently by postal-orders. The Dijon victim thus paid over sums of one thousand, six thousand, three thousand francs, and so on. He knew that he had done nothing whatever criminal under the French law—Peyrin had no real 'hold'. But the scandal was not to be faced. In this way, G—paid out to Peyrin not less than twenty-one thousand francs; until he decided, half-bankrupt, that he must turn to the law for aid. The defense of the villainous young Parisian shark was that all the money "had been given him" by G—, as merely friendly expressions of regard, as compensation for their sexual relations, and so on. The tribunal could sentence Peyrin only to two years of prison and five-hundred francs fine. G—, at last free of such bloodsucking, left for Dijon by the first train on the conclusion of the trial. One exclaims, "*Requiescat in pace!*"

Some years ago an English gentleman (a completely homosexual type) of high family, distinguished in literature, happened on an Italian instance of blackmailing "bluff." In Rome, walking one afternoon in the Villa Doria, he chanced on a handsome well-mannered young male prostitute, who mentioned himself as employed in the Villa. This was not the fact, as he had been discharged some months earlier. After half-an-hour's strolling about in the garden (which at the time had no other promenaders) the Englishman suggested that "—si diverterebbe un momentino," if the other was inclined. They turned into the shrubbery, and remained for a few minutes. (Onan. mut). Soon after, the stranger and his "friend" left the gardens; the Italian insisting on accompanying the Englishman toward his hotel. The Englishman had given his companion five lire—a liberal amount for such informal "services rendered." The Italian demanded, more, and threatened a scandal in the street. The Englishman much dreaded that turn of the situation. However he vigorously ridiculed the young rascal's charge. The circumstances had not been "public,"—to say nothing of the impossibility of the prostitute's proving a case in a court. "But the Villa is a public place, any part of it!"—insisted the other, who knew the text of Italian law better than his victim. "Pay me fifty lire, or I will also accuse you of having attempted me—forced me—though I resisted"—and so on. The Englishman, now very nervous (as several passers were in earshot and a *sicnrezza* not far) took advantage of a tram coming by him. He escaped to it, though his adversary sent a volley of abuse after him that made the passengers look at him. But the end was not there. In course of a week, he received a threatening visit from the young man, who had found out his name and address. The Englishman unwillingly went to a legal friend and stated enough of the facts to receive advice. He learned that although the. Villa gardens, like many others were indeed "public" places, just as is some lonely *impasse*, or a spot in the Campagna—nevertheless the fact of his having met his tormentor in the Villa on a day when, as was the fact, the same was not open to the public (as on other days) would be a sufficient defence, in any well-disposed court. The other charge was absurd. Fortified with this advice, he met his adversary scornfully on his second call, and so put him out of countenance, that the scamp went away silenced. The Englishman never had a word from him again, though he often saw him.

In Milan, Rome, Florence, Naples, Paris, Brussels, Geneva, many hotels of low grade, but clean enough, are used for homosexual appointments; or for ending-up the adventure of an evening. Any rented hotel-room is a legally "a private place." If no open scandal occur in it, the guests in it have a right to do what they please, so long as they are by themselves. Nevertheless, Italian courts have questioned if a hotel is ever a really "private" place. Clearly in other premises of it than the particular room hired what goes on is "under public circumstances." The prostitute sometimes uses this idea in blackmail against a stranger with whom he has gone to some hotel; he even changes the room. A knowledge of such devices and of law-codes would save homosexual men anxiety and many a skirmish: as would

Hotels and Legislation.

also would be useful the remembrance that the Italian law, like the French, in trying a blackmailer and in punishing him, does not concern itself much with questions of the relations that the parties have had. The matter to be decided is the blackmailing. The victim is not a criminal in consequence of his conduct—relatively construed.

Blackmail Carried Beyond Actual Jurisdiction. Impudent "terrorizing" by leverage of *social* opinion, can be continued when wide of the place where the incidents basing it may have occurred. Here is an example. A few years ago, a young Hew York banker of homosexual tastes, when in Venice entered into relations with a young Venetian. For some weeks such intimacy subsisted; the Italian being a passivist. The American then continued his journey. The parting was perfectly friendly; and, by the by, no great pecuniary *douceurs* passed between them, the young ephebus not demanding them. The American went to Sorrento— which pleasant resort sometimes offers much venal homosexualism, like Amalfi and Capri. His Venetian friend was kind enough to give him a line of introduction to another pleasant-mannered prostitute in Sorrento. The American utilized this acquaintance also. After this, he returned to New York. Within a few weeks, he received a visit from a third (unknown) Italian, residing in Hew York. He made a demand on the banker for a "loan" of fifty dollars. This favour was urged, indicating that the banker's social well-being lay in compliance; as otherwise his relationships with Vasco G—in Venice, and with Nazzareno S—in Sorrento, would become a topic of letters to the banker's friends, to his club, etc. The blackmailer in fact possessed indiscreet notes. The offences had been committed in Italy; there was no ground whatever for his being criminally held in America. But the social scandal was enough to chill the banker's blood! He promptly paid the sum demanded. A long history of victimizing followed. For nearly two years, the unfortunate man was mulcted, without being addressed in a single letter; but by visits, made in spite of all precautions. In vain did he try to purchase the incriminating letters—only four. The sum turned over to the impudent agent of his ex-*amorini* was to the total of thousands. At last with a request for one hundred and fifty dollars, from the representative of Vasco and Nazzareno, the banker trapped his enemy into a letter of clear blackmail. He went to the police, and stated his case as best he could. The rogue in New York was sent to prison, and the affair was kept out of publicity, even in America. This rescue of the banker was easier; for the enterprising rascal in New York had a charge of graver sort hanging about him that might have extradited him to Italy. Hence as soon as released, he disappeared.

Two recent Italian examples of audacious blackmail, through the leverage of mere social terrorizing, are as follows. In the end of March, 1909, before Section XIII of the Naples police-court, came the case of the distinguished General F—(retired) against a whole clique of young Neapolitan pederasts—Gennaro Eossi, Francesco Sarzano, Dominicis, Capezzuti and others—who had been in homosexual relations with the unlucky gentleman. They thereupon had formed a regular league of blackmail against him; threatening to publish about the city his sexual habits. The band of rascals was linked to the *Camorra* of Naples, and this gave them additional courage. During many years, General F— paid thousands of lire to his persecutors, who had compromising letters and so on, as their weapons of extortion. The victim at length decided to face the scandal. The blackmailers were sentenced to terms of imprisonment varying between six years and three months. One of them was acquitted for want of proof. In the same month, in Milan, a very well-known, man in society, the Marchese di S—, a naval lieutenant, was walking along the Corso Vittorio Emmanuele at high noon, when a young man of dubious aspect, (whom the Marchese S—declared to be absolutely unknown to him) slipped up to his side and asked for money; at the same time alluding to homosexual satisfactions. The Marchese S—turned away angrily, but his interlocutor at once became explicit and declared that if the Marchese S—would not then and there give him fifty lire he would "tell all Milan" of the intimate relations between himself and the Marchese. The Marchese S—, as his answer, caught hold of the rascal, and called tire police. The blackmailer pulled himself loose and ran away, but was arrested. He declared that he "had taken the Marchese S—for another gentleman"; but he was condignly punished.

Instances: Italian.

Quite aside from *chevaliers d'industrie*, of low degree, or audacious rogues with no social platform to be considered, numerous blackmailing scandals have occurred where the blackmailer has belonged to families and stations of high grade. To such schemes to pay their bills, or rather to add to incomes of precarious source, have descended ruined barons,

High-Class Blackmailers: an American Affair.

counts in difficulties, adventurous princes, decadent elder or younger sons and professional men of rapacious and unscrupulous types. The history of the "submerged social tenth" is abundant in such affairs. A few years ago, came before the international public a case in which a rich industrial was the victim of two individuals of distinguished social grade—titled—who had squeezed a sum running into the hundreds of thousands out their prey before they were checked; with the particularity that their victim did not know until its end that they were the real instigators of the extortion. In a provincial capital of Austria-Hungary some years ago, came much talk by a suit and a vehement counter-suit, for slander, brought respectively by two young men. One of them was of a distinguished northern family, temporarily in the city; the other was a rich young Viennese. The charge complicated mutual blackmail with mutual homosexualism. The case was such a tangle of social developments that it was finally dropped—by common consent. It was generally believed that money-difficulties of K—, one of the complainants, and his rather dramatic attempt to extort, were the original causes of the issue, especially as the other of the pair, young E—, was conclusively homosexual. This case had most bizarre lights and shadows. In fact, the old saying that almost everything in the world has at least three planes, is noted in the aristocratic blackmailers' census. *Faire chanter* is a lyrical temptation far from confined to Vulgar humanity.

Transatlantic blackmailing affairs are not often before the public. But they occur, *passim*. In America, always a practical country, occurred in the latter nineties a very curious example of a blackmailing plot, where every person concerned was of smart social position; men of culture, wealth and youth. A family living in one of the largest cities was conspicuous for fortune—a great fortune—for finance, and for religious affiliations, the line being Keltic-American. One of the brothers was noted as homosexual, had been publicly so charged. A younger one was even more famous for his effeminate beauty, his elegance, and skill as a dancer and actor in private theatricals. Humour had long united his name with several boyish "intimates" of fashionable life, art, letters, and the stage; also with an eminent clergyman of his own creed—a handsome wordly celibate, of brilliant individuality. Two clubs to which young Mr. B—belonged were almost -notoriously sprinkled with an uranian membership, of the local *jeunesse dorée*. One winter, chance threw Mr. A—into acquaintance with a fellow-townsman considerably his junior, also homosexual, extremely and rich, the heir to a vast fortune also. The two young men were at once violently sympathetic—became inseparable. The relationship took its warmest course. Unluckily, it was remarked by a third party, and then by a fourth—Messrs. C—and D—. These two, although they appeared to have plenty of money at their disposal, really were deeply embarrased and anxious. Over the head of C—hung an impending financial crash. D—also had got himself into deep water. He was being indirectly bled of cash by an acquintance of humble rank, who was not likely to be discreet if not kept in good humour by "loans"—continually asked. One night, chance happened to disclose to C—and D—unmistakeably the nature of the relationship between Messrs. A—and B—. Thy decided, in a burst of mutual roguery and confidence, to try to profit by it. They accordingly went to work to collect something like evidence, to use as a leverage—somehow. They secured what would pass very well for such; at least what would greatly disconcert their victims, who were much more hares than lions. Next, they ventured on a bold *coup*. They won over to a particular usefulness, a new ally, X—. Fairly organized, they now proceeded to threaten B—(who was the most conspicuously rich target) with anonymous letters, and so on; mentioning circumstances that B—would much dislike to have published, not to mention A—. A large sum was to be ready and surrendered, under certain circumstances—presently; or trouble would be swift for both A—and B—together. But just at the crisis, the newest partner in the game, X—became frightened. He decided to retreat. He went to the ecclesiastical friend of A—, gave him the proofs, and betrayed his accomplices. Even then it was necessary, if a social scandal were to be avoided, to use very delicate agencies for breaking-up the scheme. The high hierarchy of the church was called into help. A—and B—were both rescued, from an affair that neither of them fully had divined, and that never was fully explained to them. The actors in the drama who were its main-springs, hastily left the city. The intimacy between A—and B—was however presently completely broken, as an inevitable and prudent consequence. Later both these friends married. The entire affair was one of quite unusual social complexion, audacity and skill. It was known to some outsiders only on the death of One of the persons officially concerned in its devolution.

But we must invade deeper the Inferno of homosexual perils and crimes. We have seen that the blackguard of Uranianism may be an

The Uranian World and Murder.

able-bodied villain, disposed to assault his prey—physically. When a homosexual hints in such society that he carries valuables or cash, let him look to them; not to say to his life! Along with forcible or other robbery, can come murder. Or such murder may be matter not of burglary or robbery, but of really homosexual passions—revenge, jealousy and other motives. Such assassins are not always of base station. We have previously touched on murders by companions of princes and noblemen, high officials, and churchmen and professional men. But we are dealing for the moment, with especially the darkest paths of the homosexual labyrinth.

The reader will meet plenty of examples of "Uranian murders" in such German publications as the "Jahrbuch" mentioned; in the curious monthly bulletin of homosexual data taken from the current newspaper-press, and entitled "Mittheilungen des Bundes für Männliche Kultur," published by B. Zack, at Treptow (Berlin); and in dozens of studies dealing with homosexualism; as also in daily papers and criminal reports. In Ulrich's book "Memnon" are a classic few—now of long-ago—such as the murder of Lindemann by König; the attempt to drown a victim (already robbed) in Geneva; a series of desperate brutalities, including murder or its attempt, by the celebrated "Zürich Clique" of homosexuals and of other bad characters generally, in 1895; who lured persons of wealth into similisexual intimacies, gained access to their victims' houses, plundered them, and so on. Metropolitan police-annals abound in assassinations that are homosexual in colour. Strangers often imprudently go to the very lairs of just such assassins; have valuables on their persons; and never are seen alive again. Berlin, Vienna, London, New York, Cairo, Naples—all such large cities show this dangerous phase of the Uranian's quests and acquaintances. Here are a few such, from newspaper police-items:

"In Potsdam occurred a few days ago the mysterious murder of one Albert Schmidt, an elderly resident living for some time past in K—strasse. Schmidt was unmarried and given to peculiarly "intimate relations" with young soldiers. He had a very roomy apartment, and each week he was host to such special guests, often on short acquaintance. About a year ago Schmidt was brought into one of the criminal courts on a charge of an offence under Paragr. 175 of the Statute-Book, and the charge being-proved he was sentenced to six months imprisonment. Unluckily this affair did not 'cure' him of his eccentric habits. He was constantly to be met of an evening, in the parks or streets near the Barracks especially, "taking-up" with young soldiers, as mentioned. After four days of being missed by his immediate neighbours, he was found dead last Monday, on the floor of his sitting room, wholly undressed, and in a pool of his own blood. His skull was broken, and he had also been strangled. Evidently a hard, if curiously quiet, struggle had taken place, between Schmidt and his assailant, during an evening together. As Schmidt's purse containing 85 Marks in gold and silver, (and also his watch and valuables) were not stolen, the exact origin of the quarrel with his murderer is not clear. Several individuals, however, are suspected, including a certain young man described as wearing a light-coloured brown suit, lately much seen with Schmidt; also a soldier known to be a "friend" of the murdered man. Not long ago, Schmidt was severly chastised in the Park here one night, by three young infantry-soldiers one of whom he offended by his improper proposals. Possibly his murder completes some vengeance, with a terrible effect. Schmidt leaves a considerable estate."

In Naples, in March, 1901, occurred this characteristic affair. I cite the newspaper-account:

"A mysterious and frightful criminal occurrence has come to light, discovered last evening. About one o'clock in the morning, four officers of our police-service, Riccio, Cuomo, Stanco and Galati were informed that cries for help had been coming from the house Number 81, Via Nuova di Capodimonte, close by the Ponte di Sanità, On trying to gain access, no one admitted the policemen, and all was still. They broke open the door of the apartment in question, on the fifth floor, the residence of a certain young medical doctor named Filippo Raffaeli M—, formerly a student at our University, but lately admitted to practice, and located in the rooms mentioned. As the officers finally entered, they heard renewed groans from the darkness beyond, and at the same time were nearly knocked down by some unknown party who tried to pass them, and reach the stair, but who was captured. A direful spectacle presented itself to the officers, on lighting up the room. On the bed lay young Doctor M—perfectly naked, and bathed in his own blood, his throat cut, and faintly moaning in his last agony. He was carried to the hospital in the Via Pellegrini, but expired shortly, unable to murmur more than a few syllables. . . The other individual in the room, fortunately unable to escape, is beyond doubt the murderer of the ill-fated young physician. The circumstances are partly as follows. Dr. M—belonged to a family in easy circumstances, in Gravina, (Puglia). He was 28 years old, single, and highly talented. Lately he took into his confidential intimacy and nominal service a young Neapolitan named Vincenzo Morelli, a thorough vagabond, though not bad looking; a relative (it is said) of the concierge of the house where the Doctor was living. The young rascal had free access to the Doctor's apartments, and often slept there with his patron, it seems. Lately M—had noticed that the young man—about twenty years old—had stolen small sums from him, but nothing important came of the matter till lately when some fifty lire were missing unmistakeably through the protègé's operations. There have been several altercations since, and Dr. M—told Morelli that he would discharge him from his not very clear 'services'. It may be mentioned that a year ago the youth was arrested in consequence of public prostitution, and has Jived by such a device for part of his life. The fact that Dr. M—tolerated some equivocal associates has been unfavourable commented on, in the past. The commission of the crime by young Morelli seems to have been that partly in cupidity and partly in a fit of passionate hatred to his benefactor, he took advantage of the sleep of Dr. M—, or of other circumstances, to cut his patron's throat with fatal address, by a common razor. He slipped into the room in his stocking-feet, ready to escape after putting his victim to death and pocketing has valuables; evidently a plan long premeditated. He tells a story not in consonance however with this plain account, as indicated by the facts in the case."

In Vienna, a murder came to light, awhile ago (the victim being a citizen of respectable business connections) presenting typically uranian circumstances. The account here is abbreviated from the press:

"The mysterious murder of Herr H. K—lately noted in our columns, appears explained, although the, assassin of the merchant is still unknown positively and in at large. For two or three months, Herr K—whose habits of life and acquaintances have pointed him out as given to the class of offences referred to in Paragr. 129, of the Criminal St. B., has been especially intimate with two or three young men, all of them members of a certain well-known clique, and associated with the patrons of the notorious X—Bath establishment. One of them, not a great while ago, figured as defendant in a blackmailing case here The room of Herr H. K—was on the ground-floor, and opened directly on the street mentioned; and several times lately the police or neighbour have suspected that persons—visitors to Herr K—went in or out from the lodging at curious hours, the guests being always male. The motive of the crime appears to have been robbery, and the escape of the murderer by the window (which we have mentioned in reporting the affair a week ago) was easy enough. As the body of Herr K—: was not discovered until nearly a fortnight after he must have been knocked down, when nude, in or near his bed, as narrated—owing to the little notice fastened to his door "Gone to Brünn—will return on the 20th"—by this time the whole group of individuals suspected seems to have fled the city, to avoid examination. The arrests are not yet in sight. On Sunday—" etc. etc.

Or a brutal assault stops just at murder's threshold. As here:

"Yesterday night, Professor L—the well-known language teacher, was the victim of an impudent attempt at robbery and murder, which luckily stopped at theft, though with no light one. Professor L—was walking homeward from Moabit, at about two o'clock in the morning, when two well-dressed young men, strangers to him, accosted him near the Parliament House; and with them he entered into a conversation. Suddenly he was knocked down by them, and robbed of fifty Marks and his gold watch. As he could not save himself from falling, he fell directly down into the Spree from the sidewalk, and had the water been higher he might have drowned. Fortunately, the water was low, and Professor L—did not roll farther than the foot of the stone stairs leading down. He was found in a pitable condition and was taken home by the night-police. His injuries proved to be slight. The authors of the outrage were not identified. They belong to the worst class of social criminals.

<table>
<tr><td>Political Murders and Hoinosexuality.</td><td>In numerous examples of important political assassinations, we find that the murderer is Uranian, the blood-lust instinct perhaps being part of the perversity of his cruelty.</td></tr>
</table>

In numerous examples of important political assassinations, we find that the murderer is Uranian, the blood-lust instinct perhaps being part of the perversity of his cruelty. Thus Santo, who stabbed the Empress Elizabeth of Austria, a few years ago, and Bresci the murderer of King Umberto of Italy, were similisexual men. The instinct as in mere coincidence to many special crimes—*e.g.* Manyek, the atrocious butcher of his whole family in Vienna, in 1901, also numerous wholesale English and French affairs—may be worth remarking, even if homosexual life and passion had have nothing to do with the obvious facts.

That murders are not rare in connection with soldierhomosexualism, military prostitution, etc., was mentioned in an earlier chapter. A special example of the soldier as murderer under homosexual circumstances— already included in our references when speaking of military life and uranianism—was the shocking "Studio Affair" in London, in 1906, where a young homosexual painter, A—W—who invited only soldiers to frequent him, was discovered in his apartments, naked and dead, one morning, with his head smashed by a hammer. The evidence at the inquest was so likely to raise an appalling garrison-scandal that the affair was suppressed as quickly as possible. The murderer (out of question a soldier) was not traced. It is said that a royal command cut short the search.

A noteworthy murderous attack, in combination with a suicide— the whole affair homosexual—occurred in the vicinity of New York City, early in November, 1907. It was the subject of not only discreet legal scrutiny (not to much purpose) but also of wide local comment, on account of the high social station of the family of the younger of the two actors. The nationalities involved were rather more French in blood on the one side and Scandinavian on the other than strictly American; but the family is one identified as of America for at least three or four generations. It was a presumptively case of pederastic intrigue, ending in a bloody drama. In the luxurious summer home of the Z—family, at X—, a fashionable suburb of the metropolis, had subsisted for many months an intimacy between the young son of the house, who was a lad of about seventeen, and a valued butler named B—. To this B—, in fact, the youth (a very handsome boy) was much entrusted during the absence of the family; and in hunting-excursions, travelling etc., B—was always with him. B—was apparently in the' habit of stealing down to the boy's bedroom—quite detached, in a large villa—seeking clandestine relationships at night. The youth transferred his interest, it would seem, to a new and younger man-servant. B—, who was also alcoholic, thereupon became furiously jealous; and finally grew insanely so. One morning he got out of bed—long before daylight (probably as so often before)—threw on his bath-gown, and slipped down to the lad's room. What took place there has never been fully told. Shots were heard, awakening the sleeping household. Another servant burst open the locked door of the bedroom. On the bed—from which he had sprung up, nude—crouched the boy, with a bullet-wound in bis head, tpat just missed taking his life and which kept him unconscious for weeks. On the floor lay the man B—, naked; dead by his own hand. At the inquest, some considerable time later, the youth (as might be expected) declared that he knew absolutely nothing of what had occurred; that B—had shot him in his sleep, and that no reason could be guessed at for the affair, except that the butler was drunk or crazy. The attack was undoubtedly one of maniacal jealousy, with intent to kill.

In July 1908, occurred in Berlin a murder of distinctively homosexual accent, which made much talk. A certain Julius E—, proprietor of a café-restaurant was found strangled in his elegant rooms in Genthinerstrasse 26, the sash-cord of a window wound tight about his neck. Robbery had been the motive. E—was a notorious homosexual; during years on the secret lists of the Berlin police, and in sexual relations with many doubtful characters, including some young soldier-prostitutes of bad report. The murderer was not identified.

In 1907, 1908 and 1909, were conspicuous in the assizes of Germany several murder-cases more or less directly associated with homosexual relations between the assassins and the victims—with blackmailing, robbery and so on as also part of the story; such as the "Brühl-Forest Murder" (Guben) the murder of the insurance-agent Franke by his acquaintance Senger; the "Maagh Murder" on a railway-train—by an architect, etc., etc.

Probable Instance of Dionian Revenge on an Uranian.

Some such tragedies leave no doubt of their connection, even if not confessed or "proved." in 1900, an affair of vengeful asssassination shocked the community of a Southern town in the United States. An English artist, X—, visiting the place, to paint, had maintained a long and close intimacy with a young lad of excellent family, as his model. Gradually came gossip among the masculine population. One morning, occurred a sharp altercation between the painter and the lad. The topic was not divulged in the course of the tragic sequel. But it was mentioned that an older brother of the angry youth elicited some facts that satisfied him. At any rate, next morning, while the artist was in bed and asleep in the house of his host,' not far away, the older brother of the boy suddenly drove to the door and asked to speak with the artist— at once. He suited the action to the word; ran up the staircase, dashed open the painter's door, and with an exclamation that was explicit, shot him dead. He was promptly arrested at Y—and held for trial. The motives of his crime were explained sufficiently, under reserves of a court-room. He was acquitted of the felony.

Other Recent
Instances of
Uranianism and
Murder.

The years 1907, 1908 and 1909 were marked by notable criminal affairs before French *juges d'instruction*, or the assizes, in which homosexualism was a clear factor. Several murder-trials were strongly of such colour. In the group was the "Jobard Murder," in which the criminal, a young man, killed the youth with whom he had been sexually intimate, and also killed the lad's father in an accession of jealousy and of-fear of interruption to the intrigue, and in mania. More remarkable was the famous "Affaire Remy" at Paris, occurring in June, 1908, and before the courts, in January and June 1909. In this mysterious crime was questioned the relation to the murder of a retired banker named Remy, on the part of an elderly butler Renard, and a young valet named Courtois. Renard had been sexually intimate with one Léon E—, a young nephew of the murdered man; as also with the valet Courtois, and with others. He seemed to be a typical 'married homosexual,' in fact. He was found guilty, as was the valet Courtois, and both received heavy sentences, though not capital ones. The butler Renard nevertheless made a firm defence; claiming to he the victim of a tissue of vindictive falsehoods, by Courtois; and many arguments against his conviction were maintainable. He had a most excellent record, as a man and a servant, being already past middle life and made an excellent personal impression in the court-room. In fact, at this writing, the "Renard Case" is yet under appeal, and the two verdicts given may be set aside. All

Paris crowded to this trial—a *cause célèbre* of the year. In the notable "Albinet-Leray Affair" occurring in 1908 in the Paris Criminal Assizes, in which were tried the audacious executants of a train-robbery—"The Affair of Train 16"—a group of homosexual associates and suggestions were in evidence. Albinet, the main agent of the robbery, was uranian; and his conviction was partly on the evidence of homosexuals, one of them, a certain Duros, of evil note. In the end of March, 1909, came before examination of a magistrate the murder of a Parisian lawyer and *littérateur*, Louis Farquharson-Fleurot, of about fifty-one years of age, found assassinated in his rooms in an apartment-house at No. 8, Rue du Mont-Thabor. Fleurot, though of excellent family and superiour education, had been in bad odour as member of the bar, but not actually dismissed from the roll, and was making a considerable income by shady litigations of all sorts. He was openly and notoriously homosexual; philosyrphetic even to bringing the worst class of street-pederasts to his lodgings. He had been obliged several times to move through complaints of his landlords or of fellow-tenants. He had "adopted" one young catamite, René B—, as his son or nephew, and had kept him handsomely, till a quarrel occurred. Fleurot once or twice had had ugly misadventures—robberies and assaults—due to the sort of male prostitutes he cultivated. He had last been seen alive when he was accompanying to his rooms, at four in the morning, a young *voyou* of about twenty years, "in a brown suit and a black derby-hat," This individual could not be traced; and till now the murder is unpunished. Again in April,1909, was assassinated at Versailles, a certain Madame Barbery, who during many years had kept in the town a regular and widely-known rendezvous for homosexual guests; especially for convenience of clients who affected young soldier-prostitutes of the garrison at Versailles, or for civilists who brought Parisian catamites out to the apartment in the Rue Maurepas. She had a son in the army in Algeria, himself actively homosexual. He sent to his mother numerous regimental and other acquaintances going to Paris on leave, thus adding to her clientage an element increasingly *louche*, mixed and dangerous. Robbery was the cause of the woman's murder. This matter has not been cleared up as yet.

The fear of a scandal is often accompanied by the final courage to kill the blackmailer. Homicide—often long and carefully premeditated murder—is a kind peculiarly in key with an aristocratic and high-class

The, Uranian Victim and 'Geloso', etc., as Assassin.

desperation; with crime that is the effort of the uranian to be free of persecution. Blackmailed or otherwise menaced by scandal, his means and hopes exhausted, he takes the law in his hands. Strange "mysteries" of blood, or murderous crimes not involved in mystery, occur where some overwrought man has reached the point of "turning," with pistol or knife or poison in hand. One greatly discussed crime in France, many years ago, still is a model of this species. Another bloody family-tragedy in England, a very few years ago, was due to the fact that the homosexual criminal was in almost insane despair.

A most complicated affair came in New York City, some half-a-dozen years back, in a smart club. It involved two poisonings, with fatal results. It was a drama of homosexual jealousy, and of revengeful self-protection. The recent attempt at assassination of a German of rank by another individual of much higher station, with a terrible risk, had much the like origin. The Italian term "geloso" refers to occasional assassinations in a race which has homosexuality more or less of its tissue, and which is always keen upon homosexual relations with rich foreigners who become residents. But such strangers easily grow tired of connections useful only to the vicious protégé. A tragedy easily results.

Uranianism and Suicide: the "Open Door Out.." Not only from terror and despair under a criminal s persecution, but also m stress of sexual ignorances, we find that uranianism has a long yearly chronicle of murders that are—self-murders. Tormented to madness by his enemy, or even when merely overcome by every-day life, too weary of his riddle and burden, the victim takes the Dark Road to—liberty? He cannot endure any longer! Death is better. The mystery of his impulses, their bondage by social and legislative conditions, tyranny of a villain, the pressure of passion or of dread—enough of it all! He does not fear to meet a God—God hath *made* him as he is. He fears only humanity. With his secret he will go into the Unknown—if possible taking such secret thither.

So extends an enormous and melancholy volume of suicides, in lands where no liberal sentiments, knowledge or humane Codes aid the philarrhene. In Latin-America and Latin-Europe and so on, the proportion of self-destructions from homosexual causes is extremely small, almost *nil*—a strong contrast. It is true that the annual tale of suicides from other causes is long. Money-difficulties, domestic unhappiness of normal natures, heterosexual love-affairs, insanity, dread of other than such shames as sexual ones, griefs—all are in the common catalogue. But dread of exposure as a homosexual is a terribly potent factor. Such motives are assiduously "hushed-up." But the sexual truth is often not buried with the victim.

Before the writer of these pages there lay, not long ago, a blotted letter. Here is a transcription of part of it:

"...I cannot stand it any longer. I am what I am, and I can't change myself, and nothing can. So I am not going to try to keep up the fight any more. Sooner or later the thing would leak out about me, just as it did about poor W. S. (This referred to a homosexual scandal in the same city that had ended in the social ostracism of the person indicated.) I could never face such a disgrace and it would surely kill my father... ...I have had two narrow escapes already that you know of... I am *that way*, and there is nothing to help me... It is no use to talk to me about "God and religion." "God" could not make a man so and then let him suffer as I have, trying to crush it out of me, never to any use... I know perfectly well now that to marry any girl ever made would not change *that* in me... it would only make things worse... You must not mind if people talk about what I've decided to do, if only they don't say that it is because I was (—) But I don't think it will be much suspected... You have not suspected it, at least I am almost sure you have not. Now you know everything... They will say I am crazy but I never was clearer-headed. For anybody in my situation there is only one thing to do, that is to end it before matters are worse. *Do not let G—know*, I don't think he has ever guessed anything..."

The young professional man who wrote the foregoing letter poisoned himself a few years ago, in consequence of deep sexual bewilderment as an Uranian, and because of dread of an exposure of his homosexualism, through some possible misadventure in the future. He had been of strongly religious temper; his sexual struggles had left him almost bitterly atheistic. No word of scientific, humane interpretation of his intersexual nature had met his eyes or ears—but instead everything had darkened his views of himself and of his sex-impulses, to the final step—suicide.

One readily collects such suggestive items in the newspapers as the following—typified by extracts:

A Black List.

"—He was found dead in his bed, last evening, with a bullet in his heart. But the cause of his suicide is utterly unexplainable." "—He was found hanging, dead, to a tree in the Park this morning. The identity of the suicide who appeared to be in professional life was not established." "The hotel-proprietor, on opening the door, discovered Mr. X—dead on the sofa, with a bottle of laudanum empty beside him. A few lines stated that private worries had ruined his life. The friends of the unhappy man cannot find the least reason for his being so depressed." "—The deceased young man had been in apparently excellent spirits on the preceding evening. Nothing yet is traced in his affairs to explain his act." "In the note left his brother, the dead man threw no light one his rash act, merely stating that for many years he had been burdened with life, and was tired of it. The deceased had occasionally appeared out of sorts, but not often." "—The friend to whom the dead young man wrote the letter declines to mention its contents; he states that the deceased had long suffered from an incurable nervous disorder. But this has not ever been known to his relatives, who cannot understand the allusion."

Such are the frequent phrases of suicides not accompanied by obvious facts. Too often, not money, not disease, not woman, anxieties, disappointments nor any other reasons are at the root of the action, so much as sheer weariness of a lonely, restless or conscience-burdened homosexual life. Or perhaps dread of a blackmailer's persecution due to some imprudence; or fear of unpardonable social scandal.

Conventional Veiling of Causes of Suicides.

Indeed the pallid conventionality of terms in reporting suicides must often have struck readers of such dolorous items. In certain countries, especially teutonic ones, there has come into usage a stock of phrases that deceive nobody who appreciates the wide prevalence of homosexualism; for these phrases have now set, if recondite, meanings; "chronic disease"—"incurable malady"—"severe nervous weakness"; and above all (a conventionalism almost ludicrous)—"on account of headache" or "troubled with severe nervous headaches." One often reads between the lines of these trivial references the sombre uranian tragedy.

Thus we can group, in melancholy sequence, the following necrologic items from the papers:

"The business-acquaintances and family or other friends of the merchant S—of this city, were shocked to hear of his having committed suicide yesterday night, at his apartments, by taking hydrocyanic acid. He

Instance: Suicide to Escape Legal Process: Berlin.

left all his business-affairs in order, by various memoranda, and the suicide was most carefully carried-out. The reason is known to be the threat against the deceased man of legal proceedings in connection with a recent scandal, under the provisions of Paragraph 175 of the Criminal Code, owing to certain developments lately attracting public notice again to the affair. Herr S—leaves a large fortune. He was unmarried."

"The suicide of Mr. D—R—, a guest in the Hotel W—of this city, of which some account was given in yesterday's papers, appears to be explained beyond any doubt, by the letter left

Instance: (London) to escape Blackmail.

by the deceased to a family-friend in this city. "—I have been for two years at the mercy of a rascal, without honour or pity, who has driven me now to my death. God help me! I cannot struggle any more, and my means to keep him at bay are gone. I prefer death to disgrace." The painful affair has aroused much sympathy and surprise in the native city of the deceased, where however no such private anxieties were suspected. He was not married, but lived with his parents and sisters, in entirely comfortable circumstances."

"The well-known lawyer here, Dr. Johann B—, committed suicide yesterday by a revolver-shot, in his lodgings. Dr. B—was not married, and being in excellent circumstances had lately given up, quite prematurely compared with other men, some part of his large practice. Nothing whatever is wrong, as far as searching examinations already attest, with his affairs, and he was the last man to expect to be influenced by sentimental relations with the other sex. He has left only a note to a friend saying—"God be with you all! The reason of my suicide I shall carry along with me." Incurable neurasthenic trouble has been mentioned as the reason."

"The affair of the suicide of Captain K—, which occurred at T— two days ago is not yet explainable. The letter which Captain

K—left, bidding farewell to his comrades and to what had been till recently a promising career, is not enough to make the reason we lately printed (the failure of the dead officer to receive a farther advancement in rank immediately) the cause of his act. . . Within a few weeks he had been melancholy, in fact quite unlike his former self. It is mentioned that a severe nervous weakness only lately disclosed, and of a kind not easily to be cured, involved the young officer in painful anxieties. . . The suicide was deliberately planned."

"As the one o'clock express train from Wien arrived here last night, a young man who was a passenger entered a toilette-closet of one of the carriages, and there shot himself. In dying condition, he was brought to the nearest city-hospital, but he died at eight this morning. He was identified as Richard S—who has been missing for some days from the Finance Department here. He has lately seemed in good health, and there being no question as to money-affairs or relations of a sentimental sort, the act is a mystery to the public and his friends."

<hr />

Instance: Escape Law. To Far hack, the Year 1867, occurred a French suicide to avoid the publicity of being branded as a homosexual socially and the charge of 'public' indecorum. A popular actor of that time, Deschamps, a homosexual, was travelling one night on a railway, along with a young cuirassier named Horneck. Deschamps became sexually excited by the attractive person of the young man, and made some direct overtures to him. The latter not only repulsed them but declared that at the next halt of the train he would call an officer, and would have the actor taken into custody as "having committed an offense" in a public place—which was technically sound law. Deschamps implored mercy, but the soldier was inflexible. Deschamps opened the door of the carriage to leap out into the darkness; the train was in full speed; the angry cuirassier held him back, determined to punish his proposal, and both men in the struggle were thrown out on the track, where an approaching train at train at once struck them. Deschamps was immediately killed. Horneck lived long enough to explain the affair, and then succumbed to his injuries.

We have already, in Chapt. VIII, mentioned the suicide of Major-General Hector Macdonald, of the British Army, in Paris, in 1903.

Some years ago, the pastor of a large German parish, a man of conspicuous worth, piety, esteem and usefulness, on consulting the local physician for an ailment of importance, was obliged to confess that he was homosexual. He had never violated his physical chastity. His Uranian sentiment, though indomitable and terribly clear to him, was kept within psychic limits. But the medical man mentioned the confession. The pastor was ruined socially and professionally. He killed himself, in despair.

In London, in 1906–1907, were to be particularized two suicides; in New York City in 1908 one notable suicide; in St. Petersburg (about a year ago) another suicide—all clearly indicated by the dead men to be from similisexual causes.

A brilliant Continental capital has lately added to the record an aristocratic suicide at least open to suspicion under its veiled reference—though of this particular tragedy conflicting explanations have been current:

"Over the melancholy death of the Hon. H—G—of the. . . Legation here, which occurred through the young diplomat's suicide a few days ago, nothing further can be stated. The funeral took place at three o' clock yesterday afternoon at the M—Cemetery. Most of the diplomatic corps were represented or present. . . At the grave, was made a brief and suitable address and a prayer. . . In course of the pastor's remarks he said: "We do not come here this afternoon to sit in judgement on the act of our young brother; but as friends to show our grief for him. We all Stand or fall in life by the grace of God." As to the still unexplained cause of the sudden act. . . the only person who can throw any light on it, . . . is understood to decline to utter a word on the topic, and says that he will not under any future circumstances break the confidence reposed in him; except to state distinctly that no money-troubles, no affair connected with the other sex, and no illness brought the tragedy. The reason will probably therefore remain ever obscure, perhaps wisely so. The deceased was a reserved, quiet, well-mannered young man, living a very orderly life in handsome apartments, cared little for social gatherings, and was chiefly in company with a very few friends of his own sex, of various nationalities."

Uranian suicides occur that do not refer
to persecutions, nor to dread or criminal and
social aspects of some indiscretion. Passional
romances mix themselves in the catalogue.
Rosalind declared flippantly that "men have died and worms have
eaten them, but not for love." Uranian friends—lovers—often prove
the irony of the phrase. About ten years ago, an English Uranian,
not known to be homosexual except to a very small fraction of his
large social circle, committed suicide, while travelling abroad. It was a
deliberate suicide, but so adroitly carried out that his near relations, like
nineteen-twentieths of his friends, probably never for an instant have
thought that the tragedy was not an accident. He left no such notion
in the minds of the few persons who were in his morbid secret—some
of them, in fact, during weeks had dreaded just such a climax. He had
fallen violently in love with a man (much his junior) a type from which
no possible return of such a passion, or even toleration of it could be
expected. At the end of the second year of the acquaintance, the youth
concerned had practically quite broken off the social intimacy, clearly
because of perceiving the older man's sexual emotions. The ill-starred
Urning struggled to forget, but in vain; and at the end of a certain
week of peculiarly intense suffering and nervous disruption (as shown
by his diary) he planned and consummated his own shocking death.
An American psychiater gave to the writer a somewhat similarly
tragic history, which ended in the suicide of an-artist, advanced in
life, simply because he had nor been able to overcome his love for
another homosexual. The latter had treated the other man's passion
with indifference then coquetry, then cruel mockery and finally with
an almost brutal contempt—making sport of his admirer's unattractive
looks, his age and his individuality in general; and reading his letters
to a third homosexual who made the situation common gossip in
similisexual cliques. In the city of New York, several years ago, the
suicide of a well-known and successful business-man, conducting a
fashionable establishment, with various European, branches, referred
positively to his relationships with young man, between whom and
himself there had come about a formally adoptive connection. The
matter was hushed up assiduously. Its details were umnistakeably
homosexual—and intensely passional.

Here is an example of a double suicide, because of the mere passion
of a coming separation:

"In Werden, three days ago, occurred a painful "double-suicide." Two young men of the town, of humble life but thoroughly respectable and apparently in comfortable stations as employés in the city mentioned, have been somewhat noted in the place for their closely affectionate friendship. The elder was a certain Albert W—, the younger H—G—, and both were in good health. Recently young Albert W—received a proposal to betake himself to a distant city, to remain indefinitely. Since this matter came up, the two friends have been increasingly unhappy. Last Sunday, after a long walk together, in which they met with several of their acquaintances and rather to the surprise of these remarked that they had seen their way to leaving the place together, they returned to the modest room of young W—, being already dressed in their best clothes; and—as it would seem—when clasped tight in each other's arms, lying on the neat bed, fired simultaneously two fatal shots, each with a revolver. They had already inserted a notice in a newspaper taking a farewell of their friends. The real, motive for the tragedy is not clear."

The mutual suicides, in the artillery-barracks at Laibach, in February, 1909, of two young under-officers, Adolf Waldeck and his friend Kogei, had a strong accent of homosexualism. Such affairs are far from rare in military or civilian life.

Or suicide may be complicated with homicide—murder—because of philarrenic love and jealousy. Here are two instances:

"In the N—gasse, last evening, Herr Rudolf Wieser, hotelier, was shot and killed instantly by his best friend, one Loren/ Rotzer. The murder immediately thereafter turned the same pistol on himself, and was immediately dead also. Both bodies were found in the room of little hotel where the crime had occurred. A letter left behind by Rotzer, "for whoever might open it," stated that Wieser (who was the owner of the hotel) had made him, Rotzer "unspeakably miserable" because their relationship of a certain kind not necessary to specify here, had been "broken off," to the ruin of the writer; and the letter concluded with an appeal for forgiveness and kindly judgment. The young man also left a melancholy letter to his mother."

"A mysterious affair, which still awaits explanation, has put the residents of the Kleinseite District into much excitement. Opposite the A—Barracks, was established the shop of Johann Rak, a man of 35 years of age, unmarried. Yesterday morning the shop was not opened as usual, and a certain Joseph Rak,—not a relative, though of the same name as the owner—a clerk to Johann Rak, was not to be found. Hours passed, and the place remained closed; and neither of the two Raks was visible. Both of them lived in rooms in the building, and these rooms also were noticed as shut. On looking through a window, young Joseph Rak was seen lying on his bed, dressed. The door, was forced, and the clerk was discovered to be dead. Two half-filled glasses of soda-water were on the table by the bed, along with some confectionery. The bed of the merchant, Johann Rak, was undisturbed. The physician summoned found no traces of violence on the person of the young clerk, but there is no doubt now that he was poisoned. The body of his employer, the older Rak, was discovered in the cellar of the shop, hanging to a hook. He had committed suicide, with careful deliberation, during the night. It had been pretty generally said in the neighbourhood that the relations between the two Raks were of a criminal sort (under Paragraph 129 of the Statutes). The physical examination during the autopsy of each body afforded grounds for conclusively accepting this idea. What precipitated the murder and suicide is not clear: but it is thought that the elder Rak poisoned the young clerk and then comitted suicide. Still—this is open to some question."

Insanity as a Consequence of Persecution, etc.

The story of insanity has much, to do with the victimizing of Uranians, with their dread of the blackmailer, of the. State's Attorney, of the policeman, of the detection by society of their natures. The nerve-breaking results of forced chastity on the part of Uranians also is a terrible argument for their rescue from present-day legal and social martyrdom. The suppression of natural, wholesome, harmless desires, the terror of punishment, drives many of the finest-natured Uranians to mania. In a later chapter will be found some considerations of good or evil for the Uranian in marriage, that are not aloof from his tendency, to end violently his predicament, Frequently a married homosexual takes his own life just to break a contract that he cannot support; or to avoid entering into marital obligations—as we shall observe.

Other factors that classify homosexual suicides will be noticed in the same succeeding chapter.

So much for the Uranian as a suicide. But there are other withdrawals from battles with social prejudices, from the daily fight, from the grave mishaps more or less tragic to the philarrene. The ranks of the secular priesthood of the Catholic Church, the cells of monks, the severest Orders, incessantly enclose homosexual fugitives; those refugees who wish to forget; to vanish otherwise than in the 'foreign legions' of armies, or lower social descents. They have fled the world to avoid their daily homosexual temptations, to stifle or to root out their emotions as uranians. Let us be glad that for types of Uranians adapted to such a step it often has proved peace; an atrophy of homosexualism just as for heterosexualism. Contemplative, imaginative moral natures can succeed in such an effort. But too often we must believe that it has no good result; that on the contrary it brings more unbroken introspection; more suppressed passion, than before it. Again, the ecclesiastic who is casuistic, whose standards lower in cloister-life or as a parochial career goes on, may easily lapse deeper into the very "sin" that he quitted the outer world to avoid. An interesting suggestion of this is found in the novelist Husyman's story "En Route," with the episode of the hero's midnight observation of the monks assembled for spiritual exercises- against fleshly obsessions.

Many an Uranian, however, does bettor than to fly to any cell or altar. He throws himself into busy charities, earnest organizations, religious or secular duties where he must work hard— sometimes spend himself to death—for humanity; for the poor, the sick, the solitary, the friendless, the ignorant. If in even such noble activity he does not pass beyond temptation, he is likely to find moral and physical peace sooner than in any monastery. He sometimes resorts to certain "home" army-services; not to swell the ranks as debauché, ruffian or weakling, but as a clean-living soldier, with his secret shut within him.

Happiest of all, surely, are those Uranians, ever numerous, who have no wish nor need to fly society—or themselves. Knowing what they are,

Mysterious Disappearances, Monastic Retreats, Philantropic Self-Sacrifices, etc.

The Uranian as Altruist.

understanding the natural, the moral strength of their position as homosexuals; sure of right on their side, even if it be never accorded to them in the lands where they must live; fortunate in either due self-control or private freedom—day by day, they go on through their lives, self-respecting and respected, in relative peace.

Let us quit this part of a realm of melancholy; this demesne of human agony, of distraught souls, of infamy, of vice, of martyrdoms, of false social and legal positions—all so largely as pects of the Uranian when indeed decadent, criminal or victim. He is a human being, first of all. No social station, no philosophy, no statutes, no dangers, will hold his sexual physique in check when the passionate appetite is awake. Happy or unhappy, evil or good, he is a human fact. Intersex is intersex. King, prince, pope, cardinal, duke, statesman, tradesman, soldier, sailor, man of letters, of science, of art, of religion, workman in field or factory, nature has given to him his sexual organs and those tastes that command their use. They must be pacified, or mischief and misery result. One might as well require the Uranian to be stone, as not to yield; even if a life of cruel and unjust expiation is to be met, or death faced—as the price.

An Old Summary: Human Nature Cannot Be Eradicated.

It is in view of aspects of this practical kind, that countries whose Legislation has not till now shown due interest philosophically in the mystery of homosexuality, or humane willingness to study it legally in new lights, agitate considerable changes of paragraphs in their criminal Codes; advances on Napoleonic models or even beyond them. Such movement has received in Germany and Austria favourable popular attention. A long array of eminent physicians, psychiatric-observers high jurists, criminologists, and the general intelligent public are all alert. The recognition of the homosexual instincts as a thing to be regulated, as a troublous instinct not naturally more disgraceful than heterosexualism, has gained—vastly. Pressure on popular sentiment and legal thought has been particularly the work of Dr. Richard von Krafft-Ebing of Vienna (lately deceased); of Dr. Magnus Hirschfeld of Berlin, conspicuous as an indefatigable and self-sacrificing scientist for humanity; of Dr. A. Aletrino, of the University of Amsterdam; of Dr. Havelock Ellis and of Edward Carpenter in England; of Dr. Albert Moll, of Berlin; of many other psychiaters'

Present Legal Advances toward Uranian Protection and Privileges in Europe.

of the first rank, and of world-wide authority—although their theories of homosexualism and their ideas of its social accountability and of aspects of legal tolerance may differ. A tentative to legal reform became organized in Germany in the latter decade of the nineteenth century. It has steadily grown. Cooperation in it is in no sense particular to the homosexual, i.e. marking its participants as necesarily homosexuals; a valued proportion of the men united in the movement are heterosexual. They act simply on conviction that humanity and knowledge demand changes in forms of Statutory Law; demand sounder public notions of the case of the homosexual as a profound, urgent, appealing problem in Nature and philosophic humanism.

By the suppression in Germany of one single paragraph of the Criminal Code (often referred to here as "Paragraph 175") at some general revision of the Statute-Book, the most formidable aid to the blackmailer,—that worst barrier to the worthy and respectable Uranian's peace—will be removed, and yet no social harm will be wrought. Other changes may follow, as legal and public sentiment are clarified on the whole psychic-physic aspects of similisexualism. But the removal of express statutory clauses affecting natural, decent and private homosexualism will be a humane and legitimate gain.

The formation in Germany of a large General Committee to such ends followed, about the middle of the last nineties. From Berlin, Leipzig, Munich, Breslau and Vienna a vigorous propaganda began—in present force. An

The German "Comittee," at Berlin.

Austrian-Hungarian movement exists; less organized and aggressive than the German one, making no clearly vigorous advance toward striking-out even the particular "Paragraph 129," in the Austrian Code, that corresponds with Germany's "Paragraph 175." (In the Hungarian Statute-Book it is represented by another law even more severe and definite).

In 1897—as in 1902 and 1904—in the German Parliament, a great Petition signed by many hundred names of high distinction in German medico-psychichiatries and jurisprudence, science, letters and arts, with other professions, was formally presented;

The Petitions to the German Parliament: Herr Bebel's Plea in 1894.

asking the repeal of "Paragraph 175." A careful speech was made by Representative Bebel; and lively debate ensued. In referring to the

Petition, Herr Bebel said: "The number of these persons (homosexuals) is so great, and it joins itself so vigorously to all classes of society, from the lowest to the highest, that if here in Berlin our police did their full duty, according to law, the Government would be forced to build two new penal establishments, merely on account of offences against "Paragraph 175." This is no exaggeration. The business however goes further. We must consider whether this Paragraph does not extend to women, as well as to men, when women commit the same sort of offence. What is right in case of one sex, is right in case of the other. I tell you again, gentlemen, that if the Berlin police did their duty, why, there would come up such a scandal as never has been known in the world; a scandal in comparison with which the Panama Scandal, the Dreyfus Scandal, the Lutzow-Lectert Scandal, the Taus-Normann Scandal, all would seem mere child's play."

The reference is just'on the speaker's part, to the fact that by the Paragraph ought to be punished female similisexualism. The law does not base any argument that women should be allowed legally to gratify uraniad appetites. Uraniads are continually known to offend so, are discovered so doing, but without any legal penalty affecting them. This is of course, an old statutory inconsistency.[5]

The Petition was rejected in 1897. It was received in part with decided favour, in part with the expected very resolute opposition—and abuse. In 1898, it was brought foward, even more vigorously, with more supporters. But its fate was not any better, though there is hope that a near Code Revision will remove the specific Paragraph.[6] The Clerical Party is not friendly to any such change. More or less active and dignified attempts to similar ends iii Austria and in Hungary, aided by Protestants or Catholics, have not been to practical purport; chiefly in view of similar clerical opposition. Imperial favour is not shown to the movement.

---

5. A special attestation of this curious aspect occurred in a very recent libel suit—mentioned on a later page—in Berlin, originating in a scandal in a women's club.

6. Since the Eulenburg Trials and concurrent scandals in Germany, in 1907–8, there is noticeable in that State a serious popular reaction against even the intelligent scientific discussion of the Uranian and of uranianism; a sort of social recrudescence of sentiment against all the uranian problem; a phase regrettable on grounds of legislative justice, humanity and science, and which, it may be hoped, will not continue. Of scientific acceptance there has been no retogression, nor could there be. It is little to the Credit of Great Britain and American that of them not even so much as "action with reaction" can be said to have occurred yet.

There is some reason to argue that even as a dignified leverage to publicity in the German Parliament the association of the movement with any political party is not useful. Many persons thoroughly favouring humane and intelligent laws, will not aid in the conscientious and brilliant activities of the Committee, until it has another political atmosphere, or none. They claim that such a national movement should have absolutely no political conjunctions. The hostility of the German Emperor as to the Social Democratic element in politics is so emphasized that alliance with that faction (which includes some of the most progressive, patriotic and intellectual men in German politics) embitters the Kaiser against more liberal legislation. But it has been well said that so humane and observant a monarch as the present emperor cannot hold absolute and personal objections to the removal of a law that does his subjects no good; a law that is the cause of infinite disgraces and harm to to them.

Thus much space in this study has been given to Germany's even hesitant advance toward recognizing some human and natural rights of the homosexual, and toward freeing him from unintelligent persecution, undeserved shame and agony, because, the attitude of distinctively Anglo-Saxon social civilizations is so clearly in contrast. Hardly a shadow of any legal change in those legislations—severest of all—is manifest. Public sentiments and public ignorances in England, in her dependent States and Colonies, as in the United States of America, are against any leniences. Lawmakers will not tolerate the thought of even a legal silence as to phases of homosexualism that do not offend public morality, nor deprave innocent youth, nor exhibit other aspects always meriting legal provision. That there is any scientific view of the problem is largely unknown in Great Britain and in America. In those large dominions, with their multitudes of homosexuals, the Uranian seems likely to remain a social and a legal victim for an indefinite time to come.

To the Uraniad Intersex, the law today has almost nothing to say. Statutes are tacit, as in ages past. Respectable, discreet Uraniads are not in any really unhappy case before the world. Feminosexual relationships may be known or suspected, right and left, in all societies, in all countries. But they seldom excite open comment now-a-days, any more than of old. If a whispered

The Uraniad as Degenerate, Criminal and Victim.

and smiling contempt is shown, it does not usually much injure the social prestige of the objects. While certain crimes quite naturally are in uraniadistic ambients, the blackmailer, robber or assassin are only exceptionally met. Uraniad amours thrive and prosper, with no specters of police-courts to trouble them. Boudoirs, baths and brothels are a rendezvous, day by day; immune of penalties. Such matters as bestiality, proxenetism and other special offences are punishable; but within the pale of assenting privacy, the adult Uraniad is a free agent to do what she pleases—when, where and how her sexual passion suggests, be it nobly or indeed degenerately.

Should Not Statutory Laws Deal with Uraniads?

Here an injustice in the existing laws of all States, European, American, or what others, is plain. They tolerate-by implication—feminosexuality, while so severe against masculine relations. The Uraniad's instinct is as "unnatural," is as "immoral" and as "vicious" as is the Uranian's instinct. Inconsistence, partiality and legal injustice are obvious. Logically the Uraniad is obnoxious to prosecution and to social contempt: but her loves are tacitly licensed. Even uraniad prostitution is at liberty to exercise its activities under clandestine conditions.

Example of the "Unequal Law:" Berlin, 1909.

The propriety of an equal law as Berlin, 1909 to masculine and feminine intersexual practices and scandals, if there is to be any legislation at all concerning the matter, was strikingly illustrated very lately (April 1909) in Berlin, by a legal affair—already noted. A Berlin woman's-club, of smart class, had become notoriously one for feminosexuals. It even advertised for recruits; and admittance to it was by passwords—some of them most suggestive. A Berlin paper attacked this society of—sapphists. (One of the members had been divorced because of her intimacies in the club.) The club sued the newspaper for slander. It lost its case wholly, so convincing was the evidence that the members were lesbians—nearly all of them—and that their handsome *locale* was a regular rendezvous. Had a similar result occurred as to a club of male intersexuals, there would have been arrests right and left, as the suit ended. But as there is no law punishing feminine intercourse, the court held that the members of the club were neither legally damaged, nor to be pursued criminally. Hence the ladies turned to their own way, rejoicing in their assured freedom—if not in any other outcome of their suit.

But if the Uraniad is not nearly so much a social or legal victim as the uranian, she can suffer a natural penalty for her intersexual existence. Uraniad appetites, and the feminosexual "type," are likely to be interlinked with morbidity of

Dangerous Workings of Uraniadism on Woman's Nervous status.

psychos, with undesirable physical conditions—negative or positive—and even with organic disease. The gratification of uraniad love reacts in many instances, by obviously mischievous influences, on the Uraniad's nervous system. The uranian passion in adults, or in robust, fairly healthful youth, is not nervously harmful, per se. On the contrary, it is largely salutary; particularly, if decent, tranquil, regular in expression and idealized by circumstances. The opposite effects frequently can result by feminosexualism. Too often, by it the feminine psychos goes to pieces. The Uraniad significantly helps to fill insane asylums and sanitariums.

In an Appendix to this study will occur a comment on aspects of the Uraniad when victim of her sexual-sentimental impulses; as contrasted with uranianism.

In geographical distribution, the essentially criminal classes of Uraniads, showing moral divagations by theft, by violent behaviour (even to murderous attacks) and by prostitution with women, are most common in the latin lands.

Geographical Distribution of the Criminal Uramad.

There is, of course, a large army of the feminine intersex concentrated in Germany, in Austria-Hungary, in Great Britain, and about the Orient in general. But Italy, Spain and France, among European countries of uraniadism, specialize also her criminal types that overtly obtrude on law. France is distinctively a country of venal feminine siinilisexualism; exactly as it also a country where heterosexual prostitution is so generic. In Paris, every form of the lesbian instinct is met in prostitution. (Nevertheless, one important student of the topic estimates that in the army of prostitutes in Berlin, twenty-five per-cent are given also to uraniad intercourse, for or without a price. (Vienna is often referred to as an "uraniad capital;" where the feminosexual prostitute constantly is to be met in the streets, baths, cafés, and such resorts known for her patronage. As with the Uranian, the vapour-bath—on "ladies' days"—in Paris, Berlin, Vienna, London, and so on, are frequented by the "Sisterhood-Brotherhood" of uraniad prostitution; as by the non-venal contingent.

The Uraniad prostitute in all grades of activity is exceedingly numerous. She is frequently located

Uraniad Prostitution.

in the regular brothels of women for male clientage. Often she is a heterosexual harlot, as well—rarely is she only uraniad in nature and venal life. If her real sexual tastes are for female types, soon she has a regular clientage of them. She is also encountered, younger or older, beautiful or by no means such, as the kept-mistress to a feminosexual of wealth. Such ties are especially close and passionate. Fierce dramas arise thence, in brothels, baths, masked rendezvous, and even in private homes.

In Brothels:
Uraniadism and
Female Inmates.

The ordinary prostitute is frequently goon sated with the sexualism of men. She loses all desire, all pleasure in her trade. Exceptions apart, anon she feels indifference, horror or disgust for all her *clientèle*. Her vehicle of pleasure then becomes another Uraniad. Frequently this is a relatively young girl. In almost all large brothels, there is at least one youthful, rather refined, gentle inmate, the sexual plaything of the sisterhood, complaisant to their satisfactions. Or in contrast, some highly masculine Uraniad, her body and disposition rough and man-like, is preferred for the same offices. There is much feminine pederasty as to young gilds—even children—among respectable or depraved Uraniads, just as in the masculine world of intersex; though not of as classic background.

Uraniads and
Blackmailing.

The Uraniad, even if degenerate or vicious, is not as a class initiative in crimes of deliberation, or of audaciously "intellectual" kind. But the Uraniad now and then is met as aggressively a blackmailer. Sometimes some timid fellow-Uraniad, sometimes an Uranian, sometimes an wholly heterosexual party is attacked; into whose secrets she has been introduced. This sort of enterprise she usually conducts by letters. The feminosexual woman of high society is herself thus victimized, when her habits are suspected or her tastes noted. In all cities, such affairs occur, in higher or lower life. A great scandal of the sort came in France, several years ago. Another such affair once darkened the life of a reigning sovereign for awhile, almost with publicity. A recent example of the Uraniad as a victim of attempt at blackmail occurred in an aristocratic circle in an Austrian city. The former intimate friend and employée of a woman of rank and wealth, widowed but still youthful and beautiful, threatened to publish a romantic novel, giving a scandalous history of her victim's real "psychic" life; involving especially certain relations with a female friend of equally prominent social notoriety. The matter came to a question of whether the victim would pay the authour a handsome sum to suppress the book; or if she would refuse. The affair was brought before the criminal authorities, and the blackmailer—but not the book—was suppressed.

In the lower levels of uraniadism, the thief, the highwayman in petticoats, even the female *apache* is encountered. A small group of such amazonian prostitutes, all of the cult of Sappho, quite tolerably "terrorized" a whole street in one

Violent Crimes: Uraniads of Degraded Lives.

of the eccentric quarters of Paris, not long ago. They knocked down men and women at night; they plundered, stabbed, used revolvers, undertook burglaries, and committed homicidal attacks of serious consequences.

In the lower levels of uraniadism, outbreaks of jealousy or of revenge elicit such assaults and murders. In the *demi-mondaine* atmosphere these affairs come to notice. A few days before these lines are written, a Parisian prostitute, not at all "amazonian" or unfeminine in any external, stabbed another of her class in the brothel where they lived, dangerously wounding her victim. Interrogated by the police-judge, she answered with angry pride—"I wanted to kill her. I was not going to allow her to belong to any other girl! She was mine—I found her a traitress to our love!" The would-be murderess added intimate details of a physical and psychological clarity. A few months ago a similar crime had the same sexual motive. A boulevard *cocotte* of much beauty and elegance of dress, walked up to a "rival" in the street, and threw the classic vitriol into her face, disfiguring it forever. "She was my wife," was the excuse to the police. "I won't have her running around all the time with other women." A prostitute put a knife into the back of another of the same profession. . . "She said she was tired of men for good and all. I found she lied to me. . . I loved her. . . She had a man with her this morning. . . She was better than any man—she could make love a lot better." As a rule, however, the uraniad does not object to the "relations" of her intersexual partner when they are with men. It is only in proportion to their, occurring with "other women," with other Intersexuals of the feminine type, that the fire of jealousy rises.

A muscular and courageous Uraniad as a criminal on quite masculine lines of activity, and undoubtedly of countersexual *i.e.* intersexual type, came before the Paris police in April, 1909. A young man—or apparently such—was arrested in the Rue du Faubourg SaintMartin as a *souteneur*, while watching and aiding a young woman to pick up her clientage, as a prostitute. The prisoner was tall, robust, virile in manner, deep-voiced, had a (natural) light brown moustache, wore a neat dark suit, and actively resisted arrest. At the station-house, "he" proved to be of more feminine gender; by name one Anna Guelin, aged twenty-eight, formerly a a singer in *cafés-chantants*. In physique and sexual organs "he" was feminine, but with sundry developments toward masculinity. During eight years Anna Guelin had lived by consorting with female prostitutes. She was able to maintain sexual relations with them, had been their 'protector' in various skirmishes, and when not able to obtain an income as their "*poteau*" had turned to bi-sexual prostitution.

Sometimes the scandal as to an uraniad liaison, between types not criminal but degenerated, breaks forth on the most emphatic plane of publicity: as in the recent affair between the wife (a brilliant woman of lighter letters, internationally popular) of a well-known Parisian *littérateur* and another and titled uraniad; whose debuts in a theatrical piece provoked a stormy demonstration, that compelled their retirement from the piece.

The criminality of the Uraniad, her vicious deviations, indeed-are in key with the general aspects, of the feminine intersex; and, for that matter with women when considered in the aggregate. Uraniads suggest a lower moral nature than the uranian; and that only femininely social and physical disabilities really keep them in check from evil-doing on much the same scale as their more masculine rivals.

Uraniad Murder.
Instance.

Occasionally the Uraniad of higher social grade commits a murderous assault, or even is a murderess, through jealousy, revenge, and so on; or through less "racial" causes. In 1892, in the United States of America, took place such a tragedy between a pair of respectable young Uraniads. Jealousy was the motive. A certain Alice M—, had been from her youth a masculine type in all essentials except physical viraginity. She had grown fiercely jealous of her closest friend, Freda W—; both girls being of about the same age, nineteen years. The bond was sexual. Alice M—quarrelled with Freda W—on account of what seemed Freda's growing disposition to "desert"—i.e. to accept masculine attentions. In furious jealousy, Alice M—cut Freda's throat, in broad daylight on a public street; a hideous tragedy, shocking all the town. In the trial, the feminosexual relationship between the girls was plainly brought to light. Alice M—declared in court that she had "married" Freda W—; that the compact was solemn, "for body and soul;"

and that they had been planning to leave the town together "to pass their lives so," when Freda—had "broken faith with me." The trial resulted in the acquittal of Alice M—from murder, as being not of sound mind. She was committed to an insane asylum. Nothing indicated her as insane, by correct psychiatric judgment. She was perfectly normal in mind and body, was educated', and though neurotic in type was perfectly reasonable. She was merely uraniad in intersex.

A good example occurred many years ago, in Adèle Spitzeder, the talented, audacious founder of the sometime famous "Daschauer Bank," and the heroine of its ruin. Adèle Spitzeder did not suggest masculinity in her physique nor her attire, but she was passionately feminosexual—a thorough Uraniad; and intrigued sexually with all sorts of women and sister-Uraniads. One well-known actress was a regular mistress of the "Bankerin." She drank, smoked, gambled and so on *ad libitum*, in privacy. The letters from her, read in court at her trial, were eloquent of her sexual affairs, and of her complete moral degeneracy, as also of her masculine head for business. After she had served; her prison-term, Adèle Spitzeder organized an ambulant woman-orchestra (most of its members feminosexuals) which travelled in Europe and America with success. Her later, history is a blank.

Instance: Adèle Spitzeder.

In March, 1908, was disclosed in Vienna, by arrest and a police-court trial, a notable instance of the moral degeneracy of an Uraniad, united with vigorous bodily masculinity, much impudence, remarkable talent for shamming and a notable shrewdness in whatever related to victimizing superiour dupes. A certain "Prince Egon" X—, apparently a man in the early thirties, of brilliant social address and attractive physique, had been on the edge of smart commercial society in the city for some time; presenting himself as engaged in a law-suit against his family, for the recovery of his rights in a large estate. "Prince Egon" borrowed important sums for his affairs, from various friendly parties; led a life discreetly luxurious; and finally won the heart of a young lady of excellent family—the engagement being announced, with full consent of the parents. Suddenly "Prince Egon" was taken into custody as Margaret Erb, a woman of manlike physique and perfectly manlike manners, forty-six years old. She had been an international swindler for a long time past; had been incarcerated as a patient in an insane-asylum; and was sought

Instance: Masculine Travesty and Moral Degeneracy: Vienna.

for by criminal and medical experts. The travesty had been so perfect that the young woman to whom "Prince Egon" had become engaged, adored her fiancé, and for some time refused to believe that "he" was not a man.

Instance: Perverted Uranianism. Moral Deficiencies.

In Berlin, not long ago, came a criminal trial against an Uraniad typically ol the degenerate moral type, but of no common mind. This was the notable Frau K——; arrested as being a professional bawd in feminosexualism—sapphic. "Kupplerei" with minors—with personal sadism, masochism, fetichism, and a long category of perversities, including the use of her premises as a resort for all sexual clientages. Shocking scenes were described. She had been the associate in letters and science of many eminent scientific writers on sociology, criminology and psychiatric medicine, etc., not only in Germany but also in America and in Italy, including Cesare Lombroso. She was remarkably efficient in certain fields of literature and science. She was punished as was merited, and her career ended.

XI

The Uranian and Uraniad in Relation to Marriage as a "Cure" for Similisexualism

At least five important errors as to similisexual propensities are found to be so universal, are still so encouraged by unprogressive physicians and jurists, as by superficial observers of homosexualism, that they merit to be pointed out with pains—especially in the present chapter. Some we have already specialized. They are—that the Uranian must be physically abnormal; that he is always degenerate morally; that he is always a sodomist (in the technical sense of that term) especially as to wishing sexual satisfactions only with physical effeminates and young boys; that he is never married—at least not consenting in his heart to it; and that he is to be "cured" of his intersexual nature by systematic sexual intercourse with women. These are notions fixed in every-day popular ignorance of the topic, even among classes otherwise profoundly learned. That an Uranian in vain can try his best, for instance, to find sexual satisfactions and his "cure" by frequenting female prostitutes, by keeping a mistress, or by an apparently most happy marriage,—this is not in the popular creed.

Five Popular Errors.

We meet an error even graver, as to intercourse with women by Uranians, when we touch on the relations of the similisexual to matrimonial life, as legal husband and anon as father. By no means seldom Uranians—as do Uraniads—commit themselves to normal wedlock; and have all the responsibilities to fulfil that belong to the normal married state and to paternity. We are not speaking here of the legal marriages between Uranian and Uraniad types; though they occur, either by accident or design—and sometimes fortunately. We are considering here wedlock only between similisexuals and heterosexuals. This predicament is far from rare. Sometimes it is an almost unimportant detail of a life. Sometimes it is wholly unfavourable to the happiness and the well-being of those united; elementary to melancholy events. Physicians know most about this fact. Naturally, hardly no other class of professional confidences is more carefully kept.

Really How does such an experiment—
error—as to a marriage come about? First, the
similisexual man or woman, the Intersexual, does
not always *clearly* know himself or herself or does
not know himself or herself at all. He or she may
have been perplexed and physically, troubled, more or less severely, with
what has appeared a mysterious "contrary" sexuality. But the sufferer has
regarded it as disease, has been advised by a physician so to regard it.
Frequently a well-meaning physician prescribes matrimony (exactly as
he would advise a system of calisthienes or a set of baths) as the certain
antidote for a similisexual's unfortunate plight. Marriage often is urged
by even fairly intelligent psychiatric specialists. The intellectual and
physical attractiveness of some woman that the Uranian admires may
appear to him a certain "cure." Thus comes for him the immediately
individual appeal. Another contingent of married Uranians grows by the
important fact that dionianism and uranianism are frequently united in
one complex, human psychos. The Dionian-Uranian who still relishes
his relations with women,—or has done so—though not free from
passion as to males, may think that he has reached the end of his
similisexual impulses. Yes—henceforth he will be only dionistic! The
"risk" ahead seems slight; so he rushes upon it. Again, more openly
practical reasons urge the marriage; family-considerations, estates,
pecuniary and social advantages, debts to be paid, heirs to be begotten,
parental will, the wish for one's own household and home—and so on.

Strongly dionistic Uranians or Uraniads, in
whom the similisexual instinct is not inborn and
vigorous through sufficiently maturing years,
types whose fractional similisexuality *is* due to
superficial conditions—such similisexuals have
reason to hope to find their peace in normal
marriage. We have spoken of this possibility for
some—a few—types of relatively superficial similisexualism. But such a
grade is not over-easy to determine; and often the result is failure. It is
perniciously untrue to experience (and to sexual logic) to offer to
thousands of "(Iranians strong chances of a change in themselves by
even the most kindly marriage. Frequently the philarrene has cheated
himself, and sois involved in deeper trouble than any- he has yet known.
"Woe to Him Who Lies" is the title of one Grillparzer's dramas. Woe to
the thorough Uranian especially, if marriage has outraged his instincts!—

however gracious its other offices. He may think to play his part long and faithfully; often he does so. But Nature exacts her rights in the end. She may take even blood-revenge. She is capable of transforming the happiest of domestic relations into—hell. She is capable of continuing the punishment into coining generations.

Annals of Tragedy for Similisexuals Undertaking Wedlock. Newspapers, medical correspondence, psychiatric data, annals of criminal tragedy, bear out these statements. They pertain to the Uraniad as well as to the Uranian; but more especially and constantly to Uranians, owing to a lesser susceptibility to "curative" influences. Interrupted arrangements for marriages, engagements broken (sometimes at the last moment) vanishing bridegrooms, unhappy *ménages*, divorces, suicides, are all part of the tale. The adult Uranian who has resolved upon matrimony, in nine cases in ten expiates the step. He does not find that his intellectual sympathy with his wife suffices to overcome the *horror corporis feminae*, or warms his sexual indifference. His physical relations with her may be to her satisfaction; they are irksome or odious to him. Sometimes he can continue them only by conjuring up homosexual fancies of which she has no idea. He discovers that his experiments with women before wedlock have told him truths he was not willing to believe, or had rejected. He cannot sexually *love* his wife. He desires to be a father and beloved children are born. His wife is all that a lovely and superiour woman-friend can be. But the other Fire still smoulders; often, it blazes forth tragically.

Instances: the Uranian Unhappy in Normal Marriage: its Sad Undersides. Two instances of such purport, showing the risks of marriage for inborn Uranians, are these, cited by Dr. R. von Krafft-Ebing. In neither case was there mental or physical degeneracy or singularity, or any depraved instincts:

" . . . Mr. Z—thirty years old; wholesale merchant, states that his parents and grandparents were healthy people. He developed in his youth normally, with only irrelevant childish illnesses. At 14, came onanism by instinct, (not tuition from another lad) at fifteen he began to feel sexual passion for males of his age. Absolutely unimpressed by the female sex in a sexual way, at 24 Mr. Z—made his first visit to a brothel: but he fled from it on account of his *horror feminae nudae*. After

25 years of age, he had occasional sexual intercourse with young men of similar age. (Passionate embracings, ejaculat., occasionally masturb. mut.) On account of certain business-reasons, and in belief that he would be cured of his abnormal passion for males, Z—married a lady of 28, remarkably distinguished in person and intellect. Through calling up strong mental pictures of the good-looking young men he had met, Mr. Z—was potent with his wife, whom in a psychic way he loved with his whole heart. But this relation with a woman, contrary to his nature, made Z—very neurasthenic. After a child had been born, Z—returned to frigid sexual relations with his wife, the more because he has feared to procreate children who will be as unfortunate as himself. Every now and then, he is beset by homosexual feelings and thoughts, He has attempted to withstand them by masturbation. Lately his self-possession has had a hard proof, upon his falling love with a handsome young man. He has been victorious over the feeling; but only through the penalty of severe neurasthenia again. He has therefore turned to me, the more because lately he is sexually so excitable that he hardly can hide his homosexual inclinations, and by their disclosure might become not only ridiculous but damaged in social life,—in which he has a dignified position. Like others of his genus, Z—has taken refuge against his neurasthenic troubles in alcoholic drink, which as a fact relieves him in part; but still his sexuality increases. I have found him.an intellectual man and a fine-feeling one; outwardly thoroughly manly, of normal education, also deeply lamenting his condition, looking on his masturb. solit. with disgust, as it is contrary to his ethical nature. He is sexually appeased with a man by mutual kissings, embracings, and his happiest sexual remembrances are of this kind, beyond which he has not gone. He feels himself morally ruined. . . He is also so deeply depressed that he would have committed suicide in his terrible battle, save for consideration for his wife and child. I advised his battling-on, at any price. In the case of his not becoming 'cured', and also of the unendurableness of his situation, I advised resignation to it, with the sexual intercourse, with a man, which has been described."

The following example, from the same high source, is of rather a different type, as denoting considerable femininism of the uranian type. It is equally admonitory in its way:

. . ."Mr. P—thirty-seven years of age, married, descends from a very nervous mother, who was constitutionally *migrainée*. He himself, as a lad, suffered with hysteria; ever since then he has felt himself sexually attracted by good-looking young men. (With adspic. genitalia much excitement.) Soon after puberty came—with other men—masturb. mut. Only such types as are between 25 and 30 years of age attract him. He feels himself rather in the feminine role psychically, in sexual acts with men, with that complete glow of soul that a woman who loves possesses; and so while P—is only masculine in his corporeal relations with males, he is like an actor in a part. As a youth he was mocked at by other lads for his femininism of gestures and ideas; but girls have never made any impression on him. It was in hoping to cure his *vita sexualis* that he married, some years ago, but without any other wish to do so. He forced himself into marital coitus with his wife, and ho was potent by fancying that the act was with a young man; and he begot a child. Yet at times imagination failed, and so also his potency. After two years, he has now returned to his homosexual intimacies, such as masturb. mut. with a young man (in a public place!). He excuses this last incident by the fact that through his long abstinence from homosexual relations he was wholly thrown off his guard by adspic. genitalia. . . Mr. P—has a thoroughly virile exterior, a decorous personality; genitalia normal."

A common situation is shown in a letter to Ulrichs, from a married Uranian:

Instance: Strong Uranianism.

". . . I am well married, and to a wife who loves me passionately, and I am the father of a charming two-year old girl. But what I feel for my wife is friendship. Circumstances other than love made our match. At the mere sight of a handsome young man, I instantly feel that passionate sexual excitement (which is the only really sexual one for me) so genuinely, that since my youngest years, I have always felt the most ardent wish that marriages between men were possible. I long in vain for the man whom I secretly love. Think of it! I have never loved, I can never *love*, a woman! I am forced to appease my impulse, the masculine ideal in my mind" . . . etc. etc.

Marriage as a Useful Screen, on Occasion. Dread of disgrace is often the direct cause of an Uranian's marriage. The fact that he is honourably and normally united to a woman, is perhaps the father of children, and is a model husband outwardly, are sufficient details of social protection. Many a young Uranian has avoided thus the lightning-flash of social disgrace. It has been remarked that when a homosexual scandal occurs in a social.clique, a club or an army-circle, an epidemic of engagements and weddings can be looked-for. The precipitancy of such marriages is excused by all manner convenient fables. The *fiancée*—or the bride—is generally the last individual to suspect just *why* her hand has been asked. A clever man, a shrewd Uranian, a refined idealist readily convinces a sentimental woman of an admiration for her—hitherto a secret. A few years ago, in an American city, a similisexual scandal hung over the head of a young society-man, of notable wealth, æsthetic, and of fine intellectual and moral character. He was the last person to be supposed to make a hasty marriage. His engagement and wedding came in a trice, quite disconcerting any further gossip as to his nature—though causing much ordinary comment at the time.

A similisexual man occasionally takes his betrothed, or his wife, into his confidence—from the first; appeals to her pity, even if she cannot "understand" his sexual nature. Sometimes she is thus his good angel, his dearest *friend* through a whole life together, in which their love is without any sexualism. But many wives of Uranians do not know, or guess, or endure well such a situation. Sometimes the confidence or conduct of the husband precipitates a melancholy rupture, if not one in violence.

Timely Retreat. Or as his only safe course, however difficult, however often it may have been dismissed as impossible, no matter what the pain or the comment, the betrothed Uranian breaks his engagement—retreats in time. A pretext is concocted, even a physician's aid is called in—for a statement of importance, of real disease, and so on. This, not to speak of intelligent objection by the bride. The writer was informed of a case in France, a couple of years ago, in a family of high social mark, where the young *fiancé* convinced of the permanency of his *vita sexualis*, and of the misery consequent before him and his betrothed, advanced the hereditary insanity in one part of his family-line, as a barrier. It was effective. A London physician has furnished the writer with a more courageous instance. A young Uranian, affianced to a young lady of fine intellectual and moral qualities, decided that the best escape for unhappiness for them both was to take the *fiancée* into his dark secret. To make its gravity clear, he had to explain to her the whole problem of similisexualism—a topic little known to women. The lady was intelligently convinced, and they skilfully effected the breaking of their engagement—on a pretext from *her* side.

Historic cases of these 'escapes' are to he met. One of them involved the unlucky Ludwig II of Bavaria. We have noted such a situation as a tragedy, when speaking of the ruptured betrothal of Lenau, the distinguished poet.

Nevertheless, we continually find the homosexual entering on his engagement, after positive medical advice toward such a step.—as his "cure." But anon—perhaps at once—he finds his error. His disillusionment is pitiable. Such a well-meaning but evil counsellor is depicted in the interview with a medical specialist, included in a little psychiatric romance already cited in these pages—*Imre: A Memorandum*:

. . . "This doctor wrote of my kind as simply—diseased. 'Curable,' absolutely 'curable'; so long as the mind was man-like in all else, and the body firm and normal. Certainly that was my case! Would! not therefore do well to take that one step which was stated to be most wise and helpful toward correcting as perturbed a relation to ordinary life as mine had become? That step was—to marry. To marry immediately."

"The physician who had written that book happened to be in England at the time. I had never thought it possible that I could feel courage to go to any man. . . save to that one vague sympathizer, my dream-friend, he who some day would understand all! . . . and confess myself; lay bare my mysterious nature. But if it were a mere disease, oh, that made a difference! So I visited the distinguished specialist at once. He helped me urbanely through my embarrassing story of my 'malady' . . . 'Oh, there was nothing extraordinary, not at all extraordinary in it, from the beginning to the end,' the doctor assured me, smiling— in fact, it was 'exceedingly common. . . All confidential specialists in nervous diseases know of hundreds of just such cases; nay, of much worse ones; and treat and cure them. . . A morbid state of certain sexual-sensory nerve-centers' . . . and so on, in his glibly professional diagnosis."

"So I am to understand that I am curable?"

"Curable? Why, surely! Exactly as I have written in my work; or as Doctor So-and-So, and the great psychiatric Professor Such-a-One, proved long ago. Your case, my dear sir, is the easier because you suffer in a sentimental and sexual way from what we call the obsession of a set, distinct Type, you see; instead of a general—h'm—how shall I style it?—morbidity of your sex-inclinations. It is largely mere imagination I You say you have never really 'realized' this haunting masculine Type which has given you such trouble? My dear sir, don't think any more about such nonsense! You never will 'realize' it in any way to be—h'm— disturbed. Probably had you married and settled down pleasantly, years ago, you would laugh heartily now at the whole story of such an illusion of your nature. Too much *thought* of it all, my dear friend! Too much introspection, idealism, sedentary life, dear sir! Yes, yes—you must *marry*—God bless you!"

"I paid my distinguished specialist his fee and came away, with a far lighter heart than I had had in many a year."[1]

The Tragic Retreat: Four Instances.

But for Uranians betrothed, as for heterosexuals, withdrawals are not always easy or uneventful. So comes the tragic sort of history—with the abrupt runaway, the "missing" bridegroom—*not* to be; the suicide, the maniac, the murderer. Here is a short series of instances:

(Stuhlweissenburg, Sept 23, 1900.) "The wedding of two young people of our city, both much respected, the tailor's assistant F— with a young woman named Theresia T—was in progress, as far as the start of the bridal-procession of relatives and friends from

---

1. *cf.* "Imre: a Memoradum:" by Xavier Mayne.

EDWARD IRENAEUS PRIME-STEVENSON

the house of the bride's parents, when the bridegroom suddenly drew a revolver and shot himself through the heart. A dreadful scene of panic naturally followed. The motive of the suicide is wholly inexplicable, so far as any other previous romance, or pecuniary troubles, ill-health or what else, could be inferred. The young people were affectionate friends, though the dead bridegroom is spoken of as not being enthusiastic to marry—at all."

(Vienna.) "We mentioned yesterday the startling suicide of the teacher in the Burggasse public-school, Herr Leopold S—. The unfortunate young man committed the act only a few hours before he Was expected to meet his bride—at the altar. S—had been betrothed since July of last year. He was 38 years old, the son of a surgeon. His fiancee was a most estimable and attractive young lady of this city, also for awhile a teacher, and the daughter of a well-known architect and builder. The pair were much attached to one another, as would be supposed, but certain matters as to S— . . . (confidential to some of his most intimate friends only) have been ominous from the first. Until the engagement with the young lady, Herr S—had led the most reserved of lives, occupied only with his profession and his mother, between whom and this only son a specially close attachment existed—the admiration of their friends. In November, the mother and son took a pleasanter and larger dwelling, in K—gasse, which also was to be the home of the pair. The betrothal met with general congratulation by the friends. The wedding was set for yesterday, at half-past twelve, in the Karlskirche, and the dinner was to follow, in a hotel. S—is spoken of as having passed the preceding evening in the best of spirits, at the home of his betrothed, which he left at ten o'clock. At eight in the morning, he was found on the floor of his room with a pistol-shot in his right temple. He recovered consciousness for an instant or so, but could not speak—and died in a state of coma. The fatal shot was not heard in the house. Mrs. S—the mother was leisurely dressing for the happy event of the morning, when the news of the tragedy was broken to her. As soon as she had recovered consciousness, (but hardly within an hour) and could control her grief, she sent word to the family of the bride, who immediately countermanded the day's ceremony as best they could. The Karlskirche was decorated tastefully with flowers, and majority of the guests were already assembling there, or preparing to drive to the wedding. The news was of melancholy effect, the more as the deliberateness of Herr S—'s action was mentioned. Many guests were at different hotels in the city, and did not hear of the death till they reached the church or hotel. Among the deeply-moved friends of the teacher was one favourite pupil, a lad of sixteen, who presently came to the deceased young man's house, weeping bitterly to "lose so kind, so good a teacher" . . . It is said that S—, day before yesterday, sent a registered letter to a person in particularly close relations with him, announcing his intention. The motive of the suicide arises in certain tragic circumstances of a familiar nature. The bereaved mother is without consolation. Recently she has had grave mental anxieties, and she had hoped that henceforth her days would pass in peace. The outlook for her is sad indeed."

(Hercules Baths, Hungary):—"Yesterday Major M. C—of the S—Garrison, who has been a guest here at a well-known hotel-pension during some weeks, committed suicide by shooting himself in his lodgings. Major C—was still a young man, of excellent family, engaged to be married, in comfortable circumstances and popular with all his associates. No money-troubles existed, and in his *affaires-de cœur* are the names of none of the category of acquaintances such as frequently can make unhappiness for young men. He had come to the Hercules Baths merely for a "nerve-rest," prior to marriage with a young lady of S—. This marriage he had twice postponed. Ht is also mentioned that Major C—was long suffering from a special nervous disorder, the care of which is peculiar to psychiaters."

Or one meets other instances of suicide on the eve of marriage, such as are the subjoined. The first is from an English daily newspaper of July 19, 1908:

"Early yesterday morning a tragedy took place in a house in Lincoln-street, Brighton; a farrier-sergeant, Alfred Cecil H—, of the 2nd Dragoon Guards, shooting himself with a Service revolver a few hours before he was to have been married to Miss Alice W—, who lives next door to H—'s mother, in Lincoln-street. The wedding was to take place at ten yesterday morning at Annunciation Chiurch. Every preparation had been made for the ceremony. H—, who was stationed at Hounslow Barracks, arrived at Brighton on Friday night in readiness for the happy event; he seemed in good health and spirits, and parted with his fiancee on the best of terms. He was up soon after five yesterday morning, and went next door, where he saw Miss W-, and also her brother. He chatted in his usual cheery fashion, but said he could "do with a rest." He told Miss W—he was going out to buy same flowers for her at the market. Instead of leaving the house, he entered the front room, on the ground floor. Almost directly afterwards the inmates of the house were startled by a loud report. Miss W—, with the members of the family, ran into the room and saw H—lying on the sofa with a wound in his head. His right hand was grasping his service:revolver, in which there was a spent cartridge. Death had evidently been instataneous. Nothing was found on the deceased in any way throwing light on the tragedy, which so far is a mystery to his friends and relations."

"The suicide of Mr. T—Y—on Tuesday, at the hotel where he has been passing the week, was mentioned in this paper yesterday. It is not explained. Two or three friends of the deceased state that Mr. Y—has been out of sorts lately, and has several times confidentially intimated that he feared that his approaching marriage, which was to take place on Thursday next, in B—, was "a great mistake;" but expressly declaring that the young lady was "an ideal woman," and.that "any man who had been so lucky as to win her ought to thank God on his knees." Other remarks show the warmth of his affection for his fiancée. That there was no other "woman in the case," and no question of health or money appears conclusive. The mystery of the tragedy is deepened by the fact that Mr. Y—said to a friend some two months ago that "he knew that his marriage would be his greatest trouble"—that "there was a curse on it." He never explained this extraordinary remark."

Once bound formally, indissolubly, to the side of a woman? committed to the impossible in his marital role, the aversion of a homosexual man can become loathing till the end is a crime.

The Uranian Wife-Murderer.

Possibly there is faithlessness on his part; not with women, but with fellow-uranians. A kind of cruel pity for the wife can have a share in his fury. At any rate, he has reached the point where he will get rid of his torment; but not by suicide. Sexual hatred of his wife deepens. He does not care for gallows or guillotines? Felony and death—rather than the daily contacts that so irritate him—that drive him wild! Better his children should not live than grow up sexual unfortunates like himself! Such revolts from wedlock are labeled "insanity without cause"—"sudden mania"—"groundless jealousy;" or else unjust suspicion is cast on the wife.

One "historic" wife-murder (in the highest circles of the aristocracy of the French Second Empire) was infused with homosexualism—though the secret was well-kept. Another more recent socialtragedy, of somewhat similar kind (in England) was entirely such. In a South American city, about a year ago, a merchant killed his wife "to ged rid of her," and to resume his former sexual life with a male partner.

Earlier homosexual relations between the husband and another Uranian, adult or very youthful, can bring about violent climaxes. The lover, kept at a distance by his friend's marriage, is often capable of taking his own life, or of killing his married friend, or of destroying the woman who has separated them. Sometimes an Uranian contrives to keep his homosexual partner under the same roof with him after the marriage; more or less in their old relation. Or a new and irresistible uranian intrigue can demoralize the nuptial life. There have however been odd uranian examples of Goethe's "Elective Affinities"—in a way; the two husbands consoling each other, the two wives consoling each other, by a peaceable convention; all parties thankful that 'tis no worse. But such coincidental and four-square philosophy is not exactly common.

In the "Jahrbuch für Sexuelle Zwischenstufen" is cited a case of a wife who attempted to kill her husband, on discovering his intimacy with a young man. Failing to punish him, she took her own life. How violently can be avenged by wives the 'insult ' to their sex and to heterosexual love, when husbands are false on uranian lines of infidelity, the following examples indicate. The first is from a Berlin newspaper of May, 1908. The second is of some years ago, from an Austrian journal:—

"In Lindenfels (Odenwald) have just been arrested Herr Ernst H—of Berlin and his overseer and friend Herr H. M—, at the former's villa, on account of offenses against "Paragraph 175" of the Code. The circumstances of the case are curious. Herr H—, who has been married many years, recently built a villa in the place, in order that he could lodge comfortably his friend M—, to continue undisturbed their—special relations. Unluckily the matter became known to the wife of Herr H—, who during many years of peaceful married life has never had any cloud over her happiness with her husband.till he met Herr M—. She discovered some compromising letters that her husband had written to his friend, from Italy and Egypt. Mrs. H—turned over this delicate correspondence to the police, and her husband and Herr M—are now in custody on the grave charge indicated.

"Yesterday in Heuberg-bei-Dornbach, were discovered in a thicket, in the woods, the bodies of two young men, who beyond any doubt had committed suicide together, not a great many hours earlier. One suicide was identified as Adolf Slawiczek, of this city (Margarethen Bezirk) thirty-five years old, unmarried, and employed in a furniture-factory; and his companion was presently known as Karl Koller, twenty-eight years old, married and the father of several children, but divorced—a locksmith, in Brigittenau. Apparently the tragedy had been arranged thus: Koller had shot Slawiczek through the heart, and had then put the weapon to his own breast. Some circumstances coming to knowledge dismissed all question of there having been any quarrel between the two friends, whose close intimacy has been often spoken of by their acquaintance. They were sober and industrious, and Koller leaves a small estate. . . The motive of the act appears to be the fact that the divorced wife of Koller has recently threatened him with a criminal charge of a particular sort, involving his friend Slawiczek, whom she greatly disliked, and who in some degree was concerned in the divorce mentioned. Probably fear of this proceeding decided the two friends on their melancholy step."

Society often smiles at the reluctance, and even resentment, with which a young bachelor surrenders to marriage some special friend; his Jonathan—his David. Much deeper can be his

Marriage as an Interruption to Uranian Intimacies.

regret than their circle guesses. Often a lively girl, either in a touch of real sympathy or of merry irony, says to the "bereaved" friend "—Yes, yes, of course we all know that X—'s engagement, his marriage must be hard for *you*. You will be a regular widower after it!" Damon smiles, and caps the jest. But there is no jest when he and his Pythias are alone. This situation occurs, as the reader can suppose, chiefly when Pythias has been a Dionian-Uranian from the outset; or has become more and more dionistic, until a decisive sexual passion for some woman has conquered his heart. Here comes also the special chance of future disappointment to an Uranian who loves some dionistic youth in his teens; the man experiencing only an intenser sexual passion as the boy becomes a young man. Often grown wholly dionian, never being thoroughly an "inborn" type, the youth becomes cold toward anything but *real* friendship with his senior friend, and is more and more averse to their sexualities, Soon some one woman takes possession of his fancy. The mysterious uranian relationship falls to sudden ruin. A homosexual of refined and constant type, whose ideal is once thus met and possessed and broken, can have all the rest of his life shattered. Sometimes, at least, the Uranian has enough force of character, unselfishness of love and philosophy; and therewith he accepts his fate. He will not oppose the happiness of the being he so profoundly loves.

Jealousy, and Interference.

But the lover-friend to be deserted does not always accept the situation; nor assent to an engagement and a marriage without something more than anguish and- pleading. In an English city,, „several ago, an engagement of some social prominence was broken off, on account of a cause peculiarly unpleasing—the reluctant conviction of the *fiancé* that the young lady had misconducted herself; had been in particular intimacy with another man—deceased. But the truth came to light, out of all doubt, that the most intimate friend of the engaged man had been the calumniator and even a forger in the affair, because of homosexual jealousy; in his determination to "bring back" the deserter from their intimacy. A more tragic case of such interference, through similar jealousy, occurred in Birnbaum, in Posen, in 1903. Herr Karl T—, the presiding judge of one of the city's tribunals, a man in the early thirties, a social favourite, much respected, prosperous and well, committed suicide; apparently without reason for it. He had recently become engaged to a young lady of one of the best town-families, who loved him with all her heart, and had not any cause to doubt Herr T—'s sentiment for her. The mystery of his death was explained some months later. When a student, T—had maintained homosexual relations with a friend, also at the University. The two young men had an intense sentiment for each other in—every way. They had solemnly promised that they would never interrupt it, and that they would neither of them ever marry. T—however, being the dionistic type of the pair, for practicalities decided to marry; with expectations of happiness. The deserted friend wrote to T—, reminding him of their oath; and at the same time wrote certain facts to the family of the young lady. The match was promptly broken off. T—was involved in open scandal. He killed himself. In the eighth chapter of this book we have met a somewhat similar example, though even more tragical, in Austrian social life.

In Otto de Joux's "Enterbten des Liebesglücks," the authour describes romantically the pitiable situation of an Uranian who after a long intimacy with a young Dionian-Uranian loses the latter, as the younger man reverts to his true and normal *vita sexualis*, and is to be married:

The Anguish of an Uranian when Partnerless by Marriage.

"Renunciation and calumniation of ourselves is our lot. . . We offer our sufferings to God as a sacrifice. Our victory over the material life is greater, more exalted than that won by any other mortal. But nobody respects it, nobody knows of it. . . When I was twenty-nine, the first threatening shadow came over my life. Unfortunate creature that I was, I loved a young man, with every vein of life in me. And, after a long struggle, he—gave himself to me. I devoted myself to him like a brother, made every path in life for him smooth; it was the happinees of my life to be his special Providence, day by day. He, on his part, permitted—accepted— my caresses with a gentle but complete self-surrender. . . Only now and then came a quiet scorn across his lips. But I was not troubled by his coldness. . . Four years this state of affairs endured Then he fell in love with a young girl! Therewith he wished nothing more of my "eccentric emotion's" as he called them; they became an abomination to him. The girl returned the love of Bruno, too, and so he looked forward to a happiness beyond measure. In an evil hour we parted. . . Everything was at an end between us save friendship. All the joy that I had pictured as mine only, was now given to his betrothed; those eyes that were the light of my life, those kisses that had been mine—! Such thoughts whirled, about in my mind till I used to cry aloud in my despair. I had my Christian faith, I turned to God—but another image, my unfaithful beloved, came between God and me! . . .

I asked for one final interview. He could not refuse it. He came. We faced each other, both trembling with excitement, hardly daring to look into each other's eyes.

"What do you demand of me?" he asked. "I am certainly in duty bound to be grateful to you, and because of your great kindness to me, I wish to forget now many things that have passed between us. But do not demand too much,—what goes beyond human power! Speak!"

I caught his hand, stretched out against me. "Listen to me," I said, "you have always been my ideal of honour, my pride. That 'weakness' as you call it, which made you willing to belong to me, my own immeasureable love for you, perhaps these things have now you feel made dishonoured, lowered you in your own eyes. You perhaps think now that I have had only a lower sort of longing in seeking your love. That would be the most fearful of errors! You think that you are far higher than I, because I am your slave, your creature. But, Bruno, has not the nobler part of my love any influence on you? Oh, yes, it is a punishable passion. . . You could be guilty of a great crime; I should love you, all the same, like a god: you could draw to yourself the hate contempt and of all the world, but I should defend you against it all. . . You see how unspeakably I love you! I have no other thought, no breath of life, except—you! Bruno, this marriage of yours is impossible. It will kill me. Take pity on me" . . . Sobs choked my voice.

He was moved. In deep anxiety, I looked into his eyes,- like a criminal awaiting a sentence. Then he bent over me, and took my face between his hands, and kissed me. "You are a big, big child" he answered gently. "I shall always, always feel kindly toward you! But oh, do, *do*, get rid of this morbid mania for me. Believe me, it *must* be pathologic—curable. Recover your self-control. I have pledged my word as to my marriage. You know that I am an out-and-out *man*—I have never been able to understand your—adoration for me. Think over the whole matter. You have such a warm heart, you too must find some girl or other who will be exactly the one for you. And you must come to know my betrothed, also. She is a pure, gentle creature, she loves me so chastely—peacefully—not so stormily as you. See here now—if you had only been born a woman, why, I would have married you! I have told you that often; and *then* you only would be the mother of my children. So—why not be now at least their uncle? You are so kind—so good to me! . . . Will you not still be so?" He spoke all this in so gentle a voice, the expression in his saddened face was so beseeching and so honest, that I was utterly overcome. I covered his-hand with kisses. I said that he was free. I renounced him for ever. His children will be my heirs."

Whether pictured by merely romance or in sad fact, such episodes warn Uranians who allow their hearts to be bound-up in the affection for a much younger man; for that growing, hesitating nature which presently may swing wholly away from an immature sexual anchorage. The noble-minded type of Uranian knows that the young deserter has every right on his side. So admitting, he may accept the blow in silence; but also in an anguish never to pass away.

Here are typical examples of dramas—one in America, the other in Germany—because of passionate sensibility to the barrier and separation that must occur through marriage:

"No further explanation is given out of the suicide of Mr. C—R— which was mentioned here yesterday as a shock to a very wide circle of business and personal friends, on Sunday morning. The affairs of the deceased are all in good order, and there is lacking as yet a clue to sentimental motives. . . The body was cremated yesterday at the F—P—Crematory, in accordance with the often-expressed wish of the dead young man, repeated in the note found beside his body. It is a sad coincidence that at the wedding of his most intimate friend, Mr. W—F—of this city, last month, at which he was best-man, Mr. R—remarked in joke to several friends that "he never could survive W—'s marriage" . . . The latter cannot mention any reason for the fatal shot, unless that lately Mr. S—has been very nervous at times. He states that the letter that the deceased wrote to him contains nothing worth communicating. He says there is no ground for reports that an affair with a person of the opposite sex was the motive. This he says he knows, and he wishes some reports to the contrary positively contradicted."

"On Sunday last occurred here (Perlerberg, Germany) the funeral of Reserve-Lieutenant C—T—thirty, two years old who suddenly committed suicide some days ago. He was apparently in the prime of health and activity. The reasons for the action are curious and romantic. For a long time, Lieutenant T—has maintained an intimate friendship with another officer of his regiment, and it seems that the two had solemnly promised each other "never to marry." For all that, Lieutenant T—has lately betrothed himself, and the date of his wedding was set. Certain bitter "scenes" are said to have taken place precisely in consequence, and finally the *fiancée* of the dead officer received a letter from the friend of her betrothed, giving certain confidential facts not to her pleasure, speaking of the compact against the engagement, and putting Lieutenant T—into some embarrassment. The result has been Lieutenant T—'s suicide; and now the friend declares that he will shortly follow him to the grave."

Transmitted Similisexualism: the Uranian's Children.

We Lave printed out earlier a grave responsibility as to offspring from Uranians. Marriages by male-loving fathers are likely to be blessed, or cursed, with children that inherit homosexualism, however dionistic the influences of the mother. In his procreation the Uranian is a potent type. He "calls upon his uranian imagination, too, in sexual actions with even a perceptibly welcome wife. Not any trait of the human psychos seems more concretely transmitted than similisexualism. The boy is born, perfectly male in his physique but with the *vita sexualis* of the Uranian. If it be really "inborn" he never loses its thrill till death. This strong possibility ever must be an obstacle to trying a matrimonial "cure," on the part of a conscientious and thoughtful homosexual man, as also with any conscientious and thoughtful similisexual woman. Indeed, although a Catholic ecclesiastic can suffer life-long torture of body or soul (particularly if unaware of the scientific basis of his uranianism) the homosexual priest should be thankful that his vow of celibacy is so much more surely kept, than that one of chastity. He is alone with his God, with his sex-nature and his life; spared the danger that other confessions allow by permitting wedlock to their clergy. He is out of the track of a "cure" that is no cure, and of paternal complications of his sexual instinct.

In accepting marriage 'curatively' or otherwise, a large proportion of the feminine Intersex are in situations closely like those of Uranians. The Uraniad faces a physical and psychic predicament that often is profoundly pathetic. She cannot avoid it as easily as can the Uranian. Often she

The Uraniad and Her Marriage as a "Cure:" How Far Is It Helpful?

must begin it with interrupting her feminosexual relationships; which rupture by itself makes life a tragedy for her—that frequently brings it to a dark climax. Feminosexual friendships are shattered, or must be changed radically in quality, as the man appears on the scene. The normal nature of the Uraniad awakes, and brings separation. The wife must learn submission to the hated masculine embraces. She fears for her son for her daughter. The inner life of many women being in every way strongly emotional, the tale is worse. Neuropathic experiences can claim a vast part in her married existence. Woman is shut out from much that distracts and helps a masculine similisexual. Not only are fewer her chances of escaping anything she dreads; her opportunities of continuing uraniadistic intimacies are less favourable. One can say that the real Uraniad often is even more the *victim* of marriage than the masculine intersex. Many uraniads have not the temperaments to bear up, to philosophize, to endure the nuptial tie, to be consoled—transformed.

Differentiating the situation of the Uranias as to marriage, are also the following Dangers for Her aspects. Women (still using the word in its widest sense—including feminosexuals) have not such chances of "finding out" before they marry, or otherwise enter into sexual intimacies

The Uraniad Less Clearly Warned of Dangers for Her.

with men, how antipathetic may be a man's physical embrace. That is' to say, chaste women have not. The virtuous Uraniad is not always well acquainted with herself; her real sexualism may be quite unknown. Uranians have more opportunity to discern their homosexualism. On the other hand, emotional stress for an Uraniad who marries, or who is separated from a beloved feminine partner when the latter marries, is less often concretely tragic. Her sex-nature is likely to be shallower. Women lack the courage for suicide oftener 'than men: they are more subject to religious scruples, they are not willing to quit their children, and they dread scandal more—even if it is to be *post mortem*. Again, when married to a Dionysian, the influences of male coitus are often strong on the Uraniad. She becomes indeed "cured;" she grows truly feminine in her *vita sexualis*—as we have already pointed out in this book. "To marry, and to become a mother" is a common advice of confidential medical advisers of similisexual women, older or younger. Incontestably it is often valuable, far more so than any similar counsel given to the philarrene.

But not always. An example communicated in "Psychopathia Sexualis," by Dr. von Krafft-Ebing, is this:

"Mrs. R—thirty-five years old, of upper station in life, was brought to me for a consultation at her husband's request. Mrs. R—was of a nervous but normal family-stock. Her childhood was not of special illness, except headaches. She received a careful moral education, and showed special talent for music and languages. She became a governess and a teacher. She has always felt sexual sympathy for her own sex, and her interest in men has been at the most simply intellectual. She has never liked female work, and when a girl, preferred to play about with boys. At 27, she was much depressed and ill, having dark ideas, insomnia during five months. At 28 she entered into a sexual intimacy with a lady four years her junior, and felt a love that was adoration. The intercourse lasted five years, till the marriage (an unhappy one) of this friend occurred. After long deliberation, she now decided to marry her present husband, admiring his character, and because of his wealth and of his love for her. The result has been unfortunate. She grew deeply depressed, morally, by coitus. She had never supposed marriage to 'mean' this phase. Weariness of life, etc., ensued. The husband could not comprehend her riddlesome demeanour, and really loving his wife, did his best to calm her. Physicians gave their opinions that with pregnancy Mrs. R—would be relieved of her impressions. She was friendly toward her husband, suffered his caresses, but in sexual relations with him was from her side cold, passive, and exhausted and dispirited after coition, with spinal irritation and nervousness.

Then a journey united Mrs. R—to her former female friend. Intense and joyful excitement followed. The husband hurried a separation, finding the friendship 'peculiar.' He discovered that the correspondence between the two was exactly like that between a pair of lovers. Meantime his wife became pregnant. Her child was an abortion. Her nervous state at the time of my consultation with her was morbid, and there had occurred anatomical disorders that were discovered on exploration. Mrs. R—declare that she had married without understanding the sexualism of matrimony; that she respected and loved her husband intellectually very much, and would do anything in the world for him, if he would only spare her sexually. She had hoped for a more sexual feeling for him, in time. After the mis-birth mentioned, her status has improved. But still her future seemed 'terrible,' to her. Her highest happiness was still her correspondence with her female friend."

The following case, from the same high authority, indicates a type of considerable 'normalism' mingled with feminosexualism:

. . . "Mrs. M—forty-four years old, is a lady of superior social position, and accomplishments, as well as of fine moral nature. She consulted me in hope of benefit. She was descended from a highly-gifted family, especially in musical, literary and artistic talents. She was morbid as a child, a good scholar, and she defines herself as at this early time an Urnind. Early in her sexual development she passionately admired only young girls and beautiful women, falling into psychic love for such, and with enthusiastic friendships for them. But so naively and slowly did her actual knowledge of sex come, especially as she was convent-educated, that till she was 19, Mrs. M—had absolutely no real understanding of the sexual distinction between man and woman. Especially in consequence of this ignorance, she fell a victim to a man who passionately loved her. She married him, to live with him in "eccentric" marital relations, and bore him a child. Here her more normal self obtained, more or less. After a few years, she became a widow. Therewith she returned to her inclinations toward women, at first because she was afraid of pregnancy, etc. By this time (at 27) she nevertheless married again, but without any desire sexually toward a man, her husband being an invalid. She completely broke down nervously, in aversion to him sexually, and in effort to meet her sexual duties with him; constantly longing for appeasement, etc. She had four children. After three years, this second husband died. Her own nine-year old daughter now began to show signs of sexual insubordination, and it greatly distressed her mother. A terrible period for Mrs. M—ensued; what with her anxieties, violent sexual desires that almost distracted her, etc. At forty-four, she is now drawn to women, now to men. She is somewhat less excitable, probably by advancing maturity, but is unhappy, weary of life, etc. She has been suffering much dionistically toward a certain young man of the vicinity, whose intimacy was not practicable; yet at the same time she feels herself drawn to different younger women, and "with a nobler and higher enjoyment. Mrs. M—was wholly of feminine physique, though her extremities were not small."

Instance: Suicide after Marriage.

Some years ago, the marriage of a young English lady was followed by the suicide of her intimate friend. Both were not long past their college-days at an University. The diary of the young lady who took her own life was typical of the height to which feminosexual sufferings can mount, in such circumstances. The unfortunate Uraniad had maintained sexual relations with her friend since their earlier girlhood. She had offered no objection to the marriage, beyond a painful "scene," after her friend first had informed her that a sentimental affair was in progress between herself and a man, "likely to end in marriage"; and that she felt quite willing to marry. No doubt she did, under an advanced dionism. The deceased was cruelly surprised, but did not discuss the matter, except on this, one occasion. She began to be less intimate with Miss X—after the engagement, and finally travelled abroad. She left the young husband a note, telling him that he had been the cause of her death; but forgiving him, and wishing the pair happiness. In all details she showed deliberate self-sacrifice—followed by as deliberate self-murder. Portions of her diary were read at the inquest, and appeared in some English journals.

Does Marriage Ever "Cure"?

As a general conclusion of the relations of the similisexual instincts and normal matrimony, it is plain that favourable chances of the experiment are not to be lightly dismissed if the physician or the patient traces a considerable measure of fluctuant dionism in the individual nature; if the intersexualism is not distinctly inborn and increasing; and if.there be strongly awakened (by individual and personal attraction) the heterosexual passion, Otherwise there is danger of worse personal misery; and of its inextricably involving other lives. Obvious is the danger to *prescribe* a marriage in the case of distinctly intersexual men and women. To too many medical men, similisexualism seems "wholly a pathologic affair," a disease, a "morbid" abnormalism. They do not accept, or admit, similisexualism as the eternal manifestation of any distinct—or indistinct— Intersexes. Yet this theory alone is in full logical accord with every-day facts before intelligent minds; explains all, justifies all that puzzles in the topic. We have ever with us the physicians inclined to treat as a nervous *disease* the homosexual instinct; to urge 'curative' processes, by prayers, resolutions, medicines, hypnotism, brothels, mistresses. Uranian fire too often will not be so extinguished. It will keep on smouldering; or will—break out. For the inborn Uranian, better than any "apostolic counsel" is Hamlet's—"Nay, we'll have no more marriages! Those that are married already shall stay so. The rest shall keep as they are!"

Only one tie could ever satisfy the philarrene of inborn, passionate, mature and enduring similisexualism; the union of body and soul with those other human beings, whose sexes they

The "Impossible Wedlock.."

approach, and resemble but are *not*; who bring a psychic, magnetic, sexual completeness, to receive the only real self-surrender possible for similisexuals. *That* bizarre, sterile union is today, as a legal tolerance, only a fantastic dream of such enthusiasts as Ulrichs. It is likely so to remain, even were modern conceptions of social and sexual ethics more amenable. It abides a fantasy, not easily to be made more harmonious— even as a theory. The world revolts from such a suggestion. But if there can be no social or legal acceptance of intersexual marriage, the currents of constant and elevated uranian loves find their way the world around, century by century, in obedience to high impulses of intersexuals and of their unchartered rights. Students of them, who have religious convictions on lines of Christian theologies, can even believe that such emotions and their mystic unities refer themselves to ties more enduring, more purely spiritual than those of our earth; their essence defined by Christ when he dismissed the idea of normal marriages for disembodied spirits, in the phrase "—neither marrying nor giving in marriage but *all* are as the angels of God in heaven."

XII

Is the Uranian a Higher or a Lower Sex and Type in the Scale of Humanity?

P robably the reader will say, as he reaches this short concluding chapter, that its title presents the most vitally interesting question

A vital Question.

that can be part of such a study; a query not well left for the last. But not so. The present writer has wished to emphasize certain practicalities of the Intersexual problem and condition, and throughout these pages considerably to subordinate cross-currents of the theoretical; as also to avoid concepts essentially in dispute among psychiaters. If the supremacy of the Uranian—when at his best—were indisputably accepted by science, if in his finest examples he were popularly received in the human scheme as the much-advertised "Overman"—then his complex problem would be solved. But that is not yet the result of arguments. The Intersexual, psychically and psychiatrieally, is a disputed equation. His friends do not too often agree with each other as to his status; even his enemies do not. Sometimes he would be glad to be saved from both.

Beyond doubt, much suggests the high-natured Uranian as representing a noble and gifted species of mankind; in touch with deeper and finer secrets of human—not to say

Two Scientific Theories.

Divine—personality. The enthusiastic theorist who admires certain races eminently similisexual, who recalls the greatest names and noblest figures in the catalogue of homosexual men, is impatient that Uranistic supremacy" in the world be not conceded at once. But cautious psychology wisely keeps the interrogation-point at the end of the tempting question set at the top of this chapter. Most psychiaters will insist on keeping it there; in spite of all the amiable wishes that one could answer the query by a clear and direct affirmative.

Two great camps, so to say, yet exist in the specialists study of similisexualism. One group (including many strong names in scientific medicine and medical psychiatry) declare that the Uranian is a morbid human product, an aberration, an "abnormal." To hundreds of jurists he is indisputably a criminal; except if insane. Another group, equally dignified and firm, holds to the theory that uranianism is the manifestation of a species of natural intersex; not technically pathological. Such views, as thus outlined, naturally consider the average Uranian, in his intellectual, moral, sexual, psychic and physical attributes, not as to what is generally called vicious, decadent or degenerate, etc. In each faction the arguments are sharp. Needs not to be said, that there are numerous contingents of psychiatric observers, whose judgments halt between the two extremes, exhibiting various differences.

"Who shall decide, when doctors disagree?" The question in Shakespeare's familiar phrase is applicable here. The layman is not acccepted as arbiter, nor is often capable thereto. At this stage of our study of Uranianism, and of tracing its psychic cartography, one may do well, either as physician or layman, thoughtfully to hesitate. Far more important than analysis is giving to the unhappy intersexual man or woman the sympathy, protection and freedom that the worthy types of them deserve. The future may be trusted to decide the wrangles of science; let us imitate the Good Samaritan. The most hesitant theorist at least can care for the Intersexual meriting aid on the roadside; can drive away the prowlers that have stripped and beaten him; can bind up his wounds; can help him to continue his life-journey; all this often without stopping to discuss his place in the human or divine scheme—much less in crowning him an exiled King of Men.

"Who Shall Decide When Doctors Disagree?

This brief study will-have been written to no sufficient purport, and many far more extensive studies can be read with indifferent results, if the observer does not realize that the ranks of indisputably similisexual mankind (over and above all clearly detractive or doubtful examples) present a great list of what we call superior types, including geniuses; in their moral mental and other dignity. The world owes a vast debt to men who have been homosexual. But in contrast to these, we have an equally indisputable and disconcerting array of similisexual human beings so marked out by weakness, by depravity, by vice and crime, that the aggregate in such a review chills even a discriminating tolerance.

The Puzzling Distinction.

A summary of just this confusion and contrast may be cited here from the psychological romance already referred to in this study several times, on account of its aim at serious suggestiveness—"Imre: A Memorandum": The passage is a part of the narrative of one of the two protagonists (Oswald) in the tale, as to his bewildered reflections on contrasts in uranian types:

". . . We walk the world's ways as men. We hew our ways through it as men, with vigour, success, honour. . . *one* master-instinct unsuspected by society for, it may be, our lives long! We plough the globe's roughest seas as men, we rule its States as men, we direct its finance and commerce as men, we forge its steel as men, we grapple with all its sciences as men, we triumph in all its arts as men, we fill its gravest professions as men, we fight in the bravest ranks of its armies or we plan out its fiercest and most triumphant battles as men. . . in all this, in so much more, we are men! Why, (in a bitter paradox!) one can say that we always have been, we always are, always will be, too much *men!* So super-male, so utterly unreceptive of what is not manly, so aloof from any feminine essences, that we cannot tolerate woman at all as a sexual factor! Are we not the extreme of the male? its supreme phase, its outermost phalanx?—its climax of the aristocratic, the All-Man? And yet if love is to be only what the narrow, modern, Jewish-Christian ethics of today declare it, if what they insist upon be the only *natural* and pure expression of "the will to possess, the wish to surrender" . . . oh, then is the flouting world quite right! For then we are indeed *not* men! But if not so, what are we? Answer that, who can?"

"The more perplexed I became in all this wretchedness (for it had grown to that by the time I had reached my majority) . . . the more perplexed I became because so often in books, old ones or new, nay, in the very chronicles of the criminal-courts, I came face to face with the fact that though tens of thousands of men, in all epochs, of noblest natures, of most brilliant minds and gifts, of intensest energies. . . scores of pure spirits, deep philosophers, bravest soldiers, highest poets and artists, had been such as myself in this mystic sex-organization (or sex-disorganization) that nevertheless of this same Race, the Race-Homosexual, had been also, and apparently ever would be, countless ignoble, trivial, loathesome, feeble-souled and feeble-bodied creatures!— the weaklings—the very rubbish of humanity! Did not the widest overlook of the record of Uranianism, the average facts about one, suggest that the most part of homosexual mankind had always belonged, always would belong, to the worthless or the wicked?

"Those, *those*, terrified me, Imre! To think of them shamed me; those types of man-loving-men who, by thousands, live incapable of any noble ideals or lives. Ah, those patently depraved, noxious, flaccid, gross, womanish beings! perverted and imperfect in moral nature and in even their bodily tissues! Those homosexual legions that are the straw-chaff of society; good for nothing except the fire that purges the world of garbage and rubbish! A Heliogabalus, a Gilles de Rais, a Henri Trois, a Marquis de Sade; the painted male-prostitutes of the boulevards and twilight-glooming squares! The effeminate artists, the sugary and fibreless musicians! The Lady-Nancyish, rich young men of higher or lover society; twaddling æsthetic sophistries; stinking with perfume like cocottes! The second-rate poets and the neurasthenic, *précieux* poetasters who rhyme forth their forged literary passports out of their mere human decadence; out of their marrowless shams of all that is a man's fancy, a man's heart, a man's love-life! The cynical debauchers of little boys; the pederastic perverters of clean-minded lads in their teens; the white-haired satyrs of clubs and latrines!"

"What a contrast are these to the heroes and heroic intellects of Greece and Rome! To a Themistocles, an Agesilaus, an Aristides and a Kleomenes; to Socrates and Plato, and Saint Augustine; to Servetus and Beza; to Alexander, Julius Cæsar, Augustus, and Hadrian; to Sweden's Charles the Twelfth, to Frederick the Great, to indomitable Tilly, to the fiery Skobeleff, the austere Gordon, the ill-starred Macdonald; to great Oriental princes; to the brightest lyrists and dramatists of old Hellas and Italia; to Shakespeare, (to Marlowe also, as we can well believe) Platen, Grillparzer, Hölderlin, Byron, Whitman; to an Isaac Newton, a Justus Liebig—to the masterly Jérôme Duquesnoy, the classic-souled Winckelmann; to Mirabeau, Beethoven, to Bavaria's unhappy King Ludwig;—to an endless procesion of "exceptional men," from epoch to epoch! As to these and innumerable others, whose hidden, and inner lives have proved without shadow of doubt (however rigidly suppressed as 'popular information') or by inferences vivid enough to silence scornful denial, that they belonged to Us."

"That redeeming Rest of us! That Rest, over and over again, typified! Uranians so high-minded, often of such deserved honour from all that world which has either known nothing of their sexual lives, or else has perceived vaguely, and with a tacit, reluctant pardon! Could one really believe in God as making man to live at all,and to love at all, and yet at the same time believe that *this* love is not created, too, by God? is not of God's own divinest Nature, rightfully, eternally—in milions of hearts? . . . Could one believe that the eternal human essence is in its texture today so different from itself of immemorial time before now, whether Greek, Latin, Persian, or English? Could one somehow find in his spirit no dread through *this*, none, at the idea of facing God, as his Judge, at any instant? . . . could one feel at moments such strength of confidence that what was in him so was righteousness?—oh, could all this be?—and yet must a man shudder before himself as a monster, a solitary and pernicious being—diseased, leprous, gangrened—one that must stagger along on the road of life, ever justly bleeding and ever the more wearied, till Death would meet him, and say "Come—enough! Be free of all! Most and best thing of all, be free of—*thyself!*"

"Is our Race gold or excrement?—is it rubies or carrion? If *that* last be true, why then all those other men, the Normalists—aye, our severest judges—those others whether good or bad, whether vessels of honour or dishonour, who are not in their love-instincts as are we—the millions against our tens of thousands, even if some of us are to be respected—why they do right to cast us out of society! for, after all, we must be just a vitiated breed!.. We must perhaps be judged only by our commoner mass."[1]

Moreover the student remarks that, admitting all more solidly valuable traits and of Ethics in gifts of the Uranian, he tends to shine brightest most frequently in merely what is æsthetic, ornamental, superficially intellectual; rather than in the deepest mental or highest

The Accent of Aesthetics Rather Than of Ethics in Uranians.

---

1. *cf:* "Imre: a Memorandum: by Xavier Mayne.

ethical life. Certainly now and then we find the example that counts for much in ethics. Some Uranians are ethically on a supreme human plane. But intellectually great, superbly gifted, the Uranian tends to be not morally well-poised, not morally aggressive, not altruistic. The Uranian susceptibility in fact seems a part of the unsolveable riddle of the moral value of the Beautiful in our human life; of the eternal *duel* between our merely human ideals of Beauty and of Good.

The question of the Uraniad as tending—at her best—to present an advance toward a superior and idealized development of humanity has naturally largely the same aspects, pro and contra, as in the case of the Uranian. The transference of the problem to the feminine Intersex has however many considerations that cannot find place in the present study.

To put our query to some experienced, thoughtful, dispassionate and philosophic Uranian is not to be much enlightened. Such a type is most conservative—often. He too is likely to be gravely asking "— What is my place in the plan of Humanity?" He too reflects; and more than he asserts. Many Uranians of course never think about the matter at all; and those who do think the most are in disaccord. An extravagant confidence of being close in touch with the much-talked of "Overman," "Over-Soul" of human superiority, will be met from one enthusiast; and the humility of doubt, if not sharp deprecation, from some other intersexual equally reflective. So much depends on the personal experiences, on the individual equation—as in almost all of this Life.

The Uranian as as
a Philosopher and
Christian.

Fortunately, the Uranian does not often claim too proudly to decide his world-riddle; nor to arrogate to the masculine Intersexual, even at its best, more than is prudent; however alluring the arguments. Instead, we find his highest type anxious to make of himself the best being, morally and socially and intellectually, that he can; to live in the world and to pass from it feeling that it has been good for him and the world to be of it. The philosophic (or elementarily Christian) spirit is no uncommon thing in the male Intersex; from Socrates as from Christ, through all the ages. Instances are legion. The hours of suffering and bitterness, of relative solitude, of punishment because of the intersexual nature's Workings—all these should not weaken the Uranian's *striving* to live as a creation near to a Divine Oversoul. Human intolerance of him when society is plainly unjust, can even make him look forward to death with a calm sense of trust in it, with a philosophic welcome for it; while that mood and attitude need not urge him toward any rash act to end his mortal career. So come to the higher Uranian, and so stays, at least faith in himself and his existence, and a respect for it. Often he can live a troubled life through, and can die, with a conviction that he—or his betters in the same intersexual fellowship— are born and live nearer to the Heart of Existence, are placed for their happiness or unhappiness higher on the mystic ladder of Life, than is even the finest-natured and loftiest-lived Dionian.

Is he right? Is he wrong?

Perhaps he is right. Let us not fillip that chance from him, so far as the heterosexual's ironical smiles, scorn, or too impatient arguments, can do so—clear and decisive as may seem the opposition of various systems of logic and inference and analysis that deprecate the philarrene's higher ideas of himself. We know—the wisest, the best of us—too little of man, we guess to cloudily at a God, we are too uncertain of any abstract Right, of any abstract Wrong, of finalities in heights or depths in this life or any other, to determine such a complex and profound human and social problem. In exploring the long chain of creation that stretches out between Perfection and Imperfection, let us be willing to leave as superfluous our certitude of the relationships of the Uranian as to what is ultimate in the vast scheme of cosmic organization. Instead, let us make it our practical business, as individuals and fellow-mortals, whether Uranians ourselves or not, to climb higher with all our best wills and works—and everywhere and eternally to help human nature to climb.

Perhaps He Is Right—?

XIII

THE LIFE AND DIARY OF AN URANIAN POET: AUGUST VON PLATEN (1796–1835)

"Love devours me, and he is, coldness itself. . . O, why has Providence made me what I am? Why is it impossible for me to love women?"

"You have torn my soul from out of me, robbed me of my soul and left me only my body—a heavy, terrible burden" . . . O reader, whosoever thou mayest be, into whose hands these lines perhaps may come, lament for me, weep with me, that I should have suffered so unspeakably!"

—(From Platen's "Diary.")

August von Platen-Hallermund, by aristocratic rank a count, a member of one of the oldest of Ansbach family-lines, and certainly one of the most gifted of poets in the portrayal of what is distinctively psychologic in similisexual love, was born at Ansbach, October 24, 1796; and died suddenly at Siracusa, Sicily, in November 1835, in only the fortieth year of a prematurely-ended career. His outward life was in no case eventful, compared with many poetical existences. It was chiefly, a matter of a short military-service, a considerable University-life, and then of about a dozen years of residence or travel in Italy, during which time his literary repute in his native Germany was reaching a high measure of critical and popular recognition. As a life, however, it was in no sense monotonous or stationary. Its inner chapters are a deep psychologic drama. Born of affectionate and careful parents, in easy circumstances, the earliest outward data to be noted include Platen's severe training, for the military profession, as a mere lad in the Cadet-School in Munich, till the year 1810; when, still a youth, he was enrolled among the royal pages of honour, at the Court of King Maximilian of Bavaria. There, during about four years of service and study, his naturally quick mind advanced materially, even under the "fashionable" tutelage of the "Pagery" School. He decided to enter the army as a profession, though with no real vocation for it. From 1814 till 1818 he was not only in a regular routine of home-service in Munich, but made the march with several other Bavarian regiments into France, to join the Allies, against Napoleon. The end of the Napoleonic campaign coming before Platen's division could take part in the action, he returned to Munich without a "baptism of fire." To the period following, his military life in Munich, we shall find that some of the most characteristic of the revelations of the earlier part of his Diary belong; although not of the impressive sorts which are met in the next stage of his restive existence—his student-life at Würzburg and Erlangen Universities. For, sensibly deciding that he was not born for soldiering, and having ideas of a diplomatic life. Platen turned from the army, to pursue philosophy, literature, political history and other matters, first at Würzburg University, then at Erlangen. He was a most close and successful student. It was here, at these Universities that prolonged and notable episodes of his maturer, innermost, sentimental life are met. These quite surpass in emotional definiteness two or three affairs of a homosexual sort in his soldier-days. They include his relations to a fellow-student at Würzburg named Eduard Schmidtlein ("Adrastus"); to another student—Herman von Rotenhan; to Otto von Bulow; to the young law-student, Hoffman(?) who is named "Cardenio" in the Journal; to Justus Liebig; and to Karl Theodore German. They were all students with him, now at one time, now another, during his college-life; and successively they were central figures of the strange and affecting soul dramas that Platen has written out for us, in the Journal and in his verse.

Before the end of his student-life, Platen had attracted notice, even in high literary circles, by his poems and his brilliant satirical dramas. He abandoned his political dreams just as he had dismissed his ideas of being a soldier. He resolved to follow out what appeared to be a manifest literary destiny. His choice was justified. Though not a prolific comedy-writer nor a many-sided one, nor yet a versatile psychologic poet, still, Platen reached a high mark of popular and critical fame. The latter has not yet by any means lapsed. The Oriental poems known as the "Ghazels," the deep human feeling in the Sonnets, and the passion, rhythmic sense and melody of the Odes are always certain of admirers. As to his comedies, English readers will find them a sort of precursor of the kind of social-satire piece that W. S. Gilbert, in especial, has immortalized for the British stage—though himself modelling after Aristophanes—including the dressing-out of old theatrical figures and contentions with contemporary wit, biting irony, parody and poetic elegance. Platen's comedies do not hold the stage in Germany now; but there is no specially clear reason, as to some of the few pieces themselves, why they should not do so.

After 1826, Platen's want of personal liking for Germany, North or South, and his contempt for most of the aspects of its literary society and movements grew mordant. He became fairly Germaniphobic; a condition of temperament to which his homosexual nature contributed a good deal. At any rate, the brilliant poet's travelling in Italy became something like a residence there. In 1835 an attack of cholera, during the epidemic of that year, ended his life, at Siracusa.

Something must be premised here as to the Diary itself. From almost his boyhood, August von Platen had kept a diary. In it, with unreserved truthfulness, he wrote down not merely his educational growth and his literary studies, critical observations and much of his daytoday interests of commonplace kind; but also his deep sentimental experiences of intensively homosexual course. The Diary obviously was at first meant, like most Diaries, for only its writer's eyes. Later, Platen saw that, as the mirror of what he thought was an uncommon kind of nature and sexual life, he would do well to let posterity see his pages. We may emphasize the words "what he thought," in the foregoing sentence. For, psychologists of today know only too well that while such a history as Platen's is seldom given to the world, the sexual existences that could rival its disclosures are legion, in every land and race of civilized humanity. Several times, when Platen was reviewing his Journal, he reflects upon the increasing possibility of future readers, and even appeals to their sympathies, as in the citation heading this study. The records were written, to a considerable extent, day by day, out of hand; except as to the first two "Books" (the Diary is divided into "Books") which deal with his early years; up to October 22, 1813; which two parts are a sort of compilation made from earlier notes, but set out so as to make the biographical narrative complete. After 1813 the entries are all contemporary. During his lifetime, Platen seems not to have allowed anybody else to read the Journal, except perhaps in one unlucky instance, where one of his best friends is credited with so arriving at Platen's full measure of sexual abnormality; and with making a painful scene by what occurred in a public circle of their acquaintance. The Diary remained the truest confidant of what Platen well called "the weakness of the human heart, and a history of my own impressions." It continues past military and university days, past the first journeyings in

Italy, on and on through his long-haltings there; to the very last days of his life. There are some seventeen volumes of note-books, as we are informed by the editors.

When in Germany in 1835, Platen gave all except the latest volumes of the manuscript to a friend. Dr. Pfeufer. But after Platen's death, Dr. Pfeufer and Professor Schelling, another near friend, and also the poet's mother, were shy of publishing the complete work. Its revelations were too disconcerting. The poot's mother decided that the books would best be given to Count Friedrich Fugger, her son's intimate, confidential friend, who would use it with discretion in preparing the biography of Platen that Fugger had in mind to make. But Fugger died shortly. So came the Diary back into the hands of Dr. Pfeufer. The public had been eagerly expecting a a biography of so distinguished a literary man as Platen. Only a small, dull section of the record presently appeared, avoiding carefully all the most important psychologic history and incidents. The more suspicious part of the public were mystified, but had to be content. (This edition frequently is met now, as the complete Diary of the poet.) But the bulky original remained shut away in the Royal Library of Munich, to be seen only by privileged eyes. In 1896, on the centenary of the poet's birth appeared the volume of the complete Journal, to the extent of one large moiety; and in 1900 came the concluding volume, deciphered and edited by Herr Laubmann (of the Royal Library of Munich) and his associate Dr. L. von Scheffler. This edition is absolutely complete, word for word, line by line, with Platen's own record; except where he himself tore out pages, now and then. The Cotta publication-house, in Leipsic, issued the edition; and it is the only one that should be consulted by persons interested in its absorbingly fascinating if painful history. Various recent summaries of it, reviews, etc., in German, French and one or two other languages, are conspicuously deficient or even grossly incorrect.

A linguist of great talents, Platen wrote the Journal not only in his own tongue, but—as to considerable portions—in French, Italian or Portuguese, and with citations from Persian. German however predominates. The Journal has not been translated into English, nor is likely to be so. The two volumes now presenting it in print are a rather formidable piece of book-making—together there are some 2000 large pages to read. The last entry is at Siracusa, October 13, 1835. A few days after that date, the diarist passed from earth.

In his moral character a man of the most elevated and sensitive sort, in his religious belief a Protestant, in the daily aspects of life highly practical, possessed of an idealizing temperament that naturally shunned all that is ignoble and animal *per se*,—Platen presents a type of the ethical quite as firm as his intellectual personality. Along with this comes a third aspect—his inborn intersexualism, homosexual passion, and æsthetic uranianism, from youth upward. He was outwardly a man, a soldier; he had a virile mind in his body. Yet nevertheless only the male appealed to his sense of supreme human beauty, to his great capacity to *love*, to desire love, to his sexual longings. The surges of spiritual and bodily passion that swept over his heart, even the lighter currents of sexual admirations, the chances and changes of his ideals and his yearnings, the fleeting happinesses of love that fell to him, its jealousies, its concealments, its struggles for attainment, its uncertainties, its renunciations—always some *man* is the object and end of these matters; never a woman. And as he matured, more and more unequivocally sexual became their fire. Whole groups of his poems sprang into being solely through these homosexual inspirations. By Platen's discreet avoidance of names, of prepositions that point out sex, by Oriental colourings and so on, there is no open offence given to the reader who either knows nothing of homosexual sentiment or has a prejudice against it, even in Vergil or Hafiz or Shakespeare. Only by reading between the lines, as one well may do after perusing the Journal now before us as the master-key to Platen's poetry, do we understand that poetry. For Platen lived under the curse—at least it is seldom a blessing—which makes a man's warmest friendships into sexual loves; which makes its victim seek through the world for the sort of "friend" (so often not to be met however near at hand) who will surrender *all* to the seeker, just as the surrender of the seeker must needs be *all*; that subjection to the law of a mystic and intersexual psychos that means probably the profoundest joy or misery of which sexual human nature is capable. More than this, Platen himself, like so many thousands of Uranians, did not till comparatively late in life understand his own nature; did not succed in harmonizing its workings with his inner moral and religious convictions; did not, free himself from the specters of his mistaught conscience. This, even though he was relatively early convinced that in his sexual struggles lay nothing base or bestial. First and last, we have his fine idealizing—indeed *too* fine for his own peace—and his virile morality, in all the Diary. We may note here that he was never weakly pederastic in his instincts. He found himself drawn chiefly to the sexually mature, to the manly youth or young man. Moreover he had, all his life long many friendships that, fortunately for his tranquility and happiness, remained unaffected by his homosexual tendencies; as is the case with most intellectual Uranians. He was warmly esteemed and respected by men who were really friends—not more, and whom he thoroughly appreciated and valued. But when the attraction to another man began with the note of sexual passion, it generally proved to be such *ad finem;* and often like the old phrase of "Parrhasius" it was indeed "a mounting devil" that tortured—and lingered to torture.

The homosexualism of Platen cannot be traced to heredity here. But it seems typically inborn. Even in his boyhood, when only a royal page, amid the other lads of that aristocratic office in Munich, we find him experiencing what was a first and immature love, extremely ideal but vehement and never forgotten, for another young man, a guest at the Court, Count Mercy d'Argenteau, An even more vivid sexual-sentimental passion came to him through the charming personality of young Prince Oettingen-Wallerstein, whose untimely death on the battlefield of Hanau deeply shocked Platen. Yet prematurely strong as we shall find these experiences were, they become pale beside the chronicle of Platen's secret love for two young officers, Friedrich von Brandenburg (called "Federigo" in the Journal) and Captain Wilhelm von Hornstein; both which affairs came into progress during Platen's first military years. But in turn, these episodes seem superficial and jejune, when contrasted with the self-revelations of his passionate University-loves, during his semesters at Würzburg and Erlapgen. Here we meet with the records of, successively, his intimacy with Eduard Schmidtlein ("Adrastus"); with Hermann von Rotenhan; with young Otto von Bülow; with a student not clearly identified except as "Cardenio" (a pseudonym in the Journal); with Justus Liebig, and with Karl Theodore German. Also mentionable, as either earlier or at this time, are some other intimacies more or less homosexual in tincture, continued into his later years; though in some cases going through the mutation to "mere friendship," or else evaporating altogether from his heart and mind—those with Issel and Perglas, and with a passing military acquaintance (visiting Ansbach); with Kopisch, and so on. These however are not recorded in such graphic detail and poignant clarity.

Platen was never a woman-hater. On the contrary, he much admired the beautiful and the intellectual and the ideal-feminine in woman. All his life long, occurred intimate friendships with women. Several women fell in love with the man and poet. But no woman's beauty of physique, no sexualism in a woman ever appealed to the mature Platen. What is more consistent, even when he was a lad only once is there to be traced anything like a sentimental intimacy and feeling for any female human being. There occurred during his relatively boyish officer-days, in Munich, a superficial attraction over him from a young French girl Mademoiselle Euphrasie de B—, visiting the Court with her mother. To his own riddlement, Platen thought that "at last" he was learning what other young men do not have to learn—the falling in love with a pretty girl. But in his lines about it, we see that he had not faith in the sentiment himself, even when it occupied him in an idle way. He knew that *he* was on the wrong track for *him*, no matter what was for others the right one. We find him soon returning to his natural, passionless and 'asexual' feeling for women. Euphrasie de B—faded utterly and swiftly out of his memory. There was never any sequel to this boyish illusion.

Yet a word, before we take up the entries in the Journal—to point out that in the comedies of Platen there is hardly a trace of his homosexualism. Not in stuff, not in types, not descriptively—nowhere! If he had written some of the tragedies that he planned, doubtless he now would have yet another literary aspect. We might have had a "Conrad von Hohenstaufen," from him that would have surpassed Schiller's "Don Carlos" in its suggestions. But only in the Diary and the poems does the homosexual passion speak out. The private (and very large) correspondence of the poet is not published, will probably never be published, so far as it is now accessible extant. From that correspondence we could expect many of the same strange chords as in the passional confessions of the Journal.

Another prefatory note to be made here, is allusion to the *gradual* awakening in Platen of the physical side of his homosexualism; the long resistance on his part to physical attractions, to bodily desires toward his own sex. Only late and involuntarily in his experiences did he realize that there was no use in denying them or struggling against them—that love, *love*, it was that "devoured" him, not any merely ardent friendships; that in the phrase of "Phèdre" what burned him to the vitals was:

—"Vénus tout éntière a sa proie attachée."

In the Journal's consecutive "affairs," we trace clearly his change. He passed from a merely romantic longing for an "intellectual" relation with some young man to whom he was suddenly attracted, to the throbs of a glowing physical-sexual disturbance. Or, we may more correctly say, that we can follow the course of Platen's confessing to *himself* that his love for X or Y or Z was sexual. Not till the fifth or sixth *affaire de cœur* (that with the handsome Würzburg law-student, Schmidtlein) do we find Platen crying out that "the body has its rights as well as the soul;" and querying if "the former are more shameful than the latter?" The confession however is tardy. There are plenty of signs that he had ever struggled with the promptings of homosexual desire, in a sub-conscious way or almost so, *ab initio*. His misgivings, his very arguments with himself that are dropped out here and there, imply this. He *would* not admit the truth to himself till forced to do so; and some of his casuistry is naive; But such a vague state of mind ended when he was at the height of his passions for the beautiful Eduard Schmidtlein and for Herman von Rotenhan ("The last night we did not part, we slept together—") as with the chapters as to "Cardenio," Bülow, and German; and beyond doubt there were no more scruj pies of sexual conscience on Platen's part after Italy. Still, to the end, Platen veils the physical side of his feelings; as would any highly refined heterosexual or homosexual. The "Books" of the Diary numbered, XXI and XXII, give the clearest recognition on his side.of the power of his emotion, and of his acceptance of its full sexual conquest over him.

As regards any real revision of the Journal from Platen, after that uncertain time when he decided to think of it as suitable for other readers, we find that he has not much impaired his confessions by tinkering them. In fact, he seems to have done little more—fortunately—than to tear out some pages that he did not wish any second person ever to read. There are a good many of these tearings-out; eloquent when one notices the connections in which they occur; guesses at his courage sinking as he reviewed them. But we have enough of the long history, as it is. Many entries are of great length. A considerable quantity of verse is also met in the Journal, some of which has not yet been re-printed in the editions of his Poems. But none of this unprinted poetical matter equals what has already been transferred to his published poetry—especially the Sonnets, Odes, Ohazels, some short pieces, and the pathetic First "Epistle to Cardenio."

In the following review of from the Journal the reader must understand that not the twentieth part of actual references that would be of high interest and appropriateness can be cited here. There will be given only a relatively fragmentary series, from pages here and there; demonstrating in Platen's nature the workings of one "affair" after another—especially the maturer episodes, those at Würzburg and Erlangen. The reader will find a brief study of several of (merely) the earlier incidents set forth in an article by Ludwig Frey, in the "Jahrbuch für Sexuelle Zwischenstufen" for the year 1899. Unfortunately at the date when that study was written the most important volume of the Journal had not been given to the public. Hence the interesting article by Frey is extremely incomplete, and contains sundry more or less salient errors of judgement or statement.

On turning over the Diary we find that—as might be expected—the first entries that we seek refer to shadowy, idealistic loves; much more fanciful than grounded in personalities. Platen mentions, years later (in October 1817, when he was passing a summer at Schliersee) that a friend in the Pagery at Munich, young Xylander, "was the first object" of his homosexual emotions. But no such entries as to Xylander, occur in the proper date. Instead we find that when Platen was sixteen years old, and yet a page, he saw at a court-ball the young Count Mercy d'Argenteau, a relative of the French ambassador to Bavaria. The beauty and grace of this youth made a deep impression on Platen—deep, for it never wore away wholly. He always looked back to it with a throb of heart—the more feelingly because he felt, even to his latest years, that no physical sexualism had any share in it. Indeed Platen was spell-bound by this young d'Argenteau, merely by seeing him a few times; for he he never was presented to the young Frenchman and only two or three words—those by accident and of no importance whatever—passed between the two. But long entries in his Journal testify to his emotion. He writes later: "I wished for love: till now I had felt only a longing for friendship. . . How happy I am when near him, how my heart rises! A gentle excitement fills all my soul. Seeing him again has the same effect upon me as if out of his features, at the first glance, a new life name to my heart. . . I dreamed of him tonight—a fair and kindly dream, fair and kind as himself. . . Even if I never see him again, O, my God! let not this love be extinguished in me! It is the love for all that is Beautiful, True and Perfect. . . I will rejoice when I see him, and be sorrowful when my eye finds him not. I will think and dream and speak of him. I will love him to a passionate enthusiasm, I will call out his name in a fiery ecstasy when I am alone. . ." When the departure of young Count d'Argenteau from Munich was near, Platen's entries grow proportionately vehement: "—Is fate so inexorable? O, turn this blow from me, my protecting genius!

I will do and suffer anything if only he can be allowed to remain near me. . . I cannot be without him. I feel *that*, as an indescribable void in my life." On seeing young Mercy d'Argenteau really for the last time, at the theater one evening, Platen slips into the box that d'Argenteau had just left, and carries away the programme that probably d'Argenteau had held during the performance! Now all this state of mind was aroused by the mere physique of a young man whom Platen never knew; scarcely could say he really had met at any time! But this is characteristic, and it was to be duplicated for awhile in other sentimental attractions. Young Count d'Argenteau, we need not say, left Munich in utter ignorance of what a male adorer he left behind him.

But at this same time, or only a few months later, Platen came under the spell of another "shadow-love"; one of an even more idealistic complexion. This was his passion for a certain young Prince Oettingen-Wallerstein, a kinsman of the King of Bavaria. This Prince Oettingen-Wallerstein seems to have been of quite exceptional beauty of physique, and a fine young character withal. His traits are today traditional in the family to which he belonged. His mental and moral promise was high. Platen made no more acquaintance with Prince Oettingen-Wallerstein than with young Count d'Argenteau. But again his idealism breaks out into a not less clear and articulate love. There are several entries that sufficiently witness this, at the time, not to speak of numerous later ones. And Platen learned through this passionate fancy for young Prince Oettingen-Wallerstein what sorrow in love can mean: for the Prince was killed in the Battle of Hanau. Platen never grew indifferent to his image, nor to the painful emotion that this death excited. He was often greatly depressed by it. There are plentiful references to the deceased young soldier, and to moods that his memory inspired. Even in mature life, after all his later experiences of quite other sort, we shall find in the Journal that the Prince Occupied a special and sacred niche in Platen's heart; probably because the sentiment had been so initiative and tragic. When he heard of the death of Prince Oettingen-Wallerstein, he went so far in his grief as to write a letter to the mother of the Prince—a letter the tone of which seemed to him in after-years indiscreet, to say the least—begging the lady to send him some personal relic of her son. He never received a reply. But we can believe that he had his own sentiment in fair perspective when he wrote, by and by:—"I loved my dead, whom I had only seen three times."

Pace by pace, with the beginnings in this way of Platen's homosexual life (and but little later) were certain likings and attractions Jo young men that were more of the nature of friendships; some of these being his life-long ones, as mentioned. Yet.it is noteworthy in their connection that such relationships, no matter into what they developed, always began with a glow of homosexual love; With his being "taken" at first sight by merely the *beauty* of the young man in question; his sense of male beauty catching fire. And sometimes they balanced a good while, in a curious, a plainly homosexual and Uranian way, between friendship and love, love and friendship; till they calmed to friendship only. Or (as is so characteristic of the Uranian) he ceased to care much or at all for the originators of these emotions. Among these intimacies we have that with Messerschmied, with Count Friedrich Fugger, Gustav Jacobs, Nathaniel Schlichtegroll, Max von Gruber, Adalbert Liebeskind, Friedrich Schnitzlein, Joseph Xylander and Friedrich von Perglas. Four of these loved and valued Platen as their friend, in good and evil report, year in and year out. The still smaller circle of such true friends, including Messerschmied, Gruber and Fugger, became— more or less—Platen's lifelong confidants as to his homosexualism and its dramas. But that they were homosexual themselves, during any stages of the friendships is in no wise clear. When now and then, in after-life, that matter happens to be plainly spoken of between Platen and them, the denials on their part, plainly incidental to what they have to say to him, are not doubtful. We occasionally have sufficient reason to think that the beginning of these intimacies with Platen was on a mutually homosexual basis, in at least a psychic degree. But in any case, as time passed, these friends became "just friends," nothing more; ever invaluable as such to Platen. He was a mystery to them. They did not understand his sexualistic riddle as it matured. But they were wide-natured enough, if not experienced enough, to contemplate it philosophically and kindly, and to do what they could to guide and help their friend if he needed them. Max von Gruber and Fugger were peculiarly Platen's confidential repositories of his troubled life. They were worthy of his trust, even where.they did not—approve. The reader is particularly referred to the long entries in the Journal as to young Perglas, who was a fellow-officer; and to the records (in Book V) as to Issel, a handsome young painter. With Issel, Platen struck up a rash, enthusiastic, sentimental intimacy, full of a quality of abnormal regard. Issel and Platen became bosom-friends for some weeks; travelled about Tirol together; and then Platen found out that they were completely unsuited to intimacy! In this history, as in others, fault appears to have been not a little with Platen. Issel seems like an affectionate, impulsive fellow, while Platen was arrogant and impatient and tactless. After several trivial contentions, Issel quitted Platten at Aibling. After he had gone, Platen realized with shame that his own stupid pride and want of tact had driven a good friend away, and he laments, too late, his ill behaviour. But in the relationship with Perglas (see the many entries in the Journal) we have more curious examples of how Platen could conduct himself when mixing up friendship and love. Perglas appears to have been rather well suited to be a friend to Platen, as Platen to Perglas; especially as we cannot help surmising that Perglas was psychically homosexual—at least bisexual. But somehow neither young man was able to be perfectly straightforward and frank with the other. Neither *would* trust the other with his heart and nature. Perglas, more than once, in his sexual attitude toward women, with his plain sympathy for Platen's vaguely defined nature, hints at a hellenic sort of bond as desired by him, too. But their half-confidences and Platen's disputes and dogmatic ways, repelled Perglas. They quarrelled and made up, quarrelled again and made up again—constantly. They could not be happy apart, yet could not get along when together—in large part because of hall-confidences rather than complete ones, and also because Platen's temperament was at no time easy to meet. It was exacting, often bitter externally, in a nervous sort, of way; while all the while he might be most passionately desirous of the good-will and intimacy made almost impossible by such conduct. Bitter tears of shame and loneliness did this failing of his temperament cost him! Not till rather late in his life could he get the better of it—in part. Perglas and he were presently separated by duties. Their friendship became one by letters. Some of those from Perglas were impassioned enough; as when he declares that he "cannot exist" without Platen. Perglas died in 1820. Platen was preoccupied with other affairs at that time. We may note here that though he speaks of the absence of physical desire in any intimacy of this period, yet he uses one expression concerning his relations with Perglas that show that he was far from being quite unsophisticated or—unexpectant. But the two friends seem never to have taken what Platen termed "the last step," even in their passionally affectionate days.

Of himself, at this period Platen writes (June 1813): "I saw no women except of that artificial class that comes to a Court. These could not attract me. So may it have been that my first warmer inclinations went out to a man. I will not say that I had not any understanding of unplatonic love: still, I would rather call what I, felt an intense, inner respect than a special sexual inclination." The "special sexual" attraction for him was to become evident to him presently.

For verily his third homosexual love (distinguished from any contemporary friendships, even if ardent) was certainly of the real tincture; albeit again we have in it far more a process and spell of idealizing, of dreaming, than of interest based on even a slight personal knowledge of the object. It was a wholly one-sided sentiment, due solely to another man's beauty of face and figure. But it was a powerful and unhappy passion. It had a distinct and lasting connection with Platen's sentimental life. It entered immediately into his earlier poetical expirations. He had become an officer in Munich. As it happened, that winter found him unusually solitary, several intimate friends being on duty elsewhere. He speaks of himself as having grown especially indifferent to some recent episodes—the recollection of the young painter Issel, the little *feu-follet* glow of his feeling for Euphrasie de Boisesson both were completely past. He writes: "In this mood of ardently longing for love, it happened that at a concert on November 12, 1814, was present a young officer of the—Regiment, who caught my attention." The young officer was a certain Captain Friedrich von Brandenstein, a cuirassier. He was blond, quiet-mannered, of excellent family, and of a type that, as we find, suggested to Platen the vanished Count Mercy d'Argenteau. Platen writes: "Prom this accident developed a long love, which defied all separation, to every impression of which I surrendered myself, and which filled my heart with a cloud of dreams. The officer mentioned was that 'Federigo', who in my later pages often is so named."

"A cloud of dreams," indeed! For we find that Platen never exchanged more than a few utterly insignificant words with Captain "Federigo" von Brandenstein. He never was on terms of writing or of other real acquaintance with Branden stein; was part of the time—most of it— unknown to Brandenstein even as a street-acquaintance or fellow-officer. But Platen thus nourished, wholly by a process of idealism, what really did become a life-long love; such even amid many other realities of like sexualism. Once again Platen had met his fatal "type," in outward shape at least; and he gave himself up to an obsessive longing for it, like a woman. In reviewing this Brandenstein affair, awhile later, Platen mentions that the various occasions when he saw Brandenstein, as on the street or at parade or in a café, "served to strengthen my madness, and to establish a perfect passion in me—mild in its general characteristics (?) though often amounting to a heated longing." But he insists that in all this incoherent emotion he had not at this time "any idea that a punishable (i.e. physical) relation between two men could exist; otherwise I would probably have been frightened back from it. Some time later, I found man-to-man love outlined in several literary works, and referred to these my awakening to a notice of the topic"— and to his Plutarch readings. "But at this same date, I was still ignorant that sensual-sexual passion could come into play here—*that* unblessed secret was first clear to me by reading some indecent verses by Piron. . . Never did lust desecrate my feeling for Federigo." But whether "lust" here was present or absent, this passion for Brandenstein was the kernel of Platen's psychic life in Munich, during many months. He haunted, usually in vain, the places where he could even get a look at Federigo, could see "that divine profile." He wrote Federigo epistles (all unsent) in verse, begging sympathy and "friendship," depicting what *might* be an intimacy between them. Page after page of the Diary has Brandenstein's "dear name," with little or nothing but thoughts for him, sighs for him. Several of the shorter and earlier poems of Platen that will be met in his published works relate to his love for this almost unknown comrade. Two highly characteristic Sonnets, written seven long years later, when much else had happened to Platen's heart—as we shall see—were the result of a chance glimpse of "Federigo." Both the young men were presently obliged to quit Munich, for the last chapter of the campaign against Napoleon. There was never any.further nearing, even after each had returned to Bavaria. But that made no difference. Platen was fettered. Occasionally he fancied that Captain Brandenstein might be interested in him, in turn; and equally timid or too proud to begin an acquaintance!—a notion lacking any sufficient ground, to say least. Most likely, Brandenstein never had the remotest of what was going on in the soul of that quiet, taciturn young Platen; probably did not think a dozen thoughts of Platen during all the stay in Munich! Platen could worship in mute yearning. . . "Never were his features so attractive to me as this evening. . . I followed him through the street. . ." And later he says, writing on the night when Platen himself was ordered away from Munich, . . . "All is over. I have come from'the Court-Concert. I have seen Federigo perhaps for the last time. Oh, I see too clearly he scorns me (!)—I must go without saying farewell. . . My heart is broken. I have been ready to go away from here, I was glad to do so, but now it seems to me as if I were held fast by chains of adamant." . . . A poem of several hundred lines follows, being a romantic dialogue imagined between himself and Brandenstein. Well may Shakespeare's clown remark, "We that are true lovers run into strange capers!"

During the long marching across into France, Platen's passion for Federigo, his frequent anxieties for Brandenstein's actual safety, his hopes, longings, reminiscences, all recur. When passing through Nitry, (August 15, 1815) we have this: . . . "But the bitter certainty not even to hope for B—'s acquaintance and friendship brings me into a sort of despair. I must live days, months, years, without seeing him. . . the darling of my heart for almost a year—the eternal object of the dreams of my fancy, he whom I so deeply love, he whose noble features recall to me the image of M (ercy d'Argenteau), he whose acquaintance is the crown of my wishes. . .," etc. etc. The recurrent allusion to the haunting "type" is noteworthy for psychologists in Uranism; as so often at the base of a homosexual admiration. When Platen was back again in Munich, he breaks out (Jan. 15, 1816): . . . "O Federigo! If I am to be disappointed in you, why do I not find it out? If I am not to be so, why am I not made happy? I do not see you, I do not find you, I know nothing of you: but I love you, and if this pressure, this suspense, continue as now, the very tissue of my nerves will be torn to pieces." Here many pages of the Journal are cut out by Platen's own hand. Again. . . "O Fritz! O Federigo! Knewest thou my love and my constancy, thou wouldst reward them." Another long and impassioned entry at this time is for Jan. 28 1816 . . . "Poor glowing heart, . . ." and so on. And all this hyper-erotic state of mind was a matter of nearly complete idealism! Platen was in love, at sight, with the physique of another young man; on it he was building up a whole sentimental fabric of glowing sexual-psychic desire. But just so can be bred and nourished any sort of iove, heterosexual or homosexual; often purely such stuff as dreams are made of. As to the end of the "Federigo" affair, it never completely ended; as has been mentioned. The blessed image of the young cuirasssier of Munich remained in Platen's heart all through his career, especially in Munich. Even at the Universities, it tormented him or thrilled him. It was a sort of permanent criterion of the depth of his sentiments for his later flames.

Just at this time, in Munich, and during the march to France, Platen's love-friendship (the grade of that special feeling in Platen is hard to characterize here) with his brother-officer, Perglas was in course. As has been said, it was anything but a smooth course. Perglas and he could not part psychically, and did not, till death removed, Perglas untimely from the world; but they never came really together. There is excellent reason to believe that a certain mysterious episode in Perglas's officer-life in Munich, rather later (in the winter of 1817)—his desertion from the garrison and from duty, for some days, his disappearance and his return, in a pitiable state of shattered nerves, was a meditated plan of suicide, because of sexual depression. It was an incident in which Platen behaved to his friend with brotherly care and judgment. But to the last there is no record of a due degree of confidence between this strange pair, even when an hour of mutual disclosure might be expected.

But a new personage was now to appear on the scene for this idealistic poet-soldier. Like the matter of Mercy d'Argenteau, or of Prince Oettengen-Waller stein, or of Brandenstein, this affair, was sheer idealism, concentrated on a handsome comrade's exterior. Inasmuch as a brief personal acquaintance really was at least the finale of it, it was a trifle more concrete than its predecessors. Among the Munich officers was a certain Captain Wilhelm von Hornstein, a remarkably good-looking officer, of rather notable family, as well as being a Knight of Malta—which Order, as the reader may remember, is one vowed to celibacy, not to say to chastity of every sort. Hornstein was a man of entirely mediocre, commonplace, matter-of-fact psychos; not in the least intellectual or romantic. But unluckily Platen did not find this out till too late. Platen fell in love with him, vehemently. Between Platen's own shyness and the difference in their ranks, with some other circumstances, Platen did not meet this new idol for a considerable while. During all the interim, the Diary is a daily witness to longings, dreams, doubts, hopes, fancies, rhapsodic outbursts, and so on; exactly as in the case of "Federigo." Moreover, this Hornstein affair was growing just in the time that "Federigo" was so potent in Platen's soul. Hence we find that Platen shows a good deal of the distress and surprise, natural to any fine and inexperienced nature, that a man can be in love with two human beings at once. This appeared to Platen a sort of mysterious monstrosity! He is ashamed to discover his "inconstancy," or—capacity. He does not understand how hearts are the subjects of "type-preposessions," over and over again—simultaneously. A plurality of loves seems to him disgraceful. On February 26, 1816 he writes: "My mood was never gloomier and heavier than yesterday evening. I was filled with the thoughts of only Wilhelm. Alone and lamenting, I sat at my writing-desk in the night." And he reviews sadly how nearly he had met the beautiful Hornstein at last: "I came home and I threw myself on my bed, in a glowing longing. The sun and the new day have lightened only a little my yearning, along with a dream of Federigo. Is it not strange that I could dream of the latter, when I was so full of Wilhelm?" Then as if in self-apology, he says: "I love the first-named still—always; but I have not the least hope of meeting him, and I see him nowhere now." Platen's self-contempt for what he thought was a sort of vapourish weakness in him, apart from moral questions involved, quite filled him with unhappiness. A few weeks later, perfectly worn out with self-introspection, he went and confided the whole story of his excited heart to his good and true friend, Schnitzlein. The step was dangerous. Many friends might have cast off the confessor of such "abnormal" passions. But not so young Schnitzlein. He did not pretend to understand Platen's nature. He was wholly Dionian—we may infer. But his affection to Platen held firm. He gave him excellent advice toward proper self-restraint, resolution and silence; and generally showed himself to be a model friend. In fact, all through Platen's most detailed *grandes passions* we find that Schnitzlein and Max von Grüber were his best guides and guards.

Nevertheless, in spite of this relief by having such a confidant, Platen had many unhappy days and nights till the end of the Wilhelm von Hornstein love-passion. He came at last to a slight acquaintance with Hornstein; one of speaking terms only. He got no comfort from that, because he did not enter into any real acquaintance by it, and also because he saw no signs that Hornstein was in any wise attracted to himself. The entries of March and April, in this same year, are positively despairing. Several times Platen considers suicide. Filial duty and religion restrain him: " . . . O, if I could but mark one single sign of his kindly- interest, or even of his notice of me! I am without rest! I cannot stay in this condition!—it disgusts me. I can think of only one thing. I may be called the weakest and most contemptible of men—I cannot help that." Again we hear him exclaim (March 23, 1816) "I am lost! I see it clearly and plainly that I am lost! . . . Mock me, ridicule me, scorn me, ye men—I cannot help it. All my will, all my concentration, I have brought to bear—but only one subject can I think of, day and night. I spoke with him today, during parade—but I see only too clearly that I am nothing to him" . . . Only one means is left to guide me out of this misery—Death. Death—that means a suicide" . . .

It is superfluous to point here the evidence that what tormented Platen so fiercely was not merely the negatively "intellectual" relations with Hornstein, but the stress of sexual desire. He must have been deeply the victim of honest self-deceptions when he tried, later or at the time, to believe that no corporeal thrill, no concrete physical yearnings coloured his sentiments for Brandenstein and Hornstein. He was a robust young man; the physical passion constantly must have sought its outlet under the seethe of this sort of similisexual fire. It was not mere torturing "idealism." The outcry "I am lost!" may well point out his terror at finding that his abnormal passion was a physical one, as well as a psychic condition; a tendency never to be "cured."

Fortunately the unconscious Captain Wilhelm von Hornstein was not to trouble Platen's heart, nor to beget thoughts of suicide, or anything else for long time. Already Schnitzlein had warned Platen that if he, Platen, once came to know Hornstein—even a little—all his queer illusions about that blunt, commonplace officer would vanish; that he would find Hornstein a dull, uninteresting, rather rude type of man; no matter how handsome. Now, Platen had worried about just this possibility, more and more. He suffered; but he dreaded a broken idol. Once (March 19, 1816) Schnitzlein had even assured Platen that Hornstein was "not capable of a true friendship." Platen found this outlook "terrifying, frightful, deeply depressing." But so came the affair to an end! For, one night, Platen had to divide the watch with Hornstein; a chance he had longed for. So came their first real conversation, and his first clear impression of his Adonis. Platen found Hornstein ill-bred, vulgar, commonplace. There was no ground for any sympathetic intimacy whatever between them. From that moment, Platen's passion sunk to dullness. In a few weeks it was wholly extinguished. A few later meetings of a tame sort, friendly but not alterative at all, completed Platen's "cure" of the Knight of Malta! Platen was too honest with himself to struggle along against the real for the sake of the ideal. But he suffered much in being disillusioned. (One dolesome and long entry, that of April 9, 1816, is worth reading.) There were spasmodic fits of idealistics for Hornstein. We find Platen once kissing the sofa-pillow on which his shattered idol's "dear head" had rested. But in an entry of April 30, he says. . . "Almost my last spark of inclination for a man not worth it is now extinguished." Then, in a sort of pathetic healing-quest we find him harking back to Brandenstein (see the entries between April and June, of the year named) and there is a deal about his renewed devotion to only the beautiful "Federigo." In August 1816, occurred the odd little episode of his vain attempt to get a silhouette portrait of Brandenstein, by a thoroughly feminine ruse. But (this is significant) he now fairly had learned what great differences may exist between one's ideal of a man and the real individual. He dreads being "disillusioned" again. He applies that dread to "Federigo." ". . . O, that *he* may be the sort of man that I suppose!" Platen however never came to that knowledge. Possibly it was lucky for him. His perplexities darkened: "Father in Heaven, teach me where real happiness is I Teach me the true wisdom of life—or let me meet my end!"

The reader must not think of Platen as doing nothing but a little garrison-duty, mooning over love-affairs, writing a voluminous Journal, and inditing love-verses, during all this unhappy Munich period. On the contrary, he was assiduously studying languages, the best literatures, aesthetics; making with remarkable zeal his preparation for some sort of an intellectual life, presently to be determined on and followed. He was the soul of system in his use of every day and evening. He was already a brilliant linguist (at nineteen years!) even to writing verses of elegance and accuracy in several other languages than German. He was a solid reader, and many tranquil spare hours went for that. It is worth notice that he did not think, either now or during many years yet to come, that his poetical talents would warrant his becoming a professional man of letters. His idea was to get into diplomacy or something else intellectual. During this summer (1816) he made a tour in Switzerland alone, in June and July. In it we see how his perceptive powers and his nature judgment constantly acted. By this absence from Munich his general health, as well as his spirits, were vastly improved. On his return to military duty, he found that Brandenstein had left the city. Platen felt that this was well-timed. He seldom saw "Federigo" again. The winter passed with a good deal of depression, solitude, love-hunger, and gloom; partly through his mere reminiscences, partly because he had now earnestly to consider just what he ought to do in life if he was not content to remain a soldier in active service—as he certainly did not wish to do. There was also much correspondence, with Perglas; in course of which Perglas writes that he "finds it unendurable to be parted" from Platen. But Platen, though affectionate, is not warmly responsive to Perglas, so far as we have any word. In the autumn of this same year, 1816, Platen was for awhile on leave in Ansbach, his home. He was always delighted to return to his parents. So came during this visit of a few weeks, a new love-affair. It was not at all violent, and it was short. Still it was enough to occupy Platen's heart and his ideal-æstlmtic sensibilities for some days, and to furnish several long entries in the Journal. The object was a young cavalryofficer, indicated only as "D—A—." This "D—A—" was also on leave, visiting some Ansbach friends—the Freiberg family. Platen frankly speaks of the affair as only a sentimental "stop-gap;" a mere reaching out of his then sorrowful and empty heart for any sort of a new intimacy that would thrill it. Platen was tolerably thrilled. But now he seems to have determined to be on his guard as to cultivating any illusions only to be undeceived in a male charmer. "D—A—" was wholly a woman-admirer, not to say already in love with one of the young ladies in the Freiberg circle. So Platen "hoped" the less from him. The interest lapsed. In Dec. 21, Platen wrote that he felt himself "cured" of "D—A—." He notes: "This is the first victory of my reason over my heart." His heart had not been possessed with much ardour. He adds: . . . "Never for a moment has my inclination taken on a passionate colouring—that is to say I have never, in my inmost self, wished for D—A—'s acquaintance; I have never counted it a happiness, in a word I have never *loved* him. How much I feel ashamed that I have allowed him to gain even so much power over me!—" etc. etc. All which is tolerably loose casuistry of the erotic impulse. There is interest in observing that Platen's "type" haunted him here again: for he says (Dec. 9) that D—A—reminded him much of a certain handsome young French officer, met at Melun.

The Diary during this Ansbach visit is full of serious self-study as to weightier matters than similisexual loves; of conclusions almost always wise. Incidentally, we find Platen here lamenting his failure as a social companion, as guest, as member of a lively general circle anywhere. In truth, not till his latest years did he shake off the self-consciousness and reserve (it never was conceit) that made him a poor foregatherer in gay, commonplace circles. Indeed Platen in such relations, as in more intimate life, stands before us as most unlucky; and also as a striking lesson of how *not* to make friends, how *not* to please. Genial temperament, natural manners, spontaneity, lightness of touch and tact are so much of the secret of making and keeping one's friends! We must take pains to be lucid—or to seem lucid—or else we will be alone in the world. Platen's gradual sense of his own social defects cost him many sad moments.

He had almost determined to leave the army, as 1816 ended. But he returned to Munich (January 17, 1817) and passed the winter still in duty, though really mostly busy with hard study of literatures and languages. It is here that he speaks often (and regretfully) of being sure that, however graceful his verses have been, he has no right to think of ever becoming a real poet: The friendships with Perglas, Schnitzlein, Fugger, Lüder, and others continued. It was in this winter that the strange little episode of Perglas's escapade from duty took place—as has been mentioned in a preceding paragraph, (Febr. 2—3, 1817) Occasionally the un-met Brandenstein appeared in the city, and stirred the old fires up again; glowingly too. One entry (Feb. 15, 1817) remarks: "I doubt if Federigo be the last individual in whom I shall seek an ideal friend—whom I shall, however, never realize." This remark is eloquent of the fate of most such refined homosexuals. The- Spring of 1817 was Platen's final one of military service. He describe himself sadly as "drawing more within myself" daily; as "not having one single friend" at this time. That remark means merely that he was not in love with any young man, in spite of all his affectionate friendships; and that he was longing to be so in love! Such a status is classic. It is not badly described in a graceful trifle by Francis Beaumont,—this "Pining for Love" on general principles—and quite impersonally:

> *"How long shall I pine for love?*
> *How long shall I sue in vain?*
> *How long, like the turtle-dove,*
> *Shall I heartily thus complain?*
> *Shall the sails of my heart stand still?*
> *Shall the grists of my hope be unground?*
> *Oh, fie!—oh, fie!—oh, fie!*
> *Let the mill, let the mill go round!"*

A striking conversation on the relations of men to women (Jan. 24, 1817) occurred between Platen and Friedrich Fugger. Fugger here declared himself an emphatic "*Weiberfeind.*" In April, Platen made a pleasant acquaintance with one Captain Weishaupt, an intellectual, refined and well-mannered young officer of the artillery-corps. For a few weeks, the intimacy waxed considerably; Platen's mill-sails seem to have "gone round"—and rather briskly. But chiefly by his own inept, shy, awkward manner, his reserves and nervousness, as well as his real dread of feeling anything like a passion for another young man, the Weishaupt acquaintance fell through speedily. Platen once declares of Weishaupt that he "could trust him." That phrase, one becomes more and more sure of it, meant that he could trust his most secret nature to such a friend. But to Weishaupt he never did so. As May ended, Platen left Munich, on official leave, to spend all summer and much of the autumn at the quiet little village of Schliersee, in the near Bavarian Tirol. There he was much of the time alone, though with a few agreable acquaintances. He sent a casual farewell to Captain Weishaupt. We find him blaming himself sharply for having lost the chance to make a warm friend of Weishaupt by his badly managed relations with him, and by shy distrust.

Platen passed the time at Schliersee in incessant study, especially of the Latin classics; also in out-door life, and in writing verse, some of which is of import in his earlier published work. He continues nevertheless to feel scruples as to poetize at all, but "knows not what demon lures me to poetry-making," He has much, as usual, to observe concerning his own perplexing individuality; and—while the study of ourselves is by no means a safe guide really to knowing ourselves— doubtless Platen ripened and widened his character and cast some useful "cross-lights" on it during this Schliersee stay. Some of the retrospective passages in the Diary during this studious, solitary, summer (exactly such a summer as stimulates or depresses many and many a Uranian) have much interest, especially those in October. More striking are the memoranda, now quite positive, of Platen's realizing that he was out-and-out homosexual in his nature; incapable of loving any woman; destined to love only the male (see October entry, page 837, of the same First Volume) and his awakening knowledge that this sort of passion must needs be much a physical one, however clear its intellectual fire. He remarks at this time that he "trembles most" at discovering how his "inclination is directed toward his own sex, not to the feminine one." Yet apologetically he asks: "Can I change what is not my doing?"—the just, the eternal uranian appeal to Creative Fate. He likewise wonders whether should he marry, on a basis of friendship with some bride, sexual love for her would gradually come—another most frequent query in the mind of the similisexual of our date, and often such a dangerous illusion. Here too is a striking passage in the physical-sexualistic key: "I am at an age when love is *demanded*, which will not be satisfied with friendship. Without any sensual feeling there can be no love. Federigo has never, in any way, awakened in me a base sexual-sensual impulse. But what if that should come as to others! O, rather than that, let some chasm open, and swallow me up! I would be lost! I would waste away in misery; for *I never could attain my goal, I would shudder to reach it!* How easily a noble love can lead us to the edge of despair I know: but how fearfully a sensual fire must ruin the whole man, that I have not yet experienced, *though I have a cruel portent of it.* So much is there in the world that makes me wish that I had never been born! "The passages here italized are eloquent of Platen's obstinate, troublous fight to convince himself that he had loved and had not desired; could love and yet not desire; and that there were really great distinctions between the complexions of this or that ardent passion already "experienced." Clearly what with his "cruel portent" and many other sub-currents of emotion, he had become by no means so "idealistic," as he had kept on writing himself down to be. If favoured in any similar affairs in the future, he would not be able to hold himself in firm physical check. He knew it now. In any case, he was soon to find out just the very thing that he so dreaded, or wanted to think that he dreaded, as the "goal" of such a love.

A few months later, in the Spring of 1818, after again visiting Ansbach and returning to Munich to regulate his money-affairs and his military discharge for a term of years at least, he matriculated at Würzburg University. The writer of these pages came upon his signature, the other day, in turning over the old University Register—a clear, bold writing, however disturbed and anxious as to the future may have been the young newcomer that penned it on that now yellowed page.

At Würzburg, where Platen entered himself as a student on April 5, 1818, he found several of his older friends glad to see him, and to bid him godspeed in his next career as a student. Gruber and Massenbach were among these. Platen fairly plunged into incessant belles-lettres reading, language-study, lectures in special or regular courses in philosophy, and in other matters. Immense was his eagerness and his satisfaction of mind at being at last free to do so, and able to concentrate his mind on such work. But (the reader already will have foreseen this) he soon found that he was not happy. Mere intellectuality cannot satisfy most healthful young Uranians. Platen was vaguely longing, restless, craving, for—what? Of course, for some new sentimental predicament, for the turning-round of 'the windmill' aforesaid, whither was coming all too much grist. A new love seemed likely to center on a handsome young classmate named Döllinger (afterwards the famous head of the Old Catholic Movement) with whom he was considerably taken. Of this came "only a friendship." But in June (the entries are of June 14, 15, 18, 21, 22, 24, and July 2, 4, 6 especially) came the Awaited. Platen happened to see a young student in the Law-Department, named Schmidtlein—Eduard Schmidtlein: who, by the by, we must not confuse with Platen's old friend Friedrich Schnitzlein. Eduard Schmidtlein became almost forthwith the object of one of Platen's most vehement passions; the center of a perfect seethe of the physical, as well as of the mental, in the unlucky poet's heart; his fellow-actor in a strange and not undramatic series of sentimental incidents.

Eduard Schmidtlein is called, during all the earlier entries of the Diary, simply "Adrastus." Platen did not know his baptismal name for a long time. Schmidtlein was of a well-to-do Bavarian family, was a good routine student, and afterward became a professor of law of some distinction—rather early. For more than a year we find him the center of Platen's, whole inner existence. What is more, Platen fought with Schmidtlein the Waterloo of his battle to love "without being sensually stirred;" land presently learned, all too thoroughly, after meeting Schmidtlein, that physical surrender and bodily possesion are the very nerves of the mystic drawing to manly beauty that the Uranian feels.

There is neither necessity nor possibility in undertaking here to detail all the course of this Schmidtlein affair at Würzbürg—its leaps and bounds of growth, its frequent supposed subsidings, and its final imperiousness. The entries are in sharp contrast to the mass of those that deal with Platen's busy intellectual life at Würzburg, in the business of which it wrought now and then a nervous havoc. There are not less than three-hundred pages of memoranda about it! The main aspects and episodes are these. First, of all, not for many months did Platen get to a speaking acquaintance with his new idol. He did not began to exchange visits with Schmidtlein till within about a year. This delay was partly because of the normal slowness of conducting such acquaintances at Würzburg at the time; partly because Platen and Schmidtlein were both hard students, in totally different courses; partly because there was a difference in their social classes (the aristocratic Platen being quite superior to a "Bürgersohn" like Schmidtlein); and last, because Platen's nervous shyness kept him aloof. The hundred entries prior to May 1, 1819, call Schmidtlein only "Adrastus." But the reader will easily surmise that Platen could make his passion white-hot by his sheer idealizings as to "Adrastus," without one word of speech between them. This dangerous faculty blew the hidden fire into a perfect conflagration, within some two weeks of merely looking at the handsome young Münchener! Love, despair, jealousy, hope, melancholy speculation as to what Schmidtlein suspected of the affair or thought of him; moral, social, psychical questions—these entries surge along in a stream of homosexual sentiment for months. Above all, grew Platen's worship of Schmidtlein's "dazzling beauty," his "divine eyes" and harmonious voice. The dulcet voice of Adrastus inspired the lines "Lass tief in Dir mich lesen," and in many other poems printed in Platen's series, The person meant is Schmidtlein, though so many readers might well fancy that a girl was the object. Much of the Journal in 1818 and 1819 is written in French, Portuguese, and occasionally in English. Platen wellknew now that his ardent emotion was no vague intellectual one, but a downright sexual longing. He recognized that the mystic "goal" of which he had such fear, was what he must attain, some day,—however with agony of conscience. He cries out: "O pain without end and measure! O inexhaustible anguish! Never, never did I love thee (Adrastus) as in this moment!" . . . "He would laugh if he knew how I adore him. ". . . Then later he asks: "Has not the body its rights, as well as the soul? Are the rights of the one any more shameful than those of the other? . . ." etc., etc. Platen knew himself now, verily!

Nevertheless he is glad that "though Schmidtlein's. . ." beauty has cast a spell over me, physical lust for him has not yet polluted me." This is a queer phrase, that we can take in more than one sense. Just at this time, by the by, Platen's reading included a group of authors well-suited to enlighten him on classic and modern similisexualism and its "lust"; to-wit Anacreon, Meleager, and the Greek Anthology of erotists in general, Ovid, Tibullus, Propertius, Guarini (from whose amorous "Pastor Fido" are abundant quotations) Johannes Müller's ardently homosexual correspondence with his beloved Bonstetten, and many other such. The Müller-Bonstetten letters powerfully moved Platen; set him to sighing much—after a Bonstetten for himself.

But meantime, "Adrastus" Schmidtlein was by no means unaware of some sort of an unusual interest going on toward himself on the part of 'that young Count Platen.' This is certain, by what we afterward learn from Platen's many references to Eduard's demeanour toward himself, Eduard's glances, and so on. This knowledge—or suspicion—on Schmidtlein's side becomes plainer from what Eduard confessed much later (Aug. 22–23, 1819) when he disclosed a sexual secret as to himself, long hidden. But not coming any nearer Schmidtlein just now, Platen went to young Massenbach, who knew more or less of Platen's nature and seems to have been homosexually intimate with Platen in their earlier days, in some degree. Platen asked Massenbach to contrive to present him to Schmidtlein; as Massenbach knew the charming Eduard pretty intimately. Massenbach agreed. But though he spoke with Schmidtlein of the introduction, nothing came of the plan. Schmidtlein seems to have fended it off. Poor Platen grew more mystified and despairing than ever; for this upshot hinted at a real indifference, on the side of "Adrastus," even to their knowing each other.

But finally they met. There was no go-between. Platen broke the ice. March 17, 1819, they spoke; on the street. After some weeks, not earlier, began visits between them. Platen made the first call, with much timidity, May 1, 1819. To his relief he found that Eduard was a refined, gifted and most serious character; worthy of friendship, whatever else might come with that. The few letters from Schmidtlein that presently are quoted at full-length sketch his type, though we have no way of judging of a physical beauty that so fired Platen. But Eduard still hung back. The acquaintance stayed "roasted all of one side," like the famous Shakespearean egg. Edward did not return Platen's visits. He said that he "would call," then did *not* call; and generally he avoided Platen coldly, though'never with actual discourtesy. What is more, something like male coquetry soon appears, if vaguely, in Edward's attitude toward Platen. It is an element quite in logic with what presently we shall discover as to Eduard's psychic self. But, in 1819, we find that the two young men had become really intimate. By June, they were walking, studying, reading, talking confidentially, and so on day by day. Platen was alternately most happy and most—"unsatisfied." This is easy to understand. There is little reason to doubt that Schmidtlein now amused himself by doing what Platen expressively calls "exciting the power of his personal beauty" on Platen. Platen became only more and more aware of his own distinctly "sensual" yearnings for Eduard. Thus on June 3–8 1819, he says of Eduard: "Coming into my room, he dazzled me, like the figure of a demigod. . ."; and then we find an aspiration that has an almost comic effect, if we did not realize the moral terror underfying it. . . "If only Heaven will deign to grant me an unvarying purity of soul!" Some months earlier, had occurred already a long retrospective entry; in which Platen reverted to his still "unextinguished" love for Count d'Argenteau, for Brandenstein, and even for Hornstein, as all so much "less sensual" than this passion for Schmidtlein. By the by, in this *revue amoureuse* he does not mention his early relations with Xylander, nor those sentiments that had carried him so far with the young painter Issel. But now Platen becomes even more helpless, and hence more casuistic. On June 8th, we read of a walk with Eduard; when. . . "I held him embraced by the middle of his body, which darling burden pressed on my shoulder. One could say that this was sensually remarked; but if my soul be pure, why cannot I enjoy the sense of his beauty?" . . . Yes, certainly "one could say" that any such entry was not one of love for the mere abstract! But the tide of sexual passion was to rise much higher, and to carry both or them along with it, this time. A few days later, (June 7, 1918) sitting in a retired corner of the beautiful old Hofgarten, in Würzburg, reading together a most appropriate drama, ". . . we held each other embraced. His head rested on my breast. Our cheeks often touched" . . . Platen may well exclaim, when in a sort of *Rausch* by the memory, "These aspects. . . are joyful, but from one standpoint too dangerous. A hostile goddess can separate us, while wishing to unite us—the goddess Passion. We are young, and we love each other ardently. But I hope that God will aid us to leap over this abyss. I believe that it will be best for us to interchange frankly our ideas on this subject, and to fight off the enemy with United forces. . ." Was there ever a more amusing, pathetic, childish, and fatal policy toward mutual self-control, in any sort of love-affair? One wonders if Platen could have believed such a procedure to be of common sense! Was it practiced at all? At any rate it did not help. For a fortnight later (June 22) while alone together in a little garden, over at Heidingsfeld, near Würzburg, ". . . Eduard at last gave himself up to me with a tenderness without reserve, a tenderness equal to mine. Wo were simply one soul, and our bodies were like two trees whose branches interlace closely forever." Ah, Platen had no illusions now that his love must not be crowned with "sensuality."! But his moral conscience was in an agony. He speaks of this "surrender" in a letter, by and by to be written (mentioned in his entry of November 11 1819) to Gruber, as "the catastrophe of this melancholy history, and my crime;" which the sensible Gruber declares was merely "a betrayal through passion," adding that "although I myself detest the vice, by God and all that is holy, I do not in the least detest you for it!" But in spite of his troubled conscience, Platen exclaims that at last, once, in his life, he can say that he "has lived!" He affirms that such a state of things between him and Eduard increases, not lessens, the "ideal" qualify in his sentiment for Eduard. That delusion is as old and instinctive as the eternal war between natural and artificial ethics.

But this sudden unity was not to continue. It had to suffer a sharp defeat, for precisely that same reason which had given it such similisexual completeness. During the next few weeks, Eduard Schmidtlein avoided his new bosom-friend as much as before; causing the mystified Platen much wonderment and sorrow. What was worse, as the month was ending, Eduard wrote to Platen that he had decided that mutual relationships between them would best not be continued! An abrupt interview, and naturally a bitter quarrel, resulted: then came a reconciliation; but not a satisfactory one. "Eduard loves me," writes Platen, fresh from the embraces of his adored Adrastus, "but he is the most singular and inscrutable of creatures." Several letters are interchanged, intstead of verbal discussions. The letters of the mysterious Edward are remarkably dignified, well-expressed, manly epistles; but all are reserved as to statements *why* he had concluded that the intimacy was 'not best;' in excusing his sudden relapse to a "cold" attitude'again; Through his letters, we read how thorough had been his similisexual surrender to Platen's passion. He observes that he feels that they have misunderstood each other, and are really not suited, after all, to be intimate friends. They must part! "It is best for us," writes Eduard, "our two hearts will never fully understand each other, and I am truly sorry that I have found you one with whom I cannot as a friend get into harmony, though you have my esteem and respect in the highest degree." And now comes a pertinent, abrupt fact. A few days later than this letter, when the two were over at Kottendorf together, (Aug. 22–23) Schmidtlein confessed to Platen that he was wholly indifferent to women sexually, and was miserable because of this conviction; evidently hoping and resolving to change his nature. Of course, this rather explains Schmidtlein's conduct, both before and after this confession. Troubled by conscientious qualms or other obstacles, he would not give up the inward battle, any more than will many an Uranian today: and finding Platen to be so "like himself," recognizing Platen's uranistic nature, little by little, from the first moments, Schmidtlein had been unwilling to begin their friendship, and now was resolved to interrupt it. Schmidtlein's instincts—and Platen's passion—had betrayed Eduard farther than he had expected. At least these aspects are strongly hinted. But Eduard denied in this Rottendorf interview a physical inclination for his own sex, while also denying most positively that that he was inclined to intercourse with women. Altogether, Eduard appears to have been in a most unhappy, fairly sincere trouble of mind about himself, sexually; and sorry that he had "surrendered." Besides this, there seems to have been a strong influence exerted on Schmidtlein by a certain fellow-student and "friend," named Bannwarth, who had aimed at preventing the intimacy with Platen, as now at breaking it off. One cannot but suspect Bannwarth's hand in this whole affair; especially as we find that Eduard "told Bannwarth everything," empowered Bannwarth to act as a sort of attorney for him; and even gave Bannwarth all Platen's letters to read!—a queerly callous sort of proceeding!

In great distress, Platen writes: "Eduard is the first man, *so like myself* that there is nothing I could hide from him—and now he says that we must part. I asked him if love or virtue be the cause. He would not answer. I said that if he wished to conquer himself, I had the same intention, and so we could become guardians of each other." (!) On the 22 of August, going to find Schmidtlein early one morning (and Eduard being still in bed) after a passionate interview of farewell, full "of all our first tenderness," they agreed on a sort of compromise—not to part wholly, but never to speak of love or friendship again, and to remain on relatively distant terms. A few days later, the college-term was out. Eduard left Würzburg for Munich, and Platen, also free, went to Iphofen, a small town not distant, for the vacation. This separation brought on a painful climax to their *amourette*. On September 1, we find that Platen, much moved by absence, passion, love-longing, and so on, has written to the beloved Eduard a certain long and erotic poem, evidently full of just the forbidden topics—love, friendship and their relationships to each other. This poem originally all was transcribed in the Diary; but Platen cut most of its lines out, later. The letter which went with the poem is not cited: perhaps it too has been cut out. The poem ends:

> *Hier schmecken Küsse noch einmal so süss,*
> *Und wir bedürfen, ja, nur uns allein.*
> *Um ganz vergnügt, und ganz beglückt zu sein!"*

"Has not the body its rights as well as the soul?"—he had demanded. For some days he received no answer from Eduard to his letter and poem.

He had misgivings. He waited uneasily. "—I shall never find his like—one does not meet twice such a pair of eyes." This last touch is eloquent of the nature of Platen's sentiment. But at last came Schmidtlein's answer (Oct, 18)—"a horrible letter from Eduard," in which Schmidtlein in a stern and formal communication (addressed "Herr Graf") broke off any and all further relations between them, forbade Platen to write him, to speak to him, even to look at him on the street,—after such an evidence of his "monstrous lasciviousness." etc. etc. Platen was overwhelmed; but even now he declares that this letter is "what I have deserved." . . . "I shall never see him again: I will leave his country. . . I regard myself as a wretch who fears himself. The weight of his curse is on me." He sent his Diary, along with a full letter of 'confession' to that good and true old friend Max von Gruber. Gruber returned the Journal, with the judicious answer already cited; and also prophecied that Schmidtlein would resume friendly relations with. Platen "—even if he will never love you again." Curiously enough, Platen had sealed up part of the Diary from even Gruber; but Gruber broke the seals and read all—not to Platen's regret.

Gruber had prophecied right. Despite that robust tempest, certain brief, pacific notes were presently exchanged; and when Platen and Eduard met again, at Erlangen University, each promptly "made up" their violent difference. And the more carefully we look into this romantic bond and its episodes, between two young men not over well-suited to be too closely linked, the more its obscurities clear. There is no doubt that Eduard Schmidtlein cared deeply for the intellectual, enthusiastic Platen: but also little doubt that Eduard availed himself of a merely passing incident to break their tie because of "conscientious scruples;" as well as because he did not find in Platen the exact-type to satisfy him homosexually. The mysterious Bannwarth may have had a rôle, now past in the drama. At any rate, over in Erlangen, the two became again warm friends. Such they remained, though—so far as we can discover— they did not renew the sexual characteristics of their tie. (Eduard did not remain at Erlangen.) How aggressive Eduard Schmidtlein had been toward allowing Platen's passion to rise we divine by many allusions, including Platen's remark—after answering the "horrible letter" from Eduard—that he, Platen, did not once reproach Eduard even with what had been Eduard's fault. . . "exciting my senses *by means only too efficacious,*" etc. etc. But that their love-drama was played-through seems less of a trial to Platen at Erlangen; because Platen while there grew interested in a wholly new—and a much, much happier—homosexual intimacy, that with Herman von Rotenhan. Then, too, after Rotenhan had left Erlangen, came the even more kindly and captivating Otto von Bülow *liaison*; then Liebig; then the ill-starred "Cardenio" passion; then Karl Theodore German—and so on. Schmidtlein's real spell ended in Würzburg. Again, Platen now ceased to struggle so conscientiously with his own natural, sexual-sensual nature. He ceased to expect that innermost loves were to be mere friendships; he ceased quite to wish the attainment of a simply spiritual "goal." He had learned his lesson—that "the body has its rights as well as the soul" in such loves; though he was never gross in yielding to the conviction. To the last, Platen was an idealist. Ever he demanded beauty of psychos as well as comeliness in a young man he loved. He and Eduard Schmidtlein saw each other, by accident, for the last time, as late as 1824, in Regensburg, when Platen was otherwise preoccupied; the charming Eduard already a young law-professor in Göttlingen. But there was then no spark of the Würzburg fire.

The years at Erlangen University were most important ones in the intellectual life of Platen: and in much besides. He studied almost to excess in his daily courses. He was particularly under the instruction of the celebrated Johann Wagner and also under Schelling. He read enormously in many distinct and large literatures, occidental and oriental, classic and modern. At twenty-two, his literary and linguistic knowledge was prodigious. Better still, the life at Erlangen little by little worked a kindly change on his nature. From being shy, self-conscious, opinionated in type, he expanded now into a much more genial, companionable Sort of young man. Introspective and moody he ever was; but he brightened and clarified at Erlangen. His first general notice, as a promising poet and dramatist began here; and it decided him on literature as his real profession, not diplomacy or what else.

Nevertheless here at Erlangen, with the vibrant homosexualism of his nature as a recognized and deeply-lamented fact in his mind, ever dreading the sensual side of it but wholly unable to dismiss it, came to Platen the four or five experiences that shook him to the very center of his being, either in joy or pain. Two of these episodes, as we are glad to discover, were happy; although on the contrary, two of them were anything but that. They are none of them written-out by him at such length and detail as the Brandenstein, the Hornstein, or the Eduard Schmidtlein affairs. He grew now much more self-contained. He was not so unaccustomed to regard himself in such a light. He had less time for his Diary. But the lovedata fill many pages, and they should be read *in extenso* by any one at all interested in the study. In what remains of our summary, they must however be much condensed; I shall give only relative outlines.

The first subject of Platen's Erlangen susceptibilities was a certain remarkably handsome young student, an intellectual, amiable and dignified fellow, named Herman von Rotenhan; of a distinguished family (today well-represented) a youth who afterwards became a noted provincial statesman. Von Rotenhan lodged in the same house with Platen, in fact in the next room. Rotenhan came in November. Platen saw him standing in the passage, and fell in love with him at sight. They immediately exchanged calls. Platen discovered that Rotenhan was quite all that his attractive exterior promised—a gentleman, wholly sincere, frank, high-minded, sociable and romantic withal. So began their friendship, enthusiastically. Platen was not without immediate uneasiness, as he remarked the danger-signal of sexual feeling rising, to disturb his merely idealizing sentiment for Herman. And, just as before, so now he juggles with the evidence. On November 6th, he exclaims that he "hates love, and all its frightful caverns" (!). He has resolved that somehow he does not care "even to take Rotenhan's hand, nor to embrace him." But this state of "sinesexuality," soon passed, as we might well expect. For Rotenhan himself was decidedly ardent in sexual tendencies; was not in any ethical worriments; was a cheerful young sensualist of refined nature. He showed himself more and more inclined to be—demonstrative. Poor Platen became panicky. What ought he to do? To fly the affectionate young Herman? ". . . Can I behave otherwise than I do?," he writes. . . "Would I find rest if I let myself go back to the road I began to travel upon?" He means, of course, the "road" with Schmidtlein. "Should I not do what I feel is right? I can truly do my part toward establishing a spiritual and chaste bond with Rotenhan; but certainly *that* does not seem to lie ahead. One thing is certain, that we are neither of us unsensual: though he likely has not yet experienced to what precipices such a situation leads one. Alas, I have found that out. . . I must ward myself from any moment of self-forgetting." Platen tried this heroic attitude the more conscientiously, if only halfheartedly. He even went so far as to talk (Jan. 10, 1819) with Rotenhan of the necessity of their 'parting.' But the affectionate Rotenhan would not allow this. As it happened, there soon were various ups and downs in their intimacy; some passing differences; and they really saw less of each other temporarily. But somehow, the grew ever tenderer; and the situation ever more "heroic" for Platen. He had not made any explicit confession of homosexuality to Rotenhan, nor had Rotenhan (who was emphatically "so," but cheerfully untroubled by conscience's misgivings) said in so many words anything to Platen. But to Rotenhan, Platen wrote the little poem,—often in the minds of homosexuals when with some near friend—"Erforsche mein Geheimneiss nie." Platen's sense of his own faults of character and manner, his facility in errors of conduct with friends and the world, awakened much under association with Herman von Rotenhan. One may say that Rotenhan's love, and this special struggle, *taught* Platen a modesty not till now practised. He wondered why in the world Rotenhan ever could care so much for him—an uninteresting, moody creature, "neither rich nor attractive." But the moral struggle was over before Rotenhan had to leave Erlangen. On March 16–17, Platen remarks, in a sad anticipation of his friend's going, . . . "I tell him everything that is in my heart. . . To part from him is immeasureably sad, and the more because he has so much to forgive me., My heart bleeds, and my eyes are constantly brimming over." Then of their last nights together, he records:—"My soul demands love, I cannot be without it. Herman gives it to me. Last night I stayed late with him. We sat, or rather we Jay, embraced on the sofa, and I did not hide from him anything—how dear he was to me. . . I cannot damn this relationship; it seems to me a dispensation that has finally granted to me to find sympathy in another being, after I have so long yearned for it vainly. I did not come here with thoughts of love. I was torn to pieces in my very soul. So then let there come to us what is so innocent, especially for this short time left us. . ." The night of their parting was as long and passionate a vigil as might he expected. "We did not part, we slept in one bed . . ." Platen accompanied his friend as far as Bamberg; and there, with many kisses and embraces, they parted. Platen returned to Erlangen—"alas! I can no longer say 'to *our* house.'" Within a few days, Platen went for his usual stay at Ansbach. He and the beloved Rotenhan seldom met after these Erlangen days. Their careers, and Platen's residence in Italy, kept them apart. Rotenhan died (high in juristic honours) at his family-castle in Bavaria, in 1858.

To this affair succeeded a considerable interval of strenuous study, especially as Platen now began Persian assiduously. Also came many "merely friendly" companionships and interests, with an ever increasing development of mind and talents, along with a routine and most wholesome college-life. Rotenhan abided much in Platen's mind; he yearned mightily for him; they wrote one another constantly. But in July, 1821, came a diversion; a quick, a passionate and (luckily) peculiarly happy new love-friendship that worked well toward 'Platen's whole social nature. This was with Otto von Bülow, an ancestor lineally of the distinguished German Chancellor of our own times. Otto von Bülow was an exceedingly handsome young collegian (also an ex-officer) who came for a short course at; Erlangen. Platen loved Bülow at sight, remarking in his Diary that "it was not possible to do anything else." "The first time I saw him," he writes on July 13, 1821, "his exterior made a decidedly favourable impression on me." Also Bülow was drawn to Platen almost at once. They became warmly-beloved friends; though never did two young natures differ more evidently. Otto von Bülow proved to be presently the direct inspiration of a large part of those beautiful imitations of Persian "Ghazel" poetry, which have become specially associated with the name of Platen in German verse. The series of these, called "The Glass of Hafiz," dedicated to Otto von Bülow, was published a few months after meeting him. Platen writes: "—I glow with longing to set before the world my love and respect for Bülow"—a somewhat dangerous wish for publicity, considering the lyric tenor. And not only the Ghazels, but several other poetical matters refer directly to Bülow, as both the published verses and the Journal attest. The pen-portraits of Bülow (minute and spirited) are charming, as we meet them in Platen's records of this kindly-starred intimacy. Billow was not only handsome is, but handsome does. He was sociable, lively, sincere, open-hearted, full of practical good sense, jolly yet never trivial or unmannerly, a deservedly general favourite at the University. He often took Platen to task, in a tactful way, as to the latter's errors of temperament and conduct, and did Platen much service as his mentor. The charm of the Bülow personality exhales through the pages of the Diary. We can understand how "everybody loved" the young fellow. One winning little episode occured on July 27, 1821. There came an excursion to the Streitberg, along with Fugger; and later, at night, a talk between Platen and Bülow; when after Bülow had warmly embraced Platen, Bülow referred gracefully to a jest between them during the day, and added "—I dont believe you have made any mistake in *me*; though all the same—"I am what I am!" But the separation had to come, in September. Bülow must needs leave the University abruptly, because of military duty. Platen disconsolately accompanied Otto during some days of the journey, as far as Gottingen. They parted with many kisses and tears, expecting to meet soon again. But Bülow's plans anon were all altered. He could not return to study in Erlangen. They never dropped their affectionate friendship; and Bülow, along with almost all Platen's nearest friends (except Perglas and Gruber) long survived the poet's untimely and lonely end.

Just how far this intimacy with Bülow was "practically" homosexual is not clear. Not even so, in view of Platen's once declaring to us (after a certain night at the Streitberg) that he could praise God that he could admire Bülow's naked beauty of body without "the least desire for it mounting in me." There are contradictory passages to this calm mood. Platen begins, about this time, to be sexually reserved in his entries in the Diary. He does not analyze nor wrestle, as he did in recording his sentiments for Schmidtlein and Rotenhan. Besides, we cannot but suspect a sort of innocent insincerity, when he enters on this topic. Even after he was down, in Italy, troubled with small or no scruples of conscience as to homosexual love, he remained reticent as to the physical side of it—as we shall see.

Platen was now twenty-five years old. He had furnished his mind with a colossal, an encyclopaedic knowledge of philosophy, literature, aesthetics, languages, history, etc. etc. Already his verses and dramas were spoken of with great praise. But petty vanity never was among his weaknesses. There is no trace of this, first and last. Indeed Platen, like a great many other Uranians of genius, cared far more to be loved personally, than to be adr mired popularly for intellectual gifts. His happiness in success was in a great degree his pleasure that thus he was more an honour to his friends.

But now came a new emotional affair. In March 12, 1822, began the short but ardent intimacy between him and a student from Darmstadt named Justus Liebig, who afterward became the great chemist,—Liebig, whose name has passed into highest honour through his discoveries in laboratory-methods and preparations. Not only was young Liebig extremely good-looking. He was intellectual, cordial and refined enough to be at once drawn to Platen. More than this—there is no doubt that Liebig, in these young days of his life, was strongly uranian; certainly he was homosexual psychically, even if not wholly such physically in the Diary. The intimacy was swift. Says Platen ". . . He gave me the evidence of so decided and sudden a liking that I am really in a sort of astonishment about it. So much love has nobody shown for me; at least no one on such slight acquaintance." Then, quoting a line of Hafiz, he adds his conviction that in this strange life of ours just so much as two men come together, just so much as they try to disclose their innermost existences to one another, only the more riddlesome creatures do they become. A few days later m Nürnberg, he remarks that he and Liebig could indeed be glad that they had "found, *understood*, loved and will forever love each other. He never has seemed to me nobler, tenderer, and never handsomer than now—though he always is handsome. A slender figure, a cheerful gravity in his regular features, large brown eyes."—"What do we not say, what do we not hope?" Liebig's fineness of sexual morality charmed Platen, though "we have no shyness as to kisses." . . . do not hold ourselves at all back, and Liebig himself was the first to say that we must not show to the false and evil-seeking eye of the world that *inner feeling* which we do not reserve when we are alone." But under Platen's unfortunate star of interruption the' time that these two had together was brief. They had not met till Liebig was about to leave Erlangen for good. Liebig was much a dionian-uranian. He had become involved while at Erlangen, in a serious scrape with a married woman there, which affair he had not disclosed to Platen. Coming to learn of it now was no small surprise and disgust to Platen, though he soon got over it wholly. Liebig went to Paris to study. Platen had (more than once) a plan of joining him in Paris; partly to be with him, partly because of Oriental literature accessible in Paris. But the projects came to nothing. In course of the summer, Platen visited Liebig's city of Darmstadt; a visit that chanced to be most unlucky and disturbed, owing to Liebig's being under military "house-arrest" because of the affair just mentioned. This Darmstadt meeting turned out to be their last. They corresponded regularly and much, and Liebig's letters we know were glowing with homosexual love, jealousy, yearning for Platen and so on, to an ample degree; not to speak of Platen's missives. To the last, the bodily beauty of Justus Liebig haunted Platen. Liebig ever held a distinct post in Platen's roomy heart. Late in the Diary, we find Platen even speaking of Liebig as "the only being who ever has really loved me." The relations between Platen and Justus Liebig have formed the topic of an interesting volume (including correspondence) lately printed. It is strange to think of the eminent scientist Liebig as once upon a time so ardent a young similisexual.

We now reach the last, except one, of what we may term the series of the *grandes passions* of Platten: that is to say of what we find recorded as such by himself, and distinctively. The first is his wild, short, unhappy love for another young student at Erlangen, whom he names in the Journal as only "Cardenio," mentions in the poems addressed to him as only "Cardenio"; but who is identified with probabilty as a youth named Hoffman. "Cardenio" was, like Eduard Schmidtlein, a law-student. His beauty—merely this, for "Cardenio" was neither intellectual, interesting nor really friendly to Platen—terribly upset poor Platen for about four months. The affair has a considerable share in his verse and Diary. Of course, hero came in Platen's tendency to idealize a person whom he did not know, during a good while; and never (we are certain) would have found psychically companionable. Platen has immortalized "Cardenio" in the deeply-passionate "Epistles to Cardenio," and in the set of sonnets addressed to him, in which love, despair, hope, yearning and adoration are mingled, to all degrees. "Cardenio" first comes upon Platen's scene—for us—on November 22, 1822; Platen quotes in the entry a certain lino of poetry from the Persian Chakani, in which the old poet exclaims—"And is it really needful that I should know the name of everyone who steals my heart?" Then Platen says—"How I first came to know Cardenio has been already partially told"—though no such earlier reference appears in the Diary. It may have been torn out by Platen. Then comes a long description of the beauty of this "Cardenio," and more Persian quotations—sexual in key. Throughout the "Cardenio" affair, there come many references to Hafiz, At this time Platen was absorbed with the reading and study of that highly pederastic Persian poet.

We may note that as "Cardenio" was a mere boy, this particular love-sentiment, acutely physical, on Platen's side was eminently pederastic, like the Persian's tendency. In fact this sort of sentiment, from now on, especially when Platen was in Italy, took a clear place in his nature, as not earlier. After a considerable term of suspense, of idealizing and so on, Platen met "Cardenio." He tried hard to achieve a friendship with the beautiful boy. We can see that it was,a foolish attempt, *ab initio*. Platen was twenty-six, highly intellectual, an aristocrat in social position, an idealist; "Cardenio" was a preoccupied, boyish, untemperamental, and commonplace young collegian, dull-hearted and not too-clever. Max von Gruber once writes to Platen that "Cardenio" seemed to him (Gruber) "the most *arid* nature that I have ever met." "Cardenio" never was drawn to Platen; was unable to appreciate such a type. He did not respond to Platen's overtures. This coldness of course set poor Platen into a miserable state of mind.

Platen would have spared himself infinite distress (and the upsetting of a whole winter's plans of study) if he had never tried to cultivate that fair-faced, slender young Erlangen "student-jurist." But alack! Platen says truly of himself, as of all men and women—"I must love where I must!" So mounted a desire that blazed and smouldered alternately, week in and week out.

Before Platen had achieved "Cardenio's" acquaintance, came the end of the University-term. "Cardenio" went away. Platen, after many hesitations, decided on a most foolish step. He had planned to pass several months studying in Vienna. This mood was over. He determined instead to go and "to live alone," for those months, in the cold, dull little town of Altdorf (near Nürnberg) and there to study Greek, Persian, and so on. He went to Altdorf. The plan was a perfect failure. He was haunted by "Cardenio"; he was not well; he could not endure his miserable lodgings in such a primitive place in the winter. He realized what a folly he had undertaken, as soon as he entered on it. Worse still, inasmuch as he was not at all sure whether "Cardenio" purposed to return to Erlangen, to continue his studies, Platen was not certain for a moment whether, even if he should now give up this Altdorf exile and go back to the University, he would find there (when the terms were to be resumed) the still "unknown god" of his heart.

After obstinate weeks of solitary brooding and half-study, under winter-conditions, Platen surrendered. He returned to Erlangen. "Cardenio," the real cause of all his plight and disquiet, turned out to be there once more, for a final term. But all went amiss as to any intimacy with "Cardenio;" who now—as before—neither cared for Platen's acquaintance nor liking. They became nominally friends, but only on the surfaces of life. Platen grew fairly hysterical with love and a fierce sexual longing. In the Diary, the first of the two "Epistles to Cardenio" in verse (published in the Poems) show what a tense, agonizing, hopeless love it was:—

> "—*In Sturm und liegen wandl' ich oft bei Nacht,*
> *Zu kühlen was den Busen mir entfacht.*
> *Vor Deinem Fenster geh' ich spät vorbei,*
> *Ob wohl das Licht noch nicht verglommen sei.*
> *Oft seh' ich dann dein schönes Haupt erhellt,*
> *Als schwömm' in Strahlen eine ganze Welt;*
> *Doch trittst Du wieder einen Schritt zurück,*
> *Verlier' ich dies secundenlange Glück!*

. . . .
O dürft' ich werfen mich vor Deine Thür

Und sie betaun mit Zähren für und für!
Räum' einen Platz mir dorten gütig ein!—
Geh' ab und zu,—ich will die Schwelle sein!
Verfahre strenger mit mir jeden Tag,
Von schöner Hand erduld ich Schimpf und Schlag,
Dies einzige, nur dies, ertrag' ich nicht—
Mich nie zu nahen Deinem Angesicht!

The Sonnets are in the same boundlessly "passional" tone,—and yet more so!

We can repeat it—this passion of Platen was decidedly a pederastic sentiment, and one may suspect that his Persian readings had some share in its awakening. His health, his studies, his friendships, everything gave place to it for the time. But at last, Platen realized two important things: first that this was a case where "the glory was all in the worshipper;" and, second, that there was no hope of any intimacy. Hie mastered the emotion, in part, and in part he grew cold toward "Cardenio." They drifted apart. Platen last saw his Ganymede, by a queer coincidence, when "Cardenio" was sitting one day in August, 1824, with Eduard Schmidtlein—in another locality. But Platen's ardent emotions for both were no more!

Of Platen's acquaintance with another Erlangen, student, Peter Ulrich Kernell, a young Swede, who died suddenly, and almost, in Platen's arms, in April 1824, of another intimacy with the seductive Baron von Egloffstein; with von Stachelhausen; with the young theologian named Renner; with Reuter, Engelhardt, Hermann, and others—concerning which series we find many entries more or less homosexual and interesting—we may say that all of them belong rather to the unimportant category in our study. Some of them were indeed "merely friendships," however nearly was crossed this boundary. Besides, during the year 1824, Platen changed more and.more, for awhile at least, in his temperament; and for the better. He threw off further his introspection, self-consciousness, worriments of soul. He grew sociable, lively and even popular. His literary repute advanced. He determined on a career in letters. He also travelled much.

Nevertheless there came, before he left off study at Erlangen, what we may regard as the final articulate and recorded homosexual love. What is more, it was one that (like the Cardenio passion) has a significant place in Platen's poetry. Among the distinctively, intensively homosexual Sonnets will be found a set of not less than twenty-six, addresssed "To Karl Theodore German." The youth who inspired these is vague to us, except that he was a fellow-student, and that he came on the scene of Platen's homosexual experiences about a year later than "Cardenio;" after Platen had been travelling down in Italy and had made other considerable absences from Erlangen. (Platen often returned thither for study, during a few years.) This "Karl Theodore German" matter came after several other passions had flitted over Platen's, beauty-susceptible soul; including a flame for Reichenberger, and for a theological student named Knobel. We may note that Knobel, after beginning a most promising acquaintance with Platen suddenly and insultingly—though privately—declined to continue it; on grounds that plainly shew that in Erlangen there had been gossip about Platen's sex-nature.

Karl Theodore German, made Platen-pathetically miserable. There was no intimacy, no liking on German's side. The sonnets in question are fiercely—agonizingly—expressive of a love wholly ill-placed. But this passion, fortunately, proved to be relatively short. It was the old tale of Platen's curse—idealizing; of his being in a mood to seek a love where no basis could be maintained for friendship. The Karl Theodore German entries begin just when Platen was in a most melancholy humor, despite his recent literary successes; in the year 1826. They end in August, and German's name then lapses, for good and all. The two young men exchanged visits only once. We conclude that German was a mere lad. Platen presently was "healed of his grievous wound." But all the same, there are the sonnets "To Karl Theodore German," as the evidence of what he suffered. He writes also once in the Diary that—"Only Mercy (d'Argenteau) and Brandenstein can I put into the same category with *him*, I have loved these three above all others, and it is remarkable that all three have been blonds, with a distinct likeness of features." The psychologist smiles at Platen's use of the word "remarkable," in such ignorance of the tendency of homosexual (as of the heterosexual) love to particular physical "types."

The settled University life of Platen, and his unrecognition as a gifted dramatist and poet passed together. His profession and his fame in it appeared matters of no further doubt to him. The references in the poems themselves now and then frankly hint at this. In one of them he speaks of those who declare that there hangs already "the shadow of a laurel-wreath across his young brow." In the summer of 1824, came his first Italian tour. With this event, just at the very point where we would most naturally expect his homosexualism to speak out, when down in Italy (as later, after this first visit) his strange reserve deepens. His Diary is mute as to almost all his uranian heart-life. We may be sure that southern loves developed at once; and that no moral stresses against the sexual privileges of Italy were a check on them. We have certain discreet allusions, to such love-affairs, with beautiful young Italians. He met also down in Italy, many young Teutons and other visitors, who were homosexual, with whom Platen foregathered philarrenically. But the reticence of the Journal, generally speaking, is surprising. He seldom makes the acquaintance of a young man without mentioning that the "beauty" of the new friend had been the first attraction, a *sine qua non*. In fact, all sorts of adventures and psycho-sexual intimacies and adventures, of a greater or lesser passional sort, surely came when he was wandering and living in the land of free, humane, æsthetic man-to-man sexualism. Some of these adventures have had their memoranda in his poems. For instance, there was the unnamed young Venetian who inspired him so warmly, during his stay in the Sea-City; alluded to in the "Venetian Sonnets" numbered 48 and 51 and in the last allusion of number 43. When Platen was passing through Parma, in course of September, 1826, came the little affair with one "Luigi," a handsome soldier, who, beyond any doubt, brought to Platen a happy—and physical—love-adventure, of some days. In Florence, occurred a short, mysterious episode—a single night—of like *bonne fortune*. In Rome, he became intimate with Cochetti, a handsome member of the Papal Guard; also with a certain young German named Fries (a Berlin painter and "very good-looking") also a beautiful Roman named Ranieri; also with a Spanish artist named Lepri; and with the two Roberti brothers. These acquaintances in Italy, each in their several degrees, were tinged with sexual relationships or psychic ardours. On the occasion of two separate visits to the Church of St. Peter in Montorio, at a year's interval (see the entry for Dec. 30, 1827) we hear of his meeting and falling in love with two young Italian lads. One of them was named "Innocenzo;" the other is not named. One of them is the subject of the exquisite Ode beginning "Warm and hell, dämmert in Rom die Winternacht." Another long entry, Jan. 11, 1828 is highly expressive, the more because of its vagueness. Again, on Feb. 28, 1828 (in Rome) he records becoming acquainted with a young officer who "is the embodiment of all that I could ever see in the way of beauty"; to whom may, with some probability, be set down the origin of the "Ode 18." The person to whom is directed the passionate and jealous "Serenade" we cannot identify clearly. When down in Naples, presently, Platen achieved the interest and friendship, and unmistakeably the sexual intimacy, of a handsome young countryman, August Kopisch, a painter, living in Italy; and who, by the by, discovered or rediscovered for us the "Blue Grotto" at Capri. To him Platen addressed some verses to be found in the poems published. Kopisch was notably handsome, a charming fellow, and a good friend to Platen, first and last; though— thanks to Platen's own ineptness—their intimacy did not always run on glass, by any means. In the beginning of Platen's passion for Kopisch, we are amused to find him one night so sexually excited that he could not rest; and that instead of resorting to the monastic scourge, or to prayer he—takes a moonlighted bath in the waters of the Bay of Naples! The bond with Kopisch survived all stresses. Platen grew to account it among his happiest ties, during the short remnant of life that was left to him for ties of any kind. It seems to have been the last "love-friendship" of great inner hold over him, which he was to enjoy.

Our sense of a striking reserve of Platen's uranian confidences in the Journal constantly increases as the huge record draws to a close. Platen's residence in Italy became an unadmitted fact. He was now famous in his German Northland. But he hated its social atmosphere. Only for business, or to meet a few friends, or to visit his beloved mother (settled in Munich—a widow) had he ever inclination now to return to Germany. He found in Italy (as have found there generations of like exiles) a people who have long possessed, who ever will possess, more true, *human*, conceptions—nay, let us say more divine impulses and theories—as to life and love than any Protestant Teutonia or Anglia can understand or tolerate. He had found in Italy, as have found there so many other expatriates, his intellectual and sexual home. Silences as to his homosexualism and its adventures (apart from his reticence because the Diary would pass into other hands) became a process partly of sheer discretion, partly of his abandonment of "moral" struggles, partly because of the physical subsidence of his sexualism. The latter reason is important; for Platen's general health became gradually far from satisfactory. A chronic, malady of digestive sort beset him, and there is every evidence that his *vita sexualis* was prematurely weakened. He became more idealistic than realistic—again. He speaks in the last months of the Diary of feeling glad that the unwelcome glow of physical passion had given place to a gentle admiration of male beauty. He could wonder at it without—desire. Instead of recording loves, we find him writing page after page of the veriest "guide-book" memoranda, as to pictures, churches, art, and so on. His heart sinks wholly below the surface of his entries. We cannot hear it beat.

It soon wholly ceased to pulsate with real joy of life, did so—by a melancholy irony—there in Italy, just where it might have bounded freest! He became hypochondriac, *unempfindlich* and restless. He talked of "settling-down" in Italy. He never did so. His commonplace social records are many, but they are not written in high spirits. He seems to have grown "sinesexual," toward the end. He felt himself solitary, now bound to live and to die so. The sun was paling for him. In Germany, some of his best old friends had gone—Gruber and Perglas among them. Still, only a few days before the final entry in the Journal, before his death from cholera, at Siracusa, he speaks of noticing in Caltagirone "a remarkably handsome young man." So the ruling emotion was at least alert, to the last; if in a mechanical, tranquil fashion.

Yes, to the last—as we have seen it from the first! For Platen remains forever the type of the born Uranian of literary genius, or at least of fine talent, who is drawn sexually only toward the male, but only toward the finer examples of the male, whether physically or intellectually; who idealizes in his loving, often to his own pain and disappointment; one who "loves where he must," a philarrene who is ever the victim of an inborn, sensual-sexual temperament. He is the type of the Intersexual that is of the intellectual class of our humanity. Such Uranians must be ever in peril of sad experiences, and of worse than sad. Such must thank "whatever gods there be" for any cups of refreshment that are vouchsafed their lips, often so parched; and must not expect to be too often so blessed. They must over and over yearn for unity, fated never to find their other half. In reading such a Diary, with the poetic and epistolary matters that supplement it, which Platen has left us, we realize that the lot of the son of Venus Urania is a hazard of sorrows, rather than joys; and in thinking of Platen asleep in his quiet grave in the Villa Landolini, at Siracusa, his bright career and his sad latter days alike abruptly ended, surely we may be glad that to all such weary homosexual hearts Death, sooner or later, gives an unbroken Repose.

A Note About the Author

Edward Irenaeus Prime-Stevenson (1858–1942) was an American writer. Born in Madison, New Jersey, Prime-Stevenson was raised by Paul E. Stevenson, a Presbyterian minister, and Cornelia Prime, who hailed from a family of prominent academics. After obtaining a law degree, Prime-Stevenson embarked on a career as a novelist, journalist, and impassioned defender of homosexuality. In 1901, he moved to Europe, where he would live for the rest of his life. *Imre: A Memorandum* (1906), a novel, was published under the pseudonym Xavier Mayne in Naples, Italy. Praised for its realistic and positive depiction of romance between two men, the novel has inspired renewed interest in recent years from scholars and readers interested in the historical representation of homosexuality in literature.

A Note from the Publisher

Spanning many genres, from non-fiction essays to literature classics to children's books and lyric poetry, Mint Edition books showcase the master works of our time in a modern new package. The text is freshly typeset, is clean and easy to read, and features a new note about the author in each volume. Many books also include exclusive new introductory material. Every book boasts a striking new cover, which makes it as appropriate for collecting as it is for gift giving. Mint Edition books are only printed when a reader orders them, so natural resources are not wasted. We're proud that our books are never manufactured in excess and exist only in the exact quantity they need to be read and enjoyed.

bookfinity™

Discover more of your favorite classics with Bookfinity™.

- Track your reading with custom book lists.
- Get great book recommendations for your personalized Reader Type.
- Add reviews for your favorite books.
- AND MUCH MORE!

Visit **bookfinity.com** and take the fun Reader Type quiz to get started.

Enjoy our classic and modern companion pairings!

Classic & Modern